THE EFFECTIVE DEPOSITION

TECHNIQUES AND STRATEGIES THAT WORK

FOURTH EDITION

THE EFFECTIVE DEPOSITION

TECHNIQUES AND STRATEGIES THAT WORK

FOURTH EDITION

David M. Malone

Peter T. Hoffman

Contributing Author: Anthony J. Bocchino

Address inquiries to:
National Institute for Trial Advocacy
1685 38th Street, Suite 200
Boulder, CO 80301-2735
Phone: (800) 225-6482
Fax: (720) 890-7069
E-mail: permissions@nita.org

Library of Congress Cataloging-in-Publication Data

Malone, David M., 1944-
  The effective deposition : techniques and strategies that
work / David M. Malone, Peter T. Hoffman. -- 4th ed.
     p. cm.
  Includes bibliographical references and index.
  ISBN 978-1-60156-153-4 (alk. paper)
  1. Depositions--United States. I. Hoffman, Peter T. II. Title.
  KF8900.M34 2012
  347.73'72--dc23
                                        2012014998
ISBN 978-1-60156-153-4
FBA 1153

Printed in the United States of America

To

The Memory of
Robert F. Hanley,
My Teacher and Friend

—D.M.M.

Betty and Sarah, and in memory of Alice

—P.T.H.

For demonstration videos associated with Chapters 6–9, 11, 13, 16, and 19, please go to the following Web site:

http://bit.ly/1Ew2UxF

and enter the following password:

NITAEffDep13
(the password is case sensitive).

CONTENTS

Chapter Three: Advantages and Disadvantages of Depositions

Chapter Four: Planning and Scheduling Depositions

Chapter Five: Preparing to Take the Deposition

Chapter Six: Beginning the Deposition

Chapter Ten: Foundations

Chapter Eleven: Obnoxious or Obstructionist Opposing Counsel

APPENDICES

FOREWORD TO THE FOURTH EDITION

The first learn-by-doing deposition courses taught by the National Institute for Trial Advocacy (which may have been the first anywhere) more than forty years ago focused on the mechanics of questioning opposing witnesses to obtain new information and the procedures by which that information could be used to control witnesses at trial and obtain party statements and other evidence. We noted in the Foreword to the Revised Third Edition of this book that these goals of teaching deposition skills remained important, but were being displaced as litigation changed its shape, with trials less frequent and other approaches to dispute resolution more frequent.

Courts have less time available for trials because the trials that are held are more and more lengthy; drug arrest resolutions are more numerous and take extraordinary amounts of judicial resources; too many federal district court judgeships remain vacant; and attorneys are not persuasively taught that it is admirable and ethical to reduce the complexity of discovery and trials by eliminating issues, documents, witnesses, depositions, and trial time. We know that even complex cases—like major patent disputes, where the jurors' understanding of esoteric expert biochemical testimony will control hundreds of millions of dollars shifting hands—can be completed within the five days scheduled for trial, if the judge is strict and the attorneys have evaluated their cases rationally, prepared their cases well, and kept their egos in check. (Of course, the losing attorneys in that patent battle may avoid such streamlined trials in the future, assuming in simplistic *post hoc ergo propter hoc* reasoning that the trial was lost *because* it was short.)

Most attorneys, however, continue to believe that it is their job to grab every advantage, even if it involves delay and obfuscation. We teachers and lecturers continue to spout platitudes about the responsibility of trial counsel to be fair and ethical, the responsibility of all attorneys to seek justice and fairness in all of our dealings with clients and opponents, and the attorney's duty to act as servants of the judicial system. Yet we see little improvement in the competence of lawyers in the courtroom, little reduction in the number of ethics panel cases suspending attorneys for mishandling cases, or few proposals during pretrial that attempt to speed the civil trial process or accomplish dispute resolution while also saving money for the parties—both the parties.

As we noted in that Foreword several years ago:

> It is amusing in a way to reflect on the fact that our judicial system was itself created as an "alternative dispute resolution" system, so that trial-by-combat, trial-by-ordeal, or trial-by-oath could be abandoned

as uncivilized. Our current system of ADR is an attempt to avoid the modern trial-by-ordeal faced today by litigants in every toxic tort, product liability, or antitrust case.

Depositions and, to a lesser extent, other discovery procedures can play a role in supporting these attempts at earlier and less expensive resolution of disputes. This efficiency and cost savings are presented as though they were always good for the parties and good for the court system. Parties do not have to face the uncertainties implicit in obtaining a jury verdict, such as the "David versus Goliath" factor, or financial inequality between the parties.

Nevertheless, these savings in time and dollars themselves have a cost, because the results often represent business compromises, with no input from the community that may also have been harmed. Where a judge has retained authority to approve any settlement, the public interest may receive consideration. But consider the ADR solution to an infringement suit by the proprietary drug giant against the allegedly infringing generic competitor—the generic may receive a large payment ("large" from its perspective) in return for an agreement to remain on the sidelines for an agreed period. The public is harmed by higher prices and the absence of competition, while the two competitors split monopoly-level profits and use the court system to enforce their agreement as though it were a matter of public policy. These arrangements have their analogues in the criminal trial system, where overworked prosecutors may plea bargain in cases because they do not have the time or resources to actually present evidence at trial. Additionally, pressure from an overcrowded prison system (again, caused to a great extent by drug law violations) may compel prosecutors to deal with shorter prison terms, even for serious offenses. Not a day goes by without a newspaper report that tells of a paroled prisoner committing another crime after release by a prison system that has not discovered how to rehabilitate or has not legislatively decided that rehabilitation is an actual and achievable goal.

If it remains true for decades into the future that more than 90 percent of cases filed in both federal and state courts are resolved outside the courtroom, then we might as well admit that the trial system has been suffocated. If the system that replaces it is capable of delivering justice, serving the parties and the public, providing the best orators of our communities an opportunity to provide a true public service, then we will have achieved some valuable evolution. However, in that system or some other that we choose, the parties will still have to find ways to inform themselves about what lay people sometimes call the "true facts" of the dispute, and the best way to learn that history is still through well-taken and well-defended depositions. As the number of trials diminishes, the importance of depositions increases, because they remain the very best way to determine what happened. Even when the dispute does not go to trial, the depositions provide the controlling statements that counsel can use to persuade clients that a settlement is desirable and fair; to persuade the court that summary judgment is appropriate; and to persuade witnesses to tell the truth at an arbitration or be impeached.

We hope that this book will be of practical use to all attorneys who want to obtain the best results for their clients by mastering the facts and anticipating their opponents' proof. Those readers who are seeking a source of "black letter law," filled with dense footnotes directing the reader to seven cases for every proposition, must look elsewhere. In this book, we attempt to provide a practical and logical approach to the tactics and strategies of depositions; we depend on the rules and on logic and common sense more than we do on particular decisions that depend so often on case-specific facts. We have tried to create a resource that calls on counsel to think about what they are doing as they use depositions to help to prepare their cases. We hope that the thirty years of interest in this book are proof that practicing trial attorneys still find it useful.[1]

— P.T.H., D.M.M.

---

1. The authors take this opportunity to recognize the past contribution of Professor Anthony J. Bocchino to the Revised Third Edition.

ACKNOWLEDGMENTS

As in previous editions, most of the ideas and suggestions presented in the Fourth Edition of *The Effective Deposition* reflect our experiences through the years in taking, defending, and teaching depositions. At this point in our careers, we find it difficult to tease out what were original ideas on our part from those we have copied or borrowed from others, particularly the many talented NITA faculty members we have taught with through the years. We owe special thanks to Stuart Israel of the Michigan Bar; Tommy Fibich of the Texas Bar; Deanne Siemer, Managing Director of Wilsie Co., LLC; Frank Rothschild of the Hawaii Bar; Tom Singer of the Indiana Bar; Paul Zwier, Professor at Emory Law School; Larry Bernard, Hearing Officer at FINRA; and all outstanding students and practitioners of taking and defending depositions who over the years have shared with us and have freely allowed us to incorporate many of their of their thoughts and strategies.

Needless to say, any errors remain ours and are not attributable to others. We hope that you find the new material in this edition to be valuable and that you continue to find the older material pertinent. Please send your comments and corrections to our e-mail addresses, phoffman@elon.edu and malone@trialruninc.com.

PART ONE: THE LAW

Chapter One

The Mechanics of Taking and Defending Depositions

Mechanics will kill you.

—Trial Attorney Warren S. Radler

Few hard and fast rules control the conduct of depositions; yet you must carefully observe the few that do exist so that the product of the deposition—the transcript—is valid and useful months or years later when the witness or the witness's memory is perhaps long gone.

The mechanics of taking and defending depositions are quite simple, but to avoid mistakes you must be thoroughly familiar with the applicable rules. Small mistakes can cost money and time and prevent the use of valuable deposition testimony on behalf of your client. To avoid such mistakes, you should carefully read and study the rules and statutes applicable to discovery in your jurisdiction.

The Federal Rules of Civil Procedure that apply to depositions and discovery have been amended several times through the years. While the federal rules or some variation of them have been adopted by the vast majority of the states, a number of states have chosen to incorporate only some of the recent federal rules amendments while ignoring or rejecting others. Many states have also deviated from the federal rules by developing their own unique discovery rules that may substitute for one or more of the federal rules or may supplement what is contained in them. Because of the many variations between jurisdictions, you must carefully check the rules governing depositions in your own jurisdiction. This book will discuss how to take and defend depositions under the Federal Rules of Civil Procedure, but some of the more common state variations on these rules will also be discussed.

1.1　Whose Deposition May Be Taken?

You may take the deposition of any person, including witnesses who are not parties to the action.[1] While some other discovery devices, such as interrogatories, can only be directed to parties alone, a deposition may be taken of anyone you believe may have knowledge of relevant information. Depositions may be taken of parties, agents and employees of the parties, former parties, nonparty witnesses, organizations, and, in special circumstances, even of the attorneys of the parties.[2] A party that expects to be unavailable for trial and wants her testimony presented through a deposition may even take her own deposition, although this is unusual. In addition, it is not unusual for a party to take the deposition of its own expert witness to preserve trial testimony. Corporations can be deposed through their officers, directors, and managing agents, and organizations generally may be deposed through their designees. Note, however, that you must seek leave of court to take the deposition of a person confined in prison.[3]

The courts have crafted several exceptions to the generally unlimited right to depose any witness who has potentially relevant information. One of these—the apex doctrine—permits a court to protect highly placed corporate executives from enduring the burden of having their depositions taken on a showing that 1) the executive has no unique personal knowledge of the matter in dispute; 2) the information sought can be obtained from another witness; 3) the information can be obtained through an alternative discovery method; or 4) the deposition would impose severe hardship on the deponent.[4]

Similarly, the courts have restricted the ability to depose highly placed government officials without a showing of extraordinary circumstances or special need for the official's testimony. The rationale behind restricting depositions of highly placed government officials is to protect the official from the distraction of testifying and from the loss of time from public duties, as well as to protect the governmental decision-making process.[5] Both the apex doc-

---

1. FED. R. CIV. P. 30(a)(1).

2. Generally a deposition of opposing counsel is permitted only when the party seeking to take the deposition has shown there are no other reasonable means to obtain the information, the information is relevant and not privileged, and the information is crucial to the case. *See, e.g.,* Shelton v. American Motors Corp. 805 F.2d 1323, 1327 (8th Cir. 1986). *See also* FED. R. CIV. P. 26(b)(3) (provides for discovery of trial preparation material (or its equivalent) that the other party is unable to procure without undue hardship).

3. FED. R. CIV. P. 30(a)(2)(B).

4. *See, e.g.,* Affinity Labs of Texas v. Apple, Inc. Slip Copy, 2011 WL 1753982 N.D. Calif. May, 9 2011 (No. C09-4436 CW JL); Coupled Products, LLC v. Component Bar Products, Inc. Slip Copy, 2011 WL 1565183., E.D. Mich., April 25, 2011 (no. 09-CV-12081).

5. *See* MOORE'S FEDERAL PRACTICE 26.105[2][a]; Bogan v. City of Boston, 489 F.3d 417, 423 (1st Cir. 2007).

trine and the restrictions on deposing highly placed governmental officials do not apply when the executive or official has firsthand knowledge related to the claim being litigated and the same information cannot be obtained from other sources.

Finally, courts have restricted the right to depose a witness when the witness is so incapacitated that he is unable to answer questions or the questioning would otherwise threaten the witness's health.[6]

1.2   Rule 30(b)(6) Depositions

Many times, employees or agents of corporations, partnerships, governmental agencies, or associations such as labor unions have valuable information relevant to some issue in a case, but you may not know the identity of the particular person in the organization with that information. Or more than one person has the necessary information, with each knowing something pertinent. While a series of depositions can be taken until all persons with pertinent information have been identified and deposed, Rule 30(b)(6) of the Federal Rules of Civil Procedure provides an easier and more efficient method. The mechanics and strategy of 30(b)(6) depositions are discussed in chapter nineteen.

1.3   Timing

Under Rule 26(d), no discovery, including depositions, is permitted in most cases until after the parties have conferred to plan discovery pursuant to Rule 26(f). The purpose and timing of the conference are discussed section 4.1. Certain cases—the very unusual or the very routine, which would not benefit from having the parties confer—are exempt from this prohibition against early discovery.[7] The prohibition on discovery until after the parties have conferred can also be modified by an order within the case or by agreement of the parties. The prohibition on early discovery can also be disregarded if the notice of deposition contains a certification, with supporting facts, that the witness is expected to leave the United States and thus be unavailable for examination in this country unless deposed before the parties have conferred.[8] However, a deposition taken before the parties have conferred because the witness is leaving the United States cannot be used in a pretrial motion or at trial against a party who shows that it was unable, through the exercise of diligence, to obtain counsel to represent it at the

---

6. *See, e.g.*, Dunford v. Rolly Marine Service Co., 233 F.R.D. 635, 637 (S.D. Fla. 2005).

7. FED. R. CIV. P. 26(a)(1)(B) & (f)(1).

8. FED. R. CIV. P. 30(a)(2)(A)(iii).

deposition.[9] By the same token, depositions can only be used against parties who had notice of their taking.[10]

1.4   Priority

The concept of priority—that the party first noticing the taking of deposition has a right to complete the taking of that deposition before the opponent may take a deposition—has been abolished under the Federal Rules of Civil Procedure. Now no such priority exists in discovery, and either party may notice and take a deposition even though a previously noticed deposition has not been completed.[11]

1.5   Scheduling the Deposition

As a matter of convenience and courtesy, most depositions are scheduled by agreement among the parties. By cooperating, you can avoid conflicts in both the lawyer's and the witnesses' schedules, and you can avoid the expense of motions to reschedule the time for the deposition. Several courts, by local rules, require that before noticing a deposition, the parties must attempt to arrive at a mutually agreeable date, and many courts further require that no deposition can be scheduled when the party noticing the deposition is on notice that opposing counsel is unavailable. Absent agreement, the date set in the notice of deposition will control, unless a witness or a party objects and moves for a protective order rescheduling the deposition.[12]

A party may object to the deposition date or time by moving for a protective order and requesting the court to specify a different time.[13] A nonparty may also timely move to quash a subpoena if it "fails to allow reasonable time for compliance."[14] The motion is brought in the court issuing the subpoena (which must of course be a court that has personal jurisdiction over the intended deponent, since nonparties are not automatically subject to the jurisdiction of the forum court).[15]

---

9. FED. R. CIV. P. 32(a)(5)(B).

10. FED. R. CIV. P. 26(a)(1)(A).

11. FED. R. CIV. P. 26(d)(2)(b).

12. FED. R. CIV. P. 26(c)(1)(B). *See* chapter twelve.

13. *Id.* Rule 32(a) states that a deposition my not be used against a party who, having received less than fourteen days' notice of the deposition, has promptly filed a motion for a protective order under FED. R. CIV. P. 26(c)(1)(B) and the motion is pending at the time the deposition is held.

14. FED. R. CIV. P. 45(c)(3)(A)(i). *See also* FED. R. CIV. P. 45(c)(1) (providing for the award of costs and other relief for imposing undue burden and expense on a subpoenaed witness).

15. *Id.*

1.6   Giving Notice of the Deposition

Rule 30(b)(1) requires that the party intending to take a deposition must give written notice of the deposition to all other parties to the action. The notice must state the following: the time and place for taking the deposition; the name and address of each person to be examined if known or, if not known, a general description sufficient to identify the witness or the particular class to which the witness belongs. Further, if a subpoena duces tecum (that is, a subpoena requiring the responding person to bring stuff with her to the deposition) is to be served on the witness, the notice must include or attach a list of the materials that are to be produced at the deposition.[16] The notice of deposition may list more than one witness to be examined. Finally, Rule 30(b)(3)(A) requires that the notice state the method by which the testimony is to be recorded: stenographic, video, or audio, or by some other means that the parties have stipulated may be used. The notice for a 30(b)(6) is discussed in the chapter on that rule. Examples of a notice of deposition and of a 30(b)(6) notice of deposition are contained in Appendix B.

1.6.1   Time Requirements for Giving Notice

Rule 30(b)(1) does not require the notice to be sent a specific number of days before a deposition. Indeed, all that is required is "reasonable notice."[17] What constitutes sufficient notice depends on the circumstances of each case, but you should always check local court rules to see if they provide for a minimum number of days for notice. In the past, courts have upheld notices ranging from one day and up, but fourteen days' notice should always be safe.

1.6.2   Providing Notice of Deposition

The party taking the deposition must give notice of the deposition to every party to the action.[18] The notice must be provided to a represented party's attorney or to the party if the party is proceeding pro se. Notice may be accomplished either by personal service on the attorney or party or by first-class mail addressed to the attorney's or party's current or last-known address, or, more by custom than rule, by any other means which is reasonably intended to actually notify them, including the methods provided for formal service under the federal rules.[19]

---

16. FED. R. CIV. P. 30(b)(2).

17. FED. R. CIV. P. 32(a)(5)(A) states that a deposition shall not be used against a party who received less than fourteen days' notice of the deposition and who promptly moved for a protective order under FED. R. CIV. P. 26(c)(1)(B), if the motion was still pending at the time designated for the deposition.

18. FED R. CIV. P. 30(b)(1).

19. FED. R. CIV. P. 5. In attempting to integrate FED. R. CIV. P. 5 and 30(b)(1), relating to service, filing, and notice, we can see the efforts by the drafters to preserve the courts from

1.7 Geographic Location of the Deposition

A deposition may be taken at any location on which the parties and the witness agree. If no agreement can be reached, the geographic location depends to a large extent on whether the witness is a party or nonparty.

1.7.1 Parties

Absent other controlling rules, the deposition of a party may be scheduled for any location, subject to the court's power under Rule 26(c)(1)(B) to grant a protective order designating a different place. The burden to apply for relief is on the person wishing to change the location from that given in the notice of deposition, but the courts appear to have developed some general rules governing where depositions can be taken. In addition, several federal courts have adopted local court rules governing the place of taking of depositions.

1.7.2 Plaintiffs

A defendant may take the deposition of a plaintiff in the geographic area where the plaintiff resides, is employed, or filed the lawsuit. Corporations or organizations are generally deposed at their principal place of business. The courts have found many exceptions to this rule, and they tend to look at the realities of the situation, such as relative financial burdens on any of the parties.

1.7.3 Defendants

A plaintiff usually must depose a defendant in the geographic area of the defendant's residence or employment. Corporations and organizations must generally be deposed within the district containing their principal place of business. Again, courts usually do not enforce this general rule when to do so would result in an injustice or undue financial hardship.

---

being inundated by the filing of discovery documents: depositions, interrogatories, requests for documents and admissions, and requests for entry upon property do not need to be filed; deposition notices are "given" to the opposing party, rather than served on them. Some practitioners do "serve" notices without filing them, but if the notices are treated as part of the deposition, such service is not required by these rules. Although there is no clear statement in the rules that deposition notices are *not* filed with the court, that is certainly the common practice, and, in many courts, the local rule. *See, e.g.,* the pertinent parts of well-written Rule 26.6(a) of the District Court of Massachusetts:

> **Nonfiling of Discovery Materials.** Automatic or voluntary disclosure materials, depositions upon oral examinations and notices thereof, depositions upon written questions, interrogatories, requests for documents, requests for admissions, answers and responses thereto, and any other requests for or products of the discovery process shall not be filed unless so ordered by the court or for use in the proceeding.

1.7.4 *Corporations*

Corporate or organizational officers, directors, or managing agents usually must be deposed either in the district of their principal place of business or where the individual witnesses live. Depositions of mere employees or agents are treated the same as the deposition of any nonparty witness: their depositions must occur within 100 miles of the place where the witness resides, is employed, or regularly transacts business in person.

1.7.5 *Nonparties*

The place of deposition for a nonparty is governed principally by Rule 45(c)(3)(A)(ii), which concerns subpoenas. That rule states that the target of a deposition subpoena may be required to attend only within 100 miles of the place where the person resides, is employed, or regularly transacts business. (The subpoena would issue from whatever federal district court exercises jurisdiction over that location.)

A deposing party may always arrange—with the consent of a witness or his counsel—to have a witness's deposition taken at some place other than where the witness can be subpoenaed. Many times, it may well be more efficient to agree to pay the witness's expenses to come to another location than for the parties' attorneys to journey to the witness. But where no such agreement is possible, Rule 45 dictates the location of the deposition.

1.8 Number of Depositions

The Federal Rules of Civil Procedure impose two separate and distinct limitations on the number depositions the parties may take in a case. First, Rule 30(a)(2)(A)(i) limits plaintiffs, defendants, and third-party defendants to ten depositions per side (including depositions on written questions) unless the parties have stipulated in writing to a different number or the court has given leave for a greater number. Note that the restriction is on the number of depositions per side, not per party. Therefore, a single plaintiff would be entitled to ten depositions, but three codefendants would have ten depositions to share among them. The discovery planning conference is usually the place where the parties discuss different limitations among themselves, since Rule 29 allows the parties to stipulate to different numbers of depositions if they can do so within the court's schedule for discovery. If the parties cannot agree on a stipulation, the discovery conference with the court under Rule 16(b) may provide an opportunity to alter the number of depositions.[20]

---

20. *See* section 4.1.

Rule 30(a)(2)(ii) establishes the second limitation and states, in effect, that a witness can only be deposed once absent a stipulation or court order. (However, a witness who has acted as a designee to provide testimony in a Rule 30(b)(6) deposition may be deposed in a "named deponent" deposition without violating this provision.)

1.9   Length of Depositions

Rule 30(d)(1) imposes a seven hour, one-day time limit for depositions. Note that under this limitation, the seven hours must occur on one day rather than be extended over two or more days. The court may, by order, impose a different limitation on a specific witness or on all the depositions in a case. The parties may also alter the time limits by written stipulation. (A statement of the stipulation included in the deposition record would be sufficient to satisfy this requirement of a "writing.") Only actual deposition time is counted and not the time necessary for reasonable breaks and lunch.[21] In a 30(b)(6) deposition,[22] each designated witness's testimony is counted as a separate deposition in calculating time, but the questioning in response to a single notice under 30(b)(6) counts as one deposition, regardless of the number of designees who appear, absent some adjustment made by the court.

Additional time may be allowed by the court if required to achieve fairness or if the deposition is impeded or delayed for any reason. Parties considering extending the time for a deposition—and courts asked to order an extension—might consider a variety of factors. The Advisory Committee Note to Rule 30 suggests some of the situations in which additional time might be permitted:

- if the witness needs an interpreter, that may prolong the examination. If the examination will cover events that occurred over a long period, that may justify additional time;

- in cases where the witness will be questioned about numerous or lengthy documents, it is often desirable for the interrogating party to send copies of the documents to the witness sufficiently in advance of the deposition for the witness to become familiar with them. Should the witness nevertheless not read the documents in advance, thereby prolonging the deposition, or spends an excessive amount of time reviewing the documents during the deposition, a court could consider that to be a reason for extending the deposition; giving the witness an advance view of the selected documents may be too great a cost to pay for this potential efficiency, however;

---

21. Fed R. Civ. P. 30, advisory committee's note.

22. *See* section 1.2 and chapter nineteen.

- if the examination reveals that documents have been requested but not produced, that may justify further examination once production has occurred;

- in multiparty cases, the need for each party to examine the witness may warrant additional time, although duplicative questioning should be avoided, and parties with similar interests should strive to designate one lawyer to question about areas of common interest;

- similarly, should the lawyer for the witness want to examine the witness, that may require additional time;

- finally, with regard to expert witnesses, there may more often be a need for additional time to allow full exploration of the opinions and methodologies that the expert is presenting, even after the submission of the report required by Rule 26(a)(2)—a stipulation would be a reasonable way to handle this situation.

1.10   Compelling the Witness's Attendance

The procedure for compelling a witness to attend the deposition depends on whether the witness is a party; an officer, a managing agent, or director of a party; or a nonparty.

1.10.1   *Parties and Officers, Managing Agents, and Directors of a Party*

Any party may require an individual party to appear at a deposition by merely serving a notice of deposition on the party-deponent and the other parties. Any party may also require an officer, director, or managing agent of a party to attend its deposition by serving a notice of deposition,[23] but the notice must name or adequately describe the witness and state that the witness is an officer, director, or managing agent.[24]

1.10.2   *Nonparties*

Absent an agreement to appear voluntarily, nonparty witnesses may be required to attend their depositions only if subpoenaed.[25] The subpoena, in addition to requiring the witness to appear, may also command the witness

---

23. FED. R. CIV. P. 37(d)(1)(A)(i).
24. El Salto, S.A. v. PSG Co., 444 F.2d 477 (9th Cir. 1971).
25. FED. R. CIV. P. 30(a)(1).

to produce designated documents and other evidence.[26] The subpoena must state the method for recording the testimony.[27]

ISSUANCE OF SUBPOENA

The subpoena commanding a witness to appear for a deposition must be issued from the court for the district where the deposition is to be taken.[28] Any attorney may sign and issue the subpoena if the subpoena is for an action pending in a court in which the attorney is authorized to practice, even if the deposition will take place in another district.[29] In other words, if the case was filed in the Northern District of Texas, a Northern District of Texas attorney may sign a subpoena directed to a deponent who is within the Northern District of Texas or within 100 miles of the court. If, in that same case, a deponent is located in the District of New Jersey, the Texas attorney may still sign the subpoena, which issues from the New Jersey district court (the court having personal jurisdiction over the deponent) if the Texas attorney is authorized to practice in the forum court in Texas. A subpoena from the Texas court could not "reach" the New Jersey deponent. Clerks of any U.S. district court have blank subpoenas available. While clerks of district courts may issue signed, blank subpoenas, there is no reason to resort to this more difficult procedure when attorneys themselves may sign and issue subpoenas. The attorney taking the deposition should fill in the name of the district in which the deposition is to be taken, as stated in the notice of deposition, as well as the other requested information, and sign the subpoena to complete issuance.[30]

Examples of a subpoena and of a subpoena duces tecum are contained in Appendix B.

SERVICE OF THE SUBPOENA

Anyone eighteen years of age or older and not a party to the action may serve the subpoena,[31] but the server must take reasonable steps to avoid imposing undue burden or expense on the witness.[32] Unlike the service of the notice of deposition or even the summons commencing the action, subpoenas cannot be served by mail—only personal service is acceptable. The server must deliver the subpoena to the witness and concurrently tender one day's witness fees and mileage allowance (unless the subpoena is issued on

---

26. FED. R. CIV. P. 45(a)(1)(iii).
27. FED. R. CIV. P. 45(a)(1)(B).
28. FED. R. CIV. P. 45(a)(3)(B).
29. FED. R. CIV. P. 45(a)(2) & (3).
30. FED. R. CIV. P. 45(a).
31. FED. R. CIV. P. 45(b)(1).
32. FED. R. CIV. P. 45(c)(1).

behalf of the United States or one of its officers or agencies).[33] The witness fee in effect at the time of this writing is $40.00 per day, and the time period includes the time necessary for going to and from the place of the deposition.[34] If the witness travels by common carrier, then the most economical rate reasonably available must be paid as long as the method used was reasonable and the shortest practical route was followed.[35] If the witness travels by private car, the General Services Administration mileage rates (currently at $0.51 per mile) should be used.[36] The clerks of the U.S. district courts usually have information about current rates.

When serving a corporation or organization with a subpoena—for a Rule 30(b)(6) deposition, for instance—the server should leave the subpoena with an officer or a managing or general agent to ensure that the corporation receives actual notice.[37]

Following service, the party responsible should file a proof of service with the clerk of the district court, but in practice this is not often done unless a witness has failed to appear for the deposition and contempt proceedings are being brought. The proof of service should state the name of the person served, the date, and the manner of service, and should be signed by the person who made the service.

GEOGRAPHIC LIMITATIONS ON SERVICE

A deposition subpoena may only be served within the district of the court from which the subpoena has issued, 100 miles of the place of the deposition, or the state where the deposition is to occur if the state has a statute or court rule authorizing such service. The court may also authorize extended service of the subpoena if a federal statute so permits.[38]

1.11   Requiring Documents to Be Brought to the Deposition

Generally, you will want to have documents or other tangible evidence produced prior to a deposition so you can be completely familiar with the material before having to question about it. Rule 34 (for parties) and Rule 45 (for nonparties) establish the procedure for requiring the production of tangible evidence. The mechanics of these rules, as applied to the production of evidence outside a deposition, are beyond the scope of this discussion, but sometimes, because time is short or production will occur some geographic

---

33. FED. R. CIV. P. 45(b)(1).
34. 28 U.S.C. 1821(b).
35. 28 U.S.C. 1821(c)(1).
36. 28 U.S.C. 1821(c)(2).
37. *See* MOORE'S FEDERAL PRACTICE 44.21.
38. FED. R. CIV. P. 45(b)(2).

distance away, you will want to schedule the production as part of the deposition.

1.11.1 Parties

You can arrange the production of documents and other tangible evidence by a party witness at a deposition by agreement of the parties or by serving a request to produce pursuant to Rule 34. While some confusion exists about the issue, Rule 30(b)(2)[39] suggests that a request to produce is the exclusive mean of requiring the production of evidence by a party at a deposition. The request must be served on every party to the action and is usually served with the notice of the deposition.[40]

1.11.2 Nonparty Witnesses

You may require a nonparty deposition witness to produce documents and other tangible evidence at a deposition by using a subpoena duces tecum provided for by Rule 45(a)(1)(C) & (D). While a subpoena duces tecum can be issued and served separately from a subpoena ad testificandum issued for the taking of a deposition, the subpoena commanding the witness to appear at a deposition may also command the witness to bring and produce documents and other tangible items of evidence for inspection.[41]

The procedure for issuing a subpoena duces tecum is the same as that given above for the issuance of a subpoena ad testificandum, but the notice of deposition will be different. When a subpoena duces tecum has been served on a witness, you must attach to or include in the notice a designation of the materials to be produced as set forth in the subpoena.[42] The easiest and most convenient method of doing this is to refer to the subpoena duces tecum in the notice of deposition and attach a copy of the subpoena to the notice, which is then served on the other parties to the action.

1.12 Scope of Discovery during the Deposition

The scope of what can be discovered through a deposition is very broad:

> Parties may obtain discovery regarding any nonprivileged matter that is relevant to any party's claim or defense—including the existence, description, nature, custody, condition, and location of documents or other tangible things and the identity and

---

39. "The notice to a party deponent may be accompanied by a request under Rule 34 to produce documents and tangible things at the deposition."
40. *Id.*
41. FED. R. CIV. P. 45(a)(1)(C).
42. FED. R. CIV. P. 30(b)(2).

location of persons who know of any discoverable matter . . . .
Relevant information need not be admissible at the trial if the
discovery appears reasonably calculated to lead to the discovery
of admissible evidence.[43]

The Federal Rules of Civil Procedure do not define relevance, but the
term is defined in Federal Rule of Evidence 401, which states that evidence
is relevant if "it has any tendency to make a fact more or less probable than it
would be without the evidence" and "the fact is of consequence in determining the action." Defining the exact scope of what is relevant requires examining the pleadings in the case to determine the specific claims and defenses
alleged there and asking whether the information being sought relates in
some way to the court's resolution of the issues raised by these claims and
defenses (including matters affecting the credibility of potential witnesses).
The particular fact being sought through discovery does not itself have to
be alleged in the pleadings, but the fact must have some relationship to the
claims and defenses that were raised. In considering what is relevant, one
must also look at the substantive law concerning the claim or defense being
alleged.

The information being sought does not always directly relate to a party's
claim or defense. For example, evidence relating to impeachment of a likely
witness or information about similar happenings, organizational arrangements, or the filing system of a party is normally discoverable under the
current standard. Determining what is relevant requires looking at the particular circumstances of each case.[44]

There should be very few instances when a party needs discovery of information that is not relevant to a party's claim or defense. When this does
occur the court has the power, on a showing of good cause, to expand the
scope of discovery to "any matter relevant to the subject matter involved in
the action."[45] The exact dividing line between evidence that is relevant to a
claim or defense and that which is relevant to the subject matter of the action
is hazy at best.

---

43. FED. R. CIV. P. 26(b)(1). While the scope of discovery—relevance to a party's claim or
defense—is broad, it is actually a curtailment of what was previously permitted. The Federal
Rules, up to the adoption of the 2000 amendments, defined the scope of discovery as
relevance to the "subject matter involved in the pending action." Under the current version
of Rule 26(b)(1), the court may still permit discovery under the previous standard, but only
on a showing of good cause. The 2000 amendment was designed to curtail expensive and
broad-ranging discovery inquiries, but it appears to have had little actual effect on what the
courts are permitting.
44. FED. R. CIV. P. 26, advisory committee's note.
45. FED. R. CIV. P. 26(b)(1).

Even though the information being sought is relevant to the claim or defense of a party, the court may nevertheless limit discovery because 1) it is unreasonably cumulative or duplicative, or it can be obtained from some other source that is more convenient, less burdensome, or less expensive; 2) the party seeking the discovery has had ample opportunity through other discovery in the action to obtain the information sought; or 3) the burden or expense of the proposed discovery outweighs its likely benefit, taking into account the needs of the case, the amount in controversy, the parties' resources, the importance of the issue at stake in the litigation, and the importance of the proposed discovery in resolving the issues.[46] In short, the court may impose limits on discovery if what is being proposed is unreasonable.

1.13   The Deposition Itself

1.13.1   *Before Whom May the Deposition Be Taken?*

Depositions conducted in the United States and its territories and insular possessions may be taken before any person authorized to administer oaths either by the laws of the United States or of the place in which the action is pending or before a person appointed by the court in which the action is pending.[47] In practice, the deposition is taken before a court reporter, who is also a notary public. Although the rules permit the deposition officer and the person recording the testimony to be two different persons, the stenographer and notary are normally one person. The exception is video depositions, where the officer and the videographer are two separate individuals. The parties may stipulate to having the deposition taken before a non-notary or someone who, for instance, is an employee of one of the lawyers.[48] In other words, if the reporter does not show up for a deposition, the parties could agree that a secretary in the office could take the deposition in shorthand. Special rules, contained in Rule 28(b), govern the taking of depositions in foreign countries.

1.13.2   *Recording the Deposition*

Under Rule 30(b)(3)(A), the party noticing the deposition may choose the method of recording the testimony—normally sound, sound-and-visual, or stenographic (i.e., audiotape, videotape, and stenographic). The party taking the deposition must state the method of recording in the notice of deposition and must bear the expense of the recording. A party may also arrange

---

46. FED. R. CIV. P. 26(b)(2).

47. FED. R. CIV. P. 28(a).

48. FED. R. CIV. P. 28(a) and 29.

for a non-stenographic deposition to be transcribed. Any other party, at its own expense and after giving notice to the witness and other parties, may designate another method of recording in addition to the method given in the notice of deposition.[49] While the party noticing the deposition is free to choose any method of recording the deposition, Rule 32(c) requires that in a jury trial, the presentation of deposition testimony be by videotape or audiotape, where available and when requested by any party, unless the use is solely for impeachment. That is, if a party takes a non-stenographic deposition, that party must be prepared to present that deposition to a jury in transcript form.

The recording is usually done by the deposition officer, who is a notary public, but the rules permit it to be done by someone acting under the officer's direction and in the officer's presence.[50] Of course, as noted above, the parties can stipulate otherwise.

1.13.3   Conducting the Deposition

The rules governing the questioning, objecting, and answering at depositions are relatively few. Under Rule 30(b)(5), the deposition officer must begin the deposition with a statement on the record that gives 1) the officer's name and business address; 2) the date, time, and place of the deposition; 3) the name of the witness; and 4) the names and identification of all persons present. The deposition officer must also swear the witness on the record. In a non-stenographic deposition, the officer must recite the first three items at the beginning of each recorded unit.[51] At the end of the deposition, the officer must state on the record that the deposition is complete and must also recite any stipulations between counsel concerning the custody of the transcript or recording and of the exhibits, or about any other pertinent matters.[52] Video-recorded depositions have some further requirements that are discussed in chapter eighteen.

Examination and cross-examination may proceed as they would at trial as provided by the Federal Rules of Evidence.[53] (Of course, the first examiner at a discovery deposition is normally the opposing party, so one does not normally think of that examination as "direct"; and the examination that follows, usually by the attorney who will present the witness at trial, is not actually a "cross" examination. Some attorneys call these two examinations "the deposition" and the "follow-on examination.") Under Rule 30(c)(1), other

---

49. Fed. R. Civ. P. 30(b)(3)(B).

50. Fed. R. Civ. P. 30(c)(1).

51. Fed. R. Civ. P. 30(b)(5)(B).

52. Fed. R. Civ. P. 30(b)(5)(C).

53. Fed. R. Civ. P. 30(c)(1). The Federal Rules of Evidence apply with the exception of Rules 103 (rulings on evidence) and 615 (exclusion of witnesses). *See* Fed. R. Evid. 6.

witnesses cannot be excluded from the deposition room without first obtaining a stipulation or a protective order under Rule 26(c)(1)(e). All objections made at the deposition to the qualifications of the officer taking the deposition, the manner of taking it, the evidence presented, the conduct of the deposition, or any other objection to any aspect of the proceedings are to be noted by the officer on the deposition record, but the deposition will proceed with the testimony being taken "subject to any objections," that is questions and answers continue unless the witness is directed or advised not to answer a question to preserve a privilege or someone suspends the deposition to seek an order from the court concerning objectionable questioning or conduct.[54]

Rule 30(c)(2) requires that any objection to evidence made during the deposition be stated concisely and in a nonargumentative and nonsuggestive manner. Thus, for example, the classic objection, "You can answer, if you know," is made explicitly impermissible. Further, you can instruct a witness not to answer a question only when necessary to preserve a privilege, to enforce a previous court order limiting examination ("counsel may ask the witness about liability, but not damages"), or to seek an order limiting or terminating the deposition.[55]

Any documents or other exhibits produced during the deposition are to be marked for identification and annexed to the deposition if any party requests it. Copies may be substituted for the originals if requested, as long as copies are provided and the parties have an opportunity to compare the copies with the originals. The copies will thereafter serve as the originals. The court has the power to require the originals to be attached if there is reason for doing so.[56] Note that in modern practice, documents may be exchanged and stored electronically, and electronic versions of documents can and often are used during the course of the deposition. Of course, under Federal Rule of Evidence 1003, a duplicate is as admissible as the actual original item for nearly all purposes.

For reasons of economy, one or more of the parties may choose not to attend the deposition, but instead to serve written questions in a sealed envelope to the party taking the deposition. The party taking the deposition is required to transmit the questions to the officer conducting the deposition, who must ask those questions to the witness and record the answers verbatim.[57] As a tactical matter, such an approach is ordinarily used only when the witness is willing to cooperate with the party submitting the questions and those questions and the answers may be considered in advance.

---

54. FED. R. CIV. P. 30(c)(2).
55. *Id.*
56. FED. R. CIV. P. 30(f)(2).
57. FED. R. CIV. P. 30(c)(3).

A related procedure involves taking the entire deposition by written questions. The procedures are set forth in Rule 31 and are usually used when the witness is distant but is willing to cooperate, or the matters on which examination is to occur are routine, such as authenticating a document.

The parties may also agree, by a stipulation in writing or by a court order, that the deposition be taken by telephone or other remote means such as satellite television.[58] However, you should generally make use of a telephone deposition only when you do not think it necessary to observe the witness's demeanor and the cost of attending the deposition is relatively high. When a deposition is taken by telephone, the reporter must be located where the witness is located to verify that the answers are those of the witness.

1.13.4   Stipulations

The Federal Rules of Civil Procedure permit the parties to stipulate in writing that a deposition may be taken before any person, at any time or place, on any notice, and in the manner specified; and when so taken, that deposition may be used like any other deposition.[59] The parties may also stipulate to other procedures governing or limiting discovery, but a stipulation extending the time for any form of discovery beyond the time set for completing discovery must have a hearing or court approval. As a practical matter, the parties, if on working terms, will stipulate to many issues that arise concerning deposition problems, rather than repeatedly petitioning the court for some form of relief or protective order. In general, it is recommended that lengthy and complex stipulations be avoided (e.g., those concerning the objections that must or may be made) because of the possibility of confusion or ambiguity. The parties could instead recognize that the deposition is taken under the Federal Rules of Civil Procedure and take up stipulations on an ad hoc basis.[60]

1.13.5   Post-Deposition Requirements

Following the conclusion of the deposition, the deposition officer and the parties have several further obligations:

1. Under Rule 30(e)(1), the opportunity to review, correct, and sign the deposition transcript must be requested by the witness or a party before completion of the deposition, or else those options are waived. Once the request is made and the transcript is available, the witness has thirty days to review the deposition. Some

---

58. FED. R. CIV. P. 30(b)(4).

59. FED. R. CIV. P. 29.

60. *See* section 6.1.

states provide that the witness automatically has the opportunity to review, correct, and sign unless the parties and the witness waive that opportunity (which was the approach under previous versions of the Federal Rules of Civil Procedure). It is recommended that no party waive the opportunity to read and correct; the witness should know what binds him, and the parties should know what they have to meet at trial.[61]

2. The witness then has thirty days to make any changes in the form and substance of the deposition and to provide a signed statement of the reasons for the changes.[62]

3. Under the Federal Rules, the witness is only required to sign a statement containing any corrections to the transcript and the reasons for the changes. If no corrections are made, the witness is not required to sign anything.[63] Many states require the witness to sign the transcript regardless of any corrections unless the parties have waived signing or the witness is ill, cannot be found, or refuses to sign. In these states, if the deposition is not signed within thirty days of being given to the witness, the deposition officer will sign it and include a statement of the reasons for the failure to sign. If the witness gives a reason for refusing to sign, this must be stated as well.

4. The deposition officer must certify that the witness was duly sworn by the officer and that the deposition accurately reflects the witness's testimony.[64] Under Rule 30(e)(2), the certificate should also state whether a witness or one of the parties requested the witness to review the deposition; if so, the officer must attach any changes made by the witness to the questions or answers.

5. Unless otherwise ordered by the court, the deposition officer must seal the deposition in an envelope or package bearing the title of the action and mark it with the statement, "Deposition of [witness's name]," and promptly send it to the attorney who arranged for the transcript or recording, normally the deposing attorney. The attorney is then required to safely store the deposi-

---

61. FED. R. CIV. P. 30(e).

62. *Id.*

63. FED. R. CIV. P. 30(e)(1)(B): "if there are changes in form or substance, to sign a statement . . . ."

64. FED. R. CIV. P. 30(f)(1).

tion and protect it from loss, destruction, tampering, or deterioration.[65]

6. Under Rule 30(f)(3) the officer must retain a copy of the recording of a videotape or audiotape deposition or the notes of a stenographic deposition.

7. Depositions are not filed with the court unless used in the proceeding or the court so orders.[66] If filed for one of these reasons, the party doing so must promptly notify all other parties of the filing.[67]

8. When paid a reasonable charge, the officer is to furnish copies of the deposition to any party requesting one.[68]

---

65. *Id.*
66. FED. R. CIV. P. 5(d)(1).
67. FED. R. CIV. P. 30(f)(4).
68. FED. R. CIV. P. 30(f)(3).

PART TWO: TAKING DEPOSITIONS

Chapter Two

Purposes of Taking Depositions

Efforts and courage are not enough without purpose and direction.

—John F. Kennedy

Each side in a typical case has a number of discovery devices available: interrogatories, document subpoenas, requests for admission, requests for production, orders for physical and mental examination, informal (nonjudicial) investigations, and, of course, depositions. Depositions are the most effective of these for learning what a witness or party has to say about the facts of the case and the theories and approaches an opponent is entertaining. The opportunities provided by depositions—to follow up, to probe, and to challenge—and their ability to be used with any witness, not just parties, account for their effectiveness and popularity.[1]

Depositions can be taken for many, often overlapping, purposes. Broadly speaking, the three primary reasons to take depositions are:

1. to gather information;

2. to perpetuate testimony; and

3. to facilitate settlement.

While these purposes are not mutually exclusive, knowing the reasons or objectives for taking the deposition allows you to organize and phrase your questions in a way that maximizes your effectiveness.

2.1 Gathering Information

The most common reason for taking a deposition is to gather information. Depositions allow you to inquire into what is going on in the case, what are the facts, how the events occurred, what the other side knows, what

---

1. *See* chapter three for a discussion of the advantages and disadvantages of depositions.

information supports your version of events, what the weaknesses are in your own case, where the flaws exist in the opponent's case, what other witnesses might have useful information, and so on. In addition to gathering facts, the deposition provides information about the demeanor and likely effectiveness of witnesses at trial or some other case-dispositive proceeding. In short, the deposition is being taken for the purpose of discovery. Several different reasons exist for gathering information in a case, as is discussed below.

2.1.1　*Finding Out What You Don't Know*

One of the most important reasons for taking a deposition is to learn new information about the case. Typically, what your client and any friendly witnesses have to say about what happened will be known through informal fact gathering, but there will still be many blank spots in the facts of the case. Like a nineteenth century explorer deciding on a route by looking at a map of Africa and seeing the many vacant areas on the map, the deposing counsel seeks to fill in the gaps in the facts left by clients and friendly witnesses. Often the only ones who can fill in those blank spots are witnesses who won't cooperate or the opposing party who, of course, cannot be interviewed without permission of that party's attorney. Where was the plaintiff going before the collision with your party's car? What happened at the meeting where your client claims the defendants fixed prices? And so on. With the African explorer, the only way of filling in the blank areas is to go and look. With litigation, the most effective method of filling in those blanks (together with discovery of documents) is taking the depositions of witnesses to find out what they have to say about the facts of the case.

2.1.2　*Confirming What You Think You Know*

A second purpose for taking depositions is to try to confirm what is believed to be already known. Often, based on documents and information from clients and friendly witnesses, the attorney believes she know the facts of the case. The version of the facts from clients, friendly witnesses, and their documents is not necessarily replicated by opposing parties, their friendly witnesses, and their documents. If the opposing parties and witnesses agree with your witnesses, then you have greater confidence that this will be an undisputed area at trial. Perhaps you can even reach a stipulation with the other side about these points. On the other hand, if the witnesses disagree, you will know this before trial when there is still an opportunity to marshal the proof in favor of your version of events or to adjust case theories and themes to the new or different view of the facts. The worst possible scenario is to discover for the first time at trial, when little can be done to meet the situation, that what was thought to be undisputed is actually hotly contested. Effective depositions avoid this problem.

2.1.3 *Testing Out Legal and Factual Theories*

One objective of the discovery process is to test out whether the necessary facts exist to support a particular legal theory. At the discovery stage of a case, each side will not only be trying to figure out what happened, but also will be attempting to develop a legal and factual theory for presenting the case to the court in the most persuasive light. Because the factual story is often incomplete at this stage, a party may be considering several different factual and legal theories. Only after discovery is complete can the attorney determine which version of the facts is most likely to be accepted as true and, in turn, what legal theory or theories can be supported by those facts.

Every legal theory depends on the existence of certain key facts as well as a host of supporting ones. In the information-gathering aspect of discovery, you are seeking to elicit facts that support a favorable legal theory or theories. If a particular legal theory is not supported by the facts, you may need to abandon that theory and pursue another theory. Let's take a typical car accident personal injury case where the plaintiff claims that a collision—and the plaintiff's resulting injuries—were caused by the defendant driving at an unsafe rate of speed and failing to keep a proper lookout. The plaintiff's factual theory is that the defendant was speeding and not paying attention to the road just prior to the accident.

During discovery, each side will not only seek admissions and opposing party statements[2] that support its own legal and factual theories, but will also try to find weaknesses and flaws in the opponent's theory. The plaintiff will try to gain whatever evidence it can of the defendant's speeding and failing to pay attention to the road, as well as gain party statements (admissions) to weaken the defendant's defenses to the plaintiff's case. The defendant will do the exact opposite. For instance, the plaintiff may find out that the

---

2. In 2011, the Federal Rules of Evidence were restyled to reflect the "clear and consistent style conventions" adopted for all the federal rules (*see* Report of the Advisory Committee on Evidence Rules, at 2/480 (May 6, 2009)). The Committee clearly stated that these style changes did not constitute substantive changes. Nevertheless, the new language presents opportunities for confusion with which the authors must deal.

Specifically, FED. R. EVID. 801(d)(2), formerly entitled "Admission by party-opponent" is now entitled "An Opposing Party's Statement," but it retains its substantive purpose of defining the opposition's statements, in any context, as nonhearsay. Formerly, confusion often arose when lawyers spoke of "admissions against interest," conflating "party admissions" with "statements against interest" (a hearsay exception applying to absent witnesses who were not parties—if they were parties, it would not matter if the statement was "against interest"). Now, the confusion has been turned upside down—the word "statement" replaces "admission," but it is echoed in Rule 804's "statements against interest."

To recognize the attempt to create consistency in language style, we have chosen to label what were previously called "party admissions" as "party statements" in this new edition. Please understand that this phrase still relates to out-of-court statements, offered for their truth, made by the party, which the party can therefore not logically challenge as untrustworthy (and therefore inadmissible) because they themselves said it.

defendant was not looking at the traffic in front of the vehicle at the time of the accident and had not looked at it for the last half-block before the collision, but might also find out that the defendant was driving at the legal speed limit. From this information, the plaintiff is able to support one legal and factual theory (failing to keep a proper lookout) through a party statement, but is not able to support another (proceeding at an unsafe rate of speed). Based on this information, the plaintiff may choose to abandon the unsafe rate of speed theory and proceed only on the failing to keep a proper lookout theory. Similarly, the plaintiff will have learned which questions during cross-examination at trial will successfully support a chosen legal and factual theory and which will not.

Not only will a party test out the possible legal and factual theories to be presented at trial, but it will also look for support for bringing or defending a case-dispositive motion, such as for summary judgment. For example, in a breach of contract action the defendant may take the plaintiff's deposition seeking a party statement that the plaintiff had failed to exercise a right of first refusal in a timely manner. Similarly, the plaintiff may take the defendant's deposition in hopes of getting a party statement that the right of first refusal was in fact exercised properly. If the plaintiff is successful in getting this party statement and the defendant cannot offer any contradictory evidence on this point, the party statement can be used to support the defendant's request for summary judgment.

It may turn out, after discovery is completed, that certain key facts do not exist to support any of the plaintiff's potential theories or to weaken the defendant's theories. If that is the case, and no alternative theory remains viable, the plaintiff may have to dismiss the action or settle on the best terms available.

2.1.4   *Preparing for Trial*

Using depositions to test legal and factual theories at the same time provides the predicate for trial testimony. One of the cardinal rules of almost all cross-examination is never to ask a question to which you do not know the answer. Depositions are where those answers are found. Answers during the deposition that were favorable to your legal and factual theory point to safe areas of inquiry on cross-examination at trial. If the witness changes his answer at trial from what was given in the deposition, then the deposition is available for impeachment. On the other hand, if the answer to a deposition question was unfavorable, do not ask that question at trial.

Another rule of cross-examination is to ask only questions that ask for facts and do not contain characterizations or subjective terms. For instance, most trial lawyers would not ask a question on cross-examination of the opposing party such as, "Just before the accident, were you going very fast?" (unless it can be followed up with questions showing how fast the opponent was going). The honest answer to such a question can be "No" if the witness believes the car was going fast, but not "very" fast, or does not believe the car was going fast even though traveling well over the speed limit. But depositions are safe places to ask such questions. If the witness agrees with the characterization during the deposition, then that characterization can be the subject of trial questioning. Even if the witness does not agree with the characterization during the deposition, you can elicit facts supporting the characterization to in turn support a jury argument to that effect at the conclusion of the trial. Thus, at deposition you can ask the question, "Why don't you think you were going too fast?," get a response, and then inquire into the bases for the witness's characterization. Those bases may turn out to be illogical, or otherwise subject to attack, or patently incredible, and you can fashion a trial cross-examination to demonstrate just that.

In short, depositions are the time to try out possible story lines that both direct and cross-examination could create. Successful story lines become part of the trial theory of the case. Unsuccessful story lines will be dropped from the trial case theory, but may in fact provide insight as to what the opponent's trial theory will likely prove to be. For this reason, many trial lawyers prepare their cross-examinations from the depositions in the case, and most of them at least start their preparation with the depositions and then move to other sources for their questions. At a minimum, deposition testimony will serve as a means to lock in the testimony of witnesses so that deposition testimony that is inconsistent with trial testimony can be admitted as impeachment by prior inconsistent statement pursuant to Federal Rule of Evidence 613 and as substantive evidence pursuant to Rule 801(d)(1)(A).

2.2   Preserving Testimony

For a long time, the authors have observed how the information obtained in depositions is used has changed, even since the publication of our first edition in the 1980s. The pressure on judges, both federal and state, to clear their dockets of the hundreds or thousands of sentencing hearings required by drug cases has greatly reduced their time and patience to conduct extended civil trials. The use of pretrial procedures, especially summary judgment motions, to limit or dismiss cases has increased, and the fact today is that more than 97 percent of all filed cases are disposed of without full trial. In this edition, we intend to discuss, much more fully than in previous editions, the increased importance of depositions in supporting and opposing pretrial dispositions. How do depositions drive settlements? What is their role in summary judgment practice, and what effect does that use have on the defending attorney's decision on whether to ask his own questions at the deposition? If both sides reasonably anticipate settlement or other pre-trial resolution of the case, does that change the utility of video depositions? Questions such as these will come up in every portion of the book, and we will try to provide analysis and advice that is pertinent to modern practice.

In addition to gathering information, controlling witnesses, and supporting motions practice, depositions can be used to preserve testimony. The reasons to preserve testimony will be discussed in full below, but at the outset note that while the goals of information gathering and preserving testimony overlap to some extent, they may also conflict. For example, the purpose of deposing the witnesses for the opposing side is to prepare to attack their expected testimony at trial, not to preserve what is likely to be harmful testimony. Nonetheless, taking the deposition of a harmful witness will have the effect of preserving that testimony, both good and bad, if the witness should later prove to be unavailable for trial. One of the more unpleasant experiences a trial lawyer may have is to have taken a thorough and complete deposition of an opponent's witness, only to have that deposition used at trial as the means of presenting the testimony of an unavailable witness pursuant to Federal Rule of Evidence 804(b)(1). Although that danger exists, a party is always better off having complete information regarding the possible testimony of a witness so that it can be anticipated and attacked, than not knowing it at all.

2.2.1   Locking in Testimony

Let's face it: not all witnesses are as fully respectful of the truth as we might wish. In fact, some are out-and-out liars, while others, to be charitable, merely have memory problems. Depositions provide a control mechanism over witnesses who deviate from their prior deposition testimony by providing a means of punishing them at trial through impeachment or by encouraging truthful recollection by using the deposition to refresh their memories. Depositions freeze the witness's story so that any deviations at trial are made at the witness's peril.

2.2.2   Substitute for Live Testimony

If a witness becomes "unavailable" for any reason—death, illness, being beyond the subpoena power of the court, forgetfulness, or by claiming a privilege—the Federal Rules of Civil Procedure[3] as well as Federal Rules of Evidence[4] permit the use of the witness's deposition testimony as a substitute for live testimony. Depositions become critically important when a witness is elderly, is in danger of disappearing prior to the trial, lives a great

---

3. FED. R. CIV. P. 32(a)(4).
4. FED. R. EVID. 804(b)(1).

distance from the court, or for any other reason may not be able to testify at trial. In addition, the deposition testimony of opposing parties, as well as the depositions of witnesses containing statements attributable to opposing parties, are admissible as substantive evidence when offered as a party statement,[5] for impeachment by a prior inconsistent statement,[6] or, in more limited circumstances, as a prior *consistent* statement.[7] While often not as persuasive (or interesting) as live testimony, deposition testimony, especially when presented by video, can be a useful substitute; additionally, admissible or admitted deposition designations may be used in opening statements and closing arguments.

2.2.3 Basis for Temporary Injunctive Relief and Motions

Litigants frequently use depositions to support applications for preliminary injunctions as well as case-dispositive motions, such as a motion for summary judgment. Used in this way, depositions substitute for affidavits or declarations, which are not easily obtained from adverse parties, witnesses associated with the adverse party, or hostile witnesses.

2.3 Facilitating Settlement

Depositions facilitate settlement in at least five ways: permitting evaluation of the witness and attorney, opening lines of communication, presenting information to the opposing side, obtaining information that your client wants to consider before attempting settlement, and punishing the witness.

2.3.1 Evaluating the Witness and Attorney

Face-to-face confrontation in a deposition permits each side to evaluate the witness being deposed and make judgments about the credibility of the witness and how the judge or jury will perceive the testimony. When the witness comes across as especially believable or unbelievable, it affects the settlement value of the case. In addition, each side will also make judgments about the abilities of opposing counsel that will influence the amount at which a case will settle.

2.3.2 Opening Lines of Communication

The deposition setting provides an opportunity for counsel to talk with each other. A deposition may be the first time the two sides have had the opportunity to talk seriously other than over the telephone. If serious

---

5. Fed. R. Evid. 801(d)(2)(A–E); Fed. R. Civ. P. 32(a)(3).

6. Fed. R. Evid. 801(d)(1)(A); Fed. R. Civ. P. 32(a)(2).

7. Fed. R. Evid. 801(d)(1)(B).

settlement discussions do occur at depositions of the principals in the case, the availability of the parties will sometimes facilitate a quick settlement.

2.3.3   *Presenting Information to the Opposing Side or the Court*

The deposition can also be a time to provide favorable information about your case to the other side with the hope of bringing about a favorable settlement. A competent deposition taker will often ferret out the same information by careful and thorough questioning, but not all deposition takers are competent. Witnesses in a deposition are usually instructed to answer only what the questions ask for and never to volunteer additional information, but sometimes there is information, not otherwise discovered, that the opposing party needs to know to reach an appropriate conclusion of the case. This is especially true where the likely resolution of the case, as in most cases, is a negotiated settlement.[8] The deponent's counsel might choose to bring out such information in his own questioning that follows the opponent's examination.

Because sworn deposition testimony, subject to cross-examination, is more credible than a declaration, counsel defending her deposition testimony may want to get certain information on the record so that it is available to support or oppose a motion for summary judgment or a motion to permit or limit an expert's testimony. The witness should be prepared to give such testimony when asked for by her own attorney and to provide more detailed responses to that questioning than she did in response to the opposition's questions. She must be warned, however, that it is her lawyer's decision to ask for expansive answers and not a freedom that the witness can grant herself.

2.3.4   *Punishing the Witness*

While by itself not an ethically permissible reason for taking a deposition, a potential result of rigorous cross-examination during a deposition is that a party or key witness will find the whole experience so distasteful and unpleasant that they encourage a settlement. The witness or party may simply say it is not worth going through the same experience again at trial and may persuade or instruct counsel to settle. By the same token, a deposition may end up consuming so much of a party's or witness's time that the further demands of preparation for trial and the trial itself may not be an acceptable cost. Again, punishing the witness is not ethically permitted as the primary purpose for taking a deposition,[9] but it is frequently a by-product of a deposition taken for other, legitimate reasons. In any event, a punish-

---

8. Several methods of providing favorable information to the other side are discussed in sections 13.2.6 and 14.10.

9. Fed. R. Civ. P. 11(b)(1).

ing deposition will nearly always communicate to an opposing party with decision-making authority on settlement and settlement amount the weaknesses of their position in the lawsuit. When confronted with the stark reality of negative facts accumulated in a persuasive manner, parties often become more amenable to a faster resolution of the case.

2.4   Objectives and Questioning Techniques

As will be discussed later in this text, the objectives of a deposition will determine, to a large extent, the questioning approach for a witness. Questioning to obtain party statements is different in form, tone, and structure than questioning pursued solely to obtain information the witness knows. When multiple objectives exist, the questioning may differ in various sections of the deposition, or it may be necessary to determine which objectives are more important and then adopt a questioning approach consistent with that determination. Obviously, then, a clear understanding of the purpose for which deposition testimony is sought is a necessary prerequisite to deposition planning.

CHAPTER THREE

ADVANTAGES AND DISADVANTAGES OF DEPOSITIONS

The world is ruled only by considerations of advantages.

—Friedrich von Schiller (1759–1805)

Depositions are the most powerful discovery device available to a litigator, but certainly not the only one. If you must choose one discovery approach, you should almost always choose the deposition, but just as a shovel is sometimes preferable to a hoe, other types of discovery may be better suited than a deposition for acquiring the necessary information in a particular situation. Before deciding to take a deposition, you must determine whether the deposition of a particular witness is the best discovery device, taking into consideration the case, the type of witness, and the type of information being sought. That decision proceeds from an understanding of the advantages and disadvantages of depositions.

3.1   Advantages

There are many advantages to using depositions as a discovery device.

3.1.1   *Unfiltered Information*

Depositions provide the unfiltered story from the opposing party (or witness) in the deponent's own words, without editorial input from opposing counsel. Since a represented party may not be contacted without the permission of the attorney representing the party,[1] information about what is in the party's mind is available only through depositions, interrogatories, and requests for production and for admission. With interrogatories, opposing counsel usually gets the necessary information from the client and edits the answers to provide the least amount of usable information that is still responsive to the question. The information provided by the opposing party to its

---

1. *See* ABA MODEL RULES OF PROFESSIONAL CONDUCT R. 4.2.

attorney and what is actually put down on the paper in response to the interrogatory often have scant resemblance to each other.

On the other hand, the witness alone answers at a deposition. Defending counsel may influence the answer by carefully (or improperly) preparing the witness beforehand and giving advice during the deposition, but to a large extent you will get the witness's own answers, minimally edited by opposing counsel.

3.1.2   *Opinions, Mental Impressions, and Subjective Information*

Depositions are ideal for eliciting a witness's opinions, mental impressions, and subjective information. Contrast this with interrogatories—the other major discovery device—where the answer is edited by a lawyer and follow-up questions (through a second set of interrogatories) are cumbersome at best. For example, consider a typical interrogatory and the answer that might be given:

> Interrogatory No. 22:   Please describe how the accident occurred.
>
> Answer: The defendant's automobile collided with the plaintiff's automobile.

Nor will it help to rephrase the interrogatory to state:

> Interrogatory No. 22:   Please describe *in detail* how the accident occurred.
>
> Answer: The defendant's automobile collided very hard with the plaintiff's automobile.

Such interrogatories will almost always draw less than useful responses. Opposing counsel will often edit any response to provide as little useful information as possible. Now compare this with a deposition:

> Q: Tell me how the accident occurred.
>
> A: Well, the other car hit me.
>
> Q: OK, let's back up. Where were you when you first saw the plaintiff's car?
>
> A: I was east of the intersection of Kirby and Mattis.
>
> Q: How far east?
>
> A: About fifty feet.

Q: What lane were you in?

A: The curb lane.

Q: How fast were you going?

A: About fifteen miles per hour.

Q: Why were you going so slow?

A: The light looked like it was about to change.

And so on.

Depositions are the only useful discovery device for obtaining spontaneous, interpretive information—such as how an incident occurred, the details of a conversation, or the recollection of an eyewitness. Such matters as mental impressions, emotional reactions, or anything to do with thought processes are best obtained through depositions, which provide the opportunity and tools to probe the witness's knowledge and memory.

3.1.3   Ability to Follow Up

When an answer to an interrogatory is evasive or does not provide the requested information, the only available options are accepting the response given, bringing a motion to compel, or drafting and sending a new interrogatory better crafted to obtain the information needed—an option that is severely limited because of the limitation in most jurisdictions on the number of interrogatories that may be posed.[2] Even worse, all the questions must be composed in advance. If the answers raise facts of interest, but are incomplete, the only real way of following up is with additional interrogatories, and the answers to those interrogatories are at least thirty days away (not counting any extensions of time you have agreed to or the court has granted).

Depositions, on the other hand, allow you to immediately follow up questions until the area of inquiry is exhausted. For instance, you can quickly examine evasive or nonresponsive answers and require the witness to answer:

Q: Where were you when this conversation was going on?

A: Do you mean at the beginning or end?

Q: Let's take both. Where were you at the beginning?

A: I was over by the door.

Q: Where were you at the end?

A: I was still by the door.

---

2. *See* Fed. R. Civ. P. 33(a) limiting the number of interrogatories to twenty-five.

> Q: Did you ever move away from the door during the conversation?
>
> A: No.
>
> Q: Who started the conversation?
>
> A: It just started.
>
> Q: Well, who said the first word?
>
> A: I did.

The ability to follow up is also important when a line of questions suggests new leads. Perhaps something about the manner in which the witness answers a question or the witness's expression while answering indicates there is more there than the answer alone suggests. For instance, if a witness pauses unusually long or starts the answer in a hesitating way, this often suggests the need for follow-up questions. Sometimes the phrasing of the answer will suggest a lead:

> Q: Did she say anything about the contract?
>
> A: Not at that time.
>
> Q: Was something said about the contract at another time?

Interrogatory responses rarely provide such hints, and when they do, follow-up is difficult, for the reasons noted above.

The ability to follow up on a witness's answers also allows you to attack or attempt to weaken harmful answers. It also allows you to structure questions in a manner designed to obtain party statements for use at trial or in a motion for summary judgment.[3]

> Q: You weren't paying attention to the car in front of you when you were approaching the light?
>
> A: That's not true. I certainly was paying attention.
>
> Q: Let's see. You told me a moment ago that you had seen a boy by the side of the road, correct?
>
> A: Yes.
>
> Q: You also told me that you were worried the boy was going to run out into the street, right?
>
> A: Yes.

---

3. *See* chapter sixteen.

Q: So you were keeping your eyes on the boy in case he ran out in front of your car, true?

A: I guess so.

Q: When you were watching the boy, you weren't watching the car in front of you, right?

A: Right.

Q: You told me that you noticed the car in front of you only a few moments before you ran into it?

A: Yes.

Q: And the reason you did not notice the car in front of you until just a few moments before you ran into it is because you were watching the boy?

A: OK.

Q: You weren't paying attention to the car in front of you because you were paying attention to the boy?

A: I guess so.

Q: Actually sir, it's a fact, and not a guess, that your concern for the boy caused you not to pay attention to the car in front of you.

In short, depositions provide flexibility, allowing you to adjust to whatever the answers might be and to pursue new lines of questioning as necessary.

3.1.4 Spontaneous Answers

Depositions provide the opportunity to obtain a witness's unrehearsed response without allowing a long period of time to reflect on the answer. Contrast this again with interrogatories, where a party and the party's attorney will have a minimum of thirty days to think about how to phrase the answer in the least damaging form. Of course, witnesses can rehearse answers to expected questions in a deposition, but the ability to attack a subject from several different angles means the witness will eventually have to answer spontaneously.

3.1.5   *Fast Moving*

Depositions can be scheduled on "reasonable notice" to the other side.[4] By contrast, interrogatories, the next most commonly used discovery device, need not be answered until a minimum of thirty days after service.[5] When information is needed quickly, depositions are the discovery method to use.

Speed is particularly important when it is necessary to record a witness's story while his memory is fresh and has not started to fade. For example, in a personal injury case the recollection of a nonparty witness is almost always most accurate when closer in time to the event as opposed to shortly before trial, several months or years later. Similarly, when witnesses are likely to become unavailable, depositions preserve their stories for later use at trial, in support of or opposition to a summary judgment motion, or in some form of alternative dispute resolution.

The fast-moving nature of depositions also becomes important when discovery deadlines are close at hand. The ability to schedule a deposition quickly may prove invaluable when you need information from a witness in time to incorporate that information into the case theory. Of course, informal investigation is available at all times, even prior to filing an action, but when quick action is needed, there is nothing faster than a deposition.

3.1.6   *Face-to-Face Confrontation*

Depositions are the only discovery device that allows counsel to meet the opposing party face to face. The same is true regarding those witnesses who refuse to respond to more informal fact investigation, such as interviews by counsel or by investigators. Face-to-face confrontation in a deposition has several advantages. First, it forces witnesses to tell their stories while under oath and while facing the opposing parties—or at least the parties' attorneys. A party theoretically is also under oath when answering interrogatories, but, in reality, the oath is frequently glossed over at the time of signing. Thus, while the answers can be formally attributed to the witness, impeachment at trial with interrogatory responses is often unsatisfactory and unpersuasive— the witness muddies the water with claims of not quite understanding the lawyer's language in the interrogatories and answers; of not being precisely certain of the purpose or significance of the interrogatories; and of thinking the oath merely meant the answers had been seen and read, not that there

---

4. Rule 30(b)(1) provides only for reasonable notice. What is reasonable will vary from jurisdiction to jurisdiction and from case to case (*see* section 1.6.1), but it is usually less than the thirty days provided for answering interrogatories. Under Rule 26(d) a party cannot seek discovery from any source until after the planning conference required by Rule 26(f), unless authorized by stipulation or court order, where special circumstances exist. *See* sections 1.3 and 4.1.

5. Fed. R. Civ. P. 33(b)(2).

was agreement with every word. Although this is a clear abrogation of a party's obligations in signing interrogatory answers as well as the obligations of counsel representing the party, the jury is likely to side with the lay witness, at least to the extent that they will not give much weight to the attempted impeachment. (Where counsel crafts the interrogatory answers to avoid disclosure, this is the intentional frustrating of discovery. Counsel may also be perpetrating a fraud on the court, since such answers are being submitted as the witness's answers, when in fact they are not.) In comparison, the circumstances of administering the oath and formal questioning at a deposition often will impress on a witness the importance of truthfulness.

Second, face-to-face confrontation allows you to evaluate the impression the witness will likely make at trial. Does the witness appear shifty and disingenuous or honest and forthright? Will a jury sympathize with the witness or perceive the witness as arrogant? These questions and more regarding the credibility of witnesses can be answered, at least preliminarily, by putting the witness through the rigors of a deposition.

Third, depositions allow you to develop a personal relationship with the witness. While usually not successful with a party, a nonparty witness may be "seduced" by the taking lawyer's charm and as a result, recount the story in an advantageous way; or the witness may be intimidated by a stern manner into backing off from harmful testimony. A stern manner during a deposition may cause a witness to be more cautious at trial, even under gentler questioning.

Fourth, depositions allow you to evaluate the abilities and behavior of opposing counsel. The attorney may be passive or aggressive, prepared or unprepared, articulate or bumbling, and so on. After the deposition, you have a better gauge of how opposing counsel will perform at trial.

Fifth, depositions allow you, as deposing counsel, to demonstrate your own trial prowess as evidenced by an incisive and penetrating examination, command of the deposition room, likeable personality and, of course, polished good looks. The evaluation of counsel is a two-way street and an opposing counsel will make an assessment about your likely impact on a judge or jury.

Finally, depositions provide an opportunity to discuss settlement when the opposing attorney and client are together. Many cases are settled following a deposition because it is the first time the attorneys have met face to face and have had the chance to evaluate the effectiveness of key witnesses.

3.1.7 *Information from Uncooperative Witnesses*

Outside of court or a deposition, nothing requires a witness to answer a lawyer's or an investigator's questions. In fact, a witness can refuse to say anything to either side. When a witness does refuse to cooperate, the only discovery device available to get that person's story is a deposition. In addition, only depositions and subpoenas for the production of books, documents, and things can be used with nonparty witnesses;[6] all of the other discovery devices—interrogatories, requests for admission, notices to produce—can be used only against a party.

3.1.8 *Generate Fewer Objections*

Depositions can be contentious, with the attorneys arguing with each other and seeking the judge's assistance to referee their disputes. Nonetheless, compared to interrogatories, depositions generate fewer objections, and when objections are made they do not stop the deposition. The simple fact is that answering interrogatories is one of the most frustrating, boring, and irritating tasks a lawyer is called on to perform. As a result, it is often much easier to object to an interrogatory than to answer it, if only because of the annoyance factor of the interrogatory. An objection avoids the need to answer to the extent the interrogatory is objectionable.[7] The attorney posing the interrogatory must then bring a motion to compel to obtain a ruling on the objection. But the motion to compel comes with the risk that if the judge finds the objection to be valid, the party bringing the motion may be assessed the objecting party's reasonable expenses in responding to the motion.[8]

On the other hand, it is comparatively easy to sit and listen to a witness answer questions. Boredom may be a factor, but rarely does there arise the intense desire to engage in the sophistry that is generated by interrogatories. Even if defending counsel objects at a deposition, the objections do not excuse the witness from answering. As a result, depositions usually generate far fewer objections and yield far more information than any other type of discovery.

3.2 Disadvantages

Despite the many advantages of depositions as a discovery device, several drawbacks must also be considered.

---

6. Fed. R. Civ. P. 45.

7. Fed. R. Civ. P. 33(b)(3).

8. Fed. R. Civ. P. 37(a)(5).

3.2.1   *Failures of Memory or Lack of Knowledge*

Sometimes witnesses cannot remember or never knew the facts about which you are asking. For instance, you ask the president of the Widget Corporation how many widgets were sold in 2010, and the truthful answer is, "I don't recall." While frustrating, there is not much that can be done other than to try to refresh the witness's memory in some way. There is no right to ask the witness to look up the information, although often a polite request to do so can achieve positive results. Even more frustrating is to ask the witness the same question and have the witness respond, "I don't know," or "I don't remember," but some other witness does.

Quite simply, if a witness honestly does not know the answer to a question or cannot remember the answer and nothing refreshes the witness's memory, there is nothing you can do. Furthermore, when asked for information that is numerical in nature, such as financial data, "I don't remember" is frequently the most likely truthful answer.

To a certain extent, you can avoid these problems by advance preparation. The documents containing the necessary information or those which can be used to refresh memory may be the subject of a request to produce or subpoena before the deposition. Another alternative is to schedule a Rule 30(b)(6) deposition, requiring the corporation or other organization to designate a witness who must be reasonably prepared to testify about particular, identified matters.[9]

It must be conceded that sometimes the best approach is not to take a deposition at all, but to send interrogatories requesting the desired information (assuming the information is being sought from an opposing party). Interrogatories reach both the files and memory of a party, as well as the collective memory of an institutional party, by requiring the party to take all reasonable steps to provide the requested information. "I don't remember" will not suffice if the party can find the information with a reasonable amount of work. Files must be checked, records examined, and other employees asked to provide the necessary information. A deposition cannot do this (unless it is a 30(b)(6) deposition). However, where a search of the files is the reasonable way to find the information that answers an interrogatory, the party receiving the interrogatories may shift the burden to conduct such a search to the inquiring party where the burden would be the same for either.[10] There is no such opportunity to shift the burden when a Rule 30(b)(6) deposition is used.

---

9. *See* section 1.2.
10. Fed. R. Civ. P. 33(d).

3.2.2   *Experience with Responding to Questioning*

All but the most experienced witnesses are anxious about cross-examination. Both counsel and witness always worry that the inexperienced witness may become flustered, confused, or appear nervous. Obviously, this may cause the jury not to believe them. But all of us improve with practice, and that is what a deposition allows a witness to do—improve with practice. When the day of trial arrives, the witness will be better prepared and more effective in responding to questions as a result of having undergone similar questioning at the witness's deposition.

3.2.3   *Helps Opponent Prepare Her Case*

All attorneys, at one time or another, have had the experience of taking a deposition of a witness and watching the defending attorney scribble down every answer the witness gives. The reason for this may be thoroughness or just compulsive note taking, a "skill" often learned in law school, but often the defending attorney had not previously interviewed the witness or had not interviewed the witness with the completeness of the deposition examination. The witness's answers are as new to the defending attorney as to deposing counsel, and as such, the deposition is helping the defending lawyer prepare her case as much as it is helping the taking lawyer.

Even when opposing counsel is more conscientious and has prepared the witness, it is often the scheduling of the deposition that forced the witness and the lawyer to prepare. Absent the deposition, this work may not have been done, or at least it might not have been done at such a beneficial juncture in the litigation.

3.2.4   *Expense*

Depositions cost money. The time of the court reporter and the preparation of transcripts are costs in the litigation. In addition, the time consumed in preparing and taking the deposition must be accounted for, either against the contingent fee or as billable hours. Interrogatories and informal investigation also take time, but out-of-pocket expenses are usually less.

Depositions become even more expensive when travel is involved. Non-party witnesses and defendants must normally be deposed close to their residence or place of business or employment. Plaintiffs are usually deposed where they filed the litigation or near their residence or place of business or employment.[11] When litigation is national in scope, the travel costs can be prohibitively high. Interrogatories, subpoenas, and requests for admission, on the other hand, can be sent electronically or by mail.

---

11. *See* section 1.7.

3.2.5   *Reveal Theories*

Deposition questions often reveal the legal and factual theories of the questioning attorney's case. For instance, if the defendant's questions in a breach of contract case concern the plaintiff's efforts to exercise an option under the contract, the plaintiff's attorney will be able to guess that this will be one of the defenses raised and will prepare the plaintiff's case accordingly. Perhaps revelation of theories is not a concern because everyone involved knows from the pleadings and the facts of the case what will be raised, but if you want to try to conceal a theory until trial, depositions on that theory may be contra-indicated. Of course, this tactic means that you will not discover the opposition's response to that theory, either; as a result, we do not particularly recommend it.

3.2.6   *Cannot Obtain Legal Theories*

If the plaintiff's attorney asks in a deposition if the defendant is claiming the plaintiff was contributorily negligent, the defendant's attorney should object that the question calls for a legal opinion. Although the witness should still answer, subject to the objection, the defendant's attorney will be right. In contrast, while interrogatories cannot ask purely legal questions, they can properly ask for a party's contentions ("Are you contending that the plaintiff failed to mitigate its damages? If so, please state all facts on which you base this contention.").[12] As a consequence, interrogatories may be a slightly superior means for obtaining some additional information about the opponent's legal analysis.

---

12. Fed. R. Civ. P. 33(a)(2).

Chapter Four

Planning and Scheduling Depositions

The best laid schemes o' mice and men
Gang aft a gley . . . .

—Robert Burns

Effective discovery requires planning and coordination. For example, depositions can be combined with other methods of discovery and with each other (e.g., Rule 30(b)(6) depositions with identified-deponent depositions) to obtain the most information as efficiently as possible. Carefully planned discovery is essential in conducting successful litigation, and that planning, in turn, requires thought about what information is needed to prepare a case for trial, a motion for summary judgment, or settlement, and how best to obtain that information.

4.1   The Discovery Plan

Discovery in federal court is not left entirely to the control of the parties. Instead, in most cases Rule 26(f) requires the parties to confer about, among other things, the discovery to occur in the case and to submit the results of these discussions to the court in the form of a proposed discovery plan. This proposed discovery plan then serves as the basis for a scheduling order that includes provisions concerning the discovery in the case as well as other matters.[1]

When required, the discovery plan must specify:

1.   The changes that should be made in the timing, form, or requirements under the mandatory disclosures portion of the rules,[2] including a statement as to when the mandatory disclosures were or will be made;

---

1. Fed. R. Civ. P. 16(b), 26(f).
2. *See* section 4.2.1.

2. The subjects on which discovery may be needed, when discovery should be completed, and whether the parties should conduct discovery in phases or in waves limited to particular issues;

3. The changes that should be made to the limitations on discovery imposed by the federal rules or local rules and whether additional limitations should be imposed; and

4. Whether the courts should enter any protective orders[3] or other orders affecting scheduling and discovery;[4]

5. Finally, in the planning conference, the parties must also discuss the "nature and basis of their claims and defenses and the possibilities for a prompt settlement or resolution of the case,"[5] and how to proceed with the mandatory disclosures under Rule 26(a)(1).

The parties may also discuss other matters to be included in the scheduling order even though not listed in Rule 26(f). The parties need not agree on each of the topics discussed, but the proposed discovery plan should clearly set forth each side's position.

Unless shortened by local rule because of an expedited schedule or because the case falls within the narrow category of exempted cases, the planning conference should be held as soon as practicable, but not later than twenty-one days before a scheduling conference is held or a scheduling order is due. The parties' attorneys are jointly responsible for submitting the proposed discovery plan, in writing, to the court within fourteen days of the planning conference. The court may by local court rule shorten the time for submitting the proposed discovery plan or excuse the parties from submitting a written report and permit them to report orally.[6] Form 52 in the Appendix to the Federal Rules of Civil Procedure is an example of the type of report expected to result from the planning conference.[7]

The court will use the proposed discovery plan in issuing a scheduling order under Rule 16(b) unless the case is of a type exempted under the local rules. The scheduling order will set time limits for joining other parties and amending the pleadings, filing motions, and completing discovery. In addition, the scheduling order may modify the times for the mandatory disclosures and supplementing discovery; modify the limits on the extent of discovery; set the dates for any conferences before trial, the final pretrial conference, and the trial

---

3. Fᴇᴅ. R. Cɪᴠ. P. 26(c).

4. Fᴇᴅ. R. Cɪᴠ. P. 16(b) & (c).

5. Fᴇᴅ. R. Cɪᴠ. P. 26(f).

6. Fᴇᴅ. R. Cɪᴠ. P. 26(b).

7. A copy of Form 52 is contained in Appendix A.

date; and make any other appropriate orders. The court is to issue the scheduling order as soon as practicable, but not later than 90 days after the defendant appears or 120 days after the complaint has been served on a defendant.

Depending on the type of case, the practice and docket of the individual judge, and the results of the planning conference, some scheduling orders contain detailed timetables and directions for conducting discovery, while others do no more than set a cut-off date for when discovery must be completed. Many of the suggestions made in the following pages concerning the sequence and scheduling of discovery could be reflected in the scheduling order or could be left to the parties to develop as the litigation progresses, subject to the date of the discovery cut-off or trial.

The requirement of a planning conference in Rule 26(f) provides the trial attorneys with the opportunity to thoughtfully explore the discovery strategy to be followed in a case. Before the conference, the attorneys must think through in great detail what discovery is needed in the case. Even in jurisdictions that do not follow some version of Rule 26(f), it is still useful to consider what discovery is necessary and how it should be conducted. Some of the issues to be considered are:

- How many depositions are needed;

- What witnesses should be deposed;

- In what order the witnesses should be deposed;

- Whether to place a limit shorter or longer than seven hours on the length of the depositions;

- Whether any special rules, stipulations, or protective orders are necessary for the taking of the depositions, such as excluding other witnesses from the deposition room;

- Whether the time limits and content of the mandatory disclosures should be modified;

- Whether other discovery devices, such as interrogatories, should be used before depositions are taken;

- Whether there should be a waiver of the limitation on the number of interrogatories;

- What special orders, if any, are needed for the taking of discovery, such as a protective order concerning trade secrets;

- Whether discovery should proceed in phases, either by witnesses or topics, to avoid duplicative discovery and to set the stage for any summary judgment motions;

- Whether counsel should agree or be required to confer regularly to review and make suggestions for modifying the scheduling order.

The above is a suggested list of topics that attorneys should think about before the planning conference. A particular case may have a different list of concerns. Sometimes you may conclude that even though a topic may be appropriate to include in the scheduling order, a desire for flexibility in conducting discovery or worries about revealing litigation strategy may argue against proposing it as part of the discovery plan. This, however, in no way lessens the need to think about the topic. Effective planning requires that attorneys consider these issues at some point during the course of the case; Rule 26(f) merely requires that it happen early in the litigation.

4.2   Coordinating Depositions with Other Discovery

Coordinating a deposition schedule with other discovery requires several steps. The first of these is deciding what information is needed to pursue claims or defense. Second, attorneys must determine the most efficient or practical sources for this information. Third, they need to decide on the best method of obtaining the information. Finally, they need to decide on the order for getting the information.

Let's take as an example a case where the plaintiff is claiming lost profits as a result of a defendant's failure to purchase the number of signs required under a purchase agreement. The plaintiff is a small corporation with a president, a purchasing agent, a bookkeeper/accountant, and a plant foreman. The attorney for the defendant, based on information from her client, knows that the plaintiff is a small manufacturer of electronic signs. The contract was for the sale of a large quantity of a particular type of electronic sign manufactured by the plaintiff. The plaintiff purchases most of the component parts of the signs from various vendors and assembles them into the finished product. The plaintiff's main contribution to the product is the assembly.

At this point, one key defense is to attack the plaintiff's calculation of lost profits, and to prepare for this, the attorney intends to take whatever depositions are necessary. What information does the attorney need before taking depositions? An example list (admittedly too limited) includes:

- A list of the vendors of the parts used in assembling the signs;

- The prices and terms for the purchase of the parts;

- Any calculations by the plaintiff of costs and profits for the man-ufacturing of the signs;[8]

- Any accounting records concerning manufacturing expenses;

- The name of the employee who decided what parts to purchase.

With some thought, you could add many more items to this list, but these few illustrate the point.

Once the information needed has been identified, the next step is to iden-tify the possible sources of this information. In the example given, all of the information being sought is likely to be available from the plaintiff, but some information, such as the prices and terms for the purchase of the parts, should also be available from the different vendors who provided the parts. The defendant's attorney, of course, is not limited to seeking information from just one source if more than one is available. But in choosing a source, such factors as the cost of discovery, ease of obtaining the information, and the credibility of the source are likely to control.

The third and fourth steps are determining how to go about getting the information and planning the order in which to get it—by topic and poten-tial witness. A good approach to answering these questions is to look at the different discovery devices available.

4.2.1 Mandatory Disclosures

Absent a stipulation, a court order, or a case falling within the narrow class of excepted cases, parties litigating in the federal district courts must disclose, without awaiting a formal discovery request, certain basic information about the case. Specifically, each party must provide to all other parties in the case:

1. The name and, if known, the address and telephone number of each individual likely to have discoverable information—and identifying the subjects of the information—that the disclosing party may use to support its claims or defenses, unless solely for impeachment;

2. A copy, or a description by category and location, of all docu-ments, data compilations, and tangible things that are in the pos-session, custody, or control of the party and that the disclosing party may use to support its claims or defenses, unless solely for impeachment;

---

8. The plaintiffs will have previously provided as one of the mandatory disclosures required by Rule 25(a)(1)(A) a computation of each category of damages claimed and also made available for inspection and copying the documents or other evidentiary material on which each computation is based.

3. Computation of any category of damages claimed by the disclosing party, making available for inspection and copying all non-privileged material on which the computation is based, including materials bearing on the nature and extent of any claimed injuries; and

4. For inspection and copying, any insurance agreement that may be available to satisfy all or part of any judgment that may be entered in the action or to indemnify or reimburse for payments made to satisfy the judgment.[9]

The disclosures are to be made in writing at or within fourteen days after the planning conference, unless a party objects to making disclosures because doing so would not be appropriate for the case, or the parties stipulate or the court orders a different time.[10] While the mandatory disclosures help the discovery process, there is no requirement to identify witnesses or documents having or containing information harmful to the disclosing party's position; all that is required is the disclosure of witnesses and documents on which the disclosing party intends to rely. Therefore, while perhaps accelerating discovery, the mandatory disclosures do not relieve you of the fundamental burden of developing your own proof.

4.2.2 *Interrogatories*

Imagine the deposition of the plaintiff's purchasing agent and what could happen:

By Defendant's Counsel:

Q: Now, sir, please tell me the name of all vendors from whom the plaintiff purchases parts for use in manufacturing the electronic signs that are the subject of this action.

A: Well, let's see. We purchase most of the circuit boards from Zenith, but several of the more specialized ones come from JVC. The sign casings come from a small firm in town, Acucom, and we get some parts from jobbers.

Q: Any other vendors?

A: Oh, sure. We use over thirty vendors, but I know I can't remember them all right now.

Q: Do you have a list of the various vendors?

---

9. Fed. R. Civ. P. 26(a)(1).
10. *See* Fed. R. Civ. P. 26(a)(1)(C).

A: Yes, back at the office.

Q: Counsel, I suggest that you provide me with the list, we finish as much as we can today, and then continue the deposition tomorrow after I have a chance to review the list.

Plaintiff's Counsel: Give me a request in writing, and I will take it under advisement. Quite frankly, I see no need to continue this deposition and cause further inconvenience and expense for my client. As you know, depositions are limited to seven hours on one day. If you wanted a list of our vendors, you knew how to get it without waiting until the middle of this deposition. I will tell you now that I will resist any efforts to resume this deposition at a later time.

The defendant's lawyer could have avoided all of these problems if before the deposition he had sent the plaintiff a set of interrogatories asking for the names of all vendors supplying parts for the signs.[11] Of course, the interrogatories could also ask for any other information that would be helpful in conducting the deposition, such as a description of the parts, the purchase price, quantities, and so on.

Interrogatories are useful deposition preparation tools when used for limited purposes because, through them, an attorney can obtain information in advance. In factually complex cases, the first wave of discovery routinely consists of interrogatories sent soon after the litigation commences, with the answers to be used, in part, to help prepare for the later depositions. The advantages of using interrogatories to prepare for depositions are several:

Interrogatories can be used to identify factual data and information that a witness is not likely to recall at deposition. As illustrated above, if a witness cannot remember the correct answer to a question, there is little the lawyer taking the deposition can do except attempt to refresh the witness's memory. If, however, you have obtained such information by sending interrogatories before the deposition, you can question the witness without concern about memory failures. When a deposition witness may be questioned about objective information in the hands of the opposing party, such as data, calculations, lists, or other information that the witness will not likely recall

---

11. If the information was called for by a previous discovery request, but was not provided, the Advisory Committee Notes to Rule 30(d)(2) states "that may justify further examination once production has occurred."

easily, the deposing attorney can obtain this information before the deposition through interrogatories.

Interrogatories can help identify potential deposition witnesses and documents. Interrogatories frequently ask about all witnesses who have knowledge of the facts—who attended an event or meeting, participated in a transaction, and so on. Similarly, interrogatories often ask a party to identify all documents referring to a particular event or resulting from a transaction. The purpose of these types of interrogatories is, among other things, to identify potential deposition witnesses and documents that the opponent will be asked to produce. While the attorney can and should ask these same questions at the depositions of key witnesses as a method of confirming the accuracy of the interrogatory answers, these witnesses many times do not have comprehensive knowledge of other witnesses and documents. For instance, the plaintiff's president in our example may know others who attended the meetings that she attended concerning parts orders, but she may not know who attended other meetings when she was not present. Similarly, the defendant in a personal injury case may be unaware of those witnesses to the accident who were later located by his lawyer or a private investigator. The advantage of interrogatories over depositions in identifying witnesses and documents is that the opposing party cannot rely solely on his or her current memory of facts. Instead, the party answering the interrogatory must make reasonable inquiry of all of its employees and agents and conduct a reasonable search of all records.[12]

Interrogatories can identify who in a company or organization has knowledge about a topic. Imagine again the deposition of the plaintiff's purchasing agent in the breach of contract case. One of the facts the attorney representing the defendant wishes to know is the process and responsibility for purchasing the parts to be purchased for manufacturing the signs. An obvious method of obtaining this information is to ask about it during the purchasing agent's deposition. The response might be something like, "I am not sure, but I think it was our president." Then, when the president's

---

12. Nat'l Fire Ins. Co. of Hartford v. Jose Trucking Corp., 264 F.R.D. 233, 238 (W.D.N.C. 2010) ("The answers to interrogatories must be responsive, full, complete and unevasive. The answering party cannot limit his answers to matters within his own knowledge and ignore information immediately available to him or under his control. If an appropriate interrogatory is propounded, the answering party will be required to give the information available to him, if any, through his attorney, investigators employed by him or on his behalf or other agents or representatives, whether personally known to the answering party or not. If the answering party lacks necessary information to make a full, fair and specific answer to an interrogatory, it should so state under oath and should set forth in detail the efforts made to obtain the information." (citations omitted); Frontier-Kemper Constructors, Inc. v. Elk Run Coal Co., 246 F.R.D. 522, 529 (S.D. W.Va. 2007) (a party responding to interrogatories is under a "severe duty to make every effort to obtain the requested information"); CHARLES ALAN WRIGHT, ET AL., 8B FEDERAL PRACTICE & PROCEDURE CIVIL § 2177 (3d ed.).

deposition is taken, her answer is, "No, it wasn't me. I'm pretty sure it was an outside designer." And so goes the game of increasing expense and inconvenience. Sending a simple interrogatory before the first deposition that asks who made the decision about what parts to purchase would avoid this difficulty and greatly facilitate later discovery.

Of course, you can use a Rule 30(b)(6) deposition[13] to accomplish the same objective by specifying that the deposition will cover, among other topics, the subject of purchasing parts for the signs. Conducting a deposition for this purpose alone would be more expensive than posing an interrogatory on the same subject, but it is clear that Rule 30(b)(6) depositions work most efficiently when a list of specifications is attached so that a whole body of information can be obtained. When, the corporation or organization having the desired information is a nonparty, interrogatories cannot be used and named-deponent depositions pose the problems described above, so a Rule 30(b)(6) deposition is the only discovery method that will provide the information reliably and efficiently.

Interrogatories can be used to narrow the issues. Rule 33(a)(2) states "[a]n interrogatory is not objectionable merely because it asks for an opinion or contention that relates to fact or the application of law to fact . . . ." In other words, interrogatories may ask about an opponent's legal contentions in the case.[14] Being able to ask about an opponent's legal contentions can be very helpful in narrowing the issues. For example, in a negligence action it would be proper to ask the plaintiff, by interrogatory, to identify the acts and omissions claimed that constitute the defendant's negligence. In the breach of contract case described above, the defendant may ask in an interrogatory whether, for example, the plaintiff is claiming consequential damages as a result of the alleged breach. The answer to such an interrogatory would help narrow the issues in dispute by informing the defendant of what it will need to defend against. Because a party often will not be certain about what is being contended until after the facts have been fully explored, the court may order that contention interrogatories need not be answered until after discovery on the issue has been completed or until a pretrial conference or other later date.[15]

While interrogatories are useful at least in preparing for depositions, drawbacks do exist. Interrogatories in general:

---

13. FED. R. CIV. P. 30(b)(6). *See* chapter nineteen.

14. Interrogatories calling for pure law, divorced from the facts of the case, are still improper. FED. R. CIV. P. 33 advisory committee's note (1970).

15. FED. R. CIV. P. 33(a)(2).

- may only be directed to a party and cannot be used with a nonparty;[16]

- do not work well when asking about opinions, mental impressions, and subjective information;[17]

- need not be answered for thirty days;[18]

- are subject to a limit of twenty-five unless modified by court order or stipulation;[19]

- require careful drafting.[20]

- draw more objections than other types of discovery;

- obtain answers that are filtered through and drafted by lawyers;

- provide answers that are difficult to follow up;

- allow evasive answers that are difficult to control.

Interrogatories may alert an opponent to the areas on which there will be questioning in a later deposition. As a result, the witness will be better prepared at the later deposition. Interrogatories submitted pursuant to Rule 33(c) asking about a party's opinions and contentions are particularly troublesome (or effective for the opponent) because of the tendency to inform opponents of possible lines of defense to be taken at later depositions.

Using interrogatories may also cause delays in taking depositions, thereby allowing the opponent to gain the initiative. Under the Federal Rules of Civil Procedure, interrogatories cannot be sent until after the planning conference required by Rule 26(f), unless allowed by stipulation or leave of court.[21] Courts often grant extensions of time for answering interrogatories, particularly early in an action, thereby further delaying the discovery process. If one side delays taking depositions until interrogatories have been answered, the other side will often gain momentum by proceeding with its own depositions. Where speed and initiative are important, an attorney may well forgo interrogatories until a later stage of the litigation and commence taking depositions at the earliest possible moment.

In addition, absent a stipulation or special considerations, some courts permit only one set of interrogatories to an opponent. As a result, a party may want to defer asking any interrogatories until after all or a majority of

---

16. Fed. R. Civ. P. 33(a)(1).

17. *See* section 3.1.2.

18. Fed. R. Civ. P. 33(b)(2).

19. Fed. R. Civ. P. 26(b)(2), 33(a)(1).

20. *See generally* section 3.1.

21. Fed. R. Civ. P. 26(d)(1).

the depositions have been taken so that the interrogatories can be used to tie up any loose ends.

Like all else in litigation, no absolute rules apply to coordinating depositions with interrogatories. You must consider and handle each situation individually to decide whether any information is needed before taking depositions. If so, the next question will be whether interrogatories are the best method of obtaining that information.

4.2.3   Document Requests

Lawyers frequently use depositions to question witnesses about documents. When documents are in the hands of an uncooperative nonparty, taking a deposition in conjunction with a subpoena duces tecum was once the only method of forcing pretrial production of the documents. Now, under Rule 45(a), a party may subpoena documents from a nonparty without a simultaneous deposition. Rule 45(c)(2)(A) specifically states that a person commanded by subpoena to produce documents or things *need not appear* in *person*. Subponae duces tecum say "bring the things;" subponae *ad testificandum* say "come and testify."

For documents held by a party, the Federal Rules of Civil Procedure suggest that the only permissible method of obtaining documents beyond the voluntary disclosure under Rule 26(a) is by a request to produce,[22] but as a practical matter party-witnesses will often respond to a subpoena duces tecum without objection. One advantage of using a subpoena duces tecum is the shorter response time provided for under Rule 45 (fourteen days or fewer) than under Rule 34 (written response required within thirty days of service of the request).[23] In almost all cases, you should obtain documents—by a request to produce or a subpoena duces tecum—in advance of the deposition rather than having them produced at the deposition. Advance production gives you time to study the documents, check with other sources about information contained in the documents, and more carefully formulate questions for the deposition. Producing documents at the deposition causes delays as the documents are studied and creates the risk that the questioner may not recognize a potential area of questioning until after the deposition has concluded. Since an opponent has thirty days in which to respond to a notice to produce, and since such response period often becomes sixty or ninety days,[24] document production has to occur at an early stage of

---

22. Fed. R. Civ. P. 30(b)(2).

23. Rule 45(c)(3)(A)(i) provides that a motion to quash may be brought if the subpoena "fails to allow a reasonable time to comply."

24. The time for response often and easily transforms itself from thirty to ninety and more days: The request goes out; three days before a response is due, opposing counsel ask by telephone for an additional thirty days to respond because the responses are complex, or the

the litigation if it is not to delay depositions. (Of course, an early 30(b)(6) deposition on document creation, distribution, and storage may make your requests for production more efficient.)

But it is often difficult to get an opposing party to produce documents within the thirty days provided by Rule 34. Instead, they may resist by asking the court for extensions of time or by merely failing to respond until compelled to do so by the judge handling the case. It is usually better to proceed with depositions rather than wait for weeks and months to obtain the documents requested, reserving a right to resume the deposition if later-obtained documents create a legitimate need.

When taking the deposition of a nonparty witness, it never hurts to call the witness (or her counsel) and ask her to produce documents voluntarily in advance of the deposition. If you explain that this may help shorten the deposition, this tactic will often succeed.

4.2.4   *Requests for Admission*

Requests for admission, if successful, may help to eliminate the need to prove essential facts and may reduce discovery costs by rendering unnecessary those depositions that otherwise would be needed to establish the disputed fact. Requests for admission are particularly useful to authenticate documents in the hands of nonparties who might otherwise have to be deposed to obtain the necessary proof. In a personal injury case, for instance, copies of the medical records may be available, but if the hospital is unwilling to provide the certification allowed by Federal Rules of Evidence 803(6) and 902(11) & (12),[25] to authenticate them, you must either depose the hospital records custodian or call her as a witness at trial. If you first request that the opposing party admit the record's authenticity, you may be able to avoid the need for the deposition or, if it does takes place, to impose its cost on the party.[26]

---

computer died, or the dog died, or the dog's computer died; the extension is granted as a matter of comity, meaning the propounding attorney remembers when her dog died; one day before the extended date for response, the propounding attorney receives objections to each part of each request, with the tagline: "To the extent that this request for production is not objectionable as calling for proprietary and confidential information, plaintiff appends two documents."

25. These rules provide for the self-authentication of domestic and foreign business records by using a "certification" of the custodian or otherwise qualified person detailing facts that satisfy the requirements for the admissibility of business records under Rule 803(6), 902(11), and 902(12), and by complying with other procedural requirements contained in the rules.

26. Fed. R. Civ. P. 37(c)(2).

The drawback of requests for admission is that they are time consuming. The opposing party has thirty days in which to respond, and courts readily grant extensions of time if the requests are made early in the litigation.

Before expending the time to draft requests for admission, it makes sense to call the opposing counsel to see if a stipulation to the same topics is agreeable. A telephone call is often better received than a discovery request, and it may be more likely to achieve what is being sought.

As a practical matter, requests for admission are not really a discovery device at all, but more like a formalized request for a stipulation. A party who will not agree to stipulate to a fact is also unlikely to admit the fact in a request for admission. This is particularly true because there is usually no practical penalty for unreasonably denying a request for admission. Very few courts actually order that a fact be treated as admitted or require an opposing party who has unreasonably denied a request for admission to pay the reasonable expenses incurred in proving the truth of the fact contained in the request.

4.2.5   Self-Help

While not a discovery device provided for by the Federal Rules of Civil Procedure, self-help is often the best way of obtaining information. Conducting an informal investigation of the facts by calling up potential witnesses and asking them to explain what happened, by requesting an individual or company to voluntarily reveal documents, by taking photographs on your own, and so forth, you or your paralegal can often find out what is needed without the expense of hiring a court reporter or incurring witness fees.

There are drawbacks to such an approach. Any information you obtain is usually not made in statements under oath. (You can always ask for a sworn statement, or at least a signed statement; whether you will be successful in getting one is another matter.) The information cannot be used in court if the witness becomes unavailable, and using a pretrial statement to impeach a witness who later changes his versions of the facts is usually more difficult and less persuasive than with a deposition.

Besides typically being cheaper than formal discovery, the greatest advantage of self-help is that you will not normally be required to share the results with the opponent.[27] Contrast this with taking a deposition where the opposing attorney gets to listen to every question and answer and even ask questions, all at the expense of the attorney noticing the deposition.

Formal discovery and self-help are not the only ways to find the information necessary for preparing the case. Negotiations with opposing counsel,

---

27. There are limited circumstances when an opposing party may have access to an attorney's "work product," but they occur very rarely. *See* FED. R. CIV. P. 26(b)(3).

mediation efforts, pretrial conferences, talking with experts, the opponent's pleadings, and responses to motions for summary judgment and other types of motions are all ways of finding out information concerning your case.

4.3   Coordinating Depositions

Once you decide on an order in which discovery is to proceed (interrogatories, then requests to produce, then depositions, then requests to admit, etc.), you still must decide on the order of the depositions. Deciding on the order in which depositions should be taken depends on the facts of the particular case. However, we can at least identify the factors to be considered when making this decision.

Is it necessary to obtain evidence from one witness before deposing another witness? One view of the process of litigation is that it is similar to building a house: you must lay the foundation before you can erect the walls. Similarly, in litigation an attorney may need to obtain evidence from one witness as a prerequisite to questioning another witness. For instance, the defendant in a personal injury case who is challenging the extent and permanency of the plaintiff's injuries will probably want to depose the plaintiff about the injuries before deposing the plaintiff's medical expert about the prognosis for the plaintiff's recovery. Likewise, in the breach-of-contract action described earlier, the defendant would generally want to find out from the purchasing agent what parts were necessary to manufacture the signs before questioning the bookkeeper/accountant about the manufacturing cost.

Should key or minor witnesses be deposed first? Sometimes the attorney and the client will be unfamiliar with the facts giving rise to the dispute, the structure of the industry, or the general background to the lawsuit. For instance, in the breach-of-contract action neither the lawyer nor the defendant may know much about the sign market or the plaintiff's opportunities to mitigate damages. When you need background information, it is often better to get those facts from minor witnesses before proceeding to interrogate key witnesses.

When background information is not necessary or is already available, the general rule is to depose key witnesses before minor ones. The reason for this general rule is that deposing the key witnesses first affords less time for them to study other testimony and find opportunities to shore up defenses or spin stories in a favorable way. Also, as a matter of human nature, if the key witnesses have an opportunity to review the deposition testimony of minor witnesses or to consider the topics covered in those earlier depositions, the key witnesses are more likely to adapt their own stories to those of the minor witnesses. Minor witnesses, because they usually have less at stake, are less likely to spend the time and effort to conform their stories to the expected stories of the key witnesses. Where, however, a case has more than one key witness with similar knowledge, it may be wise to leave the deposition of one of them until close to the end of discovery. That way, if there are some unanswered questions after completing discovery of the other witnesses, there is still a key actor who can be questioned.

Again, a Rule 30(b)(6) organizational deposition would provide this same opportunity at the end of other discovery. You should consider doing *two* Rule 30(b)(6) depositions, then: one to start with, to understand the organization, structure, and processes; and one to end with (at least to end nonexpert discovery with), to clean up loose ends, unanswered questions, and the factual record (much like requests for admissions, but with useful follow-up).

When should expert witnesses be deposed? Under Rule 26(a)(2)(D), expert witnesses in most cases must provide a report of their opinions and the reasons for them, as well as any exhibits that support the opinions or summarize them, at least ninety days before trial. The report must also contain the expert's qualifications, compensation, and previous experience testifying. An expert need not be offered for deposition, and an attorney should not want to depose an expert, until she provides this report,[28] although Rule 29 on its face allows a departure from this timing. The report will provide important help when preparing for the expert's deposition. The expert's report deadline is normally at or beyond the end of the period for other discovery, with the effect that experts are normally the last witnesses to be deposed. Even with those experts who need not provide a report or in those jurisdictions where it is not required, it makes sense to wait until the end of discovery so that the expert will have fully developed the opinions to be given at trial and you have had a chance fully to understand the facts in the case.

4.4   Scheduling the Deposition

Should lay witness depositions be scheduled early or late in the discovery process? Again, this depends on the facts of the case. Early scheduling of depositions allows you to freeze the witnesses' stories before memories fade more than they already have; to put pressure on the opponent by requiring them to go on the defensive; to question witnesses, particularly parties, when they are likely to be less prepared; to discover gaps in the case while there is still time to rectify them; and to develop evidence early in the litigation that may allow a summary judgment or a quick settlement of the case.

On the other hand, if the opponent's key witnesses are likely to disappear or otherwise become unavailable for trial, the deposition may only serve to preserve harmful testimony that will benefit the opponent. Early depositions may also force your opponent to be better prepared for trial than if

---

28. Fed. R. Civ. P. 26(b)(4)(A).

depositions had been scheduled at a time when it was too late to correct any defects in the opponent's case that were revealed by the deposition. Finally, the deposition of the plaintiff's medical expert in a personal injury case often is delayed until as late in the litigation as possible to take advantage of any improvement in the plaintiff's injuries.

Rule 30(a)(2)(A) limits the number of depositions, absent a stipulation, court order, or local rule to the contrary, to ten per side. Caution dictates that you not use up all ten early in the discovery process in the event additional important witnesses are discovered later in the case. A prudent lawyer should hold at least one or two in reserve.

4.5   Duration and Intervals

The obvious answer to the question of how long a deposition should last is "as long as necessary" within the seven hour, one day constraints of Rule 30(d)(1). Of course, the hour and day limits of Rule 30(d)(1) may be increased or decreased by stipulation or court order. Depositions have no magic length; some last for only a few minutes, while others, with the appropriate stipulation or court order, last days or weeks. But depositions are an expensive form of discovery, and the longer they last, the greater the burden on the clients. When, however, the testimony is complex or presents surprises, it sometimes makes sense to slow down the process by trying to get a stipulation or court order that extends the deposition. When a deposition continues overnight or on to a later date, you have an additional opportunity to analyze what the witness has said. Be aware, however, that the longer the break, the more likely it is that the witness will also have time to reflect on the previous testimony and correct any errors or misstatements. In practice, it is common in complex cases for counsel to stipulate to longer depositions for experts and important senior executives. It can be efficient to stipulate that each side has, for example, three two-day depositions, one three-day deposition, with the remainder being one-day (seven hour) depositions. The stipulation could provide that once a two-day deposition is noticed, it is no longer available, no matter how long the deposition actually extends. This would prevent an attorney trying to force the other side into more time-intensive preparation, then rendering it useless.

The interval between depositions is often as much a function of the lawyers' and witnesses' schedules as it is of strategic planning. Where questioning counsel has the freedom to control the schedule, the time between depositions should be sufficiently long to permit review of the prior deposition testimony and to prepare for the next deposition, but no longer. The longer the break, the more complete and thorough the opponent's preparation of the next witness will likely be. Not only will opposing counsel have briefed the witness about what has occurred in prior depositions, but the witness may even have read the prior deposition transcripts. Short intervals—even taking several depositions on the same day—are not only more likely to produce unrehearsed testimony, but also put more pressure on the opposing attorney. Thus, there is no hard-and-fast answer—merely considerations that need to be evaluated.

In those jurisdictions without deposition time limits, a problem that occurs time and again is lack of agreement about the length of the deposition. Typically, the notice for the deposition will recite: "To appear at 9:30 a.m. on the 24th day of June, 2011, for the purpose of providing deposition testimony in the above-captioned matter." Then, at 4:30 or 5:00 p.m. on that day, after a long day of questioning, the deposing attorney says, "Well, let's recess for today, and we will continue tomorrow morning," and the defending attorney says, "No, you noticed this deposition for today, and it will be concluded today. We've had a full workday, so your time with this witness is over."

Unless the length of the deposition is subject to Rule 30(d)(1), to a stipulation, or to some other limitation, no rule clearly governs here, and no magic language can avoid all disputes. Certainly, the deposing attorney should have been more explicit about duration at the outset, because neglecting to do so may result in an incomplete deposition. A simple recommendation may help: counsel should be specific in the notice—don't try to hide the ball. State in the notice: "To appear at 9:30 a.m. on the 24th day of June, 2011; this deposition may take more than one day," or "to continue from day to day." A defending attorney who attempts to obtain a protective order limiting the length of the deposition at the end of the day in question cannot then claim a lack of notice and the opportunity to object before the deposition began.

CHAPTER FIVE

PREPARING TO TAKE THE DEPOSITION

Speak without emphasizing your words. Leave other people to discover what it is that you have said; and as their minds are slow, you can make your escape in time.

—Arthur Schopenhauer (1788–1860)

5.1 The Questioner's Frame of Mind

The attitude and approach taken in questioning during the deposition is governed by the intended purpose. If the questioner's primary purpose is to discover new information, then first taking time to review topics already understood, confirming old information, or displaying knowledge of the facts is contrary to the purpose of taking the deposition and wastes valuable time that could be used to gain knowledge of still unknown harmful and helpful evidence. Consider the following two approaches to questioning a witness in a product liability case:

Q: Mr. Mikionis, isn't it true that you should have used harder wood for the header in the garage that held the spring and bracket assembly?

A: No.

Q: Don't you agree that the wood was just not hard enough, or dense enough, to hold that spring and bracket assembly, given the short screws that were used?

A: No.

Q: With the wallboard installed over the wood header, the screws just didn't have enough penetration into the wood to safely hold that spring and bracket assembly, did they?

A: I don't agree.

Q: Well, why don't you tell me why you don't agree?

A: The primary cause of the failure of this spring and bracket assembly system was the use by the installer of an impact wrench to drive the screws into the header, through the wallboard. That wrench drove the screws past snug and stripped the wood, so that there was really no way that they could be relied on to hold anything, much less a powerful spring and bracket assembly like this one.

Compare that "cross-examination" style of questioning (ending with the frustrated open-ended question) with this style:

Q: Mr. Mikionis, you have studied the causes of the failure of the garage door spring assembly, right?

A: Yes, that's right.

Q: Tell me, what caused the failure?

A: The primary cause of the failure of this spring assembly system was . . . .

Q: What other causes of the failure did you find?

A: A secondary cause was the use by the installer of an impact wrench to drive the screws into the header . . . .

In the first example, the attorney had the mind-set of "knowing" the causes and merely wanted the deponent to confirm the correctness of the assumed causes. This form is fine when the questioner is intentionally trying to confirm known information or seeking a party statement. However, when seeking new information, these closed questions do not work at all. In the second example, while the attorney may have believed the causes were known, the goal was not to demonstrate this knowledge, but to find out what additional information the deponent had. Obviously, open-ended questions are more appropriate for that purpose, but the distinction to be made here is not just in the form of the question, but also in the attitude of the deposing attorney, as evidenced by the tone and inquisitive nature of the examination. Perhaps because of their superior (read "longer") education, many attorneys have come to believe they are omniscient: there are no causes, there are no effects, there are no logical arguments that the attorney has not already discovered, considered, and categorized. This kind of thinking can be fatal on cross-examination; it is almost as harmful in taking depositions.

In a deposition, every fact witness is an "expert," with a superior information base that exceeds that of the questioning lawyer—in some area, however small—because they actually know more about that area (their health, their job, their state of mind, etc.) than anyone else involved in the litigation. They may actually be "experts" under the rules of evidence, hired by the opposing side to provide opinion testimony based on education and trigonometry and carbon dating; or they may be "experts" because they know more about their business affairs or pain and suffering or fraudulent intent than anyone else; or they may be "experts" because they know better than anyone else what they saw at the intersection when the cars collided. With that thought in mind, the questioner's mind-set should be to take advantage of the witness's expertise. As with traditional experts, this mind-set should be that of an interested student, with the witness being the teacher. This alters the attorney's traditional relationship with the expert witness: from adversaries to be battled, to student-teacher. The same change can occur with fact witnesses, where the attorney's interest and an open-ended style of questioning encourage the witness to satisfy her desire to be understood and believed.

5.2   Creating the Deposition Outline

Most attorneys conduct depositions using a topic outline from which they ask questions. The outline serves as a guide to the areas of inquiry during the deposition and a method of checking, before concluding the deposition, that all important areas have been covered and nothing has been forgotten. The deposition outline is a necessary and important tool for conducting depositions, but preparing such an outline requires careful thought.

No perfect method or formula exists for creating the deposition outline. Most lawyers use more than one method and will change the combination of methods to fit the type of case for which they are creating the outline. The objective of all the techniques is to identify every useful topic for inquiry. The best way to accomplish this will vary depending on the party represented, which party controls most of the important information in the case, the size and complexity of the case, the role of the witness in the sequence of events, and many other considerations. Below we discuss some steps to follow in every case, regardless of all other factors.

5.3   Researching the Law

To state the obvious, factual inquiry will always center on the facts to be proved or disproved at trial. And, in turn, those necessary facts are governed by the legal elements of each claim and defense. Therefore, the first step in preparing the deposition outline is to research every legal issue in the case thoroughly. Only then, with a fix on the law, can you anticipate the facts underlying claims or defenses.

Many lawyers will have done the necessary legal research as part of drafting the pleadings, but a surprising number wait until just before trial to determine what each party must prove. Such delayed preparation may be too late to identify the necessary evidence. Finding out what must be proved or disproved while there is still an opportunity to generate those facts through discovery is the much better approach.

Legal research will help identify the nature and quality of the facts necessary to make a claim or defense. That research will also suggest areas of factual inquiry. If, in upholding a claim of a certain sort, the appellate courts look to certain kinds of facts, it will be important to determine whether those sorts of facts are available in *this* case. Further, the research regarding a particular claim and defense will reveal additional claims that have been made with similar sorts of facts. For example, in a claim of professional malpractice, the claim, depending on the jurisdiction, can be based on tort or contract principles. When researching the tort law in the area, the cases may reveal that a contract claim is available as well. Once an additional claim is identified, pleadings may be amended and new areas of factual inquiry in discovery may be suggested.

Discovery and preparation for trial require flexibility. It is inappropriate to lock onto one legal theory at an early point in the case (unless after careful research there is only one available). Keep as many options available as possible and identify all potentially applicable legal theories. Once discovery is completed, you can review and evaluate each legal theory to determine whether it has any viability. Abandoning a theory late in the case is not a problem, but adding theories late in the process may be difficult. The lesson is to keep an open mind until late in preparation and to remain flexible by pursuing all potential and reasonable legal theories until it is clear that one or more have no merit. Then throw that one out and keep on discovering and discarding.

5.4   Identifying All Available Facts

Once all potential and reasonable legal theories have been identified, the next step is to make an inventory of all the facts currently available. Fact sources may include clients and friendly witnesses, documentary and other real evidence, expert witnesses, information in government records, interrogatory answers, and prior depositions. Bring a creative and curious mindset to the task and consider what other possible sources of information may exist. Information gathering usually continues up to the day of trial, but the ideal approach is to gather as much information as possible before conducting discovery. This means carefully interviewing the client, talking with every witness who is willing to do so, visiting the scene of the accident, consulting with experts, reviewing every relevant document, finding out as much as possible about the opposing party and about the witnesses who will be supporting the opponent's case, and so on.

Knowing as much as reasonably possible about the facts and issues in a case before any depositions are taken enhances your ability to formulate fruitful lines of questions and challenge any inconsistencies in the witness's answers. More importantly, finding out as much as possible in advance about the facts and issues helps insure that *all* of the possible facts and issues are fully explored during a witness's deposition. Witnesses may only be deposed once.[1] Potential areas of inquiry coming to light for the first time after a witness has been deposed will have to be explored through other means of discovery—it is very unlikely a court will permit a second deposition of the same witness even though there is reason for you to believe that the witness has information about a new issue in the case.[2] Nearly every lawyer has had the stomach-knotting experience of discovering some significant fact on the eve of trial that might have changed the entire strategy of the case. If only that fact had been known earlier in the case, discovery could have been extended into a new area, and it might have been possible to develop new evidence supporting the claim or defense. Thorough advance factual investigation will help reduce these situations to a minimum.

While it is impossible to construct an exhaustive list of all the sources and types of information that should be checked before proceeding with a deposition, it *is* possible to name some of the most important:

Your Client

Clients usually know the most about their own cases. After all, what was done by or to the client is the reason for the lawsuit. Clients know how contracts were negotiated, how accidents occurred, or how their rights came to be trampled on. They often know who will be the best witnesses for their side and who will be the best witnesses for the other side. In many cases, the client will be your most important source of information.

The Deponent-Witness

It makes sense to find out everything possible about the deponent. What is their involvement in the case, what are they likely to know, what is their relationship to the parties and other witnesses, what are their personalities, and so on. "Googling"—doing an Internet search of the witness— will sometimes produce useful information, particularly if the witness is well-known, at least in the local area.

---

1. Fed. R. Civ. P. 30 (a)(2)(A)(ii).

2. The exception is where the issue was not explored in the previous deposition because of the opposing party's misconduct or wrongdoing.

Where the witness has testified or given deposition testimony in previous actions, you should review that testimony and ask the attorneys who deposed or cross-examined in those cases about what information or insights they have regarding the witness. If the witness has written any articles or books (as is obviously very common with experts), read those works (or, more reasonably, have graduate student assistants read them). If a witness has given speeches that relate to the subject of the action, which sometimes happens with company executives in complex litigation, review these as well. There are also organizations, such as the American Association for Justice (AAJ) (formerly the American Trial Lawyers Association), that collect information about witnesses in recurring types of litigation. If the deponent is one of the opponent's experts, there are many additional sources you should consult—that will be discussed in chapter twenty.

Experts

When the lawsuit involves matters requiring expert testimony, hiring a consulting expert can help counsel develop an understanding of the technical aspects of the case and can identify the facts that are necessary to be developed for expert opinions. (The use of consulting experts and the rules involving that use will also be discussed at much greater length in chapter twenty, Expert Depositions.)

Documents

It is essential that you review all documents and understand their importance, particularly those documents that directly relate to the witnesses being deposed. The categories of documents that relate to the witness include those written, received, or read by the witness; documents the witness might be aware of; documents referring to the witness or the witness's actions; and documents that refer to topics about which the witness will be asked to give evidence. Documents provided by your client are a good starting place. In addition, useful documents are often available from friendly witnesses. And of course, documents will have been identified by the opponent in Rule 26 mandatory disclosures, as well as in response to Rule 33 interrogatories and formal document production requests pursuant to Rule 34.[3] In addition, you can use a subpoena duces tecum to require nonparty witnesses to produce documents or to bring documents with them to the deposition.[4]

---

3. *See* chapter four.

4. Whenever possible, the attorney taking the deposition should attempt to obtain documents reasonably well in advance of the deposition so that they can be reviewed and incorporated into the appropriate areas of questioning. Rule 45(a)(1)(C) allows a subpoena for the production of documents (duces tecum) to be separate from a subpoena to appear and testify (*ad testificandum*).

Friendly Witnesses

Every unrepresented witness who is willing to talk informally about the case should be interviewed, at least by telephone. Even witnesses expected to be hostile should be contacted to confirm those expectations. Potentially hostile witnesses may in fact consent to an interview, the result of which might be one less deposition, or at least a deposition with a sharper focus.

Pleadings

The pleadings and other filings in the case are always a potential source of facts or of ideas on where to find facts that relate to statements made in them. Every reasonable claim or defense must, of course, be explored factually with each witness who has potential information that supports those pleadings.

Previous Discovery or Testimony

Interrogatory responses, prior depositions, and discovery in other cases involving the opposing party should be reviewed. There may be pleadings or testimony in related litigation, even in related criminal proceedings, that may be a source of information.

The Scene

In a personal injury case, visiting the scene of the accident will provide you with a better understanding of a witness's descriptions and explanations and may suggest some sort of illustrative aid you can use when you take deposition testimony. In a products liability case, visiting the factory where the product was manufactured can be helpful. In a construction case, visiting the job site may suggest a reason for the delay or failure. It makes sense to become personally familiar with the places relevant to the case and to the witnesses who will be deposed.

5.5   Constructing Your Working Theories

By the last few weeks before trial, a good trial lawyer will have decided on a theory of the case (or perhaps two theories, if the lawyer is still maintaining an alternative theory). The importance of a well thought out case theory cannot be underestimated. This case theory will govern the type of jurors selected to hear the case (or, more accurately, the type of prospective jurors who will be struck from the jury panel through the use of peremptory challenges); it will govern what is said in the opening statement; the selection and order of witnesses; the content of the direct and cross-examinations; and the arguments made in the closing. What evidence a party presents, what arguments a party makes, and every part of the trial are focused on persuading the judge or jury to adopt that party's case theory as the best explanation of what happened in the case and as a good basis for the verdict. In short, a party's case theory will structure everything that party does during the trial.

What is a *case theory*? The theory of the case is actually composed of three separate theories—1) the legal theory, 2) the factual theory, and 3) the persuasive theory. All three create the case theory. The legal theory is nothing more than the law that entitles the client to the relief being sought, regardless of whether that relief is some form of affirmative relief or the dismissal of the other side's cause of action. The factual theory is what the client contended happened in the case. Obviously, the factual theory must satisfy the requirements of the legal theory or the client will lose, perhaps on a motion going to the sufficiency of the complaint, a motion to dismiss at the close of the plaintiff's case, a motion to strike defenses, or a motion for summary judgment. Finally, the persuasive theory tells the fact finder why a party should prevail as a matter of fairness and justice, independent from the law. The persuasive theory often appeals to the judge's or jury's sense of right and wrong by attributing responsibility or blame to the opposing party.

An example of the confluence of these three theories might be a contract case where the manufacturer claims that the wholesale buyer never confirmed that he needed "extra long" golf clubs in his order for one gross of sets. The legal theory is that once the buyer specifies and confirms her order, the seller is legally required to fulfill the contract. The factual theory is that if the secretary to the seller's agent had checked on the buyer's file, a confirming letter would have been found with the details about the clubs, but the file was never checked. And the persuasive theory is that the big and experienced seller should have been responsible for paying attention to an order from a small and brand-new buyer. In terms of planning for a deposition, this integrated "case theory" suggests that in deposing the secretary, for example, questions about how he confirmed the order, where he looked for information, how he kept his files, how convenient they were to his desk, how easy it would have been to check, and so on, immediately come to the forefront of the questioner's mind.

The importance of a clear and persuasive case theory becomes evident when considering how judges and juries actually decide cases. Research suggests that a juror decides the factual issues in a trial by creating a "story" of the events, based on the evidence presented. This story is initially based on what is said by the parties during the opening statement; then, as the trial progresses and evidence is presented, the jurors will match that evidence against the story each side created. As long as a juror's story adequately explains the evidence presented—that is, it is not inconsistent with proven fact—the juror will adhere to that story. If, however, there is too great a conflict between the story and the evidence, the juror will abandon the initial story and form a new story that better explains the evidence. The story, whether the initial story or one newly formulated during the trial (or as later modified by the jury deliberations), will serve as the basis for that juror's verdict. There is every reason to believe that judges, when serving as fact finders, arrive at decisions in the same way as juries.[5]

The lesson to be drawn from this story model of jury decision making is that it is not enough for you to merely present the judge or jury with the facts and leave it to them to bring the facts together into some sort of coherent story. The judge or jury will, inevitably, create a story in response to the evidence, but it may not be the story you and your client want to have adopted. Instead, it is your task to clearly and persuasively present your *client's story* so that the judge or jury will adopt it as the template against which the evidence presented during the trial will be matched. That story is the factual theory of the case.

To summarize, what we mean by the theory of the case is the application of the law to the facts of the case, organized persuasively so as to justify a verdict in the client's favor. While simple to define, an effective case theory is much more difficult to create. It is usually impossible to decide at the discovery stage which case theory you will use at trial. Too many facts are still unknown or uncertain at that point in the litigation to allow you to craft a case theory with any certainty that the facts presented at trial will substantiate that theory. Uncertainty about the factual theory, in turn, leads to uncertainty about the proper legal and persuasive theories to assert. In short, it is usually a premature exercise to attempt to come up with a final case theory during the discovery stage.

Although too soon to decide on a final case theory, during the discovery stage you must have what are known as *working theories* of what happened. Working theories are nothing more than possible final factual theories. Imagine an African explorer in the middle of the nineteenth century contemplating a map of Africa. The explorer would have seen a map with many blank areas, areas that had not yet been explored, with no one (at least no one other than those who lived in the blank areas) knowing what might be found there. The explorer might be able to hazard an intelligent guess and say, "I suspect this area, based on what I already know, is savannah, but it could also be mountainous," but until it is actually explored, it cannot be described with certainty. The prudent explorer would, however, plan for both contingencies—savannah or mountains—rather than gambling on just one or the other.

---

5. *See* REID HASTIE, STEVEN D. PENROD & NANCY PENNINGTON, INSIDE THE JURY (2002); REID HASTIE, INSIDE THE JUROR: THE PSYCHOLOGY OF JUROR DECISION MAKING (1994).

The lawyer's situation at the beginning of discovery is similar to that of the explorer planning an African expedition—there will be blank areas on the litigator's factual map of the events underlying the case that will need to be filled in through discovery. But to conduct discovery effectively and efficiently, the trial lawyer must have thought carefully about the possible factual explanations of what happened and why, given the facts already known, that may result in a successful outcome to the case. These alternative scenarios of what might have happened are the lawyer's working theories.

The number of working theories you may have when planning discovery will depend on what facts you already know. In other words, how many and how large are the blank areas on the factual map? Regardless of the number, one of the most important functions of discovery is to test the different working theories in the case and to winnow out those that are not viable.

Keep in mind that any working theory, if it is to survive to become the factual theory of the case, must be supported by admissible and persuasive evidence—and it must be organized in a logical and understandable manner. During the discovery stage, you should evaluate the information you have gathered and the witnesses you have deposed in light of these concerns. In considering a witness's answer in a deposition, the following inquiries are appropriate: "Will this evidence be admissible; will this person make a good witness; do these facts fit into an attractive story;" and so on.

As discovery progresses and new facts come to light, some of the working theories will be discarded while others are expanded and refined. Because different factual scenarios may have different legal consequences, the legal theory must also be re-examined in light of the factual changes. By the time you deliver your closing argument at trial, only one story—one factual theory, one legal theory, one persuasive theory—should remain—the one that will be presented to the judge or jury. However, do not be too hasty in getting to that point. Keep an open mind about what happened, and explore all possible scenarios before discarding any of them.

The factual theory must be well-founded; it cannot be your wish list. The rules of ethics and fraud obviously preclude you from manufacturing evidence; the rules of case preparation preclude you from assuming that eventually some facts will be found that help. A theory unsupported by actual facts is destined to fail. To construct a sound factual theory, you must marshal the facts into a persuasive whole that will provide the fact finder with a logical and compelling story of what happened and why.

5.5.1   Timelines

Creating a visual timeline by placing the events that underlie a lawsuit in chronological order (preferably horizontally, earliest to the left, current or future to the right), may help explanations of what really happened emerge. The sequencing of events often illuminates motives and the cause-and-effect relationships among actions. Just as important, a timeline can identify gaps in the evidence that you need to fill to create an effective factual theory. In addition, inconsistencies may appear. A sequence of events that the client and witnesses give, when presented in a graphical timeline, may not make sense. That is, the story as told by one witness ("he was just outside his office at 7:00 p.m.") may be inconsistent with the stories other witnesses tell or other evidence presents ("his parking lot ticket fifteen miles from the office shows he picked up his car at 6:53 p.m."). The timeline may also suggest additional deposition questions that may fill in the gaps in the evidence.

5.5.2   Relationship Charts

A "relationship chart" is a visual representation of the interactions and potential interactions among the parties, witnesses, and institutions in the case. It is a helpful device in cases where the factual theory seeks to explain the motives of the parties for important actions. You can create the chart by identifying all the parties and ancillary actors in the case. If there is doubt about a witness's role, include that witness on the chart. A witness with what at first seems to be an apparently minor role may turn out, because of his relationship with a party or institution, to possess case-changing information about why a contract was breached, why an employee was terminated, or why an automobile steering assembly was not repaired correctly. Once you have depicted the actors and institutions on the chart, identify their relationships with a connecting line. Label each line with significant inter-relating facts. (It is hard not to think about the "perp charts" used on TV cop shows to uncover relationships among victims, suspects, and hard evidence: *See Melina Kanakaredes pull up the computer display for Gary Sinise. See Gary Sinise connect the victim to the suspect by identifying the fact that their apartments were directly across the airshaft from one another.*)

You can combine timelines that focus on the activities and relationships of individuals with complex relationship charts to introduce a chronological dimension in which to analyze those behaviors. The completed chart can reveal possible explanations of what happened, how it happened, why it happened, and who caused it to happen. From these facts, you can uncover additional questions for deposition. And from that insight, you can identify other relationships as well as other areas of inquiry during depositions.

5.5.3   *Brainstorming*

Brainstorming is a powerful analytic process of encouraging people to engage in unrestricted thinking about facts involved in a particular event. This method works best in a group, especially in a group whose members are unrelated to the case, with one person acting as a facilitator or leader. The goal is to list as many ideas as possible, and the role of the facilitator is to keep the suggestions flowing and insure that everyone contributes. Normally, the facilitator will refrain from offering ideas herself (so that others do not defer to her and eventually stop contribution). An effective brainstorming session has the following rules:

1.   There are no bad ideas;

2.   Self-censoring is unprofitable; a bad idea may provoke a good idea;

3.   Critique of another person's ideas suppresses contributions; embarrassment leads to withdrawal from the exercise;

4.   The rules of evidence are irrelevant; inadmissible concepts may suggest ways to discover admissible facts;

5.   Only facts, not conclusions, can be stated; it is not the time to argue;

6.   All suggested facts must be recorded;

7.   Evaluation and analysis of facts occurs only toward the end of the session; and

8.   The session is time-limited; participants may not volunteer for a day, but they will volunteer for forty-five minutes.

9.   The facilitator should ask certain questions at the end: e.g., "What other facts would you like to know? Why is Jones more important than Smith? What documents do you think probably exist that you have not seen?

Using these rules, the leader asks the group to state the good facts and the bad facts (or the good/bad documents, or witnesses, or legal theories, or persuasive theories (a "bad" persuasive theory would be one that worked well for your opponent, or one that did not consider all of the likely admissible facts)). After the facts have been listed, the group votes on the three or five best and worst facts. Once the voting is over, a critical look at the best and worst facts will suggest appropriate story lines that underlie factual theories for and against each party. The goal, then, of the depositions will be to confirm the good facts of the case (those supporting favorable story lines) and discredit or explain away the bad facts (those supporting unfavorable story lines). The ultimate goal is to develop for your client a coherent and persuasive explanation of what really happened and why.

5.5.4   *Focus Groups*

In modern litigation, the focus group is a fact of life. Focus groups are perhaps most commonly used when discovery in a case is complete and the matter is being readied for trial. However, pre-discovery focus groups are becoming much more common. In part this is because the cost of these groups, even when facilitated by professionals, is much more reasonable than it was even five years ago. In addition, you can learn to conduct or at least participate in your own focus groups, thereby reducing the costs even further.[6] Although a full description of focus group techniques is beyond the scope of this book, the various approaches have some common goals:

1.   Identify areas of factual inquiry (what would they like to know in addition to what they have been told);

2.   Alert the lawyers to facts a jury likely will consider as important;

3.   Identify facts that jurors will expect to exist in light of other facts in the case (*Didn't this happen? Why didn't you tell us that?*);

4.   Identify witnesses a jury would like to hear from; and

5.   Identify psychological hot issues (*Once we found out he was a child molester, well . . .*).

From the results of focus groups, you can develop potential story lines [factual theories] that can then be pursued in further discovery.

Finally, with regard to using devices for developing case theories for deposition practice, note that none of these devices is exclusive of the others. Indeed, in a proper case, all of these devices can be used to develop the alternate story lines that, after discovery, may be found to support the factual theory.

The story lines should encompass all of the characteristics of good storytelling.

---

6. It is appropriate here to disclose that one of the authors, Malone, through his company, Trial Run Inc., conducts and advises on focus groups for law firms, agencies, and companies and is a great believer in their utility.

1. A good story must account for or explain all of the known or undeniable facts. Common sense tells us that a story that contradicts the known facts will be unbelievable to a judge or jury. We will not accept an explanation premised on the world being flat; similarly, no jury will accept a story that conflicts with other facts the jurors accept as being true.

2. A good story must be supported by the details. Judges and juries are persuaded not only by the major facts in the case, but also by all of the supporting details. For instance, the credibility of a witness is enhanced if the witness can recount not just that a key meeting was held, but also where it was held, who was there, when it occurred, what words were used, etc. Of course, is not necessary to detail every fact, as that would be overwhelming and perhaps obscure the important facts; detail on important and contested key facts, however, enhances the believability of the story.

3. A good story must explain why people acted the way they did. Why was the defendant driving so fast just before the accident? Why didn't the plaintiff order substitute parts as soon as it learned the defendant was not going to deliver as promised? Why would the defendants want to fix prices? A good story must have the actors behaving consistently, spurred by motives that a fact finder can understand; or it must provide a good explanation for why they did not behave in the way the fact finder would anticipate.

4. A good story must be plausible and consistent with common sense. A story may be internally logical and even true, but if it does not square with the way jurors believe the world operates, they will be skeptical. To be believed, a story must make sense.

5. A good story must appeal to our desire for justice and fairness. A good factual theory will not only satisfy the applicable legal theory and therefore entitle you to the verdict you are asking for, but it should also make the jurors want you to win, regardless of the law, because it is the fair and just outcome. (A long-time practitioner in Georgia told the authors that he tried to find a story that would make the jurors proud to talk about their verdict.) When you identify such a story, conduct discovery to find the additional facts to support it.

5.6   Identifying the Opponent's Factual and Legal Theories

A trial is not just about proving a party's claim or defense—it is also about attacking or answering the opponent's position. However, you cannot attack something unless you know what it is. You can glean much of the opponent's theory from what is said in the opponent's pleadings, in settlement negotiations with opposing counsel, and by opposing parties and witnesses pre-litigation. Your assessment of the opponent's theory will become sharper as the case progresses, particularly when you consider the opposing counsel's questions in depositions, the information she seeks through interrogatories, and the documents and other discovery she requests. Give the same attention and diligence to researching the opposing party's possible legal and factual theories as you give to developing your client's own theories. Once you develop an understanding of potential legal theories, pro and con, you can develop questions for each deposition.

5.7   Generating Questions

You can generate topics for each deposition outline in a number of ways. As previously mentioned, most good attorneys do not rely on one particular method for thinking of topics, but will use a combination of approaches. The following is a discussion of some of those approaches.

5.7.1   *Brainstorming*

Of all of the methods of preparing for a deposition, brainstorming, as described above regarding developing potential working theories, is the best way to those identify areas where you need new information. In a large case, assemble the whole litigation team for a day; in a small case, impose on a partner and one or two others for an hour of their time. If no partner or other lawyer is available, consider including a secretary or your spouse. In any event, establish the same ground rules described above, highlighting that there will be no judgmental responses to suggestions for questions and that no proposition is too basic or too stupid to suggest.

After describing the case briefly, begin with a three-minute description of the witness or witnesses and outline their roles in the case. Then open the floor for discussion: what do people want to know from this witness that might help them understand the entire case better? Someone in the room, or several people, should be responsible for taking down all of the suggestions proposed—without editorializing or omitting seemingly trivial, irrelevant, inadmissible, or off-the-wall ideas.

A second aspect of brainstorming is bringing a healthy curiosity to the process. If there was a telephone conversation, what do we want to know about that conversation? Perhaps when it was held, the parties to the conversation, what was said, whether records were made, and so on. Or for an automobile accident, where were the drivers going, when did they see each other, how fast were they going, and so forth. Effective brainstorming depends on the participants' curiosity about the world, about how events occur, about cause and effect, and particularly about precisely what happened in the case being considered.

The key to successful brainstorming is getting everyone involved and talking. A silly question may provoke an insightful one; an irrelevant remark may lead people to recognize that the bounds of relevance for that witness should be redefined. Anyone who has participated in a brainstorming session has seen the impressive synergies that arise as several minds come at a problem or topic from different directions and with different dispositions.

If the process hits a slow spot, try to revive the energy by raising a new topic and posing particular questions: "OK, let's try this: we want to show that the manufacturer *knew* the product was unsafe in cold weather. How do we show that state of mind?" A white board, on which the main topics are displayed as they arise, helps keep those topics in the forefront. Some members of the group will dwell on particular topics while the rest of the group moves on, and often the first group will interrupt later with a series of useful questions. Any structure that promotes the free flow of ideas is useful. There are a number of books available on brainstorming, and no matter the particular subject matter, the procedures described are completely applicable to the process of developing deposition questions (as well as to choosing counts to include in a complaint, or ways to attack an expert on cross-examination, or the choice of graphics for trial).

5.7.2 Relating the Factual Theory to the Legal Theory

A good factual theory is not enough if it does not also establish the elements of a legal claim or defense. A factual theory is not constructed for its entertainment value, but to win a case. Therefore, to be successful, the facts of the story must make out a claim or defense. Keep this requirement must in mind when preparing the deposition outline.

5.7.3 Identifying Facts Missing from the Factual Theory

Once you have developed the legal and factual working theories to the greatest reasonable extent possible, the next step is to identify those facts that are missing from the factual theory. In developing the story, consider the following basic questions as a way to improve the deposition outline:

- What happened?

- Who did what?

- Who said what?

- How did it happen?

- Where did it happen?

- Who was involved?

- Who witnessed it?

- Why did it happen?

- What documents would record what happened?

- Who normally would be told about it happening?

- Who can verify it happening?

- What documents can verify it happening?

- What inferences or conclusions can you draw from it happening?

- What facts are missing from the story?

- What are the different ways this story could have occurred? What are all the possible plot variations that could occur in this story?

- If a particular fact is true, what other facts must also be true?

- If a particular fact is true, what would a normal or reasonable person have done in this situation?

- If this fact is true, what results or consequences should have been noticed?

- What evidence do you need to prove the elements of the claim?

- What do you need to refute the opponent's story?

To illustrate how you can use just one of these techniques to generate topics for the deposition outline, assume a breach of contract case. The plaintiff claims that the defendant's sales manager assured the plaintiff's president during a telephone conversation that the plaintiff would replace a missing shipment of expensive computer parts without cost even though there was no legal obligation on the part of the defendant to do so. The plaintiff is now suing because the defendant is refusing to live up to that alleged promise. In preparing for the plaintiff president's deposition, the defendant's attorney might want to think about:

- What else would likely have happened if the defendant had promised to replace the parts?

- Did the president tell anyone about this good news?

- Was a phone log record prepared?

- Was the plaintiff's purchasing or parts departments notified of the replacement parts?

- Did the plaintiff send a confirming letter of the telephone conversation? And so forth.

All of these may be useful areas on which to question the witness, and they should be included in the deposition outline.

5.7.4 *The Proof Chart*

One way to keep track of what facts are available and what facts you still need is to make a proof chart. Such a chart can be nothing more than a large piece of paper with the elements of the claims and defenses listed on one side. Nowadays, of course, it is more likely to be a table created in a computer program, providing the ability to create rows and columns and to insert and move information in boxes. In its simplest form, the proof chart has only four columns across the top: *Supporting Facts, Supporting Facts to Be Discovered, Opposing Facts,* and *Opposing Facts to Be Discovered.* As you think carefully about the facts you already know and what additional facts you need to prove or disprove each element, you can fill in the four columns. Update the chart as you receive new information. Move facts contained in the "To Be Discovered" columns to the "Facts" columns as discovery progresses. A sample proof chart for the above example follows:

	Supporting Facts	Supporting Facts to Be Discovered	Opposing Facts	Opposing Facts to Be Discovered
Representation	Jones and Smith heard	Was it said	Denial by defendant	Internal documents support
Reliance in Good Faith	No parts ordered	Plaintiff reserved parts		
Action Based on Representation	Smith told Marketing		No commission paid	

The only special thing about the chart is that it helps you focus on what information you need to prove the case or disprove the opponent's case. The chart not only helps you organize your thinking, but it also gives you a method of recording the ideas generated.

By having columns for the opponent's case, the proof chart also requires you to consider and evaluate what the opposing party will be proving and what evidence is needed to meet that proof. The information in the columns labeled "Supporting Facts to Be Discovered" and "Opposing Facts to Be Discovered" serves as the basis for the deposition outline. A computerized chart will make it easier for you to move facts from column to column and add or delete facts based on what you find in the discovery process. This chart was formerly kept on a large piece of butcher paper taped to the wall where it was available for ready reference. Even the authors of this book, both coming to the bar long before the existence of personal computers, have evolved to adopt the electronic form and the ease and convenience it presents. In reality, however, the form does not matter—the concentrated thinking about the discovery of the facts as they relate to proof requirements does.

5.7.5 Reviewing the Pleadings

If the deponent is a party, or closely identified with a party, the party's pleadings may raise numerous questions. "What is your evidence for the allegation in Complaint Paragraph 4?" is usually not a profitable question. The answer will often devolve into quibbling about what constitutes evidence, or whether this deposition is the appropriate time for a disclosure of exhibits, or whether the witness is responsible for her lawyer's choice of language, and so on and so forth.

A better question to ask is: "Do you believe that this allegation or response about control of the other car is accurate?" (or, even better, pleadings and filings aside, "Do you believe that the driver of the other car was paying sufficient attention to controlling his car?"). Then follow up with: "Why?" So when you prepare to take a deposition, review the pleadings, highlight or clip those portions that might provoke discussion, and incorporate them into the deposition outline.

5.7.6   *Documents*

Reviewing the documents in the case will usually suggest topics to include in the deposition outline. (In fact, in our live courses, we often tell young or inexperienced attorneys that the hardest thing about document analysis is figuring out what the documents do *not* say. Those things not said in a document are the subject of valuable deposition questions.) The outline should note the need to explore the contents of the documents themselves during witness examination. Questioning techniques regarding documents will be discussed in chapter nine, but when you are constructing the deposition outline, consider and include what information you are seeking about those documents.

Do not, however, view the use of the documents at the deposition as a goal in and of itself. Documents generate questions—what do phrases or discussions in the documents mean, why was the document written, who wrote the document, what happened to a document, who has seen the document, what effect did the document have on events? Nothing is gained by asking, "Doesn't this document say that the loan was discussed at the meeting?" because the authenticated document establishes its own content as well as the redundant deposition testimony would.

Chapter Nine, "Using Documents," discusses how some attorneys pile up the "relevant" documents at the start of the deposition and then end the deposition when they have reached the bottom of the pile after showing each document to the witness and authenticating it in some way. Authentication can be accomplished in many other, much less expensive ways. For example, ask in the request for production for "documents prepared and kept in the normal course of business that relate to . . . ." You will then obtain not only the documents, but also an admission that they are authentic business documents of the company. This practice saves deposition time. In preparing to take a deposition, focus on themes, theories, and occurrences, regardless of whether they are recorded in some document. The documents should be useful; they should not be controlling.

5.7.7   *Reviewing Depositions*

Prior depositions in the case are also good sources from which to prepare for the next deposition. First, your questions and a prior deponent's answers may suggest questions, but the types of questions asked by your opponent will also suggest areas for further exploration. Next, your opponent's questions will strongly suggest the legal and factual theories she is pursuing, providing you insight and ideas on how to counter those theories. Finally, periodically spending some time reviewing your own deposition transcripts will improve your questioning in the remaining depositions in the case (and in depositions in other cases as well).

5.7.8   *Working with the Client and the Expert*

Obviously, the client is one of the best sources of information when preparing any portion of a lawsuit, and preparing for the depositions of opposing witnesses is no exception. The client has a recollection of the relevant incidents obtained by living through the episode. And, although that recollection can be aided or refreshed by the use of documents, it exists independent of the documents. Therefore, before taking any depositions, it is essential that you meet with the client, perhaps with the main responsive pleading in hand, to discuss the other side's position and the facts that would have to be true to support that position. If the other side claims contributory negligence as a defense, assume, with the client, that the claim is made in good faith. What then must the opposition believe happened? Are there other facts that they must believe? Are there witnesses that you have not considered? Can your client's memory of the episode be defective or incomplete—by omitting incidents or conversations or by incorrectly remembering the sequence of events? Having such a conversation with the client allows you to pursue exactly those types of questions with the deponent. Will the opposition present additional witnesses at trial? Will they claim that the screws went in first, before the bracket was attached, instead of the other way around? Will they try to show that your client reviewed the competitor's pricing sheet before submitting its own bid, not after?

In other words, you should spend enough time with the client to understand the potential weaknesses in the case and possible holes in the client's version of the facts. You can then explore the opposition's reliance on those possible weaknesses at the deposition. Asking questions such as, "Exactly what was the sequence of events leading to the injury?" can help identify differences between the positions of the two sides, and you can follow up with additional questions, such as: "What is the significance of the screws being put in after the bracket is attached?" or "If the board did not receive the appraisal until after it approved the loan, how does that change your conclusion about the adequacy of underwriting for this loan?"

Just as the client can help identify areas for discussion at the deposition, so can the expert. Contrary to common practice, do not use the experts only to help prepare for the opposing expert's deposition; they can help identify areas of inquiry for lay witnesses as well. The expert should be used to identify those facts that must be established to support her opinions, as well as the factual assumptions on which the opposing expert's opinions must be based. These facts will then become the topics of questioning at the lay witnesses' depositions to establish the necessary factual basis for your expert's opinions and refuting the factual basis for the opposing expert's opinions.

5.8   Organizing the Deposition Outline

The deposition outline will ordinarily be organized in such a way that topics flow naturally from one to the other. Some attorneys believe it is advantageous to jump from one topic to another, unrelated one. As discussed in section 7.3, with the exception of a few planned traps, little is gained from a leapfrog approach to questioning witnesses. By systematically progressing through the materials and events—often chronologically, but also by subject matter—you can maintain control of the material and the witness.

Triple spacing the outline (whether in paper or electronic format) allows you to easily move back to the outline after you have finished an area of "improvisational" inquiry. The extra space also allows you to add topics at the last moment as new ideas develop or make very brief notations on items that you would like to come back to.

5.9   Using the Outline at the Deposition

Do not slavishly follow the outline during the deposition. Any good deposition attorney listens carefully to the witness's answers and follows where those answers lead, even if the witness's answers suggest new topics not previously considered and, therefore, not on the outline.

However, when a witness's answer suggests a new topic or an answer comes as a surprise, mark the outline and either explore the new topic immediately or merely add the topic to a list of future topics to be explored. At other times, you will abandon topics if the witness's answers show there is nothing to be gained by further exploration. Most attorneys also check off topics on the outline as they complete the questioning on that topic. Then, before concluding the deposition, they take a few moments to review the outline to make sure there are no topics left to be asked about.

Notice that we suggest using outlines of topics, not questions that are fully written out. If the outline is actually a list of questions, it will not be long before the witness's answers and the outline questions part company.

Using an outline of topics allows you to ask questions that react to the witness's answers. Using an outline of written questions does not permit this flexibility. In addition, an outline that consists of a list of questions will often restrict the topics to be explored. The rigidity of the written question format discourages conversational exploration of answers that promotes discovery of what facts a witness actually knows.

Of course, there are exceptions to the rule about not writing out deposition questions. Sometimes the evidentiary value of a question will depend on the particular wording of the question. For example, in putting a hypothetical to an expert witness, it may be necessary to be very precise with the assumptions being made. In that situation, it is much better to write out the question in advance rather than trusting to memory to pose the question extemporaneously during the deposition.

Another situation where written questions are helpful is in laying the foundation for an exhibit. Many evidentiary foundations require the use of certain "magic" words such as "fair and accurate" when laying the foundation for a photograph.[7] Rather than run the risk of forgetting to use these magic words, it is better to write them out in advance. In addition, in some cases particular words have unique legal and factual significance. Using precise phrases such as "risk of loss" in a contracts case or "substantial cause" in a torts case can provide the predicate for a summary judgment motion based on an admission extracted from an opposing party's statements. Nevertheless, as a general rule, an outline composed of words or phrases or bullet points, rather than written questions, is the best approach.

5.10   Checklist for Preparing for the Deposition

1. Review Federal Rules of Civil Procedure 26, 28, 29, 30, 32, and applicable local rules.

2. Contact all parties to see if agreement can be reached on the time and place of the deposition. *See* section 1.5.

3. If documents are needed in advance of the deposition, prepare and serve a request to produce if the documents are in the possession of a party or a subpoena duces tecum if the documents are in the possession of a nonparty. The request to produce may be served by first-class mail, but a subpoena duces tecum must be personally served. *See* section 1.11.

---

7. *See* chapter ten.

4. Consider and, if necessary, bring a motion for protective orders, such as one limiting who may be present at the deposition. *See* chapter twelve.

5. Determine how the deposition is to be recorded—stenographically or video or sound recording—and provide the proper notice. *See* section 1.13.2.

6. Reserve a room and arrange for a court reporter for the scheduled date.

7. With sufficient time before the scheduled date of the deposition (usually fourteen days or more, but check local rules) prepare and serve a notice of deposition on all parties, usually by first-class mail or facsimile. The notice of deposition must state the method of recording to be used at the deposition. If a subpoena duces tecum is to be served on the witness, the notice of deposition must include or have attached to it a list of the materials in the subpoena duces tecum that are to be produced at the deposition. Service of the notice of deposition is all that is necessary to compel the attendance at the deposition of a party or an officer, managing agent, or director of a party. *See* sections 1.6, 1.10.1. Some court reporting services will arrange for service of the notice of deposition and any subpoenas as part of the services they provide.

8. If the deposition is of someone other than a party or an officer, managing agent, or director of a party, issue a subpoena (a blank subpoena can be obtained from the clerk of the court of the district in which the deposition will be taken, or an attorney may sign and issue the subpoena if a member of the bar of the district where the appearance is compelled or of the district where the action is pending) and arrange for personal service of it on the witness. The service of the subpoena must be accompanied by a tender of the witness fee and mileage allowance. *See* section 1.10.2.

9. If documents are required for the deposition, attempt to have the documents brought to the deposition. If no agreement can be reached, *see* number 3, above.

10. Consider any stipulations to be offered to the other side. Also consider those stipulations that are likely to be offered by the opposing party and how you should respond. *See* section 1.13.4.

5.11   A Final Word about Preparation

No one is ever prepared for every question or every topic at a deposition: not the witness, not the witness's counsel, and certainly not the deposing attorney. If the progress and twists and turns could be forecast accurately, the amount of actual "discovery" would decline markedly. Therefore, instead of expending energy agonizing over inadequate preparation, listen closely to the witness, follow up on interesting or incomplete answers, and try to understand the witness's answers to uncover subjects the witness wants to avoid.

No one has ever taken a perfect deposition. Fortunately, justice does not depend on perfection from lawyers or witnesses. From a full day of deposition testimony, perhaps twenty answers will have some value and some possible use at trial; of those twenty, perhaps five will be used; and experience shows that those five are most likely to have come in response to questions that were reactions to information provided by the witness that was unanticipated in the deposition outline.

The lesson? To prepare, get ready to listen to the answers and to follow up on those answers until what the witness is saying and why she is saying it are clear in the record. Gaining an understanding of the facts is one of the most important achievements a lawyer can accomplish in litigating a case.

CHAPTER SIX

BEGINNING THE DEPOSITION

A few strong instincts and a few plain rules suffice us.

—William Wordsworth (1770–1850)

Some procedures regarding formalities and approaches apply to the beginning of every deposition, regardless of the issues in the case, the personalities of the witnesses, or the substance of the information to be discovered. An appropriate and uniform approach for most depositions can be identified. Let's review these common issues and evaluate the options.

6.1   Stipulations

Under Federal Rule of Civil Procedure 29, the parties may stipulate to nearly anything concerning depositions,[1] as long as the court's timetable is not upset. This gives the parties the power to alter such things as the:

- notices given;

- qualifications of the officer administering the oath;

- method of recording;

- time and date;

- length of the deposition;

- continuing the deposition for more than one day;

---

1. FED. R. CIV. P. 29:
Unless the court orders otherwise, the parties may stipulate that:
    (a) a deposition may be taken before any person, at any time or place, on any notice, and in the manner specified—in which event it may be used in the same way as any other deposition; and
    (b) other procedures governing or limiting discovery be modified—but a stipulation extending the time for any form of discovery must have court approval if it would interfere with the time set for completing discovery, for hearing a motion, or for trial.

- location where the deposition is held;

- order of depositions;

- production of documents at the deposition;

- handling of exhibits at the deposition;

- preserving exhibits used at the deposition;

- forms and types of objections that must be made at the deposition;

- types of objections that need not be made at the deposition;

- preserving the deposition; and

- uses of the deposition.

This is hardly a complete list of all the possible stipulations to which the parties might agree. There is nothing that prevents the parties from altering nearly any aspect of the procedure governing depositions or other discovery when it serves their joint interests to do so.

There are advantages and disadvantages to each side in altering the procedures provided by the Federal Rules of Civil Procedure. The Rules have been carefully drafted to protect the interests of both the taker and defender as well as the interests of witnesses. Stipulations have the effect of altering this carefully crafted balance. Nevertheless, it is often in the interest of both sides to agree to changes in the procedures followed during the deposition, as well as the steps leading up to the deposition and following its completion.

We sound a note of caution at this point. While stipulations can have many beneficial effects, you should never agree to a modification of the procedures imposed by the Rules without first giving careful consideration to what is being gained and what is being given up in the stipulation. A stipulation should only be agreed to when it is clearly in your client's interest to do so.

While there is hardly any limit on what can be stipulated to, there are some types of stipulations that are routinely proposed by one side or the other. These common stipulations will be considered in the following sections, along with a discussion of the advantages and disadvantages to each side. We will also give our opinions about whether it is desirable to agree to each type of stipulation.

6.1.1 *"The Usual Stipulations"*

Let us start with a type of stipulation that is frequently agreed to in many parts of the country, while being virtually unheard of in other areas—"the usual stipulations." The first thing you should understand is that there are no "usual stipulations," and there is no obligation to accept an offer to enter into them. While "the usual stipulations" may refer to a frequent agreement made in some regions of the country, or the state, or the county where it is the custom to make such a stipulation, there is no uniform definition of what is encompassed by the phrase. Attorneys may share a vague understanding of what is included within the words, even if they come from different parts of the country, but no definition of the phrase can be found in any case, statute or court rule.[2] Instead, the cases contain endless arguments about what is included within the phrase. As noted by one court, "Everyone purports to know without asking the content of the 'usual stipulations' until a dispute arises; the ephemeral nature of the parties' understanding is then quite apparent."[3]

Because of the lack of agreement about what is meant by the phrase, the first question you should ask in response to a proposal for the usual stipulations is, "What do you mean?" It may well be that the party proposing the stipulation has no idea of what is meant by the phrase and is only repeating what she has heard in other depositions. Custom is a powerful force and compels many attorneys to mimic what they have seen other attorneys do, even though they have no understanding of why the other attorneys said or did what is now being copied.

Be prepared. You will be strongly tempted to agree to the usual stipulations the first time an attorney proposes them to you. No one wants to appear clueless about proper procedures or present herself as an ignorant neophyte unaware of the meaning of a stipulation process with a long tradition among attorneys. This is especially true of newer or "baby lawyers," who fear they will be revealing their lack of experience if they should ask what is meant by the usual stipulations. As a result, you may feel a strong urge to agree to the proposed stipulations. Do not be embarrassed to ask exactly what it is that opposing counsel wants to stipulate to.

Very often, these "usual stipulations" are directed to "non-problems" or minor problems that could more easily be handled at the time they arise. Take, for example, a stipulation at the beginning of the deposition that if the

---

2. In a few jurisdictions, the term "usual stipulation" refers to a specific set of stipulations that the court reporter prepares and shows to the parties at the beginning of the deposition. These jurisdictions are a distinct minority. Caution born of experience suggests that the attorney who is not certain what the "usual stipulations" are in the jurisdiction where she is taking the deposition should specifically instruct the reporter that no stipulations have been agreed to. After making exactly that statement on his first trip to take a deposition in Des Moines, one of the authors was surprised to see two pages of stipulations show up in the written transcript, inserted automatically by the reporter. A telephone call brought a new transcript, without stipulations, to the hotel room door within a couple of hours.

3. United States v. Liquid Sugars, Inc., 158 F.R.D. 466, 473 n.8 (E.D. Cal. 1994).

witness does not say she does not understand the question, that will fairly give rise to an inference that she did understand it. That stipulation is much more cumbersome than saying to the witness, "Do you understand the question?" when she responds to a question with a blank stare. However, some of what gets rolled up into these proposed usual stipulations can be important. Suppose a "usual stipulation" in Hillsborough County, Florida, is that all objections not made are preserved (or are waived—we have heard both). This stipulation for automatic preservation makes little sense, because the purpose of stating objections at a deposition is to allow the deposing attorney to correct her questions and to cure any defect. (Where unstated objections are all waived, the result is much better; pay attention and make the objections that are important—no objections means no problems to worry about later with the transcript.)

The message is, you should not agree to something you do not understand. There is no problem, in principle, to an agreement to the usual stipulations as long as the other side is clear about what is being stipulated. "What do you mean by the usual stipulations?" should be your response to the question, "Can we agree that we will have the usual stipulations?"

6.1.2   *"Reserve All Objections Except as to Form"*

Perhaps the most common deposition stipulation—and the one with the best claim to being part of the usual stipulations—takes different forms. Depending on the area of the country in which the defender practices, it is usually phrased in one of these ways:

- "Let's reserve all objections until there is an attempt to use the deposition, or some portion thereof, at some later point in the proceedings"; or

- "Let's reserve all objections except for form"; or, finally,

- "Let's reserve all objections except for form and foundation."

This stipulation is usually proposed by the defender, since all three forms of the stipulation are to the defender's advantage.

Remember that Rule 32(d)(3)(B) requires, in essence, that any objection to a defect that can be cured must be made during the deposition or the objection is waived. All three forms of the stipulation relieve the defender of the burden of having to interpose a timely objection to the form of a question. With such a stipulation, the defender can contemplate what objections to make during the months or even years between the date of the deposition and the attempt to use the deposition at trial, in a summary judgment motion, or for some other purpose.

The degree to which the defender is relieved of this duty to object depends on which of the three forms of the stipulation was agreed to. Obviously, reserving all objections provides the defender with the greatest advantage; reserving all objections except to form and foundation offers somewhat less of an advantage, and reserving all objections except as to form confers the least benefit on the defender. But all three stipulations extend the defender's strategic position beyond what the Rule provides. Admittedly, the difference between the advantage granted by preserving "all objections" compared to preserving "objections to form and foundation" is somewhat illusory, since the vast majority of objections the defender would likely be making at the deposition are to form or foundation. But, as suggested by Rule 32(d)(3)(B), there are other objections to correctable matters that can arise in a deposition, including objections to problems in the "answer, the oath or affirmation, a party's conduct, or other matters."

While the taker gains little from the stipulation, what is given up goes well beyond what has already been suggested. Imagine an antitrust action where the plaintiff is deposing a secretary employed by the defendant. The secretary had been assigned to take notes at a key meeting of several of the defendant's employees. At the beginning of the deposition, the parties entered into a stipulation to reserve all objections. During the deposition the secretary testified about several highly damaging statements by the employees about having met with competitors to set prices in an effort to drive the plaintiff out of business. In short, the deposition was an unqualified success for the plaintiff.

The plaintiff's attorney, patting herself on the back for the brilliance of her questions at the deposition, has prepared a devastating cross-examination of the secretary at the upcoming trial based on the damaging party statements given during the deposition. Unfortunately, unbeknownst to the plaintiff's attorney, during the time between the deposition and trial the secretary has disappeared and, even if found, would likely be beyond the subpoena powers of the court. Our attorney is undaunted, however, because she recalls that she can use the secretary's deposition testimony if the secretary becomes unavailable for trial. At the appropriate point in the trial the plaintiff's attorney produces the deposition and announces to the court that she now wishes to read key questions and answers to the jury.

This is where the fun starts. In response, the defendant's attorney stands up and says to the court "You Honor, before counsel reads the deposition portions in question, I have several objections I wish to raise. We stipulated at the time of the deposition to reserve all objections. Here are my objections. On page 42, line 13 the question was . . . ." Much to the taker's consternation, the court sustains all of the defendant's objections and rules that none of the offered deposition testimony is admissible. In retrospect, the plaintiff's attorney realizes that all of the objections could have been easily cured at the deposition with some additional questions, if she had only been aware of them, but of course she was not aware of them because of the stipulation made to reserve all objections.

The moral of this story? A TAKER SHOULD NEVER STIPULATE TO RESERVING ANY OBJECTIONS. A defender, on the hand, should always propose such a stipulation, if there is any prospect at all of it being accepted.

There is one minor disadvantage to the defender that comes with such a stipulation—any objections that *are* made are obviously being used to coach the witness, since there is no legitimate need to make the objection if it has been reserved. Of course, the defender should not be attempting to coach the witness at all through the use of objections,[4] so the defender's motives in objecting become even more apparent to the judge if the questioner files a request for a protective order or for sanctions for interfering with legitimate discovery.

What does the questioner gain from such a stipulation? Such a stipulation does allow the taker to avoid the distraction caused by the defender's objections, or the distraction of having to make objections to the defender's behavior or, for example, to nonresponsive answers. But as a practical matter, the questioners usually make only a small fraction of the number of objections at a deposition as defenders do. On balance, the advantages of such a "preservation" stipulation seem to overwhelmingly favor the defender.

6.1.3   *Waiving Reading and Signing*

Another common stipulation that is often a candidate for inclusion in the usual stipulations is one waiving the reading and signing of the deposition. This stipulation is only made in those jurisdictions that make reading and signing the deposition the default position, so it would need to be affirmatively waived or else it is required. In the federal courts, under Federal Rule of Civil Procedure 30(e), a party or the witness, before the conclusion of the deposition, must affirmatively demand the opportunity to review and change or correct the transcript or recording. Otherwise, the right is waived. So, in those nonfederal jurisdictions that follow the pre-1993 version of the Federal Rules of Civil Procedure, it is very common for the parties (and the witness, if a nonparty) to stipulate to waiving the reading and signing of the deposition. Often this stipulation will be deferred to the end of the deposition, thereby giving the lawyers an opportunity to evaluate the witness's performance before making the decision whether to waive the opportunity to correct the transcript or recording. There is one problem with waiving reading, correction, and signing: No attorney should ever do it!

---

4. *See* section 14.8.

The defending party should never waive the right to read and correct the deposition transcript or recording, regardless of what rules apply. Witnesses may misspeak or make other mistakes; lawyers may lose focus and start daydreaming, causing mistakes to go unnoticed until the transcript or recording is later reviewed in the more relaxed atmosphere of the office after the deposition is concluded; court reporters may mishear an answer or transcribe a question or answer incorrectly. All of these errors strongly dictate the need for the defending attorney to seize the opportunity to review the deposition transcript or recording and make changes and corrections when necessary. In short, the defending attorney should never stipulate to waiving the right to read and correct the deposition or, in federal court, should always demand the right to read and correct. If no changes are needed after reading, the witness could sign the deposition and return it (signing is not necessary in federal court if no corrections are made) or the witness could ignore it completely, which would have the same effect as waiving reading, correction, and signing. The defending attorney gains nothing but trouble by waiving this right.

The questioning party should never waive reading, correction, and signing, either. If there are statements in the transcript that the witness thinks are incorrect for some reason, the time to hear her explanation and correction is before she takes the stand at trial. If she has had that opportunity before trial, she cannot avoid an impeachment by saying, "Well, I think that this transcript is wrong," because the impeaching attorney can in turn say, "You had a chance to sit down with your attorney and review every word of this transcript, didn't you, and you never changed this answer, right? And this is your signature back here, right, below where it says, 'I have read the above transcript, and it is true and correct to the best of my knowledge and belief.' That's your signature, right?" (Again, signing is not necessary in federal court if no corrections are made.)

This will enhance the drama of impeaching the witness if the witness should deviate from the answers given in the deposition. The following can be added to the traditional impeachment questions to emphasize the favorable, impeaching language:

Q: You also had an opportunity to read your answers over?

A: Yes.

Q: And to change your answers if they were incorrect?

A: Yes.

Q: You did correct some of your answers?

A: I did.

> Q: But you didn't change that answer on lines 14–15, where you admit you fixed prices with your competitors?
>
> A: That's correct. I didn't change it.

In state jurisdictions that still follow the pre-1993 version of the federal rules, the witness is also required to sign the deposition unless waived by the parties and the witness. There is no benefit to the defender to signing unless the witness is a nonparty who needs to be controlled, and this requirement is routinely waived (assuming the taker also agrees to do so). But signing, like reading and correcting, enhances the drama of impeachment and should never be waived by the taker ("Q: And you also signed the deposition? A: Yes. Q: And that is your signature on the last page? A: Yes."). (There may be some benefit to the nonparty witness to waive reading, signing, and correction, because that arguably provides a bit more wiggle room for the witness, but it is the rare unrepresented witness who is able to think all this through on her own.)

6.1.4   *Waiver of Notice of Receipt or Filing*

Some state jurisdictions continue to follow the provision of the pre-1993 version of the Federal Rules of Civil Procedure that requires notice of receipt of the deposition. In those jurisdictions, the parties routinely stipulate to the waiver of this requirement since both sides usually receive copies of the deposition soon after it is transcribed. Rule 30(f)(4) now requires that notice only be given when one of the parties chooses to file the deposition with the clerk for some reason. This requirement should not be waived since a notice of filing will alert the nonfiling party that the filing party is planning to use the deposition for some purpose that you might want to know about.

6.1.5   *Other Potential Stipulations*

As previously discussed, there is no real limit to the possible stipulations the parties might need and agree to in a particular case. Anything the attorneys can agree on is available for stipulation, as long as it does not delay the court's schedule. There are several additional stipulations that parties frequently make, but these stipulations are less important than those discussed above and will only be discussed briefly. Such stipulations include agreements that:

- A direction by the attorney not to answer a question will be considered a refusal by the witness to answer. (For some judges, a mere direction to a witness not to answer a question is not a sufficient basis for granting a motion to compel—the deponent must also refuse to answer the question. This stipulation eliminates the requirement that the witness herself refuse to answer the question, thereby speeding up the deposition and insuring that an inadvertent oversight by the questioner does not foreclose consideration of a motion to compel. On the other hand, absent such a stipulation, the questioner has the opportunity to ask the witness directly whether she will answer the question—and to explain the ramifications that may occur if she does not—and that may be enough to push the deponent to answer.)

- Copies of exhibits may be substituted for the originals. (This is already provided for by Rule 30(f)(2)(A)(i). There is no need for this stipulation, but it is sometimes made, probably because the attorneys do not remember the rules.)

- Where multiple parties are attending a deposition, an objection by one party will be considered an objection by all. (This stipulation obviously reduces the time consumed by multiple objections in multiparty depositions and the resulting chaos of more than one lawyer making objections. However, where one of the parties has interests divergent from the other parties, that party may choose for tactical reasons not to be bound by the objections of the other parties, either by rejecting the blanket stipulation or by entering an objection to a specific question.)

- The deposition has been properly noticed and the time and place are proper under the rules and that all objections to the notice of deposition must be in writing and promptly served. (Rule 32(d)(1).) There is no need for this stipulation, but it is sometimes made.

- The deposition officer is duly qualified. (Rule 32(d)(2) requires that objections to the officer's qualifications be made before the deposition begins or promptly after the basis for disqualification becomes known or, with reasonable diligence, could have been known. There is some utility to this stipulation, because it is possible that an objection to the officer's qualifications could arise during the deposition. This possibility is forestalled by the stipulation. The witness, however, could be affected by a defect in the officer's qualifications, if, for example, the witness is charged with perjury and a lack of qualifications to administer the oath would be a defense. A represented witness could be counseled by her attorney to agree to the stipulation. An unrepresented witness might not recognize the benefit to her of not being under oath. If the witness does not join the stipulation, it may be enforceable against the parties, but it is almost surely not enforceable against the witness.)

- Where an expert is also a percipient witness (i.e., the treating physician), the deposition on eyewitness information will be separate from the deposition regarding expert opinions. (If so, this stipulation can be made at the outset of the first deposition that is taken, without compromising the right to take the expert deposition at a later time, and the stipulation should state that no expert opinions shall be elicited during the first deposition.)

6.1.6   *A Final Note on Stipulations*

When in doubt about a stipulation, our advice is, "Don't." The Rules strike a fair balance between the interests of the taker and defender, and things usually go quite smoothly when the deposition follows the Rules. There is nothing inappropriate about responding to a request for a stipulation with the simple statement that, "We'll take it by the Rules (of state or federal civil procedure)." By making this statement, you have forestalled any later debates about the terms of any stipulations, a topic of endless appellate cases. Taking the deposition by the Rules is the common practice in many areas of the country where "the usual stipulations" are not recognized as having accepted content. There is every reason to follow the Rules in your own depositions.

However, if you and the opposing attorneys decide to enter into any stipulations, usual or otherwise, be sure the stipulations are clear on the record, preferably at the beginning of the deposition. There is nothing wrong with discussing potential stipulations off the record as long as any final agreement is clear and read into the record or reduced to writing and the signed stipulation affixed to the deposition. Take the time to make sure the agreement is exactly what is contemplated and is clearly articulated. Too many cases end up on appeal because the parties later disagree about the terms of a stipulation and what was accomplished by poorly chosen words. This problem can be easily avoided by some attention to the details of the stipulation and by making sure the stipulation is understandable and fully set forth in the record.

A final note: sometimes attorneys outsmart themselves. There is at least one case where the court has said in dicta that failing to object to the opposing party's statement that there is a stipulation amounts to agreeing that there is such a stipulation.[5] So if one side incorrectly states there is a stipula-

---

5. *See* Garcia v. Co-Con, Inc., 629 P.2d 1237, 1240 (N.M. App. 1981) ("Silence amounts to assent when one lawyer says 'it is stipulated and agreed' and the opposing lawyer remains silent.").

tion when there is none, and the other side stands mute, a stipulation on that point may in fact arise. This is a rather straightforward example of an "admission by silence." An attorney should not think that remaining silent will be construed as a refusal to stipulate. He should instead state his refusal.

6.2   Set-Up and Commitments

At the beginning of the deposition a clear record should be made that the witness understands the deposition process and his rights and obligations. Here is a typical deposition introduction:

> Q: Mr. Landsbergis, my name is Joanne Backus, and I will be taking your deposition. Have you ever been deposed before?
>
> A: Yes, I have.
>
> Q: I assume that your attorney in that case gave you some instructions about the procedures and your obligations, is that correct?
>
> A: Yes, that's true.
>
> Q: We may talk about that previous case later, Mr. Landsbergis, but for now I would like to go over with you the ground rules for this deposition so that we all have the same understanding. Does that sound fair?
>
> A: Yes.
>
> Q: Good. Now, in this deposition I will be asking you questions. My questions and your answers will be recorded by Mr. Emanuel, the court reporter at the end of the table. You understand that you need to speak up and to answer so the reporter can hear you when you give your answers? He won't be able to record a nod or shake of your head or a grunt.
>
> A: Yes, I understand.
>
> Q: Mr. Emanuel also might have trouble if we talk over each other. Therefore, it is very important that you wait until I finish my question before you begin answering, even when you think you know what the rest of the question will be. Will you do that?
>
> A: Yes.

Q: You have just taken an oath that requires you to tell the truth, the whole truth, and nothing but the truth. Do you understand that?

A: Yes.

Q: And that is the same oath you would take if you were to testify in court. Do you understand that?

A: Yes.

Q: We're interested in finding out everything you know about the events and facts that underlie this lawsuit, and for that reason we are looking for full and complete answers to the questions I'm going to ask. In other words, we are looking for the "whole truth" that you just took an oath to give. Is that understood?

A: Yes.

Q: Now, on occasion I may ask a question that I don't state very well, or for some other reason you don't understand. If you don't understand my question for any reason, don't answer it. It is my job to ask understandable questions, so if you say you don't understand, I'll try to ask a better question. OK?

A: Yes, that's fine.

Q: I want you to understand that if you need a break at any time, or for any reason, you should tell me or tell your attorney. I will finish my line of questioning, if we are in the middle of it, and then see what we can do about a break. Do you understand that?

A: Yes, thank you. That sounds fine.

Q: And you see that we have water and coffee here for you if you want. Feel free to get up and get whatever you need during the deposition. OK?

A: Yes, thank you.

Q: I am sure that your attorney has told you this, but let me reinforce it: if you want to talk to your attorney, that's fine; I just ask that if there is a question pending or if you are in the middle of an answer, you either answer the question or finish the answer before speaking to your lawyer, unless you need to talk to her about a matter of privilege. OK?

A: Yes.

Q: Sometimes it happens that you will give an answer as completely as you can, and then later on, maybe five minutes later or maybe two hours later, you remember some additional information or perhaps some clarification in response to that earlier question. If that happens to you, please tell us that you would like to add something to the earlier answer, and we will do that right then while it's on your mind. Will you do that?

A: Yes, I'll try.

Q: That's good, and I'll try to give you opportunities at regular intervals in the deposition to provide any additional information or clarification as well. Is that fair?

A: Fair enough.

Q: In addition, sometimes it occurs to people that a previous answer is not completely accurate. If that happens, will you tell me and make any necessary corrections to your answers?

A: I will.

Q: Sometimes, when you are answering, you may think of some documents that might help you remember the answer or might help you give a more accurate answer. If you do, tell us. We may have those documents right here, or we may be able to get them to help you answer completely and accurately. Is that OK?

A: Yes.

Q: Because it is so critical that we get your full, complete, and accurate answers, I have to ask you whether you are taking any medication or drugs of any kind or have you consumed any cough syrup or medicine or something containing alcohol that might make it difficult for you to understand and answer my questions today?

A: No.

Q: Are you at all sick today?

A: No.

Q: Are you currently under a doctor's care for any illness?

A: No.

Q: Is there any reason why you cannot give full, complete, and accurate testimony?"

A: Nothing comes to mind.

The primary purpose for this set of instructions, at least for the witness represented by counsel,[6] is not to ensure fair treatment of the witness, but to make a record of the fairness of the deposition process, which in turn discourages attempts at trial to avoid the effect of deposition answers[7] and, at the same time, to begin the process of attempting to develop a rapport with the witness. Let's go through this introduction, comment by comment, and analyze what is actually going on:

"Have you ever been deposed before?"

This sounds innocent enough, but if the witness answers that he has been deposed, that admission can be used later to undermine the witness's claims in front of the jury that he was confused or uncertain about the deposition procedure. For example, in closing argument:

> Members of the jury, you heard Mr. Landsbergis admit in his deposition that he attended the pricing meeting in Chicago, and then you heard him try to deny it here on the stand in front of you. He claims now he was confused about the deposition procedures and that he was very nervous. But you also heard him testify that he had been in a deposition three other times.

---

6. For the witness unrepresented by counsel, such as the nonparty witness, it is all the more important that it be clear to the jury later on that the treatment of the witness and the questioning techniques were fair. Furthermore, without getting too deep into the ethical obligations involved, deposing counsel may well have a duty of fair treatment toward an unrepresented person as well as a duty not to take unfair advantage of their lack of counsel. Where the deponent is unrepresented, the instructions concerning discussions with counsel should be amended to remind the witness that he could obtain counsel if he chooses. Further, if these questions are asked in a friendly manner, it may help convince unrepresented witnesses that you are a decent and fair person who is not attempting to take advantage of them. In civil cases, there appears to be neither an ethical or moral obligation to provide special treatment to any represented witness, regardless of the inadequacy of that representation. Thus, if defending counsel fell asleep during his client's deposition, you need not wake him, and you can refrain from reporting him to the bar until the immediate case has been resolved.

7. "Unfairness" to the witness, of course, is not an option, and the lawyer should always be fair in dealing with witnesses. The question here, however, is whether the introductory instructions have that as their primary objective; they do not. In dealing with the unrepresented witness, however, general obligations of good faith and fair dealing would seem to impose an affirmative duty to inform the deponent of the nature of the process, what is expected of him, and what he is permitted to do.

He was a veteran at depositions. He was not nervous. He was not confused. He was telling the truth at the deposition—he was at the meeting in Chicago—and his attempts to deny it here in front of you show that he is not very credible.

In addition, the fact that the witness has been previously deposed can lead to finding out about the nature of those testimonial opportunities and provide potentially relevant evidence for the current litigation. Some lawyers make the mistake, however, of foregoing the rest of the introductory instructions after getting a positive response to the query about previous deposition experience. As should become clear, given the explanations of the purposes of these preliminary questions, previous testimonial experience should never preclude making the record we suggest above and explain below.

"You need to speak up . . . ."

This does indeed help the reporter, but it may also help the attorney taking the deposition, because it keeps the witness from letting his voice trail off toward the end of an answer that may embarrass him, and it reminds the witness that his answers are being recorded. It also, of course, results in a clearer record that is easier to use at trial or on a motion for summary judgment. Some attorneys believe, however, that the attorney taking the deposition should do as little as possible to remind the witness of the fact that the answers are being recorded in the hope that the witness will be more spontaneous and less guarded. If that approach is taken, the deposing attorney should watch for nods or shakes and merely confirm their meaning with: "You are shaking your head from side to side. Is your answer, 'No'?"

"Interested in finding out everything you know, looking for full and complete answers"

Your real goal, of course, is a reliable transcript of the witness's recollection of the facts of the case. Perhaps the most common attempt to evade unfavorable deposition testimony when confronted with it at trial is the one made by a witness who expands on the facts of the case and, while not directly contradicting the deposition testimony, tries to create a different impression of the events by adding facts and nuance to make his position more plausible. It is unclear whether the phenomenon is better explained by the witness testifying to a knowing falsehood or by the witness filling in and reconstructing the events in question. That is, the witness knows what conclusions he has formed about the events and, when thinking about them, he reconstructs the events to be consistent with those firmly and honestly held conclusions. It is this reconstruction that shows up in trial testimony. When that occurs, of course, you could acceptably impeach on the theory of inconsistency by

omission. The reminder to the witness of the oath taken and the requirement of telling the "whole truth," as well as this preliminary request for full
and complete testimony, is a nice introduction to such impeachment at trial.
When the witness agrees to give full and complete testimony at deposition,
and is given every opportunity to do so, expansion at trial is more telling on
the issue of the witness's credibility. If at trial, then, the witness begins to
expand on his testimony, you could pursue the following examination:

Q: You told us on direct examination that you had a good
view of the accident, correct?

A: Yes.

Q: You claim that was so for a number of reasons, don't you?

A: I do.

Q: You said that you were forty feet from the intersection;
that there was nothing between where you were standing
and the accident; that although you were originally facing
away from the intersection, your attention was focused by
the squealing of tires; and that even though it was dark
and rainy that night, there was a street light directly behind you that illuminated the intersection.

A: That's right.

Q: In fact, Mr. Jones, there was no street light at the intersection, was there?

A: No, I remember the light.

Q: Have you always had that memory, sir?

A: Yes, I'm sure.

Q: This isn't the first time you've given sworn testimony
about this accident, is it?

A: No, there was one other time.

Q: You had your deposition taken?

A: I did.

Q: You swore at that deposition to tell the truth?

A: I did.

Q: The whole truth?

A: That's right.

Q: I told you at the deposition that we were interested in finding out everything you knew about the accident, right?

A: You did.

Q: And you agreed to give full and complete testimony, didn't you?

A: I did.

Q: You were told that if you realized that you had given an incomplete answer you could make the answer complete at any time during the deposition, correct?

A: I was.

Q: And in fact, after every break I asked you if you wanted to complete or change a previous answer, didn't I?

A: You did.

Q: You never changed or corrected any of your answers at the deposition, did you?

A: No.

Q: You also had the opportunity to read your deposition and make any corrections or changes that existed?

A: I did.

Q: And in fact you made several corrections, didn't you?

A: I did.

Q: And then you signed your deposition, didn't you?

A: I did.

Q: Let me show you what has been marked as Exhibit 77. Exhibit 77 is your signed deposition, isn't it?

A: It is.

Q: Now again sir, it's a fact, isn't it, that on the day of the accident there was no street light, was there?

A: Yes, there was.

Q: Directing your attention to page 34, line 1 of your deposition, please read along with me.

 Question: Did you have a good view of the accident?

 Answer: I did.

 Question: How is it that you were able to see what happened?

 Answer: Well, I was just forty feet from where it happened. I heard a squealing of brakes and turned and saw the accident. There was nothing between where I was standing, so I saw the whole thing.

 Question: What else gave you a good view?

 Answer: Just that. I was close and looking right at it with nothing in the way.

 Question: Were then any other reasons why you believe you had a good view of the accident?

 Answer: That's it.

Q: Have I read the transcript correctly, sir?

A: You have.

Q: At your deposition you made no mention of this street light you today claim was there, did you?

A: No.

"If you don't understand my question . . . ."

When trapped between his trial testimony and his prior answers at the deposition, the embarrassed or desperate witness often claims: "I didn't understand the question; I was confused." If the jury can see that the deposition question was in fact understandable, it may contribute further to the witness's loss of credibility. On the other hand, failing to understand and *recognizing* a failure to understand are really two separate events. Of all the preliminary instructions, this is probably the least useful.

"If you need a break at any time . . . ." "We have water and coffee here . . . ."

If the witness needs a break, the witness is going to take a break whether the deposing attorney gives this instruction or not. The instruction's purpose, however, is to show the jury that this deposition was not a "third-degree" interrogation in which the witness was questioned in the basement until exhaustion, under bright lights. This instruction may also have the benefit of relaxing the witness as well as of making a record of a fair proceeding.

The witness and opposing counsel will decide when the witness is too tired to go on, no matter what instruction you give. But this instruction sounds considerate to the jury later at trial and makes it more difficult for the witness to say: "I did give that answer about stealing from the poor box, but I was very tired and you just kept pressing me without giving me a chance to breathe."

"If you need to talk to your attorney . . . ."

This instruction may actually have some effect at the deposition, as well as at trial. When the questioning gets intense and the witness gets anxious, many witnesses will want to check with their attorney before answering the tough question. This instruction gives the questioner a bit of leverage:

> Now, Mr. Smalkus, when we started, you agreed that you would answer my question before you talked with your attorney. Please give me your answer, and then we can take some time for you to talk with your attorney.

Note that an exception is made for talking with the attorney about matters of privilege. This is, of course, the rule—witnesses may talk with their attorneys about matters of privilege even when a question is pending. But if this exception is not included, there is a risk that opposing counsel will interject: "Of course, you may talk with me while a question is pending if you need to ask about a matter of privilege." The interjection has the effect of destroying any rapport the taking attorney has achieved and generally interrupts the overall flow of the questioning.

Although certainly not a guaranteed remedy for dealing with constant attorney-witness discussions between your questions and answers, the instruction does help. At trial, the jury will again be shown the fairness of the deposition proceeding: the witness had time to talk with counsel and yet he made these incredible statements that are made even more reliable because of this instruction. That alone makes this instruction worth giving.

"If you remember some additional information or clarification . . . ."

This instruction may actually help make the information you gather at deposition more accurate and complete. Witnesses cannot be expected to know the proper procedures or what they are allowed to do at depositions. This instruction provides concrete direction on how to correct or supplement an answer. The opportunity for clarification, taken together with the request for full and complete answers, enhances the likelihood that you will get all the pertinent information from the witness you require, or, at least, you will have a reliable record that you can use with a witness who expands on or changes his deposition testimony, taking him to task as demonstrated above. Implement this instruction by giving the witness an opportunity after every break to make corrections or additions to previous answers. For example:

> Q: Alright, Mr. Smalkus, we are back on the record after our lunchtime break. Before we go ahead, are there any of your previous answers that you would like to correct or expand on?
>
> A: No, there isn't.

Be forewarned that some defending lawyers feel the need to interject something at this point by stating something to the effect of: "Counsel, we will supplement the record as required by the Rules." A better approach would be for the defending attorney, as part of witness preparation, to tell the witness to be sure to check with the defending attorney before volunteering additional information. The defending attorney should be monitoring closely what the witness is saying and should strongly discourage the witness from providing additional information without first clearing it with the attorney.

"If you think of some documents that might help . . . ."

Consistent with the goal of maximum discovery, this instruction encourages the witness to mention documents that occur to him. Of course, if a document that was the subject of a request for production has not been produced, demand that the document be brought to the deposition. If the document is not immediately produced, you should then indicate that the deposition may be reconvened when the document has been provided. If the document is still not produced, bring a motion to compel and request additional deposition time. If the document was not the subject of an earlier request for production, immediately make that request.[8] Without the instruction, the witness may not know whether he is supposed to mention those documents. At trial, the fact that he received this instruction logically precludes the witness from saying, "Well, if I had the documents in front of me then I might have remembered this other bank account."

---

8. When a "new" document is mentioned during the taking of a deposition, deposing counsel will frequently make an informal request on the record that the document be produced. Such a request has no formal value in guaranteeing the receipt of discovery material. The typical response by defending counsel is "we'll take that under advisement." Such a response is code for, "If you don't send a formal request for production, you will probably never see that document."

"Are you taking any medications . . . ."

This question and the following questions about feeling ill and doctor's care cut off excuses that a witness might give at trial to avoid an unfavorable deposition answer. Some witnesses find such questions intrusive, thus the reason for the preamble about the need for complete answers. Even so, if the witness is behaving normally, these are questions that some attorneys will choose not to ask. But we do recommend that in any personal injury or product liability cases where injuries have occurred, you should ask the plaintiff about painkillers and other medications and any effect they might be having on the plaintiff.

If you decide to ask about alcohol, particularly if the witness appears to be under the influence, it is worth asking again following the lunch break, to find out whether the witness went and had a couple of drinks over lunch to relieve her anxiety from the morning.

Of course, a witness may actually be feeling ill or a personal injury plaintiff may be on pain medication that affects his memory and so on. When this happens, find out the extent of their problem.

Q: Are you taking any medications or drugs of any kind that might make it difficult for you to understand or answer my questions today?

A: Well, I had my wisdom teeth out two days ago, and I am taking something for the pain.

Q: Do you know what medication you are taking?

A: I have the bottle here. Let's see. The label says it is Hydrocodone. I think 500 mg.

Q: When did you last take one of these?

A: At eight this morning.

Q: How many did you take?

A: Just one.

Q: Have you taken any of these before?

A: About five or six since I had the operation.

Q: What effect do they have on you?

A: They make my mouth quit hurting, and I get a little sleepy.

Q: Do they affect your memory at all?

A: Not that I can tell.

Q: You don't have any problem remembering things?

A: No.

Q: How about understanding or answering questions—does the medication cause you any problems with doing that?

A: No.

Q: How about having your wisdom teeth out? Is that causing you any pain or difficulties now?

A: Not since I took the pill.

Q: Feeling fine now?

A: Yes.

Q: Will you be sure to tell me if you feel that your teeth or the medication are causing you any problems in understanding or answering my questions?

A: Yes.

If after questioning it appears the problem will cause difficulties with the deposition—for example, if you notice that the witness seems sleepy to the point of having difficulty staying awake—your best response is to reschedule the deposition, telling opposing counsel what you intend to do and why.

"Any reason why you cannot give full, complete, and accurate testimony?"

A word of warning about the line of questions regarding doctor's care, medications, alcohol, and drug use, etc.—as mentioned previously, these questions can be very off-putting for a witness because you are asking about conduct or conditions the deponent may be embarrassed about or view as none of your business (e.g.: "Has your hemorrhoid operation caused any problems with understanding or answering my questions?"). In addition, there are reasons other than these why a witness might not be able to give full, complete, and accurate testimony. For example, over a break a witness might learn about trouble in her business, a family illness, etc., all of which might cause an unreliable deposition. For that reason, it is wise to ask the overarching question: "Is there any reason why you cannot give full, complete, and accurate testimony?" at the beginning of the deposition. Repeat the inquiry after every break by asking "Is there anything that happened over the lunch break that will prevent you from giving full, complete, and accurate testimony." This generic inquiry can help avoid the off-putting effect of the more specific questions.

6.2.1   Trouble Words

There are some words lawyers use in the set-up and commitment questions that routinely generate a contentious response from opposing counsel, at least in those areas of the country where contentiousness is a hallmark of deposition practice. Those words are "promise" and "agree." The questions usually go something like this: "Will you promise to tell me if you do not understand a question so I can rephrase it?" or "Will you agree to let me know if you later remember some additional information that should have been included in your original answer?" Opposing counsel will then roar into action, stating: "Counsel, the witness isn't here to make promises or agreements. He is here to answer questions. Now, if you have a question, ask it. Otherwise, I suggest we all go home." After such an outburst, your carefully cultivated efforts at building rapport with the witness may be completely destroyed. The solution: avoid using the words "promise" and "agree" when asking the set-up and commitment questions. The previous questions are just as effective if phrased like: "Will you tell me if you do not understand a question . . . ." or "Will you let me know if you later remember . . . ." More importantly, you have taken away an excuse for opposing counsel to act in an obstructionist manner.

Another question—or more precisely, a statement—that routinely sets off opposing counsel goes like this: "If you answer my question, I will assume you understood the question and knew the answer." Opposing counsel then interjects with "Counsel, you can assume anything you want. We're here to answer questions. Let's get on with it." It is inappropriate for the taking lawyer—opposing counsel is correct—to "threaten" the witness with assumptions that have no evidentiary value and are worthless as far as any possible later use. Avoid the problem by not making such statements.

6.3   Speculating or Guessing

Some attorneys like to advise the deponent not to speculate or guess about answers. They argue that by putting this request on the record, it is harder for the witness later to try to avoid an unfavorable answer by claiming it was a guess or speculation. These attorneys also argue that the witness can be asked to disregard the instruction and guess and speculate if that is what is wanted.

Other attorneys recommend against an instruction not to speculate because it seems counterproductive; further, most jurisdictions have no rule that guessing is not permitted at depositions. Indeed, the speculation of a knowledgeable witness may be much more valuable than the limited actual information possessed by other witnesses. For example, consider these questions to the executive secretary in an office about his boss's activities:

Q: Mr. Smalkus, how much time did your boss spend on the Century account in May?

A: Well, I'm not exactly sure. You know, I don't keep track of his every minute.

Q: Yes, I understand that. Give me your estimate of how much of his time he spent.

A: Well, it would be more of a guess, I suppose.

Q: All right, give me your guess.

Opposing Counsel: I'm going to object here. This isn't worth anything at all. I mean, all we're getting is guesses. He has already told you he's not sure.

Q: Mr. Smalkus, tell us what you know of your boss's time on the Century matter in May.

A: I don't know for sure how much time he spent.

Q: Fine. Now, give me your speculation or guess.

Opposing Counsel: Same objection. We've been through this.

Q: Answer the question, please, Mr. Smalkus. Give us your best estimate or guess as to how much time he spent on the account in May.

A: I guess it was about half of his time. I can't be sure, but we only had one other big account in the office then, and he seemed to be working on Century almost all the time. It could have been more than half.

While this testimony might not be admissible at trial, since it is a "guess" or "speculation," there is no question that it is clearly useful to know what the witness believes is the fact because this witness presumably observed "the boss" on a daily basis. Speculation such as this can certainly lead to admissible evidence, perhaps by suggesting document requests for diaries and time logs or by suggesting questions to be asked at the depositions of other witnesses, thereby bringing the request for speculation within the permissible scope of allowable discovery under Rule 26.

CHAPTER SEVEN

STYLE, ORGANIZATION, AND OTHER MATTERS

*First comes thought; then organization of that thought, into ideas and plans;
then transformation of those plans into reality. The beginning,
as you will observe, is in your imagination.*

—Napoleon Hill (1883–1970)

As the deposing attorney, you can bring many styles to the deposition and many methods of organizing the questioning of witnesses. These techniques may vary from witness to witness and from case to case, but the common thread is the need for you to find ways to encourage witnesses to talk and to tell their stories completely so that no surprises pop up at trial.

7.1   Style

At a deposition, you should be assertive, bold, controlling, deferential, effective, fair, generous, hospitable, intelligent, just, kind, lucky, magnanimous, nurturing, original, professional, questioning, retentive, studious, thorough, unexcitable, versatile, wary, xenophobic, yielding, and zealous. Caveat: reading a long list of adjectives is not preparation for adopting the proper style for taking a deposition. From deposition to deposition, witness to witness, case to case, and time to time in the same deposition, you should display many of the characteristics from this list, but there is no effective way to predict the most profitable demeanor for any given deposition.

Nevertheless, we can offer some general observations about the style and tone you should assume.

7.1.1   Style and Tone Make a Difference

Your style and the tone of voice you use when asking questions make an important difference in the way a witness responds to you, and thus the amount of information you can gain. A witness who sees you as being respectful, interested, and friendly is much more likely to provide full answers—and even volunteer information—than is a witness who believes you are too stern, disapproving, and judgmental. Note the wide differences in the responses given to the following identical questions:

Q: What was your relationship like with Mr. Salas?

A: Fine.

versus

Q: What was your relationship like with Mr. Salas?

A: We got along well most of the time. You know, we chatted a lot about things, like what he had done that weekend and what I had done. Real friendly like. But then some days he would come in and be kind of nasty. Nothing he actually said, but just his tone of voice. Real nasty, if you know what I mean.

The first answer shows a witness who does not like the questioning lawyer and is providing as little useful information as possible. The second answer is more typical of a witness who is holding a conversation with the questioning lawyer and who is willing to help the questioner by readily providing information.

What causes a witness to perceive you, the questioner, either as someone to be helped or as the enemy? The easiest way of understanding the difference between the two reactions is to ask yourself how you would respond if you were to meet these two people for the first time at a party. Imagine these two contrasting styles:

First Person

- approaches you confidently and with a smile;
- leans forward in a friendly way while talking with you;
- has a pleasant tone of voice;
- has relaxed posture;
- is courteous;
- asks open questions (about your interests) in an informal and pleasant way;
- responds with affirmation and positive feedback to your answers.

Second Person

- talks to you without smiling;

- stands or sits rigidly erect;

- uses a stern, formal tone of voice;

- has an edge to his voice;

- is abrupt, bordering on rudeness;

- asks questions using formal or legalistic language and in an aggressive fashion;

- gives no response or frowns in response to your answers to his questions; and

- interrupts.

Most of us, if we met the first person at a party, would respond favorably and react in the same fashion in which we were approached. In contrast, if we met the second person, most of us would begin immediately thinking about how to end the conversation. Yet when conducting depositions, many lawyers imitate the behavior of the second person by engaging in what could pass as a police interrogation of a suspected criminal. These lawyers come across as thoroughly dislikeable creatures and receive responses appropriate to their demeanor. For example, think of the number of times you have seen a deposition begin with the taking lawyer asking in a stern, formal voice: "State your name and address for the record?" followed by "State your occupation?" and other equally terse, legalistic questions. This is not the way to gain friends or influence people.

Coupling a pleasant questioning style with open-ended questions and starting the examination in non-threatening areas, such as the witness's background, may also help put the witness at ease.

Compare the two questions below:

Q: Was the Cadillac heading south on Kirby when it came through the yellow light at Madison?

Q: Tell us about how the accident happened.

The first question contains at least five factual statements that the witness must analyze and accept or reject before she can answer. Each factual statement involves a test of memory; one involves a test of map skills ("heading south"), and one involves judgment ("came through the yellow light"). These complicating factors reduce the witness's comfort in answering and will naturally tend to make the witness reluctant to fully answer the question in a relaxed manner, where she might provide more complete information.

In contrast, the second question asserts no facts except that an accident happened. The question adopts no version of the accident, so no version is implicitly rejected. The question gives full freedom to the witness to tell a story and sets out no "right answers" in advance that may intimidate the witness. Clearly, with a witness who is nervous or reluctant to speak in public, the second question is more useful in relieving the pressure the witness might feel and encourages the witness to engage in a conversation with the lawyer. It has the virtue of encouraging the witness to do what she does every day—have a conversation—as opposed to engaging in the unusual experience of responding to aggressive, complicated, formal, and perhaps intimidating questions. A witness, thus comforted, is more likely to provide information when she is unimpeded by the discomfort of interrogation by an unfamiliar lawyer.

The old adage "you can catch more flies with honey than with vinegar" applies as equally to depositions as to life. An important tactic in a deposition is to get the witness talking so that the questioning attorney can learn everything the witness knows that is of value to the litigation. Therefore, we strongly urge you to adopt a pleasant style in the deposition unless there are compelling reasons to do otherwise.

7.1.2   *A Pleasant Style Is Not Always Effective*

Despite the foregoing discussion, a pleasant style does not always work. Some witnesses perceive cordiality and amiability as signs of weakness and a lack of resolve on the questioning attorney's part. These witnesses, often executives and other person with positions of power, see such a style as an invitation to play with the questioning attorney and, to put it in the vernacular, to "jerk" the attorney around. Other witnesses consider the deposition to be a major inconvenience in their lives and resent the time being spent answering questions. A pleasant style has no effect on them other than to increase their sense that their time is being wasted (these witnesses are often the same as the preceding group who perceive a pleasant style as a sign of weakness). The best style with such a witness may be an assertive, no-nonsense approach to the questioning, with little time invested in pleasantries. Similarly, with a nonparty eyewitness to an accident, an assertive, official demeanor may better encourage cooperation than a friendly style.

Some witnesses react to aggressive questioning and control with something like a "whipped dog" syndrome. These witnesses become meek and malleable, willing to agree to almost anything suggested by the deposing lawyer. Sometimes you can shock the witness into this defeated attitude with difficult or embarrassing questions at the beginning of the deposition; other times by pressing the witness who is unsure of his facts into repeatedly admitting, "I don't remember." Sometimes the witness will react in the opposite manner. Through persistent and aggressive questioning, you can anger the witness until he is tempted to lash out with intemperate responses that can be quite revealing and helpful.

Finally, opposing parties or those witnesses closely associated with the opposing party are usually resistant to all efforts to be pleasant and charming (but not always). These witnesses often view the questioning lawyer as the devil incarnate whose ultimate goal is to impoverish and ruin them or someone close to them (and sometimes losing the lawsuit means just that for the opposing party). Cooperation will rarely be readily forthcoming from an opposing party and those closely allied with them. Examining the opposing party may require us to bring all our powers of control and interrogation to the questioning.

The list is too long to enumerate all of the possible styles you can bring to a deposition. It is enough to say that for a given witness, you will need to use variations on the recommended strategy of being pleasant to the witness. The point we are making is that your style and tone should suit the witness and the situation.

7.1.3   *It Is Often Necessary to Use a Combination of Styles in a Single Deposition*

Every witness will present a combination of characteristics and challenges, and you may need to try several different approaches before you achieve your goal of obtaining every shred of useful information from the witness. The dynamic of the deposition may dramatically change from when you are asking about the witness's background and other noncontroversial subjects to when you shift to issues more directly related to the merits of the case. Similarly, when you change your questioning from the open-ended questions associated with information gathering (*see* chapter eight) to the leading questions to get party statements, witnesses frequently change from being cooperative and pleasant in their answers to being more querulous and defensive. In short, it is often necessary to bring a combination of styles to the deposition, adapting your choice of style as your interaction with the witness proceeds.

7.1.4   *Start with a Pleasant Style and Then Try Other Styles*

Sometimes you can get the book on a witness before the deposition and decide on the appropriate style before the deposition begins. But usually, because of the innumerable variables that go into determining how the three or more individuals involved—the taking attorney, the witness, and the defending lawyer—will interact, it is impossible in advance to determine with any certainty what style is most appropriate to use with a particular witness. When in doubt, as we almost always are, it is wisest to start with the pleasant style and then shift, if necessary, to other styles. For obvious reasons, starting aggressively and then shifting to a more pleasant style leaves the witness doubting your sincerity when you attempt the more kind and gentle approach. At that point, regardless of your best efforts, the witness is likely to be skeptical of your new style and be more cautious in her answers. In short, start with being nice and then switch to a more aggressive or challenging style if niceness does not work.[1]

7.2   Organization: Background of the Witness

Most attorneys generally agree that some preliminary, nonconfrontational questioning is useful after the stipulations are set up as discussed in section 6.1. In a deposition, you should at least attempt to establish rapport with the witness before beginning the intrusive questioning compelled by pressing for details and before opposing counsel starts squabbling. Whether you set the tone when asking questions about the witness's background or questions on relatively unimportant introductory matters, your goal in the introductory stage of the deposition should be to draw the witness into a conversation.

With the percipient witness, determine early on (perhaps while preparing for the deposition) what background questioning will be useful. If a particular witness—normally a nonparty witness—may be more forthcoming if relaxed, you may extend the background questioning. While the answers may not be especially useful substantively, they will give the witness an opportunity to become accustomed to the deposition procedure while responding to nonthreatening, nonchallenging questions. The time you spend relaxing the witness will be repaid several-fold by the witness being more forthcoming and by your increased ability to use the remaining time more efficiently. However, senior executives and experts usually do not respond in any positive way to friendly, background questioning at the outset and, in such instances, it may be best to go directly to the heart of the issues.

In addition to relaxing the witness, a second purpose of background questioning is to assess the witness's personality, background, intelligence, and articulateness. You can make better judgments on how to handle the witness, at both deposition and trial, after you have assessed the witness's testimonial capabilities and importance to the lawsuit.

---

1. This is true for the same reasons that at trial constructive cross-examination (that does not attack the witness's credibility, but rather tries to obtain those portions of the witness's story that are favorable to the cross-examining party) should ordinarily precede destructive cross-examination (that attempts to diminish the witness's credibility).

Four factors are important when deciding how much background questioning to do with a witness:

1. **The role the witness plays in the story of the case.** If the witness merely had the bad luck to be standing on the corner when the plaintiff's and defendant's cars collided, it is unlikely that you will need to do a great deal of background questioning. On the other hand, if the allegation is, for example, that the witness is the principal perpetrator of a complicated securities fraud, you will need more background information to effectively communicate with and evaluate the witness and to place her appropriately within the litigation theory.

2. **The importance of the witness's background to the issues in the case.** When the witness's background helps prove some issue in the case, then background questioning takes on a whole new meaning, because the so-called "background" is actually a substantive issue in the case. For instance, in a securities fraud case where the broker is accused of taking advantage of a customer's naiveté, the customer's educational history is more than just background—it directly address the issue of how sophisticated or naive the customer was in relation to the information provided and consultations conducted by the alleged fraudulent broker.

3. **The size of the litigation budget.** Experienced litigators prepare a litigation budget as part of initial preparation and client counseling. You should make an informed estimate of litigation costs at the outset of the litigation and communicate it to the client early on. And, of course, as the projected costs change, you should provide those changes to the client as well. Clients do not appreciate finding out that litigation is costing more than they were initially led to believe. Attorneys operating on a contingent fee who regularly find at the end of the case that the value of the time invested is likely to substantially exceed their fees will soon be seeking a different line of work. In short, good attorneys budget the amount of time to be invested in a case and try to adhere to that budget as the case progresses. Background questioning at deposition consumes time and money and should be factored into the litigation budget.

4. **The amount of time to be spent questioning the witness on substantive matters.** The seven-hour, one-day time limit on depositions provided in Rule 30(d)(2) imposes another deposition limitation that you must factor into the calculus of the time to be

spent on background information. Unless the length of the deposition has been extended by stipulation or court order, you must decide what topics to cover during the available time and what topics to jettison if the deposition begins bumping up against the rule-imposed time limits. Questioning on the witness's background is a topic often dropped if other, more important topics are likely to take the full seven hours.

Time spent during a deposition developing the witness's background has a cost, both in dollars and in opportunity lost (it is time that cannot be used to question on other topics in the deposition, to work on other aspects of the case, or even to work on other cases). You must strike a balance between the time spent in background questioning and the expected payoff from that line of questioning. Time spent learning important, useful information is time well spent. If background questioning does not fit that description, then keep the background questioning short or omit it altogether.

As a general rule, it is helpful to know for any witness: 1) personal background, e.g., how old the witness is, if the witness is married, single, or divorced, does the witness have children and, if so, their ages, where the witness lives; 2) educational background, e.g., how far the witness went in school, what the witness's college major was, if any; and 3) relevant employment background, e.g., what jobs has the witness held, the witness's current employment, how long has the witness held this position, what the witness's duties and responsibilities are.

It is usually best to begin background questioning with basic personal information and proceed chronologically through the witness's educational background and employment history. By proceeding chronologically, you are less likely to miss a period of time or some events that the witness may not want to talk about—like the two months in the mental hospital. Once you have established the general chronology of the background information, ask the witness to supply specific dates to make sure that no period of time has been omitted, as might happen if the witness is allowed to say, for example, "Well, three years ago I left my job at American, and then I started work at Century." While it might be true that the witness left the American job three years ago, and while it is also true that his next job was at Century, carefully checking the dates of each will insure that you discover the two interim months in rehabilitation.

By asking background questions and responding to the witness's answers in an interested, conversational way, you will build rapport with the witness that carries over into the substantive portions of the deposition. While an opponent may be tempted to object that such questioning is beyond the proper scope of the deposition, or is a waste of time, you know that such objections are useless. Even if the opposing attorney objects just to interrupt, that contentiousness may backfire and further help you build rapport between the witness and yourself, since you had been getting along just fine. It is fair to say that for most witnesses (indeed, for most people), talking about themselves is a favorite past-time.

A percipient (or "fact" or "lay") witness who is a party or who is identified with a party is less likely to relax and open up just because you have asked a few background questions. The witness's counsel will be cautioning the witness throughout the deposition, and any gains you have made in building rapport will have evaporated by the time the witness and counsel return from a break in the hallway. You must be more subtle and persistent in your efforts to open up the witness. Because such a witness is less likely to freely provide useful information during the substantive portion of the deposition, and because the exploration of background is not likely to yield significant positive results, relegate background information to the end of the deposition so you can devote all available time, if necessary, to substantive matters. This is especially so in modern litigation, where the background of a person is relatively easy to find through internet research.

That is not to say that you should start the deposition of party witnesses or those associated with the opposing party with the most important matters in the lawsuit. During witness preparation, the opposing attorney has undoubtedly cast the deposing counsel (you) as evil, ruthless, calculating, conniving, and never to be trusted; a similar characterization that you probably used to describe the opposing attorney when you are preparing your client to be deposed. Because of this, the witness is likely at the outset to be wary of you. Therefore, aggressive questioning is often least profitable at the beginning of the deposition. (However, this may not be true with experts, as is discussed in chapter twenty.) To counteract this wariness, find an opportunity to engage in some form of apparently harmless discussion. For example, if the witness says that she has been deposed before, take a minute to talk about how long that deposition went and whether the case settled or she actually testified at trial. This exchange, using open questions to encourage the witness to be forthcoming, can have the same relaxing effect as questioning on background information to get a conversation started.

7.3   "The Organized Tour" versus "The 'Leapfrog' Approach"

The issue of how best to organize the remainder of the deposition presents two clear alternatives: first, question the deponent in an organized way, moving from one topic to the next related topic until the entire field has been covered; or second, jump from one topic to some other, preferably unrelated topic, and then jump again, until all intended topics have been covered.

Those who argue for the first approach contend that it leads to complete coverage of the relevant issues, with less opportunity for missing important topics or information. Those who argue in favor of the second approach, the "leapfrog" approach, urge that it keeps the witness off guard, prevents the witness from anticipating the taking lawyer's goals, and reduces the opportunity for prevarication. Let's analyze each of these arguments. As will become clear (if it is not already from the titles of the two approaches) the authors have little regard for the leapfrog approach, favoring instead what we here call the logical and organized approach.

First, the witness is more likely to relax—to be "off guard"—when he understands the nature and direction of the questioning. Conversely, the witness's defenses will be up if he is unsure and anxious about the direction of the questioning. Thus, while increasing anxiety by leapfrogging may affect the deposition in a number of ways, it will not lower the witness's guard.

Second, while leapfrogging does prevent the witness from anticipating what the next topic will be, within each topic the questions still must be related to one another and build on the answers given. If not, the deposition would degenerate into a chaotic exchange, and there would be no follow up or progression at all. Therefore, once the leap occurs from the last question on one topic to the first question on a new topic, the witness will adjust to the new topic and to some degree will still be able to anticipate the questions. In addition, counsel must then return to the methodical exploration of the relevant information within the new topic.

As a result, mere leapfrogging is unlikely to mask the deposition goals. Instead, probing the witness's answers with follow-up questions, seeking to exhaust the witness's knowledge, coming back to topics to check the consistency of information given, and asking general questions before progressing to specific events are the types of techniques that will frustrate the witness's attempts to anticipate questions and fabricate impermeable answers.

Third, the witness's opportunity to prevaricate or hide information depends more on the amount of time between his last answer and the next question—what is sometimes called the "pace" of questioning—than it does on the relationship between the topics. In other words, if the witness is motivated to shade the truth about whether the sales agreement included insurance for a shipment that has since been lost, his success in crafting a false answer depends more on how long he has to think about that answer than it does on whether the previous topic was changing the name of the business, the method of financing the sale, or the number of partners in the new operation.

Furthermore, unless it is a video deposition, there is no jury to observe the witness's demeanor when, like Perry Mason, you leap to the crucial question:

"Isn't it true that you never intended to buy the hammers?" and the witness, taken totally by surprise, stammers, "Why, I . . . I . . . I couldn't . . . I just couldn't; I never liked the hammers; I lied about wanting to buy them; I hated the hammers and everything they stood for." At the deposition, if the witness is momentarily speechless, with jaw dropping and eyes searching for help in the corners of the room, he may still recover and deliver a coherent answer (while the cold transcript reveals little of the witness's discomfort), no matter what the previous topic was—and little is gained from the leapfrogging.

Of course, gaining little is not the same as gaining nothing. If there are no negatives to the leapfrogging approach with a particular witness, it may be useful because once in a hundred times the witness's hatred of hammers will prove advantageous for the case. Sometimes witnesses *are* surprised into truthful testimony (harmful to them) or an unguarded statement that you would not otherwise have obtained, but those instances are rare. In reality, a number of negatives are usually associated with the leapfrogging approach that diminishes its value as a questioning style. First, when using the leapfrogging method, it is difficult to keep track of which topics you have covered. If you consciously avoid a logical pattern, no logic dictates what you have accomplished and what remains. Of course, this problem is mitigated by using a detailed outline and checking areas off as you finish them. However, preparing such a complete outline involves considerable discipline, and its completeness depends on "omniscience"—and few attorneys can predict in advance all the topics that will be covered in any given deposition; after all, a primary goal of the deposition is to find out information previously unknown.

The leapfrog approach also makes it difficult to ensure that you have exhausted the witness's knowledge in an area, either because such exploration would be predictable or because the witness would anticipate the follow-up questioning. Thus, in leapfrogging, you often forsake your natural inclination to follow the witness's answers with more detailed questions about that topic because of the need to leap and surprise or confound the witness. As discussed earlier, leapfrogging from one major area to another major area does not avoid predictability within the areas, and, as a result, usually offers no real strategic advantage.

Finally, the leapfrog approach reduces the likelihood of discovering unanticipated areas of knowledge, which is one of the most important goals of a discovery deposition. Because leapfrogging involves moving from one area to another unrelated area, you discard the most important tools to discovering new information: following little clues, chasing small leads, asking about odd words, pursuing hesitations, questioning illogical transitions, and insisting on some adherence to order and chronology.

Because we know that events happen in chronological order, that causes precede effects, and that motivations accompany actions, it is important to recreate and understand sequences of human behavior. By asking a deponent why something was done right after you learn that it was done, and by inquiring carefully about all of the actions surrounding an event to find the likely cause of that event, you often uncover the truth merely by following up with probing questions about the chronology—questions that disclose both sequence and failure of sequence (non sequitur, which suggests inaccuracy). If, in the discovery of the order of things, fact B follows naturally from fact A, exploring fact B after covering fact A creates the likelihood that the sequence is complete and accurate. If, however, you do not explore fact B after you have covered fact A, you will find it difficult to determine whether either fact A or B is accurate or whether there are other facts occurring between the two.

Leapfrogging, in an effort to gain the limited benefit of surprise, works against discovering those logical connections that identify patterns in human behavior. When the witness has information that you need, it makes little sense to abandon the logical tools of coherent, exhaustive questioning. Sometimes a question asked "out of the blue" will provide a valuable answer, but many more times such "shots in the dark" are merely misses and will result in leaving areas undiscovered and connections unseen. In short, leapfrogging depends on luck for its success; ordered questioning depends on thoroughness. Thoroughness is a matter of preparation and execution, both of which can be replicated with practice. Luck occurs randomly and less frequently, cannot be depended on, and is therefore less reliable. So plan to be thorough, and then hope to be inspired.

7.4   Handling Objections and Instructions Not to Answer

The most important rule for you in dealing with objections is to *listen*. Listen to the objection and make a judgment about whether it is valid. Depending on your assessment of the objection—valid or invalid—you can either rephrase the question or ignore the objection.

Let's look at the first situation where you have listened to the objection and made the decision that the objection is valid.

> Q: Mr. Vito, just a moment ago you said that as you approached the intersection, you started to brake. How far away from the intersection were you when you started to brake and how fast were you going when you started to brake?

> OC: Objection, compound question.

Q: Please go ahead and answer, Mr. Vito.

A: About 150 feet, and I was going thirty-five miles per hour.

Q: OK, let me break that apart. You were about 150 feet away from the intersection when you started braking?

A: That's right.

Q: And you were going thirty-five miles per hour when you first started braking?

A: Yes.

Notice what the taking attorney has done. First she listened to the objection and decided, correctly, that it was a valid objection. Second, rather than correcting the question immediately, she insisted on an answer to the objectionable question. In this way, she has conveyed to opposing counsel that she is not going to be thrown off track by the objection. Third, when she got an answer to her objectionable question, she went back and rephrased the questions to make them non-objectionable. She should only rephrase the question if the answer to the objectionable question was useful enough to merit rephrasing the question.

There may be times that the objectionable question is so poorly phrased that it cannot be answered without first correcting it.

Q: Mr. Vito, how long did it take you to go from here to there?

OC: Objection, vague. Counsel, we have been talking about so many "heres" and "theres" that I don't know which ones you are referring to in your question.

Q: Please answer the question.

A: I'm sorry, I don't know either.

But often you will listen to an objection and decide that the question is proper. The proper response to opposing counsel then is to politely ignore the objection and insist on an answer to your question. Assume the deposition of the opposing party:

Q: Sir, before you sent Mr. Tiltson Exhibit 1 canceling the contract, you did not telephone him to discuss the problem?

OC: You're leading the witness, counsel. I object.

Q: Your objection is noted. Please, go ahead and answer.

Note the deposing attorney did not argue with opposing counsel about the objection nor try to convince opposing counsel that the objection was invalid. The only person who can determine whether the objection is valid is the judge or magistrate, and they will only rule on the objection if you or your opponent attempts to use the deposition for some purpose such as introducing the answers at trial or for summary judgment. The witness must therefore answer the question subject to the objection, so nothing is gained by debating with counsel.

One word of caution is in order. Since the only time objections will be ruled on is if you are using the deposition at trial or to support or oppose a motion, it is critical that the objection not be sustained and important questions and answers thrown out. For example, assume that you have taken the deposition of a key witness and have successfully obtained many critical party statements. Unfortunately, the witness is dead by the time of trial, and you must introduce her deposition testimony. If the trial judge now sustains opposing counsel's objections made at the deposition, you are left without a witness and without the witness's deposition testimony. The rule, therefore, is: When in doubt, cure the objection. The perils of ignoring a possibly valid objection are too great to do otherwise.

Under Rule 30(d)(1), opposing counsel may validly instruct a witness not to answer a question only when necessary to preserve a privilege, to enforce a court order limiting discovery, or to present a motion to the court under Rule 30(d)(3) seeking to limit or terminate the deposition. If the instruction not to answer is based on a claim of privilege, Rule 26(b)(5) requires opposing counsel to expressly claim the privilege and to describe the documents, communications, or things in such a way that without revealing the claimed privileged information, the other parties will be able to determine whether the claim of privilege is valid. Therefore, whenever opposing counsel instructs a witness not to answer a question, you should ask for the basis of the instruction. If privilege is claimed, you should also insist on having opposing counsel explain the applicability of the privilege to the question being asked.

Let's look at an example:

Q: Mr. Valinces, what information did you hear about the plaintiff before you decided to terminate him?

OC: I am going to instruct the witness not to answer that question.

Q: Counsel, please state the reason you are instructing the witness not to answer.

OC: It calls for information protected by the attorney-client privilege.

Q: Counsel, are you claiming the attorney-client privilege for communications between you and the witness concerning the plaintiff?

OC: Yes.

Q: Mr. Valinces, did you learn any information about the plaintiff outside of any communications from your attorney?

A: Yes.

Q: Tell me what you learned.

7.5 The Witching Hour of 4:00 p.m.

As you prepare the witness for deposition and during the deposition itself, you should caution the witness that the possibility for making mistakes is the greatest by about 4:00 p.m. each day. Indeed, you can confidently tell the witness:

> At about four o'clock, you will make a mistake. I will make a mistake at about that same time, and so will opposing counsel. They may not be important mistakes in terms of the substance of the case, but they will be important because they will remind us that we are tired, that it is harder to concentrate, and that our patience and our listening skills have begun to run down. It probably has to do with blood sugar levels or some such thing, but there is no question that being deposed is hard work, and it takes energy, which eventually runs out.
>
> I will point your mistake out to you, and you can point mine out to me, and from that time on we will both be especially careful in our answers and statements. We won't go much longer than that. In a deposition that, by court order or stipulation, is scheduled to last more than one day, the examination might continue. If we have to come back the next day, that is better than making mistakes, because the next mistake, or the one after that, may hurt the substance of the case. If, after that time, I state that we are adjourning because it has been a long day, do not argue with me. I am in a better position to determine whether you are answering as well as you were earlier. If you disagree, we can discuss that disagreement back in the hotel lounge.

The "four o'clock mistake syndrome" is so predictable that many deposing attorneys save especially important questions for the four o'clock time period, hoping that the witness will be less guarded in his response. Knowing that this late afternoon slump is going to occur, do not commit to a specific stopping time much beyond 4:30 or 5:00 p.m., a conventional "target" time. Of course, the beginning time must be adjusted to allow the seven hours for the deposition permitted by Rule 30(d)(2). In fact, it would probably make more sense to agree to go until 4:00 p.m. and to reassess the situation at that point. When you do recess at 4:00 p.m., do not be swayed by deposing counsel's promise that "there are only one or two more areas and then we can wrap this up." Even if that is true, the witness may make mistakes in those areas that you will have to correct. And often those one or two areas drag on for another hour, lead to other areas, and may result in a deposition lasting longer than seven hours.

While we are discussing the effect of the timing of depositions on the witnesses, we should consider the situation of the witness or attorney who has come in from another time zone and has not stayed in the local time zone long enough to become adjusted. For example, if travel has been from west to east, the deposition should probably start later, so the witness or attorney begins working at about 9:00 a.m. in his home time zone. In that instance, the defending attorney should worry about 4:00 p.m. in the witness's home time zone, which may be 7:00 p.m. at the location of the deposition. If travel has been from east to west, it may be difficult to get the deposing attorney to start at 6:00 a.m.; but the 4:00 p.m. slump will hit the witness a few hours early, and the defending attorney has to caution the witness about it and watch for it.

CHAPTER EIGHT

QUESTIONING TECHNIQUES

"If one tells the truth, one is sure, sooner or later, to be found out."

—Oscar Wilde

8.1   Introduction

The types of questions asked in a deposition can take many forms. Speaking broadly, however, all of the questions can be broken down into two categories: questions that gather information and questions that seek useful and admissible party statements. Simply put, information gathering involves finding out everything the witness knows, both good and bad, about the issues in the case. In contrast, questions that seek party statements ask the witness to state specific facts that will support the taking lawyer's theory of the case or will refute the opponent's case theory. Effective attorneys know how and when to ask both types of questions.

Both types of questioning—information gathering and seeking party statements—usually occur in every deposition. The mix between the two, however, will depend on what information the lawyer already knows going into the deposition and what role the witness played in the events at issue. The more information a party has going into the deposition, the less information gathering is necessary and the more time that can be directed at seeking party statements. In general, in an information seeking deposition, the deponent is encouraged to talk at some length in responses, with little cross-examination-style leading, (e.g.: "Tell me more about how you discovered the new protein-pump inhibitor?"), while in a party-statement-seeking deposition, the deponent is encouraged to answer more concisely, perhaps one fact at a time, to provide clear party statements that are especially useful in motions for summary judgment.

As a further example, in a sexual harassment case, the plaintiff—the person complaining about the harassment—usually will know very little about the defendant company's sexual harassment policies, how complaints about harassment are handled, what other complaints have been made, how the company responded to these other complaints, and so on. Typically, the only things the plaintiff knows in detail are the facts of the particular incident. This lack of information on the plaintiff's part means that when, for example, the plaintiff deposes the defendant's human relations officer, most of the questions will be of the information-gathering type. The plaintiff will also be attempting to get some party statements from the witness, but the greater part of the questioning will be directed at filling in the blanks in the plaintiff's knowledge.

Contrast this with the defendant's deposition of the plaintiff. The company already knows most of what it needs to know. It should be familiar with or have ready access to its sexual harassment policies, and it will usually already know what the alleged victim says occurred—through internal complaints, EEOC filings, and the complaint in the lawsuit. The only thing the company may not know is what damages the plaintiff is claiming. As a result, during the plaintiff's deposition the company will usually gather some information about the incident and the damages being claimed, but many of the questions will be directed at seeking party statements from the plaintiff.

There is also overlap between the two types of questioning. When the taking lawyer is asking open-ended information-gathering questions, the answers may contain specific facts and information that help prove the taking lawyer's case or hurt the other side's case. Similarly, when the taking lawyer is trying to get the witness to give a party statement, the witness's answer may contain information that the taking lawyer did not previously know. Nonetheless, there are important differences between how a lawyer questions when gathering information and how that lawyer questions when seeking party statements.

8.2   Information-Gathering Questioning

When engaged in information gathering, you are trying to find out what relevant facts and information the witness knows about the issues in the case. You hope the answers will be helpful to the case, but you want to know what the witness has to say even if the answers contain harmful "bad facts." In short, you want to know everything the witness has to say on the topics, both good and bad.

The reasons for finding out about good facts are obvious. But bad facts do not disappear from the case merely because you don't ask about them in a deposition. If you don't ask about them during discovery, you may hear these bad facts for the first time when the other side offers them at trial or raises them in a motion for summary judgment or in settlement negotiations. By then, however, it is usually too late to devise a strategy for challenging them.

Learning about bad facts at the deposition gives you the time and opportunity to figure out what to do about them. It may be that you can attack the facts at the deposition or later through further investigation or discovery. Even if it turns out that the bad facts are unassailable, you can try to find another legal or factual theory of the case or factor that bad information into your calculations of the settlement value of the case. The rule is that it is always better to learn about any bad facts during the deposition rather than being surprised by them at some later time.

But, of course, there is an exception to every rule. The exception to this rule occurs when the opposing party is unlikely to learn about the bad facts if you do not ask about them. For example, assume you are deposing a witness who will not cooperate with either side. In that situation, you may not want to ask about potentially bad facts, but rather wait to see if the opposing lawyer asks about them. If the opposing lawyer then asks questions in follow-on examination[1] bringing out the bad facts on her own, you will have an opportunity to explore the facts when opposing counsel ends her questioning.

The risk of this strategy is that opposing counsel may be cagier than you believe and may have discovered the bad facts through means other than questioning this recalcitrant witness at the deposition. If the opposing lawyer therefore chooses not to question this witness about the bad facts, you will not have any indication at the deposition that the bad facts exist or that the opposing lawyer has this information. In that situation, you will not be alerted to the need to question the witness broadly—with nice open-ended questions—about any possible bad facts. Still, in this one situation, we believe the better strategy in the situation of a witness who will not cooperate with either side is to wait to question on bad facts until opposing counsel does so first. We would rather have them never come up than to have them come up so that we have to meet them.

8.3   The Funnel Approach

The best method of gathering new information is through the use of what is called the *funnel approach*. The name of this technique comes from its resemblance to a funnel.

---

1. "Follow-on" examination is our phrase for the apparent cross-examination that occurs after the questioning by the attorney who noticed the deposition. Because this second examination is not actually cross-examination—most often the deponent is actually represented by the second questioner—it seems more accurate to call it "follow-on" examination, abusing a phrase from British barrister friends who (rather ironically) sometimes call trial cross-examination, "follow-on" questioning.

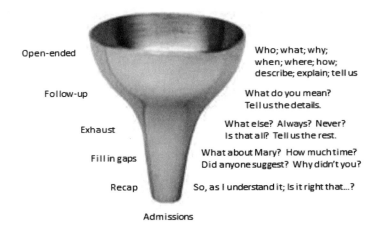

Open-ended — Who; what; why; when; where; how; describe; explain; tell us

Follow-up — What do you mean? Tell us the details.

Exhaust — What else? Always? Never? Is that all? Tell us the rest.

Fill in gaps — What about Mary? How much time? Did anyone suggest? Why didn't you?

Recap — So, as I understand it; Is it right that...?

Admissions

8.3.1   *"The Overview"*

When starting to question on a new topic, the first step should be to get an overview. This will give you some idea of what you will encounter as the questioning proceeds. It will also get the witness talking about the topic, and it encourages a discussion of those facts the witness considers important. Having some idea of what the witness considers to be important may prove to be useful information when you are determining how best to deal with the witness. Generally, the more open the question, the more you will learn from the witness. For example, in a contract action, your overview question might be:

Q: Tell me how this transaction came about?

And in a personal injury case, it could be:

Q: Tell me everything that happened to cause this accident?

8.3.2   *"Getting the List"*

The next step in using the funnel approach is "getting the list." The purpose here is to find out the breadth and scope of the witness's knowledge of a topic before finding out in detail what the witness knows about that topic. Getting the list is nothing more than staking out the limits of the witness's knowledge. Example questions are:

•   Tell me how you first learned about . . . .

•   What was your job at the time?

•   How were you involved?

•   Who else was involved?

- What did John [Mary, Hilda, Alonzo] do?
- How could it have been prevented?
- How has the process changed?
- What is the policy now?
- When were you last involved with sales?
- Why did you leave?[2]

Once you have obtained "the list" and have staked out the scope of the topics to be explored, you can then decide which items or subjects on the list are important and which can be ignored or postponed. If you are worried about time, decide which are the most important topics and pursue those first. Proceeding to ask questions on a topic without first asking an overview question and getting the list is like entering a large, dark wood without a map or guide and with no idea of what to expect.[3]

Let's take a look at how to go about getting the list in a specific context. Assume that the shipping manager at a parts supplier is being deposed about the manager's job responsibilities. An example of getting the list in that situation might look like this:

Q: What are your responsibilities as shipping manager?

A: I am in charge of all shipments going out of the company.

Q: What other responsibilities do you have?

A: If insurance is required on a shipment, I also arrange that.

Q: What else?

A: I have to arrange the type of shipping used.

Q: Any other responsibilities?

A: I have to make sure that the amount of the shipping charges is passed on to billing.

Q: What else?

A: That's everything.

---

2. It is important to note that these questions have two characteristics: they are open-ended, nonleading questions; and they generally relate to topics that are remote from the center of the controversy and therefore less likely to provoke defensive answers. The questions in the "getting a list" questioning are intended to stake out the plot of land to be examined, not to locate the stains from the accelerant in the arson case in the closet in the basement.

3. *See* Book Three, Chapter IV, "The Two Towers: Tree Beard:" "Meanwhile, the hobbits went with as much speed as the dark and tangled forest allowed . . . ." (Houghton Mifflin, pub. 1994 ed.), J.R.R. Tolkien, The Lord of the Rings Trilogy.

Now you can decide which of the duties is worth exploring and which can be ignored.

Although it may be termed "getting the list," often obtaining a chronology provides the best list. A chronology, like a list of duties, has the effect of staking out the limits of a witness's knowledge of a topic. For example, getting a chronological list from the plaintiff in a personal injury case might sound like this:

Q: I want you to take me through what happened that day from the moment you left the house until the accident occurred. When did you leave the house?

A: About 8:15 in the morning.

Q: What happened after you left?

A: I drove down 15th Street.

Q: What next?

A: As I approached the intersection with Yale Street, I saw a car stopped at the stop sign on Yale.

Q: What happened next?

A: As I was going through the intersection, the car at the stop sign suddenly shot forward and hit my car.

Q: What next?

A: I heard a big crash, and I was thrown against the door.

Q: What happened next?

A: I was in a lot of pain, and someone must have called an ambulance because I was then taken to the hospital.

In contrast, getting the list from an eyewitness to the accident might be very simple:

Q: Tell me everything you saw that day at the intersection at the time of the accident?

[followed by a series of "What else?" questions]

Notice that there is no attempt at this point to explore or go into detail as to any part of the witness's answers. It does not make sense to distract the witness from recalling information or recounting a chronology by interrupting with questions about details. The idea is to get an overview of the witness's knowledge, with the details to follow later.

8.3.3 *Top of the Funnel: Open-Ended Questions*

Once you have the list and have decided what topic on the list you will explore first, the next step is to begin questioning about the topic using open-ended questions. The questions should resemble the wide mouth of a funnel, gathering up everything the witness knows that may be relevant to the topic.

The classic reporter's questions—who, what, when, where, why, how—supplemented by "describe," "explain" and "tell me about"—will best encourage witnesses to reveal all they know. Open-ended questions force the witness to provide the information covered by the question, making it much more difficult to hide information or evade the question.

The value of open-ended questions is well illustrated by thinking about the children's game of Battleship. In the game, each side hides its ships by arranging them on a grid the opponent cannot see. Then each player drops bombs on the other side's ships by calling out a location on the opponent's grid. If the location is not occupied by an opponent's ship, it is a miss, but, if it is occupied, it is a hit. Many depositions are like playing Battleship, with the taking attorney asking a series of narrow questions, hoping for a hit on what the witness knows, but also coming up with many misses. Here is an example of such an examination in a personal injury case.

> Q: Were you driving west on Mattis Street at the time of the accident?
>
> A: Yes.
>
> Q: Were you driving within the speed limit?
>
> A: Yes.
>
> Q: Was the intersection a four-way stop?
>
> A: Yes.
>
> Q: Were you looking at the traffic ahead?
>
> A: Yes.
>
> Q: Was traffic heavy at that time of the morning?
>
> A: No.
>
> Q: Did you see the plaintiff before the collision?
>
> A: Yes.

This technique works fine as long as you ask all the right questions. But if you fail to ask a question on a topic on which the witness has information, you will have a miss, just as in Battleship. In the above example, if you fail to ask "Did you stop at the intersection?" the witness will never have to tell how she ignored the stop sign, went through the intersection, and collided with the plaintiff's car.

The results are much better when you ask open-ended questions that force witnesses to tell what they know. Instead of playing Battleship, you are, in effect, asking to look at the opponent's grid.

If we were to rerun the above example using open-ended questions, it would sound like this:

> Q: Tell me what you were doing just before the accident.
>
> Q: Where were you going?
>
> Q: Why were you going there?
>
> Q: What were you looking at?
>
> Q: What did you see?
>
> Q: What was the traffic like?
>
> Q: Describe the intersection for me.
>
> Q: What did you do when you came to the intersection?
>
> Q: When did you first see the plaintiff?
>
> Q: Tell me everything that happened after you saw the plaintiff.
>
> Q: Why did the accident happen?

Using open-ended questions is particularly important when considering how witnesses are often prepared for their depositions. A standard instruction is: "Listen to the question, answer only the question asked, do not volunteer." Open-ended questions do not permit the witness to parse the question and avoid providing information. In effect, the witness is forced to volunteer information.

8.3.4   *Middle of the Funnel: Narrowing the Questions*

Open-ended questions alone are not enough to fully explore a witness's knowledge of a topic. You also need to know the facts that underlie the answers to the open-ended questions. Your job is to flesh out the details through more narrow and focused questions. In other words, the questions are now moving down to a narrower part of the funnel. Let's take the answer to one of the previous open-ended questions and see how it can be narrowed down.

Q: When did you first see the plaintiff?

A: I saw him about 200 hundred yards away, approaching on Kirby Street.

Q: How far was the plaintiff from the intersection?

A: About 100 yards.

Q: How far were you from the intersection?

A: About the same distance.

Q: What traffic control devices, if any, were there at the intersection?

A: It was a four-way stop with stop signs at all four corners.

Q: What did the plaintiff's car do when it arrived at the intersection?

A: It came to a stop.

Q: What did you do when you came to the intersection?

A: I slowed down to about five miles per hour.

All of the questions are still open, but now they are becoming more focused on the particular topic. As the questioning on the topic progresses, your questions should become increasingly more narrow and closed-ended as detail is filled in.

8.3.5   *Bottom of the Funnel: Filling in the Detail*

You will need to start using narrow, closed-ended questions when filling in the details that the witness has not volunteered in response to more open-ended questions. The questioning is now at the bottom of the funnel.

Q: Did you come to a complete stop?

A: No.

Q: Did the plaintiff come to a complete stop?

A: I think so.

Q: Do you know whether the plaintiff saw you?

A: He appeared to be looking in my direction.

At the bottom of the funnel, most of the questions will start with verbs such as "did," "do," "have," and "had"—this type of question requires "yes" or "no" answers and obtains unambiguous answers, which may turn out to be useful party statements.

8.3.6   *Closing Off and Locking In*

One important goal at a deposition is to prevent the witness from later surprising you at trial or in a motion for summary judgment with new information that they did not testify about during their deposition.[4] You want to find out everything the witness knows about the issues in the case and to lock the witness into the answers given so there will be no later surprises. There are techniques for closing off witnesses' answers and locking in witnesses.

"Have You Told Me Everything About . . . ?"

One method of closing off and locking in the witness is to ask at the end of questioning on a topic: "Have you now told me everything that was [said, done, etc. about this topic]?" For example, if the witness, the human resources manager at a defendant company, was being examined about everything she had done in response to receiving an employee's complaint about an incident of sexual harassment, you can close off the examination on that topic by asking: "Have you now told me everything you did in response to the plaintiff's complaint to your office about sexual harassment?"

"That's All I Can Remember at this Time."

A frequent instruction during preparation of a witness for a deposition is to tell the witness that when the taking attorney attempts to pin them down by having them say that they have told everything about a topic, they should respond by saying "That is all I can remember at this time." The answer is designed to give some wiggle room if later at trial or in a declaration in support of or in opposition to summary judgment, the witness wants to add to or embellish the deposition answers. While there is no perfect response to this technique, you should try to limit its usefulness by making it difficult for the witness to claim later that she remembers additional facts.

Assume a contract dispute where the issue is who attended a particular meeting:

> Q: Have you now told me the names of everyone who was at that meeting?

---

4. Modern cases discourage the attempt to use declarations from deponents attempting post-deposition to alter their deposition testimony or to reduce its impact, so that the deposition testimony is not support for the motion. This should successfully halt the tactic in defending depositions in which the defending attorney asks no questions asking for explanations or clarifications, hoping to hide information until trial (and thereby frustrating the purposes of discovery). Under these cases, such declarations are often ruled out of order by the courts.

A: That is all I can remember at this time.

Q: Did you make any notes about the meeting?

A: No.

Q: Do you know if anyone else made such notes?

A: Nobody that I know about.

Q: Have you talked with anyone about the meeting?

A: No.

Q: Is there anything you could check—letters, emails, what-ever—about who was at the meeting?

A: Nothing I can think of.

Q: Is there anything at all that might help you remember who was at the meeting?

A: Not that I can think of.

Q: Is there anyone you could talk to who might help you remember?

A: No, I don't think anyone knows it better than I do.

Q: If all you had to do in the office tomorrow was to recon-struct who was at the meeting, how would you do it?

A: I might look for a note or something on my desk calendar for that day, but that's about all I could do.

The witness may still try to embellish the deposition answers at a later time, but any effort to do so will be much less convincing if you have made a record such as this to use to obtain control on cross-examination.

8.3.7   Going Back Up the Funnel

Questioning rarely proceeds smoothly from the top of the funnel with its open-ended questions to the bottom of the funnel with its close-ended questions calling for "yes" and "no" answers. Instead, lengthier answers may come out when you are at the bottom of the funnel stage trying to obtain "yes" or "no" statements. When that happens, you must go back to the top of the funnel to once again work down through the open-ended questions until you are satisfied that everything important about the topic has been revealed. Assume the deposition of a key witness to an automobile collision, in which the witness has earlier testified about seeing the accident occur. The questioning has proceeded to the bottom of the funnel:

Q: So, you said you were working in the service bay of the BP station?

A: Yes.

Q: What time was that?

A: About 3:30.

Q: Were you looking out at the street?

A: No, I was working on the brakes of a car that had been brought in for service.

Now you will go back up to the top of the funnel and use open-ended questions to find out how the witness was able to see the accident.

Q: What caused you to look out at the street?

A: I heard tires screeching, and that is what caused me to look out at the street.

8.3.8   *Using Multiple Funnels*

You will often find it necessary to use more than one funnel when exploring a topic. Use a new series of questions that incorporate the funnel approach each time a witness's answer contains new information that requires exploration. Imagine a single funnel being used to find out about a topic, but with new funnels within the larger funnel being used each time the witness's answer raises a new subtopic.

Assume, for example, the deposition of an insurance agent where the issue is when the agent learned of a policy holder's request to change beneficiaries. The initial funnel might go as follows:

Q: How did you learn that the plaintiff wished to change the beneficiaries on his policy?

A: He sent a letter to my office asking me to change the beneficiaries.

Q: When did you see that letter?

A: On April 3 of last year.

Applying a new funnel to the subtopic of "how mail is handled":

Q: When is the mail delivered to your office?

A: About 11:00 a.m. each day.

Q: Where does the carrier put the mail?

A: In the mailbox outside of the office front door.

Q: Who brings in the mail?

A: My secretary.

Q: When does your secretary bring in the mail?

A: He usually checks around 11:00 each day.

Continue to explore "how mail is handled" until the subtopic is exhausted. However, if the answers contain a new fact—such as "but when the secretary is not there, I usually check it"—then apply a new funnel to the second subtopic as well. Once you have exhausted the subtopic, you can return to the topic you were exploring before the witness brought up the subtopic. Alternatively, you can make a note about the new subtopic and explore it after the other potentially relevant portions of the main topic have been exhausted:

Q: Let's go back to what you were saying before . . . you know, about your secretary picking up the mail. What does he do with the mail after picking it up?

The point is that the funnel approach is rarely a smooth progression, but instead frequently requires you to go back to somewhere close to the top of the funnel and apply separate funnels to new topics that arise.

8.3.9   *Exhaustion*

You must try to obtain every important piece of information on a topic from a witness before moving on to a new topic. Some attorneys argue that jumping around between topics without first exhausting any one of them keeps the witness off guard and unable to fabricate. (A more complete discussion of the benefits and detriments of "leapfrogging" is supplied in chapter seven.) The dangers of such an approach outweigh any advantages. First, experience has shown that many lawyers who practice this approach forget to go back to previous topics to finish exhausting the witness's knowledge about those topics. Second, if you are trying to obtain everything a witness can remember, jumping around prevents the witness from concentrating on the topic and remembering everything possible about it. A better approach is to focus on one topic at a time, exhaust that topic, and then move on to the next topic.

It is a matter of judgment as to how far the exhaustion should proceed. The depth of exhaustion will depend on a number of factors, including the amount of time available in the deposition, the importance of the topic in relationship to the other topics to be covered, and the constraints of the litigation budget in the case. It is quite common, particularly in high-stakes litigation, to encounter taking lawyers who spend what seem to be endless hours exhausting the witness's knowledge about marginally relevant topics in what are known as "scorched earth depositions." Such an approach is expensive to the client and also runs the risk of losing sight of the real issues in the case. The taking lawyer's goal should be to find out everything reasonably important to understanding, analyzing, and presenting the case—not to waste time exhausting the witness's knowledge about topics that have minimal, if any, relevance to any issue in the case.

8.3.10   Suggesting New Facts

After you have exhausted a topic, suggest additional facts to see if these will trigger further recall. Generally, you will suggest only those facts that you want the witness to remember and not any harmful facts that the witness may have forgotten. If the witness remembers harmful facts at some later time, you can then impeach the witness with the deposition answers. Assume again that the shipping manager is being deposed:

Q: What happens next?

A: I often choose a shipper and fill out the shipping documents online.

Q: What else?

A: I include on the shipping documents when the shipment is to be picked up. I have the shipment ready at that time, and the shipper comes and takes the shipment away.

Q: What else?

A: That's it.

Q: Do you also arrange for insurance on the shipment?

A: Oh, that's right. I do arrange for insurance when it is needed.

Q: Is there anything else you do relating to shipments?

A: That's all I can think of.

The exception to the rule that the taking lawyer should only suggest helpful facts is that the lawyer might sometimes encourage the witness to deny the harmful facts. In this situation the lawyer is asking the witness about harmful facts *not* because the lawyer wants the witness to confirm them, but because the lawyer wants the witness will deny them.

For example, assume you did not want the shipping manager to be involved in packing the shipments, and after you asked about the shipping manager's responsibilities, no mention was made of such involvement. You could decide to close off the subject without asking about packing responsibilities. You could also wrap up the topic with something like: "So, you told us now everything you do with regard to shipments?"—with the expectation that you can impeach the witness if he testifies at trial that he is also responsible for the additional task of packing the shipments. Alternatively, you could raise the issue explicitly at the deposition, even though it is a potentially harmful topic, with the expectation (reasonably based on other information, perhaps from other witnesses or documents) that the shipping manager will deny any involvement.[5]

> Q: You aren't responsible for packing the shipment, are you?
>
> A: No, they are packed by the production division.

8.3.11   *Conversations*

Some conversations are admissible at trial and for summary judgment motions under several possible theories, including for nonhearsay purposes (e.g., notice, state of mind), as nonhearsay under Federal Rule of Evidence 801(e) (e.g., an opposing party's statement, a witness's prior consistent statement), or because the conversation falls within a Rule 803 or 804 exception to the hearsay rule (e.g., statements made for purposes of medical treatment, or where the witness is unavailable for trial, a statement against interest).

The admission at trial of testimony about a conversation requires the following foundation:

- Where the conversation occurred;

- When the conversation occurred;

- Who participated in the conversation; and

- Whether the witness was able to hear the conversation.

Of course, you can ask additional questions about the circumstances of the conversation, and the answers may increase the weight the judge or jury gives the conversation, if it is introduced during motion practice or at trial. Some of those additional questions might be what the witness was doing at the time of the conversation, what the other person and anyone else present at the time was doing, whether there are any notes of the conversation, whether there are any documents referring to the conversation, and so on.

---

5. In writing this sentence, the authors deliberated on using the word, "hope," ("in the hope that the shipping manager will deny . . .") because it was suggestive of luck or good fortune. We instead wrote, "with the expectation (reasonably based on . . .). We continue to subscribe to the deposition school that teaches, like Dante, "Abandon hope, all ye who enter here." DANTE ALIGHIERI, THE DIVINE COMEDY: INFERNO, Canto 3.

You will need to ask additional foundational questions for telephone conversations and conversations where the witness identifies the speaker by familiarity with their voice. Several trial advocacy texts, such as Lubet's *Modern Trial Advocacy*, lay out these foundational requirements. Imwinkelried's *Evidentiary Foundations* is the standard encyclopedia of foundations and is relatively inexpensive when purchased in the student edition.

If a deposition witness has given only a summary of the conversation, there is a risk the court may reject the evidence because it contains too much of the witness's interpretation or opinion rather than evidence of what was actually said. Therefore, you should ask about the actual words used in a conversation to the extent the witness can recall them.

And, in fact, witness often are unable to provide an accurate summary of a conversation after weeks or months or sometimes years have passed since the conversation occurred. Instead, like all of us, they give summaries or conclusions that place themselves in the best possible light or leave out details that appear unimportant to them, but actually have great importance to the case. When the details are examined, the conversation may appear in an entirely different light than the summary would suggest.

Consider this segment of deposition testimony concerning a conversation after an accident, as reported by a witness:

> Q: Mr. Richkus, did anyone say anything at the scene of the accident?
>
> A: Well, when the owner got there, he was really upset. You know, it sounded like the driver was trying to explain what happened, but the boss just wouldn't listen. I thought he was going to fire him. He—the boss—I mean, kept yelling and screaming about the brakes, and he was getting madder and madder. The driver finally sat down on the bumper of the truck, and he didn't say anything.

Compare that testimony with the following additional testimony where the attorney takes care to follow up to obtain actual language:

> Q: OK, let's just go through this one piece at a time. Tell me first what the driver said to the owner or boss, what words he used, and what the boss said back to him.
>
> A: OK. As best I can recall, the driver said, "The brakes went soft; they just didn't grab." And then the owner got really mad and started yelling at the driver.
>
> Q: What words did he yell at the driver?

A: I can't remember everything he said, but I remember him saying, "Don't say that to anybody; don't say anything about the brakes. Just tell them it happened too fast." I don't know, I was kind of embarrassed about hearing this, you know. I mean, obviously, they didn't know I could hear them.

Q: Did the driver say anything back to the owner?

A: No. He just sat down on the bumper of the truck and didn't say anything else that I could hear.

Q: Where were you when you heard this conversation?

A: I was standing at the back of the truck, about fifteen feet from them.

Q: Who else heard this conversation?

A: I'm not sure. Maybe the woman who was driving the Cadillac, because she was standing next to me. Both of us were waiting for the police to come.

Q: Did anyone besides the Cadillac driver overhear this conversation between the boss and the driver?

A: I don't think so.

Q: Is that all that you heard of the conversation between them?

A: Yes, then the police came, and I was talking to them.

Q: Do you remember anything else about that conversation between the boss and the driver?

A: No, that's about it.

Q: Did you make any notes about that conversation?

A: Well, no, I didn't make any notes, but I told the police officer about what I had heard, and he was writing while I was telling him.

Q: And that was Officer Davis that you mentioned before?

A: Yes.

But sometimes all you want to know about a conversation is the summary. If the summary suggests that nothing important to the case was discussed, then you may want to move on to another topic. Assume a case where the issue is whether the defendant had notice that ordered goods were required by a particular date:

Q: Did you talk with the defendant the next day?

A: I gave him a call.

Q: What did you talk about?

A: It was just a social call. I asked him if he was going to be playing in the golf tournament at the club that weekend.

Q: Was there anything said about when the goods were needed?

A: No, that didn't come up.

Q: Let's talk about the next time you spoke with the defendant. When was that?

Of course, if something important was said in the conversation, then you need to go into greater detail than can be provided by a summary.

8.3.12   The Standard Litany

The standard litany will work well for finding out what was said in a conversation. The first step in the standard litany is to lay the foundation for the conversation. Let's take a wrongful death action where the plaintiff is attempting to show the defendant, after drinking at a bar, was intoxicated at the time of the accident:

Q: Mr. Smith, were you at the Top Hat Tavern on March 4th of this year?

A: Yes.

Q: Was the defendant, Hudson Woodbridge, there that night as well?

A: Yes.

Q: Did you hear Mr. Woodbridge say anything that evening?

A: I heard him talk with the bartender.

Q: Were you able to hear what was said by Mr. Woodbridge and the bartender?

A: I was standing next to them at the time.

Q: Was anyone else there at the conversation?

A: No one else was close.

You should routinely lay the foundation for conversations to avoid any admissibility problems later on.

After the foundation has been laid, the standard litany requires that the witness be asked what was said, followed by a series of "What else?" until the witness says that's everything. Here is what it would look like in the same wrongful death action:

Q: What was said in that conversation between Mr. Wood-bridge and the bartender?

A: The bartender told him he was looking three sheets to the wind and maybe he should let someone else drive him home.

Q: What else?

A: Well, Woodbridge said, "Nah, I'm fine."

Q: What else was said?

A: The bartender said, "It's your life."

Q: What else?

A: That's it. Woodbridge walked out of the bar.

After the witness has answered that nothing more was said in the conversation, you can go back and ask for the exact words used or other details of the conversation. Do not interrupt the witness's initial recounting of the conversation with questions asking for more detail or other information; it is important that the witness not be diverted from remembering what was said. Here, once the witness has testified to everything said in the conversation, you might want to follow up with questions asking about whether Woodbridge's speech was slurred, how he appeared, and so on.[6]

8.3.13   The "Four C's" Approach to Conversations

Some conversations are so important to the issues in the case that you will want to go beyond the basic foundational requirements. Using a technique developed by Henry Hecht, a leading teacher and scholar on deposition technique,[7] called "the four C's" will insure that you will find out everything the witness knows about the conversation. Our approach is slightly modified from the approach suggested by Mr. Hecht.

---

6. Some trial technique teachers suggest using a technique they call "memory flooding," in which a witness is asked to remember what they saw, where they sat, what others were wearing, who spoke first, what they ate, etc., to draw them back to the day and time of the conversation. Once they are back "in the scene," they sometimes remember more details of the conversation.

7. *See* Henry Hecht, Effective Depositions, 761, Appendix 6.

Context

The first "C," context, is designed to do two things: 1) lay the necessary foundation for the conversation to be admissible at trial or on a motion for summary judgment, and 2) take the witness back to the time of the conversation to prod her memory about what was said.

Q: Did you ever talk with the defendant about risk of loss insurance?

A: Yes.

Q: How many times?

A: Just once.

Q: When did this conversation take place?

A: It was back in March of last year. I don't remember the exact date, but it was early in the month.

Q: Where did this conversation take place?

A: I talked with him on the phone.

Q: Where were you at the time?

A: I was in my office.

Q: Who placed the call?

A: I did.

Q: At what number did you call the defendant?

A: I called him at his office.

Q: Where did you get the number?

A: I looked it up in the phonebook.

Q: What time of day did you call him?

A: As I recall, it was in the morning.

Q: What were you doing at the time?

A: I was working on ordering the parts we needed.

Q: Was there anyone else with you when you placed the call?

A: No.

Q: Did the defendant say whether anyone was with him?

A: No.

Q: Could you hear anyone else in the room with the defendant?

A: No.

Q: Who answered the phone when you called?

A: The defendant.

Conversation

The second "C" is the conversation itself. It is useful to go through the conversation at least twice to make sure the witness has recounted as fully as possible what was said. The first run-through is phrased broadly:

Q: What did you say and what did he say in that conversation?

A: I told him we wanted the shipment to be insured, and he said that would not be a problem.

Q: What else? [*repeating this until the witness says that is everything*]

A: I think we discussed the date when we should expect the shipment to arrive.

On the second time through, you are seeking a verbatim rendition of what was said by each participant in the conversation:

Q: Let's go back. Who spoke first?

A: I guess I did.

Q: What did you say?

A: I think I started out by saying "hello."

Q: What did he say?

A: He said "hello" back

Q: What did you say to that? [*repeating this litany until the entire conversation has been elicited*]

A: I told him I needed to know when the shipment will be arriving so we could make preparations for our production run.

After the witness has recounted everything that was said, you can ask for details about the conversation and favorable facts the witness has failed to mention. Do not raise unfavorable facts unless you have a basis for expecting that the witness will deny the facts.

People tend to remember conversations as a whole rather than as a sequence of exchanges. For this reason, the first run-through is more likely to develop useful information than the second run-through. Still, the second run-through serves as a form of insurance that you have elicited everything possible about the conversation.

Close Off

The third "C," closing off, makes sure the witness has testified to everything she can remember and she cannot later add to her testimony.

> Q: Have you now told me everything you can remember about what was said in that conversation?
>
> A: Yes.
>
> Q: Is there anything that would help you remember more of what was said in that conversation?
>
> A: Not that I can think of.

Confirm

The final "C," confirming, is directed at checking the accuracy of what the witness has said by looking for corroborating evidence.

> Q: Did you make any notes of that conversation either during or after the conversation?
>
> A: I jotted down a few notes while we were talking, but I threw them away.
>
> Q: Are there any documents that refer to the conversation?
>
> A: I sent an e-mail to the CEO recounting what was said.
>
> Q: Is that Exhibit No. 3?
>
> A: Yes.
>
> Q: Did you tell anyone about the conversation?
>
> A: No.
>
> Q: Did you discuss the conversation with anyone?
>
> A: No.
>
> Q: What happened as a result of that conversation?

A: Nothing really, other than I kept waiting for the parts to arrive.

As you can see, following the "Four C's" approach can be very tedious and time consuming. It should be reserved for those conversations where knowing everything about the conversation is important.

A note of caution is in order here. If the witness starts to talk about a conversation using generalities and impressions, do not press too hard for the details unless the details are important. A common reaction from witnesses when pressed about the details of events is to retreat into "I don't know" or "I don't remember." Unfortunately, this may also be the truth rather than just an effort to avoid the hard work of recalling what was said sometime in the past. Often, it is more effective to wait until the witness has recounted a conversation and then prompt the witness to expand on the summary.

Q: You said you believed he thought your suggestion was a good one. What did he say that made you think that?

The same thing can be said about asking a witness about the exact words that were said. People rarely remember the exact wording of conversations unless the words had some sort of special significance. Of course, sometimes the answer we are looking for from the witness is "I don't know" or "I don't remember." In that situation, asking early on in the questioning about a conversation for the exact language used may be the most likely way of getting the witness to give you that answer.

8.3.14   Listening and Notes

Both types of questioning—gathering information and seeking party statements—require you to listen carefully to the witness's answers. While careful preparation is important, you should never be so heavily dependent on an outline of the questions or so intent on taking complete notes that they distract from listening to what the witness is saying.

You can always check the outline after the witness has completed answering the question. You can take notes, of course, if you think they are necessary to help you to follow up on one of the witness's answers or the witness has given names or numbers that might be difficult to remember later. But except for these limited occasions, you should be focusing on the witness while asking questions and should be watching and listening carefully to the answers being given. You can always ask the reporter to repeat a question or review the transcript later on.

Do not forget that you are paying a professional note-taker—the court reporter—to take down everything that was said. There is no reason for you to be writing a second transcript except to help you remember those areas where you may want to conduct further questioning.

Focusing on taking notes or on following an outline can easily interfere with your ability to pick up on the nuances in the witness's answers or notice the nonverbal cues the witness is giving while answering. Here is an example of an inattentive questioning lawyer missing a witness's obvious clue.

> Q: Did you talk with the defendant about what had happened?
>
> A: Not on that day.
>
> Q: Did you let your employer know what had happened? [*switching to a different topic*]

The witness's answer begs for a follow up question, a signal that the taking lawyer was too distracted to hear. The lawyer should have listened more carefully, and then asked:

> Q: If you didn't talk with the defendant that day about what happened, when did you talk with him?

If you are busy looking at notes, you will also miss nonverbal cues, such as the witness's look of distress when the questioning ventures into a sensitive area or when the witness looks at defending counsel as if begging for help in answering the question. All of these are important cues that you may be touching on important areas that require further probing.

8.3.15 *Recapitulating and Summarizing*

At the bottom of the funnel is recapitulating or summarizing the witness's answers. This can be a useful technique if used with caution.

You will sometime have difficulty following a witness's testimony or will lose track of what the witness is saying. Assume that the deposition is focusing on obtaining a list of a purchasing agent's job responsibilities. After a series of long and rambling answers, you become concerned whether the witness has given a full list of the duties. One method of bringing clarity is to recapitulate and summarize the answers:

> Q: Let me see if I understand you. You said one of your duties as purchasing agent is to determine what items need to be purchased for a production job?
>
> A: Correct.

Q: You are also responsible for determining which vendor the parts should be purchased from?

A: Right.

Q: You also have to decide on the shipping method?

A: Yes.

[*continuing until the answers have been fully summarized*]

At this point, you conclude the recapitulation and summarizing with:

Q: And there were no other duties that had involving shipping?

A: That's right.

Q: So, you have now told us all of your duties?

A: Yes.

The reason why you should use recapitulating and summarizing with caution is that a witness will often qualify or retract answers previously given if, on hearing them repeated back, he decides that he does not like what he said. Therefore, be cautious in reciting back what you think is a favorable answer if you are concerned that the witness may take the answer back. However, it is still better to hear bad answers in deposition before they hurt your position at trial, so it is a better idea to ask at deposition, and summarize or recapitulate to make certain that you understand.

8.3.16   Conclusion

Many lawyers destroy the effectiveness of the depositions they take by exclusively asking narrow questions calling for yes and no answers. We are not sure why there is this strange aversion to asking open-ended questions— perhaps a need to maintain control or a fear of a "bad" answer—but they should keep the funnel in mind as a way to organize their questioning and to maximize the opportunity to obtain all the relevant information that the witness has.

8.4   Gathering Party Statements and Testing Theories

The second type of deposition questioning, closed questioning, is used when you are seeking party statements. The difference between gathering new information and seeking party statements is that with the latter, you are trying to encourage the witness to testify to a fact that weakens or even destroys the other side's theory of the case or supports your theory. For example, in a grocery store slip-and-fall case, the plaintiff's attorney may try to have the store-manager deponent admit that he knew about the spilled may-onnaise, but just had not gotten around to calling for a "clean-up in Aisle 4." If the witness admits this, the plaintiff's case will be immeasurably strength-ened, and at least one of the store's possible defenses will be foreclosed. As another example, in a wrongful death case where the allegation is that sui-cidal thoughts were caused by the pharmaceutical company's antidepressant, the taking attorney might try to get the witness to agree that the company had never tested the challenged drug on a population of teenagers who had been diagnosed with depression.

As discussed in chapter two, there is often an overlap between informa-tion gathering and seeking party statements. When you are asking infor-mation-gathering questions, the answers may obviously also contain party statements that help your case or hurt the other side's case. Similarly, when you are trying to get the witness to state or admit specific facts that weaken or destroy the other side's theory or support your theory, the answer may con-tain information that you did not previously know. Nonetheless, there are important differences in how you question when engaged in seeking party statements from the witness.

8.4.1   *Purposes of Obtaining Party Statements*

Testing Lines of Cross-Examination for Trial

One of the most important reasons for deposing a witness with the goal of party statements is to test possible lines of cross-examination at trial. Closed, single-fact questions are useful both for obtaining party statements at depo-sition and for cross-examination at trial, because the deposition questions focus the party-statement-seeking discussion and make the answers very use-ful at trial. If the witness gives useful answers at the deposition, then those same questions can safely be asked at trial. But if the answers are not what you expected, then you will know what questions *not* to ask at trial. In short, you can test possible lines of cross-examination at the deposition to see what works and can be repeated at trial, all while trying to obtain clean statements about useful facts.

Cross-examination at trial is a difficult task under the best of circum-stances. It is even more difficult when the lawyer does not know what the wit-ness will answer. Irving Younger's "Fourth Commandment," proclaimed in his famous "Ten Commandments of Cross Examination" lecture is: "Never ask a question to which you don't know the answer." This is terrific advice, but how can a trial attorney know what the answer will be before asking the question? It's quite simple—ask the question first at the witness's deposition. And if, at trial, the witness foolishly (or deceptively) gives an answer on direct or cross that is different from the answer given at the deposition, the deposition transcript can be used to impeach the witness.[8]

Supporting or Opposing Motions for Summary Judgment

Another important reason to seek party statements at a deposition is to use those party statements to support or oppose summary judgment motions. The reality is that very few civil cases actually end up being tried.[9] Most are settled or disposed of on summary judgment or in other motions practice. Typically, in larger cases with millions or hundreds of millions of dollars at issue, both sides know the stakes are too high to risk going to trial.[10] Instead, one or both sides will conduct discovery to create a favorable settlement posture or to support a motion for summary judgment. If the summary judgment motion fails, then these cases very often settle. As a result, a frequent deposition objective is to get the witness to provide key party statements that will permit the judge to dispose of the case, or some portion of the case, on a later motion for summary judgment. Similarly, if a party is expecting a motion for summary judgment to be brought by the other side, the goal is to create a "genuine issue of material fact" by getting key party statements that create a factual controversy.

Encouraging Favorable Settlements through Negotiation or Mediation

Cases not disposed of on summary judgment are very often settled. Settlements may occur through old-fashioned negotiations between the attorneys, or, as is increasingly common, through mediation. Settlements between rational negotiators occur when the parties conclude, after doing their risk analysis after discovery, that they are likely to receive more or pay less by avoiding trial. That risk analysis includes adjusting their trial expectations based on perceived strengths and weaknesses in the opposing cases. In short, the parties and lawyers evaluate their cases and then compare what is being

---

8. And it may be used to establish the point substantively, in the federal system, because prior testimony under oath, subject to cross-examination, is a hearsay exception; in many states, the answer may not be used substantively because the state's hearsay rules do not contain that "prior sworn testimony" exception.

9. "The percentage of federal civil cases that ended in trial declined from 11.5 percent in 1962 to an amazing 1.8 percent in 2002, one sixth as many. [Footnote omitted.] Though the absolute number of civil cases 'disposed' of by trial has increased fivefold, even the absolute number of trials has declined. Similar patterns have prevailed in civil, criminal, and bankruptcy proceedings, in federal and state courts, and both jury and bench trials. The rate of decline has rapidly accelerated in the very recent past." ROBERT BURNS, THE DEATH OF THE AMERICAN TRIAL, 2 (University of Chicago Press, 2009).

10. Judges often urge counsel to redouble their efforts to settle matters by reminding them that the jurors will bring virtually no experience with the kind of sophisticated business decisions being debated at trial: "Do you really want these people second-guessing your strategies and tactics, or do you think you ought to try to work this out yourselves?"

offered in settlement with what they estimate the likely outcomes will be if the cases proceed to trial. Obviously, important party statements by key witnesses will affect both sides' expectations about the likelihood of achieving a particular verdict in the case. Of course, because risk analysis is imprecise and somewhat subjective, there is a range of uncertainty involved in the calculation, even where the apparent precision of mathematical analysis suggests that settlement ought to be possible.[11] Such human emotions as the plaintiff's insistence on retribution for how much he was offended by the price-fixing, or the defendant's anger at having been accused of competing unfairly, may skew the analysis. Attorneys themselves can introduce error in this risk analysis by overestimating their own importance in affecting the outcome—because their ego suggests that juries love them or because they mistakenly think that the judge will buy a weak argument for the admission of certain evidence simply because it comes from them. Where one party or the other is relying on poor information, estimated settlement ranges will not overlap or even come near to overlapping, and settlement will be almost impossible. Not surprisingly, therefore, the better the parties' information about their respective cases, the more likely is a settlement. Because of the strong evidentiary value of party statements, they are better information about trial proof than inferences from documents and other testimony.

Testing Case Theories

Obtaining party statements is also a way of testing potential case theories. By seeking party statements that support different case theories, the deposing attorney finds out which theories will hold up in response to a summary judgment motion, which theories will be supportable at trial, and which theories will be persuasive with a jury. Theories that cannot get past these hurdles will be abandoned.

Let's take an example. A potential client comes into the office and tells you about her involvement in an automobile accident. As the story unfolds, you hear that the client had been driving home from work when the road narrowed from two lanes to one. As the road narrowed, a car in the other lane sideswiped the client's car, resulting in a broken arm for her and damage

---

11. For example, if plaintiff believes it has a 30 percent chance of winning $1 million, a 50 percent chance of winning $300,000, and a 20 percent chance of winning $0, its settlement value could be estimated at (0.3 × $1,000,000 plus 0.5 × $300,000 plus 0.2 × $0, minus costs of trial and attorneys fees for trial = something less than $450,000. If the attorney's fees for trial and the trial costs are estimated to be in the range of $150,000, the plaintiff might well be satisfied with a settlement of $300,000, which avoids those costs and additional attorneys fees. Perhaps, by similar analysis, the defendant believes it has a 50 percent chance of paying $0 and a 50 percent chance of paying $300,000, which results in an exposure valuation of $150,000, plus trial fees and costs similar to the plaintiff's, something near $150,000, then the defendant's exposure at trial will be near $300,000; and the plaintiff and defendant may be able to reach a settlement in that $300,000 area.

to her car. While listening, you, like most lawyers, will immediately begin thinking about whether the client has a valid claim against the other driver. Some of the questions going through your head may be: "Was there a merging traffic sign giving the client the right of way?" "Did the other driver see the client's car?" "Was the other driver speeding?" "Could the other driver tell that the two cars were going to collide, but nevertheless did he continue at the same speed?" and so on.

The client may be able to answer some of these questions—was there a merging traffic sign—but many of the questions—was the other driver paying attention to the road, was he speeding, did he continue at the same speed even though he could see that the two cars would collide—can only be answered by the other driver. When you depose the other driver, you will be asking these questions and, based on the answers, as well as the other evidence in the case, you will decide which theory or theories to pursue. You will test each possible theory and decide which are the strongest theories on which to base the client's case, and which theories should be abandoned.

Bringing or Opposing a *Daubert/Kumho* Challenge

Parties often find themselves battling over the admissibility of expert testimony. One side will attempt to have the opposing expert's opinions ruled inadmissible because they allegedly do not meet the standards of Rule 702 and the *Daubert/Kumho* test; the other side will oppose such a motion. During an expert's deposition, the party bringing the challenge may seek party statements that the expert is unqualified to render an opinion, the opinion is based on insufficient facts or data, the methodology used in arriving at the opinion is unreliable, and the methodology was not properly applied to the facts or data. The side whose expert is being challenged will seek party statements from the experts for the opposing side that the challenged expert is qualified and arrived at a sound opinion based on reliable methods and adequate data. Although *Daubert/Kumho* motions to exclude do not always result in complete exclusion, their success in at least limiting experts' testimony in a case justifies the time spent in seeking party statements on these foundational issues at the depositions.[12]

---

12. Such motions are also valuable because they educate the judge about the weaknesses and limitations inherent in an expert's testimony so that the judge will give those matters some thought before they arise by way of objection at trial. Expert motions in limine should probably be motions to exclude coupled with motions to limit the testimony to specific, narrow areas.

8.4.2   *Planning for Admissions or Party Statements and Theory Testing*

Figuring out what admissions or party statements are needed from a witness is a four-step process:

1.   develop a case theory;

2.   determine the opponent's case theory;

3.   determine what facts are needed to support or discredit each side's case theory; and

4.   decide what party statements might be obtained from the particular witness.

Developing a Case Theory

The first step in preparing to obtain party statements is to have a case theory. Before you can ask questions designed to get the opposition to make a party statement that supports a theory of the case, you must have carefully thought through exactly what those theories are. Depending on how successful you are in getting the party statement, as well as in the other formal and informal discovery in the case, you may abandon or modify theories as the case progresses. We have discussed theory creation a number of times in the preceding pages.[13] At this point, we raise the topic again to emphasize that it is essential to deconstruct theories into their constituent facts so you are prepared to try to obtain those facts in clear and clean statement from the opposition. Opposing party statements that provide essential facts for your theories make your proof at trial easy.

The guiding principle is flexibility. Do not become so wedded to a particular theory during discovery that you fail to consider other potential theories. Most trial lawyers would say that by the time of trial, you should have decided on one theory—juries often find multiple theories to be confusing, inconsistent, and usually not persuasive—but during discovery it is appropriate to consider different theories to decide which ones are viable and which should be abandoned.

Determining the Opponent's Case Theories

The second step in preparing to obtain party statements is to determine, as best can be done, what case theories the other side is pursuing. Identifying the case theories of the other side is a bit like reading tea leaves,

---

13. *See, e.g.,* section 2.1.3, and succeeding sections.

but usually listening closely to opposing counsel as he makes arguments to the court or discusses the case in motions and responses, you can make an intelligent guess at what the other side is attempting to prove. As the case progresses, discovery, motions, and pretrial conferences will also give clues as to the other side's theories. (It is very likely that "relevance" objections at depositions are not really attempts at blocking discovery from the witness, but rather attempts to obtain explanations of relevance from the deposing attorney—explanations of relevance, after all, are case theories or pieces of case theories.)

Determining What Facts Are Needed to Support or Discredit Each Side's Case Theories

The third step in the process requires you to do some hard thinking about what facts you need to establish potential case theories as well as refute the other side's theories. In the simplest case, it may be that the defendant's case theory is nothing more than "the events did not happen in the way the complaint alleges." In that situation, obtaining party statements to support one side's case theory and seeking party statements to refute the opponent's theory are exactly the same. Every party statement establishing the one side's theory will by necessity refute the other side's theory. More generally, to prepare to test theories at a deposition, the deposing attorney must ask herself:

"If the opponent's theory is true, what facts must be true?"

"If this fact is true, what other facts must be true?"

"What information is available from this witness relating to these facts?"

"Who else knows about these facts?"

"What do I already know about these facts?"

Deciding What Party Statements May Be Obtainable from the Particular Witness

Having decided what facts are needed to support a case theory and to refute the other side's theory, you must then apply that knowledge to the particular witness being deposed. What party statements are wanted from this witness—what facts, conclusions, opinions, concessions, etc. do you want to hear coming from this witness's mouth?

8.4.3 Determining How to Obtain the Admissions or Party Statements from the Witness

Differences between Cross-Examination at Trial and in a Deposition

Many lawyers believe obtaining party statements in a deposition is no different in style or technique than cross-examination at trial. In fact, the process of obtaining party statements in a deposition sometimes does closely resemble cross-examination at trial, especially in the increased use of leading questions. However, there are several significant differences, and you should not believe that cross-examination and leading questions are the only methods for obtaining party statements at depositions.

Dramatic skills count for little in a deposition. Good cross-examiners in jury trials will use their voices and gestures as tools for keeping jurors' attention and impressing on them the importance of particular questions and answers. Raising or lowering the voice, using dramatic pauses and gestures are ways of injecting drama into the cross-examination. These techniques usually do not have much effect in a stenographically recorded deposition. The deposition transcript reflects only the words spoken and does not show any of the vocal inflections, gestures, or other cross-examination devices that trial lawyers regularly use. Worse, these rhetorical devices often have the effect of making a witness more aware that the deposing lawyer is trying to get the witness to say something harmful to the other side's case. A video deposition picks up voice inflection and volume to some extent, but because the camera is usually solely on the witness, much of the examiner's gestures and dramatic efforts are off camera and lost to the viewer. As a result, a firm conversational questioning style is normally the most effective way to conduct a deposition, with perhaps a bit of drama for emphasis at important points in video depositions.

Generally, it does not matter at what point in the deposition party statements are obtained or sought. In a trial, the cross-examiner will usually group together all the questions on a topic to increase clarity and to maximize jury impact. Mixing questions on different topics often makes a cross-examination more difficult to follow.

In comparison, it does not matter in stenographic depositions whether questions on a topic are grouped together or are interspersed throughout the deposition. You can rearrange the questions in any order when using the transcript later for planning cross-examination, bringing or opposing motions for summary judgment, moving to limit expert testimony, or preparing to read portions of the deposition to a jury.[14]

---

14. The only prohibition is against taking a question and answer out of context in such a way as to change their meaning. Fed. R. Civ. P. 32(a)(6) states: "If a party offers in evidence only part of a deposition, an adverse party may require the offeror to introduce any other part

It is generally a good idea in a deposition to ask "one question too many." One of Irving Younger's "Ten Commandments," referring to cross-examination at trial, is never to ask the one question too many.[15] That rule generally does not apply in depositions. If the witness has an explanation that explains away a party statement, you will want to hear that explanation at the deposition rather than for the first time at trial. Not asking the one question too many does not make the answer go away. Defending counsel has been listening to the examination, and if there is an explanation, it is likely to come out during the defending lawyer's examination of the witness at the deposition or on the witness's direct examination at trial. The only result of not asking the one question too many at the deposition is that you will now likely be surprised by whatever explanation the witness gives at trial to qualify the previous deposition testimony. There are situations where you may not want to ask the one question too many,[16] but the general rule is that there is no harm in doing so, and there is often a benefit.

It is generally proper in a deposition to ask questions to which you don't know the answer. Another of Irving Younger's commandments for cross-examining a witness at trial is "Never ask a question to which you don't know the answer." Generally, the opposite of that rule applies in deposition, where you usually do not know the answer to most of the questions being asked. One of the purposes of the deposition is to find out those answers so you will know what answers to expect when cross-examining at trial.

No judge is present during the deposition to make the witness answer. A lawyer cross-examining at trial can seek the judge's help if the witness evades a question. At a deposition, however, the judge's help is not available without first bringing a motion asking the court to compel an answer. Evasion often takes the form of the witness not directly answering a question, but instead talking about something other than what was called for by the question. Another form of evasion occurs when the witness answers the question, but then goes on to include additional information not called for

---

that in fairness should be considered with the part introduced, and any party may introduce any other parts." FED. R. EVID. 106 provides: "If a party introduces all or part of a writing or recorded statement, an adverse party may require the introduction, at that time, of any other part—or any other writing or recorded statement—that in fairness ought to be considered at the same time." Rearranging video deposition questions and answers, however, may result in a choppy presentation. Where possible, it is better in a video deposition to ask the questions and obtain the answers in the same order as they are likely to be used at trial.

15. For example, having led the defendant's witness on cross at trial to state that the defendant threw the first punch in the fight with the plaintiff, the plaintiff's attorney should not ask, "How do you know that was the first punch?" The answer may come back, "Because up to then, the fight was just the plaintiff, kicking the defendant after the defendant tripped and was down on the floor. There hadn't been any punches until the defendant managed to get up to protect himself."

16. *See* section 8.4.4, n. 15, and text at n. 17.

by the question. At trial, you can ask the judge to order the witness to answer the question asked, but there is no judge present at the deposition. When a witness evades a question at a deposition, it is up to you to get a proper answer. This can be a difficult task because both the witness and defending counsel often prefer to avoid an answer. Asking the question again, asking it again later, asking it in different language, or even asking why the witness does not want to answer it directly, are all preferable to taking the time, effort, and expense of seeking an order compelling the discovery under threat of sanction.

8.4.4   Cross-Examination Techniques

Although there are significant differences between cross-examination at trial and questioning to obtain party statements at a deposition, the two techniques share some of the same techniques. Let's turn now to what those techniques are.

Some lawyers are naturally gifted cross-examiners—they seem to have been born with a quickness of mind, an intuition for sensing weaknesses in a witness's testimony, a demeanor that compels the witness to give the answers the lawyer is looking for, and a talent for choosing exactly the right words to emphasize the problem with or significance of the witness's testimony. While trial advocacy teachers generally agree that advocacy courses cannot teach these talents, we also agree that everyone can identify and practice many of the underlying skills, and there are techniques that anyone can learn that will make her a more competent and effective examiner. A "merely competent" examiner is, in fact, a rarity among trial lawyers, because so many attorneys lack the competence to properly question at deposition due to the failure to identify goals, to build rapport, to distinguish between gathering new information and seeking part statements, to understand the rules of evidence, and to handle documents well.

At trial, the cross-examiner's goal is to exert control over the witness to compel the witness to give desired answers. That same control can be used to extract party statements from a witness at a deposition in a useful form. Control of the witness at deposition is the result of a combination of factors:

1.   the form of the questions asked;

2.   the personalities of the witness, opposing counsel, and the taking lawyer, and the interaction among them;

3.   the logic of the questions and answers; and, of course,

4.   whether the witness can truthfully give the desired answer.

Let's start with the form of the questions.

Form of the Question

Leading Questions

When you are seeking party statements, you are asking the witness to agree with specific facts that help your case or hurt the opponent's. Note that if you are instead in an information gathering mode, you will use open-ended questions, because the goal is to obtain unknown information that is useful for you to know. In contrast, when seeking party statements, you will usually use leading questions, with the witness's only role being to agree or disagree with the facts presented in the question. Of course, as has been said before, useful party statements may often be obtained in response to open questions during information gathering.

Leading questions are used for two reasons: 1) their use encourages the witness to give the desired answer in the form invited by the question; and 2) leading is more efficient because you do not have to sort through answers that may intersperse party statements with other information that is confusing or superfluous or harmful or not well expressed. With leading questions, you can put words into the witness's mouth. The questions call for "yes" or "no" answers and do not overtly invite explanation. Here is an example of leading questions at a deposition in a case where it is claimed that a work site was not properly supervised:

> Q: You work for the Lone Star Trucking Company?
>
> A: Yes.
>
> Q: You have worked there for ten years?
>
> A: Yes.
>
> Q: Your job there is to direct the loading of the moving trucks?
>
> A: Yes.
>
> Q: If you are not there the other workers cannot begin loading the trucks?
>
> A: That's right.
>
> Q: If the workers are not loading trucks they are usually just sitting around?
>
> A: Yes.

Q: You often leave the work site when there is no loading of the trucks going on?

A: I often do.

Q: That's because there is nothing for you to do on the work site when the trucks are not being loaded?

A: That's true.

Q: But you do have paperwork to do in your office?

A: Yes, there is always lots of paperwork.

Q: You often go to your office to work on paperwork when there are no trucks being loaded?

A: Sometimes.

Q: When you are in your office there is no one at the work site supervising the men?

A: They really do not need supervision if they are not loading the trucks.

Q: My question is, there is no one at the work site supervising the men when you are in your office doing paperwork?

A: True.

Through these leading questions asked of a party, representative, or person who is authorized to speak for a party, under Rule 801, the questioning attorney has established that the men were unsupervised on the work site. If the accident could have been avoided by proper supervision, this party statement takes the plaintiff's case a long way toward success.

Short Questions

Although it is a rule frequently broken in practice, questions should be short so that the facts sought in the party statement do not get obscured. Short questions also draw fewer objections (the other side can't think fast enough to make an objection), are harder for the witness to evade (because, when short, the question contains fewer modifiers and qualifiers for the witness to seize on), and are easier to understand when the question is quoted in a summary judgment motion or read to a jury.

One-Fact Questions

Asking specific leading questions to conduct "cross-examination," even at a deposition to obtain party statements, can be tedious work. The deponent usually knows where you are headed and, if aligned with the opposing party, she will want to avoid giving the answers you are seeking. Marching the witness forward toward the desired answers means reducing the witness's opportunities to disagree. One way to do this is to ask one-fact questions. The type of one-fact question being proposed is illustrated by assuming a personal injury automobile collision case in which the questioning attorney is attempting to show the defendant was speeding to avoid being late to work.

Q: The collision happened at the intersection of Westheimer and Kirby Streets?

A: Yes.

Q: The intersection of Westheimer and Kirby is two miles from your work?

A: About that.

Q: There are six traffic lights between Westheimer and Kirby and your work?

A: Around that many. I have never counted them to be sure.

Q: The accident happened on a Tuesday morning?

A: Yes.

Q: The accident happened at 8:50 a.m.?

A: I think that is when it happened.

Q: 8:50 a.m. is during rush hour?

A: Yes.

Q: You start work at 9:00 a.m.?

A: Yes.

Q: The collision occurred ten minutes before your start time?

A: Correct.

Q: If you were going to be on time for work, you had to travel two miles in ten minutes?

A: I guess so.

Q:	If you were going to be on time, you had to go through six traffic lights in ten minutes?

A:	Something like that.

Revert to Open-Ended Questions When Encountering Roadblocks

A cross-examiner at trial will know what answers a witness will give because the witness has previously been deposed. But the taking lawyer at a deposition will not know for sure what answers will be given (remember the discovery aspect of questioning) until after the questions are asked and the answers are given. (Of course, sometimes the taking lawyer can be reasonably sure of the answer because of information from other sources.) And sometimes, the answer is not what the taking lawyer expected.

When a witness gives the "wrong" answer to a leading question—that is, when no useful party statement is obtained—do not give up. Instead, find out the basis for the wrong answer by reverting to information gathering—the "top" of the funnel technique—and asking open-ended questions. Once you have determined the basis for the wrong answer, you may be able to move the witness off of the answer, or to work around it, to obtain the desired party statement. For example, the illustration of cross-examination in the previous example could have gone as follows:

Q:	The accident happened at the intersection of Westheimer and Kirby Streets?

A:	Yes.

Q:	The intersection of Westheimer and Kirby is two miles from your work?

A:	No, that's not true.

Q:	Well, how far is it then?

A:	Two and a half miles. [*Which, of course, is even better for the questioner's purposes.*]

Q:	OK. There are six traffic lights between Westheimer and Kirby and your work?

A:	Something like that.

Q:	You're not saying that there are fewer than six traffic lights between Westheimer and Kirby and your work?

A:	No, I am just not certain about the exact number.

Q: The collision happened on a Tuesday morning?

A: I wouldn't call it a collision.

Q: What would you call it?

A: An accident.

Q: The accident happened on a Tuesday morning?

A: Yes.

Q: The accident happened when the truck you were driving collided with Ms. Jones's car, right?

A: OK.

Q: The accident happened at 8:50 a.m.?

A: That's not right.

Q: What time do you say it occurred?

A: I am guessing it was more like 8:45.

Q: You're not certain about the time?

A: Not exactly.

Q: Earlier you said that the police arrived within two or three minutes of the accident?

A: Yes.

Q: If the police report states that the police arrived at 8:53 a.m., would you disagree that the police arrived at that time?

A: No, that sounds about right.

Q: If the accident happened two or three minutes before the police arrived, that would mean the accident occurred no earlier than 8:50 a.m., correct?

A: I guess so.

Q: 8:50 a.m. is during the rush hour?

A: Yes.

Q: Your work starts at 9:00 a.m.?

A: Yes.

Q: At the time of the accident you had no more than ten minutes to get to work?

A: I guess so.

Q: The lights and the traffic had to break just right for you to get to work on time?

A: Yeah, that's true.

Looping Questions

Looping is a powerful device for encouraging party statements—it incorporates a witness's favorable answer into the next question. Consider the deposition of a pharmaceutical company executive in a products liability case:

Q: In September, you were told that the drug was dangerous if taken by people with a heart condition?

A: Yes.

Q: The drug was dangerous because it can cause heart attacks, strokes, and death in users?

A: Yes.

Q: After finding out the drug can cause heart attacks, strokes, and death in users, you were concerned?

A: Yes.

Q: You were concerned about possible death, heart attacks, and strokes in users, so you wanted the company to take some action regarding the drug?

A: Yes.

The witness will feel compelled to give the desired answer by the phrasing of the question. By using looping, the witness is forced to give the "right" answer or feel foolish. Someone who is not concerned about a drug that causes death will appear foolish or heartless, and therefore the witness is more likely to answer "yes" than if the question only asked if the witness was concerned without referring to the drug causing deaths.

Sound-Bite Questions

Many depositions are driven by the quest for sound bites—those short, self-contained questions and answers in which the witness gives damaging party statements. These dramatic sound bites can then be incorporated into a summary judgment motion or read or shown to the jury.

The sound bite differs from other types of party statements in that it is designed to be a dramatic stand-alone statement—the desired information being presented in a single answer or a short series of questions and answers without being diluted by a long series of foundational questions and answers.

A sound bite's impact is greatest when captured in a video deposition. A video sound bite allows the jury to watch and listen as the damaging words come out of the witness's mouth. Video also shows the witness's nonverbal reactions to the question—his demeanor, gestures, expressions, perspiration, twitches, jitters, smirks, and other types of visual indicators that can strongly influence the jury's assessment of the answer. Let's look again at the same products liability case:

Q: A family physician out in West Texas would not be able to find out how dangerous the drug is from the package insert that comes with the drug?

A: It wasn't on there.

Q: That family physician out in West Texas would not be able to find out how dangerous the drug is from any of the literature and advertising the company sent to doctors all over the United States?

A: No.

Q: Knowing the dangers of taking a particular drug is something a physician would want to know before prescribing the drug to one of the doctor's patients?

A: They would.

Q: Without knowing about the dangers of a drug, doctors don't have the information they need to make an intelligent decision as to whether the drug's benefits outweigh its risks?

A: True.

Q: Of course, if doctors don't have information about the drug's dangers, they can't inform their patients about the risks that come with that drug such as heart attacks and strokes?

A: Correct.

Any one of these questions can later be used as a free-standing sound bite, or a number can be presented together for their cumulative impact.

To get a witness to provide a sound bite, you must carefully arrange the questions so that the witness feels compelled to give the correct answer. Sometimes, however, even an open-ended question produces a valuable sound bite if the question comes at the end of a series of leading, set-up questions. If done correctly, the open-ended question puts the witness in the awkward position of either looking foolish or giving the party statement. Consider the nice sound bite that you could obtain when an open-ended question is added to the end of the previous line of examination:

> Q: What information do you believe should have been included in the package insert to make sure a family physician in West Texas would know the risks and benefits of a drug?
>
> A: Well, obviously the package insert should have told about the increased risks of heart attack, stroke, and death that can arise with the drug's use.

"Boxing In" the Witness

Obtaining party statements would be a much easier task if every witness was completely honest and objective. You could just ask the "big" questions, whatever they might be, and receive honest answers. But not all witnesses are fully committed to the truth, and the recollection of even a reasonably honest and well-intentioned witness may be distorted by subliminal influences, like multiple preparation sessions, pressures to perform, or hopes that a friend's lawsuit will turn out well for the friend. For these reasons, it is best not to present the witness with the ultimate question prematurely. Instead, you need to build up to the important question by first establishing the necessary subsidiary facts.

The idea of cross-examination at trial or deposition is to use the logic of the questions and answers—what is known as "boxing in" the witness—to drive the witness toward the sought after party statements. At the conclusion of a line of cross-examination, the witness should feel compelled to give the "right" answer or to contradict logic and earlier answers. The goal is to force the witness to choose between truth on the one hand and foolish inconsistency on the other.

Boxing in the witness takes careful planning. You must carefully chart how to take the deponent from admitting those things about which there is little dispute to admitting facts that are harmful to the other side's case. Some of the techniques for doing so are discussed below.

Conceal Your Objective for as Long as Possible

The problem with witnesses is that too often they quickly figure out what party statements you are seeking and resist admitting facts that lead to that objective. The longer you can conceal the objective, the greater the likelihood the witness will eventually provide the party statement being sought.

Do Not React to Favorable or Unfavorable Answers

Smiling with satisfaction at a witness's answer serves as a pretty good clue that the witness has said something harmful to the party with whom the witness is aligned. Witnesses who see you reacting this way will frequently begin to backtrack or qualify the answers just given. Keep a poker face when you hear a favorable answer. Similarly, reacting negatively to an answer lets the witness know the answer was probably a good one for the witness's side.

Commit the Witness to General Principles and Undisputed Facts

Cross-examination can be viewed as a process in which the questioning lawyer starts some distance from the goal—the hoped for party statement—and establishes the general facts, principles, and propositions that the witness can easily admit. The taking attorney then slowly tightens the circle of logic, moving the witness toward the goal. It should be possible to identify the general facts, principles, and propositions in nearly every case. Start with what the witness has previously said, what others have said the witness is likely to admit, what logic and common sense suggest must be true, and facts that can be easily corroborated.

Move from Facts the Witness Must Admit to Facts You Would Like the Witness to Admit

Tightening the circle of logic means moving from those facts that cannot be sensibly denied to those facts you believe to be true. When preparing for the deposition, make a chart that contains several categories of facts: 1) facts that cannot be denied because the witness has previously written it, or said it, or was photographed doing it, or it is indisputably true; 2) facts the witness is likely to admit because they are contained in a document or can be easily corroborated; 3) facts the witness should admit because to deny them would make the witness look illogical, foolish, ignorant or a liar; and 4) facts you would like to be true that are "worth a try." The witness is more likely to testify to the party statements being sought if you start with facts that cannot be denied and then move through the different categories to end with facts you would like to be true.

Close Off Escape Routes Early

Once it is evident where a cross-examination is headed, a witness not fully committed to the truth will be looking for ways to avoid giving the sought after party statement. Therefore, think carefully about what excuses or reasons the witness might use to avoid giving the party statement and try to take those reasons and excuses away before the witness realizes where the examination is going.

Assume the party statement being sought is that a stockbroker, employed by a major brokerage house, heard a statement at an analysts meeting that a company in which the broker had been advising his clients to invest was projecting a loss for the year. The plaintiff contends that after hearing the statement, the broker failed to inform clients of this information and continued to place orders for the company's shares at their direction.

What escape routes might the stockbroker take to avoid giving this party statement? Perhaps he might say he was not at the meeting, that he didn't hear the statement, that he did not recall that his clients were investing in the company, that he did not have time to inform his clients of the news, and so on. The questioning to close off escape routes might go like this:

Q: It is part of your job to attend meetings with the investment house's analysts?

A: Yes.

Q: It's important to attend these meetings so you will know how to advise your clients regarding their investments?

A: Yes.

Q: You were at your office on May 13 of last year when there was one of these analysts meeting?

A: That's what my calendar says.

Q: You attended that meeting?

A: Yes.

Q: There was a written agenda containing the names of the stocks that would be discussed that day?

A: Yes.

Q: You look at these agendas to see if any of the companies listed are companies in which your clients are investing?

A: I usually do.

Q: Handing you what has been marked as Exhibit 1, you saw that National Computer Parts was on the agenda for the May 13 meeting?

A: Yes.

Q: You knew that five of your clients had investments in NCP?

A: Yes.

Q: The total investment of these five clients was over $1,000,000?

A: Something like that.

Q: That is a large investment?

A: I've seen larger.

Q: But it is a large investment?

A: Yes.

Q: The analysts meeting is held in the twelfth-floor conference room?

A: Yes.

Q: That's a small room?

A: Fairly small.

Q: It only holds a dozen people or so?

A: That sounds right.

Q: You can easily hear the analyst when she is making her presentation?

A: Yes.

Q: You were paying attention because she would be discussing a stock in which your clients had invested?

A: Yes.

As can be seen, the taking lawyer is closing off possible escape routes before he asks the witness whether he heard the analyst say NCP would be showing a loss for the year. Only once all the escape routes are closed off will the taking lawyer ask that question.

Get the Witness to Commit to Absolutes; Insist on Firm Answers

A party statement is worthless if the witness is able to wiggle out of it. Equivocal, ambiguous, or qualified answers offer the witness an easy escape route. When the witness says, "I usually do it that way," it is very easy to take the wiggle room offered by the answer and say that the time in question was one of the few times it was done differently. It can be very difficult to get witnesses to give unqualified or unequivocal answers, if that is what they have been coached to give (or it is the truth), but it is important to try.

> Q: Do you inform new hires of the company's procedures for reporting accusations of sexual harassment?
>
> A: Generally, no. It is something we post near the water cooler, but we do not tell them orally of this information.
>
> Q: You said "generally, no." When do you tell them?
>
> A: I can't think of any instances, but I suppose it must come up sometime when we interview new hires.
>
> Q: Was the plaintiff informed of the company's procedures for reporting accusations of sexual harassment?
>
> A: I don't think so.
>
> Q: Would anything help you remember if she was told?
>
> A: Not that I can think of.
>
> Q: Did you keep any notes of what you told her or she told you?
>
> A: No.
>
> Q: So as far as you know, as you sit here today, the plaintiff was never informed at the time she was hired of the company's procedures for reporting accusations of sexual harassment?
>
> A: That is right.

Sometimes You Have to Wrestle with the Witness

Despite your best efforts to work logically toward the party statement you want, the witness refuses sometimes to give it. It is one thing if the witness refuses to give the party statement because it is just not the truth, but it is another matter if the refusal is because the witness is not responding to the logic of the previous questions and answers. In the latter instance, you will need to wrestle with the witness by challenging and arguing with the witness's answers.

Unlike other types of examination, it is difficult to plan for wrestling with the witness because it depends so much on the witness's answers to previous questions; it is clear, however, that you must not only have complete mastery of the available facts, but you must also listen carefully.

Consider a deposition where the witness has refused to admit that the failure to tighten certain bolts in the construction of a building might cause the building to become structurally unsound:

> Q: You are saying that even if the bolts are not tightened completely, the building will still be structurally sound?
>
> A: That's right.
>
> Q: Well, let's see. The bolts are designed to hold the struts together?
>
> A: Yes.
>
> Q: The struts are necessary for the building's structural soundness?
>
> A: That may or may not be true.
>
> Q: If the struts were not installed, the building would likely collapse?
>
> A: That's true.
>
> Q: So the struts are necessary to the building's structural soundness?
>
> A: Put that way, yes.
>
> Q: The struts only work if they are connected to one another and to the upright beams?
>
> A: True.
>
> Q: If the struts are not connected, they cannot work to hold the building together?
>
> A: Correct.
>
> Q: The bolts hold the struts together?
>
> A: Yes.

Q: The plans for constructing the building indicate the bolts should be tightened to at least ninety foot-pounds of torque?

A: Yes.

Q: And you agree that the construction details specify that the bolts should be tightened to at least ninety foot-pounds of torque so that there is a solid connection between the pairs of struts?

A: Yes, that's true.

Q: Can the bolts safely be tightened to less than ninety foot-pounds and still achieve a solid connection?

A: It probably would not be as safe.

Q: And it wouldn't be as safe because there would be a possibility of the building being structurally unsound?

A: Yes.

Q: The bolts in this case were tightened to only sixty-seven foot-pounds?

A: That is my understanding.

Q: Torque of sixty-seven foot-pounds would not be as safe as ninety foot-pounds?

A: That's true.

Q: And that is because there is a possibility of the building being structurally unsound?

A: That would be true.

Q: But you don't know how unsound that difference in torque would make the building, correct?

A: I haven't run any tests.

Methods of Controlling the Witness

Eye Contact

It is more difficult for many witnesses to lie when you are looking directly into their eyes. Eye contact is an important element of control, and you should maintain it throughout the deposition, but particularly when seeking party statements.

Falling Inflections

In normal conversation, the syntax (the grammatical arrangement of words in a sentence) is a common indication that a question is being asked: "Are you aware of the problem?" as opposed to the declarative, "You were aware of the problem." Inverted subject-verb order signals a request for information. Additionally, a rising inflection at the end of a sentence also indicates a question. When witnesses hear that rising inflection or that inverted verb-noun order, they may feel invited to give an explanation in response. A lawyer cross-examining a witness, however, is not asking a question for information, but is instead making statements and asking the witness to either agree or disagree. Effective control of a witness on cross requires that the "questions" avoid the inverted verb-noun and avoid the rising inflection. Falling inflection and normal verb placement are used when making these question-statements, and the context is the clue that the statement calls for an answer.

Tone

While it is usually unproductive to become angry, to raise your voice, or to try to bully the witness into giving a desired answer, it is also a mistake to take on too gentle a tone of voice or to have a too pleasant manner when pressing for party statements in cross-examination mode. Being nice and pleasant is usually appropriate when engaging in information gathering, but when it comes to obtaining party statements, it is usually better to use a firm and level tone.[17]

Rapid-Fire Questions

The more rapidly the next question follows an answer, the less time the witness has to think about the implications of the last question and answer—and how to avoid giving the answer you want. Rapid-fire questioning does not refer to how rapidly you are asking questions, but to the length of the pause between the end of the witness's answer and the start of your next question.

Conversely, rapid-fire questioning also gives you less time to think of the next question. When you use rapid-fire questioning, you must know exactly where you intend the line of questions to take the witness.

---

17. A harsher tone may antagonize the witness, and its use, like the process of gaining party statements itself, should probably be reserved for late in the deposition. Otherwise, the price of obtaining a party statement through harsh questioning on one point may be the good-will that might have resulted in party statements on several other points. This dynamic is analogous to that which leads trial lawyers to conduct "constructive" (noncredibility challenging cross) before "destructive" cross at trial.

Be aware that the effectiveness of rapid-fire questioning is easily defeated if the witness has learned to pause before answering or if the defending lawyer constantly intervenes to delay the witness from answering too spontaneously. Spurious objections often are used in such attempts to "slow things down," and you should make a record that challenges those illicit efforts.

Other Techniques

There are a number of other techniques that you can use to extract party statements from a witness. The following list is not intended to be exclusive, but merely to present several techniques that often prove useful.

Push as Far as Possible (Usually)

Contrary to Irving Younger's "Ten Commandments of Cross-Examination" (applicable to trial), there is usually no "one question too many" concern in a deposition. At a deposition, you generally want to take the cross-examination on a topic as far as the witness will go. When the witness refuses to go any further, you then know how far to proceed with the cross-examination at trial. Trial is when the cross-examiner should not ask the one question too many.[18]

Let's turn again to a personal injury automobile collision case to illustrate this.

> Q: As you approached the intersection, you were looking straight ahead?
>
> A: Yes.
>
> Q: You were keeping your eye on the traffic light?
>
> A: Yes.
>
> Q: You wanted to get through the intersection before the light changed?
>
> A: Yes.
>
> Q: You weren't looking to the sides of the road?
>
> A: Not as much as I was looking at the light.
>
> Q: You were not looking out for pedestrians?
>
> A: That's not true. I was.

---

18. We have written briefly above about the distinction between one question too many at deposition as compared to trial. *See supra*, note 15.

Based on the deposition testimony, the cross-examination at trial will highlight that the driver was looking straight ahead, was concentrating on the traffic light, wanted to get through the intersection before the light changed, and was not looking to the sides of the road as much as she was looking at the traffic light—but the cross-examiner will not ask whether the witness was looking out for pedestrians.

When lawyers recommend not pushing beyond a helpful party statement and instead changing the subject at deposition, their reasoning is to forestall the witness from taking back or qualifying the useable party statement. The reason for *usually* pushing even beyond a successful party statement at deposition is either that sometimes the witness will give an additional, unexpected statement that you did not even hope for or the witness will provide an unexpected explanation—otherwise not discovered until trial—that destroys the impact of the party statement. "Pushing" lawyers recommend that you should always push even after getting an unexpected favorable party statement. These lawyers argue that unless the defending lawyer is incompetent or asleep, the defending lawyer will also be surprised by the unexpected party statement and will confer with the witness about it during the next break. The defending lawyer will then have the witness recant either after the break or during the defending lawyer's examination at the end of the deposition; or they may postpone the recantation to direct or re-direct at trial. Therefore, these lawyers argue, you should get the witness to firmly commit and then explore the party statement before the defending lawyer has an opportunity to talk to the witness and engage in damage control. The authors agree that pushing on after a party statement has been obtained at a deposition is the best way to solidify that party statement so that it cannot easily be wrested away by the opposing attorney.

Make Sure the Party Statements Are Admissible

Be sure to authenticate documents and other evidence and show that the witness has personal knowledge of the facts being testified to. When deposing the opposing party, this last recommendation is a matter of caution, rather than of evidentiary necessity. Opposing party's statements are excepted from the personal knowledge requirement, just as they are excepted from operation of the hearsay rule. In fact, the reasons that foundation is not required for receipt of opposing parties' statements are the same reasons that the hearsay rule does not exclude them: opposing parties cannot logically object to the inclusion in the record of their own relevant statements by claiming, "I didn't know what I was talking about."

Get Out Once You Get What You Want and Can Protect It

Even though you should push the witness as far as possible, that does not mean asking the witness to repeat favorable answers. The more opportunity the witness has to think about a particular answer, the more likely the witness is to change or qualify the answer. Once the witness has given the desired answer, and appropriate and sensible pushing has been done, move on to the next question in the sequence. "Appropriate and sensible" pushing means exploring the witness's basis for the party statement to the point where the witness and opposing counsel will have difficulty at trial (or during their questioning later in the deposition) diminishing or altering the statement. For example, if an executive admits that the company had knowledge of an important omission, follow-up questioning (pushing) could explore the witness's responsibilities during the relevant time. If those responsibilities relate only tangentially to the party statement, you could stop pushing and walk away with the party statement still intact; if the responsibilities in fact included the topic of the party statement, the pushing makes the party statement more secure against attempts by the opposition to claim that the witness really doesn't know what he is talking about. In general, in deciding how far to push on important party statements, the rule for the questioning attorney is: "Push until you believe you have exhausted the witness's information." The rule is not: "Push until you think you might get a bad answer." The "bad" answer is what you want to hear at the deposition—not for the first time at trial.

Attack Harmful Conclusions

When a witness answers in the form of a harmful conclusion, find out the foundation, or factual basis, for the conclusion. Then, if the other side finds some colorable evidentiary basis for attempting to introduce the deposition statement at trial, you will be prepared to argue against its admissibility. *"Your Honor, at the very next page the witness herself admitted that she was basing that conclusion on hearsay from sessions at the water cooler."* Many times the conclusion will be an expression of what the witness wishes to be true, but there is either no or only a weak basis for it. Of course, do not challenge helpful conclusions. Here is an example of a harmful conclusion being challenged in a personal injury case:

Q: How fast was the Buick going?

A: Very fast.

Q: How long was the Buick in your sight?

A: I saw it coming up on my left, and then the collision occurred.

Q: Where was the Buick when you first saw it?

A: About fifty yards behind me.

Q: Then you saw the Buick for one or two seconds?

A: I guess something like that.

Q: And the car was coming up from behind you?

A: Yes.

Q: Were you watching it in your rearview mirror?

A: Yes.

Q: Now, you'll agree that it is kind of hard to estimate the speed of a car in just a second or two when it is coming up from behind and you only see it in your rearview mirror?

A: I guess so.

Q: You're not really sure the Buick was going very fast?

A: Not completely sure.

Try to Get the Witness to Agree to Subjective Words and Phrases

A good trial lawyer cross-examining at trial, or leading to obtain party statements at deposition, will rarely include subjective words and phrases in questions. Subjective words and phrases can take many forms—adjectives, adverbs, conclusions, or characterizations. The problem with such language at trial is that it provides the witness with an opportunity to disagree with the proposition contained in the question. For example, a witness at trial should normally not be asked on cross-examination to agree that one of the parties was driving "very fast" at the time of the accident. Without an agreed definition of "very fast," the witness can interpret the words however he chooses. Instead, the cross-examiner's questions should suggest the party was driving very fast by eliciting facts that lead to that conclusion, but leave the conclusion itself to the closing argument.

However, an exception to the rule against using subjective words and phrases in cross-examination at trial is when the witness has already agreed to that very language during the deposition. The witness's use of those subjective words and phrases then stands as a provable, objective fact. For example, if the witness answers during the deposition that the party was going "very fast" and later refuses on cross-examination at trial to say the same thing, you can use the deposition to introduce the statement "very fast" through impeachment. Therefore, push to have the witness agree to favorable subjective words and phrases whenever possible at the deposition.

There are two methods for having the witness at a deposition agree to subjective words and phrases. First, you can ask the witness to provide the subjective words and phrases. If this method is unsuccessful or the answer is not as favorable as you hoped, then you can suggest subjective words and phrases. Let's look again at a personal injury case to illustrate how these methods are used:

Q: How fast were you going?

A: About seventy-five miles per hour.

Q: The speed limit in that stretch is fifty-five miles per hour?

A: Yes.

Q: You were going twenty miles over the speed limit?

A: I guess that's about right.

Q: How would you describe your speed?

A: I was going fast.

Q: About twenty miles over the speed limit is fast?

A: Yes.

Q: Wouldn't you say that was going very fast?

A: Maybe.

Q: In fact, you were going at a dangerous rate of speed?

A: No, that's not true.

Clean Up Messy Answers

Sometimes the party statement you are seeking is buried in the middle of a long answer that has been interrupted by objections and colloquy. Reading the entire answer to the jury, quoting it in a summary judgment motion, or attempting to impeach with it runs the risk of the judge or jury not under-standing the significance of the statement. You need to extract the favorable party statement from the surrounding answer to make it useful. But if you ask the witness to repeat only the favorable part of the answer, you are sending a clear signal that you consider it important. The better approach is to go through the entire answer and have the witness agree with each part of it. In that way, you obtain a clean party statement, and the witness is not alerted to what part of the answer you consider important.

Q: What was the road surface like at the point where the collision occurred?

A: Well, it had been sunny earlier that day, and the roads had been dry and clear ever since I passed the intersection with I-45, but then it started snowing, and there was a fair amount of snow on the ground, although I don't think the snow was the cause of the accident since I had snow tires on, so I really do not know what caused us to collide. [*The portion of the answer favorable to the taker is the statement that there was "a fair amount of snow on the ground."*]

Q: Let me see if I understand this. You said it had been sunny earlier that day?

A: Yes.

Q: The roads had been dry and clear after the intersection with I-45?

A: That's right.

Q: Then it started snowing?

A: Yes.

Q: There was a fair amount of snow on the ground?

A: Right.

Q: You don't think the snow was the cause of the accident?

A: Correct.

Q: You don't know what caused the accident?

A: True.

Many lawyers, while cleaning up a messy answer, will change their tone and inflection when they ask about the key party statement. Avoid this because it will tip off the witness to the importance of the answer. Instead, every question should be asked in the same level, routine voice.

Avoid Summarizing a Witness's Answers Unless Necessary to Clean Up a Messy Party Statement or Clarify a Confusing Answer

As previously discussed, you should recapitulate and summarize witnesses' answers sparingly. There is a risk the witness will qualify or retract some part of the answer whenever you recapitulate or summarize. Witnesses are often cued to change their answers when the defending lawyer objects that the taking lawyer is misstating or mischaracterizing the witness's earlier answer (or improperly objecting that the question has been "asked and answered").

Witnesses readily pick up on the defending attorney's suggestion and often restate their previous answers in a less favorable form.

Impeaching at Deposition

The conventional wisdom is that impeachment should be saved for trial. Where the witness is caught at deposition giving demonstrably false or mistaken testimony, the usual approach has been to postpone correction through impeachment until cross-examination at trial. The impeached witness will only recant, look ashamed, or act embarrassed once, and there is no sense in wasting that one time on the court reporter and opposing counsel (unless, of course, it is a videotaped deposition). It is better to save the impeachment until trial, where the jury can appreciate the witness's discomfort.

However, while this conventional wisdom makes sense for cases that are going to trial, *most* cases do not go to trial. Therefore, it is time to adjust deposition strategy to match modern trial practice. Today, in *most* cases, the better approach is to impeach at the deposition, where the corrected answer and the witness's diminished credibility will encourage settlement or improve the chances of winning on summary judgment.[19] If you use a document or prior inconsistent statement at a deposition to impeach, the witness will indeed be better prepared to explain away the document or prior statement at trial. But if the odds are against there ever being a trial, you have a greater chance of improving your case by including the impeachment in the deposition. Opposing counsel will have the opportunity then to attempt some rehabilitation, as he would at trial, but at least your supportive material is available for summary judgment practice.

8.4.5   When Leading Does Not Work

Leading questions sometimes cause difficulties because they alert the witness and opposing lawyer that you are trying to get the witness to give a particular answer. (Of course, by the authors' observation, most attorneys are conducting even the "new information" discovery portions of deposition by asking leading questions, so perhaps additional leading questions will not stand out very much.) Granted, an intelligent and well-prepared witness may well be aware of your objectives regardless of the form of the questions being asked, but not all witnesses are so perceptive.

The further your questions move toward leading, the greater the likelihood that the witness and opposing counsel will become aware of your objectives and will resist giving the desired answers. The increased use of leading questions often corresponds to an increase in the number of objections and

---

19. This important insight was first made by Steve Lubet in "Showing Your Hand: A Counter-Intuitive Strategy for Deposition Defense," 29 No. 2 Litigation 38 (Winter 2003).

incidents of improper behavior by opposing counsel. All of this points to the conclusion that sometimes the best approach is not to lead at all, but to use other methods of obtaining party statements. All of these methods have as their goal concealing the taker's objectives and avoiding alerting the witness and the defending lawyer to the attempt to gain party statements.

Bury Questions Where the Objective Is Not Clear

One way to conceal your objective is to bury the questions seeking party statements in a series of questions on other topics. The questions can be scattered throughout the deposition so the witness never knows your actual objective. You can then rearrange the order of the questions and answers when preparing a summary judgment motion, planning cross-examination, or impeaching the witness.

Imagine a case where the issue is whether the plaintiff's purchasing agent, at the time of placing an order for parts, was aware of the ordering procedures described in the defendant's price list. You could just ask the purchasing agent if she had read the price list and seen the language about ordering procedures. But those questions will surely alert the purchasing agent to your objective. Once aware of what you are trying to accomplish, the purchasing agent is much less likely to provide the answers you want.

Rather than using the direct approach, instead choose to bury the questions in different parts of the deposition, where the objective is not obvious. For example, you might ask the following questions at the beginning of the deposition when the witness is being asked about background matters:

Q: You said you are the plaintiff's purchasing agent, is that correct?

A: Yes.

Q: What are your duties as the plaintiff's purchasing agent?

A: I am in charge of purchasing everything the company needs.

Q: How do you decide on what products need to be purchased?

A: The different managers tell me what is needed, and I go ahead and purchase them.

Q: How do you select between the different vendors that might be selling a product?

A: Sometimes I may call them up. I will also read the catalogs and other literature the vendors send me.

Later on in the deposition, you might turn to the purchase of the parts at issue in the case:

Q: How did you decide to purchase from the defendant?

A: I checked and found out they had the parts we needed.

Q: Was price important in making the decision?

A: Yes.

Q: How did you find out about the price?

A: I checked the defendant's price list, and then I confirmed the price in a phone call with the defendant's sales manager.

Q: What about payment terms?

A: Sure, I look at those, also.

Q: How did you find out about the defendant's payment terms?

A: They were on the price list, and again I confirmed them when I talked with the defendant's sales manager.

Q: What else did you know about the defendant's sales policies when you placed your order?

A: Well, I knew about their ordering procedures.

Q: How did you find out about the ordering procedures?

A: I read about them in the defendant's price list.

By placing these questions in this order, you make it appear that you are after information other than whether the purchasing agent had read the ordering procedures. Keep your tone casual on these "unimportant" price list questions, giving any emphasis to the actual price paid, or the number of items on the price list, or who provided the price list. Anything to do with the ordering procedures should be kept low key and touched on almost as an after-thought.

Tailored Information Gathering

While not nearly as efficient for obtaining party statements as leading questions, open-ended questions on a topic can obtain useful party statements because the witness may think he is choosing the topic and direction. The witness is not tipped off to your objective. This type of questioning, when used in the context of seeking party statements, is called "tailored information gathering," because the questions, while open, are intended to encourage the witness to give party statements rather than merely to find new information. Assume the continuation of the plaintiff's purchasing agent's deposition, with the issue again being whether the purchasing agent had read about the ordering procedures contained in the defendant's price list:

> Q: Let's talk about the first order with the defendant. Take me through each step you followed in placing the order, starting with how the plaintiff decided it needed the parts, all the way to the parts arriving and being paid for. How did the plaintiff decide it needed the parts?
>
> A: The manager in charge of production told me we would need 100 gross of the parts for our next production run.
>
> Q: What was the next step?
>
> A: I selected a vendor to buy from.
>
> Q: Who was that vendor?
>
> A: The defendant.
>
> Q: How did you go about selecting the defendant as the vendor?
>
> A: I looked at the price list and catalog the defendant sent us.
>
> Q: What did you find out by looking at the price list and catalog?
>
> A: The price of the parts, whether the part is in stock, shipping and payment terms, and how to place an order.

If the witness had not provided this party statement about learning "how to order" from reading the price list, the questioning attorney would have continued with questions like, "What else did you learn from the price list?" and "How did you know what to say when you ordered?" and "When did you learn about 2 percent discount for paying cash, and conditions like that?"

Specific But Nonleading Questions

Using tailored information-gathering questions to obtain party statements can be a "hit or miss" endeavor. Sometimes the answers contain the party statements you seek, and sometimes they do not. Using specific questions is a more efficient method for obtaining party statements than tailored information-gathering questions, but the specificity of the questions has a greater probability of tipping off the witness to your objectives. You can decrease that danger by asking open-ended questions rather than leading. Start with information-gathering questions, and if they don't get the desired party statements, progress to specific open questions, and then leading questions.

Specific nonleading questions are also frequently used when there is a range of possible answers, all useful as party statements, but the taking lawyer favors one particular answer and does not know which answer the witness is likely to give. Compared to putting a question to the witness that can properly be answered with a "yes" or "no," using an open-ended question invites an explanation with the answer. As with information-gathering questions, specific nonleading questions are often coupled with "Anything else?" questions to make sure the witness is not holding back useful information that was not specifically asked about.

Q: Do you have to choose between vendors when selecting the company to buy parts from?

A: Yes, if there is more than one possible vendor.

Q: Do you look at the price of the parts in making the selection?

A: Yes.

Q: How about shipping terms, do you look at them when making a selection?

A: Yes, but that is less important than the price.

Q: Payment terms—do you look at them as well when making a selection?

A: Sure, we want the most favorable payments possible.

Q: Any other factors you look at?

A: No, that's all I can think of.

Q: Do you need to find out how to order the parts?

A: Sometimes, particularly if I haven't ordered from the vendor before.

Q: Do you get that information from the catalogs and price lists sent to you by the vendors?

A: Usually. Sometimes I have to call up and find out.

Q: Did the defendant send you a price list?

A: Yes, I got one from them before we placed our first order.

Q: Did you find out the price for the parts from the price list?

A: Yes, and then I confirmed it when I called the defendant's sales manager.

Q: Same thing with the shipping and payment terms. Did you get them from the price list?

A: Yes.

Q: And how to place the order. Did you get that from the price list?

A: Yes, and I talked with the defendant's sales manager when I called the defendant.

Leading in the Opposite Direction

Some witnesses are such contrarians that they will resist giving you the slightest concession on any topic. These witnesses refuse to admit whatever proposition is contained in the question being asked, regardless of how harmless the answer. You can sometimes capitalize on this sort of behavior by leading the witness in the opposite direction of where you want the witness to go:

Q: Your job must be very busy with a lot of responsibilities?

A: It isn't always busy.

Q: Well, as the plaintiff's purchasing agent, you must receive hundreds of catalogs and price lists and other sorts of advertising literature?

A: There's not that many that come in.

Q: Certainly too many for you to read all of them?

A: That's not true. I read them all.

[And this begins the witness's concern with defending his competence against attack, when in reality the questioning attorney is not making that attack at all. This "false attack" continues in the following questions.]

Q: You can probably glance at them, but surely you can't read all the fine print and terms and conditions in them?

A: That's my job. I am required to stay on top of that sort of information.

> Q: Well, when the defendant's price list came in, didn't you
> just glance at that?
>
> A: No, I read everything on it, front and back.

Obviously, you should lead in the opposite direction only after you have determined that the witness, out of sheer contrariness, is likely to resist any line of cross-examination.

8.4.6   *Timing*

There is no one correct answer regarding the timing of seeking party statements. It depends on the witness, the relationship between the questioning attorney and the witness, and what approach is best suited to getting the answers needed.

Sometimes it makes sense for you to start the deposition by immediately asking leading questions designed to obtain party statements. The benefit of such an approach is that the witness is unlikely to be expecting such aggressive questioning so early in the deposition. Many lawyers prepare their witnesses by telling them that the taking lawyer will start with questioning about the witness's background and only later get to asking about the merits of the case. Starting with questions seeking party statements may find the witness surprised and unprepared, which may, in turn, result in the witness more readily giving the desired answers. In fact, if you obtain enough favorable party statements right up front, you may decide to shorten the deposition substantially; however, understand that doing so depends on whether you feel that you have enough information to file a persuasive motion for summary judgment and that you are consciously taking the risk that you have limited the information that you will have to attack a direct examination at trial.

The drawback of the "hit 'em early" approach is that seeking party statements usually requires you to push the witness a certain amount to get the desired answer. As you ask leading questions and attack undesirable answers with more leading questions, your tone might sometimes become sharp. When this happens, most witnesses quickly come to view you as the adversary. If you then try to shift to information-gathering mode, employing a type of questioning that requires you to build rapport with the witness and where the witness's cooperation is important, the witness will probably be in no mood to be helpful. It is much easier to go from information gathering to obtaining party statements than the other way around.

Some witnesses, such as opposing parties, will never cooperate with the examiner.[20] These witnesses usually have a stake in the outcome of the case and consider you the enemy. With these witnesses, it does not matter whether you start the deposition with information-gathering questions or with leading questions that seek party statements. A common approach with this type of witness is for you to start with information-gathering questions to open up a new topic and then move to seeking party statements based on the answers given to the information-gathering questions. When you have exhausted a topic, you will then move to a new topic and repeat the process.

8.4.7   Conclusion

Many times you will be unsuccessful in obtaining a sought-after party statement despite doing everything possible to get the witness to give the desired answers. There are many reasons why a witness will not give the wanted answers, but one common reason is that giving the party statement would require the witness to be untruthful. Another is that the witness is unwilling to concede the truth despite your best efforts to box the witness in. Nevertheless, failing to get a witness to give a desired party statement may still provide you with useful information. You now know that a case theory based on the party statement, at least based on this witness's answers, is not viable. If you were going to use that party statement as the basis for a summary judgment motion or to plan cross-examination at trial, you know now that the deposition is complete that you'll have to look elsewhere for support. Although you were not successful in getting the party statement, you are now in a better position to select the theory you will use at trial and plan the strategy you will follow in the case.

---

20. Curiously, presidents of companies, chairs of corporate boards, and other "most senior" executives seem to recognize that the success of their lawsuit does not depend on their shaping their testimony to conceal the truth or on arguing with deposing counsel. Lesser executives, like vice-presidents or "assistants-to," are much more defensive and much less willing to concede even the most obvious truths, while they are trying to impress their bosses with their loyalty to the client. Thus, leading questions at deposition to seek party statements may be a very efficient way to proceed with senior executives and less effective with underlings who are trying to impress their bosses with their loyalty to the client.

CHAPTER NINE

USING DOCUMENTS

The historian, essentially, wants more documents than he can really use . . . .

—Henry James

In a complex commercial case where depositions alone can consume far more resources than the entire remainder of preparation and trial, attorneys taking depositions are commonly controlled and consumed by the documents produced in discovery and otherwise—they have an apparent need to get through, handle, and discuss each and every document, even though the witness's deposition testimony might replace dozens or hundreds of them. Documents should not control depositions; use documents to refresh, to direct, to encourage, but always prefer the spontaneous testimony of the witness. Once you have enough information about a document to lay the necessary foundation for its use in motions practice or at trial, focus the questioning on what is in the witness's mind, not what is in the document.

9.1   Uses for Documents in Depositions

Documents are used in depositions in several ways. Part of the careful planning process for the deposition is deciding in advance exactly what the purposes are for using any particular document you will encounter in the deposition and how best to use the document to achieve those purposes. Some of the more important uses of documents are:

9.1.1   Generating Questions for the Deposition

One of the more important uses of documents is to develop questions you will ask at the deposition. Carefully reviewing the document line-by-line before the deposition will suggest the questions you will need to ask the witness. For example, in a design defect case, a simple e-mail message from the president of the company producing the product to the company's safety officer announcing a meeting about the design of the product and requesting the safety officer to attend can generate a number of questions for the deposition.

- Was the meeting held?

- Where was the meeting held?

- How long did the meeting last?

- What was the purpose of the meeting?

- Why was the meeting held?

- Who decided to hold the meeting?

- Who attended the meeting?

- Why was each person invited to attend the meeting?

- What was discussed at the meeting?

- Were any notes made at or following the meeting?

- Were there any later discussions concerning the meeting?

- Are there any documents that refer to the meeting?

- What actions were taken as a result of the meeting?

- Why were those actions taken?

- Tell me why the safety office was invited?

- What did she contribute to the discussions?

- What other meetings were there about the safety of this product?

As you can see, documents are a fertile source of topics for you to explore and questions for you to ask at the deposition.

9.1.2   *Discovering Other Facts, Witnesses, and Documents*

Examining a deposition witness about a document in the case will often lead to the discovery of additional facts, witnesses and documents, thereby opening the way to further discovery. For example, examining the witness about the e-mail announcing the meeting about the product can lead to finding out whether there was any reply to the e-mail, the names of everyone who attended the meeting, and what was said in the meeting.

9.1.3   *Refreshing the Witness's Memory*

Just as at trial, documents can be used to refresh a witness's memory at a deposition. Of course, at trial the goal in refreshing recollection with a document is usually to bring a particular fact to the witness's mind, while in deposition, the goal is more often to remind the witness of the entire bundle of facts and sensations that relate to a meeting, decision, or event.

9.1.4   Authenticating Documents

Sometimes the whole purpose of a deposition is to have the witness authenticate documents. For example, the person in charge of managing records at the local hospital can be deposed solely to authenticate a party's medical records. Far more frequently, documents are authenticated as part of a broader examination of the witness about the issues in a case. One technique to remember is to get the witness to authenticate a nonthreatening—but representative—document. For example, use a document that perhaps the witness even supports to gain a party statement that a signature is genuine, or that a logo or trademark belongs to the company, or that it was written by someone speaking for the company at that time. Doing so will probably be enough to authenticate all other documents with the same logo, or with the same signature, or with the same author (if written at or near the same time). The federal rules regarding authentication and self-authentication (Federal Rules of Evidence 901 and 902) provide many examples and ideas for questioning at deposition to authenticate documents. Of course, when the document can self-authenticate, there may not be much need to ask many questions at deposition or trial.

9.1.5   Impeaching the Witness

When a deposition witness testifies to facts that are inconsistent with what the witness has said in a document, you could impeach the witness with the document right then (as a prior inconsistent statement). A different tactic would be to lock the witness into the answers at the deposition and save any impeachment for trial, where it will have a more powerful impact on the fact finder. However, since most cases are now resolved prior to trial, you might choose to impeach at the deposition; this way, the impeachment can influence either the settlement negotiations or the judge's response to the deponent's deposition testimony when it is used to support a summary judgment motion.

9.1.6   Testing the Witness's Candor

Impeaching with a document at deposition has other consequences besides influencing settlement negotiations or motions practice. It also lets the witness know that you have a firm grasp on the facts in the case and that there are consequences to lying. Particularly when done early in the deposition, impeaching the witness may cause her to become more truthful—if for no other reason than to avoid the embarrassment of being impeached again. And if the impeachment stings enough, she might even go along with an answer unfavorable to her party because it was suggested by the "all-knowing" taking attorney—you.

9.1.7   *Forcing Party Statements*

Documents can help you extract a party statement from a witness. The printed word has a force that evanescent oral information may not. A witness who will eagerly disagree with the testimony of another witness is usually much more hesitant to contradict facts contained in, for example, a letter written by that other witness. You can take advantage of this dynamic when seeking a party statement by first showing the witness a document that contains the answer you want the witness to adopt.

9.1.8   *Exploring Claims of Privilege for Documents*

Most lawyers will prefer, early on in the litigation, to obtain copies of documents in their opponent's possession. Thus, attorneys will routinely send requests for production of documents and document subpoenas in advance of any depositions in the case. A number of the documents requested will usually be claimed as privileged. However, not all claims of privilege are legitimate. Even scrupulously honest and ethical attorneys will and should be aggressive in claiming privilege, since a failure to do so acts as a waiver of the privilege, which is usually irrevocable. Therefore, prudent lawyers will claim privilege if there is any reasonable basis for believing that a privilege applies.

The Federal Rules of Civil Procedure and the rules of most state courts require that a privilege log be provided when documents or other materials are claimed as privileged. However, Federal Rule of Civil Procedure 26(b)(5) discusses only the process for creating and providing the privilege list (and for "clawing-back" inadvertently disclosed materials claimed as privileged), and it does not discuss how privileges should be challenged or defended. Federal Rule of Evidence 501 states that where state law provides the rule of decision in a civil case, the state law will also provide the rules of privilege. However, challenge and defense of claims of privilege are also not discussed in Rule 501 or 502. This might lead an inexperienced practitioner to misunderstand her opportunities to investigate the application of privileges. What she should understand is that depositions provide the best opportunity to explore the validity of the claim.

Therefore, when the opposing attorney at a deposition objects on the ground of privilege, ask: "Which privilege are you claiming?" Then go on to ask about when the attorney-client relationship was established; what the goal of the representation was; whether the conversations or materials took place or were created as part of that relationship; whether other people were present at the time of the conversation or ever read the documents; and so on. By obtaining answers to these questions at the deposition, you will be in a good position to argue before the court that the privilege was waived or never attached or that the materials being sought were not within any privilege. As another, simple example, if a claim is made that materials are protected by the deliberative privilege (staff communications to a governmental decision maker are protected to promote free exchange, so that the decision maker can be well informed), the attorney taking the deposition should find out whether the information was provided to the decision maker before or after the actual decision was made. If the communication (document or conversation) was after the decision, the privilege does not apply because there is no public policy reason to protect post-decision communications.

9.2   Using the Documents to Prepare

9.2.1   *Gathering All Appropriate Documents*

The first step in preparing to use documents in a deposition is to gather all of the documents that might have relevance to the examination. In smaller cases, someone—usually a paralegal or the attorney assigned to the case—conducts a "search and arrange" mission, in which all documents having any relationship to the case or the witness are pulled together and arranged in some way—often chronological or chronological within subject-matter category—that may aid in discovery questioning. Because the case is small, with few documents, the process is quite straightforward.

In the larger, well-financed corporate case, it is routine for one of the assigned paralegals to receive a notice of deposition and immediately begin to gather all the "appropriate" documents. "Appropriate" is used with some caution here because what the paralegal actually does is gather the documents called for on some generic list. Typically, that list will direct the collection of documents that the deponent wrote, received as the addressee or "copyee," or in which the deponent is mentioned. The paralegal consults the computerized database, calls up a list of those documents, and has the imaging system automatically print them out or has a file clerk pull them from hard copy files and manually make additional copies. It may be necessary to conduct supplemental searches since the witness's name will not appear on some relevant documents. For example, the blueprints or plan drawings in a construction case will not have the name or initials of the "clerk of the works" or the subcontractors, but they are certainly important at their depositions.

9.2.2 *Arrange the Documents Either Chronologically or Topically (or Both)*

Whether defending or taking the deposition, many attorneys arrange the documents they think will be used during the deposition in chronological order. It is very useful to maintain a master documents file in which the originals of all documents are maintained in chronological order. Alternatively, the documents in the master file can be maintained by Bates numbers, with a concordance list relating dates to Bates numbers. Having a master file permits easy access to the original of any document when the need arises.

Arranging the documents in chronological order for the deposition can be useful, but we believe it is usually better in a case with large number of documents to first arrange them topically, and then order them chronologically within each topic. Obviously, this reveals our bias toward questioning by topic rather than starting the deposition with questions about Day 1 and proceeding through to Day 143. Regardless, this system lends itself better to supporting questioning to exhaust the witness's knowledge in each area. This system also helps identify what the witness knows and when she knew it. (In reality, a topical organization will still result in many documents being grouped chronologically within a topic.)

Once you have all the documents pulled, you will need to:

1. Review the documents the witness has written or received within the relevant period of time to get some understanding of where the witness fits into the case. These documents show involvement that the witness may otherwise try to deny.

2. Next, consider the issues in the case that the witness's activities could have logically affected. In other words, if the witness was involved in sales during the relevant five-year period and the issues involve mislabeling and adulteration, it would be logical to ask this particular witness about complaints from customers, contacts with irate competitors, differences in price levels, and sales volumes. These topics come to mind because they involve the witness's position and the issues in the case and not because they are specifically mentioned in documents.

3. After giving thought to issues about which this witness may have knowledge, search the "unselected" documents for memoranda, letters, and the like that deal with these topics, regardless of whether the witness's name is mentioned.

4. Finally, within each topic, examine the selected documents chronologically, this time paying attention to "what happened first, and what happened next?" In other words, look for temporal relationships between statements in documents. If one document mentions "customer acceptance problems in Texas," and a document a few days later mentions the need for a trip to Texas without specifying the purpose, plan to use both documents with the witness to find out if the trip was to attempt to solve the problems or to find the source of those problems. If the witness says that the first document had nothing to do with her responsibilities, the second document putting her in Texas may help prod her memory or honesty.

    By placing the documents for each topic in a tabbed notebook or a labeled manila folder (or, just as likely in modern practice, in a computer file containing the documents in electronic format), you have them available whenever the topic arises.

Of course, when you are defending the deposition, the fact that you reviewed the documents with your witness during the preparation session before the deposition does not mean you can interrupt opposing counsel's questioning and review them again with the witness. Your hope instead is that by reviewing them in context before the deposition, the witness will be able to provide coherent answers when asked about whether and how the documents relate to one another. Because opposing counsel is likely to be prepared to question in that way, it makes sense for you and your witness to practice responses in that same way.

One final note on using documents to prepare the witness for the deposition—thorough preparation does not mean that the witness needs to be shown, and needs to discuss, every one of the several hundred documents found in the preparatory stages. The witness will not remember all of those documents or the discussion about them; indeed, that time is not only wasted—it may also serve only to make the witness more anxious and less effective. If, as we teach elsewhere, there are only fourteen documents that will have a serious impact on the case, no witness should be asked to worry about more than twenty-eight in the preparation stages. Dragging the witness through fifty-six or 112 will result in more being forgotten, not more being remembered. Focus on themes, explanations, and explanatory stories, not the contents, wording, and distribution of every one of hundreds of documents. For a witness, being prepared means understanding her role, articulating the party's positions, and appreciating the issues so she can anticipate important questions and answer them effectively. Preparation does not mean trying to recall each document verbatim from memory.

9.2.3 *Document Privilege Logs*

When you are responding to a request for document production, identify those documents that may be subject to a privilege and catalog them in a privilege log. Later, once you have gathered all the documents that relate to the witness to be deposed and have arranged them by whatever system you choose to use, you then need to go back to that privilege log and determine whether any of the pulled documents should be isolated from the rest because you may want to argue that they are covered by a privilege, usually the attorney-client privilege or work-product confidentiality. These privileged documents should not be physically segregated, but, since they are likely to be the subject of a motion for an order compelling production from the other side, it is necessary to prepare what is known as a "privilege log," listing and describing the documents.[1]

These steps are usually carried out in smaller cases by the attorney assigned to the case or by the assigned paralegal, with the attorney reviewing the log. In larger, more document intensive cases, a junior attorney will usually initially review the documents to determine which ones have already been turned over in response to a document request, and, with respect to those that have not been turned over, whether any of them contains privileged material that should not be produced to the other side or used in preparing a witness who is to be deposed by the other side.

The privilege log contains 1) the Bates number, if one was assigned to the document; 2) the date of the communication claimed to be privileged; 2) the nature of the communication (e.g., a memorandum); 3) the type of communication, e.g., letter, e-mail; 4) the author of the communication, with some indication of the author's position, e.g., "attorney for plaintiff"; 5) the recipient of the communication, e.g., president of plaintiff; 6) whether there are any copies of the document and recipients of the copies; and 7) the purpose of the communication, e.g., seeking legal advice; 8) the privilege claimed, e.g., attorney-client privilege. Some lawyers also include in the privilege log the method of communication, e.g., interoffice mail. An example of a privilege log may be found in Appendix B. If the document contains some other material for which a different protection is claimed, such as Rule 26(b)(3) work-product trial-preparation material, a similar log will be created showing the appropriateness of the claim of work-product protection. And finally, if the document contains some other material that ought to be protected from unnecessary disclosure, such as trade secrets, prepare a document claiming such protection and provide a draft Rule 26(c) protective order to the judge.

It is likely that many more privileged documents will be created after the litigation begins (for example, letters, and e-mails to and from the parties

---

1. *See* FED. R. CIV. P. 26(b)(5).

and their attorneys). Under a strict interpretation of the rules, these new documents could be considered to be covered by a document request and therefore should be listed on a privilege log. While we doubt that any court would sanction a party for failing to list such documents, it is prudent practice for the parties to stipulate that documents and files created after the commencement of litigation need not be listed and to note this stipulation on the privilege log.

An additional concern is whether exposing privileged material to a witness may constitute a waiver of the claimed privilege. If the witness is not part of the client group (those who are party to the privilege), then the risk is real, and you should consider whether the witness actually needs to see the documents within the claimed privilege. If you decide that a witness outside the client group needs to see the privileged document, you probably need to bite the bullet, send the document to the other side before the deposition, and waive the privilege. The smaller the distribution of the material claimed to be privileged, the more likely the privilege will be held to be valid by the court. If the witness does not see the document in preparation, and if it is withheld from the other party as privileged, then there is little likelihood that the witness will be questioned on it.

9.2.4   Prepare the Documents for Use at the Deposition

Many attorneys preparing to *take* a deposition write questions on the face of their working copies of the documents, which seems efficient. Once again, however, remember that confirming the information already learned from the documents is only one objective; obtaining new information is usually a more important goal. A topic outline (as discussed in chapter five), independent of the documents, that helps direct the examination is much more useful, and it, in turn, should refer to the collected documents as one part of the deposition plan. Following this method of preparation, the documents support the deposition, but do not control it.

9.2.5   Review the Documents, Not Summaries

Particularly in larger cases, it is uncommon for junior attorneys or paralegals to prepare summaries of documents for the depositions. While useful as the starting point for preparing for the deposition, we advise against using summaries as the sole basis for questioning. A summary can never capture all of the nuances of the document itself. An effective examination on a document requires nothing less than complete mastery of the documents, and this in turn requires that the lawyer who will be conducting the deposition carefully examine the actual documents, including marginal notes.

9.3 Compelling Production of Documents to Be Used at Depositions

Normally, document requests pursuant to Rule 34 or subpoenas pursuant to Rule 45 precede the deposition of key witnesses. Actually getting those documents can be handled in two ways. First, a subpoena or request to produce can direct the production of the documents weeks or more before a deposition, so you have an opportunity to analyze the documents and determine appropriate lines of questioning. Second, if there are only a few documents involved, the deposition and the document production can be scheduled for the same time (or thirty minutes or so apart if the document custodian and the substantive deponent are not the same person).[2]

You can easily determine whether a subpoena or request for production has been complied with if the subpoena or request calls for specific documents: were all of the requested documents turned over earlier or at the deposition? But where the subpoena or request is open-ended, e.g., "all documents relating to . . . . ," you would be wise to examine the witness about what efforts were made to locate and produce all the required documents. Let's take a typical examination, where the nonparty witness received a document subpoena and is not represented by counsel:

> Q: Mr. Vilas, I am handling you what has been marked as Exhibit 1, the subpoena that was served on you. Do you recognize it?
>
> A: It looks like the subpoena that was given to me.
>
> Q: Have you read the subpoena?
>
> A: I did.
>
> Q: Do you understand what the subpoena requires you to do?
>
> A: I think so.
>
> Q: Am I correct that you have brought documents with you in response to this subpoena?
>
> A: Yes. Do you want them now?
>
> Q: Thank you.

---

2. Fed. R. Civ. P. 30(b)(2) states that a notice of deposition directed to a party witness can be accompanied by a request to produce made pursuant to Rule 34. Nonparties can be made to produce documents at a deposition by a subpoena duces tecum issued pursuant to Rules 30(b)(2) and 45(a). Of course, parties can also be required to produce documents prior to the deposition by a request to produce under Rule 34. *See* section 1.11 for further discussion of this issue.

Q: Did anyone help you with the search?

A: No, I did it by myself.

Q: Let me ask you whether have collected and provided all of the documents that were called for by the subpoena?

A: I did my best.

Q: Did anyone help you in any way in complying with the subpoena?

A: I talked with my attorney about it, but that's it.

Q: Have you withheld any documents for any reason?

A: No.

Q: Do you know of any documents that were covered by the subpoena, but that you couldn't find?

A: No.

Q: When did you undertake the search?

A: Just last week.

Q: How long did the search take?

A: Only about an hour.

Q: Tell me everything you did to collect the documents called for by the subpoena?

A: Well . . . .

After the witness has fully described the search made, be sure to suggest other possible locations of covered documents:

- e-mail archives;

- computers files, including those on personal computers and servers, in back-up files, and in archives;

- documents in the possession of other individuals and entities;

- notes and diaries;

- microfilms, PowerPoint displays, and spreadsheets and other electronic files; and

- scanned documents.

It is also worth exploring whether any documents were destroyed and, if so, whether anyone would have copies of the destroyed documents. In the context of this last question, ask about document retention and destruction policies.

If the witness is represented by counsel, it is usually not worthwhile asking questions about withheld documents or whether all of the documents have been turned over in response to the subpoena or request for production. You can ask whether a privilege log has been provided, and if has been, then ask about entries on that log. Decisions on privilege are usually made by the opposing counsel, and the witness will be largely unaware of what has been withheld and what has been turned over. But it is still worth exploring how thorough a search was conducted and whether the witness has any facts relating to the existence of the claimed privilege.

If an open-ended request for production or subpoena is directed to an entity—e.g., an organization—you may need to depose the custodian of documents (or a Rule 30(b)(6) designee) on the scope of the search made. For example:

> Q: Ms. Arrowsmith, as secretary of the corporation, what responsibilities do you have for record keeping?
>
> A: I supervise all of the record-keeping procedures in the company, and all of the people involved in creating important records report to me.
>
> Q: What do you mean by important records?
>
> A: Well, the records that the company needs to operate, like sales orders, invoices in and out, bills of lading, inventory records, disbursements, receipts, everything that goes into compiling balance sheets, and other records.
>
> Q: You are talking primarily about financial records. What are the procedures for collecting and maintaining nonfinancial records, like correspondence and memoranda?
>
> A: Well, those are not quite so rigorous. We do have a document retention policy that requires each office to keep files of all correspondence and memoranda for one year, at least; then we move the files to an inactive file area, unless there has been activity within the past year. After three years in the inactive file storage, those types of documents are destroyed. Our financial records, of course, we keep much longer; some of them we keep forever.
>
> Q: What other methods are used for the retention of documents at your company?

A: None that I'm aware of.

Q: Is there someone other than you in the company who would have such information?

A: No.

And you would go through this process for electronic records as well. You can depose the person responsible for designing and maintaining the electronic document systems for the organization (generally the information and technology (IT) officer) to find out the nature of the system or systems used to maintain electronic documents (personal computers, cell phones, PDA's, and so forth), the type of electronic documents that are maintained, the method of electronic document creation, and the retention system that can track the electronic document from accessible data retention systems (e.g., hard drives) to back-up systems, archives, and final repositories. If a smaller organization does not have a technology officer, you could send a Rule 30(b)(6) notice or a subpoena that puts the burden of collecting this information on the organization as it prepares its designees.

You can use this information to fashion an electronic discovery request or to insure that the proper searches have been made to obtain relevant electronic document discovery. (This "document information" request, made through Rule 30(b)(6) deposition, would specify that you want information about the creation, litigation collection, and custody of documents. Under that approach, the opposing party or a nonparty is obligated to collect the desired information from whatever sources are reasonably available and present it through designees at the deposition.) A party's documents identified at a Rule 30(b)(6) deposition themselves should probably have been returned in response to the Rule 26(a) initial production; in response to the original, pre-deposition request for the production of documents; or in response to a second request for production, post-deposition.

9.4 Marking and Handling Documents at the Deposition

Handling exhibits at a deposition is governed by a series of rote steps that you can quickly master, but which ought to be followed faithfully if you are to avoid later problems when trying to lay foundation using the deposition at trial or in support of or opposition to a motion. The steps are straightforward and easy to follow:

9.4.1 Prepare Sufficient Copies of the Exhibits for Use at the Deposition

Do not bring just one copy of an exhibit to the deposition. Instead, prepare and bring at least enough copies to provide

- One for the witness;

- One for each party's attorney, including the attorney for the witness;

- One for the court reporter;

- A working copy for yourself, which can be marked up with notes about what questions to ask concerning the exhibit.

Some attorneys resist providing a copy to opposing counsel, thinking there is no reason to make the deposition easier for her. But, in fact, handing that copy over makes the deposition easier for the deposing attorney, too. Otherwise a time-consuming ritual occurs at the deposition when an exhibit is given the witness and opposing counsel proceeds to read the exhibit through from first word to last and then hands it to the witness with the instruction to do the same. This ritual not only slows the deposition, but also breaks the flow of questioning, often resulting in less forthcoming answers. You can shorten this inefficient ritual (but not eliminate it) if you provide copies of an exhibit to both opposing counsel and the witness so that they can simultaneously read the exhibit. ("Not eliminate" because the deponent has the right to read documents she is being questioned about, and she will have been reminded to do just that the first time that she is handed a document.)

9.4.2   Extreme Caution Teaches: "Bring the Original of Any Exhibit to the Deposition, But Use Copies to Examine the Witness"

Rule 30(f)(2)(A)(i) provides that documents and other tangible things produced for inspection during a deposition must, on a party's request, be attached by the court reporter to the deposition transcript, but that the party producing them may provide copies to be substituted for the originals. The copies may then be used in the same manner as the originals. As a practical matter, copies are almost always used instead of originals. Nonetheless, prudence dictates bringing the originals to the deposition along with the copies so that if a question arises about the accuracy of the copy, opposing counsel can compare the original with the copy. The opposing party may still, pursuant to Rule 30(f)(2)(B), move the court to require the original to be attached to the deposition pending final disposition of the case, but this is rarely done in practice. (In fact, the concept of "duplicate originals," which makes photographic, xerographic, and computer-generated copies, and other similar copies, equivalent for evidentiary purposes to the originals, renders the concept of "an original" rather antiquated, and few disputes on such points survive into modern practice.)

One of the reasons copies are used at the deposition instead of originals is that a witness is often asked to mark on the exhibit—for instance, to circle where in a contract the delivery date is specified or the exact location on a diagram of a defective part. If it later becomes necessary to introduce the original at trial,[3] you will need to explain the markings put on the exhibit at the deposition. You can avoid these inconveniences by using a copy of the exhibit at the deposition.

9.4.3   Premark the Exhibits or Ask the Court Reporter to Mark the Exhibit

The first step in using an exhibit at a deposition is to have the exhibit marked. Just like at trial, documents used at the deposition need unique names—exhibit numbers—so documents can be specifically identified. Not only do the people at the deposition need to know what piece of paper is being referred to at any particular time, but people using the deposition later (at a summary judgment motion, at another deposition, or at trial) also need to know whether the piece of paper they are looking at is the same piece of paper the deposition witness was testifying about.

Where an exhibit consists of several pages, it is wise to assign an exhibit number to each one of the pages. This often consists of assigning a number to the first page of the exhibit and then using a letter suffix for each individual page. As an example, the first page of a multipage contract would be marked as Exhibit 4-A, the second page as 4-B or 4B, and so on until each page in the contract has its own unique identifying mark. Alternatively, if the document pages have already been Bates stamped, the Bates number can be used.[4] In modern practice, Bates numbers are often mentioned at deposition when the document is first introduced to the questioning and a new exhibit number is provided. From there on, usually only the exhibit number is used. (Prepare a concordance list between Bates numbers and the exhibit numbers, to be used when the provenance of a document is desired.)

Exhibits can be premarked before the deposition begins or marked at the deposition. If you are marking the exhibits at the deposition, simply ask the court reporter to mark the exhibit when the exhibit is first used by handing the exhibit to the court reporter and making the request: "Please mark this as Exhibit Number 3." The court reporter will then affix an exhibit sticker to the exhibit (often one color for plaintiff's exhibits and another color for

---

3. *See* FED. R. EVID. 1001 *et seq.*, the "Best Evidence Rule."

4. These are called "Bates numbers" because Bates is the manufacturer of a popular number stamping machine and a piece of software that is often used in document control systems to affix sequential numbers, identical numbers, or "duplicate sequential" numbers, that is, two copies of a document in a row with the same number, and then the next two with the next sequential number. Computer imaging systems can number documents automatically (with the Bates or other software), and then print the documents with or without the assigned number. Even when done by computer, these are often called Bates numbers by force of habit, which habit is then passed to each new generation of attorneys.

defendant's) and write in the number and the date. Some court reporters use a stamp and then fill in the exhibit number and date. If you are using premarked exhibits, mark them before you appear at the deposition or ask the court reporter do the marking at some point before the witness is sworn.

There are two advantages to premarking deposition exhibits. First, premarking saves time during the deposition that would otherwise be consumed by the court reporter marking the exhibits. Where time is at a premium and many exhibits are being used, the time saved by premarking can be significant. Second, as discussed below, premarking permits the numbering system to coordinate.

9.4.4   *Have a System for Marking Exhibits*

There is no particular magic to how exhibits are premarked unless there is a court rule or order dictating how it should be done. In many jurisdictions, court reporters when marking exhibits at trial or in the deposition customarily use exhibit stickers with different colors for plaintiff and defendant. If this is the practice in your jurisdiction, it is probably wise to conform to that custom so that premarked exhibits will resemble other exhibits that are marked for the first time at the deposition or at trial. But there is usually nothing remiss in merely writing the exhibit number on the exhibit without using an exhibit sticker.

The great majority of courts today require, by pretrial order or otherwise, that documents for trial be premarked. Doing so greatly enhances the efficiency of using exhibits at trials and in motion practice. The same exhibit number for each exhibit might then be maintained throughout the litigation—Exhibit 17 will be the same for every witness and in every deposition. As a result, gathering information for any use—a motion in limine, summary judgment motion, trial, and so forth—is easier and substantially more efficient. This is especially so when deposition testimony is transcribed in a more easily accessible digital format. For example, in a case where there is a question about whether a particular document should be admitted over a hearsay objection, the lawyers need only search the deposition transcripts by exhibit number and all testimony necessary for making or opposing the motion is readily available.

Of course, to make this system work, you will need to reach an agreement with opposing counsel on how premarking will proceed; you could be responsible for assigning numbers to your documents, and she would be responsible for hers. This is important because many documents will be the subject of inquiry by both parties with the same or different witnesses. One approach, mentioned in another context earlier, is to put all of the documents in piles according to topic as described above and then in chronological order within each topic. In most "big document" cases, the bulk of documentary discovery occurs before substantive depositions begin. If for some reason that is not the case, chronological numbering of the exhibits should be postponed until after all or most documents have been exchanged.

Of course, this system will leave blanks in the sequence at trial where documents are not offered, but that is not a problem except to the most compulsive record keepers or judges. Nevertheless, some court rules and judges require exhibits used at trial to be numbered sequentially in the order in which they are offered. The reason for this preference is not clear. No instruction reminds the jury that "the numerical order of the documents provides a means of recalling the order of events at trial," nor would that be at all useful for any purpose. Furthermore, the order of events in the "historical" scene that the trial is examining—the actions between the parties that gave rise to the dispute—is the important order. Therefore, documents that are arranged by topics and numbered consecutively give some meaning to the numbering system, but not enough to worry about. Of course, no matter what their number, documents will still be used at trial and elsewhere in the order that suits the story being told by the witnesses, whose appearance one at a time normally prevents a straight chronological retelling of the events underlying the dispute.

Even if the court requires the exhibit numbers to follow the order of their use at trial, ordering and numbering documents chronologically for the depositions is still useful because it provides a reference among the documents and gives them their unique names.

As a final thought, using numbers for exhibits usually works better than letters. Some courts require that one side use numbers and the other side use letters, but if the choice is up to you, choose numbers. A sequence of numbers can extend infinitely, but after 26 letters the sequence must start over, usually with a doubling of the letters, e.g., AA, BB, CC or AA, AB, AC, and so forth. If a case involves hundreds, or even thousands of documents, a system using letters becomes cumbersome and inconvenient.

9.4.5   If Necessary, Create a Concordance of Exhibit Numbers

Some attorneys, for what we consider insufficient reasons, like to number the documents anew for each deposition: Jonas Deposition Exhibit 1, Jonas Deposition Exhibit 2, Sugis Deposition Exhibit 1, and so forth. However, this approach can cause some confusion unless care is taken. Often, a document is used at several depositions. Thus, Jonas Deposition Exhibit 39 may also be Sugis Deposition Exhibit 3. The attorneys on both sides must keep a meticulous "table of concordance," which, before computers, often provided a paralegal or secretary with many wearisome hours of work to produce a document that would appear as follows:

TABLE OF CONCORDANCE
SUGIS-JONAS DEPOSITION EXHIBITS

Sugis 1	=	Jonas 17
Sugis 2	=	Jonas 4
Sugis 3	=	Jonas 39
Sugis 4	=	Jonas 1

* * * * *

SUGIS-JONAS DEPOSITION EXHIBITS

Jonas 1	=	Sugis 4
Jonas 2	=	Sugis 9
Jonas 3	=	Sugis 42
Jonas 4	=	Sugis 2

If there are only two deponents, only two lists have to be prepared, with two columns. With the big document case, and the client who can support such extensive pretrial preparation, more record keeping is necessary. If there are three deponents, three lists are necessary with three columns, and so forth. With the current easy access to computers, a database program can take care of this record keeping rather easily, although the burden of putting the information into the database still exists. (Again, all of this work is avoided if one set of numbers is used throughout the plaintiff's or the defendant's depositions.)

After each deposition, someone must track what exhibits were used and what numbers they were given. If an imaging system is used for the documents, and all the transcripts are put on the system, then when the exhibit number is entered in the system as associated with a particular document, the concordances can be produced automatically. If a manual hard-copy system for the documents is used, the pages of the deposition transcripts at which documents are used are often included in the document control database or in a special exhibit control database, or at least in a word identification table at the back of the deposition. Then, once trial numbers have been assigned and that information is in the imaging system or the database utilized, the concordance has another column that shows the trial numbers. The final pretrial product, after all depositions are complete and all trial numbers have been assigned, looks like this:

FINAL CONCORDANCE

Exhibit Number	Sugis No./Used Tr.	Jonas No./Used Tr.
DX-1	73 / 153–157	14 / 43–44
DX-2	74 / 168, 179	3 / 10
DX-3	5 / 23	72 / 198–199
DX-4	15 / 68	31 / 97, 201
DX-5	46 / 109	62 153

If you want to relate to a witness's deposition testimony when you use it at trial, you will need to take an additional foundational step to relate the deposition document to the trial document:

Q: Ms. Vardas, you then wrote a letter to the president of the Shadis Company, didn't you?

A: I'm not sure what you are referring to. I don't think I ever wrote to him.

Q: In the same deposition we have talked about, Ms. Vardas, I asked you this question, didn't I? Page 73, counsel: "Isn't Vardas Deposition Exhibit 15 a letter from you to the president of the Shadis Company?" And you answered, "Yes, I wrote that to him." Wasn't that your answer?

A: Yes, I said that.

Q: Ms. Vardas, let me show you what has been marked as Defendant's Exhibit 142. That's the Deposition Exhibit 15 we've been talking about, isn't it?

A: Yes, it looks like the same letter.

Obviously, it makes a much cleaner trial examination if only one set of numbers is involved—yet another reason to assign trial numbers before the depositions of significant witnesses.[5]

---

5. Once trial begins, you can supplement the computerized concordance to track rulings on admissibility of exhibits and transcript pages where witnesses testify about exhibits. In the 100-document cases, this may sound trivial. In the 30,000-document cases, it is not.

9.4.6   *Providing Exhibits in Advance to the Witness*

The Advisory Committee Notes to Rule 30 suggest that the impact of the seven-hour time limit on depositions can be lessened by the taking attorney sending copies of exhibits to be used to the witness before the deposition. The idea is that the witness can then review the documents before the deposition and thereby avoid the time consumed by the witness reading each document during the deposition.

There are several problems with providing the witness in advance with copies of the exhibits. First, any element of spontaneity by the witness is lost. Admittedly, a well-prepared witness is unlikely to be surprised by any document asked about during the deposition. But not all witnesses are well-prepared, and a certain amount of uncertainty, even with those witnesses who are well prepared, will give you a psychological edge. Second, providing the documents in advance provides a roadmap to the other side about your case theory and strategy. A legitimate privilege objection can be made if the taking lawyer asks about what documents the witness's attorney showed the witness as preparation for the deposition.[6] This suggests that it is unwise to show the witness in advance of the deposition the documents the taking attorney will be asking about. However, it may be appropriate in a particular case for you, as questioning counsel, to expedite the deposition by providing the witness in advance with copies of any documents that you will be asking about at the deposition

9.4.7   *Identify the Exhibit for the Record and Hand the Exhibit to Opposing Counsel and the Witness*

If the court reporter is marking exhibits during the deposition, the reporter should hand the exhibit to the witness once the exhibit is marked. As the reporter is doing so, the questioning attorney should say: "Mr. Smith, would you please hand the marked Exhibit 13 to the witness" or "Mr. Witness, the reporter has just handed you a document that has been marked Exhibit 13." Once the exhibit is handed to the witness, the next step is for the questioning attorney to hand a copy of the exhibit to opposing counsel, saying, "Mr. Mouth, here is a copy of Exhibit 13 for you." If other parties are represented at the deposition, copies should also be given to them at this point.

While handing the exhibit to opposing counsel and the witness, you should give a short, non-argumentative description of the exhibit. If there is ever any confusion at some later point about what exhibit number was assigned to a particular exhibit—when the same exhibit number is inadvertently assigned to two separate exhibits, for example—the description can clear up the confusion. This description can merely be something like: "The

---

6. *See* section 9.6.

exhibit that you have been handed, Exhibit 4, appears to be a letter from Mr. Vardas to Ms. Jones at the Shadis Company, dated January 13, 2010. Do you agree? Let me know when you have finished looking at Exhibit 13."

Patience is required at this point as opposing counsel and the witness will usually take their time carefully reading the exhibit from beginning to end. Once the witness and counsel have looked up from reading the exhibit, you can begin your questioning.

9.4.8   Lay Any Necessary Foundation for the Exhibit

As discussed before, depositions are frequently used to support or oppose motions for summary judgment or for preliminary injunctions; they are also used at trial as a substitute for the testimony of an unavailable witness. But the deposition testimony may be inadmissible for any of these purposes if you failed to lay a proper foundation for the proffered testimony and the defending lawyer raised a valid objection at the deposition. The motion or trial may be lost for lack of the necessary proof unless there are alternative methods available for establishing the facts for which the deposition was being offered. Under the Federal Rules of Civil Procedure, a foundation objection is treated as curable and therefore must be made at the deposition or is waived, a topic that is discussed more fully in chapter ten. For our purposes now, it is necessary to emphasize the importance of laying any necessary foundations at the deposition to avoid the later possibility of deposition testimony being excluded because no foundation has been shown.

9.4.9   Ask if Anything Is Missing from the Document

Always check to see if anything is missing from the document that was there when the witness saw the document on previous occasions. These questions are usually asked as part of laying the foundation for the document: "Is the exhibit in the same condition as when you saw it at any time before the deposition? Is there anything missing from the exhibit that was there when you saw it at any time before the deposition?"

9.4.10   Keeping Track of the Exhibits at the Deposition

When paper documents are being used at the deposition, many attorneys will put their pile of documents right up on the conference table, shifting them from the "to be asked about" pile to the "already asked about" pile as the deposition wears on. Beware, however, that this two-pile arrangement has the tendency to allow the documents to control the course and content of the deposition. This also may signal the defending attorney and the witness about how much of the deposition is left, since they can watch the "to be asked about" pile dwindle. One simple solution is to put the "already asked about" documents back under the "to be asked about" pile whenever there is a break and opposing counsel and the witness are out of the room. Another is to keep the documents in a file box below table level, so only you know how many documents are left to ask about. An attorney with a sense of humor, like one of the authors, might add pieces of paper to the bottom of the pile "to be asked about," so that it actually grows during the deposition.

9.4.11 Referring to Exhibit Numbers during the Deposition

Once an exhibit has been given to the witness and identified for the record, include the exhibit number in every, or nearly every, question about the exhibit. You can do this without any particular formality or cumbersome phrasing, beginning with a statement for the deposition transcript that identifies the document:

Q: Ms. Vardas, let me hand you what has now been marked as Vardas Deposition Exhibit 43, which appears to be a letter from you to Ms. Jones at the Shadis Company dated January 13, 2010. Counsel, here's another copy you may use. Would you look at that, please, Ms. Vardas?

A: Yes, this is the letter we were talking about.

Q: And is Exhibit 43 the same letter that you say you wrote after rejecting the Shadis Company offer?

A: No, there's another letter that I was thinking of.

Q: Let me show you another letter. Mr. Emmanuel, would you please mark this document as Vardas Deposition Exhibit 44, which appears to be a letter from Ms. Vardas to Ms. Jones at the Shadis Company dated January 26, 2010? Now, Ms. Vardas, take a look at Exhibit 44. Counsel, here's an extra copy for you. Is this the letter you wrote after receiving the Shadis offer?

A: Yes, that's the one.

Q: Exhibit 44 is dated January 26, 2010, isn't it?

A: Yes.

Q: Now, could you tell us how this letter, Exhibit 44, relates to your rejection of the Shadis offer?

A: Yes, I can explain.

Q: Please do.

Any lawyer who has worked on a summary judgment brief or attempted to use deposition testimony at trial will understand the importance of using the exhibit number in as many questions as possible. It is cumbersome and awkward to cite to a question that reads, "After you received this letter, what was the next thing you did?" and then go back several questions or even pages to find out what letter is being referred to. You can avoid all of this effort by the simple expedient of using the exhibit number in every question inquiring about an exhibit. In short, a clear record makes everyone happier, including judges and senior partners.

Later, perhaps at trial or when the parties are presenting their summary judgment motions, this care in keeping documents straight by using their "proper names" will allow all counsel and the court to know exactly what document the attorney and the witness were talking about.[7]

As previously discussed, if a document has more than one page, it is important that each page have some unique identification. Otherwise, the witness may come back later and claim that she was referring to a different page. Sometimes, to save time, the reporter is asked to mark only the first page of an exhibit. When the taking lawyer wants to examine on a page within the exhibit, the document's internal pagination will then be used to identify the particular page ("the page marked 53 of Exhibit 13"). The record should always show the exhibit number along with the page number to which the question or answer refers.

9.4.12   Referring the Witness to a Portion of the Document

You will often find it necessary to direct a witness to a particular portion of an exhibit as part of questioning the witness about the document. For example, in questioning a witness about a contract, you might ask, "Why did you include in the contract a right of first refusal for the development of variations of the plug?" To insure that the witness is looking at the same portion of the exhibit as you, refer the witness to that portion containing, for example, the right of first refusal. The preferred method is to read into the record that portion of the exhibit to which the witness is being directed:

Q: Ms. Vardas, would you please look at the fifth page of Vardas Deposition Exhibit 57. That's the page that begins with the language "and to tour the plant with Jonas and his employees." Do you have that page in front of you?

A: Yes, I have it.

---

7. The availability of transcripts electronically has created another reason to properly refer to documents by their numbers—when the transcript database is being searched for references to the document, you will pick up more occurrences if the number has been used instead of "this document," "that letter," or "the first memo."

A variation on this approach when referring to one or two sentences in the document is to quote that portion verbatim: "Do you see the sentence in the fourth paragraph of Exhibit 14, the letter from you to Mr. Smith, that reads, and I quote. 'I expect you to respond to this letter immediately'?"

Many lawyers use a less preferred method of asking the witness to read aloud a particular sentence or paragraph in the document. If you ask the witness to read silently the sentence or paragraph, there is no way of knowing if the witness is reading the correct portion of the exhibit. And if the witness reads the sentence or paragraph aloud, they often read the wrong paragraph or sentence.

> Q: Ms. Vardas, please read aloud the fourth paragraph of Exhibit 23, the notes you made of your telephone conversation with Mr. Wycliff.
>
> A: He asked me [*interrupted*]
>
> Q: No, I meant the paragraph below that one.

This happens frequently enough that it makes much more sense to read the portion to which the witness is being directed rather than having the witness read it: "Ms. Vardas, do you see the fourth paragraph in Exhibit 23, which reads . . . ."

9.4.13   Quote Exactly When Referring to a Portion of an Exhibit

If you attempt to summarize a document or a portion of the document, you will frequently draw an objection that you are mischaracterizing the exhibit or, as it is sometimes made, "the document speaks for itself." There is no reason to take the risk that a court will sustain this objection. (There is actually no such evidentiary objection as "the document speaks for itself." Professor and friend Jim McElhaney believes that this spurious objection results from attorney confusion between the rule excluding hearsay and the little-understood "best evidence" rule. Documents may be hearsay, but they can still be quoted and analyzed during discovery, and the "best evidence" rule does not require the best evidence—instead it asks, with respect to relevant documents, "Where is the original?") All that is necessary is to quote the document exactly, or that portion of the document, to which reference is being made.

9.4.14   Do Not Read Long Portions or Entire Documents into the Record

For reasons unknown, some lawyers insist on not only showing an exhibit to the witness, but also reading aloud the entire document, or some portion of it, so it will appear verbatim in the deposition transcript. The only person who benefits from this exercise is the court reporter, who is enriched by transcribing the number of pages required by the recitation. There is no legitimate reason to engage in this time consuming and expensive behavior. If there is any question about what exhibit is being referred to or to the contents of the exhibit, merely ask the court reporter to have it affixed to the deposition transcript, something that can be done as a matter of right under Rule 30(f)(2)(A). These document-reading lawyers may be trying to bind the witness more tightly to the language of the document, as though by hearing it all, they are sponsoring it all.

9.4.15   *Identify for the Record any Markings on Exhibits*

If you ask a witness to mark on an exhibit, make sure the record is clear as to exactly what marking is being made. For example, assume you are examining a witness about where a structural defect occurred in a support beam in a building:

Q: Would you please take this red pen and mark where the beam was cracked?

A: Yes, sure. It was right about there.

Q: Could it have been up here a bit further? [*Indicating.*]

A: It may have. It could have been up to here.

Q: Here? Or are you saying as far as there?

Q: No, here.

A: Thank you.

This is not very helpful because readers cannot follow that discussion, even with the document in from of them. Instead, ask:

Q: You have put your initials near where the beam cracked. Could that break have been further up the beam, nearer to where I am placing this X?

A: Perhaps. It might even have been up to there.

Q: Would you please place a Y where you have just indicated as "up to there"?

A: Yes.

Q: Do you mean it was where you have placed the Y on Exhibit 13, or could it have been as low as this spot, where I am placing a Z?

A: It was not as low as your Z. I think it was where I placed my initials.

All of these decisions on how to handle documents at a deposition are intended to reduce the possibility of confusion in the record. As with so many other areas of depositions, there are virtually no "rules" about how to mark exhibits—common sense is quite enough, once the goal is understood. Over time, however, it is preferable to develop a system for dealing with documents that is replicated, as a matter of habit, in every deposition, no matter the case or the witness. Habitual conduct has the advantage of creating consistently complete and accurate records of the use of exhibits during the deposition and for later use in motion practice, ADR, or at trial.

9.5   Questioning on Documents

9.5.1   *Determine the Purposes of Examining on a Document*

As stated in section 9.1, there are a number of reasons for using a document in a deposition. The first step in deciding whether to use a document is to consider all possible case theories, for both your own and your opponent's case.[8] Fortunately, having done this once, you don't need to do it again, no matter how many documents are involved, unless further discovery reveals theory-changing facts. Then decide whether a particular document contributes in some way to establishing one of your possible case theories or refuting one of your opponent's possible case theories. If it does not help one of you then there is no reason to question on the document. But if it does in some way support or refute theories in the case, you need to decide exactly how the document should be used with this particular witness to advance these objectives. Are you merely seeking to authenticate the document so that it can be later introduced at trial or used to support or respond to a summary judgment motion?[9] Are you using the document to box in the witness in an effort to compel the witness to give a needed party statement?[10] Is the purpose of the document to impel the witness to provide new, as yet unknown information?[11] Whatever the purposes—and there may be multiple purposes—you must know those purposes in advance of the deposition.

The purposes for using the document will, in turn, determine when and how the questioning on the document should occur. If the document is being used to box in the witness in an effort to extract a key party statement, what facts must first be established before showing the witness the docu-

---

8. *See* section 2.3, *et. seq.*

9. *See* chapter sixteen.

10. *See* chapter eight.

11. *See* chapter two.

ment? If the document is being used to direct the witness to provide new information, when in the questioning should this occur? And so on. Equally important is the issue of what questions should be asked to achieve the goal for which the document is being used and what should be the form of those questions. If the goal is simply to authenticate the document, leading questions will usually be the most efficient and expeditious method of asking the necessary question. On the other hand, if the goal is to obtain new information, open-ended questions and the previously described funnel approach usually work best.[12] Whatever the goal, you must give thought to when and how to use the document to achieve the purpose (or multiple purposes) for which the document is being used.

9.5.2   Questioning on the Document

The questions you ask about a particular document will be determined largely by the document itself. How does the document fit into the larger case theories? Given the size of the universe of cases, theories, documents, and witnesses, it is impossible to even begin to suggest a list of appropriate questions. Nonetheless, there are certain recurring situations and categories of questions that will help you prepare the deposition outline.

Using Documents as Part of the Story

As has been mentioned earlier in this chapter, it is common to see a lawyer conducting a deposition by starting out with a stack of documents and proceeding to work through the stack by taking each document, handing it to the witness, and asking a series of questions that runs as follows:

> Q: I am handing you what has been marked as Exhibit 1 and ask if you recognize it?
>
> A: I do.
>
> Q: Is Exhibit 1 a letter that you sent the defendant on June 3, 2010?
>
> A: Yes, it seems to be a copy of that letter.
>
> Q: I am now handing you what has been marked as Exhibit No. 2 and ask if you recognize it?
>
> A: I do.
>
> Q: Is Exhibit 2 the letter you received from the defendant on June 7, 2010, in response to Exhibit No. 1?
>
> A: It is.

---

12. *See* chapter eight.

> Q: I am now handing you what has been marked as Exhibit
> No. 3 and ask if you recognize it?

And so on until the pile has been exhausted.

The taking attorney has succeeded in authenticating all of the documents in the pile and confirming that the taking attorney is correct in her understanding of each document. But beyond these two very limited objectives, little has been accomplished. The taking attorney has certainly not learned any new information about the documents and, more importantly, the taking attorney has not found out what the witness's version of events consists of or added anything to the taking attorney's understanding of those events.

It is far better practice for you, the taking attorney, to *first* find out what the witness knows about the events in question by having the witness tell the story of those events. Then you can lock the witness into the story if it is favorable or attack the story if it runs counter to the story you want to be told. The documents will come into play to confirm or contradict the witness's story as it unfolds in response to your questions and to prod the witness to add or explain additional facts. Instead of the predictable and unrevealing use of documents described above, the sequence will now look something like the following:

> Q: Tell me how the agreement between you and the defen-
> dant came about?

> A: I wrote him a letter back in June of this year asking him if
> he was interested in selling me his business.

> Q: I am handing you what has been marked as Exhibit No.
> 1. Is that the letter you wrote the defendant?

> A: Yes.

> Q: That letter is dated June 3, 2010?

> A: Yes.

> Q: In Exhibit 1, you state that you are interested in buying
> his business for $1.2 million, is that correct?

> A: It is.

> Q: How did you arrive at the value of $1.2 million as the
> price for the defendant's business?

And the questioning would then continue on after the taking attorney had learned everything of value about the offer for the business. In the extreme example of the use of the "story, then document" approach, you would bring out no documents until you have exhausted the witness's memory of events.

If you use documents before that, the witness's memory becomes confined to what is shown in the documents, and new information is not revealed.

The approach of asking about documents only after the witness has told her story, instead of treating the documents as a discrete and separate part of the deposition, is much more likely to contribute to developing a full understanding of the events in question; this approach tends to reveal information of which you had no previous knowledge. If, at the end of hearing the witness's story, there are still documents remaining to be discussed, you will know that there are gaps in the story that you must explore. Finally, with a more complete understanding of the story, you will be in a better position to attack the unfavorable aspects of the story. Using the initial approach of merely working through the stack of documents is unlikely to bring any of these benefits.

9.5.3   *Testing the Witness's Memory*

Some lawyers think it is appropriate to test the witness's memory of what is contained in particular documents. Their questioning runs something like:

> Q: You received a letter from Mr. Smith in April of last year?
>
> A: Yes.
>
> Q: What did that letter say?
>
> A: I don't know. Wasn't it a solicitation for bids?
>
> Q: Tell me exactly what it said as best you can remember?
>
> A: It was just the usual solicitation letter.
>
> Q: What did it say about how the bid should be submitted?
>
> Counsel for Witness: You have the letter. Why don't you just show it to him or put it in the record?
>
> Q: I want to know what you remember it said about how the bid should be submitted.

This testing of the witness's memory serves no useful purpose and is merely a waste of everyone's time. Nothing the witness says will alter in any way the contents of the letter. Nor does the witness's current memory, or lack thereof, change in any way what the witness did, said, or thought about the letter at the relevant time. In fact, it is impossible to think of any relevant purpose to the witness's current memory, or lack of memory, of the contents of a document that exists and could be easily shown to the witness, other than to demonstrate a willingness on the taking attorney's part to engage in what are basically unfair tactics. A defending attorney who encounters such a situation should always request that the witness be shown the document in question. Making such a request will make the record clear that the questions are directed to the witness's memory of a document rather than to what the document actually says. If this type of questioning is used as a tactic to exhaust, annoy, or harass the witness, an appropriate objection should be made and a direction or suggestion on that basis should be made.

9.5.4   *Exploring Claims of Privilege*

It is likely that some of the documents requested by a subpoena or a request for production were claimed as privileged and not turned over, either before or at the deposition. Instead, a privilege log could have been provided, listing the documents and the basis for the privilege claim.[13] While many claims of privilege are valid and legitimate, be sure to question the witness about the privileges claimed for any documents with which the witness is connected and on which you have doubts. At a minimum, it is worth exploring whether there has been any waiver of the privilege and whether the document was for the purpose giving or requesting legal advice. Explore the waiver issue by asking about everyone who has seen the document and the efforts taken to protect the document's confidentiality. While it is unlikely that the defending lawyer will permit questions about the details of the content, you may ask whether the document contained any information unrelated to the case or to the giving or receiving of legal advice (in which case the court may direct the production of a redacted copy of the document).

9.6   Inquiring about Documents Used to Refresh the Witness's Memory

A favorite question of deposing attorneys is: "What documents have you reviewed in preparation for this deposition [sometimes adding, "to help refresh your memory"]?" The witness may then disgorge a list of various types of documents ("the letters from the government about the spill site, internal memoranda concerning the clean-up efforts, diagrams and maps of the area . . . ."), and defending counsel will make no objection. The attorneys in such an instance believe they are applying the provisions of Federal Rule of Evidence 612. Indeed, if the documents have not already been produced, defending counsel will often agree to produce them, without regard to whether they were required to be disclosed under the mandatory disclosure requirements of Federal Rule of Civil Procedure 26(a)(1)(B) or were called for by any subpoena or document production request.

There is no question that Federal Rule of Evidence 612 impacts what must be revealed about documents that are shown to the witness as part of

---

13. *See* section 9.2.3.

preparing the witness to testify at a deposition (since that is before trial), but the extent of that impact is very unclear and may vary from judge to judge and from jurisdiction to jurisdiction. As stated by one court, "A review of the cases in general . . . indicates that courts have been grappling with the scope of Rule 612 with varying degrees of clarity."[14]

Rule 612 often is debated in the context of selecting and using documents covered by the work-product doctrine or the attorney-client privilege to prepare a witness to testify at a deposition. The tension is between the need for the examining attorney to be able to cross-examine on how refreshing the witness's memory affected the deposition testimony and the need to protect the work-product status of the defending attorney's decision to use these documents in preparation. We will deal separately with the issues raised by each of these concerns.

Is the taking attorney entitled to learn the identity of those documents that opposing counsel has selected to show the witness in preparing the witness to testify at the deposition? Generally, the identity of documents assembled by counsel, but not otherwise privileged, is not protected by the work-product doctrine. "[T]he mere assembly of documents, without more, does not indicate that the attorney placed special weight on those documents as opposed to documents that were not obtained, and does not reveal which of the assembled documents the attorney deems important."[15] But where the attorney has selected a few documents to show the witness from the thousands in the case, the choice of particular documents may well be considered the attorney's work-protect, albeit only ordinary work-product and not opinion work-product. "In cases that involve reams of documents and extensive document discovery, the selection and compilation of documents is often more crucial than legal research."[16] The selection of the documents to be shown to the deponent during preparation will, in all likelihood, reveal the mental impressions of the lawyer as she prepares the case. Neither the documents nor the fact that the witness reviewed them are privileged in and of themselves, but "the selection process itself represents . . . counsel's mental impressions and legal opinions as to how the evidence in the documents relates to the issues and defenses in the litigation."[17] If the witness's testimony establishes that the document actually refreshed his memory, however, many courts have held that Rule 612 requires the witness to identify the document regardless of whether the selection process is work product.

---

14. Suss v. MSX Int'l Eng'g. Servs., Inc., 212 F.R.D. 159, 163 (S.D.N.Y. 2002).

15. Kartman v. State Farm Mut. Auto. Ins. Co., 247 F.R.D. 561, 564 (S.D. Ind. 2007).

16. Shelton v. Am. Motors Corp., 805 F.2d 1323, 1329 (8th Cir. 1986). *See* Disability Rights Council of Greater Wash. v. Wash. Metro. Transit Auth., 242 F.R.D. 139, 144 (D.D.C. 2007).

17. Sporck v. Peil, 759 F.2d 312, 315 (3d Cir. 1985).

When faced with this situation, the courts have come to three different conclusions. On one end of the spectrum, if the witness has reviewed documents in preparation for his testimony, some trial judges issue a blanket order that all such documents must be produced. These judges reason that it is impossible to determine in any reliable way whether a document that was reviewed actually "refreshed memory" or not, so in fairness, if the deponent reviewed it, the document is certainly relevant to the deponent's testimony and it must be produced. In these circumstances the "right" to production of the document occurs once the deponent responds that such a review took place and the documents are identified by the witness.

The middle position appears to be that if the deponent testifies that she reviewed a document and that it helped her recall the events surrounding the lawsuit, then all such documents must be produced, at least to the extent that they refreshed memory. That is, if a ten-page document was reviewed and only the middle two paragraphs on page six actually refreshed memory, then all that need be produced is some identifying information regarding the document (e.g., Memorandum of August 10, 2009, from J. Smith to D. Jones) and the two paragraphs from the document on page six. In this construct, before the document must be produced the witness must testify that her recollection had been refreshed regarding the matters underlying the lawsuit and the document must then be identified.

On the other end of the spectrum, before a document must be produced pursuant to Rule 612, it must be shown not only that the document refreshed the memory of the witness about the events underlying the lawsuit, but that the document refreshed the memory of the witness about testimony actually given at the deposition. These judges reason that unless there was actual testimony about the topic that was refreshed, there is no reason for the document to be produced under the rubric of Rule 612. Under this view of the law, then, the witness usually testifies first about a topic, and then if she responds that there was a document that refreshed her memory about the topic about which she has testified, that document (or portion of document) must be produced.

No matter which view a court holds on the refreshing documents that must be produced, another evidentiary issue concerns refreshing documents subject to privilege. Imagine that before the deposition a party witness has reviewed copies of letters she had sent her counsel concerning key facts in the case, and the letters refreshed her recollection about what occurred. Many courts have held that this may, pursuant to Rule 612, justify production of documents that would otherwise be protected under the attorney-client privilege.[18] This should serve as cautionary warning that a client should

---

18. *See, e.g.*, Derderian v. Polaroid Corp., 121 F.R.D. 13 (D. Mass. 1988).

never be provided documents for refreshing recollection that are privileged documents that should be shielded from discovery. In fact, the best "rule" regarding documents provided to a witness in preparation for deposition testimony is to provide only those documents that either have already been produced or present no tactical disadvantage should they have to be produced to opposing counsel.

In addition, inquiries about documents selected by counsel and used by the witness in preparing to testify can often be parried. For example:

> Q: What documents did you review in preparation for this deposition?
>
> Defending Counsel: Counsel, Mr. Shadis reviewed a number of documents with me as we prepared for this deposition. That review, and the identity of the documents we reviewed, is protected work product as trial preparation material under Rule 26(b)(3). You may of course ask about whether he has seen particular documents before, and he will answer you as fully as he can without waiving the privilege.

Or:

> Q: Mr. Shadis, are there any documents that you reviewed in preparation for your deposition testimony or otherwise that assisted in refreshing your recollection about the matters about which you have testified today?
>
> Defending Counsel: Counsel, Mr. Shadis has only reviewed documents that have already been produced in discovery, so you have already received them. Any selection from those documents by me is protected work product.

Of course, this last objection does not deal with the problem of identifying those documents that actually refreshed recollection of topics dealt with at the deposition. The mere fact that all have been received does not reveal whether any had an effect. You should pursue that information from the witness until the witness refuses to answer. And, of course, you can ask about documents the deponent reviewed of his own accord—that is, without having been directed to do so by his counsel—and about documents used to refresh recollection on particular topics.

9.7   Requesting Documents Identified during the Deposition

Often during depositions, witnesses will refer to documents that have not yet been obtained by the opposing party, and deposing counsel then turns to defending counsel:

Deposing Counsel:	Vito, will you provide us with these documents we've been talking about?
Defending Counsel:	Well, I don't think they were on any of your requests to produce, Ann, and they certainly weren't among the documents subject to mandatory disclosure under Rule 26(a)(1)(B).
Deposing Counsel:	I'm not saying they were. I'm just asking whether you will agree to provide us with the file of letters and the other materials, the memoranda that Mr. Shadis has referred to in the last hour or so.
Defending Counsel:	We don't have them here.
Deposing Counsel:	When can you produce them?
Defending Counsel:	I don't know. I'll have to get back to you.
Deposing Counsel:	Well, it's going to have to be soon, because you can see that we're probably going to have to have some more time with Mr. Shadis after we get the documents.
Defending Counsel:	I'm not going to agree to that. You could have asked for the documents before you scheduled this deposition. We're not going to just hold it open and let you keep coming back again and again.
Deposing Counsel:	Well, we scheduled the deposition to fit your witness's schedule, and you know that. If you've held back some documents we have to ask him about, then we'll get an order for him to return.
Defending Counsel:	Ann, we'll look at the transcript when we get it and do the best we can, con-

sistent with our need to represent our client's best interests and to avoid subjecting him to harassment through repetitive depositions.

In fact, this unproductive colloquy occurs so frequently we ought to just give it a number, or a nickname, and whenever this situation arises we could just announce, "Document production argument number three," and it would be understood that all of the above worthless verbiage was intended. Why is it worthless verbiage? Because it neither created nor waived any legal obligations. Defending counsel has merely agreed to look at the transcript and make a decision. If, after two months, he then decides not to produce the documents, he has not violated any agreement, stipulation, or order, and no motion to compel discovery is appropriate. In fact, all that is appropriate is a request to produce documents (or a subpoena, if it is a nonparty deponent)—the same request to produce that would have been appropriate immediately after the deposition if none of this discussion had occurred. In other words, the exchange between counsel is really code for defending counsel saying, "File your document request motion" and deposing counsel responding, "You'll have it tomorrow."

Many times a less contentious counsel does agree to produce the requested documents, but often the record is not crystal clear on what documents must be provided, nor within what time period. If, a month later, a few memoranda have been produced, the record supporting a request to the court for an order compelling further production is not as clear as it ought to be.

A more likely scenario is that following the agreement to produce the documents, the deposition proceeds and both sides promptly forget about the matter. Only months or even years later, when reviewing the deposition transcript in preparation for trial, do both sides recall that they had made an agreement.[19] Which party a court will side with at that point—the party who failed to live up to the agreement or the party who failed to move for enforcement in a timely manner—is a matter of conjecture.

How should the attorneys have handled the situation?

| Deposing Counsel: | Counsel, I don't think that document has been produced to us. Will you provide it without a formal request for discovery? |

If defending counsel knows the document and is comfortable agreeing to release it without further review for privilege, he can agree at that time, since the scope of his obligation is clear. All that remains is to clearly identify the

---

19. Such an agreement is an enforceable stipulation. FED. R. CIV. P. 29.

document to be produced. But to avoid the problem of both sides promptly forgetting the agreement until sometime in the future, the deposing counsel should make a note to follow up the agreement with a letter sent immediately following the conclusion of the deposition reminding the other side of the agreement. Similarly, the defending counsel should make a note to remind herself to provide the requested document. This is obviously one of the main reasons that Post-It Notes were invented.

Depending on the degree of cooperation existing between the parties, and whether the document is readily available, it can be produced immediately to obviate a later squabble over reconvening the deposition to explore the document in question. More competitive counsel may choose to respond to a request to provide a document with a response of "Write me a letter to tell me exactly which document you want, and we'll review it." We estimate that no follow-up letter is ever sent in over half the times this response is given. Again, we cannot overemphasize the importance of Post-It Notes.

But if the requested document is covered by an existing request to produce and the defending party inadvertently failed to turn it over, the most appropriate response is to produce the document immediately before the deposition concludes. If necessary, have the document expressed or couriered over to the deposition. Taking counsel is in a much stronger position to demand that the deposition be continued or resumed at some future time, and even demand costs for doing so, if the reason is the failure to comply with a valid earlier request to produce.

Some attorneys insist on a request for production in place of a letter after the deposition, although the advantage is not clear. We can hope an attorney's agreement to treat a letter as though it were a formal request for production would be sufficient, without any need for judicial intervention to determine the mutual obligations. Nevertheless, it is possible that attorneys find it easier to get their clients' attention if they can tell them, "These documents are subject to a request for production," than if they have to say, "Well, they wrote me a letter asking for them." Even if counsel does insist on the request for production, deposing counsel should not debate the point. If the documents need not have been produced in response to earlier discovery requests, another request is appropriate; if the documents should have been produced earlier, then a motion to compel may be appropriate. In either event, arguing about the matter at the deposition achieves nothing.

One final note is in order. Threats to force the witness to come back for further deposition because of the need for additional documents are counterproductive and should be ignored. As discussed in section 21.3, your right to call the witness back for further deposition does not depend on what counsel says, but rather on whether you have had a fair opportunity for a complete deposition. Only the court reporter, who gets to transcribe additional pages of deathless attorney prose, benefits from the debate on this point.

9.8   Refreshing Recollection

To be certain that a witness's knowledge has been exhausted at the deposition, it is sometimes appropriate to try to refresh the witness's recollection about a topic or event about which the witness testifies he has no memory or an incomplete memory. When attempting to refresh with a document (as it usually is), however, do so with care, because once a witness is shown a document, it may indeed refresh the witness's memory, but it will likely have a limiting effect on it as well. In other words, if a deponent testifies that he remembers only three subjects discussed at a meeting, and then you show him a memorandum that lists four subjects, the witness will adopt those four as the complete meeting agenda, regardless of how many more subjects were actually discussed. The key to avoiding this premature closure is to keep the document in reserve for as long as possible. Use the information in the document to probe the witness's memory, but bring the document out only at the end of that portion of the examination. Here is an example, based on a document that shows that the prime contractor met with the roofing subcontractor at least three times about the change order on the roofing material. The subcontractor is being deposed for discovery:

> Q: Now, Mr. Strongis, when did you discuss the materials with the prime contractor, Mary Jonas?
>
> A: Well, we had one meeting on the site, and that would have been around the first of April, I suppose.
>
> Q: Who was at that meeting?
>
> A: Just me and Mary; oh, and maybe the clerk of the works, Harry Barker.
>
> Q: What did Mary say about the roofing material at that meeting?
>
> A: Well, I remember we discussed using a rubberized membrane covered with gravel instead of the roofing felt shown in the drawings.
>
> Q: What did you say in the conversation?
>
> A: I can't remember anything specific—we just talked about the potential change in the plans.
>
> Q: What else was discussed at that meeting?

A: Nothing else.

Q: Were there other meetings about the roofing material?

A: Yes, I think there was one in the middle of May, because the membrane we wanted to use was not available.

Q: Who was that meeting with?

A: Someone from Mary's office, probably John Forsythe, and me.

Q: Who said what?

A: Well, I told John that the membrane from the Harrelson Company wasn't available when we needed it to dry in the building—you know, seal the roof—so we really should plan on some substitute.

Q: What did John say?

A: He told me to write up the proposed change and submit it as soon as possible, and I gave it to him that day, or maybe the next day.

Q: Was there more to that conversation?

A: No, that was about it.

Q: Were there any other meetings about the roofing material?

A: Yes, I remember we talked once more about it, after we laid the roofing membrane. The question came up whether we needed to use more gravel, and we decided that we didn't.

Q: Who talked about that?

A: I think that this time it was Mary and John Forsythe and me. That was near the end of the entire outside job, so it would have been in August sometime.

Q: Who said what at that meeting?

A: Again, I don't remember specific words that were said, but I did say, in so many words, that I thought that the gravel in the plans was sufficient, and they asked about the lighter weight of the new membrane, and I told them that really wasn't a problem because we were putting down a lot of gravel anyhow. That was about it.

Q: Were there any other conversations or meetings about the roofing material?

A: You mean, before this lawsuit came up?

Q: Right.

A: No, I think you've got them.

Q: Do you recall that there was a meeting at the end of July, about ordering more gravel?

A: Oh, yeah, but that . . . well, that wasn't more gravel so that we'd have more per square foot; that was more to cover a projection that had been added, over the front entrance. We kept the per-square-foot number the same.

Q: Who was present at that meeting?

A: That was just me and John, I think, because it was no big deal.

Q: Who said what?

A: Well, just what I told you. I told John that we needed more gravel to cover the area that wasn't in the original plan, and he said go ahead and order and submit a change order right away. So we did.

Q: What other meetings or conversations occurred regarding the roofing material?

A: None.

Q: Let me show you what has been marked as Strongis Deposition Exhibit 15, which appears to be a letter from Mary Smith in your office to the Smith Construction Company dated September 14, 2010. Is Exhibit 15 a letter that your office sent to the general contractor at the end of the job?

A: Yes. Oh, yeah, I looked at this last night.

Q: This letter lists one more meeting about the roofing materials, doesn't it?

A: Yeah, it has the two meetings that I mentioned, and then there's a meeting mentioned in here where the owner actually came down, in early July.

Q: Who else was at that meeting?

A: Well, Pierson, the owner, and me, and Mary Jonas, and I think the architect, Penn Sharp, was there, too.

Q: And who said what at that meeting?

A: Well, of course, the owner, all he wanted to talk about was when we'd be finished—you know, when the building would be dried in. Sharp and Mary were looking at the weight limits for the roof. All I wanted to know was whether they would sign off on the subroof so that we could finish up, since the new membrane had come in, and we were ready to go.

Q: What happened as a result of that meeting?

A: Oh, it all got worked out. The weight was good, and the subroof passed, so we could start.

By using the document in this way, the whole equals more than the sum of the parts: the deponent remembered three meetings; the document had two of those meetings, plus a fourth the witness did not initially recall. If the document has been used at the beginning of the inquiry about the subject, the information might have been limited to the three meetings referred to in the document. If the document wasn't used at all, the information would have been limited to the three meetings that the witness initially remembered. By holding back on the document until the witness's recollection was exhausted, information was obtained about all four meetings.

CHAPTER TEN

FOUNDATIONS

*He who has not first laid his foundations may be able with great ability
to lay them afterwards, but they will be laid with trouble
to the architect and danger to the building.*

—Niccolo Machiavelli

There is no requirement that in a deposition you must lay a foundation before, for example, asking the witness about what was said in a conversation the witness overheard. But if you do not at some time lay the necessary foundation, a court later may prohibit you from using that portion of the deposition at trial or in support of or in opposition to a motion, *provided* that the defending lawyer raised a proper objection at the deposition. An objection to the failure to lay a foundation is a "curable" objection and must be made at the deposition or it is waived. (*See* chapter fourteen for a discussion of curable objections and the need to make them at the deposition.) A prudent questioner therefore will always lay any necessary foundations for testimony or documents that she likes at the deposition to insure its later admissibility if the need should arise in the future to offer that testimony at trial or in support of or opposition to a motion. (If the lawyer does not like the testimony, she should not lay foundation; why do the work for the other side? There, it is recommended that the answer be taken and then a decision can be made on whether to lay foundation.)

Every trial lawyer knows the importance of being able to lay a "foundation," but there is little agreement about what is meant by that term. Some commentators and judges limit the definition of foundation to establishing that an item of evidence is authentic—i.e., that it is what its proponent claims it to be.[1] In other instances, the term is used more broadly to mean the proof

---

1. FED. R. EVID. 901(a): "To satisfy the requirement of authenticating or identifying an item of evidence, the proponent must produce evidence sufficient to support a finding that the item is what the proponent claims it is."

of any fact that is a prerequisite to admissibility.[2] Used in this broader sense, to lay a foundation, you must establish that an item of evidence:

1. is **authentic** under Federal Rule of Evidence 901 or 902;

2. is not **hearsay** by the rule excluding hearsay, Rule 801, or fits within a hearsay exception under Rule 803 or 804,

3. is an **original** as defined by Rules 1001 and 1002, or other evidence of the contents is admissible under Rule 1004,

4. is **relevant** under Rules 401 and 402;

And that the witness:

5. has **personal knowledge** of appropriate underlying facts supporting conclusions 1–4, above, as required by Rule 602; and

6. is **competent to testify to such facts,** pursuant to Rule 601.

Note that while relevance is often considered to be embraced by the concept of foundation, it is specifically excluded by Federal Rule of Civil Procedure 32(d)(3)(A) from those matters that are waived if not raised by objection at the deposition. This means that silence from the defending attorney is not a waiver of the "foundation" objection to an asserted lack of relevance, and the objection can be raised for the first time when the deposition testimony is offered in motions practice or at trial.

Listing the foundational facts for all of the different types of evidence is beyond the scope of this book. We will discuss the foundational requirements for several kinds of commonly recurring evidence, but those seeking a more detailed discussion should refer to those portions of any of the major trial advocacy treatises[3] for their discussions of relevance, authenticity, hearsay, best evidence (or "original document rule"), and the competence of witnesses. There also exists a superb "encyclopedia" of evidentiary foundations by Edward J. Imwinkelried with the catchy title of *Evidentiary Foundations*. This unexcelled reference book is compact enough to be taken along to depositions and is available in an inexpensive, paperbound "student" edition. A companion to it is Imwinkelreid's *Criminal Foundations*.[4]

---

2. Black's Law Dictionary (8th ed.) defines "Laying a Foundation" as "Introducing evidence of certain facts needed to render later evidence relevant, material, or competent."

3. An excellent trial advocacy treatise containing a chapter devoted to foundations and exhibits is Steven Lubet, Modern Trial Advocacy: Analysis and Practice, 4th ed. (Nita 2008). Other trial advocacy texts contain similar chapters.

4. Imwinkelreid's evidentiary credentials are remarkable, as shown by his participation as a consultant to the *Daubert* family in their appeal to the Supreme Court in *Daubert v. Merrill*

10.1 Foundations for Real or Tangible Evidence or Documents—Rule 901(b)(1)

How an exhibit is authenticated depends on the purpose for which it is being offered.[5] If Exhibit 47, a letter, is being offered to prove that the witness wrote it, then the examination must establish by direct ("I wrote that") or circumstantial ("That's the stationary he uses") evidence that the witness is the author of the letter. On the other hand, if the exhibit is being offered to establish that it was received by the addressee, you must establish that some witness or the addressee herself recognizes the exhibit as the letter that she received. Depending on the type of exhibit and the purpose for which it is being offered, you can establish the foundation for real or tangible evidence by several different methods.

10.1.1 *Real Evidence—Unique or Recognizable Objects—In General*

Real evidence can be authenticated by a witness testifying that an exhibit is what it purports to be.

Elements

- The object is unique—it can be distinguished from similar objects. (Says the cop: "I scratched my initials on the butt of the gun, and there they are.")

- The witness has previously observed the object at or near the relevant time and is familiar with its uniqueness. (An eyewitness says: "I have seen him sign other documents, and this is that same signature.")

- The witness can identify the exhibit as the object by its uniqueness. (The eyewitness says: "I never saw another football that said 'Willie Mays Model' on it, so I knew it was my father's. And right here, on the end, that's where my son chewed on it when he was teething.")

Dow, 509 U.S. 579 (1993), and his invitation to submit an *amicus* brief in *Kumho Tire Co. v. Carmichael*, 526 U.S. 137 (1999)—both on the issue of the foundation for admissibility of expert testimony.

5. In modern practice, it is probably true that most exhibits are stipulated as authentic on "document day," when the judge sits to make decisions on objections to documents and deposition extracts, or are admitted into the trial record because no objection to authenticity is raised when the document is offered. Nevertheless, counsel should know how to authenticate evidence, so that she can recognize and object to baseless offers, where the document is sufficiently important. At deposition, know how to lay foundation; at trial, know when to object and when to hold off.

- The object is in the same or substantially the same condition as at the relevant time, or any differences can be explained or are not material to its use at trial. (The lab tech says: "Yes, that's the bag I opened, sampled, closed, and initialed, but it has less cocaine in it now.")

Example

Q: Mr. Woodbridge, I am handing you what has been marked as Exhibit 14, which appears to be a contract between you and Mr. Morganfield for the sale of your mobile home. Do you recognize it?

A: Yes.

Q: What is Exhibit 14?

A: It is in fact the contract Morganfield and I signed for him to buy my mobile home.

Q: How do you recognize Exhibit 14 as the contract for the sale of your mobile home?

A: Well, I got the form out of a book a friend had of business forms. That's my signature right above the "Seller" line, and I saw Morganfield sign it right above the line marked "buyer."

Q: Is Exhibit 14 in the same or substantially the same condition as when you and Mr. Morganfield signed it?

A: Yes.

10.1.2   *Real Evidence—Witness Recognizes Handwriting—Rule 901(b)(2)*

Federal Rule of Evidence 901(b)(2) states that a writing or document can be authenticated by "[a] nonexpert's opinion that the handwriting is genuine, based on familiarity with it that was not acquired for the current litigation." Please note the requirement that the familiarity cannot be acquired for purposes of the litigation. In effect, this means that the familiarity must have been acquired before the dispute arose.

Elements

- The witness is familiar with the writer's handwriting.

- The witness recognizes the handwriting on the document in question.

- The document is in the same or substantially the same condition as at the relevant time, or any differences can be explained.

Example

Q: When did you receive the letter in question?

A: Christmas week of last year.

Q: Are you familiar with Mr. Jones's handwriting?

A: Yes.

Q: How are you familiar with his handwriting?

A: I worked with him for ten years. I saw many notes and letters he wrote over that time. I've seen his handwriting at least several hundred times.

Q: Are you also familiar with his signature?

A: Yes.

Q: How are you familiar with his signature?

A: Same way. Over those ten years I must have seen him sign more than a thousand letters and documents.

Q: I am handing you what has been marked as Exhibit 4 and ask if you recognize it?

A: Yes, this is the letter I received.

Q: Do you recognize the writing on that letter, Exhibit 4?

A: I do.

Q: Whose handwriting is it on Exhibit 4?

A: Mr. Jones.

Q: Do you also recognize the signature on Exhibit 4?

A: Yes.

Q: Whose signature is it on Exhibit 4?

A: Mr. Jones.

Q: Is Exhibit 4 in the same or substantially the same condition as when you received it?

A: It is.

10.1.3 *Real Evidence—Circumstantial Evidence—Rule 901(b)(4)*

Sometimes you can identify the creator of a document or writing through circumstantial evidence. For example, in the prosecution of Alger Hiss, an FBI agent testified that transcriptions of certain government documents were typed on a typewriter owned by Hiss. This testimony was based on the unique characteristics of the letters produced by the Hiss typewriter. Similarly, if a letter contained misspellings unique to the alleged author, this would be circumstantial evidence that the note was written by that person. Or, as another example, if a letter referred to facts that only the alleged author would likely know, this again is circumstantial evidence of authorship.

The Reply Letter Doctrine, adopted in some states, is a variant on the use of circumstantial evidence to establish authenticity. This doctrine states that if a letter is sent to a particular person and in the due course of the mail the witness receives a reply purportedly signed by the person to whom the first letter was sent and the reply letter refers to or purports to respond to the first letter, this is sufficient circumstantial evidence of the authenticity of the second letter.

Elements

- The witness is familiar with the first letter.

- The first letter was placed in a properly addressed envelope, stamped with the proper postage and mailed.

- The first letter was addressed to the alleged author of the second letter.

- A second letter was later received in the due course of the mail.

- The second letter referred to the first letter or was responding to it.

- The second letter contained the alleged author's name.

- The witness recognizes the second letter and the circumstances under which it was received.

- The second letter is in the same, or substantially the same condition, as at the relevant time or any differences can be explained or are not relevant.

Example

Q: Did you ever notify the defendant of your concerns?

A: Yes, I wrote him detailing my complaints.

Q: How did you do that?

A: I typed up a letter, signed it, put a first class stamp on it, and took it down to the post office where I mailed it.

Q: What address did you put on the letter?

A: The one in the ad he sent me.

Q: When did you send this letter?

A: It was that very day, August 3, 2010.

Q: What happened after that?

A: I got a letter back.

Q: When did you receive that letter?

A: About two weeks later.

Q: Did that second letter have a signature?

A: Yes, the defendant's.

Q: Did the letter you received refer in any way to the letter you sent?

A: Yes, it responded to the concerns I raised in my letter to the defendant.

Q: I am handing you what has been marked as Exhibit 8. Do you recognize it?

A: Yes.

Q: What is Exhibit 8?

A: This is the letter I received from the defendant.

Q: How do you know that is the letter, Exhibit 8, you received?

A: I read it at the time, and also it has the defendant's name on it.

Q: Is Exhibit 8 in the same or substantially the same condition as when you received it?

A: It is.

Example

Assume that the witness is testifying about a purported letter from Chester Burnett that was received after a discussion between the witness and Mr. Burnett.

Q: Did you ever have a discussion with a Mr. Chester Burnett about purchasing baseball bats from him?

A: Yes.

Q: Where was that discussion?

A: We were both attending a preseason game between the Cubs and the White Sox.

Q: When was that discussion?

A: I don't remember the exact date, but it was in the spring of this year.

Q: What was said in that discussion?

A: Burnett offered to sell me 1,500 of his top of the line bat for $27.00 each. I told him I would get back with him.

Q: Did you ever hear from Mr. Burnett again?

A: Yes, I received a letter from him at the end of March offering again to sell me the bats.

Q: I am handing you what has been marked as Exhibit 2. Do you recognize it?

A: I do. This is the letter that Burnett sent me.

Q: Is the letter, Exhibit 2, on letterhead?

A: Yes, it is on the letterhead of Big Bat, Inc., Mr. Burnett's company.

Q: How do you know that's his letterhead?

A: I have conducted business with his company before, and he used that letterhead.

Q: Is the letter, Exhibit 2, signed?

A: Yes, Burnett's signature is above the signature line marked "Chester Burnett, President."

Q: How do you know that is his signature?

A: I recognize it from other dealings with him where I have seen him sign things.

Q: Does Exhibit 2 refer to the meeting between you and Mr. Burnett that was held at the Cubs-White Sox preseason game?

A: Yes. It says right here that he enjoyed meeting me at the game and that he is renewing his offer to sell me 1,500 bats for $27.00 each.[6]

Q: Have you discussed the conversation between you and Mr. Burnett with anyone else?

A: Only my lawyer.

Q: Is Exhibit 2 in the same or substantially the same condition as when you received it?

A: Yes.

Now, these examples are a bit unrealistic, because normally only a couple questions on "how do you know" are necessary, and you don't need to discover every last bit of authenticating evidence. At a deposition, you may want to be cautious, but there is more to life and lawsuits than authentication, so don't overdo it. Chapter 9 of the Federal Rules of Evidence, and especially Rule 902, provide a nonexhaustive list of additional examples of both authentication and self-authentication, with which you should be familiar.

10.1.4   Real Evidence—Business Records—Rule 803(6)

Federal Rule of Evidence 803(6), Records of a Regularly Conducted Activity—familiarly known as the Business Records Rule—is an exception to the hearsay rule and is not a rule of authentication. Nonetheless, establish-

---

6. It is not permissible to have a witness read, or show to the jury, the contents of an exhibit until the exhibit has been received in evidence. If the contents themselves are being offered to establish the authenticity of the exhibit, the court should make its ruling on admissibility. Then the authenticating portions, along with the remainder of the document, can be shown to the jury so that it can exercise its function as final fact finder and decide whether it finds the document authentic. Authenticity, being a matter of fact, is conclusively decided by the jury, and it does not have to accept the preliminary finding of authenticity made by the court as it considers admissibility. This is true for all elements of foundation, all the way "up" to a finding that an expert's testimony is authentic ("reliable" under *Daubert* analysis: the court may admit it as relevant and reliable, but the jury may refuse to accept it and therefore reject the opinion). Incidentally, the judge's initial preliminary finding of a foundational fact applies the lowest threshold in the law: Could a reasonable jury conclude that this document is in fact authentic? Not *must* they so find, which would be a directed verdict standard, but only *can* they so find, based on the evidence presented.

ing the exception also establishes the authenticity of the business record—
that is, that it is in fact a contemporaneous record of the company or person.

Elements

- The exhibit is a memorandum, report, record, or data compilation, in any form.

- The record is of acts, events, conditions, opinions, or diagnoses.

- The record was made at or near the time of the acts, events, conditions, opinions, or diagnoses that it reports.

- The record was made by a person with knowledge, or from information transmitted by a person with knowledge, of the acts, events, conditions, opinions, or diagnoses.

- The person with knowledge had a business duty to report the information (this requirement is not explicitly contained in Rule 803(6), but is imposed by case law) or the information being reported falls within some other exception to the hearsay rule, such as a statement of a party opponent.

- The record was kept in the course of a regularly conducted activity.

- Making the record was a regular practice of that activity.

- The record was not prepared in anticipation of litigation (this requirement is not explicitly contained in Rule 803(6), but is imposed by case law).

- The above elements are shown by the testimony of the custodian of the record or by an affidavit complying with Rule 902(10). Note that the witness does not have to have personal knowledge of the making and keeping of the particular record being offered, but only of how records of this type are made and kept.

- The record is the same or substantially the same condition as when taken from the files.

Example

The business records foundation, when established by the testimony of a witness, is commonly accomplished in two ways—the litany version and the prose version. (It can also be done by a written declaration or certification from the keeper of the records, as is also true for domestic public documents not under seal, foreign public documents, certified copies of public records, acknowledged documents, and foreign "business records," all as discussed in Rule 902 as part of self-authentication.)

The litany version mirrors the requirements of Rule 803(6):

Q: Are you the custodian of records for Nita Memorial Hospital?

A: Yes.

Q: Are you familiar with the making and keeping of the medical records at the hospital?

A: Yes.

Q: Are those records made and kept as part of the regularly conducted business activities of the hospital?

A: Yes.

Q: Are those records made at or near the time of the events recorded in them?

A: Yes.

Q: Are those records made by, or from information transmitted by, persons with first-hand knowledge of the events recorded in them?

A: Yes.

Q: Did the person reporting the information have a business duty to do so?

A: Yes.

Q: When you came to court today, did you bring with you the medical records for the plaintiff, John Smythe?

A: Yes.

Q: I hand you what has now been marked as Exhibit 14 and ask if you recognize it?

A: I do.

Q: Is Exhibit 14 the hospital's medical record for John Smythe?

A: Yes.

Q: Is Exhibit 14 one of the records whose making and keeping you have just described?

A: Yes.

The prose version is more jury-friendly. In ruling on the adequacy of the foundation provided by deposition testimony concerning a business record, many judges mentally check off the elements for a business record as they hear or read the above testimony. If there is testimony on each of the elements, the exhibit will be received. But you can well imagine what a jury thinks when they hear this testimony—bunch of legal mumbo jumbo. Where the goal is not only to get the exhibit into evidence, but also to persuade a jury (to whom the deposition questions and answers are being read) of the accuracy of the record, it will be necessary to supplement the litany version with the prose version:

Q: What is your position at the Nita Memorial Hospital?

A: I am the custodian of medical records.

Q: What does the custodian of medical records at Nita Memorial Hospital do?

A: I am responsible for making sure that all the hospital's medical records are properly prepared and stored at the hospital.

Q: Please tell us how these records are prepared?

A: The nurses and doctors make entries on a patient's medical chart of all information concerning the patient's treatment. For instance, when a doctor prescribes a medication, this is put on the chart; or when the patient's temperature is taken, that information is also put on the chart.

Q: Who makes these entries on the chart?

A: The nurses and doctors treating the patient.

Q: When are these entries made?

A: When the treatment is given. For example, when the patient's temperature is taken, the nurse will write the temperature on the chart right after taking it.

Q: How are these records kept?

A: When the patient is discharged, all of the patient's records are sent to the Medical Records Department, where we put them in a file and keep them.

The business records foundation may also be established by an affidavit prepared by the person who would otherwise be testifying to the foundation at trial. The form of the affidavit is contained in Rule 902(11).

10.1.5   Real Evidence—Public Records—Rules 803(8), 901(b)(7), & 902(1)–(5)

While it is perfectly proper to obtain deposition testimony to lay the foundation for a public record, it is usually not necessary to do so. Rule 902 provides for most public records to be self-authenticating. The requirements for self-authentication depend on whether the record is that of a foreign government or a United States governmental unit and whether the document bears a seal of that governmental unit. Nonetheless, usually the most convenient method of authenticating a public record is by certification.[7] It is not necessary to ask any questions to lay a foundation when an exhibit is self-authenticating and otherwise satisfies the hearsay exception for public records.[8]

10.2   Substantive Visual Evidence—Photographs, Maps, and Diagrams

The foundations for photographs, maps, and diagrams are very similar in their requirements.

Element

- The witness recognizes the photograph, map, or diagram as being the relevant scene. ("That's what I photographed when the policeman asked me to 'shoot' the intersection that night.")

- The photograph, map, or diagram fairly and accurately depicts the scene at the relevant time.

- The photograph, map, or diagram shows the scene to scale, or not to scale. It is not necessary for the photograph, map or diagram to be drawn to scale, only that the judge knows whether it is. (A photograph that is not drawn to scale is more often called "distorted," and the extent of distortion may affect its admissibility; e.g., "The angle of this photograph makes the man in the foreground look much, much bigger than he actually was.")

- There is no evidentiary requirement that the photograph, map, or diagram be supported by testimony from the person who took it or created it. Familiarity with the "scene" that is shown is sufficient, so that the witness has a basis for comparing reality with the image. That comparison, however, can be provided by a different witness. For example, the photographer could say, "This was taken by a camera in the desert that I triggered remotely," while another witness could say, "That looks just like the patch of desert I saw where I found the wrecked car."

---

7. Fed. R. Evid. 902(4).
8. Fed. R. Evid. 803(8).

Example

Q: Are you familiar with the intersection of Kirby and Richmond?

A: I am.

Q: How did you become familiar with that intersection?

A: I drive through that intersection nearly every day.

Q: Are you familiar with the way it looked in December of last year?

A: Yes. It hasn't changed much since then.

Q: Are you familiar with the way it looked when you are facing north?

A: Sure, that's the way I drive through it going to work in the mornings.

Q: I am handing you what has been marked as Exhibit 12 and ask if you recognize what is shown in the photograph?

A: I do. That's the intersection of Kirby and Richmond.

Q: Does Exhibit 12 fairly and accurately show the intersection of Kirby and Richmond as it appeared during the month of December last year?

A: Yes.

Q: Does it fairly and accurately show the intersection as it appeared when facing north?

A: Yes.

10.3   Oral Evidence—In General

There are several methods of authenticating oral statements.

Elements

•   The witness was able to hear the statement.

•   The time, place, and surrounding circumstances of the statement are known.

Example

Q: Do you know Mr. Shrackle, the defendant?

A: I do.

Q: Were you present during the month of May 2010 at a conversation in which Mr. Shrackle participated?

A: I was.

Q: Where was that conversation held?

A: It was at my house.

Q: When was that conversation?

A: On May 10 at about 3:00 p.m.

Q: Who else was present?

A: It was just me and Mr. Shrackle.

Q: What did Mr. Shrackle say?

A: He said that he was ashamed of how he behaved last night.

10.3.1 *Oral Evidence—Voice Identification—Rule 901(b)(5)*

Sometimes the listener is not in the presence of the speaker when the speaker makes the statement, as, for example, during a telephone conversation. One way to identify the speaker and authenticate the statement is to show the witness's familiarity with the speaker's voice.[9]

Elements

• The witness is familiar with the speaker's voice.

• The time, place, and surrounding circumstances of the statement are known.

• The witness recognized the speaker's voice.

Note that the familiarity with the speaker's voice can be acquired after the statement was made and can even be acquired for purposes of litigation, unlike familiarity with handwriting.[10]

---

9. Fed. R. Evid. 901(b)(5).

10. *See* Fed. R. Evid. 901(b)(2).

Example

Q: Are you familiar with Ms. Holton's voice?

A: Yes.

Q: How did you become familiar with her voice?

A: I dated her for a number of years.

Q: Did you receive a telephone call on June 8, 2010?

A: I did.

Q: Did you recognize the voice of the person calling?

A: I did.

Q: Whose voice was it?

A: Ms. Holton.

Q: What did Ms. Holton say?

A: She said she was going out of town.

10.3.2   *Oral Evidence—Outgoing Telephone Calls—Rule 901(b)(6)*

Elements

- The call was made to the number assigned by the telephone company to that person or company.

- In the case of a person, circumstances, including self-identification, show the person answering to be the one called.

- In the case of a business, the call was made to a place of business and the conversation related to business reasonably transacted over the telephone.

Example

Q: Did you ever place an order with the defendant company?

A: I did.

Q: When did you do that?

A: On Thursday of that week, sometime in the morning.

Q: Where did you get the number?

A: I looked it up in the phone book.

Q: When you called, how was the phone answered?

A: It was a man, and he said "Cut-Rate Order Department. May I help you?"

Q: What did you do?

A: I placed my order.

10.3.3 Oral Evidence—Circumstantial Evidence of Speaker's Identity—Rule 901(b)(4)

As with documents, circumstantial evidence can be used to establish the identity of a speaker. For example, if the speaker talks about information only the claimed speaker would know, this is circumstantial evidence of the speaker's identity. The elements and example of this type of foundation are the same as for circumstantial evidence of the author of a document.

10.4 Laying Foundations Efficiently

Laying the foundation for a piece of evidence can be time consuming and is easily frustrated by a hostile witness who refuses to cooperate. Nonetheless, you have techniques available to reduce the time consumed by this exercise.

10.4.1 Use Leading Questions When Permissible to Establish the Foundation

It is usually more efficient to use leading questions to establish a foundation with an adverse party, an agent or employee of an adverse party, or a hostile witness, then it is to try to get the same information by inviting them with open questions to tell "the story." Although Rule 104(a) states that a court is not bound by the rules of evidence when determining the admissibility of evidence, courts display varying degrees of tolerance to leading, even in this circumstance. Because of the uncertainty of how a judge will react, it is best to avoid leading questions when establishing foundations when it would be otherwise improper to lead the witness in questioning on the merits. But where leading questions would be permitted—with an adverse party, for example—leading is a quick and efficient method of establishing any necessary foundations.

Q: I am handing you what has been marked as Exhibit 13, what appears to be a letter the witness sent to the plaintiff. This is a letter you wrote, correct?

A: Yes.

> Q: You wrote that letter, Exhibit 13, on June 30 of last year?
>
> A: Yes.
>
> Q: And you mailed that letter, Exhibit 13, on that same day?
>
> A: Yes.

10.4.2   Lay Foundations for Groups of Exhibits

You can frequently save a great deal of time discussing categories of documents rather than laying the foundation for each exhibit separately:

> Q: Mr. Shadis, with regard to Exhibit 76, is that document an example of a form used by your company?
>
> A: Yes, it is.
>
> Q: And Exhibit 76, this form document with "Shadis Co." in the upper right-hand corner, and "Invoice No." with a blank in the left corner, and then spaces for entering items and amounts, is that your standard form of invoice for bulk purchases of Shadis construction materials?
>
> A: Yes, that's the form we use.
>
> Q: And would all of your company invoices be in the same form?
>
> A: Yes, they would.

After getting that answer, there is no need to ask about the form every time one of them occurs as a deposition exhibit. Similarly, you can authenticate the form for internal memoranda in an organization generically: "Was Exhibit 102 an internal memorandum, using the form you previously told us about?" This obviates the need to ask about it with each exhibit that is a memorandum in the company form.

10.4.3   Ask for the Basis for a Foundation Objection

If a foundation objection is made and you're not sure what your opponent believes is missing, ask. There is no sense in floundering around attempting to figure out what question you failed to ask. If the opponent refuses to reveal the basis for the objection, it will be harder later, under Rule 37(d)(3)(B), for him to argue that the objection was preserved. It is virtually impossible to cure a lack of foundation if the objector refuses to identify what is lacking in that foundation.

If an objection is made, be sure its basis is clear and address whatever infirmities can be cured during the deposition. (A further discussion of making and meeting objections at deposition appears in chapter fourteen.)

10.4.4   Do Not Offer the Exhibit

There is no judge attending the deposition and therefore no need to offer an exhibit after laying a foundation. If that portion of the deposition testimony and the accompanying exhibit are used at a later time, the judge will make a ruling at that time about the admissibility of the exhibit. Offering the exhibit at the deposition will produce either confusion or bemusement on the part of opposing counsel. (However, it is at the same time bemusing to note that those same smug attorneys who wait to pounce on innocent errors by young or inexperienced counsel at depositions are often the same attorneys who make objections like, "Objection, assumes facts not in evidence," even though, of course, there is no evidentiary record, since that is not created until trial.)

10.5   Negative Foundations

In addition to using deposition testimony to lay the foundation for the admissibility of a document or oral statements, it is likewise appropriate to use the deposition as a vehicle for laying what can be called a "negative foundation." During the course of document production, opposing counsel will often produce a document that is particularly probative of the opponent's position, but may suffer from some evidentiary infirmity. During the deposition of the creator of the document or another witness who is usually part of the same entity as the creator of the document, you can show the inadmissibility of the document and lay the foundation for a motion in limine to exclude the document from use in later proceedings. For example, consider the situation where a company has been sued for gender discrimination. As a precursor to the bringing of the action, a complaint was filed with the Equal Employment Opportunity Commission, which in turn requested a reply from the now-defendant company. In response to the request, the defendant company's human relations department conducted an investigation and then prepared a report that disclaims any discrimination on the part of the company and asserts that the now-plaintiff was discharged for poor work performance. The following, in pursuit of a "negative foundation," occurs at the deposition of the human relations officer, Ms. Wilson, by plaintiff's counsel:

> Q: Ms. Wilson, were you the person who investigated my client's claim of gender discrimination at the Acme Paper Company?
>
> A: Yes, I was.

Q: Did you prepare a report of your investigation for Acme's Vice President for Personnel?

A: I did.

Q: Let me show you a six-page document that we have marked as Exhibit 23, which appears to be a memorandum prepared by you on January 28, 2010, and sent to Joyce O'Toole, Vice President for Personnel at Acme Paper Company. Do you recognize Exhibit 23?

A: Yes, that's the memorandum I just told you about that contains my report on your client's complaint.

Q: Why was Exhibit 23 prepared?

A: As I understand it, your client had made a complaint of gender discrimination against Acme, and we had been asked by the EEOC to respond to that complaint.

Q: So when you conducted your investigation you knew that a complaint had been made by my client to the EEOC?

A: Yes, this has happened a few times in my ten years at Acme—someone complains to the EEOC, they ask for a response, and we respond.

Q: In the past when this has happened, has there ever been a lawsuit filed against Acme by the person who complained to the EEOC?

A: Yes, that has happened several times.

Q: Were you aware of that when you prepared Exhibit 23?

A: Yes.

Q: In addition to sending Exhibit 23 to Ms. O'Toole, does Exhibit 23 show that any copies were sent to anyone else, and I refer you to the last page, page six of Exhibit 23?

A: Yes, a copy was sent to Jack Burns, Acme's General Counsel.

Q: Why was that?

A: Because there is always a possibility of litigation when an EEOC complaint is made.

Q: Am I correct then, that Exhibit 23 was prepared for two purposes—one, to respond to the EEOC, and two, in anticipation of possible litigation?

A: That's right.

With this "negative foundation," Exhibit 23 can likely be excluded as hearsay if offered by the defendant company. (The plaintiff, of course, could always offer Exhibit 23 as a party statement.[11]) Although it was part of the business of Acme to respond to EEOC inquiries, the memorandum was prepared in anticipation of litigation, which in all likelihood would disqualify it as a record of regularly conducted activity (business record) of Acme.[12]

This provides one example of a "negative foundation," that is, questioning to demonstrate that the foundation for the admission of a document or other piece of evidence does not exist. In general, the questioner analyzes the basis on which such a piece of evidence might be offered and then attempts to obtain deposition testimony that the facts do not support such an argument for admissibility.

---

11. Fed. R. Evid. 801(d)(2).
12. Fed. R. Evid. 803(6).

CHAPTER ELEVEN

OBNOXIOUS OR OBSTRUCTIONIST OPPOSING COUNSEL

[The enemy] must be hounded and annihilated at every step and all their measures frustrated.

—Joseph Stalin

Some attorneys believe it is their job in defending a deposition to prevent the discovery of information at virtually any cost. At least three reasons account for such behavior: first, the attorney is ignorant of the issues and unprepared to defend the deposition—therefore, he is desperate to avoid the substance of the case; second, the attorney is inexperienced in defending depositions and he therefore lacks the confidence to allow the facts to come out; and third, the attorney does not accept the premises of the Federal Rules of Civil Procedure that pretrial discovery of the opponent's information is favored,[1] and that trial by ambush, obfuscation, and surprise is disfavored.[2]

Most obstructionist attorneys are more likely to prey on young or apparently inexperienced lawyers who appear vulnerable to intimidation, but some attorneys will try these tactics on any attorney, from the newest to the most experienced, and in any deposition, from the small tort case to multidistrict commercial litigation.

Obstructionist behavior takes a number of forms. The most common of these are:

---

1. "The Federal Rules of Civil Procedure . . . are designed to prevent trial by ambush." Yohannon v. Keene Corp., 924 F.2d 1255, 1259 n.4 (3d Cir. 1991). The goal of the discovery rules is to promote "free and open" exchange of information between the parties and to prevent surprise and delay. *See, e.g.,* Davis v. Romney, 55 F.R.D. 337 (D. Pa. 1972); United States v. I.B.M., 68 F.R.D. 315 (S.D.N.Y. 1975); Wiener King, Inc. v. Wiener King Corp., 615 F.2d 512 (C.C.P.A. 1980).

2. From time to time, it seems that a "fourth category" attorney is discovered—the "absolute jerk"—but like the "new" dinosaur that turns out to be the scrambled bones of previously known dinosaurs, the "jerk" usually turns out to be an energetic combination of two or all three of the previously known categories.

- speaking and meritless objections;

- argumentative objections or statements of a condescending, denigrating, or intimidating tone;

- distracting coughing, throat clearing, signaling, mumbling, and so forth;

- distracting physical movements; and

- baseless instructions not to answer.

Because this sort of behavior interferes with the legitimate goals of discovery, it has been the topic of numerous criticism and proposals by the organized bar, trial judges, rule makers, and others. And because the making of spurious objections and instructions not to answer and the manner in which these tactics were used was the primary form of obstructive behavior, the Federal Rules of Civil Procedure contain clear dictates regarding how and under what conditions objections and instructions not to answer may be accomplished legitimately. Rule 30(c)(2) provides:

> An objection must be stated concisely and in a nonargumentative and nonsuggestive manner. A person may instruct a deponent not to answer only when necessary to preserve a privilege, to enforce a limitation directed by the court, or to present a motion under Rule 30(d)(3) [seeking a limitation on the deposition].[3]

Strict adherence to this rule would prevent 90 percent of the obstructive behavior that occurs at depositions, and judges, especially those in the federal courts, are more and more often insisting on just that. Individual federal districts and state courts have gone even further. The local rules in many districts severely limit the form of objections that can be made. For example, local rules in several districts limit to stating the word, "objection," or to a limited range of permissible objections such "objection, form." No grounds may be stated, other than those specifically permitted, such as "form," unless questioning counsel requests the basis for the objection so it can be cured.

Finally, individual judges have fashioned discovery orders that severely limit defending counsel from any communication with the deponent while the deposition in ongoing. These rules are designed to prevent defending counsel from consulting with the deponent during the deposition. However, these discovery orders usually do—and properly should—allow appropriate consultation with the client to discuss a potential claim of privilege or the

---

3. Objections and instructions not to answer questions will be discussed more fully in chapter fourteen.

ethically required remonstration with the client when the defending lawyer believes that the deponent has given false testimony.

It is the authors' impression that these efforts are showing results. The increasing number of cases in the past few years in which attorneys are sanctioned for obstructionist behavior and improper coaching at depositions demonstrates that the courts, in general, are making a genuine effort to curb these types of behavior. Similarly, attorney behavior is being affected by local and state rules limiting the types and forms of objections that are permissible at a deposition, and imposing sanctions for violations of the rules. We believe that the problem of obstructionist lawyers is diminishing with time, but certainly it has not been solved. Therefore, it is important for counsel to know how to deal with these attorneys when they show up across the table at a deposition.

A few simple techniques will help you control the obstructionist attorney; if these techniques do not control him, at least they will help you, the reasonable attorney, complete your deposition despite the interference.

11.1   Irritating or Obstructing Behavior

The first step in dealing with the defending counsel is to decide whether the behavior is merely irritating, thereby making the deposition more difficult, or is actually obstructing and defeating your ability to obtain information from the deponent. In one situation, opposing counsel may make long, speaking objections that do not actually have the effect of coaching or cueing the witness. Or the lawyer may ask for unnecessary clarifications of questions without instructing the witness to refuse to answer. In the second situation, opposing counsel may whisper in the witness's ear while a question is pending or instruct the witness to refuse to answer merely because of relevance or form, with no mention of privilege. The effects on the deposition from the two types of behavior—irritating and obstructing—are different, and your response to the two should reflect that difference.

11.2   The Irritating Opposing Counsel

First, let us examine the first situation described above—the irritating opposing counsel. The following are a few tactics to deal with this type of interference.

11.2.1   *Size Up the Defending Counsel*

Some lawyers actually are "jerks," while others sometimes behave like jerks as a calculated strategy. Remember, however, that every instance of opposing counsel asking for a question to be clarified or conferring with the witness while a question is pending does not automatically translate to jerk-like behavior or engaging in irritating or obstructionist tactics. Some lawyers ask for clarification because your question has genuinely confused them. They believe that the witness may be similarly confused or that the question is likely to lead to a misleading transcript on a matter of some importance to the lawsuit. Some lawyers confer with the witness while a question is pending because a legitimate issue of privilege must be cleared up before the witness can answer. Some objections are made because they are valid and legitimate, and the lawyer is trying to handle the problem as best she can.

Unless there were previous bad experiences with the opposing counsel or the lawyer has a reputation as one of the hated breed of obstructionists, you should assume, until proven otherwise, that opposing counsel is acting in good faith. Responding with the nuclear option to a polite request for clarification of a question is guaranteed to turn the deposition into an unpleasant experience for all involved. More importantly, it is also likely to interfere with your ability to obtain the maximum amount of information from the witness.

Treating opposing counsel as the enemy every time she makes an objection or inserts a comment may also result in you ignoring a valid objection that you ought to cure to get the sought-after information in the most usable form. Consider the objection carefully, while ignoring the tone or volume, to determine if the question or the record can be improved. If it later becomes necessary to offer the deposition at trial or to use it as support for a summary judgment motion, you may have important favorable evidence available because you adjusted the question in response to the grumbled or shouted or otherwise nastily made objection. Opposing counsel was being a jerk, but a legitimate objection may have been cloaked in the melodramatic conduct. Make this decision on an objection-by-objection basis and do not rely on assumptions. A hundred loud chants of "objection, irrelevant and compound and complex" may be irritating, but some of those questions probably are compound or complex, and they actually can be improved by changing them into two or three separate questions. In short, if the opportunity still exists to obtain information from the deponent, and if objection has any chance of improving the questioning, be reasonable in conduct and tone and consider whether a changed question might do a better job. A pleasant, courteous response on your part may engender the same sort of behavior from opposing counsel when later in the litigation the roles of counsel are reversed.

11.2.2   Keep the Deposition Goals in Mind

In all discovery depositions the primary goal is to obtain information, helpful or harmful, to better prepare for the disposition of the case. To state this goal more succinctly, both the goal and the process of the deposition is to ask questions and receive answers. As we have said before, the ultimate goal of every deposition is to exhaust the witness's information about the case.

To accomplish this goal, especially because depositions are time-constrained, counsel must operate efficiently. By engaging in irritating behavior, the opposing attorney is inviting you to behave inefficiently by arguing about objections, engaging in worthless debate on procedural points, or calling on deposing counsel to refine and further refine questions that are understandable at first asking.[4]

Therefore, whenever anything is occurring at the deposition other than the asking of questions and the receiving of answers, it is probably also true that the goals of the deposition are not being advanced. Unless the "extracurricular activity" is more important than discovering facts and information from this witness (something that is extremely unlikely), a return to asking questions and receiving answers is wise. The "cue" for analyzing the situation is clear and important: if you, as deposing counsel, are addressing opposing counsel instead of questioning the witness, you have abandoned the primary goal of obtaining information.

11.2.3   Do Not Play Opposing Counsel's Game: Act, Do Not React

This point is closely related to keeping the primary goal in mind. For whatever of the reasons that motivate the unacceptable behavior, the irritating defending attorney does not want the flow of information at the deposition to go forward. In other words, opposing counsel's primary goal is directly opposed to your primary goal. Responding to objections; debating points with counsel and the witness; unconsciously switching from open questions to closed, cross-examination style questions (as often occurs in response to a myriad of objections); becoming formalistic, objecting to routine and legitimate conferences between the witness and defense counsel that are not actually interfering with the deposition; and other such behavior on the part of deposing counsel all are good evidence that the irritating counsel is achieving the goal of preventing the flow of information, and that deposing counsel has lost focus on the goal of the deposition.

---

4. Fed. R. Civ. P. 30(d)(2) advisory committee's notes, limiting depositions to seven hours and one day: "if the deponent or another person [opposing counsel] impedes or delays the examination, the court must authorize extra time."

Instead of playing this game, simply ignore the annoying behavior by literally refusing to acknowledge the conduct in any way or even to look at opposing counsel. By so doing, and thereby demonstrating the futility of the conduct, you may make the annoying attorney eventually tire of the game and become much more docile. In short, behave as if opposing counsel were dead and no longer involved in the deposition. This approach requires discipline and patience, however, and it undoubtedly will throw the deposition off track somewhat because the witness may well be confused about what is happening as the objector screams to be recognized. ("Won't you even give me the courtesy of looking at me and answering my question about why this is relevant?") Nevertheless, demonstrating the futility of irritating behavior at the outset will result in a much more effective remainder of the deposition.

It is easier to tell you to ignore opposing counsel when irritating behavior begins then it will be for you to follow this advice. The problem is that a normal person's blood pressure begins to rise when opposing counsel launches into a five-minute harangue about your purported inability to ask proper questions and insistence on pursuing information that has nothing to do with the issues in the case. It is often not long before you explode in anger at defending counsel's behavior, threaten to call the magistrate judge, actually call the magistrate judge, and then take other steps further down the path to filing motions for protective orders, motions for failure to make discovery, and motions to impose sanctions. (Notice that none of this activity has anything to do with directly obtaining answers to questions about facts in the case, which means that defending counsel has won this round, no matter what the outcome is in the motions battle.)

The taking lawyer who becomes angry and engages in arguing with opposing counsel is the only one who suffers in the exchange. The defending lawyer has accomplished the goal, at least temporarily, of preventing the taking lawyer from obtaining information—the witness gets a rest while the attorneys squabble, and the court reporter is making money by transcribing each side's testy retorts. Worse, arguing with or berating opposing counsel accomplishes nothing. There is not one recorded instance in the entire history of the legal profession of one lawyer convincing another lawyer of the other lawyer's wrongheadedness (or of the irrelevance of a line of questions, or of the fact that a question was asked and answered earlier, or that it is remarkable that the opposing lawyer ever actually graduated from law school).

The answer to how to handle irritating opposing counsel is quite simple. Imagine the chair in which opposing counsel is sitting is empty, that opposing counsel has died and gone to the place where lawyers of that type spend eternity, and that all of opposing counsel's speeches are nothing but "white noise." Since white noise does not affect the deposition questions and answers, counsel should not pay attention to it. In short, ignore, do not respond.

Some lawyers will disagree with this advice, based on a belief that it is important to establish that the taker is in control of the deposition. We agree with this premise when the alternative is to permit obstructionist opposing counsel to restrict the flow of information from the witness, a matter discussed in the next section. But where the witness is answering your questions without surrendering to coaching by the defending lawyer, you have little to gain from an abstract battle over control. You are getting what you need from the witness, and that is what counts.

Too often the arguments between lawyers at a deposition resemble nature documentaries, where two bull elephant seals square off on the beach, smashing their chests into each other until one of them waddles off into the sea. Put grey suits on them and brush their whiskers down, and they fully resemble full-blown trial lawyers of the obstructionist species. Such behavior in seal society may preserve order and establish entitlement to attractive mates; in the deposition room, however, it accomplishes nothing useful and should be avoided. As long as uncoached answers are being received, the best tactic is to ignore opposing counsel. The lesson is to keep your eye on the prize. Everything else is unimportant.

Let's look at an example of this tactic of ignoring an irritating opposing counsel:

Q: Now, Ms. Adomaitis, what makes you believe that your broker was not handling your stock account properly?

Objection: Well, wait; let's just get our time periods straightened out here before we all get confused. What are you talking about? When she first believed that he was churning, or what?

Q: Mrs. Adomaitis, please answer the question.

Objection: Counsel, now, you haven't answered my question. I don't know when we are talking about here, and I'm sure that the witness doesn't either. That's just not the way to take an intelligent deposition, and I'm surprised your senior partners didn't tell you that, because maybe you just don't know. But you've got to have a time period for all these things.

Q: Ms. Adomaitis, do you remember the question?

A: Well, no, I'm not sure that I do.

Q: All right, let me ask it again. What makes you believe that your broker was not handling your stock account properly?

Objection: Counsel, you are just trying to confuse the witness now, by not telling her when you are asking about her knowledge. Clearly, she knows a lot of things today that she didn't know back when this guy was handling her account, and it's not fair for you to just ask about what she knows or what she knew without saying "when." So, why don't you ask a better question?[5]

Q: Ms. Adomaitis, please answer the question?

A: Yes. I think that I was first, you know, a little suspicious when I saw some interest charges on my monthly statements, and he wasn't very direct when I asked him about them.

The important things to notice here are that the attorney taking the deposition never responded to the challenge by the defending attorney and continued to press the witness for an answer. If we were watching this little drama, we would have seen that the taking attorney's eyes were kept on the witness at all times, never looking at defending counsel. No attention at all was paid to defending counsel's inappropriate comments; taking counsel did not even say, "Your objection is noted," or "The question is proper," or make any other comment indicating that defending counsel's words were being heard. The objection will be in the record whether taking counsel acknowledges it or not; the question is either proper or improper regardless of what either side says—comments and argument add nothing to the record. By ignoring the comments, the questioning lawyer will take almost all of the fun out of his game for the defending lawyer. The proof of this is often seen when, after receiving no visible reaction to a tirade, opposing counsel eventually decides to give it up and sit quietly. It is no fun to put on a show if the audience does not react at all. By watching the witness throughout defending counsel's comments and then immediately asking the witness, "Please

---

5. "Why don't you ask a better question?" or "Why don't you ask the witness . . . ?" are apparently among the most potent needles a defending attorney can jab into a deposing attorney. There are reported instances of attorneys getting into physical wrestling matches in the deposition room, spilling out into the hallway, over who has the right to suggest questions at a deposition; and there is one instance, transcribed in what has become a famous page of transcript in Washington, D.C., where the attorneys end a series of bitter exchanges about "suggested" questions with the taking attorney shouting at the defending attorney, "___ you, I'll ask whatever questions I want to!" This is probably not the most efficient way to obtain information from the witness.

answer the question?" you clearly send the message that those interruptions will not succeed in hiding information and that the witness should not gain any courage from them.

The implicit message to the witness from deposing counsel is: "I will stay here until next Tuesday if it's necessary because of the jerk sitting alongside of you; so you decide—do we do this the easy way, or do we do this the hard way, because we *are* going to do it." Where the witness cannot really understand why the objection is important, or even understand it is being made at all, this sort of tactic has a good chance of success, where success is defined, of course, as obtaining information from the witness and discouraging opposing counsel from continuing this behavior.

Having said this, sometimes merely acknowledging that opposing counsel has made an objection will cause the deposition to move forward. If opposing counsel feels it necessary, for reasons of ego or otherwise, to receive some sort of recognition of their comments and statements, and none is forthcoming, the disruptive behavior may continue until that recognition is given. If opposing counsel does not soften his disruptive stance after being ignored for fifteen minutes, questioning counsel might consider a simple response, without looking at counsel, "Your objection is noted. Now, Ms. Adomaitis, please answer my question." Remember, the objective is to get answers to questions, not to fight with opposing counsel.

11.2.4 Ask Good Questions

One of the most effective ways of limiting the impact of irritating counsel, who is waiting to pounce on every minor flaw in questioning, is simply to ask good questions. While certainly every question cannot be planned in advance, it is always appropriate to spend some predeposition time preparing matters like the form of questions and the proper document handling. If you follow the advice of chapter eight and ask simple, open-ended questions, frequently beginning with "who, what, where, why, when, how, tell us, describe, and explain," you will provide little opportunity for legitimate objection. These questions not only frustrate obstructionist counsel because there is little opportunity to object, but they also send the message that you are a competent and professional attorney.

If, in the alternative, opposing counsel has a legitimate reason to object to questions on the grounds that they are compound, for example, arguing in defense of those questions is merely a further waste of time; correct the problem with the form of the question by asking two questions instead of one. But there is no doubt that this type of success encourages the irritating opposing counsel. In reality, there is nothing obstructionist (although it may be "irritating") about opposing counsel making legitimate objections.

It is incumbent on you, the questioning counsel, to take away that opportunity by asking unobjectionable questions, thereby frustrating the defending lawyer who is intent on disruptive behavior. And, of course, if you take the allegedly irritating behavior to the court, it does not help your position when opposing counsel proves to have made a legitimate objection.

11.3   The Obstructing Opposing Counsel

While the approach for dealing with the merely irritating opposing counsel is to ignore the behavior, this tactic does not work with the obstructionist, who actually precludes you from obtaining necessary information. Ignoring opposing counsel who coaches the witness's answers or who improperly instructs the witness not to answer rewards what is clearly improper behavior. The question is how to control such behavior.

Obstructionist behavior can take many forms:

- Making objections that inform the witness of how the question should be handled.

- Whispering in the witness's ear, while the question is pending, about how to respond substantively to the question.

- Signaling the witness by nudging, kicking, or otherwise physically contacting the witness.

- Making hand signals to the witness on how to respond to a question.

- Pointing out portions of a document to help the witness answer a question.

- Writing notes to the witness.

- Sending messages to the witness via cell phone or Blackberry.

- Making "helpful" suggestions to the taking lawyer on how to ask a question, but actually coaching the witness (e.g.: "Why don't you ask the witness whether she ever, even once in her life, had anything at all to do with even the slightest instance of price-fixing with her competitors?").

- Engaging in the rehearsed charade of "Objection, vague," followed by the witness saying, "I don't understand the question."

- The similar charade of "Answer only if you know" followed by the witness saying, "I don't know."

These are some of the more common examples of obstructionist behavior, but hardly a complete catalog. The creativity and ingenuity of opposing counsel in behaving inappropriately limits our efforts to come up with a definitive list of everything that can be done to obstruct the flow of information at a deposition.

11.3.1   Relate to the Witness

One tactic for controlling obstructionist behavior is to try to develop a relationship to the witness. Even when the witness is the chief executive officer of the opposing company, you may well be able to develop a relationship that will help you (and ultimately the witness, when their time is an issue) when opposing counsel becomes obnoxious and unreasonable. For example, when a simple question is asked and opposing counsel claims that it is actually as complicated as the Theory of Relativity, the witness may be too honest or too embarrassed to agree. Consider the following exchange, which is rather common:

> Q: Ms. Lemontas, how long have you been in charge of sales for the Crabtree Company?
>
> Objection: Counsel, you have got to be more specific than that. I mean, what are we talking about in terms of "in charge" of sales? That could mean, "How long has she been involved in selling any products for them?" or "How long has she supervised anyone in sales?" or any number of things. You have to ask a better question.
>
> Q: Ms. Lemontas, do you understand my question, "How long have you been in charge of sales for Crabtree?"
>
> A: Well, yes, I think that I do.
>
> Q: Could you answer the question, please?

One might think that the responsible executive, as well as the lowly corporate employee, would carefully follow the defending attorney's lead in such a situation, but in fact the relationship is just not that simple. First, at the human level, the witness may feel a bit offended by being told by his own lawyer that she does not understand something, especially when that something seems perfectly clear and understandable. Second, while the witness may be willing to sit quietly while the lawyer makes a speech about simple things being complicated, it is quite another thing to be called on to agree. That direct question, "Do you understand?" calls on the witness to lie or to tell the truth, under oath, on the record, and that requires more deliberation than just sitting and letting the lawyer makes noises. Third, as the witness may already have learned in this deposition, the net effect of these kinds of arguments is that the information is eventually obtained, but it just takes longer. It wastes the witness's time (and the company's money). This last consideration is especially persuasive with executives and professionals, who have a healthy estimate of the value of their own time. Sometimes this fact can be brought home to the witness rather forcibly:

Q: Doctor, I am sure your time is worth more than mine, but it appears that at the pace we are moving it will not be possible to finish up your deposition this morning. I will do my best, however, to tie it up by three o'clock or so this afternoon. So let me again ask the question I just asked and to which your counsel objected. We would prefer to avoid having to go to the judge to ask for an extension of the deposition.

11.3.2   *Making Your Record and Escalating the Response*

Every once in a while it is useful to demonstrate to opposing counsel that you are aware of the tactics he is using and that those tactics are being tracked for later discussions with the court. Obviously, if objections about "ambiguous" or "compound" or "confusing" are having little effect on the witness's answers and your ability to gain information, there is no sense at all in having any discussion with opposing counsel. In such situations, treat the lawyer on the other side as merely an irritant and stick with rule number one: Ignore.

Sometimes, however, such obstructionist tactics cause trouble; they may not completely halt the flow of information, but they do slow it down or affect the quality of the information so the effect is felt. You can easily note each obstruction to the free flow of information on the record for later reference by saying something such as, "Let the record reflect that Mr. Barkauskas is again conferring with the witness before the witness has answered the question, and please mark this exchange for transcription for later motions."

If the interruptions continue and become more serious in their disruptive effect, and the low-intensity "note-for-the-record" approach does not discourage them, the next approach is to escalate the response and draw a line. A typical series of escalating responses is to:

- Note for the record the improper conduct in which counsel is engaging: "Let the record reflect that counsel is conferring with the witness while the question is pending."

- Have the court reporter mark the point in the record where the offending conduct is occurring: "Counsel, this is the third time in a row that you have conferred with the witness while a question is pending. You know that is improper, and I am asking the court reporter to mark the deposition."[6]

- Threaten to seek the assistance of the court: "Let the record reflect again that counsel is conferring with the witness while a question is pending. Counsel, if this conduct persists, you will leave me little choice but to ask the court for assistance. Of course, if I am forced to do that, I will also ask that your client be held responsible for costs and expenses and that."

- Actually seek the assistance of the court. After a sufficient record of obstruction has been created, tell opposing counsel that you are suspending the deposition to seek a protective order from the magistrate judge. Ask the reporter to mark offending sections of the transcript and to be prepared to read those sections if the phone call or meeting with the judge can be arranged. Call the magistrate and ask for a very short hearing in chambers or for permission to state the problem over the speakerphone. Keep your presentation short and to the point. Don't whine. Request a protective order directing opposing counsel to obey the rules and to refrain from making the improper objections or counseling with the witness before an answers unless privilege is involved.

- Take a break and talk with opposing counsel away from the witness. Counsel cannot afford to back down in front of the client—that is not the way to maintain good client relationships. Sometimes a reasonable request made in the hallway, apart from the client, will have better prospects for success: "Bill, this is getting out of hand. I don't want to break this off and see Magistrate Jones—you're busy and so am I, and the judge won't like it—but you are putting me in a corner. If you don't stop the conferring and interruptions, I am going to have to call her."

- Note on the record the time consumed by the obstructionist counsel taking breaks, conferring while a question is pending, and other disruptive contact: "Let the record reflect that counsel and the witness took a break while a question was pending and were gone for seventeen minutes."

---

6. Most court reporting machines have a key that places a mark in the margin of the tape or electronically marks the point where the behavior occurs. The purpose of this is so the reporter can quickly locate a particular question or answer.

The Advisory Committee Notes to 31(d)(2), the rule limiting depositions to seven hours on one day, state that the court must grant additional time if the witness or counsel engage in inappropriate, time-consuming conduct. In fact, computerized transcription equipment has become so sophisticated that the amount of time in the deposition devoted to legitimate purposes (asking questions and receiving answers) and obstructionist conduct can be calculated so that the full seven hours of deposition testimony can be guaranteed.

11.3.3   Use the Discipline of the Rules

While it may not always be evident, many lawyers feel somewhat constrained when they are confronted by a clear statement in the law that certain kinds of conduct are prohibited. Bringing to the offending lawyer's attention the prohibitions of Rule 30(d)(1) may control the improper conduct.

Taking Counsel: Counsel, that last objection was argumentative and suggestive and clearly designed to coach the witness. You know that Rule 30(c)(2) of the Federal Rules of Civil Procedure states that "an objection must be stated concisely in a nonargumentative and nonsuggestive manner." Please do not violate that rule again.

11.3.4   Record the Deposition on Video

The most effective method for controlling inappropriate behavior is a video deposition. Even if the deposition was not originally noticed as being a video deposition, counsel subjected to improper behavior can announce, perhaps just before the lunch break, that the remainder of the deposition will be recorded on video. Opposing counsel can object, but under the rules the video recording should go forward, subject later resolution of that objection. If, before the deposition, you know that opposing counsel has a reputation for obstructionist behavior or previous experience with this lawyer makes it likely that improper behavior is likely to occur, the original notice should announce that it will be a video deposition. Video recording the deposition may stop the behavior before it starts. Rule 30(b)(3) gives the noticing attorney the option of video recording, voice recording, or stenographically recording the deposition. For whatever reasons, lawyers who engage in the most outrageous conduct when only a court reporter is present tend to be on their best behavior when their actions are being video recorded.[7] Perhaps their knowledge that the video can be shown to the judge or magistrate accounts for this, but, regardless of the reasons, it works. For those opponents who obstruct not merely by objections and instructions not to answer, but by coughing, sighing, making faces and gestures, and other activity not shown on the transcript or on the head and shoulders shot of the deponent used in most videotaped depositions, a second camera, operated by a second videographer, can be brought to the deposition and aimed at the opposing counsel at all times, or at taking and defending counsel and the witness. This turns the process into a rather expensive deposition, but if the witness is important, enduring this expense for a half day may be well worth the cost. In this way, there will be indisputable videographic support for a claim that opposing counsel had been engaging in obstructive behavior.

11.4   The Blocking Opposing Counsel: The Special Problem of Instructions Not to Answer

Instructing a witness not to answer can be a perfectly proper response by opposing counsel to a deposition question, if:

- the question calls for privileged information, or

- the question inquires into an area that the court has previously ordered off limits (by discovery order or protective order), or

- opposing counsel is adjourning the deposition to seek an order terminating the deposition because of improper conduct.

A problem arises, however, when opposing counsel gives the instruction, not because of one of these legitimate reasons, but because he is concerned (or knows) that the answer will be unfavorable to his case.

An instruction not to answer is a complete frustration of the ability to obtain information, at least on the topic covered by the question. The first step in dealing with such an instruction is to request opposing counsel to state the reasons for the instruction.

> Q: Mr. Glietus, when did you first learn about the problems with the computer design?
>
> Objection: Hold on. I have no idea of what you mean by first learning about the problems. You make it sound like all of sudden he learned this. He could have gradually learned about it.
>
> Q: Please answer the question.

---

7. *See* section 1.13.2.

Objection: No way. I am not going to let him answer that question the way you are asking it.

Q: Again, please answer the question.

Objection: Are you deaf? I am instructing the witness not to answer.

Q: Mr. Glietus, are you going to follow your lawyer's instruction and refuse to answer?

A: Yes.

Q: Counsel, I ask you to state the reason for your instruction not to answer.

Opposing Counsel: Because your question stinks.

Q: Rule 30(c)(2) states that an attorney may only instruct a witness not to answer in order to preserve a privilege; to prevent the violation of a protective order; or to adjourn the deposition to seek an order limiting or terminating the deposition based on harassment, annoyance, or embarrassment of the deponent. Which one of these are you relying on?

Opposing Counsel: I don't have to tell you that.

Q: Are you refusing to give the basis for your instruction?

Opposing Counsel: Yes.

Q: Counsel, I am sure you are aware that Rule 26(b)(5) requires that if you are claiming privilege as the basis for your instruction, you must "expressly" claim the privilege and describe the documents, communications, or things in a manner that will allow the opposing attorney to determine the applicability of the privilege. Rule 37(a)(1) also requires that we confer to see if I can obtain the information called for by my question without seeking court action. Do you see any way for me to get that information or to get around this problem?[8]

Opposing Counsel: You guys who sit there and spout off rules make me sick. If you don't have any more questions, I suggest we end this deposition now.

---

8. It would be a good idea for lawyers to copy the paragraphs comprising this statement about claims of privilege to include them in the notebook that is taken to every deposition so that rule sections can be quoted effectively.

Once an instruction not to answer has been given, it is difficult for opposing counsel to now permit the answer without losing face. The attempt is worth making, however, but a likely, more successful approach is to caucus with opposing counsel out in the hallway away from the witness. If you have been unsuccessful in getting the deposition back on track, make a record of the effort after returning to the deposition room.

If opposing counsel will not bend on a particular point, it makes sense to try to exhaust other topics before seeking the assistance of the court. In fact, most judges do not want to hear from counsel regarding discovery disputes until the deposition has been completed on all other topics. Assuming that the deposition continues on to other matters and proceeds with less acrimony, it may even be possible to get an answer to the question that engendered the illegitimate instruction not to answer. Attempting to finish before going to the judge is also a good idea—if the deposition is adjourned to seek an order compelling an answer and the court refuses to grant the order, opposing counsel may oppose resuming the deposition. Finishing the deposition also allows you time to calmly consider the legal merits of the instruction outside the heated atmosphere of the deposition room. Merely state that you are going to proceed to other topics and are not waiving your right to return to the problematic topic or to seek an order compelling discovery. Be sure to make the motion to compel discovery reasonably quickly after the deposition is adjourned or suspended so that the offending party cannot muddy the water by arguing that you waited too long before moving and was trying to gain some illegitimate advantage by sitting on your hands.

Note that if the instruction not to answer is based on belief that the question is intended to harass, annoy, or embarrass the witness,[9] the rules require the instructing lawyer to terminate or suspend the deposition to allow a protective order to be sought from the court. It is usually in neither side's interest to terminate the deposition at this point. (One side wants to finish questioning, the other side wants to have the witness released.) The problem can be solved by the parties agreeing to continue with the questioning and then to decide at the end of the deposition whether the matter should be brought to the judge or magistrate for a ruling on whether the witness will answer the question. Of course, after the deposition is completed on everything but the contested question, the dispute will disappear if you withdraw the question because you no longer need the answer.

11.4.1 Try Again Later

Many lawyers are in a feisty mood at the beginning of the deposition, but become increasingly subdued as the day drags on. Lawyers who are quick

---

9. *See* Fed. R. Civ. P. 30(d)(3)(A).

to make objections and give instructions not to answer become increasingly interested in just getting the deposition over and done with. This means that sometime around four in the afternoon, it is worth again asking the question that earlier in the day drew an instruction not to answer. It is best to phrase the second attempt differently than the first try, but is possible that the question will now be answered without any interference by opposing counsel because she does not recognize the question as being the same, because she just does not care anymore, or because she realizes she has no basis for opposing an answer.

11.5   Obstructing Behavior That Is Not Obstructing Behavior

There are several common deposition tactics that at first glance appear to interfere with your ability to obtain information, but with experience are easy to deal with. Let's look at several of these.

11.5.1   *Objection, Vague*

Certainly, it is an acceptable tactic to ignore objections that do not coach the witness, unless, of course, they are valid—in which case the question should be reconsidered and, perhaps, rephrased. Sometimes, however, opposing counsel and the witness have worked out a code or routine, particularly for questions that have been objected to as vague, which effectively stops the flow of information. Here is an example:

> Q: Ms. Lemontas, how large is the sales department at the Crabtree Company?
>
> Opposing Counsel: Objection, vague.
>
> Q: Ms. Lemontas, do you understand the question?
>
> A: No, I can't. I don't understand it.

When this pattern is repeated every time opposing counsel makes a vagueness objection, it may indicate that opposing counsel and witness planned and rehearsed this routine. Here are some tactics to handle this situation. First, do not ask the witness whether the witness understands the question. Most likely the witness will say "no," or, alternatively, you will have succeeded in putting the idea in the witness's mind that saying "no" is an easy way to avoid giving an answer. Instead, merely ask the witness to answer the question. Second, if the witness does respond by saying, "I don't understand the question," the easiest method of dealing with this tactic is then to ask the witness, "What it is about the question you don't understand?"

Q: Ms. Lemontas, what is it that you do not understand about the question?

Opposing Counsel: She doesn't know whether you are talking about the number of employees in the sales department or how big that physical area of the company is.

A: That's right.

Q: I am asking about how many employees. How big is the sales department?

A variation of the vagueness game is when, as above, opposing counsel argues that the question can mean one of two or more things. A quick way of punishing this behavior is always to ask for all of the alternatives.

Q: Ms. Lemontas, what is it that you do not understand about the question?

Opposing Counsel: She doesn't know whether you are talking about the number of employees of the sales department or how big that physical area of the company is.

A: That's right.

Q: Well, let's take both of them. First, tell me the physical size of the sales department.

A: About 2,000 square feet.

Q: And how many employees does the sales department have?

A: About thirty-six.

Q: And what were the sales made by that department last fiscal year?

Opposing Counsel: Objection. Are you talking net sales or gross sales or sales before or after interest, taxes, depreciation, and amortization?

Q: Ms. Lemontas, what were sales dollars last fiscal year before interest payments were deducted?

A: About 420 million dollars.

Q: And what were they before interest and taxes were deducted?

A: About 570 million dollars.

Q: And what were they for the last fiscal year before interest and taxes and depreciation deductions?

A: They were about 620 million dollars.

Q: And what were sales last fiscal year through the sales department before interest, taxes, depreciation, and amortization?

A: EBITDA—that's earnings before interest, taxes, depreciation, and amortization, for the last fiscal year, were about 670 million dollars.

This tactic by defending counsel will cease when she realizes that every time all of the proposed "ambiguities" are raised, you will follow with more questions and learn even more information.

11.5.2 Dictionary

Sometimes witnesses play this game without any help from defending counsel. Sometimes counsel plays it alone. Here is an example:

Q: What procedures does the purchasing department follow in placing orders for computer parts?

A: What do you mean by "procedures"?

Q: Well, I mean what does the purchasing department routinely do when it buys computer parts?

A: What do you mean by "routinely"?

Q: I mean regularly. Do you have a regular practice for ordering parts?

A: I am not sure what you mean by "regular" practice.

It could be that the witness may well be genuinely confused by the meaning of the questions, although, in the example given above, that is unlikely. Here it is more likely that this is a sharp witness who is attempting to lure deposing counsel into playing the game of dictionary, in which the witness tries to divert attention from a question the witness would prefer not to answer. The way to respond to this game is to turn it back on the witness.

Q: Mr. Vitar, what precautions did you take when you learned that the boiler was overheating?

Opposing Counsel: Objection, vague. What do you mean by precautions?

Q: Mr. Vitar, are you familiar with the word "precautions"?

A: Yes.

Q: What does that word mean to you?

A: Well, I guess it means what you do to prevent problems.

Q: OK, using that definition, what precautions did you take when you learned that the boiler was overheating?

If the definition used by the witness differs from yours, then first get the information using the witness's definition. Then you can insert your definition and ask the question again.

CHAPTER TWELVE

PROTECTIVE ORDERS AND APPLICATIONS TO THE COURT

They say that the first inclination an animal has is to protect itself.

—Diogenes Laertius

12.1   Protective Orders

Problems that occur at deposition can sometimes be anticipated, and proactive motion practice can eliminate them. If the deposition has been noticed for an inconvenient time or place; or if privilege issues are likely to arise; or if there may be questioning that exceeds the permissible scope of discovery or a court-ordered limitation; or if opposing counsel's past behavior in the case suggests improper behavior may occur at this deposition; or if there is concern that trade secrets will be revealed during the course of the questioning, then one of the parties or the witness should seek a protective order in an effort to resolve the problem before the deposition is convened.[1] It is often less costly and more convenient to resolve anticipated problems before they arise, either by stipulation or court hearing and order, than to attempt to do so after the problems show up during the course of the deposition.[2]

Rule 26(c) gives an indication of the wide variety of problems that may be the topic of a protective order. Under this rule, a court may "issue an order to protect a party or person from annoyance, embarrassment, oppression, or undue burden or expense," including one or more of the following:

---

1. It would be unusual for an unrepresented, nonparty witness to apply for a protective order. An exception is the nonparty 30(b)(6) designee, who is likely to be represented by the organization's counsel, and that counsel will understand the opportunity to seek protection from improper treatment or questioning. Another exception might be the deposition of an additional competitor in a lawsuit between two firms in an industry; there, everyone will be represented and more than adequately protected (or over-protected).

2. In fact, if you fail to obtain a protective order in advance, you may not be allowed to object to the discovery during the deposition. Mitsui & Co. (U.S.A.), Inc. v. Puerto Rico Water Resources Authority, 93 F.R.D. 62 (D.P.R. 1981).

(A) forbidding the disclosure or discovery;

(B) specifying the terms, including time and place, for . . . discovery;

(C) prescribing a discovery method other than the one selected by the party seeking discovery;

(D) forbidding inquiry into certain matters, or limiting the scope of . . . discovery to certain matters;

(E) designating the persons who may be present while the discovery is conducted;

(F) requiring that a deposition be sealed and opened only on court order;

(G) requiring that a trade secret or other confidential research, development, or commercial information not be revealed or be revealed only in a specified way; and

(H) requiring that the parties simultaneously file specified documents or information in sealed envelopes, to be opened as the court directs.[3]

A protective order can be sought from either a court in the district in which the action is pending or the district where the deposition is to be taken. Under Rule 26(c), however, a certification must be filed with the motion that there has been a conference or a good-faith attempt to confer with other affected parties in an effort to resolve the dispute without court action. Many of the jurisdictions following the pre-1993 version of the Federal Rules of Civil Procedure also have rules imposing a similar requirement. The risk of bringing a motion for a protective order is that if the motion is unsuccessful, the court may order the moving party or lawyer to pay the opposing party's reasonable expenses, including attorney's fees, in opposing the motion. Conversely, if the motion is granted, the opposing party may be required to pay the reasonable expenses, including attorney's fees, for bringing the motion. The parties should therefore try to resolve the dispute during their conference. (As an aside, clients are often upset when called on to pay costs and fees because their own counsel was thought to be engaging in improper conduct, especially when the client sees no benefit to such conduct.)

While protective orders have traditionally been used defensively—to ward off anticipated improper conduct—they can also be used offensively. For

---

3. Fed. R. Civ. P. 26(c).

example, you can seek a protective order in advance of the deposition that specifically allows you to inquire into certain topics on which you anticipate that opposing counsel will be raising objections and directing the witness not to answer. This use of the motion for protective order promotes efficiency because it resolves the issue and allows the parties and witness to prepare for what will actually occur. Some time, expense, and inconvenience at the deposition may be saved. You may also seek protective orders for affirmative relief if problems arise once the deposition has begun.

Motions for protective orders are generally based on facts, rather than on extensive legal analysis. The basis for a protective order should take three sentences to state, not three paragraphs or three pages, and it certainly should not take thirty pages. A written motion for a protective order can be simple in form and ordinarily does not require the support of lengthy case authority. Rule 26(b)(1) provides the primary authority for a motion for a protective order granting permission to inquire into an area. This rule allows discovery into all matters, not privileged, that are relevant or are reasonably calculated to lead to the discovery of admissible evidence. Thus, the best support for a protective-order motion seeking permission to inquire into an area is a strong factual argument that the area is directly relevant to the case or may reasonably lead to admissible evidence.

A motion for a protective order seeking to preclude inquiry into an area should, conversely, demonstrate that the material sought to be protected is either privileged or is so clearly irrelevant that it could not reasonably lead to admissible evidence. If a protective order is sought barring certain conduct because of the opposing attorney's previous improper behavior, attach relevant transcript excerpts and video clips from previous depositions to the motion. Matters of privilege aside, the question of whether topics are open to discovery is essentially a preliminary question of fact to be resolved by the court by comparing the issues in the case to the materials sought to be discovered or protected. The court may engage in an in camera review of material where the anticipated questioning involves a claim of privilege, a request for protection of trade secrets, or harassment, annoyance, or embarrassment amounting to invasion of privacy by bringing up sensitive personal matters. Sometimes the court will permit outside counsel for the party seeking discovery to participate in the in camera inspections, while excluding the inside counsel. This inspection would be governed by rules of confidentiality, which outside counsel must obey. The counsel producing the documents for in camera review should be on guard in this circumstance, even if discovery is ultimately denied, because the mere act of inspection by opposing counsel may provide leads for other discovery and therefore confer an advantage (like a "fruit of the forbidden tree" problem in criminal law). This advantage may occur even if counsel seeking discovery does not violate confidentiality rules, because what counsel has seen and discussed with the court may, even subconsciously, influence later requests and decisions on further discovery. In arguing against participation by discovering counsel in any in camera inspection, opposing counsel should make the court aware of these concerns. At the least, counsel opposing discovery should argue that any in-house counsel appearing in the case should not participate in the review and is not permitted to discuss the review with outside counsel.

12.1.1   The "Meet and Confer" Requirement

Rule 37(a)(1) requires as a prerequisite to any discovery motion that the parties meet and confer in an attempt to resolve the problem on their own without court intervention. Many courts, by local rule, require the filing of a certification that this meeting has occurred and has not been successful. Always check the local rules of the court in which the motion is being filed to determine how compliance with the meet and confer requirement can be satisfied. Even in the absence of such a requirement in the particular jurisdiction, it makes good sense to discuss the possibilities of resolving the problem with opposing counsel before appearing before the judge or magistrate. Counsel gain an advantage if the court becomes convinced that the lawyers are capable of behaving like grown-ups, or at least polite adolescents.

12.2   Applications to the Court

Modern discovery is intended to function largely without judicial intervention. But when you believe you must seek help from the court because of instances of misconduct or anticipated misconduct, you have several approaches available.

Where permitted by courts, you can resolve many problems through a telephone conference with opposing counsel and the judge or magistrate. Telephone conferences are a quick and efficient method of resolving disputes without burdening the court's docket, and they are preferred by many judges and magistrates over formal in-court hearings with written motions and supporting briefs. Telephone conferences also can quickly end problems and allow the deposition to reconvene without waiting the weeks, or perhaps months, for a written motion to be drafted, placed on the motion calendar, heard, and finally resolved. Although "Let's get the judge on the phone!" is usually wielded more often as a threat than a real suggestion, a request to the court for a telephone conference, where permitted, should be the first line of attack in resolving problems occurring during the deposition where discussion with opposing counsel has failed. Some judges and magistrates, however, will not hear discovery disputes over the telephone. Before breaking off the deposition to call the judge, be sure to first check to see if the judge or magistrate is willing to take such calls and is actually available to do so. At the pretrial conference under Rule 16, you could ask the judge or magistrate about the court's willingness to accept such telephone calls, and, when dates for depositions are scheduled, ask the court's clerk about the court's availability.

For all of the motions listed below, it is still necessary to comply with the meet and confer requirement discussed in section 12.1.1 above. Do not neglect to do so.

12.2.1   Rule 30(d)—Duration, Termination, and Suspension

Under Rule 30(d)(3), or Rule 30(d) of the pre-1993 version of the rules, a party or the witness may suspend the deposition to move for a court order to terminate or limit the deposition as provided in Rule 26(c) (or move for such an order without suspending the deposition), because the deposition is being conducted in bad faith or in such an unreasonable manner as to annoy, embarrass, or oppress the witness or party. The motion can be made either to the court in which the action is pending or the court in the district where the deposition is being taken. If either court terminates the deposition, only the court in which the action is pending may permit it to resume. Under the provisions of Rule 37(a)(5), the court can award expenses to a party for the cost of either bringing or defending the motion.

12.2.2   Rule 30(d)(1)—Deposition Time Limits

Rule 30(d)(1) permits the district court to issue an order in a particular case to alter the time limits for conducting a deposition, which otherwise is one day of seven hours.[4] The rule also permits the court to extend the time for a fair examination (for example, where the subject matter is especially complex) or because the witness or another party has impeded or delayed the examination. The motion is made to the court in which the action is pending and, if the court finds that one of the parties has impeded, delayed, or frustrated the fair conduct of the deposition, it may impose sanctions on that party. It is for purposes of motions such as these that modern electronic court-reporting systems have the ability to track the actual time during which examination of the witness is occurring (by recording starting and ending times of questioning sessions on the tape or electronic recording), and have this recorded separately from the time expended for breaks, arguing objections, conferences with the deponent by defending counsel, or any other interruption. Most courts and the Advisory Committee view the seven-hour time limit as the time during which the actual questioning of the deponent by the examining lawyer is occurring.

---

4. To avoid wholesale "opting-out" within a district, these orders must be case specific and are not to be incorporated into "rules of court" applying across the board, as the Advisory Committee's Notes make clear.

12.2.3   Rule 30(g)—Failure to Attend

If the party noticing the deposition fails to attend and proceed with the deposition, or if the party fails to subpoena a witness who then fails to attend the deposition, the other parties attending the deposition may ask the court in which the action is pending to award them their reasonable expenses, including reasonable attorney's fees. (Parties often stipulate that each party will assure the attendance of its employees who are not sufficiently senior in the organization to be summoned by a mere notice of deposition. Of course, such a stipulation would not bind the recalcitrant employee, who may insist on a subpoena.)

12.2.4   Rule 32(d)(4)—Errors in Preparing, Signing, and Certifying

Federal Rule of Civil Procedure 32(d)(4) permits the deposition, or a portion thereof, to be suppressed because of errors and irregularities in the transcribing, preparing, signing, certifying, sealing, endorsing, transmitting, filing, or in the way in which the officer is otherwise dealing with the deposition. The motion to suppress must be made with reasonable promptness after the defect is, or with due diligence might have been, ascertained.

12.2.5   Rule 37(a)—Refusals to Answer and Failures to Designate

If a witness refuses to answer a question at a deposition or if a party fails to make a designation under Rule 30(b)(6), the questioning party or, in the case of a failure to designate under Rule 30(b)(6), the noticing party, may move for an order compelling an answer or designation. Rule 37(a)(4) treats an evasive or incomplete answer as a failure to answer. Under Rule 37(a)(2), any motion concerning a party is made to the court in which the action is pending, while motions concerning the witness are made to the court in the district where the deposition is being taken (because that is where the witness is subject to the court's power). Under the pre-1993 version of the rule (still in effect in many state jurisdictions), motions concerning parties could also be made to the court in the district where the deposition was being taken. The court may award expenses for unsuccessfully bringing or opposing the motion pursuant to Rule 37(a)(4).

12.2.6   Rule 37(b)—Failure to Obey an Order Compelling an Answer or Designation

If the court issues an order under Rule 37(a) compelling a witness to answer a question at the deposition or compelling a party to designate a witness pursuant to Rule 30(b)(6), and there is a refusal to obey the order, the court may impose a variety of sanctions against the witness or party. The court in the district where the deposition is being taken may hold a witness in contempt if she refuses to obey an order to answer. The witness may also be held in contempt for refusing to be sworn. A party who refuses to answer a question or to designate after being ordered to do so is subject to the further sanctions listed in Rule 37(b)(2). A party failing to abide by the order, the attorney advising the party, or both can be required to pay the reasonable expenses, including attorney's fees, caused by the failure.

12.2.7   Rule 37(d)—Failure of a Party to Appear

If a party or an officer, director, or managing agent of a party, or a person designated to testify pursuant to Federal Rules of Civil Procedure 30(b)(6) fails to appear at the deposition after being served with notice, the court in which the action is pending may make whatever orders are just, including imposing any of the sanctions listed in Rule 37(b)(2)(A)–(C). The court can also require the party and the attorney advising the party, or both, to pay the reasonable expenses, including attorney's fees, caused by the failure to appear. That the discovery is objectionable is no defense to the motion unless the party has already filed a motion for a protective order.

12.2.8   An Example

Let's see how one kind of these disputes actually arises during a deposition and review the process for obtaining a hearing over the telephone:

> Q: Mr. Steponkis, let me ask you a few questions about the early days of your corporation. Who were the original shareholders?
>
> Opposing Counsel: Objection. That was ten years ago. It has nothing at all to do with this case. Let's try to stick to relevant questions here, Adrian.
>
> Q: Mr. Steponkis, will you answer the question, please? Who were the original shareholders?
>
> Opposing Counsel: Adrian, I just objected to that question. Now, you're not going to try to play hardball here, are you? Why don't you move on?
>
> Q: Are you going to answer the question, Mr. Steponkis?
>
> Opposing Counsel: I'm sorry, you are being so unreasonable, Adrian. I'm going to instruct the witness not to answer.

Q: Mr. Steponkis, will you answer the question, please?

A: No, I am going to follow the instructions of my lawyer.

Q: Well, let me ask this, then. Were the shares originally held by more than ten people?

Opposing Counsel: Again, this just has nothing to do with the issues here, and I instruct Mr. Steponkis that he need not answer this question.

Q: Mr. Steponkis, how many people held the shares originally?

A: I'm not going to answer the question, on the advice of my attorney.

Q: Counsel, are you claiming some sort of privilege here? You realize, of course, that under Rule 30(d)(1) a witness may be instructed not to answer only to preserve a privilege, or because I am violating a protective order, or because you are adjourning the deposition so you can seek an order terminating or limiting the deposition. Which one of these reasons are you relying on?

Opposing Counsel: I'm claiming that these questions have nothing to do with the claims or defenses in the case, or with discovering admissible evidence in the case, and are far beyond the scope permitted of Rule 26. So, the witness does not have to answer them.

Q: Mr. Steponkis, let me see if I can get at the information in another way. There is some question whether the owners on the certificate of incorporation were all of the original owners. Let me show you that certificate, which is Steponkis Deposition Exhibit 13. Are those all of the original owners?

Opposing Counsel: Same objection. You are way out of line here, Adrian. Just ask relevant questions, and we will have no problems, but you're just not going to snoop around on some fishing expedition.

Q: Mr. Steponkis, will you answer my last question about the certificate?

A: No, I am going to follow my lawyer's advice and decline to answer the question.

Q: Counsel, this is important to me, so before I call the magistrate, let me confer with you, as required by the rules,[5] to see if there is anything further I can do or if there is some agreement or arrangement we can make so that I can get the information I need.

Opposing Counsel: I think I have made my position very clear. I am not budging.

Q: Well, since this is the last area I need to question the witness about, I might as well see if we can get the magistrate on the phone right now rather than waiting until the deposition is concluded.

Since the deposing attorney has now asked about the same subject matter in three different ways, a solid record has been made demonstrating that discovery in that area is being precluded by directions to the witness not to answer. Counsel also has specifically asked whether the instructions not to answer were premised on a claim of privilege, and the defending attorney refused to claim privilege or any of the grounds permitted under Rule 30(d)(1), relying instead on a "beyond the scope of Rule 26 discovery" argument. Arguably, a question exceeding the proper scope of discovery is designed to oppress, embarrass, or harass. Let's return to the deposition room.

Counsel: Mr. Reporter, would you please mark those last few pages, where I am asking about the original owners of the corporation and the certificate of incorporation? Then, let's just go off the record until I can get the magistrate on the telephone.

[After the magistrate is on the telephone:]

Your Honor, we have a problem here in the Smith case, Docket Number C-93-1443. Plaintiff is taking the deposition of Mr. Julius Steponkis, the vice-president of the defendant corporation, and we have asked who the original

---

5. Fed. R. Civ. P. 37(a)(2)(B).

	shareholders were and how many there were. The defendant has instructed the witness not to answer on the grounds that the information being sought is beyond the scope of discovery under Rule 26. Let me now orally certify, as required by Rule 37(a)(2)(B), that I have in good faith conferred with opposing counsel in an attempt to avoid the need for court action, but that has been unsuccessful. We have the reporter here, prepared to read the questions and objections, if you would like.
Magistrate:	No, counsel, not at this point. Let me talk to defendant's counsel.
Opposing Counsel:	Your Honor, what plaintiff's counsel has been doing here is egregious. These questions about original ownership have nothing to do with the issues in this case, and he knows it. He is just trying to fish around to see if he can bring other people into this controversy, people who have nothing to do with the problems that his client has experienced, so that he can inconvenience and embarrass them. Besides that, I know that he is working with other counsel in a different case against my client, and he may very well be intending to share the answers in this deposition with that other lawyer to give her an advantage in that other lawsuit. That's why I had no choice but to direct the witness not to answer these improper questions.
Magistrate:	OK, let me hear the questions from the reporter. [*The questions are read back from the paper tape by the reporter.*]

Counsel, put me on the speaker phone, so you and the witness can all hear my ruling. The witness is directed to answer these questions, and other questions reasonably related to them. There is nothing privileged here, and, as I understand it, defense counsel is not arguing privilege. These questions may not be on matters directly part of the claims or defenses in the case, but they are reasonably intended to lead to the discovery of admissible evidence, such as the identity of witnesses with knowledge of the initial purposes and profit-sharing structure of the company. If counsel in some other lawsuit can take advantage of these answers, that has nothing to do with whether the answers should be given in this case. Their use in the other case depends on a determination of the judge in that matter on the relevance of the information to that other case.[6] I find that these questions present a legitimate area for discovery, and, counsel for the defendant, you will not interfere by directing this witness, or other witnesses who may be asked about these topics, not to answer. Are there any other problems now, counsel?

Both Counsel: No, your Honor.

After closing the telephone conference with the magistrate, counsel can return to the deposition table and resume questioning. Deposing counsel should, of course, start right back into the deposition with the questions that were the subject of the application to the magistrate and which the

---

6. However, the magistrate or judge ruling on this application has the discretionary power to order deposing counsel not to release the information obtained during the deposition to anyone, including counsel in another case. *See* Scott v. Monsanto Co., 868 F.2d 786, 792 (5th Cir. 1989). Generally, courts find this "gag-order" power relates only to matters obtained through discovery and may not be used by courts to restrict the dissemination of material that counsel has obtained during pretrial from sources other than discovery under the rules. *See* Seattle Times v. Rhinehart, 467 U.S. 20 (1984); Rodgers v. United States Steel Corp., 536 F.2d 1001 (3d Cir. 1976); International Products Corp. v. Koons, 325 F.2d 403 (2d Cir. 1963).

witness refused to answer. Counsel may also want to "push the envelope" a bit, i.e., press into areas where the defendant may have something to hide or may claim privilege, under the assumption that the defendant's counsel is unlikely to provoke another hearing before the magistrate so soon after a loss. On the other hand, the magistrate may not be prepared to rule in favor of the plaintiff if another dispute arises immediately after the first ruling, either because the magistrate thinks that the plaintiff is pressing his luck or the magistrate is alternating favorable rulings between the parties in an effort to appear even-handed. The best approach is to ask the questions that you had intended to ask and not get caught up in discovery "gamesmanship."

PART THREE: DEFENDING THE DEPOSITIONS

Chapter Thirteen

Preparing the Witness to Be Deposed

Oh the nerves, the nerves; the mysteries of this machine called Man!
Oh the little that unhinges it: poor creature that we are!

—Charles Dickens

According to our preferred method of research (called "casual empiricism," where we have a few beverages together and try to remember how many times we personally have seen some particular thing happen), perhaps 40 percent of attorneys prepare witnesses for deposition by extensively reviewing the substantive facts of the case; and maybe another 40 percent prepare the witness by reciting an inordinately long list of "do's" and "don't's" that even attorneys cannot remember (and therefore those instructions are provided to the witness in writing, or on videotape, for the witness "to take home" and read for herself after the last preparation session). That leaves only 20 percent of attorneys who realize that neither of these approaches deal with the primary factor affecting the witness's performance at the deposition—his level of confidence about his ability to perform in the unfamiliar deposition environment.

No matter how well prepared the witness is on the substance of his testimony, he will not give clear and persuasive testimony unless he remains calm enough to understand the questions and to respond appropriately and cautiously. His demeanor must reflect his confidence in the truth of his testimony. Your primary goal in the preparation sessions should therefore be to take burdens off of the witness's shoulders so he can focus only on the substance of his answers.

As a general rule, hold a preparation session with the witness on the substance of the dispute before (and on a different day, if possible) preparing him on the procedures of the deposition. Sometimes, however, the witness's role is so minor or the witness is located at such a distance, or the witness makes so little time available, that it makes good economic sense to combine the two sessions on the same day; in that case, substance should still precede process. If you have only two hours with the witness, spend the first hour on substance and the next hour on process.

Separating substance from process allows you to provide better preparation for each. It also gives you some idea of the witness's personality, intelligence, confidence, and anxieties before attempting to prepare the witness on the procedures of deposition. The logic of this order of preparation should be clear. The witness knows what she is testifying about—she knows her business; she remembers what happened at the meeting; she can tell everyone why her father left her the company when he died. What she is much more likely to have problems with is the pace of questioning, or what to do when she does not understand the question, or how to handle aggressive counsel who interrupts her or repeats the questions or talks over your objections. Finally, conducting separate preparation sessions, one on substance and then another on process, allows you time to follow up any questions or issues about substance that need to be addressed before you conclude the preparation for the deposition.

Therefore, we will deal with these two preparation topics separately—and in the proper order. First, let's discuss preparation on the substance of the deposition.

13.1 Preparing the Witness on Substance

13.1.1 *How to Handle Documents in Preparation*

In the reasonably small case where there are twenty or thirty crucial documents, you should carefully review those documents with the witness before her deposition. Witnesses are sometimes unnerved by facing documents relating to their testimony that they have not seen in months or years. The predeposition review assures the witness that her testimony will be consistent with the important documents and that letters written long ago will not trap her out on a limb. Those documents also provide a check on reconstructed memories that build up over time, often with inaccuracies that seem perfectly real until contemporaneous documents reveal the truth. Organize the documents chronologically within a topic or issue so that the review helps establish cause and effect: "Oh, I see. I called him on the tenth because he sent me this e-mail on the eighth asking if we could fill his order. I wondered about why I called."

Larger cases pose a different problem, however. Faced with hundreds or thousands of documents from the company records or obtained from the opponent during discovery, the witness will not be able to use them in any effective way to prepare for the deposition. Even if the witness had the time and energy to read through—or even just scan—each page, she could not retain all that information in an organized way, so when she is shown Exhibit 153 at the deposition, she remembers that it is related to Exhibit 791. In a complex case, therefore, you must cull the documents to those that are most important to the witness's testimony. This means giving the witness *only* the key documents relating to her expected testimony and not overwhelming her with boxes of material of limited importance.

We recommend applying the "fourteen document rule" at both deposition and trial. Because human beings have good, but not faultless, memories, it is not reasonable, as stated above, to expect that a witness will remember 100 documents accurately; and certainly not 1,000 or 10,000. It just will not happen. No matter how well organized the documents are—by topic, by recipient, by author, by copyees, by chronology—the witness will not be able to handle any large number of documents. Therefore, you must reduce the number.[1]

Some lawyers also provide witnesses with summaries of what other witnesses have said in their depositions. This practice has some attendant risk because if the witness's recollection of the events about which testimony will be given is refreshed by these lawyer-prepared summaries, a judge may very well order that those memoranda be turned over to opposing counsel pursuant to Federal Rule of Evidence 612.

Simply giving documents to a witness for review does not, of course, ensure she will actually look at them. Therefore, you must still go through the documents with the witness at the preparation session. Here, the task falls to you to organize and review those documents and to prepare the witness by leading her through the events, using the documents to assist where necessary.

Assuming that there are several issues on which the witness is likely to be questioned at her deposition, choose the fourteen documents that you and your colleagues believe are most important to the witness's testimony or the

---

1. And, of course, jurors have no greater ability to handle documents that a deponent; if you give the jurors 150 medical records, or spreadsheets, or invoices, or miscellaneous memoranda, they will try to find a shortcut for their use: perhaps they will pick one from each week or year; maybe they will consider every tenth out of 100 invoices to be a sufficient sample; maybe they could just look at documents from May. Since you know the jury will be looking for help, you should give it to them. Have a witness identify three or four of the documents from the pile as good summaries for the entire group; have the witness point out that the records from the first day of the twelve-month period give a good idea of the production levels; ask the witness to select the three memoranda that best show the company's plans for growth in the third quarter. Then, when the jurors begin to deliberate, they will pay attention to the documents that the witness emphasized. Do not go beyond fourteen documents; at least, do not go beyond fourteen documents in any topic area. Too many documents encourage the jury to just ignore them all—even your summary graphics that were so persuasive when you presented them individually in your focus groups.

party's story. Go through those documents with the witness to determine whether the witness agrees to their selection. When you have your fourteen, arrange the documents chronologically within each issue. (In a complex case, you may have to rely on fourteen documents for each issue. In that situation, you may want one witness to handle no more than two issues. This will keep the presentation within each witness's capabilities as well as make the eventual trial presentation more interesting.)

The documents will help you prepare an outline that you can use as a road map to the preparation session for each issue. (This same outline, obviously, can become the primary basis for arranging the witness's direct examination at trial.) During preparation, ask the witness to describe the events pertinent to each issue and have the witness clarify when her description seems at odds with the documents. After this exercise, the witness should have some confidence that she has not forgotten something important shown in the documents. The more complex the case and the more issues the witness has information on, the longer the preparation will take. Sessions can extend for days. One rule of thumb for both deposition and trial preparation is three hours of preparation for each hour of anticipated testimony. Preparing in this fashion may be time-consuming for you, but it greatly eases the load on the witness.

As has been discussed elsewhere, a standard question at depositions is: "Have you reviewed any documents in preparation for this deposition?" This question is based on the rule that at trial the questioner is entitled to know whether the witness has used documents "at or before trial" to refresh her recollection. This logic fails to justify this question because "reviewing a document" and "refreshing recollection" are different activities. If a witness reviews a document under the direction or in consultation with her attorney and the witness finds the document to be consistent with her recollection or finds that she still has no recollection, then the document has not been used to "refresh her recollection." Thus no basis exists, at deposition or trial, to reveal that those documents were reviewed with the attorney's assistance. That review remains protected work product.

Be sure to discuss this issue with the witness in the preparation session. In response to a question about document review, she should answer truthfully, "Yes, I have reviewed documents with my attorney in preparation for this deposition." However, you should meet any follow-up questions about specifically which documents were reviewed with a direction to the witness not to identify particular documents (on the grounds of attorney work product) unless the questioning attorney can establish that some document did in fact refresh her memory on some relevant point. (And it is not sufficient that the witness has said, "Some of the documents refreshed me on some topics." The questioner should identify specific topics on which the witness will say, "Yes, there was a document that helped me remember those negotiations.")

Having selected the documents on which the witness should focus, there are just a few rules on what the witness should do when presented with a document at the deposition. This falls somewhere between "substance" and "process," so we will handle it here. For every document given to the witness, she should apply the following steps:

1. The witness should examine the document to be certain that it is complete and that it is not two documents mistakenly stapled together.

2. The witness should make certain that she knows the date and author of the document and whether she received it.

3. The witness should look through the document or any table of contents to refresh her memory on what it covers.

4. If the questioner directs the witness's attention to one portion of the document, the witness should look at related portions to guard against things being taken out of context.

5. If the witness recognizes that there are other portions of the document that change the meaning of statements she is questioned about, she should point those out to her counsel.

6. The witness should listen carefully to opposing counsel's characterization of the document before she agrees that it is correct.

7. If the document in the question is inconsistent with "her fourteen," she should read the entire document to determine if and why it is inconsistent.

13.1.2   *Practicing Answering Questions*

The heart of witness preparation is having the witness actually practice answering questions. Only through practice will the witness fully understand how to phrase her answers to get her meaning across accurately, how to respond to an aggressive cross-examination style, how to behave during the deposition, how to apply the instructions given about the form and content of answers, and how to deal with the many other nuanced situations that occur during the deposition.

You will not be able to rehearse every likely deposition question, nor is it necessary to do so. It is important, however, to identify the key areas on which the witness is reasonably certain to be examined and to have the witness practice answering questions on those topics. But remember, this is not just a time for practicing answering, but also a time to refine and improve the language of the answers by helping the witness with word choice, chronology, and accuracy. While the substance must come from the witness, you are entitled—even obligated—to help the witness's delivery so she is correctly understood. Listen to the witness's answers and give suggestions about how they can be phrased to better state the witness's knowledge. Then have the witness practice answering again until the response is accurate and clearly states what the witness intends. Here is an example of what should occur:

> Lawyer: OK, let's imagine again I am the lawyer for Hospital Pathology, and let me ask you some questions about your efforts to generate pathology patients. Ready?
>
> Lawyer: Dr. Unitas, please tell me all of the things you did to get pathology patients of your own.
>
> Witness: Well, I contacted all of the hospitals and told them I had left Hospital Pathology and was now accepting patients of my own. And I also sent a letter to all of the primary care physicians telling them about the availability of my services.
>
> Lawyer: Is that all?
>
> Witness: That's about it.
>
> Lawyer: OK, let me become your lawyer again. Those were good answers, but I think we can phrase some of it better. Didn't you tell me that when you went out on your own, you sat down and tried to figure out the best way of generating patients?
>
> Witness: That's true.
>
> Lawyer: And as I recall, you also did some research on how to start your own practice and made some phone calls to doctors to let them know you were now taking patients?
>
> Witness: That's true.

Lawyer: Did you ever tell other doctors at parties and medical association meetings that you were now out on your own and accepting patients?

Witness: Sure, it would come up, and I would let them know.

Lawyer: Let's see if you can incorporate this information into your answers. Here is an example of what I mean. If you were asked the question of what did you do to generate patients, based on what you've told me, a more complete and accurate answer would be this:

When I started my own practice I thought about the best way of getting patients, so I did a lot of reading on the subject in publications such as books and articles in medical economics journals. I also talked with other doctors who were practicing on their own and received a number of suggestions about how they were able to generate patients. Another thing I did was to carefully study how Hospital Pathology went about getting patients. When I went into practice, I systematically visited all of the hospitals in the area, where I met with the surgeons and other hospital staff to let them know of my availability. I explained my background and experience to them even though I had worked with many of them through the years and they were well familiar with my skills. I also sent a personally signed letter to all of the primary care physicians in the area, again explaining that I was available to take patients and about my experience. Finally, when I determined that a personal contact would be helpful, I followed the letter up with a phone call to the physician, in which I emphasized the same things.

I think you have told me in previous interviews everything I just included in that answer, but you can add other things you did that I left out or subtract anything I got wrong. OK?

Witness: Yes. That's a better answer. That's what I really meant.

Lawyer: Let's try it again. Imagine again I am the lawyer for Hospital Pathology. Tell me everything you did to generate patients when you went out on your own.

Note what is going on here. The lawyer is actively suggesting how the answer should be phrased and is not relying on the witness to think of what should be said. The lawyer is being very careful to suggest only those facts the witness has previously related or has confirmed as true. The information must come from the witness or documents, otherwise the danger of improper "coaching" arises. Most importantly, the lawyer does not just suggest a better way to answer, but has the witness actually practice until the lawyer is satisfied.

The witness's answers during the deposition will never be as perfect as they were during the preparation session, but they will be better for having been practiced. Even if not phrased exactly the same way as in the witness preparation session, the witness is now better aware of what facts should be included in the answer and is more likely to give the information in a persuasive manner when asked the question.

In the above vignette it was assumed that the preparing lawyer would first assume the role of the deposing counsel and from time to time step out of that role to help the witness complete and formulate answers. This process can be confusing to the witness and, of course, takes the preparing lawyer out of the role she will ultimately play at the deposition—that of defending counsel. For that reason, whenever possible, the role of questioning counsel during the preparation session should be assumed by another lawyer. Preparing counsel can then stay in the role of defender and stop the questioning whenever the witness needs help in the manner or content of answers. This process is much easier on the preparing lawyer as it makes the witness's answers (and not the next question to be asked) the clear focus of the session, thereby making the preparation session qualitatively better and more efficient. Finally, it is during this preparation session that the witness can be given suggestions on to how to insert in her answers the information that the opponent, or some later decision maker, needs to know to make a fair evaluation of the case. These answers should be carefully planned so that when the opportunity arises during the deposition, the witness will give opposing counsel the bad news about the small likelihood his client has of prevailing in the lawsuit.

13.1.3 *Getting Used to Aggressive Cross-Examination*

The witness should not suffer the shock of an aggressive cross-examination for the first time during the deposition. Instead, let the witness get comfortable with this type of questioning during the witness preparation session so the witness will be more comfortable when it actually occurs during the deposition. If the witness knows what to expect, she is less likely to become angry or intimidated when the opposing counsel tries this tactic. If another lawyer is not available to role play for the entirety of the preparation practice session, make every effort to use one for this limited exercise of acclimating the witness to an aggressive examination. To the extent possible, the person playing the role should be as much like deposing counsel as possible in style and demeanor. Consider the following example:

Lawyer 1: Sometimes aggressive questions may make you upset. The important thing for you is not to get angry or intimidated by what is happening. Just remain cool and answer the questions as best you can. Let me show you what I mean by this. Pretend we are at the deposition and Mary, my partner here, is opposing counsel. Go ahead, Mary.

Lawyer 2: Now Doctor, you never ran any advertisements in the Nita Medical Association Journal saying you were available to accept patients?

Witness: No.

Lawyer 2: You know every doctor in the area receives a copy of the Journal?

Witness: Yes.

Lawyer 2: A three-by-five-inch ad would only cost $250?

Witness: I don't know what the advertising rates are.

Lawyer 2: You never checked?

Witness: That's right.

Lawyer 2: You would agree this is an inexpensive way of making sure all of the physicians in the area would know about your services?

Witness: Well, quite frankly, I don't think many doctors read those ads or take them seriously. I have talked with lots of doctors through the years, and I have never heard of any of them bothering to read those ads. And when I talked with other doctors who had started their own practices, none of them thought it was a good idea to run an ad like that.

Lawyer 1: OK. Let's take a break from the questioning for a moment and talk about what just happened. You are doing the right thing. Just remain calm and answer the questions. But in the last question, Mary asked whether you would agree that the ads are an inexpensive way of making sure all of the doctors know about your services. If you don't agree, just say "I don't agree." What you did was natural. You wanted to explain why you didn't think so. Don't give the explanation unless it is asked for, OK?

Witness: Yes. I am afraid I was starting to get angry.

Lawyer 1: Yes, and you know that anger won't help you. It won't help you focus. You may say more than you should, and more or less than you mean, when you speak from anger. Keep calm and listen to the question.

Keep the examples of aggressive cross-examination short. Even though the witness understands intellectually that your colleague is merely playing the role of opposing counsel, being treated in such a hostile fashion is still irritating. The idea is not to make the witness angry with her own lawyers, but only to prepare her to deal with this type of questioning. Using one of your colleagues to conduct the cross will reduce the possibility of any damage to your relationship with the witness.

13.1.4   Using Video to Prepare

Some witnesses require intensive work to prevent speech habits or mannerisms that distract from their testimony—first at deposition, then at trial. While they might not always believe your comments about their demeanor or speech habits, they will find it difficult to argue with a video showing those problems. Stuffy corporate executives, pompous experts, and mumbling fact witnesses can all markedly step up their performances if they are shown video of the problems.

Lengthy recording sessions are not necessary; the witness will most likely improve his delivery by recording a fifteen-minute segment, reviewing and discussing it, and then recording another segment with further suggestions for improvement. For key witnesses, communications consultants can help identify and cure problems that interfere with the witness effectively presenting his evidence.

The question arises, of course, whether such video rehearsals are discoverable: they are, after all, verbatim statements by the witness. Nevertheless, the better rule is that these videos, just like an attorney's notes taken during preparation sessions, constitute attorney work-product and are protected from discovery. The order of questioning, the subjects prepared, the suggestions from the attorney or consultant all reflect the attorney's approach to and preparation of the case. The fact that video technology provides an especially effective way of preparing does not reduce the protection courts should accord such effort by the attorney. While courts should uphold a claim of work product protection, make sure your client is prepared to discuss such preparation if the court decides otherwise.

A more subtle question is whether using video to prepare a witness for deposition or trial makes that witness more vulnerable to effective cross-examination at trial on the use, if not the content, of video preparation. Assume that your opponent has discovered the use of video (or suspects its use) in a witness's preparation session; consider the following approach to cross-examination on such "rehearsals," which questioning counsel can attempt at no risk during the deposition of the witness.

> Q: Mr. Shadis, you spent quite a good deal of time reviewing and preparing your testimony with your lawyer before you came to court, didn't you?
>
> A: Yes, I did, I suppose.
>
> Q: And you went over and over that testimony, your story, because you wanted to get it just right, isn't that true?
>
> A: Well, we did go over it several times, yes.
>
> Q: Several times, until your attorney thought it was just right?
>
> A: Well, until she was satisfied that it was clear.
>
> Q: In fact, you gave these answers again and again in your attorney's office, so you could get them just the way she wanted them?
>
> A: Well, as I've said, we went over my testimony.
>
> Q: And then she actually recorded you on video giving your answers, didn't she?
>
> A: Yes, we used video to prepare.
>
> Q: And then you reviewed the video and looked at what you said, and how you said it, and what words you used, and how you looked while you were answering, right?
>
> A: We did review the videos, yes, but I don't see anything wrong with that.
>
> Q: Then your testimony here this morning is actually the result of very careful rehearsal, isn't it?

A: I don't think I would use the word rehearsal.

Q: You prepared as though you were playacting and delivering lines that had been written for you, isn't that right?

A: No, no, I think that presents the wrong picture entirely.

No matter how the witness protests, the impression that the jury receives when this same examination is performed at trial is that they have somehow been "conned" by having a set piece of theater presented when they thought that they were hearing the spontaneous testimony of the witness in his own words.

The witness can dispel this impression, however, if he makes it clear to the jury why this video preparation was necessary:

A: No, no, I think that presents the wrong picture entirely. I am nervous about testifying here; I've never done it before, and I don't speak in public often. I don't think that it would be fair if that nervousness made me mix up my testimony or kept me from telling the jury what really happened. So my attorney and I decided that we would try to do everything that we could, including going over my testimony several times on video, to get the truth of what happened across to the jury.

The simple fact is that if a witness needs the help that video-recorded practice can provide so effectively and efficiently, the concern about disclosure at trial should not by itself be a sufficient argument against that assistance.

13.2 Preparing the Witness for the Deposition Process

13.2.1 Reducing the Witness's Anxieties

The first task in preparing a witness for the deposition process is reducing the witness's anxieties. Many witnesses dread the prospect of giving testimony at a deposition or trial. Anxiety and worry can overwhelm the witness as she conjures up scenes from "Law and Order" or "Boston Legal" or "Harry's Law," and as she remembers what happens to such witnesses on such overly dramatic and unrealistic shows. If the witness is a party or has her employment on the line, her worries and concerns become even more heightened. In short, testifying at a deposition is not perceived as a pleasant experience, and witnesses often grossly overestimate how unpleasant it will be.

This anxiety prevents witnesses from focusing on those things they must remember. When a witness is thinking about some embarrassing questions that might be asked instead of concentrating on what you[2] are saying during the preparation session, she has gone far astray. Anxiety interferes with the witness's ability to understand and remember your advice. Therefore, if the session is going to serve its purpose—preparing the witness to testify—you must confront and ease the witness's nervousness and worries about what is going to happen.

Start the witness "process" preparation session, even if conducted after the witness has been previously prepared on substance, by asking whether new or different substantive facts have come to light since the last communication. Has her story changed? The witness might have remembered more information, discovered or looked at a new document, or talked with another person who has knowledge of the event between the substantive preparation session and the process preparation session. Complete this "information gathering" after initially addressing the witness's nervousness, but before preparing the witness on the procedural and any remaining substantive matters relating to the deposition. The following discussion of witness preparation, however, assumes that you are confident that the substance has been sufficiently covered and that there is no new information that must be analyzed. As a result, the focus is on the manner in which the witness will answer at the deposition, rather than finding out what will be said in those answers.

13.2.2 The Wrong Way to Reduce Anxieties

As a comparison, we start with a portion of a "conventional" preparation session. We do not recommend this approach:

Q: So, John, how do you feel about this deposition coming up? You're not nervous about it, are you?

A: Well, I guess I am, a little. I'm not sure exactly what to expect, you know. I don't want to make any mistakes.

Q: Well, that's right, it's important that you don't make any mistakes, so I thought that we would go over your testimony again, what you know about the facts in this case. All right?

A: Sure, that seems like a good idea. But, you know, I was just wondering—are they going to try to make me look stupid or forgetful or anything? I'm just not sure what to do if I get confused about what they're asking.

---

2. By using "you," we do not intend to limit this chapter to situations where the deponent is your client; we are merely using this word, "you," to refer to the attorney who is preparing her and who will sit on her side of the table during the deposition, whether she is the client, an employee of the client, a designee of the client, or even a nonparty with whom counsel has talked with about the deposition.

Q: Well, it is very important that you be sure about what they are asking. Don't answer any question that's unclear to you or that is ambiguous. They may try to make you look forgetful, so watch out for that.

A: Well, you'll be there, right?

Q: Yes, of course, I'll be right there, and I can object if they try to take advantage of you. Make sure that you pause, maybe take a deep breath before every answer, so that I have time to object if I think it's necessary. Then pay attention to what I say in my objection, because there may be something in the question that I think is unfair or improper, and you should be aware of that when you answer.

A: Are they allowed to ask unfair or improper questions?

Q: Lawyers do it all the time. They ask questions that have a double meaning, or they try to get the witness to admit things that he really doesn't mean, or they only put in part of the story: those kinds of things. So we have to watch out for them and only answer fair questions. Now, another thing for you to remember is not to volunteer information. By "volunteer," I mean answering with more than you were asked for. If the other attorney asks you, "Where do you work?" your answer should be "Strongis Ironworks," not "I've worked as a foreman at Strongis for the past seventeen years." You see, he didn't ask, "What is your position?" or "How long have you worked there?" So just answer what is asked; answers that go beyond that just cause trouble.

Let's just pause here to take a moment to examine whether the attorney is actually helping the witness. The attorney asked whether the witness was nervous in a way that suggested that it is wrong to be nervous. This caused the witness, at the outset of the preparation process, to feel like he is not doing the right thing. When the witness answered that he was nervous because he did not want to make any mistakes, the attorney emphasized that it is important not to make mistakes. That certainly did not reduce the witness's anxiety level. Instead, the witness might be comforted to hear the following:

I know that you don't want to make any mistakes, but you should not worry too much about that. First, we have already gone over what I think will be the substance of the other lawyer's questions, and I am impressed by how well you know the facts. We even did some practice deposition questions and answers, where one of my partners came in and asked questions as though she was the opposing counsel, and you handled that very well. And let me tell you, you will have a chance to read this deposition over once it is typed up, and I'll read it with you. If we see any mistakes, we can correct them. You really shouldn't feel that you need to be perfect. You'll make some mistakes, I'll make some mistakes, and the attorney on the other side will make some mistakes, but they just won't matter when we get to trial. Besides that, I'll be at the deposition, and if I think that anything is important enough to need correction right at the deposition, I'll make a note of it, and I can ask you questions after the other attorney is finished. You'll do fine.

The whole idea here is to reduce the witness's nervousness. No one has ever given a mistake-free deposition, no matter how much he was cautioned not to make mistakes, so we might as well tell the witness that there are procedures for fixing mistakes and that we, the attorneys, will worry about identifying mistakes that need to be fixed. In addition, it is usually helpful to let the witness know that most people are nervous when they have their deposition taken and that it is natural to feel that way. In follow-up questions, probe the basis for the witness's nervousness. If you give the witness the opportunity to express his concerns, you can address them. There is an additional benefit to such an inquiry—at times the nervousness of the witness about a particular area of testimony will be a signal for you to pay special attention and carefully prepare the witness in that area.

Next, the witness expressed concern that the other side would try to make him look stupid or forgetful, and he said he did not know what to do if he got confused. Instead of providing reassurance, the attorney said, "Watch out for that." In other words, "You are right, they may confuse you, and if that happens, it's your job to avoid it." The attorney could instead have said:

> I'm going to be there to deal with any objectionable questions, so you don't have to worry about them. I don't think they will try to be unfair, because they just want to know what you know about this case. But I will deal with objectionable questions, and I will tell you what to do at that time. That's my job, and [said with a smile] I am very good at it.

Further, you should tell the witness directly what to do if he feels confused by a question. "Don't answer" is not sufficient because, absent an instruction from you not to answer, the witness will be pressed by opposing counsel for an answer and will likely become more confused. In preparing the witness, instruct him that if a question is confusing he should simply say, "I don't understand the question," and not feel embarrassed about doing so. Tell him it is then the questioner's job to ask a question that he does understand.

Next, the witness in the example asked, "You'll be there, right?" Clearly, this question signaled the witness's lack of comfort with the proceedings. By responding that she will be there to object "if they try to take advantage of you," the attorney actually caused more problems than she solved. "Take advantage of you" is an ominous phrase, and like other such phrases it raises the specter of more problems than the witness has already imagined. The attorney then burdened the witness further by telling the witness to "take a breath" before every answer. Now, besides worrying about the content of his answers and losing some undefined "advantages," the witness must worry about timing as well. Then the attorney told the witness to interpret any objections before giving his answer. This did not lift burdens from the witness's shoulders, but instead added more.

Finally, in the example, the attorney reminded the witness that lawyers ask unfair and improper questions all of the time but, again, she failed to give the witness any tools to deal with such questions. By instructing the witness not to volunteer information, and failing to provide any rationale, the attorney suggested to the witness that there are hidden rules with hidden purposes. Again, none of this puts the witness at ease.

13.2.3 *Burden-Reducing Preparation*

Let's start the "process" preparation session all over again. This time, the focus will be on taking burdens away from the witness and allowing him to focus only on the testimony.

> Q: Good morning, John. Thanks for coming in for a final session about this deposition. How do you feel today about the deposition?
>
> A: Well, I guess I'm a little nervous.
>
> Q: Well, that's natural. It's just a little bit of extra adrenaline pumping, getting you ready to do your best. I feel the same thing every time I go into a deposition or a courtroom, and that tells me I am ready to do a good job. Is there anything in particular that you are nervous about?
>
> A: No. I mean, I've never been deposed before, and I guess it's just fear of the unknown.
>
> Q: That's understandable. Why don't I start by explaining the set up for the deposition. It will be in the offices of

plaintiff's attorney, but I want you to come here one hour before the deposition so we can go over there together. We'll take a cab from here so we don't have to worry about parking. Is that all right with you?

A: Yes, that's fine.

Q: They have a comfortable conference room, very similar to this one, and there will be water and coffee throughout the deposition. And there will be a court reporter there. Do you know what a court reporter does?

A: Yes. I've seen them on "Law and Order."

Q: Right. The court reporter will be there to place you under oath and to record the questions and the answers. There will also be a video operator, to record the deposition digitally. Later on, the stenographic reporter will type up the questions and answers, and the video reporter will prepare the disk, and they will both send them to us so that we can read and watch them and correct anything that we don't think is accurate. Any questions so far?

A: No, I don't think so.

Q: I will be sitting right alongside you at the deposition, and anytime you think that you need to talk to me, you just tell me. We can talk right there if we turn away from the table and talk softly, or we can leave the room. You just tell me you want to talk with me, and I'll take care of it. Is that all right?

A: Yes.[3]

Q: If you have any questions at any time please feel free to ask. Sometimes we lawyers don't fully appreciate how foreign this process can be to nonlawyers.

A: I will, thanks.

---

3. Of course, when a question is pending, the witness normally should answer before he talks with counsel. On the other hand, because the witness must be given the opportunity to discuss questions of privilege with counsel before being compelled to answer, this rule must have some flexibility. In general, as long as you do not abuse this procedure, it should be permissible for the witness to check with you if a particular question raises a concern in his mind. Where appropriate, you can prevent that interruption from becoming an issue by explaining, on the record, why the witness had a problem with the question: "Ms. Jones asked me whether we were still talking about the first transaction or had jumped ahead to the second transaction. I told her that I would ask you." Or, "Ms. Jones asked whether this last question got into a privileged area, and I told her that she could answer."

The above instruction starts the preparation session by immediately putting the witness at ease about several of his concerns. First, he knows that his anxiety is natural. Next, the logistics—where the deposition is and how he will get there—are taken care of. The witness is also told that it is appropriate for him to ask questions during the preparation process. With this backdrop, counsel can then talk about what a deposition is, explain the deposition procedures to the witness, and assure the witness that counsel will be with him during the entire process.

How long this part of witness preparation lasts and what is said depends on the witness. Some witnesses have had their depositions taken before or are quite experienced with the way litigation works. Others are just not the nervous or worried type. For a third group, the deposition is not a significant part of their responsibilities. But many witnesses are entirely ignorant of the whole process and are scared almost to muteness. Be sure you tailor the witness preparation to meet the individual needs of the witness.

A caveat: false or insincere reassurances do not work. Comments like, "Don't worry, everything will be fine," do nothing to comfort the witness when the witness fears that the wrong answer may cause him to lose his job, his house, and everything else he holds dear. Far better to be honest, but upbeat and confident. Avoid false promises.

13.2.4 *Making Witness Preparation Stick*

Before we get into other specifics about witness preparation, a word about style is appropriate. Too often, witness preparation consists of the lawyer giving the witness a long, uninterrupted lecture that may go on for up to an hour and contains a set of so-called "rules" for the witness to follow during the deposition. At the end of the lecture, the attorney asks the witness if he has any questions and then sends him on his way. The attorney is then surprised to see the witness quickly forget everything discussed during the process preparation session and start violating all of the "rules" the attorney thought she had so carefully impressed on the witness.

The question is how to make all of the suggestions made during the witness preparation session stick with the witness during the deposition. The answer is to follow five important rules of witness preparation:

1. Confirm that the witness heard and remembers the instruction.

Think back to your law school days and recall how interested you were in listening to the professors' lectures. For most of us they were boring. Remember how your mind wandered during the lectures and how much you retained without going back and studying your notes. The same is true of witnesses. Straight lecturing is boring, and not much of what is said will be remembered. But if the witness preparation session is more of a discussion with give-and-take between counsel and the witness, then it is more likely the witness will internalize and remember what was said.

2. Assure yourself that the witness understood the instruction in context.

Assure means constantly checking with the witness to assure yourself that the witness understands what is being said and that the witness does not have any questions.

3. Repeat the instruction a number of times.

Repeating information several times makes it more likely that it will be remembered than if the information is mentioned only once. Therefore, give key instructions three or more times, with different examples and practice drills (and, during the substantive preparation, go through the important facts three or four times). Remember, effective repetition does not mean merely saying the same thing twice. Instead, phrase the instruction differently, but make the same point each time—who can predict which phrasing or example will stick in the witness's memory?

4. "Emphasize" the instruction or guidance.

Have the witness practice following the instructions given. This helps impress the instructions on the witness and makes it much easier for the witness to recall and apply the instruction during the deposition. Usually, emphasis involves pointing out to the witness that he has violated an instruction, but it should also mean having the witness practice answering the same questions, but in the correct way. Constantly reminding the witness of deposition preparation instructions will make it easier for him to remember the instructions during the deposition.

5. Describe situations where the instruction will assist the witness.

"Describe" a situation where the advice might be useful. Give an example (not too frightening). This will make the instruction much more understandable to the witness.

13.2.5   *Addressing Questions about the Preparation Session*

Whether a lawyer's conversation with a particular witness is covered by the attorney-client privilege is somewhat beyond the scope of this section.

Be sure to research your jurisdiction's interpretation of the federal or state rules of procedure. Your study of the local rules and decisions should allow you, well before the witness preparation session, to decide whether the other side will be able to discover what counsel and the witness say to each other. If the sessions with the witness are covered by the attorney-client privilege (because she is the client or essentially a spokesperson for the client), the witness should be told this:

> Let me tell you right now that whatever we say to each other in getting you ready for your deposition is confidential. The other side is not entitled to learn about what we say here, so I want you to feel comfortable in saying whatever you wish during our preparation here. Do you have any questions about that? I need to know what you know.

If the sessions with the witness are not covered by a privilege, you should also explain this:

> I want you to understand that whatever we say here can be asked about during the deposition, and you will have to tell them what you remember about our conversation. What this means is that we should not talk about anything or say anything to each other we would not want the other side to hear. But understand this: at no time am I telling you what facts or story to tell. On the history of this dispute, tell the truth. The two things we are talking about here are the procedures of the deposition and whatever you can tell me about how this dispute developed.

More important than the explanation of what the witness can or cannot say is counsel not revealing client or attorney confidences to a non-client witness when those confidences would better be kept confidential.

13.2.6   *The Process of Answering Questions*

Now, as part of the process preparation session, let's address how to answer questions (what facts to provide in an answer is obviously part of the "substance" preparation). The following is one form of the classic instruction intended to keep the witness from volunteering too much information:

> At the beginning of the deposition, you will be asked to swear to tell the truth, and then the plaintiff's attorney will start his questioning. The only thing that you have to remember during this whole time is to give the shortest correct answer to each question. Let's just take a minute here for me to explain what I mean by the shortest correct answer. There are seven answers

that are the best response to 90 percent of the questions asked at deposition. Those seven are:

1. "Green," "Two o'clock," "In the basement";

2. "Yes";

3. "No";

4. "I don't understand the question";

5. "I don't know";

6. "I don't remember"; and

7. "I'd like to take a break."

Then explain each of these answers individually.

1. "Green." "Two o'clock." "In the basement."

Tell the witness:

> If you are asked what color your car is, or when you came home in the afternoon, or where you keep your canceled checks, short answers are best. You don't have to worry about what the questioner really wants to know or where he is going. If he wants more information, he will ask for it. The main reason that short answers are best is that attorneys are trained to chase down any paths that appear, just in case there is something relevant at the end. We don't have any desire to prolong this deposition unnecessarily, so it helps us if we keep the answers short and to the point and don't create new paths

2. and 3. "Yes" or "No"

Tell the witness:

> You will find that most of the time the attorney will ask questions that let you answer "yes" or "no." When he asks those questions, go ahead and answer that way. If he wants more information, it's his job to ask for it. If I want you to explain some answer more fully, I will talk to you at breaks, and we can ask some questions of our own at the end of his questioning; or I may ask you to expand on your answer right then. Let me

worry about that. Just remember, it is not rude to answer with a simple "yes" or "no."

4. "I don't understand the question"

Witnesses frequently will answer questions without fully understanding what information is sought. Therefore, tell the witness:

5. "I don't know"

This is often the hardest answer for witnesses to give, because they feel somehow as if they should know all the answers. Tell the witness:

> You just don't have to feel that way. We haven't told the other side in this lawsuit that you have all the answers, and our case does not depend at all on you having all the answers. What you do know, tell them; what you don't know, don't worry about. Just say, "I don't know." There is no need for you to try to guess what the answer is, or to try to figure out what it probably is, unless they ask you to do that.[4] If you don't have the answer in your mind, say, "I don't know."

6. "I don't remember"

Witnesses also find it hard to use this answer, perhaps because no one wants to admit that his memory is not perfect. The following assurance is often helpful:

> You are not expected to have every answer or to remember every fact that the other attorney wants to ask about. If you don't remember at the deposition, and then later something reminds you of the answer, we can correct the transcript of the deposition or we can explain at trial that you remembered if the question even comes up at trial. But if you are asked for information that you can't remember at the deposition, just say, "I don't remember." Then, if the attorney wants to try to help you remember by showing you documents or suggesting answers,

---

4. Some attorneys in preparing witnesses for deposition tell the witness, "Don't speculate." There is only one problem with this advice: it's wrong. There is no rule against seeking the witness's speculation in a deposition, as long as that speculation is reasonably calculated to lead to the production of admissible information. For example, suppose the question is: "Who was the last person to adjust the temperature settings on the boiler?" The witness answers, "Well, I'd really have to guess, based on who was there." The next question could quite properly be: "OK, what's your guess?" There is no basis here for directing the witness not to answer since there is no question of privilege or harassment and the question is not patently beyond the scope of proper discovery. Yet if the witness is told during preparation that he should not speculate, he may be confused when speculation is properly called for at the deposition itself.

he can do that. If those things help you remember, that's fine; if they don't, you just say, "I still don't remember."

7. "I'd like to take a break"

Finally, the witness needs to appreciate and learn to use the request for a break appropriately. Tell the witness:

> Sometimes in the deposition you may need to use the rest room or make a call to check on your kids or on a meeting back in your office; sometimes you may be asked a question that you think is too personal and you just are not sure what you are supposed to do. Maybe you think the answer should be private; maybe you just need a chance to stretch and collect your thoughts; maybe you think something is privileged and you want to talk to me. If, for any reason, you want to take a break, just tell me or tell the other attorney, and we will take a break. I'll worry about whether it's a good idea or not. It is much better to take a break and talk together—to either figure out how to make you comfortable with going forward or to decide whether the question is objectionable—than it is to go forward and perhaps give the other side some information that really is your private business or that they are not entitled to. So if you legitimately think that you want a break for what seems to you to be a good reason, talk to me right then and say, "I'd like to take a break." If there is a question pending, the other lawyer may try to insist on an answer to her question before the break, but, if you really think that you need a break, just say so, and I will make it happen.

These seven "shortest correct answers" are intended to simplify the witness's job—to reduce his burden at the deposition. When giving these instructions, continually reassure the witness: "It is not your job to wonder about the procedure or what the other attorney might say or do—that is why I'm there; I'll take care of all those matters, so you don't have to worry about them. All you have to do is give the shortest correct answer."

13.2.7   *Better Deposition Answers When Trial Will Not Happen*

The first three best answers assume that there will be a trial, and they date from the time when trials of civil cases were common. Consider, however, modern litigation, where trial is only a remote possibility and settlement or some sort of assisted mediation is most likely. Today, it must be assumed that deposition responses may be the only opportunity for opposing counsel to get the information she needs from the witness to value the case. If both sides are interested in achieving a successful negotiated or mediated resolution, they will have a different attitude about exchanging information and restricting answers to the minimum. To achieve pretrial resolution, some of these rules governing deposition responses may have to change.

When you do not anticipate trial, and it seems most likely that settlement, motions practice, or other resolution of some sort will end the dispute, answers one, two, and three ("green," "yes," and "no") will not be the "best" answers that can be given to a question, because the goals have changed. If in fair response to a question, an opportunity is provided to inform opposing counsel—and put in the record—facts that are helpful to the deponent's position in the matter, take that opportunity. In addition, especially if the deposition is recorded on videotape, the short "yes," "no," "green" answers that do not volunteer any information can appear to be evasive.

Recall the deposition of President Clinton. Deposing counsel was required to ask a number questions to obtain even the most basic of information. When that performance was played before the public, the clear message was that the President was lying. (Of course that impression was aided by the denial of certain activity that was later recanted.) In another well-known example, Bill Gates's deposition testimony in the case of *United States v. Microsoft* was marred by his constantly stating that he could not recall information, even though there was a document, later shown to be known to him, that would have refreshed his memory. The clear impression left with the judge in that matter was that the witness was being intentionally evasive.

For the above reasons, the "best" answer in modern litigation may well be the answer that provides fairly responsive information to the question. A fair response to the question, "Did you go to college?" is not "Yes" but rather, "Yes, I graduated from State University in 1994 with a Bachelor of Science degree in civil engineering." This sort of response has several benefits.

- **First**, the more casual response is the sort that a person would give to such an inquiry if it occurred outside of a deposition, so it is an easy (more comfortable) way for the witness to respond, unencumbered by a lawyer's instruction to act in an artificial and defensive way.

- **Second**, the answer may eventually save time, because it requires one question by the lawyer, not four.

- **Third**, the witness's credibility can be better evaluated by a later decision maker, just as if at trial. Certainly the question about college will not receive the answer "Yes" on direct examination of the witness at trial.

- **Fourth**, any reader of a transcript or viewer of a video deposition will perceive that the information was being given in a forthcoming and natural way, and that enhances the credibility of the witness.

- **Fifth**, the response sounds unguarded and complete and may provoke less probing by deposing counsel.

All witnesses (except perhaps experts paid by the hour) want to shorten the deposition process. As a result, they may eventually begin to respond in a natural, more expansive way to reasonable and relevant questions from deposing counsel. At that point, defending and questioning counsel may find that with the witnesses' help, they have stumbled on the right way to use depositions.

Even if the likely end-game for the litigation is a trial, there are exceptions to the giving of the first three responses as the "best" responses. First, if the deposition is of a party or a witness whose statements are attributable to the party as party statements, a more complete answer will make its use more difficult by the opposing counsel at trial. When looking for party statements, as described in an earlier chapter, deposing counsel is seeking short, specific answers that can be read or shown to the jury during the trial. The more expansive answer is harder to dissect and then use as a party statement, and it is more likely to contain information helpful to the witness's sponsor. With these witnesses, it will usually be best to prepare your witnesses to answer fully, with appropriate explanatory material, to all of the most important questions in the lawsuit. In this way, even if a fact can be isolated as a party statement, Federal Rule of Evidence 106 will allow you to provide the jury with explanatory material regarding the claimed party statement. Second, if the witness is your witness and one who will likely be unavailable at trial, remember that the jury will either be read or shown her deposition testimony—so you should depose her in a preservation (or *de bene esse* or trial) deposition, where you capture the direct examination, complete with choreography and documents. Prepare her to give complete answers where those answers are helpful to the party sponsoring the witness. There is no advantage to having such a witness fail to disclose helpful information. In addition, for trial purposes the demeanor of the witness should communicate that the witness is being open and forthcoming. These witnesses should be prepared, then, just as if they were being prepared for trial, and counsel who would normally call this witness at trial should be ready to conduct what is essentially the direct examination during the course of the deposition.

Finally, as will be discussed later in this chapter, when a deposition is recorded by video, it is more likely that the "best seven" responses to opposing counsel's "cross-examination" will be viewed as evasive. If there is a chance that the video will be played in any substantial part at a trial, the more complete, fair response is usually preferable to the short responses dictated by the "best seven."

13.2.8 Explaining the Issues

Witnesses who have an interest in the outcome of the case will naturally try to give answers helpful to the side they support. This does not mean they will be dishonest or less than fully truthful, but they will probably try to phrase their answers in the most helpful way possible and to emphasize those facts they believe contribute to a winning outcome. In addition, during the course of a dispute, most witnesses reconstruct the events in question. During this reconstruction, the witness has a natural tendency to supply information to fill the gaps that is consistent with the witness's point of view about the case. The reconstruction therefore unintentionally shades the facts so they become part of a more seamless story. Recognize, however, that these witnesses are not fabricating. They would all pass a lie detector test.

The danger exists that witnesses may misunderstand or not fully grasp the position of the side they wish to help. As a result, they end up emphasizing facts that actually help the other side and do harm to their own side's position. To avoid such problems, be sure to spend some time explaining the issues in the case and each side's position regarding each issue. This does not mean giving a long legal explanation or getting the witness to your level of understanding. Instead, the goal is to help the witness develop a basic grasp of what the case is about.

If the witness is also the client, you will undoubtedly have educated her on the issues early in the case and updated her many times since as issues are eliminated or sharpened. But in corporate and similar cases, lower-level employees and others not directly interested in the outcome may have only vague ideas of what the lawsuit is about.

Explain the case issue by issue. Long summaries are not necessary; the discussion should cover manageable amounts of information by focusing on one issue at a time. Then, for each issue, give each side's position or what it is trying to prove. If the witness's role in the events giving rise to the litigation is limited, limit the discussion just to those issues in which the witness was involved. Like every other aspect of witness preparation, you should tailor the explanations of the issues to fit the witness's comprehension. Do not make the explanation more complex than the witness can understand and remember. The following is an example of an explanation of the issues to a nonparty witness:

Lawyer:	Let's now talk about what this case concerns and how you fit into it. As you know, this is an antitrust action. Dr. Rimard is claiming Hospital Pathology, Inc., has unfairly taken all of the pathology business for itself and has prevented Dr. Rimard from getting any of the business. Have you heard about that?
Witness:	Yes, there has been a lot of talk in the doctors' lounge about the case.
Lawyer:	The reason your deposition is being taken next week is to find out whether Hospital Pathology uses general practitioners such as yourself to steer pathology patients to themselves and away from Dr. Rimard. Dr. Rimard is claiming that when a patient requires pathology work, the hospital automatically refers the patient to Hospital Pathology without letting the patient or the patient's primary care physician know about alternative sources of pathology services. Hospital Pathology, on the other hand, is claiming it and the hospital always give a patient and the primary care physician a choice about what pathology services to use.
Witness:	OK.
Lawyer:	Your deposition is being taken today because you are a primary care doctor, and Hospital Pathology wants to find out what your experience has been with the referral of patients for pathology services. Does this all make sense?
Witness:	Yes.

13.2.9   *What to Do When Objections Are Made*

In a preparation session, witnesses often ask what to do if a particular topic comes up, or if the opposing counsel asks irrelevant questions, or if she asks the same question over and over again. The attorney's typical response is: "Well, if she does that, I'll object." Unfortunately, the attorney usually does not tell the witness that he will have to answer the question anyhow.

You must tell the witness that he must usually answer the question, even if it is objectionable, and that when appropriate, you will specifically direct or advise him not to answer. Discuss privilege issues with the witness and describe the ways in which such issues could come up. Tell the witness that if he has any question about whether an answer will involve privileged matters, he should request to speak with you before he answers so that he does not inadvertently reveal the privilege.[5] If you see a privilege problem that the witness does not, you should make the following objection: "Mr. Smith, objection; there may be a matter of privilege involved here; give me a moment with the witness, please." Then you can consult with the witness.

During the preparation session, tell the witness that if privileged matters come up, you will object and then instruct the witness not to answer based on privilege. Also let the witness know that some other questions you consider seriously objectionable may prompt an objection and a direction not to answer, but they will be rare. Those are questions that are designed to harass, annoy, and embarrass the witness, and the witness may be instructed not to answer so you can seek a protective order (although it is probably counterproductive to get into a detailed description of such questions with the witness). Finally, be sure the witness knows that if a question calls for information covered by a protective order already in existence, you may have to instruct him not to answer.

At that same point in the preparation session, inform the witness that opposing counsel will frequently follow up on a direction not to answer by asking the witness whether he will answer the question. The witness should be prepared to state, "On the advice of my counsel, I decline to answer the question."

Beyond these three situations, however—privilege, harassment/annoyance/embarrassment, and protective orders—the witness needs to understand that he is expected to answer all questions truthfully, and preferably in accordance with the approach outlined above, even when an objection has been made.

Defending counsel may sometimes object, "Assumes facts not in evidence." This objection is often heard at depositions, even though, technically, nothing is yet in evidence because this is still discovery. Therefore, this objection, if taken literally, could probably be made to all questions at depositions. Often, however, the objecting attorney is concerned about a question that is in some sense compound—that is, it contains within it the suggestion

---

5. Of course, as mentioned earlier, the questioning attorney may object strenuously if the defending attorney consults with the deponent while a question is pending. Because there is no better way to protect legitimate privileges, however, this consultation before the answer is given is appropriate. If the deposing attorney raises such a fuss that you cannot consult with the witness effectively, you can take a break and take the witness out in the hallway to discuss the possible privilege. Sometimes we call this the "elbow rule," since you take the witness by the elbow and lead him out of the room; normally, this effectively prevents the witness from giving answers until he has had adequate time to obtain advice about the privilege from counsel.

that a certain fact has already been established by the testimony of this deponent. Then, in answering the explicit question, the witness seems to be giving approval to or adopting the implicit fact. For example, a witness might be asked, "Well, when your company was doing so poorly with respect to environmental compliance in the late 1980s, you were still in charge of the governmental regulation group, weren't you?" By answering that she was still in that position, the witness seems to be accepting the characterization of the company's environmental performance. Putting the burden on the witness to avoid such an interpretation by giving a two-part answer ("We weren't doing poorly, and yes, I was still in the government regulation group.") is patently unfair. Perhaps a better objection would be "compound" or "complex" (or even "misleading," in the manner of, "are you still an environmental criminal?"), but "assumes facts not in evidence" certainly calls attention to the problem, although somewhat inartfully.

Too frequently a witness will listen to a question, decide the information that the questioning counsel is seeking, and begin to answer almost before the question is completed. This, of course, is how conversations occur, and it is difficult for a person to change a life's worth of conversation experience for the purpose of a deposition. This phenomenon creates several problems. First, the witness will frequently answer a better question than what was going to be asked. Second, if the answer begins immediately as the question ends, the witness may be rushing and not thinking about her answer sufficiently. For that reason, tell your witness that the process of answering questions in a deposition has four steps:

1. Listen to the question;

2. Think about what information the question calls for, and specifically consider the important words in the question;

3. Think thorough the answer silently, putting it in sentence form in your mind; and

4. Answer the question.

A witness should not be told to "wait a moment before answering to allow an objection," because that heightens, rather than reduces, the witness's burdens and anxieties. Witnesses should be given less, not more, to worry about. Slowing down the process of answering questions is almost always beneficial to the witness, and the four-step process described above should accomplish just that. In a deposition that is recorded in a written transcript (as opposed to on video), the immediate audience is a piece of paper. Silence between the question and the answer is not shown. Once the witness understands this fact, the opportunity to provide clear and precise answers is greatly enhanced.

13.3 Final Instructions

Conclude the witness preparation sessions by taking care of a few of the remaining necessary housekeeping details.

13.3.1 What to Wear

As discussed in section 2.3.1, depositions influence the settlement value of a case by giving opposing counsel a chance to assess the impression a witness will make on a judge or jury. A strong favorable witness—a witness whose testimony is believable and who can withstand the rigors of cross-examination—will cause the opposing party to demand less or pay more in settlement than a witness who vacillates, is tentative, has memory problems, or otherwise makes a poor impression.

The witness's appearance is one of the factors affecting the impression a witness makes. If the witness is attractive (not so much physically attractive as pleasant in demeanor and manner of speech) and is dressed appropriately, this will enhance the witness's credibility. The clothing appropriate for a particular witness depends on the image you want him to project and deserves careful thought—for both video and non-video depositions. Whatever the image you desire, instruct the witness on how to dress for the deposition, perhaps after consulting with a professional communications consultant.

13.3.2 What to Bring

When defending a deposition, one of an attorney's less pleasant experiences occurs when a witness suddenly reaches into his pocket and pulls out a set of notes that you've never seen before. That in itself is an unwelcome surprise, and it gets worse when you discover that the witness has scribbled in them all sorts of damaging comments about the strength of the case. If the witness uses the notes to refresh his memory, little can be done to keep them away from opposing counsel.

The scene just described happens more times than defending lawyers wish. Often, after the witness preparation session, a witness will go home and start worrying about what questions will be asked the next day. The witness logically thinks that a few notes will help him keep events straight. Then, if he forgets, he can also refer to the notes during the deposition. The witness may also figure it would not hurt to write down counsel's comments about some of the problems in the case.

The easiest way to prevent this scenario from occurring is to instruct witnesses to bring nothing to the deposition—no notes, documents, or anything else. Do not, however, rely only on these instructions. On the day of the deposition, be sure to ask whether the witness has any notes or other papers and, if he does, take them away before the deposition begins.

(There are some witnesses who will be presenting especially complex testimony at trial, and you may want these witnesses to use extensive notes during their testimony, including timelines and source notes describing the genesis of spreadsheets or scientific calculations. If those notes have been thoroughly reviewed to make sure that they do not contain your or other counsel's instructions or privileged or confidential communications, there is no reason to avoid them, because opposing counsel, even if they obtain them, will learn little that they should not learn.)

13.3.3   *What to Look At and Who to Talk To*

To enhance the settlement value of the case, the witness wants his testimony to be accepted by questioning counsel as rational and credible. Whether the deposition is video recorded or not, the witness needs to have an appropriate amount of eye contact with the questioner. If it is video recorded, however, looking at the questioner means looking away from the camera (and from the judge or jury who will eventually be seeing the witness through the camera's perspective). Therefore, instruct the witness that the normal approach for an answer that is more than a few words long is to start the answer by looking at questioning counsel; then, for the second or third sentence on, to turn to the camera and provide the expansion or explanation of the answer. This "TV weatherman" approach ("Yes, Brittany, we could use a break from this heat—TURN TO CAMERA—and folks, that is just what we'll be getting this next Tuesday and Wednesday") appears natural and draws the fact finder into the conversation. (At trial before a jury, this same approach can be used by experts on direct and cross-examination. In a bench trial, because judges tend to avoid eye contract, the witness should just look at and talk to questioning counsel.)

13.4   Practicing Your Theme with the Witness

With any witness, lay or expert, the deposition preparation should include a discussion of how their testimony helps support the theme of your case. As an example, with an expert, tell the expert the theme or themes that you are evaluating for your presentations at trial. In a patent case, perhaps your themes are, "Dr. Madison was the first to think of a flexible coronary stent and use it to save lives," and "The defendant corporation took Dr. Madison's invention, without pay, without permission, and made $500 million by selling it as their own." In preparing for the deposition, you want the witness to practice answers using key words that invoke those themes: "They had nothing like this," "They promised they would not steal it," "Save lives,"

"I first thought of it," "They took it," "It was very profitable for them." Identify the core principles of your case—the ones that you must prove to have an effective presentation—and emphasize to the witness how he cannot let these be diminished by crafty questions that lead to weak statements by him. There may be other facts or positions that he can give up when pressed, but he cannot give up your thematic elements.

13.5   Conclusion

In summary, the basic rules for preparing a witness to be deposed are simple:

- Review the substantive testimony until the witness is comfortable with phrasing, chronology, with the history she is telling, and with the fourteen most important documents.

- Explain the deposition process overall.

- Try to reduce the witness's anxieties by narrowing their concerns: "Tell the truth briefly."

- Try to assure the witness that you are there to handle any legal matters (not "problems") that might come up.

Persuade the witness that any procedural problems will be minor and will not interfere with effective testimony.

CHAPTER FOURTEEN

DEFENDING THE DEPOSITION

They have no lawyers among them, for they consider them
as a sort of people whose profession it is to disguise matters.

—Sir Thomas More

The attorney defending the deposition has many responsibilities, including supporting and protecting the witness, preserving certain objections in the record for the court's later ruling, and protecting against the disclosure of privileged and other confidential information.

14.1   Advance Preparation

Just as the taker must carefully research and be familiar with the legal issues in the case, so must the defending attorney. As defending attorney, you must also be completely familiar with the facts of the case and with what the witness knows. You will not know whether your witness in answering a question has misspoken or has decided to change the story previously told during preparation unless you are familiar enough with the story to know when the witness has deviated from it. Similarly, you will not know when you need to correct the record unless you know the correct story.

There are two other pieces of information you must know in advance of the deposition: 1) the law, including the local rules, governing the taking and defending of depositions for the jurisdiction controlling the deposition; and 2) the predilections of the judge or magistrate who will be hearing any discovery disputes arising in the case. What do the law and the local rules say about conferring with a witness while a question is pending? Are there any limitations on the types and forms of objections that can be made? Is the judge/magistrate someone who applies the rules of procedure strictly or are the parties given more latitude than the rules would appear to permit? Does the judge/magistrate permit speaking objections and other sorts of misbehavior to go unpunished or are sanctions immediately levied? Will this judge/magistrate entertain telephone hearings if a dispute should arise during the deposition, or are discovery disputes noticed and heard in the same way as other non-discovery motions? You need to know the answers to these and many more questions about the law and the judge/magistrate before the deposition begins.

14.2   Determining Whether the Witness Is a Client

How you defend the deposition depends on whether the witness is your client, is represented by somebody else, or is unrepresented. Determining whether a witness is a client is usually quite simple: Has the witness retained you for purposes of representation? More difficult problems arise, however, when you are retained by a party that is a corporation and the deponent is an officer of the corporation or, at the extreme, is a low-level employee at the bottom of the organizational chart. Even though these individuals may not be clients, they may nevertheless be covered by the corporation's attorney-client privilege and work-product protections.

Whether a corporation's attorney-client privilege extends to corporate employees or employees of a collective entity such as a labor union or an organization depends on whether the question is being asked in what is known as a "control-group" jurisdiction or in what is labeled as an "*Upjohn*" jurisdiction, or in a jurisdiction following some variation of these two tests.

In a "control-group" jurisdiction—constituting a dwindling number of states—the attorney-client privilege extends only to those individuals in the corporation or collective entity who can make legal decisions on behalf of the organization or have the authority to bind the organization in any way. Many of these jurisdictions limit the "control group" to such persons as the directors or officers of the organization. In contrast, *Upjohn* jurisdictions (so named after the 1981 Supreme Court case of *Upjohn Co. v. United States*[1]) extend the attorney-client privilege to communications between counsel and *any* employee of the corporation or collective entity, from the lowest to the highest, as long as the communications are to obtain information or provide legal advice, which in turn is necessary to provide legal representation for the organization. In both types of jurisdictions, the privilege belongs to the organization and may only be waived by those persons within the organization with the power to make legal decisions on behalf of the organization.

The employees covered by the organization's attorney-client privilege may also have their own separate and independent privilege. For example, the CEO of a corporation may be represented by the CEO's own attorney. Communications between the CEO and the CEO's attorney will be protected by the CEO's attorney-client privilege. At the same time, the corporation may

---

1. 449 U.S. 383 (1981).

have its own attorneys with the communications between them protected by the corporation's attorney-client privilege.

What privilege applies, if any, depends on the court in which the action is pending. If the action is pending in a federal court, Rule 501 controls.[2] Privileges in actions based on a federal question and federal criminal proceedings are governed by federal common law, which means the court will follow the *Upjohn* rule discussed above. Privileges in diversity actions, in contrast, are controlled by the laws of the state providing the rules of decision in the action. Only occasionally do choice of law issues arise in litigation. In most state court cases, the law of the forum state will apply and will provide the attorney-client privilege to be applied. While the issue of which privilege rules apply in a particular case can be difficult, the answer is to research the applicable law when in doubt.

When the witness is a client or someone covered by the client's attorney-client privilege, any meetings between the attorney and the witness to prepare the witness to testify at the witness's deposition are privileged. Similarly, the witness can consult privately with counsel during the deposition and any discussions between them are also privileged. The following sections discuss what you must do to adequately represent the interests of clients and witnesses protected by the attorney-client privilege. Even when the witness is neither a client nor covered by any attorney-client privilege, many of the same roles apply in the deposition room that you would perform on behalf of a client or a witness covered by the attorney-client privilege. The important difference between witnesses covered by the attorney-client privilege and those who are not is that the uncovered witness may have to disclose the contents of any conversations between herself and counsel in response to questioning by opposing counsel.[3] Unless otherwise specifically noted, the remainder of this chapter assumes that the deponent is being represented by counsel or is otherwise covered by the attorney-client privilege.

---

2. FED. R. EVID. 501 states:

> The common law—as interpreted by United States courts in the light of reason and experience—governs a claim of privilege unless any of the following provides otherwise:
> the United States Constitution;
> a federal statute; or
> rules prescribed by the Supreme Court.
> But in a civil case, state law governs privileges regarding a claim or defense for which state law supplies the rule of decision.

3. An attorney does not have the right to instruct a nonclient to refuse to answer a question at the deposition, but she may tell the nonclient that he has the right to refuse to answer in some circumstances and to seek counsel of his own.

14.3 Preparing the Witness to Testify

Of all the tasks the defending lawyer must perform, preparing the witness to testify is by far the most important. If done well, there will be little for the defending attorney to do during the deposition. The issue is so significant that we have devoted a separate chapter, chapter thirteen, to the subject.

14.4 Supporting and Protecting the Witness

Anyone who has ever been deposed can attest that it is almost always a stressful, anxiety-provoking, unpleasant experience. Most deponents are justifiably nervous about the prospect of being deposed. If witnesses are parties, they are worried about whether they are answering correctly or in a way that might cause them to lose the case. Even when not a party, they may be concerned that their answers might cause them to lose their jobs or that people whose opinion they value may think they did something wrong. The interrogating attorney often challenges and argues with the witness, asks personally embarrassing questions, and even suggests, directly or indirectly, that the witness is a scoundrel and a liar. In short, being a witness at a deposition can be a horrible experience.

One of the most important tasks you have as defending counsel at deposition is to provide emotional comfort and support to the witness. The job is to make an unpleasant situation as bearable as possible and to keep the pressures of the situation from interfering with the witness's attempt to give accurate and effective deposition testimony. In large part, you can do this merely by insuring that the deponent recognizes that you are there to look after the deponent's interests. Your witness is relying on you to make sure that nothing bad happens.

This is not just a matter of handholding and client service. A witness who feels secure and protected will feel more comfortable in defending her actions, fending off the questioning attorney's efforts to shake her story, and avoiding unfortunate party statements. It is not only good client service, but also good deposition strategy to have the witness see you, defending counsel, as a guardian during the deposition. Keep in mind, however, that there are limits to what you can do to protect a deponent. Witnesses are frequently called on to answer proper questions that may be embarrassing or, more likely, call for information about the case that is harmful to their position. Take care to tell the witness during preparation of such possibilities. If you do not warn the witness properly, the protective relationship you have built with the witness can break down when you cannot prevent the witness from answering a question that she would rather avoid.

At the deposition, sit next to your witness, with the questioner across from both of you, and put yourself between the witness and the reporter. To participate effectively in the deposition, take a position slightly forward of the deponent, that is, closer to the table, so you are always in the deponent's view. When you take that position, the witness will constantly be aware of your presence, thereby giving her some degree of comfort. Being seated slightly forward of the witness also permits you to stop the witness from answering merely by slightly raising a hand, thereby preserving the opportunity to make objections or to instruct the witness not to answer before she blurts out an answer. You may want a moment before the witness answers to give yourself a moment to think about the question and its propriety and ramifications. By holding up a hand in front of the witness and saying, "Give me a moment, please," you gain some reasonable time to consider whether an objection or direction not to answer is called for. No rule requires that counsel must, without thought, immediately object to a question being asked; just as the questioner is entitled to pause and consider between an answer and the next question, so should a defender be allowed to think about possible objections to questions.

By staying up at the table at the witness's elbow, you will also stay much more involved in the deposition, and the witness is less likely to fall into a "conversation" with deposing counsel that can lead to ill-considered volunteering. When you make objections, the witness will be able to both see and hear you and will more readily understand the significance of the objection.[4] In that position, at the witness's elbow, you are also positioned to exercise two of the most important—albeit, limited—rights available to the defending attorney: the opportunity to consult with the witness at the table

---

4. In the authors' opinion, attorneys in trial or deposition may not object for the primary purpose of coaching a witness or otherwise substantively affecting the witness's testimony; but a good-faith objection—that is, one that has an arguably valid evidentiary basis—does not become improper merely because the witness, on hearing it, may adjust an answer.

For example, consider a good-faith objection that a question is ambiguous:

Q: Tell us about the regular procedure.
DC: Objection. At what time, counsel? The question is ambiguous. I object. The witness will certainly review the "regular procedures" in his mind to determine whether there have been changes since the relevant time. That review by the witness does not render the objection improper or unethical. On the other hand, an objection clearly intended to cue the witness, and for no valid evidentiary purpose, is improper.

Q: Did your company earn any profit the first year of operation?
DC: Objection. I don't understand the question. I don't see how anyone could understand the question. It's completely ambiguous as to what you mean by "profit" and "operation." Can you understand the question, Mrs. Banis?

A: No, I don't understand the question.

See Fed. R. Civ. P. 30(d)(1).

and the ability to recess the deposition for a brief period to confer with the witness outside the deposition room.[5] Protection of the witness also extends to the time before the deposition begins and during breaks. Never plan to meet the witness at opposing counsel's office. Although the vast majority of attorney's will not take advantage of the opportunity to question the witness if the witness arrives before the witness's attorney, some attorneys are not so scrupulous. Avoid this problem by agreeing to meet at your office and to go together to opposing counsel's office.

Also be cautious about allowing the witness to talk with opposing counsel before the deposition begins, while everyone is filling up their coffee cups and getting comfortable. Even if your witness does not disclose anything of substance, these casual moments with opposing counsel tend to cause her to lower her guard. As a corollary to this, never leave the witness alone in the deposition room. Follow the rule that the witness is never left without counsel: if you must leave the room for a telephone call or a restroom break, take the witness out of the room as well. During restroom breaks, instruct the witness not to speak with anyone—opposing counsel, paralegals, friends, strangers, or secretaries. Even though it is clearly inappropriate, deposing counsel frequently try to engage the witness in conversation when defending counsel is absent or occupied. Although deposing counsel always tries to defend those conversations as "merely trying to make the witness comfortable," they are improper when the witness is represented.

14.5   Entering into Stipulations

The wisdom of agreeing to various stipulations has been discussed in section 1.13.4.

14.6   Preserving the Record

Depositions usually result in a transcript or video recording of the testimony that can be used for various purposes, including use at trial.[6] Like an appellate record, the deposition transcript may be clear and understandable or a muddled jumble of words incomprehensible to both judge and jury. The question you must answer as the defending attorney is: "Which is better—clear or muddled?" Is the client's best interest served by a clear record, or is the client better off if the transcript created by opposing counsel is a mass of confusion? The answer to this question may change with the topics under examination and also with whether the deponent's answers are favorable or unfavorable to the client's position. Given the choice, helpful answers should be clear and understandable; harmful answers are better left obtuse

---

5. *See* section 14.7.

6. *See* chapter sixteen.

and incomprehensible. To make this decision—clear or muddled—you must be alert during the deposition and listen carefully to the answers being given.

Such answers as "It was from here to there," or "It was right here at this point on the map that I first saw the other car," are likely going to be useless if the deposition is later used at trial. Even though everyone in the deposition room could see exactly where the witness was pointing when these answers were given, the judge or jury will be left without a clue as to where "here" and "there" are or to which point on the map the witness was referring.

If that is the way you prefer it—the judge and jury in the dark—because the answer is harmful to your claim or defense, sit quietly. However, if the answer is helpful, then you should state for the record what the witness is doing: "Let the record reflect that the witness is indicating from his chair to counsel's chair, a distance of approximately five feet," or "Counsel, let's have the witness mark with the letter A where he is pointing on the map, which has been marked as Deposition Exhibit 12." However, it must be absolutely clear that while you as defending counsel have no affirmative duty to clarify a record that is muddied by deposing counsel's ineptitude, you may not contribute to such muddiness by baseless objections, inappropriate demeanor, improper preparation of the witness, or other unethical behavior.[7]

14.7 Conferring with the Witness

Another reason to sit next to the witness is to allow you and the witness to confer quickly and easily about a question or answer when necessary and appropriate. Assuming you do not abuse such conferences in an effort to obstruct the deposition, there is no limit on the frequency or number of times you and the witness can confer, unless, of course, such conferences are precluded by a discovery order or local rule. More and more judges are issuing discovery orders that do not allow conferences between the defending lawyer and the witness during the pendency of the deposition, even during breaks and recesses, except when necessary to discuss whether to assert a privilege or when required as a matter of professional responsibility to ensure that the witness is not committing perjury.[8] Some courts accomplish the same end through local rules. Assuming, however, that such conferences are permissible for other reasons, and your relationship with opposing counsel has been a professional and courteous one, the following can occur.

---

7. *See* chapter eleven for extended discussions of ethical problems arising due to interference by defending counsel.

8. *See, e.g.,* Hall v. Clifton Precision, 150 F.R.D. 525 (E.D. Pa. 1993); Chapsky v. Baxter Healthcare, Mueller Div., 1995 WL 327348, 1995 U.S. Dist. LEXIS 2609 (N.D. Ill. 1994). *Hall* represents perhaps the extreme constraints on counsel at deposition, where the court felt that it had to impose draconian restrictions to prevent counsel from fighting like little children over the smallest disputes.

After the witness has answered a question, you can lean over and remind the witness not to volunteer information beyond that called for by the question, or not to argue the case, but merely state facts. This conference is off the record because it is whispered and inaudible to the reporter and opposing counsel. Obviously, if you follow every important question and answer with this type of conference, deposing counsel should begin to "make a record" by commenting on each conference. Then the witness may grow uncomfortable and the judge, if asked to rule on this behavior, may grow skeptical. As long as you use this limited "right" to confer judiciously and not for the purpose of obstructing legitimate discovery, it can be an effective and proper means of controlling the witness so that her answers are responsive without being overly generous.

Even where some topics are off-limits in a deposition because they are privileged or because the court has previously issued a protective order prohibiting questioning on the topics, you can use a "mini-conference" to remind the witness that the questions are getting close to those topics. This may prevent the witness from inadvertently providing protected or privileged information in an answer to a question that approaches such topics; if such information is inadvertently provided, the protection of the order or the privilege may be waived.

Occasionally at a deposition, a witness will need some lengthier counseling on procedures. Having forgotten the basic rules of listening to the question and answering accurately and briefly, the witness has adopted the role of advocate rather than witness, or is allowing the deposing attorney to provoke intemperate statements. In such situations, after an answer is completed, you should invoke the "elbow rule": take the client-witness by the elbow, state, "We're taking a break here," and go into the hallway or a vacant office to straighten things out.

Deposing counsel will probably try to prevent this interruption by saying something like, "You can't do that," or "You can take a break after I finish this line," or "Let's break after this next question," but no response to those suggestions is required. Deposing counsel cannot prevent you and the witness from leaving. Use the "elbow rule" as soon as the witness is starting to get out of control. At a minimum, deposing counsel will get no information from the witness while the witness is out of the room.

As stated, these conferences can be held *sotto voce* at the table or out in the hallway without much concern that they will lead to a ruling by a judge that discovery has been illegitimately frustrated. Sometimes, however, you and the client-deponent must confer before an answer is given—when privileged information might be disclosed in an answer or when the witness is unsure about how to answer without divulging confidential or personal information. In such a case, there is little choice but to confer with the witness while the question is pending to determine whether the witness should be instructed not to answer the question on grounds of privilege.

In fact, this conference adds no interruption to the proceedings because the alternative would be for you to object to the question and instruct the witness not to answer—then you and the witness would hold the exact conference just discussed.

It is important to emphasize that there is no right to confer with the witness while a question is pending except regarding a matter of privilege. To do so is to risk the possibility of sanctions, and you should not do it.[9]

14.8   Taking Breaks

Answering questions at a deposition is exhausting work, made more so by need for the witness to be constantly alert to the wording of the questions and the need to give complete and precise answers. Defending a deposition is also difficult and tiring (albeit not as tiring as for the witness). Both the witness and the defending attorney will find themselves becoming increasingly fatigued as the deposition wears on, and, therefore, it is essential that breaks be taken periodically during which both can relax and prepare themselves for returning to the deposition room. Do not rely on the witness's protestations that they are doing fine and do not need a break. Nor should you be tempted to think that it is better to just get the deposition over rather than taking a break. People—you included—need breaks if they are to maintain alertness. Do not forgo them.

How often you should take breaks is open to debate. Our advice is the deposition should go no longer than one and a half hours at a stretch without a break. In the afternoon, the period without a break should be reduced to once each hour. But, of course, you should be constantly monitoring the witness's performance as well as your own and taking breaks, regardless of the amount of time since the last one, whenever it appears that fatigue is setting in. Sloppiness in wording answers, yawning, rubbing eyes, looking haggard, and so on, are all reliable signs that you or the witness is in need of a break. Take one.

Breaks can be handled in several ways. The two sides can agree at the beginning of the deposition to a break schedule to be followed or either side can call for a break whenever needed. Breaks in most depositions are handled both ways, that is, by following a schedule and supplementing the schedule with additional breaks as needed.

---

9. *See* Calzaturficio v. S.C.A.R.P.A. s.p.a. v. Fabiano Shoe Co., Inc., 201 F.R.D. 40 (D. Mass. 2001); McKinley Infuser, Inc. v. Zdeb, 200 F.R.D. 648, 650 (D. Colo. 2001); In re Stratosphere Sec. Litig., 182 F.R.D. 614, 621 (D. Nev. 1998); *see generally* United States v. Phillip Morris, 212 F.R.D. 418, 420 (D.D.C. 2002).

14.9   Stating Objections

The process of making and responding to deposition objections probably consumes more energy, causes more frustration, and wastes more time than any other aspect of discovery. Perhaps because of their lack of confidence in their own knowledge of the rules of evidence, or because they are unsure about what objections are waived and what objections are preserved, attorneys at depositions object and battle over objections, by actual count, at least one million times more than is necessary to represent their clients properly. Most deposition disputes could be avoided by the parties paying more attention to the requirements of the Federal Rules of Civil Procedure and the Federal Rules of Evidence. The following is a review of what objections should be made at a deposition and how to make them.

14.9.1   Objections That (Usually) Do Not Have to Be Made at the Deposition

Rule 32(d)(3)(A) states that objections to competency, relevancy, or materiality need not be made at the deposition unless by doing so the grounds for the objection could have been cured. Similarly, Rule 32(d)(3)(B) states that only curable objections are waived by failing to make them at the deposition. In short, you need not assert any objection that cannot be cured at the deposition, but can assert them for the first time when one of the parties attempts to introduce the objectionable portion of the deposition at trial, in support of or in opposition to a motion, or for some other purpose.[10] While it is possible to imagine circumstances where additional questions might cure the objection, the reality is that most objections to competency, relevancy, or materiality cannot be cured.

What kinds of objections cannot be cured? Again without attempting to be exhaustive, the usual noncurable objections are:

Relevancy (including materiality)

Relevancy and materiality are defined in Rule 401:

Evidence is relevant if:

(a)   it has any tendency to make a fact more or less probably than it would be without the evidence; and

(b)   the fact is of consequence in determining the action.

The common-law term "material" is not used in the rule, but the concept of materiality is encompassed within the phrase "the fact is of consequence

---

10. At least one court has said that it is improper to make objections at the deposition to competency, relevancy, and materiality. *Hall*, 150 F.R.D. at 528, n.3.

in determining the action." In short, materiality means the evidence being offered must go to proving or disproving to an issue that is provable in the case.

Obviously, relevance and materiality are matters that cannot be cured by further questioning or by rephrasing the question; they may be disclosed, but they are not cured. They depend solely on the relationship between the facts sought and the issues in the case. Furthermore, Rule 26(b)(1) allows discovery of relevant information and defines it to include information that may not itself be admissible, but which is reasonably calculated to lead to the discovery of admissible evidence.

Prejudicial

Whether, under Rule 403, the probative value of the evidence is outweighed by the danger of unfair prejudicial effect cannot be determined until trial, when the evidence is weighed in relationship to all of the evidence in the case.[11]

Hearsay (unless the testimony can be placed within a hearsay exception)

Hearsay is normally not a curable objection, and therefore it is not waived if not made at the deposition. If a statement is hearsay under Rule 801, no amount of further questioning will convert the statement into nonhearsay. If, however, the hearsay statement can be placed into one of the hearsay exceptions of Rule 803, 804 or 807, then the objection can be cured. Whether the statement is admissible under a hearsay exception depends, of course, on the particulars of the statement.[12]

Confusion of the Issues, Misleading to the Jury, Undue Delay, Waste of Time, or Needless Presentation of Cumulative Evidence

As with unfairly prejudicial evidence, these objections under Rule 403 can only be evaluated in the context of trial or a motion in limine and not at the

---

11. *See generally*, Old Chief v. United States, 519 U.S. 172 (1997).

12. The conventional wisdom is that a hearsay objection is not curable regardless of whether the hearsay fits into a hearsay exception. We believe the conventional wisdom is incorrect. It is well worth arguing to the court that if defending counsel had interposed a timely hearsay objection, it would have been possible for you to lay the necessary foundation for the hearsay to fall within an exception. Of course, be sure you can articulate the applicable hearsay exception and what likely evidence would permit it falling within that exception. As defending counsel, there is no harm in making an objection to make certain that you are preserving possible hearsay objections, assuming that you have a good-faith belief that such an objection is appropriate.

discovery stage. Therefore, these objections are not waived by failing to make them at the deposition.

Competency

Rule 601 provides that every person is competent to be a witness unless otherwise provided in the rules.[13] However, when state law supplies the rule of decision for an element of the claim or defense, then the competency of a witness will be determined in accordance with state law. Rule 32(d)(3)(A) expressly states that objections to a lack of competency are not waived by failing to make them at the deposition.

14.9.2   *Objections That Must Be Made at or before the Deposition*

Objections to problems in the notice and taking of the deposition that can be cured must be made or they are waived. Neither the taker nor the defender should assume an objection to improper questions or procedures raised for the first time after the deposition will be considered by the judge; a timely objection must have been made at or before the deposition.

Objections as to Notice

Rule 32(d)(1) states that all errors and irregularities in the notice of deposition are waived unless a written objection is promptly served on the party giving notice. The purpose of this provision is to prevent technical irregularities from destroying the utility of depositions at trial. If the irregularities are not corrected and they substantially affect the deposition, the objecting party should seek a protective order directed at correcting the complained of defect.[14]

Counsel will usually have agreed to a time and place for the deposition, and the fact that the witness showed up is usually a demonstration that the notice has been adequate. Sometimes, however, the notice should contain some additional information—the subject of a 30(b)(6) deposition, the method of recording the testimony, or the specifications of the subpoena *duces tecum* served on a non-party witness—on which counsel may not agree. Because these are matters of notice that can be corrected—cured or obviated—they must be raised by an objection before the deposition is taken or any such objections is waived.

---

13. Fed. R. Evid. 601: "Every person is competent to be a witness unless these rules provide otherwise. But in a civil case, state law governs the witness's competency regarding a claim or defense for which state law supplies the rule of decision."

14. *See* chapter twelve.

Objections as to Qualifications of the Officer

Rule 32(d)(2) states that unless an objection is made before the deposition begins, or as soon thereafter as the disqualification becomes known or could be discovered with reasonable diligence, any objection to the qualifications of the officer before whom the deposition is being taken is waived. Occasionally, the reporter provided by the reporting service is not a notary in the jurisdiction in which the deposition is being taken. Sometimes this occurs because the notarial powers are granted for limited geographic areas, like counties, and the reporting service was not aware that the deposition was across a county line. Nevertheless, this defect can be easily cured by having a notary come in to swear the witness. As a technical matter, the "officer" notary would then have to remain in the room, because the deposition is to be recorded "in the officer's presence."[15] By stipulation, of course, the parties could waive this requirement so the officer/notary could then leave.

14.9.3 Objections That Must Be Made at the Deposition

In addition to the specific objections mentioned in Rule 32(d)(3)(A), Rule 32(d)(3)(B) provides that errors or irregularities of any kind occurring at the deposition that might have been corrected if promptly raised at the time are waived by failing to make a timely objection at the deposition. This includes, but is not limited to, errors in the taking of the deposition, in the form of the questions or answers, in the oath or affirmation, or in the conduct of the parties. The vast majority of deposition objections are made under this provision.

There are a number of objections that traditionally are not made at a deposition because the conventional wisdom is that the objection cannot be cured. While in most instances this is correct—the objection cannot be cured—it is too simplistic to say they can never be cured. It is very possible to imagine situations where these "noncurable" objections are in fact curable. Subject to this caveat, what follows is a collection of the objections that are generally considered to beyond cure and therefore do not have to be made at the deposition.

Objections to Form of the Question

Most objections to questions at a deposition are directed to the form of the questions. Sound objections to the form of a question are always curable by merely rephrasing the question. Such an objection is therefore waived unless made at the time of the deposition.[16] The following are the generally

---

15. Fed. R. Civ. P. 30(c).

16. Fed. R. Civ. P. 32(d)(3). Objections to questions at a deposition are made appropriate by Rule 30(c), which provides that the examination of witnesses may proceed as if at trial.

recognized objections to the form of the question. Note that except with regard to leading questions, there is no Federal Rule of Evidence governing these objections. They are all derived from the general authority of the court to regulate the mode of witness questioning.[17]

Leading

A leading question is one that suggests the desired answer to the deponent in such a way that there is concern it is the lawyer who is testifying. Rule 611(c) states that leading questions should only be used on direct examination when the witness is hostile, an adverse party, or identified with an adverse party. In the context of a deposition, there is no doubt an adverse party, employees or agents of an adverse party, and others closely associated with an adverse party may be examined by using leading questions. The examination at the deposition is the equivalent of a cross-examination or adverse examination at trial.

But the examination is more akin to a direct examination if the witness is a nonparty and not associated in any way with a party. In such situations, the questioning is the equivalent of a direct examination at trial and should be conducted with nonleading questions. Some witnesses, while nonparties and not associated with a party, may nonetheless behave in a hostile way to being questioned. With such witnesses, the examining lawyer must first establish through the witness's answers or attitude that hostility exists. The witness's nonverbal hostility in a stenographic deposition may require the taking lawyer to describe for the record the behavior being displayed. Once the hostility is established to the taker's satisfaction, and hopefully later to the court's satisfaction as well, the examination may proceed through leading questions.

An example of leading questions is the following interrogation:

Q: Mr. Smith, on June 6 of last year, you were driving north on Kirby Street, is that correct?

A: Yes.

Q: That would have been around eleven o'clock in the morning?

A: I think so. About then.

Q: You were going to your office?

A: Yes.

Even though questioning counsel can ask leading questions of adverse parties and those identified with them, as well as of hostile witnesses, defend-

---

17. Fed. R. Evid. 611(a).

ing counsel should remember that leading questions are not an efficient method of learning new information, and defending counsel should hesitate before helping questioning counsel by objecting to leading by questioning counsel. Leading questions should generally be reserved for obtaining party statements from the witness.[18]

An objection to a leading question can be cured by questioning counsel by rephrasing the question to be nonleading or by demonstrating that the leading question is necessary to adequately develop the testimony of the witness. Tactically, it may well be advisable not to object to leading questions, even though legally appropriate, since it is likely that a judge or jury reading or hearing the deposition testimony at some later point in the proceeding will conclude it is the lawyer who is providing the answers for the witness through the form of the questions being asked. But if defending counsel suspects that the witness would not be providing the same answers if required to answer nonleading questions—that the lawyer is actually feeding the correct answers to a friendly witness—then defending counsel should make a timely objection.

If defending counsel chooses to ask questions of the witness at the end of the taking counsel's questioning, those questions should normally be nonleading unless the deposition is of the adverse party, a witness closely associated with the adverse party, or a hostile witness.

Ambiguous/Vague/Unintelligible/Complex/Confusing

All of these terms, which are often used interchangeably, describe questions that do not advise the witness in a clear and understandable manner what information is being sought by the questions. In particular, an ambiguous question is one that is susceptible to at least two interpretations. A vague question is so unintelligible as to make it likely that the witness does not understand what is being asked for in response or confuses the deponent. The rest of the listed terms are self-explanatory. A typical example of a vague question would be:

Q: How large is the Acme Corporation?

A: I'm sorry, but I don't understand. Are you asking for the annual sales, how many employees work for the Acme Corporation, the square footage of the building, or something else?

Most courts will not sustain objections on the listed grounds if the witness claims to understand the question. A simple, "Do you understand the question?" followed by a "yes" is usually enough to obviate the objection.

---

18. *See* chapter eight.

On the other hand, it is usually a mistake to ask this question immediately following a vagueness objection—witnesses often pick up on the defending attorney's objection and reply that they do not understand the question even though they have a perfect understanding of what is being asked. It is often better to follow a vagueness objection with, "Please go ahead and answer the question," and put on the witness the burden of claiming a lack of understanding. If the witness says in response to the command to answer the question that the question is not understandable, then follow up by asking what is it about the question the witness does not understand. But if the witness does answer the question, oftentimes the answer will provide useful information even though not it was not what the taking attorney was hoping to find out through the question. The taking attorney can then ask further, better phrased questions to obtain the sought-after information. The objection can also be cured by rephrasing the question to make it more clear and understandable.

Tactically, the listed objections should, as a general rule, always be made. Unless you conclude it does not matter how the witness answers the question—all possible answers are harmless—it is always better for the witness to understand exactly what is being asked. Otherwise, there is a possibility that the taking attorney was asking for innocuous information, but the witness will misunderstand the question and provide a harmful answer.

Argumentative

An argumentative question is one that is asked not for the purpose of obtaining information from the witness but rather to make an argument, in the guise of a question, regarding the facts of the case and hoping that the witness will agree. The question is a conclusion by the interrogator and argues or comments on the evidence rather than asking a true question. An example of an argumentative question is: "That was very reckless driving on your part. Weren't you worried you might have an accident?" The objection can be cured or avoided by rephrasing the question so that it is clearly seeking facts rather than inferences. Tactically, you should always object to an argumentative question.

Asked and Answered

A defender may object to a question as asked and answered when it appears to ask the same question again. The objection to such a question is sometimes also stated as "cumulative." This objection is fundamentally improper because it interferes with the spontaneous testimony of the deponent.

It is often a tactic for the taking lawyer in a deposition to ask in a different way an already-asked question to test the credibility of both the witness and the information that has been provided. Judges will only rarely sustain an asked-and-answered objection made in a deposition, and then only when repetition constitutes harassment. If the answer is different the second time the question is asked, that pretty much defeats the objection. But defending lawyers rarely make the objection with the expectation that it will be sustained. Instead, the usual purposes of the objection are to throw the questioning attorney off track and to alert the witness that the question has been answered before and the answer this time should be the same as the previous time. Both of these are impermissible grounds for making an objection. Best advice to the questioner: As usual, tell the witness that she may answer the question and do not engage with the defender.

Assuming Facts Not in Evidence

A question is objectionable if it assumes facts that have not already been proved through the testimony of the deponent or by other competent evidence. The objection is cured by asking the witness about the fact that was assumed in the objected-to question and verifying that the witness knows the fact. The main body of the objected-to question can then be asked in a subsequent question. For example, the question, "When you went to the store, what did you buy?" might assume that the deponent went to the store although she has not testified about going to the store. It could be improved by asking, "Did you go to the store? What did you buy?"

If the defending attorney knows the assumed fact to be true and the witness will readily admit it, little is to be gained from objecting that the question assumes a fact not in evidence other than to annoy the taking attorney. The taking attorney will easily cure the objection by asking whether the assumed fact is true. But an objection should always be made if there is there is any uncertainty about the truthfulness of the assumed fact. Some attorneys will deliberately place contested facts in questions as assumed facts with the hopes that the witness and defending attorney will not notice this verbal sleight of hand and will answer the question without focusing on the assumed fact. In this way the assumed fact becomes an admitted fact.

Compound Questions

Compound questions are actually two questions combined into one, making it difficult to tell to which question the witness is responding. An example of a compound question is: "You were driving on the left side of the road and were driving at 45 miles per hour?" If the witness answers "yes," it is unclear whether the witness was driving on the left side of the road, driving at 45 miles per hour, or both. Objections to compound questions are easily cured by breaking the question down into two or more separate question: "Were you driving on the left side of the road?" "Were you driving at 45 miles per hour?"

Again, you must use judgment when deciding whether to object to a compound question. Failing to object may result in a judge or jury concluding that a "yes" answer applied to all the separate elements combined into the one question. Where the question can be answered with a simple "yes" or "no," it therefore makes sense to object. But a different calculus applies when the question calls for the witness to narrate facts. As a practical matter, witnesses often respond to compound questions that require the witness to provide information by responding to only the last part of the question. For example, a witness asked to answer the question "When was Mega Corporation formed and how is it organized?" will often respond by either describing the organization of Mega Corporation or, less frequently, the year the corporation was formed. Less-than-alert taking counsel will not notice that only one part of the question has received an answer and will move on to the next question. Objecting to the question as compound, however, would usually require the taking lawyer to back up and ask two separate questions, thereby resulting in more information being revealed, but a clearer record.

Misleading Question

A misleading question is a trick question. There are two primary forms of misleading questions. One is the two-part question, which when answered provides erroneous information to the trier of fact. The classical example of this type of misleading question is, "Have you stopped beating your horse?" If the witness answer is "yes," the implication is that the witness did at one time beat his horse. A "no" answer makes it sound as though the witness is continuing to beat his horse. By seeking a "yes" or "no" answer to such a misleading question, the questioner does not permit the witness to explain that he has never beaten his horse. Such a question is objectionable and may also be the subject of a direction not to answer under Rule 30(d)(4) as a question being asked in bad faith or in such a manner as unreasonably to annoy, embarrass, or oppress the deponent. If the witness is instructed not to answer such a question, you must also adjourn the deposition and seek a protective order from the court[19] or seek a stipulation that you are not waiving your right to adjourn by allowing further questions on other topics.

The other form of a misleading question is one that asks the witness to accept certain facts as true when they are not. For example: "Mr. Kaunas, we have already talked to many witnesses who believe that your car was over the center line. Now, don't you agree that you were not in your lane?" If the deposing attorney has not, in fact, talked to many witnesses and obtained

---

19. *See* section 12.2.5.

this information, the question misleads the witness and is a breach of ethics to boot. These questions can be cured by changing their form. They should always be objected to when asked.

Misquoting the Witness

A question is objectionable when it includes a factual predicate purportedly based on previous testimony by the deponent, but in fact misstates the previous testimony of the deponent. An example of misquoting the witness is the following exchange:

> Q: How far from the intersection did you start braking?
>
> A: About 500 feet away.
>
> Q: When you started braking 300 feet or so from the intersection, how fast were you going?

The objection can be cured by having the witness repeat earlier testimony or by having the witness's previous testimony read back to clarify what was said.

Narratives (Questions and Responses)

You can object to a question that is unfocused because it is overbroad: "Tell me everything you know about how the contract with Mammoth came about." That puts too great a burden on the deponent to identify what the questioner wants to know; it is probably ambiguous.

Speculation

Although some courts have held to the contrary, asking the witness to speculate is not objectionable since the speculation may lead to the discovery of admissible evidence. It is objectionable, however, not to make clear that the witness is being asked to speculate. An example of a question asking the witness to speculate is: "What did the defendant think when you told him that you could not deliver the parts as originally scheduled?" The question, as phrased, is asking the witness to read the defendant's mind.

One way the questioner could improve the question is by asking the witness to give the basis for the speculation:

> Q: Did the defendant say anything about he what thought when you told him you could not deliver the parts as originally scheduled?
>
> A: Yes.

Q: What did he say?

A: He said he did not think it would cause any problems.

The other way of asking the question is to invite the witness explicitly to speculate:

Q: What did you *believe* the defendant was thinking when you told him that you could not deliver the parts as originally scheduled?

The inappropriate objection to speculation may motivate questioning counsel to bring out the basis for the speculation, and this may not be what defending counsel wants. It may be better just to make certain that the witness identifies the answer as speculation in the re-examination by the defender and then to object at trial when opposing counsel tries to introduce the speculation, which, in the normal course, is not admissible at trial.

Unfair Characterization

An unfair characterization occurs when the questioner characterizes a previous answer while asking another question:

Q: How fast were you going?

A: 50 miles per hour.

Q: When you were speeding at 50 miles per hour, were you looking ahead of you?

Objecting to an unfair characterization is related to objecting to misstating prior testimony, but with a slightly different slant. In practice, either objection will usually suffice to preserve the objection. The defect can be cured by either omitting the characterization from the question or by asking the witness to agree with the characterization: "Were you speeding?" Unfair characterizations should always draw an objection.

Calling for a Legal Conclusion

It is objectionable to ask a witness about the legal significance of actions or words or documents. For example, it is objectionable as calling for a legal conclusion to ask a witness: "Was it negligence for the defendant to be driving at 75 miles per hour in a 25 mile per hour zone?' Nor is it proper to ask the witness to testify about what the law states: "Tell me what 'mitigation of damages' means?" You can ask a witness, however, about what the witness believes to be the law or believes to be the legal significance of some act, statement or document. The question asking for a legal conclusion, which should always be objected to, can be cured by couching the question in terms of belief: "Do you believe that was an appropriately careful way to drive in that area?"

Calling for an Improper Lay Opinion

Rule 701 permits certain types of lay opinions, but when the question asks the witness for an impermissible lay opinion or an opinion that can only be given by an expert, it is objectionable: "Do you have an opinion about whether the failure to administer blood thinners contributed to your stroke?" Depending on the type of opinion being elicited, it may or may not be curable, but the objection should always be made.

Calling for an Opinion beyond an Expert's Qualifications

A physician qualified to give an opinion in the field of hematology should not be required at deposition to express an opinion about the prognosis for the patient's fractured femur unless separately qualified to give that opinion as well. If the expert can be so qualified, the objectionable issue is curable. Such an objection should always be made.

Calling for Hearsay

A question that is objected to on the grounds of hearsay is by conventional wisdom thought of as noncurable: "What did the bystander you spoke to say happened?" But if the hearsay statement can be placed within the exceptions of Rule 803, 804 or 807, then the objection is arguably addressed: "Did the bystander appear excited?" A prudent defending lawyer will object to questions calling for hearsay, either to keep the answers out of the record or to understand the potential exceptions to the hearsay rule that might be cited.

Objections to Questions Calling for Privileged Information or Work Product

If defending counsel fails to object to a question that seeks privileged information and fails to instruct the deponent not to answer, those failures will likely result in the waiver of the privilege. Immediately after such a question is posed, defending counsel should make an objection, instruct the deponent not to answer, and seek a recess to discuss with the deponent the propriety of claiming a privilege. Most questioning counsel will honor such a request for a pause, but even if there is a protest, you must take a recess. Although the privilege belongs to the client and can be waived by the client, always assume that the deponent will want to invoke her privilege and act accordingly. Follow the same procedure to protect trial preparation materials[20] from discovery during the course of the deposition.

Once the client decides to invoke a privilege, defending counsel must allow the witness to provide sufficient information for the questioning counsel to determine whether the assertion of the privilege is proper, and for the judge to have sufficient information to rule on either a request for a protective order to enforce the claim of privilege or a motion to compel to overcome the claim of privilege.

Federal Rule of Civil Procedure 26(b) provides:

> **(5) *Claims of Privilege or Protection of Trial-Preparation Materials.***
>
> **(A)** *Information Withheld.* When a party withholds information otherwise discoverable by claiming that the information is privileged or subject to protection as trial-preparation material, the party must:
>
> > **(i)** expressly make the claim; and
> >
> > **(ii)** describe the nature of the documents, communications, or tangible things not produced or disclosed—and do so in a manner that without revealing information itself privileged or protected, will enable other parties to assess the claim.

For example, suppose a case where the plaintiff claims that the defendant defrauded him in a contract for the sale of goods. At deposition, plaintiff's counsel asks the deponent/defendant whether he spoke to anyone before he decided to enter into the contract that underlies the cause of action, and the defendant responds that he spoke with a lawyer. Defending counsel should object to any attempt to determine the content of that conversation, and additionally she should instruct the deponent not to answer the question. If, after conferring with her client, defending counsel asserts the attorney-client privilege on behalf of the deponent, defending counsel should be prepared to allow the witness to provide the following information:

1. the name of the client;

2. the name of the person spoken to;[21]

---

20. *See* FED. R. CIV. P. 26(b)(3) (limiting discovery of documents and other tangible things prepared by or for a party in anticipation of trial) *and* FED. R. CIV. P. 26(b)(4)(D) (limiting discovery relating to consulting expert witnesses).

21. This information will insure that the person spoken to was either a licensed lawyer or an agent of a licensed lawyer.

3.   the date of the communication and the date that the attorney-client relationship began;[22]

4.   the place of the communication;[23]

5.   people present during the communication;[24]

6.   any person to whom the subject matter of the communication was given either orally or in writing;[25]

7.   the general nature and purpose of the communication (e.g., oral or written communication for the purpose of obtaining legal advice.);[26]

8.   whether the communication was recorded and, if so, to whom the record was disclosed and where it currently is kept.[27]

Once she gets this information, deposing counsel can ask questions about any of the factors listed above, and others, to attempt to show that the communication does not fall within the attorney-client privilege because of a waiver or because it comes within an exception to the privilege. Defending counsel may want to raise a continuing objection on privilege grounds to make it clear that the substance of the communications is still being protected. Armed with the information about the circumstances of the communications, questioning counsel can seek a motion to compel disclosure of the substance of the communication as not privileged or seek in camera inspection of a written communication (or a recording of an oral communication) by the judge to determine whether the privilege is properly claimed, if there has been waiver, or if an exception to the privilege exists.

The same process would be used regarding a claim that the information sought during the deposition is not discoverable because it is trial preparation material pursuant to Rule 26. Defending counsel, after objecting and

---

22. This information will help determine whether the attorney-client relationship existed at the time of the communication.

23. This information will help determine whether the communication occurred in a place where there was a reasonable expectation that it would be confidential (e.g., in the lawyer's office as opposed to a crowded restaurant).

24. This information will help determine whether there were people present during the communication whose presence might negate the privilege.

25. This information will help determine whether the privilege was destroyed by the communication of the alleged privileged information to someone outside the privilege.

26. The communication must have been one that sought legal advice and may not have been for a purpose that destroys the privilege, such as preparing or furthering a crime or fraud.

27. The provision of a record of the communication to an entity outside the privilege, or the failure to keep it safely, may be evidence that the communication was not intended to remain confidential.

instructing the witness not to answer, must allow questioning counsel to obtain sufficient information about the nature of the trial preparation material claim for protection so that deposing counsel can ask questions aimed at undermining the validity of the claim, and so that a judge can make an appropriate ruling should there be a motion to either protect against disclosure of the material in question or to compel its production.

In addition to attacking the validity of objecting counsel's claim that the material or information sought are indeed trial preparation materials, questioning counsel may also try to show that there are valid reasons for invading the claimed trial preparation materials protection. The protection of these materials from discovery can be invaded on a showing of (1) substantial need for the material; and (2) the inability, without undue hardship, to obtain the substantial equivalent of the materials by some other means.[28] A typical situation is when one party has obtained a statement from a witness who has unique information set and who has since become unavailable or whose location cannot be determined after a diligent search.

Objections to Lack of Foundation

Foundation is an elastic concept that encompasses several distinct prerequisites to the admissibility of evidence. In its narrowest form, it covers the authentication of evidence as contemplated in Rules 901 and 902. Used in a broader sense, it also covers such concepts as showing that a witness has personal knowledge about the subject of the witness's testimony,[29] or that the best evidence rule has not been satisfied.[30] The concept of foundations is discussed in greater detail in chapter ten, but we turn now to the subject to discuss it as a basis for objections.

All foundation issues can be cured merely by laying the necessary foundation. Whether a foundation objection should be made depends on whether the questioner can in fact lay the necessary foundation and whether the witness's testimony for which the foundation is being laid will be made admissible or more persuasive as a result. We will now discuss the major types of foundation objections.

Authenticity

Federal Rule of Evidence 901(a) states:

> To satisfy the requirement of authenticating or identifying an item of evidence, the proponent must produce evidence suf-

---

28. Fed. R. Civ. P. 26(b)(3).
29. Fed. R. Evid. 602.
30. Fed. R. Evid. 1001 *et seq.*

ficient to support a finding that the item is what the proponent claims it is.[31]

In short, before a witness may testify to some fact—e.g. a statement made over the telephone by the defendant—there must be sufficient testimony that the witness heard the telephone conversation and is able to identify the speaker as the defendant. Rule 901 gives examples of how to authenticate several types of evidence, a matter more fully discussed in chapter ten. The exceptions to the requirement of a showing of authenticity are the types of evidence listed in Rule 902 as self-authenticating.

Again, an objection to a failure to show authenticity can be answered by laying the necessary foundation to show that the proffered evidence is what the witness claims it to be. Whether such an objection should be made depends again on whether the proponent can lay the necessary foundation and, if so, whether it will make the witness's testimony more persuasive as a result. Defending counsel may not want the testimony to be more persuasive; if it hurts, even though it is from defending counsel's own witness, do not press for foundational support.

No Showing of Personal Knowledge

Rule 602 requires that "[a] witness may testify to a matter only if evidence is introduced sufficient to support a finding that the witness has personal knowledge of the matter." The testimony of experts and statements of a party-opponent are the two exceptions to this rule. Before lay witnesses can give testimony about an event, they must show that they have firsthand knowledge about the topic of their proposed testimony. An example of a situation where no showing of personal knowledge has been made would be if a witness was asked what was said a meeting without first establishing that the witness was present at the meeting and in a position to hear what was said. The requirement of personal knowledge extends to all forms of evidence. For example, a fact witness must be able to testify to hearing, seeing, or experiencing that about which she will testify; a character witness must establish sufficient familiarity with the person about whom character evidence will be given; a witness testifying to a habit or routine must show a familiarity with the habit and routine about which he is testifying; and so on.

If you make an objection that a witness lacks personal knowledge, questioning counsel can have the witness testify about the time, place, and cir-

---

31. This is the lowest evidentiary threshold in the law: "Based on this evidence, could a reasonable jury conclude that this item of evidence is what sponsoring counsel purports it to be?" The test is not, "should the jury," but merely "could the jury. "Should the jury" would be equivalent to the standard for a directed verdict on that particular evidentiary point: the judge would order the jury to find the fact to be true.

cumstances under which she acquired firsthand knowledge, thus showing the testimonial prerequisite is met:

Q: Did you attend the meeting?

Q: Were you able to hear what was said at the meeting?

Whether you, as defending counsel, should object to a failure to show personal knowledge depends on whether the necessary foundation can be laid and, if so, whether doing so will make the witness's testimony more or less useful to your side.

Best Evidence Rule

The Best Evidence Rule, found in Federal Rule of Evidence 1001 *et seq.* (also known as the rule requiring the production of the original document), requires that to prove the contents of a document (including writings, recordings, electronic records, or photographs) where the contents of that document are directly in issue, the proponent must produce an original of the document, unless its production is excused.[32] The obvious way of answering a valid Best Evidence Rule objection is by producing the document, photograph, or recording at issue. Once produced, the witness may then be asked questions about the contents. If the original cannot be produced for a legitimate reason (it was lost or it is in the uncooperative hands of a party or nonparty, for example), substitute evidence, such as testimony or an unsigned carbon copy may be introduced. Accurate duplicates, like xerographic or digital copies, are typically treated as "duplicate originals" and are as admissible as originals unless some injustice will occur.

An important reason for making a Best Evidence Rule objection when a witness is asked to testify about the contents of a writing, photograph, or record is that the answers are more likely to be accurate if the witness is first given the opportunity to view the document, photograph, or recording. Therefore, the prudent approach is to always take the opportunity to make a valid Best Evidence Rule objection.

Objections to the Answer

Objections to a witness's answer can be dealt with just as objections to a question. Much as a question can be rephrased in response to an objection, a witness can be asked to rephrase an answer to remove the objectionable portion of it. Thus, objections to a defect in an answer that can be cured must be

---

32. Fed. R. Evid. 1002 states that "[a]n original writing, recording, or photograph is required in order to prove its content unless these rules or a federal statute provides otherwise." Although the term is not used in the rules, this requirement was known at common law as the best evidence rule.

made at the deposition or the objection is waived. For example, if the witness has answered, "I don't know about the process in this case, but in another case against these same people, I remember that we settled with two parties who were never sued in court," the defender (or perhaps the questioner) might say: "Objection to the portion of the answer relating to another case, and I ask that it be stricken. Mr. Watkins, would you please answer the question again, but restrict your answer to what you know about this case."

If the objectionable answer is the result of the question calling for objectionable testimony, the objection should be to the question, not the answer. For example, if the question calls for the witness to provide a legal opinion, an objection should be made to the question rather than to the answer to the question. To be timely, any objection to the question should be made before the witness has answered. But witnesses sometimes give answers, unprompted by the question, that contain objectionable material. For example, a fact witness may volunteer what would be considered expert opinion about someone's financial position ("Yeah, I thought that he was seriously undercapitalized—just my opinion as a grocery clerk, you know") when the question did not call for such.

Many of the objections to questions discussed above are equally applicable to answers. Thus, answers given in response to unobjectionable questions that demonstrate a lack of firsthand knowledge; contain opinion; are directed to the contents of a writing, recording, or photograph covered by the Best Evidence Rule; contain (trial-) inadmissible hearsay; etc.; are subject to objections. The objection will be waived if a timely objection is not made.

There is one objection that is unique to answers, and the defect that prompts it is curable and therefore waived if the objection is not made in a timely manner:

Nonresponsive Answers

A deponent's answer that exceeds the scope of the question or fails to respond to the question is subject to objection and a motion to strike by questioning counsel. If, in fact, the witness's answer was nonresponsive, but provided relevant information, defending counsel can ask about those matters at the end of the deposition. It would be unusual for defending counsel to object on the basis that the answer is unresponsive.

Many courts permit only the attorney asking the question to make a nonresponsive objection, while some courts will permit either party to object. Some courts also expect the objection to be accompanied by a motion to strike (even though there is no one at the deposition to rule on the motion).

The witness can cure by limiting her answer to the information called for by the question; or opposing counsel can elicit the same answer when given an opportunity to question the witness.

As noted, the questioner almost always makes the objection that the answer is nonresponsive. The objection, especially when accompanied by a motion to strike, often has the same effect as a slap across the witness's face. All cooperation from the witness usually ceases when the objection is made. Therefore, you should only make the objection if the witness is persistent in refusing to answer the question or in adding nonresponsive information that renders useless the responsive portion of the answer. If the witness is adding information that does not have the effect of making the responsive portion useless, objecting usually accomplishes nothing—defending counsel, when the opportunity to question arrives, will typically ask the necessary questions to bring out the information that was the subject of the objection.

14.10   The Form of Objections

Since the exceptional case of *Hall v. Clifton Precision Tools* in 1993,[33] the manner and form of objecting at depositions has received increased scrutiny from judges, commentators, and rule makers. The courts, legal commentators, and the bar have frequently condemned lawyers for using objections as a method of coaching witnesses about the answers to be given. Similarly, the once common practice of using unjustified instructions not to answer legitimate questions has been harshly criticized. The result has been amendments to the Federal Rules of Civil Procedure, further regulation in the district courts by promulgation of even more restrictive local rules, and the fashioning of discovery orders by individual judges that govern the conduct of counsel during the taking and defending of deposition testimony.

The Federal Rules of Civil Procedure have made clear the proper manner for the making of objections and the limited circumstances in which a lawyer defending a deposition can instruct a witness not to answer. As to the making of objections, Rule 30(c) provides:

> (2) ***Objections.***
>
> * * * An objection must be stated ***concisely and in a non-argumentative and nonsuggestive manner***. (Emphasis added.)

This rule envisions that objections be made by stating the word "objection" and then giving a brief statement of the specific legal grounds for the objection. For example, an objection to a compound question would be stated as "Objection: Compound question." Similarly, an objection to a confusing question would consist of "Objection: Complex" or "Confusing." In

---

33. 150 F.R.D. 525 (E.D. Pa. 1993).

this way objecting counsel makes clear the basis for objection without coaching the deponent, and questioning counsel has a fair opportunity to cure.

A last caveat: It is important to always check the local rules of the court controlling the litigation. Many U.S. district courts, as well as several state courts, have adopted rules that would prohibit even the simple objection, described above, of "Objection: Compound question." These jurisdictions prescribe the permissible objections that can be made in a deposition, usually limiting them to "Objection: Form" or something similar. An example of such a rule is that found in the local rules of the U.S. District Court for the Eastern District of Texas:

> Objections to questions during the oral deposition are limited to 'Objection, leading' and 'Objection, form.' Objections to testimony during the oral deposition are limited to 'Objection, nonresponsive.' These objections are waived if not stated as phrased during the oral deposition. All other objections need not be made or recorded during the oral deposition to be later raised with the court. The objecting party must give a clear and concise explanation of an objection if requested by the party taking the oral deposition, or the objection is waived.[34]

In addition, there are individual discovery orders incorporating similar restrictions on the form of objections routinely issued by judges in jurisdictions where the local rules are silent on the subject.

14.11   The Calculus of Deciding whether to Object

Not every objectionable question or answer deserves an objection. The defending attorney should do nothing more in response to some potential objections than sit quietly. Other potential objections require action and perhaps more, including a direction to the witness not to answer. A defending attorney must engage in a sophisticated calculus, weighing the advantages and disadvantages of objecting, before deciding what to do. And this calculus must usually be performed in a fraction of a second if the objection is to be timely. What we will do now is describe that calculus.

14.11.1   Step One: Decide whether an Objection Is Required

You are not required to object to every objectionable question or answer at the deposition. You can make many potential objections for the first time when the opposing party attempts to use the question and answer at trial, on a motion for a summary judgment, or for some other purpose. As discussed in previous sections, there is no need to make any objection when the

---

34. Local Rule CV-30.

problem cannot be cured, including objections to competency, relevancy, materiality, hearsay that does not fit into a hearsay exception, and any objection under Rule 403 (prejudice outweighs relevance). If you determine that a potential objection is one that need not be made at the deposition to be preserved, you need to do nothing more than sit quietly and let the deposition proceed. (But as noted earlier, resist the temptation to agree to a stipulation that objections to form need not be made, unless you calculate that somehow you will obtain a clear advantage.)

14.11.2 Step Two: Decide whether the Advantages of Objecting Outweigh the Disadvantages

The rule for making objections at a deposition is basically the same as for trial: only object if you will gain by the objection. Objections come with advantages and disadvantages. You will need to decide whether those advantages outweigh any disadvantages before making any objection.

Before discussing those advantages and disadvantages, it is necessary to reiterate an important point—the vast majority of objections made at a deposition will never be ruled on. A court will only rule on an objection if one of the parties tries to use a question and answer to which a timely objection has been lodged. The judge must rule on an objection if, for example, one of the parties offers the deposition testimony as a substitute for the live testimony of a witness who is unavailable to testify at trial. Similarly, the court must rule on objections made during the deposition if a party offers that portion of the deposition in support of or in opposition to a motion for summary judgment. But as a practical matter, the vast majority of objections made at a deposition are never brought to the court's attention at trial because no one ever tries to use 99 percent of the deposition for trial purposes. The obvious advantage of objecting to a question or answer at a deposition is that potentially harmful evidence may be excluded at some later point in the proceedings if the opposing party tries to use them. This alone is usually sufficient justification for making an objection. The more damaging the evidence, the greater the incentive to object when an objection that sounds significant can be found. (This is actually true for any objection, proper or not, which leads most questioning lawyers to recognize that when defending counsel gets the most pompous and bombastic in her objections, the questioning has obviously come close to important information.)

The corollary to this is that where the question and answer will have little or no effect on the outcome of the litigation, there is little reason to object. If you think back to the depositions you have taken and defended, you will quickly realize that the vast majority of the questions could, in retrospect, have been skipped entirely without changing the outcome of the litigation in any way. The reality is that many questions are asked at a deposition for reasons having nothing to do with the merits of the dispute—background, gaining an overview of the subject matter, attempting to ingratiate the interrogator with the witness, helping the questioner understand the facts of the case, filling the time until the questioner can think of some useful questions, and so on. Many questions are also asked with the hopes of gaining useful information, but the answers end up showing that the facts are contrary to what the questioner hoped to hear. Defending counsel, being familiar with what the witness will testify, knows before the answer is given that nothing harmful will be said.

If defending counsel knows that nothing useful to the other side will result from the question, then nothing will be gained by objecting to the question or answer. Objecting to questions and answers where there can be no discernible effect on the outcome of the litigation is a waste of time for all involved and will do little to enhance your reputation as a litigator.

Objections may also have the effect of improving the persuasiveness of harmful testimony. Examples of this are objections to the form of a question or to a lack of foundation. As has been previously discussed, objecting to the use of leading questions with a neutral witness may cause the interrogator to shift to nonleading questions, resulting in the witness telling a more persuasive story than would have occurred if the lawyer's leading questions were providing the necessary facts. Similarly, an objection to a lack of foundation may cause the questioner to lay the foundation, thereby making the witness's testimony more believable.

Another example that occurs frequently in practice is where the questioner fails to specify a time period in the question when asking about events that extend over time. Imagine a situation where the interrogator is asking about the procedures for processing orders at the defendant company, but fails to specify the time period for which the information is being sought. If the witness then testifies to a different procedure at trial, the impeachment of the witness with the deposition testimony might proceed like this:

Q: Let's look at page 23, line 16 of your deposition to see how you described the order processing procedures at your company. I asked you the following question: "What were the procedures for processing orders?"

And your answer, under oath, was, and I quote, "Sometimes I would review the order, and sometimes I would leave that to my secretary." I read that correctly, didn't I?

A: Yes, but I was describing our procedures in 2008. We changed those procedures in 2009, and since then I have

> reviewed every order before it is processed. My secretary
> now never reviews the orders. The plaintiff's order was
> placed in 2009, and I reviewed it before it was processed.

It is at times like this that you fervently pray for the earth to open up and
swallow you. And it is also why defending counsel may not object to the
interrogator's failure to specify a time period in a question. The lack of a time
frame creates an ambiguous record, and that provides the witness with wig-
gle-room if the deposition is ever used to attempt to impeach the witness's
trial testimony. For the same reasons, defending counsel often chooses not to
ask for clarification of questions with too many pronouns or questions, thus
creating a muddy or ambiguous record.[35]

Objections are sometimes also used for impermissible purposes, such as to
misdirect or intimidate new or inexperienced questioning lawyers, to needlessly consume time, or to coach witnesses. Nothing more about these uses
needs to be said except that you should not be the attorney who engages in
such improper tactics. Finally, it is worth noting here that objections do not
count against the seven hour time limit of Rule 30(d)(1).

14.11.3   Step Three: When In Doubt, Object

Often during a deposition, there is no time to make the fine calculations
necessary to determine whether the advantages of objecting outweigh the
disadvantages. By the time you have gone through the pros and cons, the
opportunity for making a timely objection has passed because the witness
has answered. Our suggestion is that your default rule should be: *When in
doubt, object.* There is no requirement that having made an objection, you
must assert it if the other side attempts to use that portion of the deposition
at some later time. But if you fail to make the objection and it is waived,
you will never have the opportunity to consider whether or not to assert
the objection. Therefore, prudence suggests that when in doubt, it is better
to object than not. (As suggested earlier in this chapter, you could ask for a
moment to consider the question before the witness answers; as long as this
tactic is not abused, and as long as there is no communication with the witness during this pause, this pause is not itself objectionable.)

14.11.4   Step Four: Make a Timely Objection

Objections have to be timely to be valid. To be timely, an objection to a
question has to be made before the answer is given. Objections to an answer
have to be made before the next question is asked.[36] But the objection should

---

35. *See* section 14.9.3

36. *See* Charles Alan Wright, et al., 21 Fed. Prac. & Proc. Evid. § 5037.1 (2d ed.)
(an objection must be made as soon as the ground of it is known).

not be made until the questioning attorney has finished asking the question or the witness has finished answering the question. Do not be rude and interrupt the question or answer with your objection. If the witness has answered or the next question has been asked before a timely objection has been interposed, you should still make the objection and note the reason for the delay for the record.[37]

Making a record of the inability to make a timely objection is quite simple:

> I am objecting on the grounds that the question called for speculation. Let me note that the witness answered so quickly that I did not have time to object to the question before the answer started.

14.11.5   Step Five: Make a Correct and Specific Objection

Objecting on the wrong grounds or failing to object with specificity can constitute a waiver of the objection.[38] Therefore, make sure any objection made is the correct one and is made specifically. One way to protect yourself, at least partially, from making the wrong objection is to object, within reason, on all the grounds that come to mind. For example, when in doubt about the correct grounds, you could object as follows: "Objection: Calls for speculation, lack of foundation, and no showing of personal knowledge." You can further protect yourself by keeping a list of common objections in front of you when defending a deposition. But do not expect to have much time to consult the list before making the objection. A final safeguard is to quickly state "Objection," but then take several moments to decide what grounds to state. Your opponent may attempt to hurry you along in completing the objection, but do not be rattled. You are entitled to think about the grounds for a reasonable time. Bear in mind that merely reciting a list of all objections that you know, regardless of whether they apply to the question at hand, is a sure way to lose credibility with the court on any discovery dispute. Treat objections seriously: they are intended to improve the record and warn opposing counsel of problems with her questions so that they can be fixed. They are not intended to show off your wit, to rescue the witness, or to smuggle your favorable facts under cover of darkness into the record.

The specificity of an objection is a matter of degree, but sufficiently specific objections may require something more than the mere statement "Objection." Similarly, unless required by local rule or court order, a generic statement of "Objection: Form" is usually thought to be insufficient. In both these circumstances, questioning counsel can ask for more information, and that is to be preferred over making an objection that is argumentative or

---

37. This is known as the "fast lip" excuse.
38. WRIGHT, *supra* note 36 at §§ 5036–5036.4.

suggestive. The objection should be specific enough for the taking lawyer to know what the claimed flaw in the question is or answer the objecting lawyer is complaining of.[39] Otherwise, the opportunity to cure would be meaningless. Similarly, the judge is entitled to know what the objecting lawyer is complaining about. While specificity is required and "suggestion is deplored," courts normally allow something akin to "Objection: Compound question."

14.12 Instructions Not to Answer

When defending a deposition, one of the most difficult decisions to make is whether to instruct or direct a witness not to answer a question. Rule 30(c)(2) sharply curtails the situations in which such an instruction is proper: "A person may instruct a deponent not to answer only when necessary to preserve a privilege, to enforce a limitation ordered by the court, or to present a motion under Rule 30(d)(3)." Rule 30(d)(3) refers to adjourning the deposition to seek an order terminating or limiting the deposition because it is being conducted in bad faith or in such a manner as unreasonably to annoy, embarrass, or oppress the deponent.

The decision whether to instruct is difficult because if you make the wrong choice, the penalties can be great. If you instruct the witness not to answer a question that the court later determines is proper, the attorney or the client can be required to pay the reasonable expenses, including attorney's fees, of the questioning attorney in obtaining the order compelling an answer.[40] On the other hand, if you allow the witness to answer the question, you risk both losing the protections of the privilege or court order, at least for that question, and waiving them for the future as well. (Of course, if you instruct the witness not to answer and the next day decide that was a mistake, you could call opposing counsel, admit the mistake, and offer some additional deposition time in person or on the phone. Apologies to all if this seems too reasonable.)

The calculus of deciding whether to instruct the witness not to answer runs as follows:

1. If I instruct the witness not to answer, how likely is it that opposing counsel will bring a motion to compel?

2. If opposing counsel brings a motion to compel, how likely is it that the court will sustain the motion and compel an answer?

---

39. *Id.* at § 5036.1 ("The objection should be specific enough to alert the trial judge to the proper course of action and to enable the opponent to obviate the objection, if possible.").

40. *See* sections 12.2.1 and 12.2.5.

3. If the court sustains the motion, how likely is it that I or my client will be required to pay the reasonable expenses of opposing counsel for bringing the motion and resuming the deposition?

4. How important is it to prevent discovery of the information to which the question is directed compared to the amount of the opposing attorney's expenses and the probability of having to pay them?

If you are giving the instruction not to answer with adjourning the deposition to seek a protective order as the next step, then your calculation must focus on how badly the protective order is needed and the prospects of the court granting it.

If you decide to instruct the witness not to answer, the actual instruction should sound like this:

Q: Now, Mr. Vasys, did you ever receive any advice from your attorney concerning whether it was proper to terminate the contract?

Defending Counsel: I object to the question on the grounds that it asks for information covered by the attorney-client privilege, and I instruct the witness not to answer.

Q: Mr. Vasys, will you answer the question, please?

A: No, I'll follow my counsel's advice.

Several additional comments are in order on the topic of instructions not to answer:

- One of the matters that must be covered when you are preparing a witness to be deposed is what to do when an instruction not to answer is given. You must instruct the witness not to answer the question, and if asked whether an answer will be given, her response should be "No."

- You should gain eye contact with the witness ("John, this is important. I am instructing you not to answer this question on the grounds of attorney-client privilege.") If the witness then starts to answer, interrupt him and tell him he should not answer on the grounds of privilege.

- Rule 26(b)(5) requires that when instructing a witness not to answer based on a claim of privilege or work product, you must do so expressly and "describe the nature of the documents, communications, or tangible things not . . . disclosed—and do so in a manner that without revealing information itself privileged or protected, will enable other parties to assess the claim."

- Be alert to questioning counsel's tactic of coming back later in the deposition, often toward the end when everyone is tired, to an area about which you have instructed the witness not to answer. Unless you have decided that the previous instruction not to answer was a mistake, you should persist in closing off the inquiry by repeating your instruction to the witness.

- You may instruct the witness not to answer for purposes of adjourning the deposition for many different reasons. The questioning attorney may be engaged in abusive behavior by yelling at the witness, the questions may be asking for trade secrets, the questioning attorney may be asking questions about matters that have absolutely nothing to do with the issues in the case ("beyond the scope of discovery under Rule 26"), the witness may be asked a misleading question in the nature of "have you stopped beating your wife," and so forth. While Rule 30(d)(3) suggests that you should immediately adjourn the deposition to seek a protective order, the lawyers often agree to complete the deposition before filing their motions. An exception occurs when the questioning lawyer engages in abusive tactics; then you should adjourn the deposition immediately.

The "beyond the scope of Rule 26" problem mentioned above often occurs when, at least in the eyes of the defender, the questioning attorney has gone so far beyond the scope of the complaint and answer that the information sought no longer "appears reasonably calculated to lead to the discovery of admissible evidence," which is the outer bound for discovery defined in Rule 26(b)(1). Problems arise when what the questioner believes is "reasonably calculated" is seen by the defender as unreasonable and intrusive. The result is the type of argument between counsel that probably accounts for much of the heat and none of the light at depositions.

The practical solution is this: defending lawyers counsel should recognize their own biases in favor of a narrow interpretation here, and therefore should give the questioners a bit of latitude; questioning attorneys should recognize they need not turn over every rock in the field to find the worms they need to go fishing.[41] As long as no privileges and confidences are involved in the

---

41. Controversies on scope can be better understood if we recognize that attorneys at a deposition take such positions in large part because they believe their clients expect them to, and not because they believe in the need for the discovery or the protection. Thus, the deposing attorney is intent on pressing her inquiries to the limits of reasonableness because she does not want her client (or senior partner, or government supervisor) to think she gave away

answer, the preferable course is to state the "beyond the scope of reasonable discovery" objection, but avoid any instruction not to answer. Alternatively, the areas could be postponed by stipulation until the defender can bring the matter to the court in a motion for a protective order.

14.13   Questioning and Clarifying and Correcting Answers

Traditionally, defending counsel did not ask any questions at the deposition of his own party or of a friendly witness. The reason was simple. If the witness was friendly or a client, the best place to ask questions is in the privacy of the lawyer's office where opposing counsel could not overhear what was being said. It was thought that there was no sense sharing information with the other side when there was no requirement to do so. But all of this assumed that the end game of the litigation was a trial, when undiscovered information could be used to surprise the opponent and when there was less time to construct a theory to answer this surprise evidence.

Despite the arguments against defending counsel asking questions of the party being represented or of friendly witnesses, there are a number of situations where you will want to do exactly that—ask questions following the conclusion of the taking attorney's questions. There are several reasons for doing so.

14.13.1   *Favorably Influence Settlement*

In modern practice, as discussed in previous chapters, the end game for most litigation not resolved by a dispositive motion is a mediated or negotiated settlement. Deposition testimony is frequently used by the parties as leverage points in mediations and negotiations. It is often better to reveal favorable information in a deposition setting rather than waiting to spring it on the other side for the first time in a mediation or negotiation. In this way, opposing counsel can be satisfied about the strength of information revealed, something that cannot be easily done in a mediation or negotiation. Therefore, witnesses are often primed by the defending lawyer, as discussed in chapter thirteen, to take any opportunity during their depositions to reveal favorable information in an effort to influence later mediation and negotiation efforts. If, however, the opportunity to reveal the favorable information does not arise during the taking attorney's examination, then defending counsel should be prepared to ask the questions necessary for the opposing counsel to appreciate the strength of your client's case.

---

the store; the defending attorney has the same concerns about allowing too much latitude. In fact, these are exactly the kinds of judgments trial attorneys get paid to make, and if their focus were on the genuine needs of the litigation, rather than on how their actions would be second-guessed later on, the purposes of discovery would be better served.

14.13.2   *Obtaining Information from Uncooperative Witnesses*

When a witness (normally nonparty) refuses to cooperate or to be interviewed informally, defending counsel should question such a witness at the deposition for the same reason that the other side is asking questions: to find out what the witness knows. When the witness is uncooperative with both sides, both have an incentive to ask questions. Even though the other side has noticed the deposition, defending counsel may also question the witness.

14.13.3   *The Witness Will Be Unavailable for Trial*

Defending counsel will also want to question a deposition witness, even though friendly, if the witness is expected to be unavailable for trial and the deposition will be the vehicle used to get that witness's information to the jury. In such a circumstance, interview and prepare the friendly witness in the same manner as preparing for trial testimony, even if opposing counsel has noticed the preservation or *de bene esse* deposition.

Sometimes the opposing party will notice the deposition of its own party or of a witness friendly to that side. This usually indicates that the witness will be unavailable for trial and the deposition is being taken to preserve his testimony. Where you cannot interview or prepare the witness (as mentioned in the preceding paragraph), prepare to question (cross-examine) the witness in the same way you would prepare if you were noticing the deposition.[42]

14.13.4   *Clarifying Ambiguous Answers*

Defending counsel should also question a friendly witness when that witness is likely to testify at trial, but has given answers at the deposition that are unclear or capable of several interpretations, one of which may be considered inconsistent with the trial testimony that the witness is expected to give. In that case, asking clarifying questions is wise because as part of the deposition transcript, those clarifications can be read to the jury pursuant to Rule 32(a)(6) if opposing counsel tries to impeach the witness at trial—they are part of the same writing or recording and should be considered contemporaneously with the evidence they clarify.[43] In addition, once the witness has clarified the supposed inconsistency, opposing counsel will likely avoid a losing battle at trial and not bother to attempt the possible impeachment.

---

42. *See* section 17.3.

43. Fed. R. Civ. P. 32(a)(6) states: "If a party offers in evidence only part of a deposition, an adverse party may require the offeror to introduce other parts that in fairness should be considered with the part introduced, and any party may itself introduce any other parts."

14.13.5   *Correcting a Wrong, Confusing, or Incomplete Answer*

Finally, defending counsel may want to correct a witness's answers given previously in response to questioning by the taking attorney. Before doing so, confirm with the witness during a break that the previous answer was a mistake and confirm what the correct answer should be. Preface the clarification with a statement such as:

> Earlier in the deposition you stated in a response to a question by Ms. Jones that you first began considering design modifications in 2009. Was 2009 the year you starting considering a design modification, or was it earlier or later? Why did you say 2009 earlier?

The questions should also ask why the witness gave a mistaken earlier answer.

A second method of correcting a previous answer is merely to have the witness announce a correction on the record (having first confirmed during a break what the correct answer should have been): "Let me correct an answer I previously gave." And then the witness gives the correction.

Examining counsel may follow up on questions by defending counsel with a "redirect" examination, to be followed by "recross" and further redirects and recrosses until everyone reaches the point of exhaustion or the seven or more hours have run out.[44]

14.14   Concluding the Deposition

Under Rule 30(e), the deponent or a party must demand before the conclusion of the deposition the right to review the deposition transcript or recording and to make corrections. As discussed elsewhere,[45] it makes little sense to give up the right to correct mistakes the witness has made in answering or the court reporter has made in transcribing the testimony. Therefore, if not demanded at the beginning of the deposition, defending counsel should always demand the right to make corrections before ending the deposition. No statement by either is necessary to "formally" end the deposition, other than, "I have no further questions." The court will be the ultimate arbiter of whether further deposition time is to be allowed, and it will not be swayed by "magic language."

---

44. FED. R. CIV. P. 30(c) provides that "[t]he examination and cross-examination of a deponent [should] proceed as they would at trial under the provisions of the Federal Rules of Evidence . . . ."

45. *See* chapter fifteen and section 6.1.

CHAPTER FIFTEEN

REVIEWING, CORRECTING, EDITING, AND SUPPLEMENTING THE TRANSCRIPT

You can't always get what you want,
But if you try sometimes,
Well you just might find
You get what you need.

—The Rolling Stones

15.1 Reviewing, Correcting, and Editing

Under Rule 30(e), a party or the deponent must request before the completion of the deposition the right to review and change the deposition. If this request is not made, this opportunity is waived. It is imperative that this demand be made clearly and before the conclusion of the deposition.[1] We discussed earlier the stipulations often requested at the outset of the deposition and the fact that most were not very useful. In contrast, this stipulation or request for reading, correction, and signing, is very useful. Therefore, you should put this on your checklist of things to do right at the beginning of the deposition, when you are at your freshest.

After the demand has been made and the deposition transcript has been delivered to her counsel or the deposition officer has given notice that the deposition transcript is available for review, the deponent has thirty days to carry out the review and to make and sign any changes. (In those state jurisdictions following the pre-1993 version of the Federal Rules of Civil Procedure, if the parties and the witness say nothing at all about the requirement to review and make corrections to the deposition, then the witness must review and correct. In those jurisdictions, a failure to have the witness join in the waiver may make the deposition unusable at trial even though the witness is now unavailable. Obviously, if the deposition is of a party, then only the parties' counsel need waive. No penalty attaches under either the current rules or the pre-1993 version of the rules if the witness fails, within

---

1. *See, e.g.,* EBC, Inc. v. Clark Bldg. Sys., Inc., 618 F.3d 253 (3d Cir. 2010).

the thirty-day period for doing so, to review and correct the deposition or, under the pre-1993 rules, to sign the deposition; the court will treat it as being as admissible as if the witness had reviewed it and, when necessary, signed it. Normally, both sides have an incentive for the witness to review the deposition, a matter more fully discussed in section 6.1. We recommend that no one—witness, plaintiff's counsel, or defendant's counsel—waive these rights. Claim them affirmatively and unequivocally at the outset of the deposition—"We request review, correction, and signature"—and do nothing to suggest that you waive them in any way.

In practice, the correcting and editing process usually begins when the reporter creates the transcript and sends it to the attorney who defended the witness at the deposition. Nowadays, transcripts can be created and delivered within two days, or even less. That attorney then arranges for the witness to read the transcript, either at the attorney's office or at a convenient location for the witness. If the witness reviews the transcript without the attorney present, proposed changes should be noted and later reviewed with the attorney. Preferably, the witness should sit with the attorney so that they can discuss the possible changes together.

The courts are split as to whether the right to make changes under Rule 30(e) extends to substantive changes to the answers given or whether the witness may only correct mistakes made by the reporter or transcriber. The majority view apparently is that the witness may make any kind of change, while a minority of courts have held that the changes may not alter the substance of the deponent's testimony.[2] There is a further split as to whether those courts that otherwise permit substantive changes to the testimony may examine the explanation given and strike any changes if the justification given for the changes is not convincing. The majority view is that substantive changes are permitted even if the changes are not supported by convincing explanations.[3] Finally, some courts apply a different standard to changes in a deposition used in a summary judgment context than when used at trial. Akin to the "sham affidavit" doctrine that is applied in the summary judgment context (used to strike affidavits that contradict previous deposition testimony), this doctrine justifies striking any changes to the substance of the deposition testimony.[4] The courts remain concerned with attempts to sandbag opposing counsel who is relying on sworn deposition testimony. The unsettled state of the law makes it imperative that the case law for the particular jurisdiction be carefully researched before any substantive changes are made to a witness's deposition testimony.

---

2. *See* Aetna v. Express Scripts, Inc., 261 F.R.D. 72, 75 (E.D. Pa. 2009); Agrizap, Inc. v. Woodstream Corp., 232 F.R.D. 491, 493 & n. 2 (E.D. Pa. 2006).

3. *See* Wright & Miller, Federal Practice and Procedure § 2118.

4. *See, e.g., Clark Bldg. Systems, Inc.,* 618 F.3d 253.

If substantive changes are made to a witness's deposition testimony, this does not make the original answers disappear from the case. The original answers are still preserved in the transcript, and they may still be used to impeach the witness. If the deposition was of a party-opponent, the original answers are party statements that can be offered at trial for the truth of the matter asserted,[5] as well as for impeachment, with the corrections or changes being available for arguable rehabilitation. Further, if the changes are substantial enough, a court may permit resumption of the witness's deposition to permit exploration of the changes and the justifications given.[6] Exercise caution before allowing the witness to make changes in deposition answers and avoid making wholesale changes in the deposition transcript. Changes in the original transcript are treated as though they resulted from examination by counsel for the witness at the deposition. Thus, the deposing attorney can obtain an order permitting further examination of the witness.[7] Moreover, the additional examination may inquire into the reasons for the changes.[8] The deponent may also bear the costs and attorney fees associated with re-examination.[9]

In practice, the standard procedure for correcting the deposition transcript is for the witness and defending counsel to review the transcript and create a sheet—or use one provided by the court reporter—that notes the page and line numbers of the deposition testimony and the corrected testimony. (This is known as an "errata sheet.") The witness then signs the errata sheet and, depending on the jurisdiction, may also have the signature notarized. The errata or corrections sheet is then returned to the officer or reporter who, under Rule 30(e), will attach the sheet to the certification under Rule 30(f)(1). The certificate will also indicate whether any changes were made. The corrections are included in the final bound transcript of the deposition. A typical errata sheet under either version of the rules looks like the following:

Corrections to Vardas Deposition of May 17

Page 17, ll. 2–5:

> "should have been considered a possible sort of supplier, but never really came to a close on supplying," should read, "should have been considered a possible source of supply, but never really came close to supplying."

---

5. *See Express Scripts, Inc.*, 261 F.R.D 72.

6. *See* Colin v. Thompson, 16 F.R.D. 194 (W.D. Mo. 1954).

7. *See, e.g.*, De Seversky v. Republic Aviation Corp., 2 F.R.D. 113 (E.D.N.Y. 1941); *Colin*, 161 F.R.D 194.

8. Sanford v. CBS, Inc., 594 F. Supp. 713, 715 (N.D. Ill. 1984).

9. *See, e.g.*, Lugtig v. Thomas, 89 F.R.D. 639 (N.D. Ill. 1981).

Page 43, l. 13:

> "now that I see a difference" should read, "not that I see a difference."

Page 51, l. 20:

> "Harry Schmidt and Russell Trover" should read, "Harry Schmidt, Russell Trover, and Jane Vilnius."

Page 73, ll. 15–18:

> "and lumber. I cannot remember the other person at the meeting. It may have been George Estus, but I am not certain" should read, "and lumber. The other person at the meeting was George Estus."

Page 114, l. 10:

> "No" should read "Yes."

Page 165, ll. 7–10:

> "if you understand the document, and I can read it to you and we'll discuss" should read, "if you understand the document, and I cannot, read it to me and we'll discuss."

The reason for any changes, necessary to satisfy Rule 30(e), should also be given after the new answer even though the reason for the change is readily apparent from the context and the change itself. Failure to give the reasons for any changes may lead opposing counsel to move to strike the corrections. For example, the page 114 change above might read:

Page 114, l. 10:

> "No" should read "Yes." Reason: The deponent did not understand that the question had been phrased in the negative.

Some attorneys prefer to provide the changes in a brief form that requires the reader examining the changes to refer back to the original transcript more often to understand the context. For example, two of the above changes in this case would instead be:

Page 43, l. 13:

> "now" should be "not"

Page 165, ll. 7–10:

> "I can read it to you" should be "I cannot, read it
> to me"

A better practice, however, is to include enough of the unchanged material that the reader can understand the significance of the change without referring back.

An important point that some attorneys do not appreciate is how corrected answers are used at trial. In impeaching the witness or presenting a party statement, the deposing attorney is entitled to read the original, uncorrected transcript. The defending attorney can then request, under Federal Rule of Civil Procedure 32(a)(4) and Federal Rules of Evidence 106, that the corrected response be read immediately thereafter so that the trier-of-fact can hear the answers in context and determine what to accept.

15.2   Supplementing the Deposition

The Advisory Committee Note to Rule 26(e) clearly states that with two exceptions, a witness has no duty to supplement deposition testimony by correcting or adding to the answers given. The first exception applies to depositions of expert witnesses. The depositions of such experts must be supplemented if the answers are in any way incomplete or incorrect, provided that the new information has not previously been made known to the other parties during the discovery process or in writing. Second, the court may also order any witness to supplement the witness's deposition if the court deems it appropriate.

Of course, as with almost all discovery rules, the parties can stipulate to different obligations for supplementation.[10] Therefore, when defending a deposition, counsel should recognize that a casual agreement—to provide further information, to produce additional documents, or to check on the accuracy of an answer—does in fact impose an enforceable obligation.

---

10. FED. R. CIV. P. 29.

PART FOUR: USING DEPOSITIONS

CHAPTER SIXTEEN

USING DEPOSITIONS IN MOTIONS AND TRIAL

How use doth breed a habit in a man!

—William Shakespeare

Testimony from depositions, especially that of parties to the lawsuit, can be used in many ways, both pretrial and trial. Deposition testimony can be used to support or to oppose motions (such as summary judgment and other motions), as a source of party statements, as a substitute for the testimony of absent witnesses, to control witnesses at trial, and to prepare for trial. Therefore, using depositions primarily as a source of impeachment material fails to extract the most value from the process.

There at least seven ways to use depositions at trial, although many lawyers seem to be comfortable with only two or three. Most attorneys know that a deposition can be a substitute for the testimony of a witness who is unavailable for trial due to illness, death, or being beyond the reach of the court; and they also know that prior testimony from a deposition can be used to impeach a witness who deviated materially from the deposition testimony. And many may understand that deposition testimony can be used to refresh memory, or to support pre-trial motions, or to serve as a basis for making a proffer to the court (to demonstrate, for example, that a good-faith basis exists for posing a suggestive question). But it is the rare attorney who has mastered four or five or the seven or more uses of deposition testimony.

16.1 Motions for Summary Judgment

Witness statements from depositions are commonly used like affidavits to support or oppose motions for summary judgment.[1] Deposition testimony consists of statements made under oath, so those statements have all the

---

1. *See* FED. R. CIV. P. 56(c) (the court will consider depositions along with the affidavits, pleadings, admissions, and responses to interrogatories in determining whether a genuine issue of material fact exists). *See also* Weldon v. Kraft, Inc., 896 F.2d 793 (3d Cir. 1990); C. WRIGHT & A. MILLER, CIVIL PROCEDURE § 2142 (West 1994).

trappings that give weight to an affidavit; therefore, logically, they should be regarded in the same way.

Some attorneys are concerned about asking open questions at depositions of the opposing party's witnesses because they feel this gives opposing counsel the opportunity to create a record to use in a motion for summary judgment, and perhaps in some small part because they believe that if they do not discover unfavorable information, the other side will not discover it either.

In simple fact, opposing counsel has the opportunity to create a favorable record in any event, either through her own questioning at depositions or through affidavits from the party or friendly witnesses if the subject is avoided at the deposition (although some courts see post-deposition affidavits to oppose motions as sandbagging and will not permit it). Therefore, there is no impediment to proceeding with the normal "funnel" approach at the discovery deposition, using open questions to try to uncover all the witness's relevant information. The idea that unfavorable information can be left undiscovered should be discarded. The safest assumption, especially when dealing with witnesses who are parties or closely identified with parties, is that the opposing attorney already knows all of the information they have that hurts the client, and deposing counsel might as well find it out, along with any additional information that may lessen its impact.

Occasionally, when one side has to defend a motion for summary judgment early in the pretrial schedule, depositions are scheduled explicitly to permit response to the motion.[2] At such a deposition the deposing attorney's focus is clearly on discovering "material facts" that are "genuinely disputed." The emphasis, however, remains on "discovering," since relying solely on a cross-examination style with narrow, leading questions may leave entire areas of dispute unrevealed. Just as in a normal discovery deposition, the last portion of the deposition may be used to sharpen positions and issues with more leading questions, so that the answers are narrower and the court may see the "genuine dispute" and the "materiality of the facts" more clearly. The approach for summary judgment or simple discovery is the same.

Deposition testimony can always be used to support or oppose any motion where the court would consider affidavit evidence. As previously noted, a deposition, being under oath, resembles an affidavit and courts will generally give the same weight to the two.

---

2. Rule 56(d) specifically provides, among other things, that where it appears that a party opposing a motion needs discovery beyond affidavits to support its opposition, time for depositions may be allowed.

16.2   Preparing for Trial

Perhaps the most important use of depositions is in preparing to cross-examine witnesses at trial. The late Irving Younger, in his famous lecture, *The Ten Commandments of Cross-Examination*, gave as his fifth commandment, "Never ask a question to which you do not already know the answer." ("If you didn't see him bite it off, how do you know my client did bite off the plaintiff's ear?" "I saw him spit it out.") One of the ways to know the answer is through the witness's deposition.

Many trial lawyers construct their cross-examinations based on the answers given in the witness's deposition. At trial, however, those deposition questions can be reorganized to make the intended points in the most effective way possible on cross-examination. For example, a critical point for trial may not have been covered until toward the end of a deposition, but nothing prevents beginning the cross-examination with this point. Not only may the order of points and questions be changed, but unimportant or harmful information in the deposition may be deleted and inartfully phrased questions may be rephrased.

When dealing with important party statements by a witness, the cross-examination questions should mirror the deposition questions as closely as possible in meaning, if not actual wording, so that an attempted impeachment will present clearly inconsistent answers to the judge or jury. A minor change in wording between the deposition and trial may permit an intelligent witness to avoid the sting of impeachment and may make the cross-examiner look foolish in the process. Consider the following example:

> Q: Isn't it true, sir, that you never even bothered to read the contract?
>
> A: No, that's not true.
>
> Q: Are you telling this jury that you did read the contract?
>
> A: Yes.
>
> Q: Well sir, do you remember having your deposition taken?
>
> A: Yes.
>
> Q: Showing you that deposition, do you see on page 14, line 6 that you were asked, "Did you read the contract before you signed it?" and your answer was "No"?
>
> A: Yes, but that's different than what you just asked me. You asked whether I had ever read the contract, and I did read it about two weeks after the signing.

Q: Well, then, let's move on.

When preparing both their direct and cross-examination outlines for witnesses, many trial lawyers will annotate the outline with the page and line of the deposition that confirms the expected answer. Such an outline—this one for cross-examination—might look like this:

> Was going approximately 50 mph as approached the intersection. (28:16)
>
> Started braking about 200 feet away. (30:14)
>
> Baby was crying in the back seat. (12:4)
>
> Was expected to be at work at 8:00 a.m. (72:12)
>
> Was running late that morning. (73:19)

Thus, if you need to refresh a witness's memory on direct or impeach a witness on cross, you can quickly locate the exact page and line of the deposition. In modern deposition practice, deposition transcripts are often created in a digital format, in which the answers that form the basis for cross-examination can be bar-coded. If the witness varies his testimony, a simple swipe of the bar code can display the deposition transcript on monitors throughout the courtroom. Similarly, if the deposition is recorded using digital video, the video can be bar-coded so the witness can be seen and heard delivering his self-contradictory testimony.

To help prepare for motions and trial, summarize or create abstracts of the depositions shortly after they are taken. Doing so will also help you locate impeaching answers in the heat of trial. Paralegals or new associates usually do the abstracting, but experienced attorneys also do it as a way of becoming more familiar with what was said during the deposition. Clients are more likely to read abstracts than full transcripts, and they may be able to participate in trial preparation more fully as a result.

There are a number of methods of abstracting depositions, including the full summary method and the subject method. The first is a straight summary of the deposition; the second organizes the summary by topics. Some attorneys, instead of abstracting, now rely on computer searches for key words and phrases, having used a reporting service that provides a searchable word-processing file of the deposition on a disk or flash drive. This method is more expensive and requires bringing a computer to trial, but in modern practice many courtrooms have installed equipment that merely requires plugging in a laptop computer that has the relevant information stored on disk or hard drive, or that allows access to the electronic files in your office.

Of course, as with any technology, you should have back-up computers and, if all else fails, hard copy of the deposition transcript or summary. Use of the available technology can sometimes be quicker and more efficient than reviewing a lengthy abstract. A typical summary abstract might look like the following:

14:6   Formed own construction co. after graduation from college.

14:12   Had only 5 to 10 employees for 1st 10 years.

14:16   Now has 50 employees.

14:20   Does all engineering work and bidding on contracts.

A typical subject abstract of the same topic would look like this:

Formed own company after college (14:6) where he does all the engineering and bidding work on the contracts (14:20). The company has grown from 5 employees to 50 in 10 years (14:12, 14:16). He has plans to grow it to 100 (43:25) and then to sell it to his younger sister and brother-in-law (45:13).

Witnesses will often be testifying at trial months and even years after they gave their deposition testimony. It is not uncommon for their trial testimony to change in minor ways from what they said at the deposition, not because of any intent to lie or deceive, but because memories fade. Nonetheless, these deviations in the hands of a skillful attorney can be used to discredit a witness's integrity and honesty, along with their memories.

You can avoid many of these problems if you ask all witnesses expected to testify in a trial or other proceeding to review their depositions carefully before they take the stand. When preparing each witness for trial, emphasize the dangers of changing their testimony from what they said in the deposition

16.3   Using the Deposition Testimony at Trial

How deposition testimony is presented to the trier of fact is very much a matter of local custom and procedure. In a bench trial, the offering party usually will merely designate the pages and lines that the court is to consider, and the judge (or the judge's clerk) will read the testimony at some later time. In a jury trial, however, the testimony is almost always read to the jury, and the actual deposition transcript is never given to the jury to consider during its deliberations.

The procedure for reading the deposition to the jury also varies from jurisdiction to jurisdiction. Some courts have the bailiff read the designated portions to the jury, while in others it is one of the attorneys for the offering side who reads it. The preferred method with many attorneys, however, is to have a person—an attorney, a paralegal, even an actor—sit in the witness box to read the deposition answers while another attorney reads the questions. This makes the deposition reading resemble actual trial testimony as much as possible. Some attorneys select an associate or other person who presents the desired image to the jury.

Before the deposition can be presented at trial, two steps are necessary: first, editing; and second, ruling on objections.[3]

Deposition readings are invariably a tedious experience for the jury. One study of jury comprehension noted that "[t]he jurors' response to reading of depositions into evidence was uniformly negative. They found it boring, difficult to follow, and uninformative."[4] The more mercifully brief the experience, the more likely the jury will understand, remember, and be persuaded by what they hear. If lawyers will be reading the testimony, they should animate their voices and, within reason, emphasize those questions and answers they particularly wish the jury to focus upon. While the reading of depositions is boring, reading in a monotone turns it into torture.

A mistake many lawyers make is reading the entire deposition to the jury, not because all of it contributes to their cause, but because they want to give context or convey completeness. Do not do this. Instead, carefully edit the deposition so that you present only those questions and answers that will help the jury's understand and be persuaded. The other side can request that additional portions be read, but whether this occurs as part of counsel's reading or during the opponent's case is at the judge's discretion.[5] Brevity should be your guiding principle.

Most of the above applies equally to the presentation of deposition testimony that has been recorded on video. There are, however, some significant differences. Video recorded depositions are treated fully in a separate chapter, but, in summary, in the video deposition, demeanor matters; both the demeanor of the witness and the demeanor of the lawyer. All those factors important to demeanor at trial apply to the video deposition. The witness must look at the fact finder. In a video deposition, that is the camera. It is for that reason that the examining counsel will frequently sit in a position so the camera is directly over counsel's shoulder. In that way, when the witness naturally speaks to the questioner, she is also speaking to the jury through the eye of the camera. Proper courtroom attire, at least for the witness, is

---

3. *See* section 16.5.

4. Special Committee of the ABA Section of Litigation, Jury Comprehension in Complex Cases, 37 (1990).

5. Fed. R. Civ. P. 32(a)(4).

required and should be consistent with the witness's place in the litigation and the image sought to be portrayed of the witness. Unlike in a paper transcript, pauses between questions and answers appear on the video as being evasive, as they do in trial. Attorneys "appear" in video depositions through their voices. Questions must be clear and precise, with inflection appropriate to the information being solicited.

The judge must rule on objections only if objections have been made in the designated portion of the video. Usually the judge's ruling is done as part of the pretrial conference or during the trial.[6] As to objections, most videographers ask, and many judges require, that counsel state the word, "objection," whereupon the video stops and the nature of any objection and response is recorded in a paper transcript. Once the judge rules on the objection, the video is edited to be consistent with the court's ruling.

Although better than reading a deposition, head-and-shoulder shot video depositions are not scintillating. Consider using visual aids and other devices that enhance the jurors' interest and understanding at trial. And above all, if the option arises, it is almost always preferable to have the witness actually appear at trial.

16.4   Seven Ways to Use a Deposition at Trial

Whether you have originally taken a deposition for discovery or trial purposes, you can use it at trial in many ways. Among the most common uses are:

1.   as the testimony of an absent witness;

2.   as a basis for a proffer;

3.   as a source of party statements;

4.   as a means of refreshing recollection;

5.   as the testimony of a witness who is unable to testify because of lapse of memory;

6.   as a means of impeaching a witness; and

7.   as a means of accomplishing a "phantom" impeachment.

Each use of a deposition has a different foundation, deriving from the evidentiary rules that control that use. Since depositions are out-of-court statements the attorney may be offering for their truth, the rules restricting

6. *Id.*

the use of hearsay are often involved in determining the proper foundation. Here are examples of each use of a deposition at trial.

16.4.1   The Testimony of an Absent Witness

By the time of trial, some witnesses will have become unavailable, even though you may not have anticipated this when the absent witnesses' depositions were taken. In that event, the depositions may be used to replace the live testimony of the missing witness under Rule 32(a)(4) and Federal Rule of Evidence 804(b)(1). Here is what that process would sound like in court:

Plaintiff's Counsel:	Your Honor, Mr. Theodore Barker was scheduled to be our next witness, but he has been called out of the state due to an illness in his family. Counsel for the defendant has been kind enough to stipulate to Mr. Barker's unavailability and to the fact that this is his deposition testimony.[7] In place of Mr. Barker's live testimony, we would like to read certain limited portions of his deposition testimony for the jury. In total, there are about fifteen pages, Your Honor.
Court:	That's fine, Mr. Moreland. I presume that these portions have been redacted pursuant to the pretrial rulings?[8]
Plaintiff's Counsel:	Yes, your Honor, and defendant's counsel also has had an opportunity to review the portions we intend to read. And with the court's permission, we would like to have Mr. Richkus, a paralegal who works with us, read Mr. Barker's answers from the witness stand as I read the questions.

---

7. By reciting the stipulation, counsel has laid the foundation for use of the deposition under Fed. R. Evid. 804: the witness is unavailable, not through the fault of the proponent of the evidence, and this is in fact his deposition. If opposing counsel refuses to stipulate, you may have to offer evidence establishing the witness's unavailability.

8. Normally during the pretrial proceedings parties will have designated the deposition portions they intend to use and have presented objections for ruling by the court. In addition, any objection to the witness's unavailability would have been raised as part of the mandatory pretrial disclosure scheme. *See* section 16.4. The portions that the court has ruled inadmissible are "redacted," or deleted.

Court:	All right. There being no objection, you may proceed.
Plaintiff's Counsel:	Mr. Richkus, if you will go up to the witness stand, we can start with page 27, at line 17.

Q: (By defendant's counsel) Mr. Barker, what was your position with Vitas Industries in 1992 and 1993?

A: I was the vice-president for purchasing for the company.

Q: What were your responsibilities in that position?

A: I oversaw the purchasing of all materials that we required to manufacture all of our products. That included everything from the copper wire that we wound around the cores, to make the armatures for the generators, to the decals that we put on the transformer boxes telling about the high voltage.

Q: During that time, from whom did Vitas Industries purchase refined copper?

A: We had several suppliers, but the main ones for those two years were Chilean Copper Conglomerate, Incorporated, and Python Industrial Metals.

Plaintiff's Counsel:	Now, Mr. Richkus, will you please turn to page 43 in the deposition of Mr. Barker? We'll begin with line 4.

Q: Mr. Barker, why do you think that Chilean Copper and Python Industries were engaged in some kind of agreement to fix copper prices to your company, as is alleged in the complaint in this case?

A: Well, during that time, I often tried to get one or the other of them to give me a better price, you know, to bid against a price I had from the other. But they'd never break the line. Right in lockstep, all the time. On my other metal purchases, I could make deals by going from one supplier to the next, but on copper, those two never gave even a penny off.

Defendant's Counsel:	Your Honor, at this point, we ask that the next two questions and answers be read, pursuant to Rule 32(a)(6), because they contain material which, in

fairness, the jury ought to be allowed to consider along with this last answer.

Court: Well, let me just look at that material for a moment. Yes, I agree, we'll have that read at this point, please, Mr. Moreland.

Plaintiff's Counsel: Yes, your Honor.

Q: Mr. Barker, isn't it true that there was a terrific demand for copper during that period and a shortage of supply due to unrest in the government of Chile?

A: Well, there were some political problems down there that made the supply of copper a little less predictable. But we were getting all that we needed.

Q: And isn't it also true, Mr. Barker, based on your experience in the purchase of metals, that no one discounts their prices on metals during periods of shortage, because they can clear their inventories without price reductions?

A: Yes, I suppose that is true in general, but I still think that Chilean Copper and Python were fixing prices.

The process continues until all selected portions of the deposition have been read. At that point, opposing counsel may read in as her cross-examination additional portions of the deposition, either with another "witness" on the stand, or perhaps with this same one to lessen the likelihood that jurors would get confused.[9]

Some courts rule, erroneously, that 32(a)(6) material can just as well be presented during cross-examination. If the conditions of these rules have been met—that is, that the proffered material is so closely related to what has already been read, the jury "ought in fairness" to consider the two selections together—then the two selections should be presented together, not separated by the remainder of the main examination. These rules promote the jurors' understanding of the evidence; the fact that the additional material could be presented on cross-examination does not mean that is the best way for the jurors to understand it.

---

9. The use of Rule 32(a)(6) deserves comment. This rule allows additional portions of depositions to be read into the record that "in fairness should be considered with" portions that have been read by the other side.

16.4.2   As a Basis for a Proffer

Often you must persuade the court that certain evidence is relevant or certain lines of questioning have a good-faith basis. Sometimes you can use depositions to provide this foundation for going forward. Consider the following example from a cross-examination:

Q: Mr. Taras, isn't it true that you never saw the plaintiff before he went into the hospital?

A: No, that's not true at all. I saw him several times. We were good friends, and we visited a lot.

Q: Mr. Taras, you were good friends a year before the plaintiff's car accident, weren't you?

A: Yes, yes, of course.

Q: And you are good friends now, aren't you?

A: Yes, that's true, of course.

Q: But at the time of the accident, you and the plaintiff were not even on speaking terms, were you?

A: I don't understand what you're saying. He's my friend, and I see him all the time.

Q: Mr. Taras, you used to play poker with the plaintiff once a week, didn't you?

Plaintiff's Counsel: I object, your Honor. This is irrelevant and prejudicial, and I request that counsel be directed to move on to another area.

Defendant's Counsel: Your Honor, may we approach the bench?

Court: Yes, step up, counsel. Now, where are you going with this, Mr. Kaunas?

Defendant's Counsel: Your Honor, based on this witness's deposition testimony, which I can show you here at pages 34 and 35 of the deposition transcript, I believe that he will testify that he and the plaintiff used to play poker once a week, but that two weeks before the accident they had an argument over a poker hand and that they didn't speak to one another for several months. That testimony impeaches his testimony on direct that he visited with the plaintiff in the weeks after the accident and could see the pain and limited movement that the plaintiff now claims he had.

Court: Let me see the deposition. All right. Based on this deposition testimony, I am going to overrule the objections and permit the questioning. You may proceed, Mr. Kaunas.

Defendant's Counsel: Mr. Taras, the question is, didn't you and the plaintiff play poker once a week before the accident?

A: Yes, but he was never very good.

Q: But just a week or so before the accident, you stopped playing poker, right?

A: Yes, that's true.

Q: You had an argument about a poker hand, didn't you?

A: Yes. He never had a pair of aces. He had one ace, and he took the other from his pocket.

Q: And because of that argument, you and the plaintiff didn't talk to each other for almost a year?

A: Yes, that's the truth. It was silly. I've had aces in my pocket, too.

Q: And you didn't spend time with him and visit with him right after the accident, did you?

A: No, I didn't. But he has told me that he was really in a lot of pain then.

16.4.3   *As a Source of Party Statements*

You can introduce party statements in a deposition under Rule 32(a)(3) as though the statements were given as live testimony from the stand. Rule 32(a)(3) specifically authorizes using the deposition of a party, an officer, director or managing agent of a party, or a person designated to testify under Rule 30(b)(6). Further, Federal Rule of Evidence 801(d)(2) defines an opposing party's statement to include not only the party's own statements, but also statements made by the party's agents, employees, and persons authorized to speak on behalf of the party. All of these statements are classified by the Federal Rules of Evidence as nonhearsay and are admissible as substantive evidence.[10]

Thus, a plaintiff may use portions of the defendant's deposition to establish the plaintiff's prima facie case without calling the defendant as an adverse witness. Assume in the following assault and battery case that an element of plaintiff's case is the fact that the guard was an agent of the company at the time of the assault.

> *(Questioning by Plaintiff's Counsel)*

Q: And what was the defendant Sugis wearing when he came out of the building and struck you with the nightstick?

A: He had on a guard's uniform—you know, like a rent-a-cop kind of outfit—that said, "Ace Security" on a patch on his shoulder.

Plaintiff's Counsel: Your Honor, at this time we would like to read a section of one page of the defendant Sugis's deposition, which is an opposing party's statement under Federal Rule of Evidence 801(d)(2). The depositions have been stipulated as authentic.

Court: With that stipulation, you may proceed, but let's keep it short, since you have this witness on the stand.

Plaintiff's Counsel: Yes, your Honor. The portion appears on page 17 of the deposition. Quote:

Q: Mr. Sugis, when you saw the plaintiff marching down the street with the group carrying the antiwar signs, what were you doing?

A: I was at my desk in the lobby of the Metropolitan Building.

---

10. Rule 32(a)(1) states that depositions can be used for any purpose permitted by the Federal Rules of Evidence. Opposing party's statements (under Rule 801(d)(2)), direct or vicarious, should not be confused with "statements against interest," which are defined by FED. R. EVID. 804 as exceptions to the rule excluding hearsay if the declarant is unavailable. This confusion has probably persisted much longer than it otherwise would have because of the unfortunate habit of some courts of using the hybrid phrase, "admission against interest."

Q: Why were you there?

A: I was on the job; that's my responsibility, to provide security for the clients of the company.

Q: You say, "the company." Is that the Ace Security Company?

A: Yes. That's who I work for, Ace Security.

Of course, use of a deposition as a party statement is not limited to matters that are elements of the prima facie case. You can use selections for any purpose, as long as they are relevant and otherwise unobjectionable.

Rule 32(a)(6) applies to this use of depositions also. Thus, in the above situation involving Ace Security, counsel for the company might say:

Defendant's Counsel: Your Honor, may we read the next two questions and answers, under Rule 32(a)(6)? Let me give you a copy.

Court: Well, let's see. Yes, I see what you're saying. Yes, you may read the next two questions and answers.

Defendant's Counsel: Thank you, your Honor. Let me quote:

Q: Mr. Sugis, what time was it when you went out onto the street and had this confrontation with the plaintiff?

A: Well, it was about 9:30 in the morning.

Q: And what shift were you working for Ace Security at the Metropolitan Building?

A: I was on the midnight to eight shift, but, you know, I heard there was going to be this demonstration, so I kind of stayed around so I could see these people with their signs and things.

16.4.4 *As a Means of Refreshing Recollection*

You may refresh a witness's recollection with anything from a simple leading question to a photograph, a snatch of song, or a letter from Mom. The question the court must decide is not, "What was used to refresh recollection?" but rather, "Is the witness actually testifying from refreshed recollection?" Depositions are useful tools to refresh recollection because they have often been taken months or years closer to the relevant events. The foundation at trial for using depositions in this way is essentially the same as that for any attempt to refresh present recollection:

Q: Now, Ms. Vardas, what was the next step in trying to persuade United Lumber and Hardware to finance the expansion of your business?

A: Well, I think that I met with Mr. Shadis at the bank. No, that wasn't it. Maybe . . . . I'm sorry, I'm just not sure what was next. There were a number of meetings.

Q: Is there anything that might help you remember?

A: I think that we discussed this, you know, at my deposition. It seems to me that we went over this in the deposition.

Q: OK, let me hand you your deposition and ask if you would turn there to page 73. Read that to yourself, please, and tell me when you've finished.

A: All right. Yes, I've read it.

Q: Now, just let me have the transcript back, please. Having read that portion of your deposition, do you now recall what the next step was in trying to negotiate financing through United Lumber and Hardware?

A: Yes, I do. I met with their accountant, and brought my accountant and architect with me. It was at that meeting that United told me, "Go ahead with obtaining the permits and negotiating with your general contractor. We'll work something out."

Notice Rule 32(a)(6) does not apply here, since no deposition, writing, or other recorded statement is being offered; only the refreshed memory of the witness provides the evidence.

16.4.5 As the Testimony of a Witness Whose Memory Cannot Be Refreshed

When a nonparty witness[11] or your own client testifies at trial and cannot remember what color the traffic light was even though the witness testified in her deposition that the light was red, another method of introducing the statement, other than impeaching the witness with the deposition testimony, is available. Federal Rule of Evidence 804(a)(3) defines a failure of memory as unavailability for purposes of admitting statements that would otherwise

---

11. We focus here on nonparty depositions because the deposition of an adverse party can be used as a party statement, regardless of his present recollection or his availability, as we have discussed above.

be hearsay.[12] The witness's deposition testimony then becomes admissible as substantive evidence under Rule 804(b)(1), the provision allowing the use of "former testimony."

The foundation under Rule 804(a)(3) and 804(b)(1) is quite simple. You merely need to show that the witness's memory is currently inadequate for the matters on which the deposition is being offered and that the deposition was in fact given. Here is an example of cross-examination (but the same thing could also occur on direct examination using nonleading questions) using the deposition testimony in this way:

> Q: Now, isn't it true that as his friend, you were advising the defendant not to break this contract with the plaintiff?
>
> A: Well, I don't remember doing that.
>
> Q: You don't remember having a conversation where you told Mr. Shadis that you thought it was a fair contract and that he shouldn't breach it?
>
> A: No, I don't remember that.
>
> Q: Mr. Barker, in that same deposition we discussed earlier this morning, you were asked this question and you gave this answer—page 46, counsel: "Question: What did you discuss about the McLean contract? Answer: Well, I told Shadis that he seemed to be getting his money's worth, and that it looked to me like Vardas was doing a good job. I mean, he asked if I thought it was a fair deal, and I said, 'Yeah, it looks fair to me'." That was your answer, wasn't it, Mr. Barker?
>
> A: Yes, that's what I said.

16.4.6   *As a Means of Impeachment*

Under Federal Rule of Civil Procedure 32(a)(2) you can also use depositions as prior inconsistent statements to impeach a witness at trial. In fact, under Federal Rule of Evidence 801(d)(1)(A), deposition testimony used to impeach a witness with a prior inconsistent statement is classified as non-hearsay and may be considered by the judge or jury as substantive evidence as well as reflecting on the witness's credibility.[13] Such testimony may also qualify under Rule 801(d)(2)(A) as an opposing party's statement.

---

12. Rule 32(a)(1)(B) states that a deposition may be used by any party for any purpose permitted by the Federal Rules of Evidence.

13. In contrast, prior inconsistent statements not under oath can be used only for impeachment, i.e., reflecting on the witness's credibility, and cannot be considered as substantive evidence.

Early on, we discussed the commitments extracted at the outset of the deposition in some detail and made the point that those commitments were made to aid in control and impeachment at trial. Now, presented with the opportunity to impeach at trial, that groundwork comes into play. A full-blown impeachment of a nonparty witness at trial, at the first time an impeachment of the witness has been necessary, follows:

Q: Mr. Lapitis, on your direct examination you said that you saw the traffic signal when the defendant's Cadillac started into the intersection, is that right?

A: Yes, sir, I said it, and it's true. I saw that light.

Q: Isn't it true that the light was red for the defendant?

A: No, like I said, it was green for him. No question about it.

Q: No question about it?

A: No question about it.

Q: Mr. Lapitis, you remember coming to my office a few months ago?

A: Yes, I remember that.

Q: You came there to have your deposition taken, right?

A: Yes. Well, I got a subpoena, so I showed up like I was supposed to.

Q: And the defendant's attorney was there, wasn't she?

A: Yes.

Q: In fact, you met with her before the deposition, didn't you?

A: Well, yes, she asked me to come to her office the day before, so I went in and talked with her.

Q: When you came to my office for your deposition, we met in a conference room; do you remember that?

A: Yes.

Thus, if the defendant's running of a red light is an element of the plaintiff's prima facie case, a letter in which the witness wrote, "the light was red" can impeach his testimony that the light was green, but it cannot prove the light was red to satisfy the plaintiff's burden on that point. A deposition from the same witness in which he previously testified the light was red can impeach his trial testimony that the light was green and can also provide the necessary substantive element that the light was red.

Q: And the defendant's lawyer sat right next to you during the deposition, didn't she, and talked with you?

A: Yes, she was very nice.

Q: I told you that you could have breaks when you wanted them, and we had coffee and water there for you, isn't that right?

A: Yes, it was very pleasant.

Q: There was a court reporter there who gave you the same oath that you took here in court today?

A: Yes, that's right.

Q: And you promised then to tell the truth?

A: Yes, I swore to tell the truth as best I could.

Q: And you did tell the truth in your answers, didn't you?

A: Yes, I did.

Q: And after the deposition was over, the court reporter typed up my questions and your answers into a booklet, and he sent you that booklet, didn't he?

A: Yes, I went over it with the defendant's lawyer.

Q: And after you made corrections of some errors, you signed the corrections and sent the booklet back to the court reporter, right?

A: Yes.

Q: Let me show you that deposition, Mr. Lapitis, and I'd like you to look at page 76, the correction page. That's your signature right there at the bottom?"

A: Yes.

Q: Mr. Lapitis, at that deposition, page 16, line 32, I asked you this question and you gave this answer: "Question: Sir, what color was the traffic light for the westbound car, the defendant's Cadillac? Answer: For the Caddy, let me see . . . for the Caddy it was red." I have read your answer correctly, haven't I, sir?

A: Well, yes, that's what I said then.

> Q: And you did not change that page of the deposition when you read it later with the lawyers, did you, Mr. Lapitis? Take a look at the page of corrections here.
>
> A: No, we didn't change it.

That completes the impeachment, and under Federal Rule of Evidence 801(d)(1)(A) that puts in front of the jury the substantive evidence the light was red for the Cadillac, as well as the evidence that this witness has told two different stories under oath.

Sometimes, especially when there is nothing about the stories to distinguish them—that is, to make the favorable deposition statement apparently more truthful than the later, trial testimony—impeaching counsel might want to provide the motive:

> Q: Mr. Lapitis, since the deposition, you have met with the defendant's counsel a couple times, haven't you?
>
> A: Yes.
>
> Q: You met with her to review the deposition, and you met with her to prepare for your testimony today in court, isn't that right?
>
> A: Yes.
>
> Q: And both those times, you discussed what you were going to say here today, didn't you?
>
> Defendant's Counsel: Objection, your Honor. This calls for hearsay and attorney work product.
>
> Plaintiff's Counsel: Your Honor, these are conversations with a nonparty witness. There's no privilege here. And these conversations are relevant and admissible for impeachment, and therefore they are not hearsay.
>
> Court: Objections overruled. Please answer the question, Mr. Lapitis.
>
> A: Well, yes, we discussed what was going to happen at trial, and what questions I'd be asked.
>
> Q: And you practiced your answers to those questions, didn't you?
>
> A: Well, yes.[14]

---

14. One caveat is appropriate here, however. The success of this impeachment for bias depends on the latent (or patent?) mistrust that lay jurors have for attorneys—their belief

16.4.7   As a Means of Accomplishing a "Phantom" Impeachment

The "phantom" or "ghost" impeachment is so-called because no impeachment actually occurs, but the witness answers truthfully because he thinks impeachment is possible. The success of this tactic depends on convincing the witness at trial that the cross-examiner has absolute mastery of the facts in the deposition, coupled with ability to call them up virtually instantaneously.[15]

Some attorneys put the witness's deposition in a booklet with bright covers, with the witness's name two inches high across the front so that, perhaps during the direct examination, but certainly during the cross, the witness comes to recognize the cross-examiner has that deposition transcript readily available. Using this technique when impeaching during the cross-examination, you will make conspicuous use of the brightly bound volume, moving from your notes directly to the right page and line without fumbling.

After a number of such impeachments, the witness will become "disciplined," that is, will be much less willing to fight over testimony. At that point, you may be able to force the witness to tell the truth by making apparent use of the deposition, even though the deposition does not contain testimony on the point in question. If you have a good-faith basis for believing a particular fact is true—for example, that the witness's breathing problems started before his work at the asbestos brake removal company—but that fact is not in the deposition, you might conspicuously leaf through the deposition, settle on one page, appear to read it for a moment, and then say to the witness who has been watching:

> Q: And, sir, your breathing problems started long before you began work at Dustco Brake Manufacturing Company, didn't they?

The witness, now believing that the date of onset of his problems is pinned down in the deposition because the attorney has not been wrong yet, would rather admit the truth of earlier onset than lie and be impeached again.

---

that an attorney can make a witness say that red is green. If the cross-examiner establishes this as a premise, he indeed weakens that particular witness's testimony, but he also weakens the testimony of all of his own witnesses. And, since he is an attorney, he risks weakening his own credibility as well if the jury analyzes this form of impeachment logically.

15. In *The Art of Cross-Examination*, Francis Wellman writes, "A witness, in anger, often forgets himself and speaks the truth." WELLMAN, THE ART OF CROSS-EXAMINATION, 4th ed. at 135 (Macmillan Publishing Co. 1962). A similar phenomenon occurs with the phantom impeachment.

16.5   The Designation Process and Obtaining Rulings on Objections

Discovery depositions, unlike examination at trial, contain many misstatements, false starts, irrelevancies, and arguments between counsel. The procedures for cleansing the transcript of such problems have arisen not so much from the rules of procedure as from common practice and common sense. The designation and counter-designation conventions are intended to avoid arguments at trial about objections and to provide all parties with the opportunity to respond to deposition testimony that has been selected for use at trial.

If the case is sufficiently complex, at some point before trial most courts will order the parties to designate those depositions or portions of depositions each intends to offer at trial. In federal district courts, Rule 26(a)(3)(A) requires as part of the mandatory pretrial disclosures that each party designate those witnesses whose testimony is expected to be presented by means of a deposition, except for impeachment testimony, and, if the deposition was not recorded stenographically, also to provide a transcript of the deposition portions to be used. Each party must make these disclosures at least thirty days before trial unless the court orders otherwise. Each party then has fourteen days, unless the court sets a different time, in which to file any objections to the use under Rule 32(a) of the deposition testimony designated by any other party. You must be careful to include all objections you intend to urge since any not listed are waived. The only exceptions are for objections made under Federal Rule of Evidence 402 (relevancy) and 403 (prejudice, cumulative, and so forth) or if the court permits the objection to be added later for good cause shown.

In those jurisdictions following the pre-1993 version of the Federal Rules of Civil Procedure as well as those following the current rules, no required procedure for the actual designation and ruling on objections exists. Some general observations apply, however. Simultaneous designations are common: first, each side identifies the portions of depositions it intends to offer, either by making a list of witnesses, pages, and lines (the procedure under the current Federal Rules) or by marking on a copy of the transcripts with a particular color; red for plaintiff's designations and green for defendant's designations, for example. The parties then exchange the lists or transcript volumes and make counter-designations, either with additional lists, or by marking with additional colors; blue for plaintiff's counter-designations, yellow for defendant's. (Of course, the parties keep duplicate color-coded copies so that each can know what it designated and counter-designated and what the other side designated and counter-designated.) That normally is the end of it—counter-counter-designations normally do not occur.

Once the designation and counter-designation process has occurred, the court will usually order a submission on objections to any designated portions and then may hold a hearing to resolve those objections. Some judges prefer to postpone a ruling on the objections until trial, but that does not provide the attorneys with any certainty about what portions will be admitted. On the other hand, ruling pretrial on all objections to the designated portions can be very time-consuming and will result in the court spending time on objections to portions that may never be used at trial.

The best procedure may be to ask the court to review designations a few days before their intended use at trial, after the jury has left for the day. That will be close enough to the presentation for the attorneys to have a relatively firm idea of what they actually want to use at trial, and yet far enough in advance from them to formulate a plan based on the judge's rulings.

As a practical matter, however, courts are very unwilling to set aside time for ruling on these objections to designated portions and seem to hope that if they postpone looking at the designations long enough, those designations may never surface at all. To a great extent this is true because, far in advance of trial, attorneys tend to designate more than they will ever need. By refusing to turn to rulings on designations until near trial, or during trial, the courts may be dealing with the attorneys when they are able to evaluate their needs more realistically.

After the parties have made their designations and registered their objections, no other designations or objections should be considered by the court for party statements or testimony of an absent witness. (Uses for impeachment, proffers, and refreshing recollection of course remain unaffected.) Even for use of the depositions under Rule 32(a)(6), those materials ought to have been counter-designated, since that rule deals with use in response to an opponent's original use. The court should allow additional deposition material to be used only on a showing by the proponent that the need to use that portion of the deposition could not reasonably have been anticipated.

16.6   Presenting Deposition Testimony at Trial

We have already discussed one method of presenting written deposition transcript in court—having an associate or paralegal read the answers from the witness stand.[16] Although suitable for lengthier portions of the written deposition, this method is much too cumbersome for short excerpts and, of course, is inapplicable to video-recorded depositions.

Using an associate to read answers from the stand, however, is clearly preferable to the attorney standing and reading pages to the jury Even though it

---

16. *See* section 16.4.1.

is a "re-enactment," the give-and-take of questioning of a live witness has a dramatic content that is not present in a straight reading. You should consider, however, some subtle problems.

The court will expect the deposition readers, attorney and employee, to avoid inserting emotional content into the deposition through exaggerated intonation or pauses. Nevertheless, the jury itself will "add" content to the deposition reading by reacting to the appearance and personality of the witness-reader. In the instance where a friendly witness is unavailable and you are reading his deposition, you will want to select a witness-reader who presents an appropriate and attractive demeanor in terms of age, appearance, and bearing. Thus, if your absent witness is a middle-aged executive, select a middle-aged reader dressed in a suit and tie; if the witness is an assembly line worker, select a reader who looks as though he could make a living with his hands, and perhaps have him wear a sports coat and open-collared shirt; if the witness is a woman who owns a small business, select a reader who presents the appropriate appearance of experience, competence, and success.

Obviously, the opponent must guard against abuse by the attorney presenting the reader. If the actual deponent is a twenty-five-year-old high school dropout who happened to be present when his boss discussed contract terms, it is misleading to present to the jury a reader of his deposition who looks and speaks as though he has a graduate degree in business administration. The opponent should object, under Rule 403, that use of that particular reader will mislead and confuse the jury by inviting it to associate greater credibility with the testimony than would have occurred had the actual witness been available. The court may have a hard time appreciating this objection because it will not have seen the actual deponent, but the objecting attorney could present the educational background of the witness from the deposition, helping the court understand her concern.[17] Sometimes you suspect your opponent is taking the deposition because the witness will be unavailable for trial and is deliberately choosing to stenographically record the deposition because the witness would be less persuasive on video. While expensive to do so, you can defeat your opponent's strategy by arranging under Rule 30(b)(3) for the deposition to be recorded on video. At trial, when your opponent presents the deposition to a jury, you have a right under Rule 32(c) to insist on having the jury see the video rather than your opponent's associate or actor reading the stenographic version.

The opponent of the deposition testimony may have no advance notice of the identity of the reader selected by the other side, so it would be wise for

---

17. As mentioned, courts already understand that the weight given the testimony can be affected by the manner in which it is read, and they will instruct readers to avoid adding any emphasis or drama. The same concern logically applies to adding substance or weight by selecting readers from "Central Casting."

you to keep a "generic" bench brief in your trial notebook. This brief would remind the court of its power to control the mode of presentation of this deposition testimony and of the need to prevent confusing and misleading the jury.

CHAPTER SEVENTEEN

TAKING AND USING PRESERVATION DEPOSITIONS

It took me forty years on Earth,
To reach this sure conclusion:
There is no Heaven but clarity,
No Hell except confusion.

—Jan Struther

17.1   Preparing to Take the Preservation Deposition

Any deposition can be used at trial as a substitute for the live testimony of a witness if for some reason the witness is unavailable when the trial occurs.[1] One inherent risk of taking a deposition of a potentially adverse witness is that if the witness later becomes unavailable to testify at trial, portions of the deposition taken for discovery purposes may end up being read into evidence by opposing counsel. Thus, questions asked to gather as much information as possible later come back to haunt deposing counsel when the other side uses the answers. This becomes an even greater problem when deposing counsel has refrained from aggressively cross-examining the witness during the deposition, planning to reserve such attacks until trial to avoid giving the witness experience on how to respond. If the witness has become unavailable, then the other side can present the deposition testimony to the jury mostly unchallenged.

But depositions sometimes are taken specifically in anticipation that a witness, particularly a friendly witness, will not be available at the time of trial. These are called "preservation depositions," "trial depositions," or "depositions *de bene esse*." The plan is to present the witness's direct testimony through deposition testimony, often video-recorded deposition testimony. For instance, if a friendly witness is moving to another state or is expected to die before the trial, the deposition may be taken primarily for preservation purposes, and only incidentally, if at all, for discovery purposes (since it is assumed that a friendly witness will talk to counsel during trial preparation

---

1. FED. R. CIV. P. 32(a)(3); FED. R. EVID. 804.

and compulsory process and deposition under oath are not needed to discover what the friendly witness knows). Despite the risk of preserving unfavorable testimony, you will often find it necessary to take a witness's deposition in anticipation that the witness may be unavailable for trial. Preparing for and taking these depositions is sometimes more so important than taking a discovery deposition, because a preservation deposition is intended to support your affirmative case. You can prepare friendly witnesses for their depositions in the same way you would have prepared them to testify at trial. Occasionally, however, a witness is known to have important information that may be favorable, but neither side is quite sure and the witness refuses to be interviewed. When it is expected that the witness will be unavailable for trial, the hard decision must be made whether to take the witness's deposition to preserve what may be favorable testimony, or forgo taking it because of the risk that the testimony will turn out to be unfavorable and the deposition will ultimately be used to the client's detriment.[2] Of course, the other side can short-circuit any of these plans by noticing the witness's deposition (although it has to go through the same analysis). If a nonparty witness allows an interview, that may be preferable because the results of the interview need not be shared with the opposing party. If counsel thinks the witness will not need to be controlled by a deposition transcript at trial, the interview may be sufficient discovery of the witness's information.

When a witness refuses to be interviewed or when it is otherwise impossible to pin down a witness's story in advance, the deposition must be a combination of discovery (finding out what the witness has to say) and perpetuation (putting the testimony in a form that can be used for trial). The risk, of course, is that all of the information will be harmful and there is little affirmative testimony to use in presenting the case at trial.

Schedule the deposition of the potentially unavailable witness as early in the discovery plan as possible, especially if the witness is in precarious health or is known to be planning to leave the country.

When preparing to take a deposition for purposes of perpetuating the witness's testimony for later use at trial, remember that reading the deposition testimony almost always renders juries slightly comatose. Even placing a colleague in the witness box to play the role of the witness only minimally increases the interest level of the jurors. Thus, if finances and logistics permit, consider video recording the testimony.[3] When useful portions of the video are played back in court, the jury's attention span and retention are likely to be much greater than with the use of a stenographic deposition.

---

2. In some states, attorneys control this risk by conducting a discovery deposition first, then proceeding with a "trial" or *de benne esse* deposition if the evidence is favorable and should be preserved.

3. *See* chapter eighteen, "Video Depositions."

If the witness is friendly and cooperative, you can use the same process to prepare for the deposition as used for trial. Carefully explore the witness's story and try to resolve any internal discrepancies or weaknesses. More importantly, review the expected questions and the witness's answers and make suggestions for improving the presentation through better word choice, order, or emphasis. Incorporate documents and graphics into the presentation—it will serve as the direct examination. Discuss potential cross-examination topics and give the witness a flavor of what it will be like to endure cross. At a preservation deposition, the opposing party of course may conduct cross-examination, which can be presented if the deposition is used as the direct examination at trial. That "preserved" cross-examination may well be incorporated in a discovery deposition that the opposing party schedules to precede the preservation deposition once notice is received that the preservation deposition is to be taken. Remember, however, that the preparation conference with the witness will not likely be privileged unless the witness is a client or an agent or designee of a client. Finally, carefully control the witness's appearance at a video deposition; both dress and demeanor are as important here as they are in an appearance on the stand in testifying at trial.

17.2   Taking the Preservation Deposition

Conduct the examination of a witness whose deposition is being taken to *preserve* testimony as if the witness were testifying at trial. First, because the jury or judge will not have an opportunity to observe the witness's demeanor in person, explore other indices of veracity. The most important is a longer and more complete accreditation of the witness. Providing details about the witness's personal background is helpful, such as whether the witness is married, has children, and has lived in the community for a number of years. Similar information about the witness's education and employment history may also help the judge or jury. If the witness's testimony relates to his or her job, some detail about the job and the witness's experience will add to credibility. Finally, if the witness is neutral and has no ties to either side of the dispute, emphasize this.

Because you will have no opportunity to ask the questions again at trial, your questions and the answers must be clear and understandable. By carefully thinking through the best method of explaining complex matters and even writing out the questions, you will help ensure that the jury or judge will understand the witness's testimony when it is read at trial. An effective trial lawyer learns how to "self-monitor." In other words, you must learn to listen to your own questions and the witness's answers and judge whether they are clear, understandable, and persuasive in bringing out all of the witness's important information. Paying particular attention to the order in which facts are presented, usually adhering more closely to a chronological approach, will pay off by helping the judge and jury follow the story, even when the witness is not present.

If the deposition is not videotaped, the witness's tone of voice, gestures, and facial expressions do not convey meaning—they are not reflected in stenographic depositions. If you must present testimony from a written transcript of a deposition, make sure that all the questions and answers are understandable as they are on the page, without reference to these visual and aural factors. If the witness must give distances or illustrate movements, plan in advance how to do this in such a way that the jury listening to the testimony later will understand what is going on. Thus, you should clarify all hand gestures and descriptions, such as "from here to there," by stating such clarifications as, "let the record show that the witness has pointed to an object ten feet from the witness chair." As questioning counsel, you may do this because opposing counsel is there to correct any misstatements. ("We'll stipulate that the object is at least eight feet away from the chair.")

When opposing counsel makes an objection at a deposition being taken for discovery purposes, you will normally not respond in any way to the objection except to request that the witness answer the question. Where there is no intention ever to introduce the testimony at trial or use it for a summary judgment motion, it does not really matter that the question was objectionable; the only interest is the answer and the facts provided by that answer. However, this is not the case with a deposition being taken for use at trial.

At deposition, answers are taken "subject to objection," meaning that when an objection is made, the witness still answers the question, and the court can rule on the objection later if the answer is ever offered for use at trial. Deposing counsel in a preservation deposition might want to respond to many objections by adjusting the question to avoid the situation where an objection is sustained by the court at trial, and there is no longer a witness available to answer an adjusted question. If in doubt about the basis for the objection, do not hesitate to ask opposing counsel to state the grounds. If she refuses to provide the basis for a general objection, it is almost certain that the court will not sustain the objection; if she provides a basis, you are in a better position to decide whether and how to reframe the question. Even if the objection is of doubtful validity, take the answer, then rephrase the question and get a second answer. Then, if the objection ultimately turns out to be unfounded, you can choose which of the two phrasings you will use at trial. If the objection is sustained when "pressed" at trial, the second, improved question and answer will still stand.

Sometimes you will need to take a deposition for use at trial even though you have had no opportunity to interview the witness in advance. In those situations, you may need to first ask discovery-type questions to find out what the witness knows. Once you have explored the witness's knowledge, you can them formulate questions that cover the desired information in a form more suitable for trial presentation. For instance, if the witness, in answering a question about what happened, provides a long answer with a lot of neutral information and a few items of importance, ask several additional questions that highlight the favorable information. That the useful questions are separated by several questions and answers with unhelpful information does not matter. When you have the deposition read at trial, you can omit the irrelevant questions and answers and present only the useful ones.

Remember also that leading questions are only permissible in limited circumstances: preliminary matters, an adverse party, a witness identified with an adverse party, a witness who has demonstrated hostility, or when leading questions are necessary to develop the testimony of the witness, such as with a child witness or with an expert witness where leading questions may be necessary to translate "heteroskedasticity" from statistics into English. There should be no question about who is an adverse party, but you will need to establish through questioning that a witness is hostile or identified with an adverse party. The foundation for asking leading questions is usually laid at the beginning of the trial deposition, or, as it is in trial, at the beginning of that portion of the testimony, where the witness's hostility begins to affect the answers.

17.3   Defending the Preservation Deposition

Nothing in a notice of deposition indicates whether the deposition is being taken for use at trial, for discovery, or for both. But any time a notice of deposition is received from the other side for a witness who is known to be friendly to the side giving notice, the deposition is probably being taken to preserve testimony. It generally makes no sense to take the deposition of a witness who can be interviewed out of the presence of opposing counsel unless the witness is likely to be unavailable for trial. If this occurs, as defending counsel, you should be prepared to cross-examine the witness in the same way you would at trial.

Witnesses friendly to the other side will probably not consent to being interviewed prior to the deposition (but try), and therefore the "defending" lawyer is going into the deposition blind, not knowing what the witness's testimony will be.[4] Thus, before the proponent of the witness conducts the deposition to preserve direct testimony for use at trial, opposing counsel may

---

4. In the deposition of a friendly witness, the taking attorney also defends the witness during the other side's questioning, including guarding against overly aggressive behavior, attempts to obtain privileged information, and so forth.

notice a deposition for discovery purposes so that cross-examination can be conducted and preserved. Since a witness may only be deposed once, absent a court order or stipulation, serving a second notice of deposition is likely to cause the lawyer who noticed the preservation deposition to seek a protective order limiting this witness to only one deposition. The argument may be made at that time about the unfairness of having only one deposition, but be forewarned that judges usually only permit one deposition. (As noted above, however, in some jurisdictions it is common for one party to conduct a discovery deposition before the other party conducts a preservation deposition, so that the follow-up "cross-examination" at the preservation deposition can be based on information discovered by the opponent.)

The usual procedure in preparing to cross-examine a witness who cannot be interviewed and whose deposition is being taken to preserve testimony is to conduct information-gathering questioning after the preservation questioning—goal here is to determine what the witness knows and to develop possible areas for cross-examination and impeachment during the follow-on questioning. While a lawyer would normally worry about preserving unfavorable testimony, such information is likely to be brought out on direct examination, unless opposing counsel is equally ignorant of what the witness will say. In this situation, your task is to discover the testimony favorable to your client that opposing counsel may fail or has failed to bring out, as well as all information that tends to discredit the witness. Then take a break to plan a trial-type cross-examination, which you will execute before concluding the deposition. When the deposition is read or (in the case of a video deposition) played at trial, you will deliver only the trial-type examination to the jury. Remember, however, that after a portion of a deposition is offered, Federal Rule of Civil Procedure 32(a)(6) and Federal Rule of Evidence 106 permit the other side to offer additional, related portions of writings, including depositions, to be introduced for consideration by the judge or jury, if fairness requires. These are often called "rules of fairness and completeness," and they are used to put the entire portion of the story in the record at one place so the trier-of-fact can more easily understand the totality of the record. (While in theory the court can order the party who offered the first part to read in the second part, it is more normal for the judge to tell the "completing" counsel to offer and read the second part herself.)

Appropriate objections must also be made during the deposition of a witness friendly to the other side and whose testimony is being taken for presentation at trial. Since any objection to a problem that can be cured is waived if not made, you must be alert in the role of opposing counsel. The transcript will be read at trial, and this is your only opportunity to make curable objections.[5] Naturally, the same strategic considerations that govern objections

---

5. *See* section 14.9.2.

at trial also govern in defending the trial deposition; therefore, you will not make some objections for tactical reasons. For instance, objecting to a lack of foundation is rarely helpful unless the questioner cannot establish the necessary foundation.[6] Otherwise, the opposing lawyer is likely to ask the necessary questions resulting in the evidence being more persuasive than it would otherwise be.

---

6. *See* section 14.11.1.

CHAPTER EIGHTEEN

VIDEO DEPOSITIONS

"A picture may instantly present what a book could set forth only in a hundred pages."

—Ivan Sergeyevich Turgenev[1]

Presenting a witness on video gives that witness's testimony much greater impact than a dry reading of the deposition transcript. This is true whether the testimony is offered for impeachment or in place of the live testimony of an absent or adverse witness. Because of that greater impact, you need to take special care at the deposition to create a visual record that conveys the message you want the fact finder to take away. As a corollary, in defending the video deposition, the deponent must be protected from sometimes subtle techniques that can unfairly diminish or distort her performance and credibility.

18.1   When to Take a Video Deposition

Presenting testimony from a live witness in the witness box is almost always preferred to presenting evidence through reading or showing depositions. A witness on the stand answering questions not only holds the jury's interest better, but is more understandable and persuasive than listening to the reading of a deposition. Jurors also expect that the testimony of key witnesses, particularly the testimony of a party, will be presented live. If it isn't, jurors can easily assume that a party or witness must not think that the case is very important if they are not willing to come to the trial. This preference for live testimony is reflected in the requirement in most jurisdictions that deposition testimony may only be used as substantive testimony if the witness is unavailable.

---

1. Ivan Turgenev (1818–83), Russian novelist, short-story writer, and playwright; major work, the novel *Fathers and Sons*.

By definition, a witness is unavailable for trial when she is seriously ill or elderly; she is out of the country or jurisdiction; or, at the time of trial, she has insufficient memory of the events.[2] Expert witnesses present a special problem. The best usually have full schedules, complicated by teaching and patient obligations, and their time is very expensive. The problem of coordinating the expert's schedule with the court's is often insurmountable, and the expense of having an expert witness waiting to testify is more than many clients can bear. In such circumstances, the expert might be found to be unavailable. Nevertheless, when any of these witnesses are important to the proponent's case, that attorney will want the testimony to have as much impact as possible.

Other times, it is the party adverse to the witness's position who wants to use video to enhance the impression that the witness makes. That party thinks that the witness's party statements may be clearer and more convincing, or the witness's disorganized story will be less believable, if the judge and jury can actually see the testimony, even if it is not live. Again, this is a place where video may serve the attorney well.

Through video, the judge and jury can observe the witness's demeanor while testifying as well as hear what the witness is saying. The jury can evaluate the witness's demeanor and credibility almost as well as they could if the witness were in the courtroom sitting in the witness box. In short, video technology now provides the ability to virtually bring distant witnesses into the courtroom and have the jury hear their testimony as if the witness were testifying live.

18.2   Advantages of Video Depositions

Just as live witnesses are more interesting and persuasive than video deposition testimony, so are video depositions more interesting than stenographically recorded ones. Consider the following advantages of video depositions:

Video depositions permit jurors to see the witness's demeanor. Video allows jurors to evaluate a witness's sincerity and trustworthiness based on the witness's demeanor almost as well as they can with live testimony at trial. Reading selected portions of a stenographic deposition to the jurors deprives them of this opportunity.

Video depositions allow jurors to see the witness's physical condition. A video deposition can capture the physical condition of a witness who is terminally ill and who is expected to die soon or who has become too infirm to

---

2. During the "Watergate Hearings" in the early 1970s, many Nixon administration witnesses testified repeatedly, to the point of nationwide laughter, that they "had no present recollection at this point in time." Those witnesses would have been declared "absent" had the matter ever wound up in federal court, and if the Federal Rules of Evidence had been in place at the time.

testify at trial. For example, a video deposition of a plaintiff with asbestosis[3] allows the jury to see the effects of the disease on his health in a way the bare transcript of a stenographic deposition cannot.

Video deposition testimony is more entertaining and easier to follow; reading stenographic depositions is often the most boring part of the trial. Stenographic deposition testimony is usually presented by one or two lawyers reading the questions and answers to the jury. No matter how well it is presented, juries repeatedly confirm that the reading of transcribed deposition testimony leaves them confused and bored. While not as easy to follow as live testimony, video depositions are an improvement over having depositions read. Jurors get to watch as well as listen to the witness and are more likely to follow the testimony and remain interested in what is occurring. It is well known among social sciences that information presented to two senses (sight and hearing) is much easier to comprehend and believe than information presented to the ears alone.

Video depositions allow exhibits to be presented better. Consider what happens in a stenographic deposition when a witness refers to an exhibit—an anatomical diagram about which a doctor is testifying, for example. The witness might say, "The fracture occurred here," and the lawyer will then attempt to make the record clear by saying, "You are pointing to the upper portion of the ulna?" and so on. If the deposition is read at trial, a copy of the exhibit must be shown to the jury with the hope the jury can understand from the deposition testimony what part of the exhibit they should be looking at. The procedure is cumbersome, and there is always a risk that the jury will not understand what part of the exhibit the witness is referring to.

A video deposition solves most of these problems because the camera can take a close-up of the exhibit and show the viewer exactly where the witness is pointing when she testifies, "The fracture occurred here." The video view of the exhibit could also be taped separately by the videographer and inserted into the video of the witness's testimony at the appropriate point, as indicted by the attorney's instructions at the deposition. If the court later rules that the exhibit is not admissible, it can be removed from the selection of the video to be used, just as objectionable questions and their answers can be removed if an objection is sustained by the court.

Video depositions permit the witness to demonstrate large pieces of equipment, work with materials, and show a scene when these cannot be brought into the courtroom. Sometimes counsel in a product liability case

---

3. Asbestosis is an occupational lung disease, caused by inhalation of asbestos during long-term or intensive exposure to asbestos fibers, normally occurring in workers installing or removing asbestos or asbestos-containing products used in shipbuilding, insulation installation and removal, brake removal and installation, and mining in asbestos-bearing seams. Asbestosis can result in mesothelioma, a cancer that is almost always fatal.

may want the jury to see how a piece of equipment was operating when the injury occurred, or how, for instance, a piece of scaffolding was assembled. When the exhibit is too large or inconvenient to bring into the courtroom, the best way of helping jurors understand the witness's testimony is through a video deposition taken where the witness can demonstrate exactly what happened. Similarly, a video deposition permits the witness to visit the scene of an accident or a construction site to point out where events occurred, perhaps while the witness provides a "voice-over" describing the scene. If the deposition is being taken by opposing counsel, her questions can be directing the witness's descriptive comments. (Of course, videos can also be prepared as exhibits to be used during trial to illustrate the witness's testimony or as substantive evidence when the proper foundation is laid: "It fairly and accurately depicts a relevant scene at a relevant time," stated by someone who is familiar with the relevant scene at a relevant time.)

Video depositions can show tests and experiments being conducted in the laboratory when they cannot be shown in court. Where an expert witness has conducted experiments, but will be unavailable to testify at trial, or the experiments cannot be conducted in the courtroom for reasons of safety or practicality, a video deposition permits the jury to see exactly what the expert did and what results she reached if the experiments are included on the video with the witness's commentary.

Video depositions can be more effective for impeachment because jurors can see as well as hear the prior inconsistent statement and the witness's reaction to being confronted with it. The dramatic impact of impeachment is heightened when jurors can both hear and see the witness confronted by or actually speaking the words of the prior inconsistent statement. Modern technology has made it much easier to use the video deposition (because the video is recorded in a digital format and the sections likely to be used are easy to find quickly). Under the Federal Rules of Evidence, this video would constitute extrinsic evidence of a prior inconsistent statement, which need not be shown to the witness on the stand at trial, but must be disclosed to counsel on request. The video itself will not be admissible unless the witness denies the statement, is shown the video, and opposing counsel has the chance to question her witness about it.[4]

Video depositions highlight an opposition witness's evasion, fumbling, or pause before answering. Some witnesses do not perform well in the deposition room. They come across as evasive or disingenuous, and their counsel may conclude that they will perform just as poorly in the courtroom and that the jury is not likely to believe their testimony. This is wonderful if they are important opposing witnesses. Presumably, counsel defending the

---

4. Fed. R. Evid. 613.

deponent in this situation will make the same evaluation of the witness and, if the witness is beyond the subpoena power of the court and is not considered part of the "party" (when they might be compelled to attend), they may be unavailable. Their own counsel could present them by stenographic transcript, reducing the negative image the witness presents, but opposing counsel, of course, can nevertheless use a video deposition, thereby allowing the jury to see the witness and make almost the same judgment about the witness's credibility as if it were live testimony.

Video depositions can be edited to use during the closing argument and, with the court's permission, during the opening statement. During opening statement and closing argument, courts are increasingly permitting the use of selected portions of video depositions that have been admitted in evidence during the pretrial process or that the proponent reasonably believes will be admitted during trial. The effect on jurors of actually showing them a key question and answer in the deposition during opening—to introduce the theme or so that the witness is placed in the desired light before even appearing to give testimony—is significant. This technique introduces foreshadowing[5] into the theatre of the trial, with its considerable dramatic impact. When used in the closing, video segments can rouse clear memories of significant witness testimony just as the jurors are ready to make their decisions.

Video depositions are more likely to control the behavior of disruptive opposing counsel. As noted earlier, lawyers who are willing, in front of a court reporter, to disrupt the deposition and act completely inappropriately are often much more reluctant to do so when their actions are captured on video. Even for those lawyers who are not deterred by the presence of the camera, the existence of the tape will make it much easier when you request sanctions against opposing counsel's behavior at deposition, as the judge will be better able to evaluate obstreperous counsel and the effect of that behavior on the discovery process. When you anticipate misbehavior, notice the deposition as a video deposition. If the misbehavior arises for the first time at the deposition, advise the misbehaving counsel that the deposition will be video recorded from lunch or the next break and then make the appropriate arrangements with the reporting service. If the offending lawyer does not agree to the switch to video, she can object (as with other disagreements she may have), but the objection is merely recorded in the record, and it does not prevent the video recording from proceeding.[6]

---

5. "Foreshadowing" is the literary technique of alluding to future events to heighten suspense and drama. In a trial, the opening statement may state that a witness will testify in a certain way, so the jurors look forward to it or begin to draw inferences before the testimony actually is introduced.

6. Fed. R. Civ. P. 26(c)(2).

*The Effective Deposition: Techniques and Strategies That Work*411

18.3   Disadvantages of Video Depositions

While video depositions have many important advantages over steno-graphic depositions, they also have some drawbacks. When considering whether a deposition should be taken stenographically or by video, think about both the advantages and disadvantages of each and decide which method provides the greater benefits in light of the objectives of the deposi-tion and its potential later use. The drawbacks of video depositions include the following.

Video depositions are usually more expensive than stenographic depo-sitions, require more effort to arrange, and may involve editing costs. As a general rule, video depositions are more expensive than stenographic records, although this becomes less of a factor each year. In addition to the cost or rental of the equipment, an operator must be paid, a larger room may be needed, and the video may require editing before it can be presented at trial. Rules 26(a)(3)(A)(iii) and 32(c) as well as the deposition rules of many states require that a transcript of the stenographic record be prepared of the portions of the deposition to be offered at trial to make it more convenient for the court to make rulings on objections and to ensure accuracy. Attempts to save money by having the lawyer acts as the operator of her own equip-ment may seem like a good idea, but in fact the deposing lawyer has more important duties, like asking intelligent questions and listening to the depo-nent's answers. Problems with a "self-generated" transcript and video may result in inaccuracies that make both the video and the written transcript partially useless, and which present additional costs in time and money.

Video depositions are more likely than stenographic depositions to have technical or mechanical problems. Video equipment occasionally breaks down or malfunctions, the operator forgets to turn on the machine at the proper time, or no one notices the batteries have died. The results can be disastrous, particularly if the malfunction or error is not discovered until the deposition is completed and the witness has departed. Carefully checking the equipment before the deposition begins and using a monitor while the depo-sition is occurring help minimize the problem, but the risk is always present.

Video depositions are more difficult to use for trial preparation. One of the important uses of depositions is to help prepare for trial. They can be used to review what evidence is available to support or oppose a position, to plan the witness's cross-examination, or to sketch out the closing argument. Using a stenographic deposition is often more convenient than reviewing a video when preparing for trial. Of course, normally a typed transcript is also prepared, so this review can be done from that transcript. It takes more time to review the video (reading is faster than speaking), but the necessary video equipment must be available and the attorney has to develop some facility with it. It is more difficult with video to go back to an earlier question and answer, and the attorney cannot put colored sticky-notes on the video at important points. It is harder with the video to keep track of what has been said. A stenographic transcription can be prepared and ordered, but its preparation will add to the deposition's expense.

Video depositions are a waste of money if the deposition is being taken for discovery purposes only. You don't need to incur the expense of a video deposition if discovery is the only anticipated purpose for the deposition. The strength of video is in presenting evidence at trial or to a mediator or arbitrator. Usually, however, if you have no intention to show the tape at the trial or other proceeding, then a stenographic deposition is easier to take and even easier to use for trial preparation. One exception to this rule, of course, is where the video is being used to record or control the behavior of an obstreperous opposing counsel.

Video depositions require special equipment and extra arrangements when used in court. Reading a stenographic deposition in court does not require any special preparation or equipment, but the same is not true of video depositions. Video monitors or projection equipment need to be ready and situated so that they do not interfere with movement in the courtroom during trial, but can be put in position immediately to support viewing of important testimony or impeachments. Apparently, an infinite number of extension cords is required for any electrical equipment in the courtroom. Furthermore, you must allow for equipment malfunction (backups of everything), and everything must be set up and running before the video can be shown. Regardless of your belief that you are technically competent, have a technical assistant available.

Video depositions allow the opponent's witnesses to hone their performances if they later testify at trial. When a video deposition is taken of an opposing party's witness for discovery purposes, it may wind up helping the witness practice for trial. If the witness made a poor impression on video because of poor eye contact, hesitations, fumbling with documents, or appearing evasive when answering questions, she can use the video as a guide on how to improve.

Video deposition witnesses may not talk or film well. Remember Richard Nixon in the 1960 Presidential Debates—poor preparation and hot lights made him look like a gangster and may have lost him the election. And then there was the performance of President Clinton's deposition during the Monica Lewinsky investigation, whose projected false sincerity increased his problems (among them, perjury). The video of the deposition of Bill Gates in the *United States v. Microsoft* case, in which he appeared distracted and ill-informed, has become a textbook on how not to perform on a video deposition.[7] When a witness cannot testify at trial, you must consider how they will appear and sound on the tape. Evaluation of a witness's demeanor works both ways: some witnesses are more persuasive and credible if the jury cannot see and hear them. Reading a stenographic deposition will not give any hint of a witness's halting answers, furtive looks, and nervous manner, but a video deposition reveals all these flaws and more.

18.4   The Law

The Federal Rules of Civil Procedure allow video depositions to be used in trials, but also require that stenographic depositions be available. Under Rule 32(c), on the request of any party, if video deposition testimony is available and is offered other than for impeachment purposes (usually, that is, as the testimony of an unavailable witness), it must be presented in non-stenographic form, unless the court for good cause orders otherwise. In bench trials, deposition testimony may be offered in stenographic or nonstenographic form. Whenever a video deposition is used at trial or in support of a motion for summary judgment (or other such motion), the offering party must provide the court with a transcript of the portions being offered.

Rule 30(b)(3) states that video depositions may be taken as a matter of right unless the court orders otherwise. The only requirement is that the notice of deposition must state that video will be used to record the testimony. The cost of the video is borne by the taking party, but any party may arrange for a transcription to be made from the video. Any party may also, after giving notice to the witness and other parties, designate another method, in addition to the noticed method, for recording the testimony. In short, even if the taking party states in its notice that the deposition will be taken by stenographic means, any other party may, as of right, require that the deposition also be recorded on video. The requesting party will be responsible for both arranging and paying for the video recording.

Rule 30(b)(5)(B) specifically instructs that the appearance or demeanor of the deposition witness must not be distorted through camera or sound-recording techniques. In other words, the recording must be fair and accurate. Rule 26(a)(3) states that if a party intends to use video deposition testimony at trial, this fact must be disclosed to opposing counsel as part of the required pretrial disclosures at least thirty days prior to trial or by a date set by the court. In addition, a transcript of the pertinent portions of the deposition testimony must be provided to the other parties.

---

7. In fairness, Gates needed better preparation by his counsel, although he would have had to make time available for the additional preparation. Obtaining enough preparation time is a common and serious problem with senior executives, although more with ambitious vice-presidents and "assistants-to" than with confident chief executives.

Many states have adopted specific rules concerning video depositions, but in those jurisdictions following the pre-1993 version of the federal rules, the parties may stipulate in writing or the court may on motion order that a deposition be taken by video. The stipulation or order must also designate before whom the deposition is to be taken; the manner of preserving and filing the deposition; and other provisions necessary to assure that the recorded testimony will be accurate and trustworthy.

18.5   Scheduling the Video Deposition

Video depositions are scheduled in the same manner as other depositions, but, as previously noted, the video may need to be edited before being used at trial. Also, the potential for mechanical or technical problems is always present. Therefore, take the deposition sufficiently in advance of trial to leave adequate time for any necessary editing or to retake the deposition if technical difficulties do interfere with an accurate recording.[8]

18.6   Preparing to Take the Video Deposition

If you plan to use extensive clips from the video depositions at trial (and here "extensive" may mean three or four minutes or more), remember that the video deposition portions should be both entertaining and persuasive, whether they are offered as direct testimony or as impeachment or rebuttal. If the direct examination on video drags on, is poorly organized, or is filled with jargon, the jury will not follow the story or chronology and the intended points will be lost. If the impeaching segments are not crisp, or take too long to set up the contradiction, the jury will not see the inconsistency or appreciate its significance.

Effective video depositions must be carefully planned productions. Keep in mind that when the video is being shown, the jury is concentrating on every word and action occurring on the screen in a way that does not occur

---

8. If a notice of a video deposition is received from the party sponsoring the witness, it should be anticipated that it is a preservation-trial-*de bene esse* deposition and that the witness will be unavailable for trial. Therefore, counsel will need to be fully prepared to conduct any cross-examination of the witness at the deposition. To prepare adequately for cross-examination, counsel must consider all discovery that might provide her with potential sources of cross-examination before the deposition occurs. Counsel may even want to try to postpone the video deposition either by agreement or by requesting a protective order from the court until document discovery and other preparation are complete. While expensive, counsel resisting the preservation deposition may want to notice her own discovery deposition to be taken sometime before the preservation deposition (even the morning of the same day), either by agreement or with the court's permission. Since such a discovery deposition would normally be held before trial testimony, this "discovery then preservation" schedule would be the procedure if the witness were to be testifying at trial. A strong argument can be made that a similar procedure should be followed when a preservation deposition is noticed.

with live testimony. When counsel is examining a witness at trial and briefly stops to search for a document, the jury can look at the judge, opposing counsel, the witness, or entertain itself in other ways as long as the interruption is short. With a video deposition, the television monitor becomes the center of attention and on-screen that same pause to find a document will seem to last forever.

18.6.1   *Hire a Capable Operator to Conduct the Video Deposition*

By using an experienced and capable video operator to conduct the deposition, you can avoid many of the difficulties that can occur with video. An experienced operator can provide guidance in planning room setup, lighting, positioning the camera, post-production editing, and many other considerations that do not exist with a stenographic deposition, but which are crucial to taking an effective video deposition. Most court-reporting firms now have good video capability, but before making the decision on which one to hire, be sure to check on what actual experience they have had. Ask for the names of several lawyers they have worked for in the past, and check with these lawyers on the quality of the work.

18.6.2   *Decide on Recording Options*

Distance, Width, and Objections

Most video cameras have zoom lenses, which permit a range of shots from wide-angle to close-ups. Even without a zoom lens, the camera can be positioned to capture a range of shots from the entire room to a close-up of the witness's face. Before deciding on the recording distance or field-of-view, check whether local court rules or practice require a particular method. Depending on the opponent, you may also want to get an agreement before the deposition on how the camera will be placed and what will be included in the field of view. Once you are satisfied with the shot and what is included in it, instruct the video operator to maintain that shot until you tell him to change it. Opposing counsel, of course, is perfectly entitled to inspect the camera settings, including who is included in the frame, but if he is unhappy because he is included along with the witness and deposing counsel, his only recourse is to make an objection on the record, or to bring in his own videographer, whom he would then control.

Microphones and Their Arrangement

Be sure to consider the number and arrangement of microphones before the deposition. Often there is one microphone for each participant, but sensitive table microphones have come into use that can pick up more than one participant. Always check the microphones before the deposition to ensure they can adequately pick up the voices of all the participants. Directional microphones attached to the camera, formerly the standard, are not sufficiently sensitive and should be considered inadequate. If the witness is some distance from the camera, or if someone off the line of the camera is speaking, the voices may not be picked up clearly and it may be difficult to identify who is speaking.

18.6.3   Select a Suitable Location for the Deposition

Unlike a stenographic deposition, the jury will see the room in which a video deposition is conducted. As with everything else connected with a video-recorded deposition, the surroundings should present the witness in the best possible light. For instance, a cluttered or messy foreground, with stacks of documents and files and paper cups, looks unprofessional and distracts the jury—it may even cause the jury to think less of the witness's testimony. When the deposition is to be conducted in a city where neither firm has an office, the court-reporting firm may have a room where the deposition can be conducted, or the deposing lawyer may have a friend at a firm that will provide a conference room out of courtesy. Even where the opposition is conducting a discovery deposition on video, an offer by defending counsel to provide the office for the deposition of her witness may be accepted, allowing some control over the surroundings.

Size

The room should be large enough to permit all of the participants to be comfortably seated and to hold all of the necessary equipment. Allow adequate room to position the camera and for the operator to move about.

Lighting

Always check whether the lighting is adequate, whether the lighting causes glare, whether curtains or shades should be open or closed, and whether additional lighting is necessary.

Temperature

If the deposition room is too hot, the sweat on the witness's brow will show on the tape and may cause the jury to believe it is because of nervousness or lying. A room that is too warm also makes everyone, including questioning counsel, drowsy by the time mid-afternoon rolls around.

18.6.4 Planning the Questions

Whether it is a preservation deposition or a discovery deposition, the video deposition stands in the stead of live testimony at trial; therefore, carefully organize the portions of deposition testimony that you think you might use at trial (for direct or for impeachment and cross) as you would if you were actually in front of a jury. A video deposition is not the place for stream-of-consciousness questioning or for asking questions on the fly. The goal is to present the fact finder a clear, persuasive, and memorable piece of testimony. To do so you must carefully plan the questions.

Dynamic Questions and Visual Aids

The usual video deposition shows what the television industry calls "talking heads," and talking heads are boring. Make every legitimate attempt to enliven the testimony without sacrificing the witness's credibility. Putting more energy in questions, in both form and delivery, making the questions as dynamic as possible, is one method of doing this; But do not stray far from normal courtroom demeanor or the video may appear false or contrived. Practice your deposition (and courtroom) delivery on video to identify these problems and work to correct any underplaying or overplaying.

Exhibits and visual aids help make otherwise flat testimony more interesting. If possible, keep the jurors' interest to the end by distributing exhibits throughout the testimony. Concentrating exhibits at one point in the examination can be as boring as uninterrupted testimony.[9]

Exhibits should be arranged so they are quickly accessible during the deposition and are in the order in which they will be used. Avoid delays during the deposition by premarking exhibits and having extra copies for opposing counsel and the court reporter.

Minimize Objections

Objections during the deposition can be edited out before the video is presented at trial, but such editing can be expensive and can make the testimony appear choppy. Therefore, carefully review planned questions and expected answers before the deposition to avoid objections. While an excessive number of objections may cause the judge to place the editing costs on the objecting party, the party offering the deposition most often will bear the cost, particularly if the objections are sustained.

---

9. Edward Tufte, noted speaker and author on visual evidence, has been heard to say that a display of exhibit after exhibit is just "one damn thing after another," although he was commenting also on presenting visual exhibits without simultaneously providing a base exhibit with which an audience can make comparisons.

18.6.5 *Preparing the Witness*

Factors that are not important in a stenographic deposition may become critical in a video deposition. For instance, a stenographic deposition does not show the witness's dress or demeanor, the tone with which questions are answered, or a witness's movements and nervous habits. However, to minimize your witness's anxiety and improve the impression she will make on the jury, explore these factors a few days or more before the actual video deposition, just as you would for trial testimony.

Dress

Usually dark jackets and business shirts or blouses in light colors film best, but run a test shot to be sure. The belief that white shirts will "flare" on camera no longer applies, because video technology has improved. Checks and small prints still cause distracting *moiré* problems.[10] In general, the witness should dress as if for court.

Demeanor

Rehearse responding to all questions in a courteous and responsive manner. Jurors will readily see on the video any evidence of evasiveness, particularly in answering difficult, cross-examination style questions. Similarly, while mostly hidden in a written transcript, jousting with opposing counsel and displays of anger or irritation will come across clearly on the video. Work with the witness to avoid being drawn into this type of conduct. In general, the deponent should exercise the same manners and restraint at a video deposition as you would want from her when in front of the jury and judge during direct and cross at trial. And don't forget that the witness's demeanor must remain consistent across direct and cross-examination so that it does not appear that the truth of her testimony depends on who is questioning her.

18.6.6 *Preparing the Operator*

Without close cooperation between you, as the questioning attorney, and the video operator, a video deposition can quickly turn into a disaster. Meet with the operator well before the time set for the deposition to make sure that he fully understands his role and what you particularly need from him to make the presentation as accurate and useful as possible.

---

10. Moiré is a cloth (sometimes pronounced "mwar") or a pattern of interference of light waves passing through grids or weaving (then sometimes pronounced "mwar-ay").

Check Equipment in Advance

Have the operator thoroughly check all of the equipment in advance to make sure it is in operating condition. Waiting until a few minutes before the deposition to discover that a key cord is missing is courting frustration.

Camera Set-Up and Lighting

Discuss the lighting in the room with the operator so that the camera shot does not include glaring windows or dark shadows on the deponent. Consider whether the light and shadows will change as the sun moves, necessitating a shift of camera location by mid-afternoon. As part of the review, test how well all of your exhibits, especially those like x-rays and photographs, show on video If some exhibits present problems, you may need to create enlargements, positive images of x-rays, or duplicate exhibits with a change of colors in diagrams and graphs so that these problematic exhibits come across clearly on the video.

Arrange Operator Cues

You can instruct the operator to zoom in on a particular exhibit at a specific point in the question—the jury obviously knows that the operator is present and controlling the camera, so you don't lose realism by such instructions; this is not a movie, trying to recreate reality—it is a recording of a legal proceeding that has certain necessary limitations. If your directions are few, no harm is done by allowing them to be heard on the tape—they are the same kind of things that occur in the courtroom: for instance, when the witness points to an exhibit, it will appear quite natural for you to say, "Why don't we get a close-up of where you are pointing on Johnson Deposition Exhibit 17?"

Arrange for a Deposition Officer

As a matter of economy, the camera operator should also be a notary public, able to serve as the deposition officer. If a stenographic transcript is being prepared simultaneously, the stenographer could instead be the notary. Even then, the videographer or other deposition officer must state, on the record, her name and address; the date, time, and place of the deposition; the deponent's name; the fact that the witness has been placed under oath or affirmation; and the identity of all persons present in the deposition room.[11]

---

11. Fed. R. Civ. P. 30(b)(5)(A).

18.6.7 *Working Out Stipulations and Agreements*

Resolving as many matters as possible with opposing counsel before the deposition will not only help you avoid unnecessary disruptions of the deposition—and the associated expense—but it also helps facilitate future use of the deposition at trial. Get agreement on such matters as the schedule for the day, the handling of exhibits, and the order in which counsel for multiple parties will question. Other topics to cover are:

- All the participants should avoid speaking while another participant is still speaking. The lawyers should avoid stepping on the witness's answers.

- Objections should be made only after the examining attorney has finished the question or the witness has finished the answer.

- Distracting noises should be avoided.

18.7   Conducting the Video Deposition

Most details of conducting the video deposition can be worked out during the preparation stage, but spending some time thinking through how the deposition will actually progress is important to its success. As noted earlier, many of these issues may be decided by local rule concerning the manner and mode which video depositions must take.

18.7.1 *Beginning the Deposition*

Instructions to the witness at a video deposition are no different from instructions given in a stenographically recorded deposition. Begin the video deposition by instructing the deponent, at the very least, on how to indicate that a question has not been understood, how to request a break, and the need to answer pending questions before breaks are taken. You can deal with other matters, such as the possibility that the deponent is under the influence of some substance that will impair her ability to answer truthfully and fully, at the beginning of the deposition or at such time as a related problem arises.

18.7.2 *Questioning*

Maintaining Interest

Remember that long questions are difficult for a jury to follow and understand. Therefore, keep questions short and simple as you would in a stenographic deposition. In a discovery deposition, long answers are encouraged, as long as the witness is being responsive. Remember that in a video deposition, your tone of voice is captured as well as that of the witness, so even when you get frustrated by a nonresponsive witness, you must remain polite, calm, and interested. Otherwise, questioning at the video deposition proceeds just as it does in a stenographic deposition, discussed in detail in earlier chapters. To recap briefly, with a video discovery deposition, first ask the information-gathering questions necessary to find out what the witness knows. Once you get familiar with the witness's story, focus on the helpful information that you would like to present at trial, and ask leading questions to draw party statements in a form that is easy for the judge and jury to understand at trial.

Counsel's Demeanor and Conduct

As noted just above, take care to present a pleasant and authoritative image, just as you would in the courtroom. Displays of irritation or anger are rarely appropriate. The jury will appreciate your courteous approach even more if the witness or her counsel is acting in an obnoxious manner. The jury will also be favorably impressed if you ask appropriate and logical questions and maintain a suitable pace. Long pauses and a disorganized approach may prevent the jury from following important testimony.

Going Off-the-Record

Whoever is paying for the reporter controls what is on and off the record by virtue of the contractual relationship with the videographer and stenographer. One way to control interruptions and delays on the video record is to go off-the-record when it appears the witness will need to look for an exhibit, read a long document, or otherwise slow down the questioning process. When coming back on-the-record, give a short explanation of what happened: "While we were off the record, Doctor Mathis, you reviewed the plaintiff's x-rays. Let me ask a couple questions about them." Counsel defending the witness may object to this procedure, because it leaves the deponent working (reviewing documents, evaluating x-rays, etc.) while everyone else takes a break, and the time the witness works would apparently not be part of the seven hours since everyone was "off-the-record." This point is fair. Whether in a stenographic or a video deposition, if the witness has been asked to spend time on certain tasks by questioning counsel, that time should count as part of the seven hours of deposition, regardless of the fact that it may be off the record.

18.7.3   *Concluding the Video Deposition*

Rule 30(b)(5)(C) requires that at the end of the deposition, video or stenographic, the officer must state on the record that the deposition is complete and set out any stipulations made by the parties.

18.7.4   *Post-Deposition Review*

Under Rule 30(e), if the witness or one of the parties makes a request before completion of the deposition, the witness will have thirty days after having been notified by the deposition officer that the deposition was available for review to note proposed changes or errata. As a general rule, counsel should have a transcript of the video deposition made simultaneously, and the witness should review that written transcript to create the errata sheet. If a stenographic record of the video deposition has been created, that transcript can be corrected using the standard rules and procedures for a written deposition transcript. This will save money in the long run, because it obviates the need for repeated real-time viewings of the video during the review process. There is no way to correct the video of the deposition without redoing the challenged portions, and that is not realistic. Nevertheless, with party statements and impeachments involving "corrected" testimony, deposing counsel has the advantage, because she can show the video as it was originally recorded, with gestures, pauses, and nervous coughs, while defending counsel has only the written errata to present to the jury. The visual testimony clearly has more impact.

18.8   Preparing to Use the Video Deposition at Trial

18.8.1   *Transcribing*

In those jurisdictions that require a stenographic transcription to be prepared, you will need to have the videos transcribed or arrange to have a court reporter attend the deposition (who can also serve as the deposition officer). It is usually cheaper to have the transcription made from the videos or from audio recordings made simultaneously with the videos. A stenographic transcription is useful even when not required. Taking a simultaneous audio recording of the proceedings will permit secretarial staff to prepare a transcription at a lower cost than having a court reporter prepare one.

18.8.2   *Editing*

While video depositions are more entertaining and will hold the jurors' interest better than stenographic depositions, even the best video deposition can be terribly tedious. Keep the jurors' exposure to all depositions, both video and stenographic, as short as possible, consistent with the jurors hearing the necessary testimony and being persuaded of its truthfulness. You can do this through prudent editing. As a practical matter, many more questions are asked at a deposition than are necessary for the effective presentation of that evidence at trial. In selecting the testimony to be presented at trial, whether from stenographic or video recording, critically examine each question and answer with an eye to deleting any that do not advance the theory of the case. Create a concordance between transcript pages and video counter numbers so that the court can easily go from one to the other when it is called on to rule on objections.

18.8.3   *Ruling on Objections*

The pretrial conference is the usual and best time for the court to rule on objections to documents and to deposition designations, but this is a matter of local practice and court rules. Whatever procedure is used, be sure to suggest that it be done sufficiently in advance of trial so that any portion of the video ruled inadmissible can be deleted or a new video can be created with only the unobjectionable designation portions. Of course, to preserve the matter for appeal, a complete original tape or disk of the testimony, without deletions, must be maintained.

Having the judge watch the tape to rule on objections is a time-consuming and wasteful procedure, and most judges will refuse to do so unless the objection is to the taping or the counsel's or the parties' conduct during the deposition. But if the objection is to a question or answer, the court can much more conveniently make these rulings by examining a stenographic transcription of the tape. Once the excluded portions have been edited, be sure to review the tape to ensure that the editing was done correctly.

18.9   Using the Video Deposition at Trial

The usual method of showing a video deposition to a jury is to position a monitor and playback unit (often a video camera itself) in front of the jury box for viewing. In very modern courtrooms (or retrofitted courtrooms), monitors may be built into the jury box, often between pairs of jurors, with video being fed into a master control unit, all under the ultimate control of the judge, who has a "kill" switch that permits her to instantly stop the playback and darken the monitor screens. Like all other aspects of the trial, showing the video should proceed as smoothly as possible. A few simple steps will make this possible. Perhaps a week or two before the trial, with the assistance of the court clerk's office:

- Check the equipment to make sure it is in proper working order and compatible with any equipment being brought in;

- Know how to operate the equipment or have a competent operator present;

- Unless multiple monitors are already installed in the jury box, check in advance to determine how far away from the jury box the monitor should be positioned, where the electrical outlets are located, whether you will need extension cords, and whether glare on the monitor screens or other problems might cause the jury difficulty in viewing the video;

- Determine whether the judge already has or will require a separate monitor.

Try to show the video following a regular break, like lunch or the mid-morning or mid-afternoon breaks, so you have an opportunity to set up the necessary equipment without disrupting the trial. Before the actual showing, ask the judge to explain to the jurors that they are about to see: either a piece of testimony from a video deposition that one side is offering as being inconsistent with testimony that the witness gave in court, or a substantial amount of testimony from a video deposition that is being offered as the testimony of a witness who cannot attend the trial because she is dead, ill, or unavailable for some other reason. If you are sponsoring the video deposition testimony, ask the court in its post-trial instructions to tell the jury that the video testimony may be considered in the same way that live testimony is considered and that the jury is to judge the weight of weight of all of the testimony, live, written, and video. Leave the courtroom lights on during showing unless darkness is necessary to prevent glare on the television screen. A dark room and the hypnotic effects of television are too much of a temptation to sleep.

18.10   Defending a Video Deposition

We have previously discussed some of the considerations concerning defending a video deposition. For instance, if the opponent schedules a video deposition of a witness before defending counsel has had an adequate opportunity to prepare the witness, defending counsel should consider asking for a continuance of the deposition. The major concern in defending a video deposition is to ensure the taping is fair and is not done in such a way that would make either the witness or counsel appear in an unfair, unflattering, or deceptive light. Be vigilant and correct distorting camera angles, close-ups of the witness that show the pores on their noses and every drop of perspiration, and other such tricks. Finally, while you should make appropriate objections, courts have been known to saddle the defending attorney with the cost of editing out an excessive number of objections. Somewhat draconian is the practice of some courts of not permitting the tape to be edited, but instead allowing the jury to see the behavior of the defending attorney. Therefore, be particularly aware of how objections may appear to the judge or jury.

CHAPTER NINETEEN

RULE 30(b)(6) DEPOSITIONS

*"He who would propagate an opinion must begin by making sure of his ground
and holding it firmly."*

—Samuel Butler (1835–1902)

Depositions taken under Federal Rule of Civil Procedure 30(b)(6) are the most powerful and efficient discovery tool available to the lawyer involved in complex litigation. Pursuant to a single notice naming an organization of virtually any sort and listing topics for the deposition, that organization must gather information from the organization's archives, data repositories, and retired employees; and must produce deponents, perhaps many of them, to provide that information in response to deposition questioning. The organization, if necessary, must conduct a reasonable search for responsive information and then educate the designees to answer on the topics identified in the notice; the designees are not required to have personal knowledge of any of the information they provide in their answers. Designees can be questioned on other topics as though they were named and noticed or subpoenaed for a normal deposition. Nonparty organizations can also be deposed under Rule 30(b)(6) by their designees.

Party designees create party statements when they answer questions that are within the noticed topics; nonparty designees, of course, do not create party statements. The organization's search for information must only be reasonable; micro-bits of information may remain hidden by the shrouds of time, because finding that information would require an unreasonable search. If a designee answers "I don't know" at the deposition to a question within the specified subjects, and a reasonable search would have disclosed the information if it existed, the organization is bound by the answer and cannot later claim, in any part of its case, that it does know and has additional evidence to present on the point.

Rule 30(b)(6) deposition questioning can therefore take the place of interrogatories, thus bypassing those nonresponsive, lawyer-written answers and their virtually unending time extensions; they can take the place of written requests for admissions, which do not allow easy follow-up to remove ambiguities; and they can take the place of normal, "named-deponent" depositions, a long string of which may be required to find an appropriate person who has personal knowledge of the topics. Indeed, there is nothing in Rule 30 that prevents a party from taking more than one 30(b)(6) deposition— one at the outset of deposition discovery to gain an understanding of policies, procedures, structure, and history of the organization, and one at the end to wrap up loose ends in certain fact strings and to try to obtain party statements that will eliminate issues and shorten the trial.

Pursuant to Rule 30(b)(6), the deposition of an association, a corporation, a partnership, or a governmental agency may be noticed.[1] The notice of deposition specifies the matters on which examination is requested, without naming a particular person to be deposed. The organization must then designate, prepare, and produce one or more witnesses who are knowledgeable about the matters specified in the notice of deposition, so that the witnesses can give complete, knowledgeable, and often binding answers. This duty to designate and produce such a knowledgeable witness exists, even if there is no one currently with or employed by the organization who has knowledge or memory about the particular matter. A witness still must be prepared to testify about the topic or topics based on a reasonable search (both of documents and the minds of available persons, including past employees or other sources. If the organization produces a witness as the designee on a topic and that witness is not knowledgeable about the designated matters, the organization may be required to prepare and produce another witness and may also be subject to Rule 37(d) sanctions. In other words, the organization must make reasonable efforts to find and present the requested information through the witness or witnesses of its choosing.

---

1. When government entities are the targeted organization, there are exceptions to discovery rules that must be considered. "Tuohy" regulations (32 C.F.R. 721–25), for example, require some different procedures to obtain materials that the military's litigation manuals consider attorney-work product but which are not within the classic work-product definition. In such situations, a subpoena may need to be sent to the appropriate office of the government agency to obtain the materials which that agency typically but erroneously considers part of attorney-work product, such as documents that the agency possesses that the attorneys have collected and read as part of their own investigation. These government approaches are probably as numerous as the agencies themselves; they may be found with the Freedom of Information Act ("FOIA") agency regulations, and the litigation "hold-outs" are often enforced or interpreted by the same personnel who enforce FOIA compliance.

19.1   Rule 30(b)(6)

The text of Rule 30(b) reads as follows:

> **(6)** *Notice or Subpoena Directed to an Organization.* In its notice or subpoena, a party may name as the deponent a public or private corporation, a partnership, an association, a governmental agency, or other entity and must describe with reasonable particularity the matters for examination. The named organization must then designate one or more officers, directors, or managing agents, or designate other persons who consent to testify on its behalf; and it may set out the matters on which each person designated will testify. A subpoena must advise a nonparty organization of its duty to make this designation. The persons designated must testify about information known or reasonably available to the organization. This paragraph (6) does not preclude a deposition by any other procedure allowed by these rules.

The rule has three main parts—one describing the obligations of the party seeking discovery, one describing the obligations of the party responding to the discovery notice, and one describing the obligations of the designated witness.

For the Party Seeking Discovery

> In its notice or subpoena [to a nonparty], a party may name as the deponent a public or private corporation, a partnership, an association, a governmental agency, or other entity and must describe with reasonable particularity the matters for examination . . . . A subpoena must advise a nonparty organization of its duty to make this designation.

For the Party Responding to the Notice

> The named organization must then designate one or more officers, directors, or managing agents, or designate other persons who consent to testify on its behalf; and it may set out the matters on which each person designated will testify.

For the Testifying Designee

> The persons designated must testify about information known or reasonably available to the organization."[2]

According to the Advisory Committee's Notes, the change in deposition practice authorized by Rule 30(b)(6) was intended to ease the noticing party's burden of finding information in a large organization and someone to explain it, and the organization's burden in providing personnel to respond:

> A new provision is added, whereby a party may name a corporation, partnership, association, or governmental agency as the deponent and designate the matters on which he requests examination, and the organization shall then name one or more of its officers, directors, or managing agents, or other persons consenting to appear and testify on its behalf with respect to matters known or reasonably available to the organization. [Citations omitted.] The organization may designate persons other than officers, directors, and managing agents, but only with their consent. Thus, an employee or agent who has an independent or conflicting interest in the litigation--for example, in a personal injury case—can refuse to testify on behalf of the organization.
>
> This procedure supplements the existing practice whereby the examining party designates the corporate official to be deposed. Thus, if the examining party believes that certain officials who have not testified pursuant to this subdivision have added information, he may depose them. On the other hand, a court's decision whether to issue a protective order may take account of the availability and use made of the procedures provided in this subdivision.
>
> The new procedure should be viewed as an added facility for discovery, one which may be advantageous to both sides as well as an improvement in the deposition process. It will reduce the difficulties now encountered in determining, prior to taking of a deposition, whether a particular employee or agent is a "managing agent." *See* Note, Discovery Against Corporations Under the Federal Rules, 47 Iowa L. Rev. 1006–16 (1962). It will curb the "bandying" by which officers or managing agents of a corporation are deposed in turn but each disclaims knowledge of facts that are clearly known to persons in the organization

---

2. Of course, this "burden on the designee" should actually be seen as a further burden on the organization, because it is the party that must conduct the "reasonable" search to find the information that will be presented through the designee.

and thereby to it. Cf. *Haney v Woodward & Lothrop, Inc.*, 330 F.2d 940, 944 (4th Cir. 1964). The provision should also assist organizations which find that an unnecessarily large number of their officers and agents are being deposed by a party uncertain of who in the organization has knowledge. Some courts have held that under the existing rules a corporation should not be burdened with choosing which person is to appear for it. *E.g., United States v Gahagan Dredging Corp.*, 24 F.R.D. 328 (S.D.N.Y. 1958). This burden is not essentially different from that of answering interrogatories under Rule 33, and is in any case lighter than that of an examining party ignorant of who in the corporation has knowledge.

19.2   Deciding to Take a Rule 30(b)(6) Deposition

19.2.1   When and Why

Taking a Rule 30(b)(6) deposition of an organization makes the most sense either at the beginning or near the end of discovery. You can use a 30(b)(6) deposition at the beginning of the discovery program to identify the important players; to gain an understanding of the organizational structure; to learn how documents are created, kept, and destroyed; and to learn how and why significant decisions were made. You can also use it even before document discovery to get a better understanding of the organization's structure, document retention and destruction policies, and lines of actual authority, as well as the identity of decision-makers. Because the organization must exert reasonable efforts to find the information and select a witness to communicate that information at the deposition, there is little risk of encountering frustrating "I don't know" answers, since that answer is a party statement that the organization does not know and cannot reasonably find the information. That party statement will normally be treated by the court as a reason to preclude the organization from offering related information itself. Therefore, it can be called a "binding" party statement that cannot be rebutted with any evidence, or at least with evidence that would have been responsive to the specifications in the notice.

You can use a Rule 30(b)(6) deposition to force the opponent to gather information that would be very difficult for you to find and collect. Suppose, for example, that you want relevant policies that were in effect twenty years earlier. Without the 30(b)(6) deposition, you would have a harder time finding that information than would the organization possessing it, even it is buried in the archives, because you might have to serially depose a number of past or present officers or agents or record keepers before you found someone who knows about the policies. Instead, the organization is responsible for making a reasonable effort to locate the information and then either educating a designee on the policies or choosing a designee who already knows about them.[3]

Such a 30(b)(6) deposition would take the place of interrogatories and named-witness depositions that are normally used to gain fundamental facts, locate documents and understand document procedures, and identify the people who actually participated in the event that gave rise to the lawsuit. An early 30(b)(6) deposition might provide information that will be a basis for moving to quash counts or eliminate issues. That would simplify all remaining discovery in a way that is not achieved by cumbersome and clever interrogatory responses, which are prepared in actuality by the opposing attorney.

Near the end of discovery, before the discovery cut-off and before the expert depositions, you could take another 30(b)(6) deposition of the opposing party organization instead of sending out a written request for admissions. The party statements you get from a 30(b)(6) deposition (through the agents of the party) have the same status as admissions obtained in the written admissions process, as long as the questions are within the topics of the specifications; however, you gain an advantage because you can ask immediate follow-up questions, and the responses do not get filtered through the lawyers before the questioner hears them.[4]

---

3. As the deposing party, you are not entitled to select the person to be produced as the organization's Rule 30(b)(6) designee—that is the prerogative of the organization. Therefore, a 30(b)(6) notice that includes language like "shall designate witnesses, including Robert W. Baldwin, Vice-President, to testify to the specified topics . . . ," has no effect on the selection or identity of the designee, and the organization can safely ignore the "Robert W. Baldwin" language.

4. There are a few significant differences between 30(b)(6) opposing party's statements and Rule 36 admissions: First, Rule 36 admissions are limited in their use to the proceeding in which they were obtained (Rule 36(a)(1) and Rule 36(b)). In fact, Rule 36 repeats the limitation to the instant proceeding twice. There is no such limitation on party statements obtained through a 30(b)(6) designee, so those party statements may be used in other proceedings (just like other statements made by a party). Rules of statutory construction dictate that where the legislature made a distinction in one instance, its failure to make a similar distinction in another instance is evidence that it had consciously rejected that distinction for the second instance. *See* "Congress Knows How to Say..." (Congressional Research Service, "Statutory Interpretation: General Principles and Recent Trends," http://www.fas.org/sgp/crs/misc/97-589.pdf). These Rule 30(b)(6) designee statements obtain their status as party statements from that fact that the designee is "a person whom the party to make a statement on the subject . . . ." (FED. R. CIV. P. 801(d)(2)(C).)

A similarity between the two "admissions" rules is that both require a reasonable search to be conducted: a denial under Rule 36(a)(4) must be preceded by a reasonable search, and an answer by a designee under Rule 30(b)(6) must be preceded by a reasonable search. Logic would indicate that an answer under 30(b)(6) that was clearly harmful to the organization should not require a search, just as an admission of harmful information under Rule 36(a)(4) does not require a search.

Further, Rule 36(b) states that an admission is conclusively binding unless the court permits it to be withdrawn or amended where there is no prejudice to the opposing party and

The organization receiving the notice under Rule 30(b)(6) is obligated to designate the persons who will convey the information requested in the specifications; therefore, when taking the Rule 30(b)(6) deposition, you *do not have to* send a notice to some specific corporate official and then put up with the frustration of having one official after the next say, "I don't know about that area; the vice-president for human resources probably knows." It was precisely to avoid that waste of time and resources through this sandbagging—a tactic that is called "bandying"—that 30(b)(6) was created in its present form in 1970. Rule 30(b)(6) also permits a large organization to avoid having dozens of its executives tied up in depositions when a single representative could have provided the information, but that is a relatively minor benefit compared to the advantages gained by the party taking the 30(b)(6) deposition.

19.2.2   How

To start the process, the party seeking to use 30(b)(6) sends a notice to opposing counsel that in form looks just like a notice for the deposition of a named officer or employee, except that the organization itself is named as the deponent and a list of specifications is attached. If only a portion of the organization is involved in the suit, like the sales division or the human resources division, the notice could be directed to that division. The object of the deposition need not be incorporated or a separate profit center, or have independent legal status.

19.3   The Specifications

As part of the notice for the 30(b)(6) deposition, you must include a list of specifications so that the opposing organization can designate its witnesses. The most common mistake made in drafting these specifications is to make them too broad—they may cover too much time or too many topics. A fifteen-year period may be too long if the central issue in the case is whether

---

where it will serve the presentation of the merits. There is no such provision in Rule 30(b)(6). The Advisory Committee's notes to Rule 36 indicate that a party statement under that rule is only as binding as a stipulation between counsel, as opposed to an evidentiary admission of a party. Thus, by the Advisory Committee's logic, while Rule 36 admissions are binding until withdrawn or amended with the court's approval, Rule 30(b)(6) opposing party's statements are binding without opportunity for withdrawal or amendment.

Except, logical or not, that does not seem to be the rule. All of these factors taken into consideration, the current majority rule appears to be that testimony by 30(b)(6) designees are indeed "admissions" by the party through its designees; but that binding nature simply makes it more difficult for the organization to contradict them at trial, by having to show some reason that it should be allowed to introduce opposing evidence on the point. State Farm Mut. Auto. Ins. Co. v. New Horizon, Inc. 250 F.R.D. 203 (E.D. Pa. 2008). However, as said elsewhere in this section, such a rule diminishes the value of the 30(b)(6) deposition, without any benefit other than allowing a recalcitrant organization to avoid making full discovery.

employment discrimination caused the firing of a particular worker. Similarly, specifications may be too broad where they involve all branches of a multinational company when the issue is whether a single branch defectively manufactured a product.

If the parties cannot agree on limitations of the specifications, the responding party may need to move for a protective order, asking the court to limit the time or scope covered. The showing required here is not that the information is completely unavailable, but rather that the burden in collecting and conveying the information is too great. That showing should be made in advance of the deposition, rather than presented as an objection at the deposition. If such an objection is left to the time of the deposition, the parties will have wasted time in travel and preparation that could have been avoided. Of course, the responding organization would have to conduct some investigation on how much effort would be expended in gathering and conveying the specified information, and it should be prepared to support that claim of burden with declarations or affidavits: an attorney's representation is not as persuasive as statements by records custodians or IT coordinators. If a test search has been conducted, for example, at one company division out of twelve, the attorney should be prepared, with a declaration from a party representative, to describe that search and to state what can be estimated about the resources required by a full search.

19.4   Finding, Preparing, and Defending the Rule 30(b)(6) Designee

In deciding whether she wants to designate one or seven people as the 30(b)(6) designees, defending counsel should look at the scope of the specifications and at the possibility that questioning counsel will go beyond those specification into other areas. The topics in a 30(b)(6) list of specifications depend almost entirely on the complexity of the case, and large financial, securities, antitrust, patent, and insurance coverage disputes could reasonably generate lists of specifications that have scores of topics. In such cases, multiple designees are, as a practical matter, the only way to respond, so the burden of designee preparation is commensurately greater. Defending counsel will have an easier job if she can combine topics and reduce the number of designees, but the individual designee's preparation may be harder, having to cover multiple topics. Defending counsel will have to find a way to strike a balance in each case.

If defending counsel does choose multiple designees, the time for the deposition may be expanded dramatically. As mentioned earlier, according to the Advisory Committee, each designee is treated as a separate witness; thus, the questioning attorney is entitled to a separate seven-hour questioning session for each of the designees. The routine 30(b)(6) deposition could then very easily become a thirty-five-hour deposition, as five designees are questioned about forty or fifty specifications.

Of course, the organization might seek a protective order, arguing that the specifications are too numerous and impose too great a burden in time and money on the organization and that the deposition(s) should be limited to seven or fourteen hours. The success of this argument will depend on 1) how well the party noticing the Rule 30(b)(6) deposition has drafted her specifications, and 2) whether the judge thinks that the organization has loaded up with designees to create an appearance of burden to hinder legitimate discovery under the rule. However, when naming a number of designees, perhaps to frighten opposing counsel, the organization must also keep in mind that each additional witness multiplies the possibility that the testimony of people who supposedly speak for the organization will contain inconsistencies; each witness requires time to review documents and prepare; and it may be hard to find designees who have no knowledge of other important areas, which leaves them open to being led into trouble by questioning that goes beyond the specifications, as discussed above.

Defending counsel should choose a designee who has the time and motivation to prepare. For each day of deposition testimony, preparation may require as many as three days. If the potential designee cannot spare that time, or is not interested in working with defending counsel for that long, she may not be the right designee at all. Of course, defending counsel may reduce the preparation time by finding a designee who already knows about the dispute—perhaps was a participant in it. That may ease preparation, but it may also introduce the designee's personal biases into the case, perhaps taking the deposition well beyond the "organizational knowledge" into the designee's personal opinions and speculation. Because the designee's testimony is a useable party statement, defending counsel must be aware of the possibility of this expansion.

In deciding who will serve as a designee, the organization's counsel is not limited to current employees.[5] Counsel can designate nonemployees or former employees, if they are willing to serve as designees; she can even designate outside advisors. It is not advisable, however, to use a lawyer as a designee. Doing so could result in waiver of attorney-client privilege on the specified topics. In *Motley v. Marathon Oil Co.*,[6] the court held that such

---

5. In fact, there is nothing in Rule 30(b)(6) or the other, related rules that requires designees to be or to have been employees of the organization; they could be past employees, consultants, experts, or even actors. 29 LITIGATION 20, 23–24 (ABA Winter 2003). *See* Ierardi v. Lorillard, Inc., 777 F. Supp. 420 (E.D. Pa. 1991).

6. 71 F.3d 1547 (10th Cir. 1995).

waiver had not occurred, but noted that if the lawyer had claimed privilege for communications to and from the witness, waiver was a possibility:

> Further, the mere fact that it designated a lawyer, pursuant to FED. R. CIV. P. 30(b)(6), as its corporate representative at one deposition, is a wholly insufficient ground to hold that Marathon waived its attorney-client privilege. Although Miller's counsel did state at the deposition that he would not allow questions regarding the two privileged documents, Miller did not otherwise assert the privilege a single time at his deposition.[7]

In *Adler v. Wallace Computer Services, Inc.*,[8] where the lawyer-designee was not so careful and answered some questions, but then claimed privilege to refuse to answer other questions on the same topic, the court found that privilege was waived. That case also shows how an organizational designee is more than just a witness for the organizational client: the designee *is* the client, and as such, she can even waive privilege.[9]

A recently retired senior executive who was not involved in the dispute leading to the lawsuit may make the best designee. She would have knowledge of the corporate structure and the lines of authority, so her preparation would be more efficient, and she would have an interest in doing a good job for her old company. Defending counsel would have to be confident that she was happy while she still worked with the company and that there are no outstanding issues between her and the human resources people, like some argument over the amount of retirement pay. Obviously this has to be decided on a case-by-case basis.

Counsel preparing to defend a Rule 30(b)(6) deposition can be confident that questioning counsel will ask the witness about preparation. The rules on witness preparation for a Rule 30(b)(6) witness are fundamentally the same as the rules on preparation of any deponent, and those are fully covered in chapter thirteen. With a Rule 30(b)(6) witness, however, the preparation sessions may well be when the designee obtains most of her substantive infor-

---

7. *Id.* at 1553.

8. 202 F.R.D. 666 (N.D. Ga. 2001). In *Adler*, the vice-president and general counsel of the defendant, as a 30(b)(6) designee, discussed some information within the attorney-client privilege, but refused to answer all questions on those topics fully. The court held that the privilege is waived (1) when a client testifies concerning portions of the attorney-client communications; (2) when a client places the attorney-client relationship directly in issue; and (3) when a client asserts reliance on attorney advice as an element of the defense. [Footnote omitted.]

The court also said that the designee was speaking for the corporation under the rule, and therefore had authority to waive the privilege. *Id.* at 674–75.

9. The *Adler* court also said that the designee was speaking for the corporation under the rule and therefore had authority to waive the privilege. *Id.* at 675.

mation about the topics—from interviewing or being present for interviews of knowledgeable people with (or formerly with) the organization or from reviewing relevant documents.

The designee's interviews of knowledgeable people are not protected by any confidential status or privileges, except to the extent that the deposition questioner asks: "Who did counsel interview or suggest that you interview during your preparation?" Although sometimes it seems to be a distinction without a difference, the designee can be directed not to answer that question on the grounds of the attorney-client privilege or the attorney work-product doctrine; however, the designee must answer the question: "To whom did you speak, other than counsel, in preparation for your role as designee?" There is a slight, but important difference between the two questions: The first question—who did counsel interview or suggest that you interview?—would reveal counsel's thoughts and plans, which are classic work-product that have long been protected. The second question—who did you talk to?—does not reveal the attorney's thoughts, at least not directly. It seeks only the sources that have been used by the witness to obtain the information the designee is going to convey.[10]

With respect to questions about what documents were reviewed by the witness, the analysis is the same: questioning about what the attorney said or what documents she chose is not allowed; questioning about what documents the witness reviewed to refresh recollection or to gain information is allowed, even if those documents happened to be provided or selected by counsel. Again, the only reason to review these areas specially during the preparation of the Rule 30(b)(6) designee is that these people and documents are presumably the source of most of her information, and they are therefore

---

10. A district court in New Jersey recently held that a defendant drug company had failed to provide a proper 30(b)(6) designee when it produced a witness whose only access to (supposedly) corporate knowledge came from a notebook of information written by the outside counsel to the company. At the deposition, the designee was limited by company counsel to reading from the notebook; he was directed not to answer questions without reading from the book; and he was further directed not to answer any questions about his preparation for serving as a designee, outside of reading the notebook, on work-product grounds. In re Neurontin Antitrust Litig., 2011 U.S. Dist. LEXIS 62032 (D.N.J. June 9, 2011). The district court affirmed the magistrate's orders on both the inadequacy of the 30(b)(6) witness and work-product. The district court quoted the magistrate with approval:

> Magistrate Judge Schwartz also concluded that "the use of an outline created entirely by litigation counsel contradicts the purpose of Rule 30(b)(6) and turned the witness here into something even less than a "mere document gatherer . . . ." Further, "the outline and conduct of [outside litigation] counsel during the deposition reflect that the corporation and its counsel have inverted their respective roles and duties . . . . [I]t appears that [outside litigation] counsel have 'manufacture[d] the corporation's contentions' rather than having the antitrust defendants designate a person to speak about the facts and their contentions."

Neurontin, at 12 [citations omitted; ellipses in the original.]

more important than in the normal deposition taken under Rule 30(a). If the witness reviewed documents that did not refresh recollection or provide new information, then there is no basis in the evidentiary rules for identifying them to opposing counsel.[11]

If the designee is shown privileged material to prepare her for a 30(b)(6) deposition, it is very likely that the privilege is waived. The analysis here follows the familiar "sword and shield" form—the preparing party cannot gain the advantage of preparing the designee with the information while simultaneously shielding it from the other party. [12]

There are times in litigation when an organization must prepare a designee to testify about activities, policies, and decisions that occurred so long ago that no one can be found who has personal knowledge of them. Nevertheless, the designees may not claim lack of their own personal knowledge in refusing to answer or in answering, "I don't know."[13] Logically, because hearsay is discoverable, the reasonable search for information required by Rule 30(b)(6) would extend beyond personal knowledge of the designees or the organization. When the information is not directly available, the organization has to undertake the task of recreating it, using reasonable resources, from archived material, whether stored in the basement or in off-site storage facilities. Both the designee and the attorney should take notes of all of these efforts to find information, which will make for better and more accurate presentations when requesting the court to grant relief from at least part of the burden. The expense and scope of the search shows not only that the organization has been reasonable, but also that so many resources would be required to complete the search that the 30(b)(6) specifications should be severely limited.

As a final item in preparation, counsel should remind the designee once again that she will be speaking for the organization, not for herself. When she is asked, "What did you think of this person's work?" she must answer with the understanding that "you" in the question means, "the organization." Most of the time, it is unclear whether an ambiguity on this point creates

---

11. Fed. R. Evid. 612.

12. There has in the past been debate on this point, but it has been largely resolved. For example, in *Audiotext Communications Network, Inc. v. U.S. Telecom, Inc.*, 164 F.R.D. 250, 252 (D. Kan. 1966), the court stated, "The selecting and grouping of information does not transform discoverable documents into work product." This minority opinion is perhaps explained by the court's failure to distinguish between the information in the documents, which is not and does not become work product, and the attorney's activities in selecting the data, which may well reveal that attorney's approach to the case, which is indeed classic work product. This distinction explains why the question, "What documents did you look at that refreshed your recollection?" is allowed, while the question, "What documents did the attorney show you?" is not allowed. The *Audiotext* decision has been both criticized and ignored.

13. Banco Del Atlantico, S.A. v. Woods Industries Inc., 519 F.3d 350 (7th Cir. 2008).

a transcript that is more favorable or less favorable to the organization, but counsel for the designee and the organization cannot take a chance. If such ambiguities do crop up during the deposition, an objection should be made; or a follow-up question should be asked to remove the ambiguity ("When you answered the question about "how you liked Jackson's work," did you understand that the "you" meant 'the ABC Company,' your employer?"); or the transcript should be corrected when it is reviewed after the deposition is over.

19.5   How to Ask Questions

Questioning at a 30(b)(6) deposition is a little bit different. At a 30(b)(6) deposition, you do not have to worry much about foundation for the answers—the organization has supplied that foundation by designating the witness as a company spokesperson, which turns all of the relevant answers into party statements, as long as the organization is a party opponent. (When the organization is *not* a party opponent, the designee's answers have the same evidentiary status as answers given by a nonparty deponent in a normal deposition—they can be used to impeach or refresh, they can replace live testimony from an absent witness, they can form the basis for a proffer—but they don't come into evidence at trial without some additional foundation, especially including a demonstration that they are within an exception to the rule excluding hearsay (usually, "witness unavailability," under Federal Rule of Evidence 804). In comparison, Rule 30(b)(6) deposition answers, when within the specifications, are party statements under Rule 801, and face no hearsay problems.[14]

At the deposition, remember not to ask questions that leave the source of the information requested ambiguous. Do not ask: "What were you trying to achieve by changing the blueprints for the brake pedal attachment." Instead ask: "What was Aston-Martin trying to achieve . . . ." Such ambiguities may lead a judge to think that the answer might have been an expression of the designee's own opinions rather than a statement of the corporation's agent. By avoiding this kind of ambiguity, you can get the full benefit of the 30(b)(6) process—party statements. Similarly, watch for answers like "My personal feeling is . . . ," or "Well, in my opinion . . . ," or "I think . . . ," so the court does not interpret those answers as expressing something other than what is within the organization's knowledge. Therefore, if you like the information or opinion that the witness gave, and you want it attributed to the organization, but its source is somewhat ambiguous, follow up with questions that establish that the opinion or feeling is based on the designee's

---

14. In the federal system, under FED. R. EVID. 801(d)(2), and in many states, party statements are defined as "nonhearsay." In the remaining states, party statements are considered hearsay, but are within a "party statement" exception. In either case, the result is the same.

review of organizational information or was developed during her work with the organization and is being provided as information from the organization's designee. That "work information" would then be seen as part of the organization's information and the answer may be a favorable party statement.

19.6   Questioning on Topics within the Specifications

In a 30(b)(6) deposition of an organization that is a party opponent, the answers to questions that fall fairly within the specifications will usually be treated as binding statements by the party. A binding party statement is one that the opposing party will not be allowed to challenge. If it is relevant, it will come into evidence without further foundation, and the party that made the statement will not be allowed to introduce evidence to oppose it. In fact, if the designated witness says "I don't know" in response to a question within the specifications, the organization may well be precluded from introducing any evidence on that topic at the trial, because the designee was supposed to be prepared with *all* of the information possessed by the organization.

If 30(b)(6) answers are used in motions practice to eliminate issues, to argue for summary judgment, or to preclude or limit expert testimony, then the responding party that produced the designee should not even be allowed use contradictory declarations from the deponents or any other people and should not logically be allowed to argue from documents to counter the 30(b)(6) answers. The organization's knowledge, as evidenced by the designee's sworn answers, should supersede these other sources of evidence. If the binding nature of 30(b)(6) testimony is to have any meaning, then the statements on matters within the specifications should end any dispute on that topic. Otherwise, crafty lawyers will render the 30(b)(6) procedure a sham by producing designees who have shirked their duties and are prepared to answer "I don't know" to all of the questions.

When deposing occurrence or "eye" witnesses, it is relatively easy to get information on what they believe occurred—how the concrete forms were poured, how the records of the promotion panels were kept, how the inspection criteria for the building were established. It is much more difficult to find people—especially when selecting from a roster of clever executives—who will say that they can answer the "why" questions: Why did the organization adopt this policy? Why was an employee fired? Why were prices raised in the fall? The 30(b)(6) deposition was intended to remove a lot of that difficulty, but the specifications must call for information about the reasons that certain steps were taken, or that certain procedures were established, or that certain decisions were made. So in a 30(b)(6) deposition, with proper specifications, the deposing attorney can ask questions like:

- Why did General Propeller change the aircraft engine design?

- What was the company's goal in acquiring the competing plastics extrusion company?

- How did the company hope to meet its supply obligations under the oil contract?

- Could the company have run three shifts? Why didn't it?

- Give us the reasons that the archived documents for the division were purged every three years.

- What was the purpose in giving European office directors information about U.S. competitors' prices?

In providing the attorney the ability to put these "why" questions to a designee, without "bandying," the 30(b)(6) deposition is exactly like deposing the full board of directors (and a very well-informed chief executive officer and all the other high executives) when they cannot easily claim lack of knowledge or forgetfulness. The decision makers' reasons are within the organization's reasonably available knowledge, and that is all that matters.

19.7   Questioning on Topics beyond the Specifications

Cases within the last ten years or so have established a majority rule that a 30(b)(6) designee may be asked questions beyond the areas covered by the specifications.[15] The rationale is that the specifications impose an obligation on the organization—to provide appropriately knowledgeable designees—but not a limitation on the questioner. (Therefore, such an argument would go, simply because the noticing party made it *easier* for the organization to respond, the noticing party should not be penalized by a limitation to the specifications. This somewhat circular reasoning is partially resolved when courts rule that answers to questions beyond the specifications do not constitute party statements, as is discussed in a later section of this chapter. However, the "easier" part of this argument only makes sense if the responding party does not have to worry about preparing for questions beyond the specifications.) Additionally, courts are apparently hopeful that allowing questioning broader than the specifications will avoid the need to bring the designee back to give additional testimony as a regular deponent.

A better rule would be that because the questioner is the one who drafted the specifications, she should be limited by their scope. This approach would

---

15. *See, e.g.*, Am. Gen. Life Ins. Co. v. Billard, 2010 WL 4367052, 2010 Dist. LEXIS 137804 (N.D. Iowa Oct. 28, 2010). In *Billard*, the court held that deposing counsel would be allowed to question beyond the specified topics; King v. Pratt & Whitney, 161 F.R.D. 475, 476 (S.D. Fla. 1995).

be consistent with the discussion in the Advisory Committee Notes in 1970 that state that the requirement of specifications in 30(b)(6) is intended to make it easier for the organization to select a designee on appropriate topics. Nevertheless, the majority rule today is that questioning beyond the specifications is fair, but answers to those questions may not constitute binding opposing party's statements by operation of 30(b)(6) and 801(d)(2). If there is some other basis for claiming that those answers are party statements—for example, if the party has chosen a managing agent as the designee or has chosen an employee who is authorized to speak within the scope of her employment and is therefore an agent under the federal rules—then the answers to questions beyond the specifications may become binding party statements.

As a matter of tactics, it may make sense for the designating party to avoid the possibility that the court may consider "beyond the specifications" answers as party statements by using a designee who has no attachment to the organization and no involvement in the controversy. Thus, if the witness is prepared only for the specifications, she will only be able to answer questions about those specifications—she will not be able to answer questions beyond the specifications (at least not beyond the extent of her personal knowledge) because she has not been prepared for them. Again, the taker may try to turn the answer into a party statement by asking follow-up questions to establish a connection to some specification or by asking questions intended to establish that the witness is speaking as an agent or authorized speaker on that topic. There are some cases out there suggesting that counsel defending the deponent could state on the deposition record that answers to "beyond the specification" questions are not intended as statements by the organization. Of course, this is a matter of law on which the courts or the Rules Advisory Committee should try to agree.

As a collateral matter, in many of these cases courts have considered the question of whether it is ever permissible to direct the witness not to answer on the ground that the question is outside the specifications. As might be expected, since such questioning is allowed, the direction not to answer is logically not allowed.[16] Even if there were some question about the propriety of such questions, the courts say that the better approach is to suspend the deposition to seek an in limine ruling on a request for a protective order or for the parties to stipulate that the objection to the question is not waived while the parties continue the deposition on other topics. This latter approach is preferable, so the witness can be used efficiently while she is available and additional objections that arise later can be resolved by the court at the same time.

---

16. *Billard, supra* note 15, contains a clear and recent holding that directions not to answer—on the grounds that the question goes beyond the Rule 30(b)(6) specifications— are improper primarily because the rules only authorize such directions when the questions involve privilege, a court order, or suspension to file a motion for a protective order to limit or approve questioning. *See also* FED. R. CIV. P. 30(d)(3).

19.8   The Number and Identity of Designees

When you notice a 30(b)(6) deposition, you should informally request that the organization indicate whether they will produce more than one designee and, if there is more than one, to identify the specifications to which each designee is intended to provide responsive answers. This is not required under the rule, but it is reasonable and courteous to exchange that information. If the opponent refuses to identify the designees, by name or number, and which designee will speak to which topics, ask the first designee, on the record, to correlate designees with topics. (Of course, to avoid any "beyond the specifications" delays, put that topic in the original list as the last specification.) At the beginning of the deposition make certain that when all the designees are identified, at least one is assigned to each of the specified areas. It has happened that when the opponent has not been called on to make such an identification, the last designee is asked about the remaining three specifications, only to have the opposing lawyer say, "Oh, that's a question you should have asked designee number one; he's the one who was prepared to speak to that." This problem is easily enough avoided—just start each designee's deposition by asking what specifications they are prepared to respond to and make sure that the landscape is covered. It is terrifically embarrassing and inconvenient when you forget to have the designees identified and allocated to the specifications.

In the typical case, if the organization chooses to use multiple designees, you will be entitled to multiple days of seven-hour deposition questioning. According to the Advisory Committee, each designee is considered a separate witness. However, if your specifications are very broad, the opponent may be able to persuade the court to cut the specifications down and also to limit your deposition time to less than a day per designee.

Another tactic occasionally seen from opposing counsel in response to a 30(b)(6) notice is informing deposing counsel that she, deposing counsel, has already deposed, as named deponents, the people the organization considers the most knowledgeable on the specified areas—thus the 30(b)(6) deposition of those same people as designees would just be duplication. "Perhaps," she suggests, "you would just like to stipulate that their depositions will be treated as 30(b)(6) depositions." Clever, but a very bad idea for deposing counsel.

First, deposing counsel does not have to settle for individuals who personally are the *most* knowledgeable; counsel is entitled to *all* of the reasonably available knowledge of the organization, regardless of whether there is even a single person remaining at the organization who personally possesses that information (before preparation as a designee).[17]

Second, when those individuals were deposed previously, they had no obligation to search for the knowledge available to the organization; they were answering from personal knowledge, supplemented by whatever documents they were given or people to whom their attorney had them speak. As a result, those deponents could answer, "I don't know," and there would be no binding party statements created from such personal statements of lack of knowledge. Since Rule 30(b)(6) procedures are available, deposing counsel should send a 30(b)(6) notice, so she can obtain the party statements she is entitled to from designees selected and produced by the opposing party. Deposing counsel should also remember that she has the option to conduct "regular" depositions of managing agents or authorized speakers of the organization under normal deposition procedures, thereby creating party statements from the answers given by those deponents, and then to notice a 30(b)(6) deposition to compel the organization to produce designees for all the topics in which lack of knowledge was claimed by those individuals.

The discovering party's only option in the 30(b)(6) notice process is to state the specifications. The choice of persons to designate belongs to the organization. Some counsel in their 30(b)(6) notice call for the organization to designate a specific person, either by name or by title: "Notice that we intend, under FED. R. CIV. P. 30(b)(6), to depose IBM Corporation by its designee, Walter Von Trapp, Vice President for Alpine Computer Sales." Despite such language, IBM remains free to designate and prepare whomever it chooses.

19.9   How Do Nonparties Respond?

The Rule 30(b)(6) deposition process creates three differences between parties and nonparties. First, the nonparty is entitled to a subpoena compelling the appearance of designees at the deposition; second, the answers of the designees presented by the nonparty obviously do not create party statements; and, third, the party sending the subpoena must explain the Rule 30(b)(6) obligation to select, educate, and provide witnesses, which includes explaining the duty to take reasonable steps to search for information to use

---

17. In some jurisdictions (*see* CAL. CODE CIV. P. § 2025.230), state rules of procedure permit "Person Most Knowledgeable" or "Person Most Qualified" depositions, which are essentially more limited Rule 30(b)(6) depositions. Under these rules, the organization is compelled to provide designees (more than one, if necessary, despite the adjective "most") who can provide the specified information to the extent it can reasonably be found by the organization. In general, it seems that the designees are intended to be employees or agents (like the accountants), and not outsiders. In other respects, these rules seem to function exactly as FED. R. CIV. P. 30(b)(6) depositions do in the federal system.

to prepare the designee. Of course, the nonparty's designees are entitled to have counsel present at the deposition, and the opposing party in the lawsuit is entitled to notice of the deposition and to participate through objections and questioning.

CHAPTER TWENTY

EXPERT DEPOSITIONS[1]

An expert is someone from out of town who carries a briefcase.

—Anonymous

20.1   Preparing to Depose the Expert

Begin your preparation for the deposition of the opponent's expert with a review of the expert report and the "voluntary disclosures" required under Rule 26(a)(1)–(2). Much of the information underlying an expert's report and testimony may be beyond your understanding or that of your team of paralegals and assistants; if so, look to graduate students at local colleges who can provide inexpensive and talented sources of support for the preparation. Despite tantalizing anecdotal evidence,[2] the expert's curriculum vita is least likely to provide effective cross-examination material, and the information in the "CV" can be easily checked outside the deposition. Indeed, this kind of an assignment is perfect for graduate students in the appropriate discipline. Therefore, it should probably be left until late in the deposition plan or outside formal discovery entirely.

Conferences with your own consulting and testifying experts, on the other hand, provide rich sources of questions for the deposing expert at the deposition. Two timelines—one that shows the historical events giving rise to the lawsuit and the other that shows the history of the opposing expert's involvement from first contact through the completion of the work and the submission of the expert report—are important tools during preparation and

---

1. Portions of this chapter have been adapted from DAVID M. MALONE AND PAUL ZWIER, EFFECTIVE EXPERT TESTIMONY, 2nd ed. (NITA 2006).

2. Stories of attorneys forcing the expert witness to admit, during cross-examination that her c.v. is wrong because she never attended Harvard or did not author articles attributed to him are probably exaggerations or, at the most, iterations of a single episode that have been passed along from lawyer to lawyer and generation to generation. We can all dream that someday we will enjoy such an unearned victory; in the meantime, however, we will have to continue to earn our victories over experts by studying their works and methodologies and by using depositions to force them to reveal their weaknesses and flaws.

at the deposition itself. Consider less traditional sources of information as well, such as lunch with attorneys who have opposed the expert in different litigation or telephone calls to other experts who have debated the opposing expert or written articles critiquing her work. As mentioned above, an important use of consulting experts is to provide advice to the attorney (not to counsel's testifying expert) on what approaches can be taken toward the opposing expert.

20.1.1   Expert Discovery

Depositions are clearly the most useful tool available to discover an opposing expert's opinions, bases, and methodologies. As you begin to plan discovery of the facts in the case and the opinions held and bases relied on by the opponent's experts, do not overlook the other discovery devices that are available in addition to depositions. The Rule 26(a) voluntary disclosures provide some information about the expert, and expert reports provide much more information about the expert's opinions and bases (if they have been done properly). Of course, you will not receive those expert reports until perhaps ninety days before trial, and therefore you cannot rely on them to guide other discovery efforts or trial preparation. Interrogatories are a poorly conceived device for obtaining useful information, from both lay witnesses and experts, for two simple reasons: 1) there is no practical opportunity for follow-up questioning, where incomplete or less useful answers could be clarified; and 2) the responses, while signed by a party, are prepared by attorneys. Recognize that just as one party's word processor creates the interrogatory set, the other party's word processor creates the response to that interrogatory set. This litigious society is rapidly reaching the time when lawyers' word processors will merely shout electrons at one another and accomplish useless interrogatory discovery without the cumbersome intervention of attorneys. Requests for admissions are minimally useful before the expert deposition ("minimally" because "yes" and "no" answers are such an awkward way to learn new information), but they can be somewhat useful in pinning down specific opinions, assumptions, and bases if more specificity is needed for trial.

Again considering the use of graduate students and their role as low-level consulting experts, one technique you can use early in the case is to assign some of the students the role of preparing a "mock-up" of the opponent's expert report. With the help of the consulting expert, if there is one, the student would research the facts and the issues from the perspective of the opposing party and then provide you with questions, learned texts, and treatises the opposing expert may use in preparing her report. Read summaries or abstracts of these texts and treatises so you can gain the expertise to effectively question the opposing expert in the deposition—thus all of the preparation does not have to be crammed in between the receipt of the report and the first day of trial. The mock expert report can also help you fully complete the depositions of fact witnesses, because the opposing expert's opinions will have to be consistent with those facts. If you can develop facts that do not comport with the opposing expert's underlying bases or assumptions, those inconsistencies can undermine the opposing expert in front of the trier-of-fact. Graduate students are also useful because they provide an inexpensive source of sophisticated labor to review the transcripts of prior testimony, which have been identified through the Rule 26(a) disclosures.

Especially with the availability of computerized legal research, do not feel limited by the four-year period for which Rule 26 mandates that the opposing party must disclose expert trial or deposition testimony in other cases. The mandated contents of the report are a "floor," not a "ceiling," for disclosures. Four years' worth of such testimony must be voluntarily disclosed, but there is no limit (other than burden or beyond the limits of appropriate discovery under Rule 26's "reasonably calculated") on the number of years of testimony that may be discovered through deposition or otherwise. Later, at deposition, feel free to ask the expert about testimony given beyond those four years, just as you may ask about publications authored beyond the ten-year period stated in Rule 26.

Before the deposition—if the budget permits—direct the graduate students or other assistants to investigate earlier testimony and earlier publications and then read them all with the issues of the present case in mind. If you have been so fortunate as to make contact with other counsel who have opposed the expert in their cases, they may be able to provide not only transcripts, but also copies of exhibits prepared by that expert, or at least used by the expert, which may mirror the expert presentation that you will likely face at deposition and trial. This informal discovery is conducted "outside the rules," to the extent that it is not governed by rule-imposed deadlines or limitations, and it does not require notice or legal process.

Graduate students or other assistants can also create a complete curriculum vitae for the opposing expert even before one is received through the discovery process. Publications by the expert, available in specialized libraries, normally provide substantial biographical detail; Web sites maintained by educational institutions often proudly boast of the credentials of their faculty; and prior testimony is likely to contain sworn statements or adopted exhibits detailing the expert's credentials. Thus, before you receive a formal curriculum vita from the expert, your informal discovery may have provided you with even more complete information. All of that information can then be run down by graduate students to determine its truthfulness and accuracy. As a result, the trial lawyer's dream of unmasking the expert as never having graduated from Hometown U as claimed has perhaps a slightly increased chance of becoming reality than it did twenty or thirty years ago, but the foundation for such deadly cross-examination will have been laid months before formal discovery even began. (To avoid the nightmare of having the same cross-examination happen to *your* expert witness, consider having your graduate students conduct the same kind of search on the credentials of experts you are considering or perhaps have already hired.)

Use online research to find additional instances in which the opposing expert has testified as well as find additional cases where the same expert issues have arisen. For example, using Google and LexisNexis, there are a number of ways to search cases to get information dealing with:

- the opposing expert's actual testimony;

- for whom she usually testifies;

- whether her testimony has ever been refused;

- other experts who may have given opinions on the same subject;

- copies of various (and varying) resumes that may have been sub-mitted electronically as exhibits to dispositive motions.

A thorough Internet search (including news and public record sources) may also turn up additional information, including where the expert works or teaches; lectures she has given and books she has edited; and professional licensing information, both past and present, current and suspended. Lex-isNexis also has a verdict and settlement reporting feature that may con-tain information on a given expert or area of expertise. In addition, Google searches may reveal Web pages that contain resumes or other publication information not provided in discovery.

From such information, you can often identify material you can use on deposition and cross-examination—changes on a resume or exaggeration of credentials, the identity of other experts who disagree with the approach being taken, the existence of literature from reliable authorities that contra-dicts assumptions or approaches being used, and even data problems that challenge the opposing expert's basis for drawing the conclusions she is pre-senting. As an example, in the renowned *Daubert* case, the expert for the unsuccessful plaintiffs, Dr. Done, had amalgamated data from several studies that had been found by experts in other cases to be insufficient as a basis for epidemiological analysis. Done's ability to reach valid conclusions based on the agglomeration of otherwise inadequate data became the central issue in the appeal. These individual prior cases might have been discovered by com-puter searches directed at the issues rather than at Dr. Done. LexisNexis has a "*Daubert* tracker" feature that can greatly help you find updated informa-tion relating to *Daubert* issues that have been raised in the subject area of the expert's field of specialization. For instance, you can find cases that will not only help you prepare a *Daubert* motion, but also prepare for a deposition of your opposing expert that will help you gain party statements that may keep the expert from testifying.

Clearly, if you are already committed to having a testifying expert of your own, then you will spend substantial time with the expert before expert deposition are taken, learning the areas of the field that are relevant to the case and understanding the adversary's position. Your own expert is of invaluable assistance in helping you understand the opposing expert's position, relating bases to methodology and opinion, reducing the opposing expert's advantages, shaping the case, and preparing for all phases of discovery.

Federal Rule of Evidence 703

An expert may base an opinion on facts or data in the case that the expert has been made aware of or personally observed. If experts in the particular field would reasonably rely on those kinds of facts or data in forming on opinion on the subject, they need not be admissible for the opinion to be admitted. But if the facts of data would otherwise be inadmissible, the proponent of the opinion may disclose them to the jury only if their probative value in helping the jury evaluate the opinion substantially outweighs their prejudicial effect.

20.1.2   Location of the Deposition

Normally, the expert deposition is held in the office of the questioning attorney, just as lay depositions are. If possible, however, as taking attorney, you should consider holding the deposition in the expert's own office or building. The deposition may be interrupted from time to time as the expert's regular work intrudes, but you will have the opportunity to learn more about the expert, her approach to matters, and her other interests. The titles of books on the expert's shelves, the identity of her colleagues down the hall, the photographs of handshaking politicians on the wall—all of these give some additional clues to the personality and allegiances of the witness. They may not amount to much—if anything at all—but once again, why give up a possible advantage, no matter how small?

An additional reason to hold the deposition at or near the expert's office is that her files will likely be more accessible, and you may have the opportunity to see and ask about underlying materials at the deposition for which you would otherwise have to wait. Certainly, the normal exchange of expert interrogatory responses and Rule 26(a) and (b) data may provide a good deal of material before the deposition, but you should not be interested only in what the expert and the opposing counsel have concluded are the underlying data—it is also quite enjoyable and profitable to review the material that the expert considered, but rejected because it did not provide support to the expert's opinion. If you are in the expert's office, you are more likely to obtain such materials.

On the other hand, if you are insecure about your own level of knowledge, there are advantages to bringing the expert to you. Protecting the session from interruption and having your own support people available can lead to a more in-depth examination of what the expert has to say. You may not want your consulting expert in the deposition room (because there is no reason to reveal even her existence to the opponent), but you may appreciate having her upstairs for advice at breaks and lunchtime.

A party who identifies an expert as a likely witness at trial will normally be obligated to present that expert for deposition within the jurisdiction of the forum court or at the expert's normal place of business. By agreement (including the expert's agreement), the expert deposition may be held almost anywhere. If faced with a dispute, the forum court is likely to defer to the expert's convenience, especially if the expert is only occasionally a witness and is normally engaged in the practice of her profession. In other words, it is appropriate for the deposing attorney to choose her preferred location for the expert's deposition and to negotiate to gain that location, but she is limited in her ability to insist on it.

20.1.3   Preparing to Take the Deposition

There is a lot you can do to prepare yourself to take an opposing expert's deposition. Not later than two or three weeks before the opposing expert's deposition, you should begin your preparation by immersing yourself in the relevant information—the data, the reports, the statistics, the conflicting data, the depositions of the fact witnesses, the expert's writings, the expert's teachings, the materials from her own experts, the findings of the graduate students—all the information that may provide grist for the deposition mill. You should participate in discussions with the consulting expert and assistants, graduate students or others, in which they raise possible lines of deposition inquiry and expert response, so you not only practice following up, but also becomes familiar with the "scientific, technical, or other specialized knowledge" that is the subject of the expert's opinion. In further preparation, review the potential legal theories, which have probably by this point been sharpened by motions to dismiss and motions for summary judgment. On the defense side, the elements of the affirmative defenses should be analyzed.

In addition, research the law of evidence to determine whether there are any particular standards of admissibility that must be met by the opinion of the opposing expert. For example, in a medical malpractice case, must the opinion include knowledge of the local standard of care, or, in a legal malpractice case, must the opinion display knowledge of the level of practice within a particular legal specialty like antitrust or products liability prosecutions? There may be cases where the methodology to be employed by the expert is dictated by statute or prior cases. In a patent case where she is calculating damages due to infringement, the expert may be required to state the damages in terms of reasonable royalties that were lost by the patent-holder.[3]

With a lay witness, reviewing legal theories would be sufficient for that portion of deposition preparation, but with an expert, you must proceed to review the "scientific, technical, or other specialized" theories being offered by both her expert and the expert to be deposed. This presents a great part of the challenge and charm of dealing with experts: for a short time during the deposition, your goal is to be as expert as the expert in the narrow slice of her field that is involved in the case. You should indeed adopt the persona of the ignorant, but interested student as you depose the expert, but that ignorance hopefully is largely feigned. You must be sensitive to the nuances of the expert's methodologies and opinions, to those small changes in assumptions or facts that could result in major changes in conclusions, and to those studied choices of words that are an attempt to mask weaknesses or unfavorable alternatives. You are seeking to become attuned to the relevant science to the point where you can identify occasions when the expert has substituted judgment for knowledge, assumptions for facts, faith for understanding, or opinion for truth. The consulting expert is the great ally; the testifying expert may be less useful because of concerns about exposing her to worries about unfavorable theories and marginally provable fact, or involving her in discussions about material touching on the attorney-client privilege or attorney work-product.

The newly amended Rule 26(b)(4) allows discovery of facts or data that the expert received from any source, with limited protection against disclosure of—or discovery into—"work product-type" communications between attorneys and testifying experts that do not contain facts or data. Thus, an attorney's opinion, disclosed to a testifying expert, that the attorney is concerned about a certain part of the case, or that in the attorney's opinion the acquired company would have gone into bankruptcy within a year, are not discoverable since they are not facts or data, but merely speculation or opinion. One can wonder, however, had the attorney told the expert that she believed the facts were too weak to support one part of the expert's testimony or that the financial records in fact showed serious weakness in the company, if these conversations would still be protected. There is some concern that

---

3. *See* Georgia-Pacific Corp. v. U.S. Plywood Corp., 318 F. Supp. 1116, 1121 (S.D.N.Y. 1970), *modified*, 446 F.2d 295 (2d Cir. 1971).

allowing the attorney's manner of speech to control discoverability of expert foundations leads to quixotic results. A better test, embodied in earlier versions of the same rule, evaluated whether the information "considered" had the potential to affect the expert's testimony or opinions. Using that test, the phrasing of the lawyer's communication would be unimportant. Nevertheless, the rule has been changed, and there now exists a safe harbor for attorneys to directly expose the testifying expert to the persuasive force of the attorney's musings, suggestions, and opinions.

Despite the new rule formulation, as the questioning attorney at an expert deposition, you should thoroughly probe the source and substance of all communications on the subjects of the lawsuit received by the expert from anyone. Just as with other claims of privilege that intrude into discovery, these "non-fact expert communications" claimed by counsel may overstate and overreach, and you should carefully map out their real boundaries so that the expert's thought processes and methodologies do not remain unduly shrouded by the fog of whispered words from an attorney.

In developing this very narrow but intense understanding of the relevant science, you must position yourself to unmask what is non-science, the concern of *Daubert*—those factors of judgment and discretion, of bias and prejudice, of interest and ignorance that allow the opposing expert to disagree irrationally with the another expert while wrapping that disagreement in a cloak of apparent scientific certainty. Because the trier-of-fact, judge or jury, cannot always (or often) distinguish science from mythology and fiction, you must work to do so and to create a sound foundation on which that distinction can be presented at trial.

20.1.4 *Brainstorming on the Experts*

One device you can use to get to that level of preparation is to brainstorm the case with your trial team—legal assistants, graduate students, associates, and consulting experts. Brainstorming is described more fully in section 5.7.1. In this context, brainstorming is the free-flowing and relatively unconstrained discussion of ideas about the case, and it would include questions such as:

- What factual bases does the opposing expert rely on?

- Where do those facts come from?

- What sources of facts have not been used?

- What separate theories are involved in the methodology?

- How is it known that the methodology is accurate?

- What alternative methodologies exist and were tried?

- Who selected documents and other sources of information?

- What limitations were placed on the expert's work?

- Who participated in applying methodologies to facts?

More questions are suggested in the article, "The *Daubert* Deposition Dance," reprinted in the appendices.

20.1.5 Timelines

After the brainstorming has been completed, organization begins. One way to organize the facts, opinions, data, and approaches is to place the material on a timeline, a horizontal array of information organized chronologically and displayed from left to right. The timeline can be constructed according to when key facts occurred in the case; it can reveal when opinions were reached by the opposing expert in relation to the acquisition of information about these facts, thereby perhaps disclosing a rush to judgment. Timelines are also useful for telling you what you know and what you do not know. You can look at the time line and ask what caused the events to occur when they did, and also what facts and approaches do not appear or were not used by the expert or by the party on the other side. Policies and procedures, which may have been in place but not followed, should be included on the time line, to signal you to ask about whether those policies and procedures existed.

During deposition preparation, prepare a timeline and redraft it until you are comfortable that it displays known and relevant information organized correctly by date. You can then reduce the timeline to a size that you can keep available during the deposition, so when the expert refers to events, you can locate them on the time line easily, add them to the time line if necessary, and note their relationships to the other historical incidents that make up the dispute being litigated. *Post hoc ergo propter hoc*, "after which therefore because of which," is indeed a logical fallacy (just because bullfrogs come out after it rains does not mean it rained bullfrogs); however, causes do precede effects (bullfrog eggs precede bullfrogs), and until the chronological relationship of events is understood, the cause-and-effect relationship may remain undiscovered. One additional reason to prepare a time line is that you can use it as a starting point for creating a storyline—what you will tell the jury that will appeal to their common sense as to what happened, why it happened, and how it compares with their intuitions and experience. Preparing a two-paragraph, chronological statement that answers the questions, "What is the case about?" and "Why do we care what happens here?" encourages you to focus on the forest and not on a selected tree or two.

20.1.6   The "Fourteen Documents" Rule

To further prepare for taking the opposing expert's deposition, you must review and become intimately familiar with the important documents in the case—those that support your client's position and those that challenge it. Especially where you are working with documents recording scientific information—laboratory notes, chemical analysis, engineering diagrams, critical path flow charts, econometric calculations, medical charts—you will find extraordinary comfort in having at the deposition a well-annotated copy of the document in question, where the annotations are a result of careful review by you and your consulting expert. Such review begins with the consulting expert explaining the document line by line, entry by entry, number by number, describing sources for each entry and providing meaning to each entry. As the consultant guides you through the document, annotate your copy, so eventually you are able to present an explanation of the document in the same detail as the consultant. At deposition, your goal is not to disclose your thorough knowledge of the documents; but that thorough knowledge allows you to recognize instances where the opposing expert has inadequate or mistaken knowledge and may have arrived at consequently mistaken conclusions.

When the entire case is presented to the jury, there should be no more than fourteen documents that will sway the jury's verdict—in part because it is too difficult to consider more documents than that and to keep them separate; in part because the jury will be satisfied to select one document from a group as representative of the case and will use it while ignoring the others; and in final part because, while lawyers tend to overcomplicate cases, juries act to reduce them once again to their proper (or, perhaps, "convenient") dimensions. (In other words, some cases are as simple as, "who hit who first?") In preparing for the deposition, you must deal with more than the ultimate fourteen documents—you probably will not be able yet to identify which fourteen those are—but you should not overcomplicate your preparation or the deposition by attempting to master and then question the expert about all aspects of all documents. Clearly "all documents" will not be the subject of cross-examination at trial. Life is too short!

Expert Depositions in a Nutshell

- Opinions

- What did you do; why did you do it; how did you do it; what result did you get; what effect did that have on your opinion?

- What learned treatises do you recognize in your field?

- What assumptions did you make?

- What did you not do?

- Curriculum vitae

20.1.7   The Goal in Deposing an Expert

As a final step in preparing to take the deposition of the opposing expert, you must determine the goal. There are times when you will be asking questions at the deposition purely for discovery—to learn the opinions, bases, methodology, and conclusions that the expert is preparing to state at trial. When such pure discovery is the goal, remind yourself that open questions are your sharpest tool: who, what, when, where, why, how, tell us, describe, and explain. These questions force the expert to speak in more than monosyllables and, in the best of deposition worlds, encourage the building of a rapport between you and the opposing expert as you play your role of ignorant, but interested student.

Another goal—not inconsistent with pure discovery, but normally pursued after the discovery portion of an expert deposition—is theory testing: laying before the opposing expert different portions of the client's explanations and opinions to learn in advance of trial the opposing expert's avenues of challenge or to produce party statements, concessions, and narrowing of issues.

For example, you could ask the opposing expert: "Professor Jones, am I correct that you have no fault with the use of a critical path methodology in determining the cause for the construction delay? Instead, your only disagreement with plaintiff's expert involves the proper reading of the blueprints to determine the number of structural steel units that should have been purchased?" In a medical malpractice case, where the question is whether the plaintiff's epilepsy was caused by a motorcycle accident, you might ask the opposing expert: "Doctor, your opinion is the plaintiff's epilepsy is idiopathic—of unknown origin. Of the factors that are potential causes of epilepsy, which factor do you believe is the most likely cause of the plaintiff's epilepsy, even though you cannot select one as the cause?" You might then ask a follow-up question: "Even though you say that your opinion is that the cause of the plaintiff's epilepsy cannot be known with scientific certainty, do you agree that the most likely cause was traumatic head injury?"

A third reasonable goal in taking the deposition of an opposing expert is to test cross-examination—that is, to try part or even all of a line of questions that challenges the expert in her credentials or her opinion testimony. The benefit is that you can learn about the defenses the expert may have during cross-examination and then try to avoid those defenses during trial. The detriment is the expert is alerted to that possible line of cross and will be more prepared to meet it at trial. If, however, you have weighed these possible outcomes and determined that the line of cross is too tenuous to use without some confirmation that it will work, then you have little to lose by testing it during deposition.

In addition, the purpose of the cross could be to persuade opposing counsel to settle the case by demonstrating the weakness of her expert. Finally, in the best of all worlds, the deposition cross can lead to success in a motion for summary judgment, which may dispose of the case.

Occasionally, counsel will seek to punish an opposing expert during the deposition by extending its length or increasing its heat, as though the expert has committed some crime by daring to appear for the other side or daring to hold contrary opinions. The theory seems to be that the witness will rethink her decision to testify because the deposition was so unpleasant and cross-examination is yet to come. A strong argument exists that deposition questioning designed with this goal in mind is improper and perhaps unethical because the purpose of discovery is to uncover information that may lead to the further discovery of admissible evidence; it is not a proper role for counsel to delay the proceeding, to sanction witnesses, or to take a position merely to harass, annoy, or embarrass the witness.

20.1.8 *Expert Party Statements*

Using the deposition of the opposing expert to confirm known facts serves the purpose of limiting the dispute—at least the dispute between the experts—and perhaps facilitating a settlement or accelerating the end of the trial. Creating a record at the expert deposition of the facts on which the expert relies as being true for the purposes of her analysis makes it virtually impossible for the opposing party to contest those facts during motions practice or at trial. (Indeed, a close reading of Federal Rule of Evidence 801(d)(2), especially sections C and D, has persuaded a number of courts that a deposition statement made by a party's expert is "an opposing party's statement" as defined by the rule. The expert is, after all, "a person whom the party authorized to make a statement on the subject."[4] As a technical matter, facts accepted as true by the opposing expert at her deposition need not be the subject of requests for admission under Rule 36 because they would already be an opposing party's statement by operation of Rule 801(d)(2).)

20.2   Deposing the Expert: Strategies

Open questions seeking new information remain the recommended approach for expert depositions. While experts possess some advantages over lay witnesses at trial, you can often turn those apparent advantages to your own use. Experts often feel constrained by factors beyond the lawsuit, such as a need to maintain their credibility and reputation in their profession, which you can use to bring them back from extreme positions. By making the expert think of you as an ignorant, but very interested student, you will encourage the expert to teach you what you need to know.

20.2.1   *Keeping an Open Mind*

A good piece of advice on deposing the opposing expert is "Do not assume you know any answers the expert will give." When Albert Einstein was asked, "What do you consider the most powerful force in the universe?" anyone at all familiar with Einstein and his work might reasonably have guessed that his answer would be "gravity" or "mass times the speed of light squared"—or, if one were of a particularly philosophical bent, "the human mind." All are consistent with general knowledge about Einstein, and yet all would be incorrect. Einstein's actual answer: "Compound interest." The interesting thing about the Einsteinian answer is that it tells more than just what Einstein saw as a potent force—it tells about Einstein himself, about his sense of humor, his perspective on himself, his work in relation to common people and their problems, and his ability to differentiate between the abstractions of a relativistic universe and the unavoidable financial realities of everyday life.

By asking Einstein at deposition, "What do you consider the most powerful force in the universe?" instead of, "Is it your opinion that gravity is the most powerful force in the universe?" the attorney creates an opportunity to see into Einstein's mind. "The human mind is dark to those of us who attempt to look into it and to most of us who attempt to look out from it."[5]

---

4. Fed. R. Evid. 801(d)(2)(C).
5. Carl Gustav Jung, Swiss psychiatrist (1875–1961).

How presumptuous of attorneys to believe they can accurately predict the answers to complex questions as analyzed by experts with opposing viewpoints, when those who study the human mind suggest people cannot even understand their own motivations.

20.2.2   *Expert's Advantages*

As the attorney approaches the opposing expert to take the expert's deposition, the expert should recognize that just by virtue of being an expert, she has some substantial advantages to bring to the process—advantages the attorney can sometimes diminish or turn to her advantage at deposition and trial.

Expert's Advantages

- Experts are experts.

- Experts are not intimidated by the process.

- Experts can hide behind their expertise.

- Experts may be more highly educated than lawyers.

- Experts like to teach.

One of the expert's primary advantages is she has superior knowledge in her field—superior to the deposing lawyer, superior to her own counsel, and superior to everyone involved in the case (except, perhaps, the opposing expert). If the examination at trial had as its purpose to allow the jury to decide whether the lawyer or the opposing expert were the better geologist, endocrinologist, cabinet maker, or mathematician, there would be little contest (and little purpose to holding the trial at all). But that is not the purpose of the trial or of the expert's testimony at the trial. Instead, she is there to offer her specialized assistance to the trier of fact, who will attempt to resolve a dispute that touches on some small portion of her field of expertise. And in that very small portion, for a very short time, while the attorney and expert face one another, the attorney may be equally expert.

You can improve your chances of holding your own by carefully choosing the areas of confrontation on cross-examination—and that is where you should focus the deposition. You have no obligation to examine the expert on every facet of her knowledge or even on any facets that support her opinions in the case. As the attorney who is working in your own arena, you are entitled to ask questions limited to those areas in which the expert is factually ignorant, mistaken, or poorly prepared. If you have been able to identify such areas through deposition and other discovery, you have negated the expert's advantage of superior overall knowledge in the field.

A second advantage possessed by the expert is that she is not intimidated by the discovery and trial process. Either she has gone through it before and understands that it is normally not fatal or she has thoroughly discussed the process with the counsel who is presenting her. Or, because she is educated and intelligent, she recognizes that her exposure to inconvenience, embarrassment, or ridicule will be limited. While the lay witness approaches cross-examination with some trepidation (except for business people with the phrase "assistant to" in their titles, who seem to believe they are the embodiment of all business acumen), the expert generally looks forward to the trial, relishes the intellectual challenge, and often prefers the excitement of the courtroom to the perceived drudgery of the classroom, laboratory, or doctor's office. (There are some experts who are wary of the process because they have learned how public the deposition can be. They have learned that what they say in one case can come back to haunt them in another. These experts are not intimidated by the deposition process, but they can become overly cautious and overly concerned about choosing the right words and as a result may appear hesitant and evasive.)

The fact that many experts are not intimidated by the deposition or trial process, however, is not an unmitigated advantage to them. That intimidation caused by fear or concern in lay witnesses serves to make those witnesses more cautious about allowing the deposing attorney to develop a rapport or to encourage them to speak freely. "Unintimidated" experts, on the other hand, may lose sight of the deposing attorney's goal, which is to find means to diminish the expert's credibility or to challenge the bases for the expert's opinions. Because they think they understand the questioning process, they think they cannot be seriously challenged. And because they think they are safe within their own field, experts at deposition may be more willing to provide explanations and lengthy answers, to volunteer information, and to educate their ignorant, but interested student. So if you can remember to smile, nod, lean forward, maintain eye contact, and ask open questions in your genuine search for illumination from the expert, the expert may allow her teaching instincts and her passion for her subject to overwhelm the caution that her counsel has been advising for the previous three months.

Experts may also derive some comfort from their belief that if they encounter a question they do not want to answer, they can hide behind their expertise by using jargon, by insisting on hyper-technical definition of terms, or by discussing the premises and conditions they claim to see as being built into the question, to a point where the examiner has forgotten what the question was and has literally lost her ability to determine whether it was ever answered at all. For example, when asked whether the assumed shape of the curve showing the receipt of profits for a project was more an ascending ramp than a descending ramp, an econometrician might answer:

> Well, counsel, that question presumes more information than is readily available from the few facts you seem to be implying, and without engaging in substantial efforts at crafting a regression equation that produced a large enough R^2 to give us some comfort, an acceptable degree of confidence, perhaps at the 95 percent level, we will be unsure whether we are dealing adequately with problems of heteroskedasticity or multicolinearity.

However, you can deal with an expert's use of jargon to avoid answering a question and turn it to your advantage. The expert, in using such jargon, is counting on your unwillingness to show your ignorance by asking for explanations. The expert presumes (with some good reason for many trial attorneys) that your ego will keep you from admitting that you are unable to determine whether she has answered your question and you will therefore go blindly forward.

But because you are already playing the role of the interested but admittedly ignorant student, you should feel no shame in admitting your ignorance—when faced with jargon and other expert-speak, you should say: "I'm sorry. I don't understand that last answer. Can you help me? What do you mean by regression analysis? What do you mean by R^2? What do you mean by large enough R^2? What do you mean by heteroskedasticity? Why should we be concerned about that in your analysis?" Continue with your line of questioning until you have required the expert to define all of the terms and have demonstrated that you have the patience and intent to cure your apparent ignorance with detailed questions.

Whether the expert has been intentionally trying to dissemble by hiding behind the jargon of her expertise or has merely forgotten that English is the language in which she is normally expected to converse, the lesson will eventually become clear to her: this is your arena, and she will answer the questions eventually, and neither your ignorance nor your desire to get on to other topics will prevent you from slicing through the expert's attempts at obfuscation.

Jerry Seinfeld joked in his eponymous TV series: "A recent survey stated that the average person's greatest fear is having to give a speech in public. Somehow this ranked even higher than death, which was third on the list. So, you're telling me that at a funeral, most people would rather be the guy in the coffin than have to stand up and give a eulogy."

The normal American may worry for days about her need to make a presentation to a committee at work, the parent-teacher association, or the library board. (Trial lawyers, of course, relish the opportunity to speak in public and abuse it as often as possible; therefore, counsel's own experience as a trial attorney should not be taken as indicative in any way of the experience or concerns of human beings.) Expert witnesses, like trial lawyers, have largely overcome the fear of public speaking. They have put themselves in a position in their professions that requires them to make public presentations—not only in the trial courtroom, but more routinely in the classroom or before professional organizations. While some may still get the sweaty palms and racing pulse that adrenalin can produce, many of the experts the attorney encounters in the courtroom are as comfortable as she is at presenting their viewpoints from the stand. In sum, they like to teach.

The fact that experts like to teach may give them an advantage at trial, but if you can successfully encourage them to teach at the deposition with you in the role of student, the experts will ultimately give more information than their counsel would prefer. Giving the expert a whiteboard at deposition[6] to use to explain her analysis may also encourage her to drop into a teaching role. Instead of remembering that you are seeking material to use to diminish her credibility and undermine her opinions, she may come to think (correctly) it is her responsibility and obligation to answer the questions fully, and thereby to repeat, to simplify, to analogize, and to instruct until she is confident the attorney understands even the most esoteric and sophisticated aspects of her methodology and conclusions. Then she would have delivered the "whole truth" demanded by her oath. Once the expert begins teaching at the deposition, the expert's advantage has been turned into yours.

---

6. There is no legitimate objection to asking the expert to use a whiteboard or blackboard or pad at a deposition. The objection has been made (as it was to requests for the witness to draw on a pad) that "she is here to answer oral questions, not to draw pictures"), but courts recognize the general rule that if it can be asked by her counsel at trial ("Dr. Jones, would you please step down, with the court's permission, and sketch the entry wound on the outline of the skull shown on the pad?"), it can be asked by opposing counsel at the deposition. Another objection that is sometimes made is that the drawing on the board will not be included in the record. With the universal availability of digital cameras and the common use of video depositions (so that the camera operator can include the drawing by capturing it at a break), this no longer remains a concern. Furthermore, and more importantly, this concern is logically a concern of the questioner, not the defender; if the questioning attorney is satisfied with the completeness of her record, she can move on. If she wants the drawing or outline or diagram or illustration included, once she sees what the expert has drawn, she can copy it, photograph it, or take whatever other steps she believes are adequate. At the least, if a drawing on a board or pad is copied, it is simple enough to sketch it again at a break and then have the witness authenticate it as a fair copy and then initial it when the record is reopened.

20.2.3 *Expert's Vulnerabilities*

Expert's Vulnerabilities

- Experts are in the lawyer's arena.

- Experts cannot resist teaching.

- Experts don't know the power of FED. R. EVID. 803(18).

- Experts' time is finite, and the universe of facts is infinite.

- Experts must rely on assumptions.

- Experts are concerned about consistency.

- Experts worry about facts they don't know.

Experts have vulnerabilities that should be exploited at deposition. An important one is that their time to devote to this particular engagement is finite, while the universe of information for it is infinite. Therefore, experts must always admit there is more that they could have done and more that they could have known. While they may claim it is only a remote possibility that their opinion would be changed if they had done those undone tasks or knew those unknown facts, you may be able to present a sufficient number of such facts and tasks to make it appear to the jury as if the experts have left their job unfinished.

As an example, at the deposition in a wrongful death action, the damages expert is asked to identify all the people she has talked with in gathering information to calculate the future income stream, which is then to be reduced to present value. The expert answers that she has talked to the decedent's superiors at work, others in the same field of work, professors who were familiar with the decedent's potential, and other experts who studied the decedent's field of employment to determine the likelihood of its economic growth. She is then asked if there were any others to whom she spoke, and in various forms she is asked again and again. The expert finally states clearly and without condition that she has identified everyone to whom she spoke, but the questioning attorney recognizes that the expert has not identified the decedent's husband. With that deposition foundation, the attorney is prepared for cross-examination at trial, which makes the apparently undone task seem significant and inexcusable:

Q: Professor Delaney, I understand from your direct examination that you spent approximately 217 hours working for plaintiff's counsel in this matter.

A: Yes, I believe that's correct.

Q: And of those 217 hours, I imagine you spent, what, perhaps twenty-four hours—that is, three work days—talking with Sheila Foley's husband? That would be three days out of about twenty-six?

A: No, I didn't. I . . . .

Q: Well, is it fair to say you spent at least one day talking with the husband, Carl Foley?

A: Well, no, what I'm trying to say is . . . .

Q: Well, if not one day of conversation, then I presume you had some substantial correspondence with Mr. Foley. Letters back and forth, asking him for information, is that right?

A: No, I talked to Sheila Foley's bosses and co-workers and professors. I talked to people in her computer science field . . . .

Q: So, Professor Delaney, the simple fact is in all of those hours—those 217 hours—that you spent trying to figure out how much money you think the plaintiff should get from the hospital, you never even spent five minutes talking to her husband about her plans to work or have a family or make other decisions about her life, like changing jobs or going back to school? Is that correct?

A: I never talked to him.

Q: Well, Professor Delaney, who decided you wouldn't talk to Sheila Foley's husband? You or the attorneys you were working with?

Another problem for experts that makes them vulnerable to cross-examination is that some information, necessary for their work in the case, is simply not knowable. As an example, Professor Delaney in the wrongful death case is attempting to calculate the present value of the future income stream. Part of that calculation involves future interest rates, future inflation rates, and future discount rates. While these can be estimated, they cannot be known with certainty.

A typical approach for an expert in such a position is to look at those same values for a similar past period; if she is projecting income for a twenty-year period in the future, she may take the average inflation rate (or discount rate or interest rate) for the immediate past twenty years. But this is not the same as knowing. The average is almost certain to be incorrect when compared to the actuality (twenty years from now), and any reasonable expert will always admit this. Nevertheless, experts have little choice but to assume that the past average (or some other proxy) will be a sufficiently close approximation to the future actual rate that the figures generated will be reasonably close to accurate. There is no other way to do the calculation. And the expert's attorney will have to figure out how to explain this uncertainty to the jury.

In such a situation, the expert cannot logically be faulted for relying on assumptions; indeed the questioning attorney's own expert may have to rely on assumptions, albeit different and (from the attorney's perspective) more reasonable assumptions. One connection between expert testimony and the overall theme of the case is whether the expert has made an unreasonable assumption. The unreasonableness of that assumption can affect not only the credibility of the expert on the damages calculations, but also the overall credibility of the opponent's case. The trial lawyer can eventually argue if the expert is wrong about damages or if her assumptions are fanciful, what else is she making up to support the story she is telling?

Of course, the attorney may have already made the decision that she is not going to present an expert—this is normally more an option for a defendant's counsel than for a plaintiff's counsel—because she does not want to lend credence to the "pseudoscience" being hawked by the plaintiff. For example, presenting her own expert to challenge plaintiff's expert witness who seeks to testify about the emotional distress damages suffered in a sex discrimination case be seen by the jury as lending weight to the methodology or approach.

When using a deposition to prepare to challenge an expert, you must remember that there are many ways to diminish the opposing expert's testimony without putting your own expert on the stand. Sometimes, where you do not want to present your own phrenologist to challenge their phrenologist—because you do not want the jury to think that your side believes in phrenology in any way—you may instead consider challenging:

- the accuracy of the facts the opposing expert is relying on;

- the reasonableness of alternative assumptions she could have made;

- the sources of data she did not consult;

- the learned treatises that do not support her conclusions;

- her sketchy record of publications; and

- the dependence of her conclusion on the honesty and truthfulness of those who have reported the facts to her (e.g.: "So, if your client didn't tell you about all of the episodes of dizziness, your opinion could be based on inaccurate facts? And it could be wrong?").

In other words, the psychologist testifying in a case alleging sexual harassment depends to an extraordinary extent on the truthfulness of statements made by the claimed victim, as that victim purports to describe her experiences; the child abuse expert must rely on the truthfulness and memory of young children as they are encouraged to describe unpleasant experiences; the damages expert testifying for the plaintiff in a patent infringement case must accept as accurate the plaintiff's statements regarding the success with which she would have marketed the product had the infringement not occurred.

Be wary about how far you go in refusing to give credence, however. In the well-known *Texaco-Pennzoil* case, the defendant wanted to avoid a damages presentation of its own because it did not want the jury to think that any damages were appropriate. When the jurors found the defendant liable, they felt that they were left with no alternative but to accept the plaintiff's enormous damage figure.

The good news is that you can ameliorate this problem in several ways:

- by using cross-examination of the opposing expert to present alternatives;

- by identifying other assumptions and introducing recalculations through that opposing expert based on those other assumptions;

- by identifying information the expert did not take into consideration, and then asking the expert to agree that such information might well reduce her damage calculations;

- by pointing out to that expert instances in which a conclusion crucially depended on the truthfulness of a single witness; or

- by showing other circumstances that put the expert's figures in doubt, thereby providing the jury with an alternative figure or an indication of the direction of appropriate change.

Where an expert's client has the burden of proof on a damage issue and argues that there should be a change in its damage calculations, but fails to specify the direction of change, it should be relatively easy to persuade a jury that the opposing party has essentially failed in its proof. If the opposition does not quantify the change, the jury could be justified in concluding that the change would be insubstantial.

Unlike lay witnesses, experts bear the burden of belonging to a profession; they feel themselves to be part of a larger whole, and while they may wish to stand out as superior when compared to their colleagues, they have no desire to stand out *because* they are outliers—that is, because they are espousing such extreme positions that few, if any, of their colleagues agree with them. Thus, as much as they are able while fulfilling the terms of their engagement (which, by the time of deposition, they interpret as implicitly requiring them to support their principal's case), they will try to remain consistent with the mainstream beliefs and approaches in their field. For example, you may be more likely to get the opposing expert to agree that the texts and treatises your expert relies on are authoritative (for purposes of Rule 803(18)) if you ask about them in general, perhaps as a group. In fact, if the opposing expert believes you are examining her credentials by asking about her familiarity with authoritative texts, she may be more willing to demonstrate she has a broad knowledge of authoritative literature in the field—much more willing than she will be if you foreshadow your intention of reviewing that literature to determine whether the expert was being consistent with it.

A further aspect of the expert's desire to appear consistent is her constant concern that she not say anything in the case that contradicts something she has said in another case or in some of her own publications. As a result, while you are focusing on three pages of transcript and four pages from two articles that you have identified as possibly useful on cross-examination, the expert is worrying about all twenty-three of her articles and the four cases in which she has given both deposition and trial testimony, and she is wondering whether she should have her graduate student assistant review them all again or perhaps cancel her vacation and review them herself.

20.2.4   Daubert *and Deposition Strategy*

Suppose your consulting or testifying expert tells you that the opposing expert's report fails on its face to contain sufficient facts, data, or reasoning to support the opinions it presents or that the opinion either is irrelevant or is the product of an unreliable or misapplied methodology. Then you are presented with the strategic choice of either challenging the witness before trial by a motion *in limine* to preclude testimony or trying to discredit the witness at the trial by cross-examining on the deficiencies. This second choice—"sandbagging" the opposition by waiting to challenge the expert until the expert's opinion is offered at trial—may surprise the opponent, but it may also surprise you when you learn for the first time (and too late) why this expert believes that *Daubert* has been satisfied and why the data are sufficient and why the methodologies are reliable. If this unsuccessful "surprise assault" comprised all or most of the cross examination, the expert may win a huge victory.

Even if you are so confident that your *Daubert* arguments will succeed that you seriously considering taking the risk of avoiding *Daubert* issues at the deposition, don't do it. If you have that strong a challenge before the deposition, you should realize that the answers to your *Daubert* questions would likely strengthen your in limine motion to preclude the expert's trial testimony, and that greater likelihood of success is worth the disadvantage of revealing your tactics by questioning at the deposition. Most courts want evidentiary issues handled pretrial, before the jury is in the box and the witness is on the stand so that the trial runs smoothly and jurors are not inconvenienced. Therefore, the judge wants to learn ahead of time if there are *Daubert* challenges that require resolution. It is also within the court's discretion to let the expert supplement her report and allow further deposition if the court believes the interests of justice are served by it.[7] In the final analysis, if you believe that there are serious *Daubert* problems with the expert's report or deposition testimony—problems serious enough to warrant preclusion of all or part of the expert's testimony—make those areas the subject of deposition questioning and a motion to preclude before trial.

20.3   Deposing and Defending the Expert: Tactics

The seven most useful answers still pertain to experts, and you must caution your expert to tell the truth, briefly, unless the need to show that *Daubert* has been satisfied requires lengthier answers.

When taking the opposing expert's deposition—especially today when the time available for depositions is limited by rule, court order, expense, or all three[8]—extract the expert's opinions and bases as early in the deposition as possible. Ask the expert to describe her opinions, methodology, and bases in detail and to articulate fully all the indicia of reliability that might be interesting. The funnel technique,[9] which moves from wide-open questions seeking new information, to confirmation of known information, to testing of theories, is especially valuable in deposing experts. Opposing experts may be encouraged to lecture about their opinions and methods if they think of the deposing attorney as an ignorant, but interested student.

---

7. FED. R. EVID. 102.

8. Where expert issues are complex, it has become common in modern litigation for the parties to stipulate that expert depositions may be taken over two or three days, or even more. The parties should discuss this in their conference pursuant to FED. R. CIV. P. 16. Such a stipulation could even allow, for example, for one three-day deposition per side, for use only on an expert; two two-day depositions per side, for important executive witnesses of the deposing party's choice; and the remainder of the depositions all being seven hours or fewer. A logical extension of this stipulation would be an agreement that once a multiple-day deposition was begun, that "two-days" or "three-days" was no longer available for other depositions, regardless of whether it actually consumed the full two or three days.

9. Described *supra* in chapter eight.

20.3.1 *Deposing Experts: Tactics*

Many attorneys start the deposition of the opposing expert with a detailed examination of the expert's background.[10] Other attorneys spend a great deal of time taking the expert through a chronological recitation of how they were hired, what they were shown, what they were asked to do, and what they did before reaching their opinion. There are several disadvantages to both of these approaches. In these days of limited time for depositions and increasing expense, both especially important in expert depositions, you should postpone questioning about those areas that are less likely to give you good information, are less likely to lead to material for cross-examination, or have a greater tendency to antagonize the expert and keep the expert from becoming the teacher. Additionally (especially with respect to the credentials), this material is easily checked by graduate student assistants outside of the cumbersome and expensive deposition or discovery process, as has earlier been discussed in this chapter. Finally, when preparing for the deposition, opposing counsel told the expert: "They'll probably spend the first hour or so, maybe two, asking about your resume, when we first contacted you, and what we told you. That's fine; it gets us almost all the way to lunch before we have to deal with any hard stuff." If you behave as predicted, you increase the expert's confidence in both herself and her counsel.

Instead, choose another topic, an important topic, the one that the expert is most likely concerned about and one that must concern the expert's attorney also. Ask that most important question first. In other words, right at the outset, ask the expert for her opinions. Her opinions are what distinguish her from a lay witness and from the opposing expert. Her opinions are information you absolutely must understand to prepare for trial. Her opinions are something she would much rather postpone explaining until after she has settled into the process and become accustomed to your techniques and tempo. Her opinions are *not* what she wants to talk about immediately; therefore, you should ask her to talk about her opinions immediately.

Begin the opposing expert's deposition by asking her for all of her opinions. Ask her to list them all before going back to ask about the bases and details of any individual opinion. Oil exploration teams look at the topography of the surrounding land before they choose a particular place to drill down. Similarly, you should see the entire landscape of opinions before choosing the order in which to question on them. Some experts are savvy enough, or have been trained well enough, to start the list of their opinions

---

10. Some attorneys call this a curriculum vita, even when they are referring to it in front of the jury. Casual empiricism suggests many jurors no longer speak Latin; some attorneys avoid the problem with Latin by referring to this as a resume; indeed, French is not Latin, but it is not plain English, either. "List of credentials" may derive from medieval Latin, but jurors now accept it as modern English.

with the least significant of them, hoping to entrap the questioner into drilling down on unimportant opinions and their bases without even finding out about the existence of more important opinions. If, however, you have discovered the entire set of opinions before drilling down, you are in the position to choose where to start. Questioning on the most important opinions then gets the time it deserves.

You must learn the expert's opinions and bases at the deposition, even if you learn nothing else; you can forego learning about aspects of the expert's credentials or publications, or about her familiarity with the literature in her field, or about the details of her initial engagement if time restraints require that you leave some questions unasked. Of course, you go in armed with the expert report, which in theory contains the expert's opinions and identifies facts and data being utilized, and you have the assistance of your trial team, your own testifying expert, and your consulting expert (if you have one). The danger of leaving the deposition with opinions undisclosed is therefore somewhat reduced. Nevertheless, it is dangerous to rely on the opposing counsel and her expert to present a report that contains an adequate and informative statement of the expert's opinions. Because you choose the order of examination at the deposition, you can ask the expert for all of her opinions first and then insure that those opinions are no more and no less than the opinions disclosed in the expert report.[11]

20.3.2 *Key Questions to Ask Experts*

Here are the most important questions to ask at the expert deposition, beginning with the key question and its follow-up:

What opinions have you reached in this matter?

Before even putting the expert's report on the table, get the expert's statement of each of her opinions and satisfy yourself that the expert's knowledge of those opinions has been exhausted:

Are those all your opinions and conclusions?

You stated four opinions. Are there any more?

---

11. The expert report required by FED R. CIV. P. 26(a)(2)(B) is not intended as anything more than a discovery aid to counsel opposing the expert. It is not typically admissible if offered by the expert's counsel, because it is hearsay ("out of court statement offered for its truth"); relevant portions could be admissible if offered by opposing counsel, because it is an opposing party's statement (the expert is a person or agent authorized to speak for the client, under FED. R. EVID. 801(d)(2)).

Is there anything that would help you recall whether there are other opinions?

Did you make any notes on your opinions?

Then go back to the first (or most important, or most interesting) opinion, restate it for the record, ask the expert to agree that it is her opinion, and then ask for the bases for that opinion, again to the point of exhaustion.

In questioning about the bases, the next five questions are recommended. (The first four are useful in having any witness describe any process.) Indeed, they are the same four or five questions you would use on direct examination to have an expert describe how she came to her opinions.

What did you do?

Why did you do that?

How did you do that?

What result did you get?

What significance does that result have to your conclusion?

Ask these same five questions to get the bases for each opinion. Ask the expert whether she has any additional bases. Are these all the bases? Did she make any notes on her bases? These questions make certain that you have exhausted the expert's knowledge on relevant points.

There are many checklists in the literature that claim to anticipate and cure all problems that might be encountered in expert depositions. Some are interesting; some are even useful. Nevertheless, there is no real substitute for careful preparation, thoughtful questioning, attentive listening, and intensive follow-up. If you are reading your questions to make sure you cover all that is needed to depose an expert witness, you are in danger of becoming wedded to that list and of being unable to respond to the cues, the body language, the voice tone, and the pauses that would signal you to follow up on areas not included in your notes. Further, you will not project the attention and animation that characterize the interested, but ignorant student. When used properly, reasonable checklists can stimulate memory or imagination, but always be aware of the danger that the checklist will become a crutch, depriving you of creative leaps and useful insights. If the deposition on oral examination could be actually reduced to a checklist, it would be called "deposition on written interrogatories," and you could just mail it in.

Nevertheless, for those who would like a memory aide for expert depositions, make a short and pithy checklist from the questions above ("What are your opinions? and the follow-up exhaustion questions, then the five bases follow-up questions) and add the four following questions. Together, these questions comprise a reasonably effective ten-question deposition of an expert:[12]

1.   What are your opinions?

2.   What did you do?

3.   How did you do it?

4.   Why did you do it?

5.   What result did you get?

6.   What significance did that result have to you opinions?

7.   What are the reliable authorities in their field?

8.   What assumptions did you make in your work?

9.   What tasks did you not do?

10.   Is this your current and accurate list of credentials?

Because preliminary questions of fact are determined by the judge, who is allowed to consider hearsay and other evidence not admissible under the Federal Rules of Evidence and most state rules, a party may be allowed to support an expert's qualifications to testify through a declaration or testimony at deposition. Therefore, at the deposition of your own expert, you should ask enough questions to lay that foundation for admissibility of the expert's testimony—perhaps not as extensively as you would at trial, but at least to the extent that you generally establish the expert's knowledge in the field. Then, if the court requires that only a very brief foundation be established at trial, you can offer the deposition or a brief statement culled from the deposition. Of course, as long as the expert is available, a brief direct examination on qualifications will satisfy most courts.

---

12. These ten questions are not intended to present the be-all and end-all of thorough deposition questioning of an opposing expert. They are not intended to capture all the nuances of subtle and sophisticated questioning of an expert, which may reveal hidden biases, untold assumptions, or imperfect calculations. They are intended to remind the attorney of the main areas that should be covered in any expert deposition (and then followed up with all of the areas of questioning illustrated by the "funnel," described in earlier chapters).

If there is a *Daubert* hearing to exclude or limit an expert, an affidavit[13] or deposition excerpt may help the court make a quick ruling. Parties are allowed to supplement testimony at Federal Rule of Evidence 104 conferences with affidavit testimony—just as one can in a summary judgment motion. In addition, today most judges will not take the time to hold a hearing. They will instead order the parties to fully disclose the experts and present the depositions as their basis for opposing or supporting expert opinions. In other words, if you have support for your expert, you should present that support during the expert's deposition. Be sure that the declaration or deposition testimony touches on the *Daubert* requirements, including things considered, reliability of methodology, consistency of application, and sufficiency of data. In other words, where the court may treat the deposition as part of the basis for the *Daubert* ruling, conduct the "follow-on" questioning of the expert as though it were a preservation or trial deposition. The goal is to preserve the foundational portion of the expert's testimony for trial—to the extent that the opposition does not ask those questions—and to give the expert a chance to establish her credentials and her adherence to the principles of *Daubert.*

---

13. Nowadays, to avoid sandbagging with post-deposition affidavits, many courts are holding that only affidavits consistent with deposition testimony may be submitted. *See* section 15.1 on correcting a deposition.

**A Different List of Useful Questions
for Expert Depositions**

- Who in the field agrees with you?

- Who in the field disagrees with you?

- What did you review and choose not to rely on?

- Who selected the documents you reviewed?

- Did you ask for anything you did not receive?

- Have you published peer-reviewed publications?

- What is the error rate in your methodology?

- Is the methodology accepted in the field (*Frye*)?

- Is your methodology testable?[14]

- Is your opinion relevant?[15]

- Is the methodology reliable? (Does it generate scientifically valid results?)[16]

- Are there learned treatises which you accept?

- Have you testified as an expert before?

- Do you make your money by testifying or by working in the field of your expertise?

---

14. "Is your methodology testable?" at its simplest level means: "If you do it again with the same data, do you get the same results? If you do it again with different data, do you get proportionately different results? If someone else does it again, do they get the same results that you did?" However, "testability" also means: "Can this methodology be tested to determine the truth or falsity of the underlying premise?" This aspect of testability is called, "falsifiability," and it essentially asks whether we possess the ability to test the methodology and results for truth. Some hypotheses, like, "The universe expands two-fold and contracts to one-half every second" is not falsifiable, because we cannot test to see if it is true (or false). We have no test, no unchanging yardstick, because everything we know is contained within the universe, and we are left without a constant measure. Hypotheses that are not falsifiable therefore cannot form the basis for a methodology on which courts should rely; they are at least as likely false as true.

15. Relevance here is defined as: "Does this opinion assist the trier of fact in resolving an issue that is important in this case?" "Does it *fit* the issue in this case?" is another way that this is sometimes expressed.

16. As "fit" relates to "relevance," "foundation" relates to "reliability." Do we have a reason to accept the opinions (the results from the methodology) as likely providing us with the truth; not always, but a preponderance of the time?

Of course, all of the questions in the box above require follow-up and exhaustion. If the expert says that her methodology is testable, we want to know how to test it, if it has been tested, and where the results of those tests are shown. If she does not know the error rate, we want to know why not and whether she is still comfortable relying on the methodology. And so on, down the funnel.

20.3.3   Rule 803(18): Learned Treatises as Nonhearsay

Federal Rule of Evidence 803(18) is, on its face, merely another exception to the rule excluding hearsay statements. Statements from treatises by authorities in the scientific area are hearsay and cannot be admitted in court unless a certain foundation is laid. In practice, Rule 803(18) has become much more than that. It is now a powerful tool for cross-examining and impeaching expert witnesses because, when it is demonstrated that the author of the publication is indeed an authority, relevant segments may be admitted on direct or cross-examination of an expert as substantive evidence—material on which the trier-of-fact may rely in drawing conclusions (that is, not merely as part of witness impeachment). This is worth repeating. *Rule 803(18) permits the introduction of relevant material from written sources that have been demonstrated as being reliable, either by the testimony of the proponent's expert, testimony of the opposing expert, or through judicial notice.*

The deposition provides an excellent opportunity to find out whether the opposing expert will concede the existence of reliable sources in the field, which can be obtained and reviewed for use on cross-examination.[17] The beauty of this approach to cross-examination is that the author of the materials, although functioning as a source of expert information in the case, is never hired, paid, deposed, or cross-examined. Indeed, a book's author may not even earn a royalty on the book, because the book itself does not come into evidence, but is merely read in pertinent part (and then can be returned to the library, where only overdue charges are paid).

At the deposition, ask the opposing expert what sources she consults when she has a question in her field and wants a second opinion; ask about materials she directs graduate students to if she is a teacher; ask about publica-

---

17. Introducing Rule 803(18) material during the testimony of the proponent's own expert requires little effort. Show your favorable expert the book or article, ask whether she recognizes the author, ask her opinion of the author or the work (since courts do not always distinguish between those questions), and then read the relevant portion into the record (with the court's permission). The expert on the stand need only testify that she relied on the material; the expert on cross need only be present when it is read (so that it is "called to her attention"). If you are tempted to introduce the material on the direct of your expert instead of the cross of the opposing expert because it is so easy to do, reflect on the pleasure and impact of introducing material that contradicts the opposing expert while that expert is actually sitting there on the stand.

tions by colleagues in her company or college department—especially if she considers them useful. Her counsel may have warned her about the phrase "reliable authority," so she may shy away from providing useful answers to questions that use that language, but other language such as "useful," "well researched," or "important" will suffice at trial. Putting the language aside, if the expert admits to using a publication in her own work, she can hardly argue at trial that the work was not a "reliable authority." A question that is always useful at expert or lay depositions may be particularly appropriate in the learned treatise context: "How would you find out?" Ask where the expert would look for other approaches, where she checks her approach, where she looks for additional issues or to find more sources of help. If she needed help in understanding, where would she go? Did she cite sources in her last article because she thought their science was sound? Would she incorporate footnotes to sources for her writings where she thought the foot-noted sources were unreliable? So the opposing expert indeed did rely on all of those materials, and therefore, under Rule 803(18), the court should consider all of them reliable

Then, on cross at trial, call her attention to a portion of a text that is in your favor, reminding her that at the deposition she considered the writing to be sound or authoritative. With that foundation, when the excerpt is read into the record, it comes in as substantive evidence, whether the opposing expert agrees or not. Remember, there is no need to ask: "Do you agree with that statement that I have just read?" Her own attorney can do that if that attorney knows how to do that and understands that she is allowed to do that. All you need to show the judge is, first, that there is evidence (from which a reasonable jury could infer that this is reliable material—a very low threshold, indeed); and, second, that the "authoritative work" has been called to the opposing witness's attention (which is accomplished by the question, "Have I read that clearly enough so that you could hear it?").

THE IMPACT OF *DAUBERT*

The *Daubert* decision has arisen so frequently in this discussion of ways to question opposing experts at deposition that it seems appropriate to take a moment to reflect on its importance. *Daubert* and its progeny have changed expert deposition practice substantially. In supporting expert testimony, the attorney must demonstrate the relevance of the opinions and the reliability of the methodology; in challenging expert testimony, the attorney has new license to question the methodology and the expert's competence at using it. All of this adds new importance to the question of why an expert did a particular study or took particular steps, because that "why" provides the connection (or exposes the lack of connection) between what the expert did and the results and their utility, between the expert's methodology and the expert's opinion.

In examining the reliability of methodology, counsel is looking for the reasonable causal nexus between what was done and the opinion reached. When the logic of that connection is lacking (as when the astrologer opines the angle between Saturn, Jupiter, and the sun makes Sagittarians prone to impulsiveness in matters of both love and highway driving), the court is likely to find that the reliability of the methodology has not been shown. Where an analysis of the logic is beyond the capability of a nonexpert court (as where the attorney is dealing with questions of subatomic physics), counsel may profitably utilize substitutes to stand in for an understanding of the causal relationships. For example, *Daubert* suggests that the lawyers and trial courts look at whether a methodology has been subjected to peer review before publication. The concept here is that peers will understand the process and point out errors when they read about it. Attorneys can question whether there is a known or knowable error rate; and they can argue that if the error rate is known, it is too high to allow the results of the methodology to be accepted as reliable evidence, even without knowing what resulted in that error rate. The point here is that the deposition is the opportunity to gather information for *Daubert* challenges and to prepare counsel's own expert to defend the reliability of her methodology.

20.3.4   Expert Witnesses: Preparation

Just with lay witnesses, you must prepare your own expert witness for her deposition. Although most expert witnesses have had substantial public speaking experience—in the classroom, at professional meetings, or even in the courtroom—they still may suffer some anxiety at the thought of giving a deposition in front of lawyers in a very formal and artificial environment. Therefore, as with lay witnesses, you need to spend some time with the expert early on to reduce her anxiety about the process so she is able to perform to her potential. One of the best ways to reduce the witness's anxieties is to simplify the witness's task: be sure she understands that her only task at the deposition is to tell the truth briefly. "Telling the truth briefly" means providing accurate answers to questions—after she understands (and, if necessary, clarifies) them—and then stating those accurate answers in as short a way as possible without unnecessary adverbs, adjectives, parentheticals, footnotes, analogies, cute stories, asides, qualifications, and other unrequested information.

Many expert witnesses are at first frustrated by the direction to abstain from volunteering additional information. You will hear statements like: "Why can't I just tell them what I know? Won't that shorten the whole process?" Or "I know where they're going. Why don't I just tell our side of their case?" In fact, the more volunteered information the expert includes, the longer the deposition will be.

When trying to persuade the expert witness that volunteering will not shorten their deposition experience, keep in mind, and perhaps even share with the experts, the story of Sir Richard Francis Burton (the British explorer—1821–1890; not the Welsh actor, Richard Burton—1925–1984) and John Henning Speke, two noted explorers from the United Kingdom who are credited with exploration of the Nile to its source at Lake Victoria. (Sir Richard gained considerable fame for the discovery of the source of the Nile as Lake Tanganyika, although subsequent disclosures reveal he may have turned back before the source was found and left John Henning Speke to continue the trip up the White Nile to its eventual source in Lake Victoria. Speke, in fact, was seriously wounded by natives during these travels, apparently being shot with arrows in both arms and legs and pierced through his body with a spear. Nevertheless, he journeyed on.) Each time the Burton-Speke party reached a fork in the river in their travels, they had to establish a base camp and send part of their party to explore what seemed the less-likely branch of the river. When that less-likely branch was found to end in a back-water (so that it obviously was not the source of the Nile), that portion of the party returned to the base camp, and they all packed up and continued their exploration up the other branch of the river.

This is exactly how attorneys have learned to ask questions. Every time the witness uses an adjective or adverb or supplies additional, unanticipated information, the questioning attorney feels compelled to inquire about those forks in the testimony. For example, if the question is, "What color is your car?" the witness should answer, "Green." If instead the witness, expert or lay, responds, "I have a green Buick," then the questioning attorney is faced with a fork: should she ask about why the color green was chosen or why a Buick was chosen, or will the questioning attorney already know enough to recognize that the Buick does not transport her into any relevant waters? In the diagrams on the accompanying page, note the similarity between a map of the Nile and a "map" of a typically volunteered answer to the question, "What color is your car?" When preparing your witness, find a way to use the Burton-Speke story or your own example to persuade the expert witness that she does not want to help turn her deposition into an endless trip of exploration. You, as counsel for the expert, do not want to spend weeks and months at the deposition—only hours or perhaps a day.

At this point in the litigation, you have already reviewed with the expert where she fits into the case and how her opinions support the theories in the case. For plaintiffs in particular, the expert may have the task of establishing certain essential elements in the case through her testimony. For example, a causation witness must be prepared to testify at the deposition that she believes to a reasonable degree of certainty in her field that there is a causal relationship between the plaintiff's injury and the alleged conduct of the defendant. Be careful not to overstate your "do-not-volunteer" instructions to the expert—you do not want the expert to be hesitant about testifying fully and completely about her opinions on the causation elements or the elements upon which you have the affirmative burden of proof.

Role-playing is a good tool to help your expert witness distinguish between answering with responsive facts and volunteering nonresponsive facts. However, role-playing takes a fair amount of time. It involves analyzing what questions are likely to come from the opposing counsel and then asking the follow-up questions opposing counsel is likely to ask once the answers are given. In play-acting the role of the questioning counsel, fully explore the answers the expert is giving to questions that touch on the essential elements of the case, and press the witness to expand on the answers she gives—this way, the expert can be truly prepared for the skepticism of the opposing counsel. The practice sessions can show the expert the dangers of unnecessary volunteering and can encourage the expert to be as forceful and direct as possible in those areas where her testimony is crucial to the case.

Map of the Nile

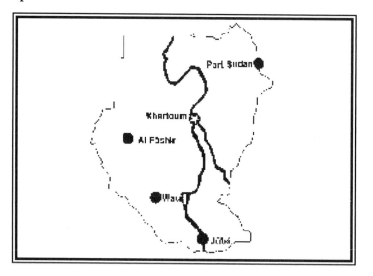

Car-toum

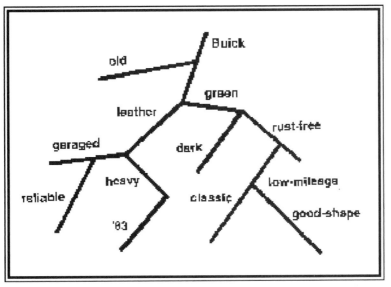

In role-playing, your job is to diagnose what type of expert witness you have. Is the expert a "master of the universe" type, who comes off as arrogant and over-confident—which might show that she has lost her objectivity as she has become more involved in the case? Or, on the other hand, is she overly hesitant, too concerned with making a mistake, and worried she may have said things in earlier testimony that will be used against her either in this case or in her professional arena? As you gauge where this expert falls in the spectrum between the "master of the universe" and the "overly-hesitant" witness, your next job is to bring her to the middle—confident where she needs to be confident and careful where she needs to be careful.[18]

As you prepare the expert witness to be examined at deposition, you should also review important documents, but here "important" has a slightly different meaning. The expert has some responsibility to explain to the

---

18. In role-playing with the witness, be aware that it can be confusing to the witness to have you, whom the expert has come to rely on as her guide through the process, adopt a cross-examination mode—more strident tone of voice, more piercing eye contact, more insistent demeanor—as she assumes the role of opposing counsel at deposition. When role-playing, you should go to the opposite side of the conference table to emphasize that you are pretending to be the opposing attorney. After the moot questioning session, return to your seat beside the witness, where you will be sitting at the actual deposition. If you have adequate support, consider asking one of your colleagues or member of the litigation team to assume the role of examining counsel while you sit right alongside the witness as you will at the deposition, providing physical and moral support. That way at the deposition, where the room and some of the people will be different, at least the important things—the attorney's physical and supportive relationship—will be the same.

opposition the interpretation and significance of the various documents she has considered as part of her analysis. Many of those documents will be much less important than the core set that the expert intends to use in her trial testimony, but to protect her credibility, she must be able to demonstrate a familiarity and comfort with all of them as opposing counsel asks her to explain them. Therefore, in preparation, you will have to spend more time on documents with the expert than you would with a lay witness. Have the expert explain the documents until she fully understands them. Then have the expert explain them again. The expert should make notations—even if they are decipherable only by her—on her copies of the documents if she feels making such notations will make her more comfortable and less likely to forget the relationship between various figures, entries, numbers, formulas, or other documentary content. Although you should recognize that such notations may be discovered at the deposition as opposing counsel sees the expert referring to them, the presence of such notes is not improper, and the expert should have little concern about using them. Acting as an expert in deposition and trial is not a memory test; it is a means by which "scientific" knowledge is provided to the court through an expert who can employ and explain modern technologies. The need to use notes does not diminish the expert in performing this task. The expert should understand, however, that these should be minimal notes, two or three words here or there, and not major dissertations or caveats written in margins or along the bottom of several succeeding pages. Often, the best notes merely remind the expert of other worksheets or related documents that need to be considered with this particular document or spreadsheet.

If the expert is asked at deposition if she reviewed documents in preparing for the deposition, her answer will obviously be "yes." Almost invariably, the opposing counsel will ask the witness to identify the documents reviewed. If you know those documents have already been turned over to opposing counsel as part of the voluntary disclosure of expert materials or as attachments to the expert report, or in the remainder of documentary discovery, there is little harm in allowing the expert to identify the documents she reviewed, although it is probably a good idea to explicitly state that no waiver is being made regarding attorney work product by allowing these documents to be identified. There is no need to confuse an expert with some procedural battle. If you still intend to argue that the identity of the documents remains attorney work-product even though it has been revealed to the expert and is therefore "considered" by her, then you must make your objections at the deposition and direct or advise the witness not to answer the question; otherwise the attorney work-product immunity from production will be lost.

The introduction of the word "considered" to the expert discovery obligations in Rule 26(a)(2)(B) (by way of the 2003 amendments) created a significant distinction between the law relating to lay witness preparation and the law relating to expert witness preparation (in addition to expanding the expert disclosure obligations from "relied upon" to "considered" [in any way, even if not relied upon]). With respect to the lay witness, documents that were reviewed but did not refresh the witness's recollection—either because they were not effective in refreshing recollection or because the witness's recollection was already sound and did not need recollection— are not subject to production simply because they were reviewed. They may be subject to production because they were called for under requests for documents or subpoenaed or for other reasons, but their review in preparation for the deposition does not, in and of itself, make them subject to production. However, since the adoption of the rule amendment using "considered" instead of "relied upon," that is no longer the case with expert witnesses. The expert's review of the document in preparation for deposition, by itself, puts that document in the category of all the other documents she has "considered," and considered material must be produced, subject to the exceptions in jurisdictions that still permit some protection of materials that were considered but are also attorney work product.[19]

One goal of the role-playing process it to provide your witness with an opportunity to answer questions in a deposition context. Therefore, the questioner (you or a colleague) should probably use open questions—questions beginning with who, what, where, when, why, how, tell us, describe, or explain—and some closed or leading questions. By asking the expert open questions, you force her to think about framing an answer and to provide content to it without unnecessary volunteering. As has been mentioned, this is also your opportunity to talk to the witness about the need for her to state

---

19. Under Rule 26(a)(2) as amended December 19, 2010, discussions by the expert with the attorney are not discoverable as information that was considered, subject to the exceptions provided. The exceptions (that is, information that may still be discovered) are communications on the topics of "facts or data," the expert's compensation, and assumptions that the expert was told to make. In other words, discovery of discussions of the attorney's legal theories, or factual hypotheses ("Here's what I think happened . . . ."), or concerns about the case—even concerns about the expert's testimony and report—is not allowed. The "facts or data" that the attorney may transmit will still be discoverable. Rule 26(b)(4) provides that there shall be no discovery concerning draft reports, apparently because the Advisory Committee, the Congress, and the Supreme Court have concluded, on some basis not coherently set out in the Advisory Committee's Notes, that such discovery is too time-consuming and expensive. Before they came to that conclusion, it is hoped that those bodies at least considered the availability, under Rule 29, of stipulations to refrain from such discovery, which have been used many years by attorneys who are in a position to assess their client's need for discovery and ability to afford it. In fairness, where there is a disparity in the resources available to the parties, such a stipulation may be unavailable, as one party attempts to retain its financial advantages over the other, smaller party, by complicating and extending discovery. In such a case, however, under the old or the new rule, recourse could be had to the court for a protective order.

each of her opinions[20] clearly and succinctly, so they will be clear to the judge if this record is used as support in dispositive motions.

However, because of the way most attorneys ask questions at deposition, you and the expert can expect that the overwhelming majority of questions asked will be closed (did you, do you, have you, were you, was he, and the like) or small (what color was your car, where is your office, what was his name). The expert needs guidance on how to answer these closed questions, so you should still train her how to answer closed and small questions. Therefore, review with the expert the same "seven answers to most deposition questions" that you provide to lay witnesses.

The Seven Answers to Most Deposition Questions

- Yes.

- No.

- Green.

- I don't know.

- I don't remember.

- I don't understand the question.

- I need a break.

These "best" answers have been discussed earlier, in the context of preparing the lay witness.[21] With regard to preparing the expert witness, there are a few additional issues to consider or emphasize. The fourth suggested answer to most deposition questions is "I don't know." This answer is particularly hard for experts to give in depositions simply because they are experts, and, as experts, they believe they are under some obligation to know everything that touches on the subject matter of their expertise, case related or otherwise. After all, the experts are thinking, no self-respecting expert is ignorant, and the answer "I don't know" discloses ignorance. You must assure the expert during preparation that she is not obligated to know everything;

---

20. The expert's bases can, of course, be explored fully at the deposition, but the expert is probably better off if she finds a brief, truthful way to state those bases, without expanding beyond the specific questions asked. Bases for opinions come up less often in pretrial motions, and a full explanation of bases is therefore less likely to be needed by the proponent of the expert's testimony in responses to motions for summary judgment or exclusion or limitation of expert testimony.

21. *See* section 13.2.6.

in fact, there are things not related to her analysis of the case that she legitimately does not know; there are matters she was not asked to investigate and therefore does not know; and there may be other evidence or information in the case on which she will not testify and which she therefore does not know. The best answer in such circumstances is, "I don't know," and you need to tell the expert that this is the appropriate answer in those circumstances. If the expert needs further persuasion, ask her to consider the alternative answer. If the expert answers that she does know, when she does not, nothing but trouble is ahead of her. Therefore, she must be authorized and persuaded to state, "I don't know," when that is the most accurate answer.

A closely related answer at deposition is number five above: "I don't remember." This answer is distinguished from "I don't know" because it suggests the witness once had the information being sought, but can no longer remember. If that is true, this is the best answer for the witness, lay or expert. If the expert says that she does remember certain information, when she does not, she will not be able intelligently to deal with the follow-up questions that are sure to come. The way to avoid those embarrassing follow-up questions at deposition is to admit without embarrassment "I don't remember." It is worth emphasizing here that many modern cases depend crucially on expert testimony and that if the trier of fact finds the expert less than fully credible, the case may be lost on that fact alone. It is far better to have the expert admit that she has forgotten something on one point at deposition than it is to have proven that she does not have the knowledge and memory of facts that she claims.

With regard to the sixth answer in the list, no witness, lay or expert, is obligated to answer a question she does not understand. Experts, however, are asked more complex questions that incorporate terms of art, countertheories, and convoluted fact hypotheticals. Tell the expert witness that she is not obligated to answer any question she does not fully understand and that if she is asked a question she does not understand, she should say, "I'm sorry. I don't understand your question." You should also tell her to resist what for an expert is an understandable temptation—suggesting ways in which the question could be fixed so she could understand and answer it. The likelihood is if she attempts such repairs, she will simply create more forks in the river—forks the questioner would never discover for himself and will feel compelled to explore, further extending the deposition.

Once the experts tells deposing counsel that she does not understand the question, she should wait for the questioner to take the next step. He may rephrase the question; he may ask a different question; or he may ask her what she does not understand or whether she has used the offending word or phrase herself in other contexts. If the questioner's use of a particular term is confusing or inappropriate, the expert could tell the questioner that the term is the source of the problem. If the question seems to be built on assumptions that have not been fully stated, the expert could say "I don't understand all of your assumptions," or "I don't have sufficient facts to answer that question." The important rule is simply that the expert should wait for a different question, new or revised, that she understands well, before she provides a substantive answer.

The seventh best answer to most deposition questions is simply, "I need a break." If the expert witness for some reason believes that she cannot continue the deposition or if she is not comfortable without taking a break—a break to talk to her attorney, a break to call the office, a break to check on matters at home, a break to use the facilities, a break merely to walk up and down the hall, or a break to stretch and to reflect—then she should say, "I need to take a break." She should say it on the record, either to opposing counsel or to her attorney. In either event, the result should be the same. You, as her sponsor, should say "We're taking a break" and take the witness out of the room for a break. Almost inevitably, opposing counsel will object, especially if the break is requested while a question is pending. It is much better deposition practice for the witness to answer the question before taking a break, and both in preparation and in the private discussion with the witness before leaving the room, you should discuss that with the witness. When the witness asks for a break with a question pending, ask her in an aside if she feels she must take the break before answering the question because there is something about the answer that concerns her—for example, the possibility of a privilege being involved. However, if the witness insists that she have a break before she provides an answer, then you have little choice other than to take that break.

Until you know that the answer would not involve a protected matter, you must allow the break and deal with questioning counsel when you and the expert return to the room. You may have to apologize, perhaps by saying: "I apologize. The witness was concerned that she had forgotten to provide instructions on an important matter back in her office, so she felt she had to call them." Or, if the expert had a concern about privilege, the attorney might say: "Sorry. Dr. Jones was not certain if she was allowed to talk about her other client's financial data on which she has done a similar analysis. She needed a moment to talk to that client's attorneys. She is now ready to answer your questions on that data."

In one sense, there is an eighth "best answer" available at deposition to expert witnesses. An expert may be frustrated by what may fairly be characterized as trick questions, such as questions that ask whether she considered factors that are completely irrelevant to any legitimate analysis. For example, an expert in diamond appraisal may be asked whether she considered prior ownership in assessing the value or whether she spoke with the woman who was wearing the diamond when it was last photographed—or whether she had ever considered a relationship between the two words, "carat" and "carrot." Instead of allowing her to grow increasingly upset with such patently irrelevant questions, you should prepare her to come back to her "core" positions, if they are at all responsive. She might say: "Those matters need not be considered because my opinion depends solely on the factors I have mentioned already, including cut, clarity, color, country of origin, carats, the demand in the market for diamonds of this particular quality and size; and the retail availability of such diamonds within a reasonable distance from the location of the purchaser. These items are so important, so overwhelmingly important, that other matters are either trivial or, like the ones you mention, facetious or completely irrelevant from a gemologist's point of view. Cut, clarity, color, country, and carats; demand; and availability: that's what you need, and that's all you need."

Thus, instead of trying to defend against whether the suggested additional factors can ever play a role and sometimes must be considered, she emphasizes her core positions and brings the discussion back to a focus with which she is comfortable. In a car accident case, a reconstruction expert, when asked whether she considered the location where the hubcap was found, in a field off the road, might say: "The debris field was wide; nevertheless, the locations of the cars' frames and engines, the heaviest parts, in relation to the skid marks, provided us with sufficient and persuasive data from which to reconstruct the movement of the cars before and after the impact. The location of the hubcap alone could not alter the conclusions we drew from the much more important information about the location of the tons of components we considered, all of which showed that your client's car crossed the center line and then struck the plaintiff's car." Thus, instead of debating whether this or that small piece of evidence, perhaps aberrational, refuted her conclusions, the expert returns the focus to the mass of much more persuasive evidence that supports to her opinions.

During the deposition preparation, press the expert to identify the "pillars" that support her opinions. These are the items of evidence that provide the foundation for her opinions and analysis. Identify these pillars by asking the expert: "If I negated this particular fact, or the support of this particular fact witness, would you continue to hold the same opinions with the same degree of certainty?" When the expert has to answer "No" with respect to a particular basis or fact, you have identified a pillar. Other facts may provide additional support, but the essential facts constitute "pillars." As long as those pillars remain intact on deposition and cross-examination, the expert need not worry greatly about bits and pieces of less important evidence, and she should not risk her credibility by trying to argue that, yes, she implicitly considered this, and yes, she implicitly considered that. She should instead think about whether challenges in questions go to her the pillars, her core concepts, or whether they are an attempt to get her to testify as though some minor difference might be a major theoretical or methodological dispute. It is when the expert tries to explain everything—the location of every hubcap and license plate screw, the behavior of every diamond-buyer in the market—that she risks overreaching and introducing inconsistencies. Have her practice saying: "I don't know, and it really doesn't matter, why the hubcap wound up in the middle of the field; but I have spent 300 hours determining why 7 percent of the mass of the cars wound up trying to occupy the very same spot on US-95 at 3:04 a.m. on September 30, and the answer is that your client, Barry Smith, crossed the center line at seventy-nine miles per hour."

20.3.5   *Conclusion*

Preparation of an expert can no longer be conducted by the "seat of the pants." If an expert is being deposed to refute a *Daubert* challenge, the seven "best answers" are not sufficient. But if the expert is a "master-of-the-universe" type and an egoist, likely to get herself into trouble by her arrogance and verbosity, or if she is too nonassertive to protect her important opinions and bases, then you need to thoroughly prepare her using role-playing sessions until she is comfortable and consistent in giving short and truthful answers. There are many tools available to protect the expert's opportunities to state her opinions and methodologies, at deposition and trial, in a coherent manner; and there are just as many tools available to the opposing attorney to deconstruct and examine the expert's approaches. In this *Daubert* world, the proponents of expert testimony should remember that even when all of the expert credentials and methodologies are in the record, it is the expert's personal credibility that will persuade the jurors to believe her, even when they have not mastered the science; and opponents should remember that attacking scientific testimony is only effective if errors and omissions and inconsistencies reflect the witness's inadequacies as a truth-teller. In cases where the science is not challenged as hucksterism, the expert's personal credibility is the key.

CHAPTER TWENTY-ONE

CONCLUDING THE DEPOSITION

It ain't over till it's over.

—Yogi Berra

Normally there is only one opportunity to depose the witness; once the deposition is concluded, it is difficult to persuade the opponent or the court to call the witness back to reconvene the deposition. Therefore, you must review all areas of examination or important questions to be certain that you have not overlooked anything important.

21.1   Insuring Completeness

Before concluding the deposition, call a recess to consider whether the goals of the deposition have been accomplished as well as possible, given the available time and the number of issues presented. Review the deposition outline to check off what has been covered and see what remains. If there are friendly others present (a client, co-counsel, paralegal, and so forth), check with them as well. Be sure to reserve time to review what you have accomplished at the deposition, so you can make a well-founded decision on whether it is time to conclude. Attorneys often ask a set series of questions at the end of the deposition:

> Q: Now Mr. Tilts, are there any answers to my questions that you wish to change before we close this deposition?
>
> A: Not that I can think of.
>
> Q: Is there any information I asked about that you remember now, but you didn't recall when I asked the question about it?
>
> A: No.

Q: Is there anything that you would like to add to what you have told us so that we can understand your perspective or viewpoint more clearly?

A: No.

Q: Do you have anything to add that would allow me to present your side of this dispute to my client that would make your position more reasonable?

A: No, I don't think so.

Q: Is there anything you can tell me, before we finish, that would make settlement of this matter without trial more likely?

A: No, I have told you what I think are all the facts.

Q: Thank you.

A witness rarely remembers anything new or changes an earlier answer. The value of these questions becomes apparent if you need to later impeach the witness:

Q: Mr. Tilts, on your direct examination, you said that the disk player in the car was off.

A: Yes, it was off.

Q: You remember that I asked you questions before trial, at your deposition?

A: Yes.

Q: You were under oath to tell the truth?

A: Yes, I remember that.

Q: And I asked you then, under oath, if the disk player or radio was on at the time of the accident?

A: Yes.

Q: And you told me then that the disk player was on? That you were playing "Bad Romance" by Lady Gaga?

A: Well, I, uh, I may have said that.

Q: And before we ended that deposition, I asked if you remembered anything more, or wanted to change any answers, right?

A: Yes, I remember.

Q: You were happy with those answers at the deposition until you came to court today to give your direct examination?

A: Yes, I guess so.

Q: But now, today, you wanted to change that earlier, truthful testimony?

A: Well, I don't know. I mean, I guess the disk player was on. I play a lot of Gaga.

If a witness attempts to avoid the consequences of an impeachment, you can show that you gave the witness an opportunity to correct and change any of his answers during the deposition. Having given this opportunity to expand at the deposition makes it easier to hold the witness to the breadth and depth of his prior, inconsistent, impeaching testimony.

21.2   Arrests and Convictions

Under appropriate circumstances, a witness can be impeached by criminal convictions.[1] The court also has discretion during the cross-examination of a character witness to allow inquiry about arrests and other bad acts of the person whose character is being attested to. This kind of questioning attempts to impeach the credibility of the character witness by showing either that the witness does not really know the subject of the character evidence or, in the alternative, that the character witness has a faulty notion of what is means to have good character. For some strange reason, however, most deponents become quite resentful when asked if they have ever been arrested or convicted of a crime. You may reasonably assume that the witness will cease cooperating once you begin asking about criminal convictions. Therefore, while you should normally ask a witness about arrests and convictions, and about civil violations of regulations like environmental rules, reserve those questions until the end of the deposition, when cooperation no longer matters. But you should ask. In this day and age of numerous regulatory crimes, the possibility of a criminal conviction is more likely than one might think. Even if the information is not worth bringing out at trial, the mere possibility that testifying may bring about the revelation of a prior undisclosed conviction may induce the opposing party to settle the case.

---

1. FED. R. EVID. 609.

21.3   Completing, Adjourning, Recessing, Terminating, Ending, Continuing the Deposition: When Is It Actually Done?

In those jurisdictions that have not adopted the Federal Rules of Civil Procedure limitation of depositions to seven hours on one day, or some similar limitation, the deposing attorney at the end of the deposition normally selects "appropriate" language from this shopping list of stock phrases:

1.   The deposition is adjourned until next month.

2.   It is suspended until a time to be identified in the future.

3.   It is adjourned until such time as the court issues its rulings on certain outstanding motions.

4.   It is terminated pending further discussions between the parties on the production of documents.

5.   It is suspended to permit a motion to be made for an order to compel discovery.

6.   It is concluded, subject to the right to recall the witness for further questioning should that be required.

7.   "I have no further questions at this time."

What is the legal effect of using phrase four as opposed to phrase two? Young attorneys, or attorneys inexperienced at deposition, have probably spent collective centuries worrying over this question. In fact, none of these phrases has any specific legal effect at all. Unless there is an agreement to continue the deposition or a court order to continue the deposition exists, Rule 30(b)(5)(C) requires the officer to state on the record that the deposition is complete and to set out any stipulations made by the lawyers.

All of these phrases, and any other similar phrases that regional creativity has brought into local practice, accomplish the same thing: the witness is excused to go home with no obligation to return unless ordered by the court or requested by agreement of counsel. (If the witness is not a party to the suit, even such a stipulation between counsel would probably be insufficient to compel the witness to attend an extension of the original day of deposition.) In this matter, there is no arcane ritual to be followed to achieve a certain effect—no magic language to preserve the client's rights and opportunities.[2]

---

2. In fact, Rule 30(d) is the only section of the Federal Rules that touches on the procedure for concluding a deposition: on the grounds of bad faith, annoyance, embarrassment, or oppression of the deponent or a party, the court in which the action is pending or where the deposition is held may terminate the deposition (or may place limitations on its continuation).

But what about the situation where the deposing attorney has done all that she can, but she knows that new documents are on the way? Or that later witnesses may provide information that justifies further questioning of this witness? Or that rulings from the court on claims of privilege may open new areas? What should she do to protect her right to come back later for further deposition questioning? And what about the defending attorney who believes that the deposing attorney is trying to "hold open" the witness's deposition just to irritate or discomfort the witness with the threat of having to return? How can that defending attorney protect the witness without exposing either the witness or herself to paying the costs of a motion to compel discovery?

The right to have a witness return to answer more questions is governed not by whether the deposing attorney selected the proper phrase at the end of the day, but by whether there is some justification for calling the witness back. In other words, if the court is later persuaded that it should deny the witness's privilege claims and orders the deposition to resume, the witness will have to come back regardless of the language used at the "end" of the last deposition session. Conversely, if the deposing attorney cannot demonstrate a sufficient reason for resuming the deposition, then the witness does not have to come back, no matter how careful the attorney was to say at the deposition: "Adjourned, subject to my right to recall."

Rule 30(a)(2)(A)(ii) requires court permission or a stipulation before a witness can be deposed a second time. If the attorneys disagree about whether the deposition was completed, the simple and safe approach is to seek an order permitting the witness to be deposed again. When the deponent is a party (or party surrogate of some sort, such as a Rule 30(b)(6) designee), a slightly more risky approach is simply for the deposing attorney to notice the deposition again, thereby putting the party in the position of either appearing for further deposition, applying for a protective order, or failing to appear. If the witness fails to appear, the matter is brought to the court on a motion to compel discovery. In any event, this process will resolve the question; arguing about the particular litany used at the "end" of the deposition does not.

If a party to the deposition demands suspension so that a motion for such an order may be made, the deposition "shall be suspended." Under Rule 37(a)(4), the court may impose costs of making or defending the motion upon the unsuccessful party or witness.

CONCLUSION

When the authors started trying cases more than forty years ago, depositions were used to discover facts to present at trial and to create transcripts to use to control trial witnesses through impeachment. Now depositions are also used to gather information for use in mediation, arbitration, settlement, and nontrial resolution, such as summary judgment and other motions practice. Then, *Daubert* was still some twenty-five years in the future, and expert practice generally was much less sophisticated, with no expert depositions allowed. Back "in the day," filed cases most often resulted in trials, while recent figures suggest that only some 3 percent of filed cases, state and federal, are resolved by trial today. Finally, in the '60s and '70s, most witnesses were probably deposed by the senior attorneys who intended to present them at trial, with younger attorneys learning deposition skills by sitting second chair; today, attorneys learn deposition skills by taking and defending depositions and trying to show off for the client along the way. The world of the trial attorney has changed.

In your authors' attempt in this Fourth Edition to create new approaches to these modern challenges, we found that every time we wrote or revised a page, section, or chapter, we encountered more questions to answer and new deposition practices to analyze, evaluate, and critique. Some of these new questions seem to have no answers yet in reported cases; for example, under the 2010 changes made in the federal rules relating to expert discovery, some expert product (like draft reports) is protected under the work-product doctrine; yet there is no guidance given in the rules on whether draft reports must be listed on the privilege log or preserved, although not exchanged, so the court can evaluate the claims of protection from discovery. In short, can you destroy draft expert reports without committing spoliation? Some other questions have answers, but they are not completely satisfactory; for example, while it is now the majority rule in federal courts that questions beyond the Rule 30(b)(6) specifications must be answered, this seems to be a rather arbitrary position. If the questioner wanted to ask questions in additional areas, why couldn't she just put those additional areas into the list of specifications so that answers in those areas would be given by a knowledgeable designee?

In this new edition, we provided our best thinking on these and other new areas of deposition practice, and we hope that you found these discussions useful to consider. Please send us accounts of your deposition experiences with these modern developments. We would find it useful to hear about the different approaches to resolving such questions that you hear from judges and colleagues at bar meetings and (probably more likely) cocktail parties. As must be obvious to you readers from our changes from edition to edition, we have no corner on deposition knowledge; we just have a fascination with the process by which attorneys work in a formal setting to get new information from eyewitnesses and experts in some useful form, without normally resorting to hitting and name-calling (except, as motions for sanctions still show, as perhaps a second resort).

In addition to trying to deal with new issues and rules, we have tried to make this Fourth Edition more friendly to practicing attorneys by re-ordering the chapters more logically and by expanding some chapters (like "Preparing the Witness to Be Deposed" and "Rule 30(b)(6) Depositions") so that space devoted to them more closely matches their importance in modern discovery. Other chapters may deserve expansion, also, and we would like to hear about them.

When we were new authors working on the First Edition, we may have thought that we were creating a definitive rulebook for taking and defending depositions (or that at least one of the five editions, counting a revised Third Edition) would be definitive. How silly. Laws change, lawyers change, and problems change. We realize that we should instead view our book as a snapshot of deposition practice at a single point in time. Therefore, we will probably be back in a few years, begging your attention and indulgence once again, as we try to find new ways to help practicing attorneys be more effective in their deposition efforts under new rules and circumstances.

In the meantime, please write to us about mistakes, recommendations, and requests for additional content. As noted in the Introduction, the mistakes are ours; and the recommendations and requests will all be seriously considered by our publisher and us.

—P.T.H.

—D.M.M.

APPENDIX A

A.1   Federal Rules of Civil Procedure, Rule 26

Rule 26.   **Duty to Disclose; General Provisions Governing Discovery**

  (a)   **Required Disclosures.**

    (1)   *Initial Disclosure.*

        (A)   *In General.* Except as exempted by Rule 26(a)(1)(B) or as otherwise stipulated or ordered by the court, a party must, without awaiting a discovery request, provide to the other parties:

          (i)   the name and, if known, the address and telephone number of each individual likely to have discoverable information—along with the subjects of that information—that the disclosing party may use to support its claims or defenses, unless the use would be solely for impeachment;

          (ii) a copy—or a description by category and location—of all documents, electronically stored information, and tangible things that the disclosing party has in its possession, custody, or control and may use to support its claims or defenses, unless the use would be solely for impeachment;

          (iii) a computation of each category of damages claimed by the disclosing party—who must also make available for inspection and copying as under Rule 34 the documents or other evidentiary material, unless privileged or protected from disclosure, on which each computation is based, including materials bearing on the nature and extent of injuries suffered; and

          (iv) for inspection and copying as under Rule 34, any insurance agreement under which an insurance business may be liable to satisfy all or part of a possible judgment in the action or to indemnify or reimburse for payments made to satisfy the judgment.

        (B)   *Proceedings Exempt from Initial Disclosure.* The following proceedings are exempt from initial disclosure:

          (i) an action for review on an administrative record;

          (ii) a forfeiture action in rem arising from a federal statute;

          (iii) a petition for habeas corpus or any other proceeding to challenge a criminal conviction or sentence;

          (iv) an action brought without an attorney by a person in the custody of the United States, a state, or a state subdivision;

(v) an action to enforce or quash an administrative summons or subpoena;

(vi) an action by the United States to recover benefit payments;

(vii) an action by the United States to collect on a student loan guaranteed by the United States;

(viii) a proceeding ancillary to a proceeding in another court; and

(ix) an action to enforce an arbitration award.

(C)   *Time for Initial Disclosures—In General.* A party must make the initial disclosures at or within 14 days after the parties' Rule 26(f) conference unless a different time is set by stipulation or court order, or unless a party objects during the conference that initial disclosures are not appropriate in this action and states the objection in the proposed discovery plan. In ruling on the objection, the court must determine what disclosures, if any, are to be made and must set the time for disclosure.

(D)   *Time for Initial Disclosure—For Parties Served or Joined Later.* A party that is first served or otherwise joined after the Rule 26(f) conference must make the initial disclosures based on the information then reasonably available to it. A party is not excused from making its disclosures because it has not fully investigated the case or because it challenges the sufficiency of another party's disclosures or because another party has not made its disclosures.

(2) *Disclosures of Expert Testimony.*

(A)   *In General.* In addition to the disclosures required by Rule 26(a)(1), a party must disclose to the other parties the identity of any witness it may use at trial to present evidence under Federal Rule of Evidence 702, 703, or 705.

(B)   *Witnesses Who Must Provide a Written Report.* Unless otherwise stipulated or ordered by the court, this disclosure must be accompanied by a written report—prepared and signed by the witness—if the witness is one retained or specially employed to provide expert testimony in the case or one whose duties as the party's employee regularly involve giving expert testimony. This report must contain:

(i) a complete statement of all opinions the witness will express and the basis and reasons for them;

(ii) the facts or data considered by the witness in forming them;

(iii) any exhibits that will be used to summarize or support them;

(iv) the witness's qualification, including a list of all publications authored in the previous 10 years;

(v) a list of all other cases in which, during the previous 4 years, the witness testified as an expert at trial or by deposition; and

(vi) a statement of the compensation to be paid for the study and testimony in the case.

(C)   *Witnesses Who Do Not Provide a Written Report.* Unless otherwise stipulated or ordered by the court, if the witness is not required to provide a written report, this disclosure must state:

(i) the subject matter on which the witness is expected to present evidence under Federal Rule of Evidence 702, 703, or 705; and

(ii) a summary of the facts and opinions to which the witness is expected to testify.

(D)   *Time to Disclose Expert Testimony.* A party must make these disclosures at the times and in the sequence that the court orders. Absent a stipulation or a court order, the disclosures must be made:

(i) at least 90 days before the date set for trial or for the case to be ready for trial; or

(ii) if the evidence is intended solely to contradict or rebut evidence on the same subject matter identified by another party under Rule 26(a)(2)(B) or (C), within 30 days after the other party's disclosure.

(E)   *Supplementing the Disclosure.* The parties must supplement these disclosures when required under Rule 26(e).

(3)   ***Pretrial Disclosures.***

(A)   *In General.* In addition to the disclosures required by Rule 26(a)(1) and (2), a party must provide to the other parties and promptly file the following information about the evidence that it may present at trial other than solely for impeachment:

(i) the name, and if not previously provided, the address and telephone number of each witness—separately identifying those the party expects to present and those it may call if the need arises;

(ii) the designation of those witnesses whose testimony the party expects to present by deposition and, if not taken stenographically, a transcript of the pertinent parts of the deposition; and

(iii) an identification of each document or other exhibit, including summaries of other evidence—separately identifying those items the party expects to offer and those it may offer it the need arises.

(B) *Time for Pretrial Disclosures; Objections.* Unless the court orders otherwise, these disclosures must be made at least 30 days before trial. Within 14 days after they are made, unless the court sets a different time, a party may serve and promptly file a list of the following objections: any objections to the use under Rule 32(a) of a deposition designated by another party under Rule 26(a)(3)(A)(ii); and any objection, together with the grounds for it, that may be made to the admissibility of materials identified under Rule 26(a)(3)(A)(iii). An objection not so made—except for one under Federal Rule of Evidence 402 or 403—is waived unless excused by the court for good cause.

(4) *Form of Disclosures.* Unless the court orders otherwise, all disclosures under Rule 26(a) must be in writing, signed, and served.

(b) **Discovery Scope and Limits.**

(1) *Scope in General.* Unless otherwise limited by court order, the scope of discovery is as follows: Parties may obtain discovery regarding any nonprivileged matter that is relevant to any party's claim or defense—including the existence, description, nature, custody, condition, and location of any documents or other tangible things and the identity and location of person who know of any discoverable matter. For good cause, the court may order discovery of any matter relevant to the subject matter involved in the action. Relevant information need not be admissible at the trial if the discovery appears reasonably calculated to lead to the discovery of admissible evidence. All discovery is subject to the limitations imposed by Rule 26(b)(2)(C).

(2) *Limitation on Frequency and Extent.*

(A) *When Permitted.* By order, the court may alter the limits in these rules on the number of depositions and interrogatories or on the length of depositions under Rule 30. By order or local rule, the court may also limit the number of requests under Rule 36.

(B) *Specific Limitations on Electronically Stored Information.* A party need not provide discovery of electronically stored information from sources that the party identifies as not reasonably accessible because of undue burden or cost. On motion to compel discovery or for a protective order, the party from whom discovery is sought must show that the information is not reasonably accessible because of undue burden or cost. If that showing is made, the court may nonetheless order discovery from such sources if the requesting party shows good cause, considering the limitations of Rule 26(b)(2)(C). The court may specify conditions for the discovery.

(C)   *When Required.* On motion or on its own, the court must limit the frequency or extent of discovery otherwise allowed by these rules or by local rule if it determines that:

> **(i)** the discovery sought is unreasonably cumulative or duplicative, or can be obtained from some other source that it more convenient, less burdensome, or less expensive;

> **(ii)** the party seeking discovery has had ample opportunity to obtain the information by discovery in the action; or

> **(iii)** the burden or expense of the proposed discovery outweighs its likely benefit, considering the needs of the case, the amount in controversy, the parties' resources, the importance of the issues at stake in the action, and the importance of the discovery in resolving the issues.

(3)   *Trial Preparation: Materials.*

(A)   *Documents and Tangible Things.* Ordinarily, a party may not discover documents and tangible things that are prepared in anticipation of litigation or for trial by or for another party or its representative (including the other party's attorney, consultant, surety, indemnitor, insurer, or agent). But, subject to Rule 26(b)(4), those materials may be discovered if:

> **(i)** they are otherwise discoverable under Rule 26(b)(1); and

> **(ii)** the party shows that it has substantial need for the materials to prepare its case and cannot, without undue hardship, obtain their substantial equivalent by other means.

(B)   *Protection Against Disclosure.* If the court orders discovery of those materials, it must protect against disclosure of the mental impressions, conclusions, opinions, or legal theories of a party's attorney or other representative concerning the litigation.

(C)   *Previous Statements.* Any party or other person may, on request and without the required showing, obtain the person's own previous statements about the action or its subject matter. If the request is refused, the person may move for a court order, and Rule

37(a)(5) applies to the award of expenses. A previous statement is either:

(i) a written statement that the person has signed or otherwise adopted or approved; or

(ii) a contemporaneous stenographic, mechanical, electrical, or other recording—or a transcription of it—that recites substantially verbatim the person's oral statement.

(4) *Trial Preparation: Experts.*

(A) *Deposition of an Expert Who May Testify.* A party may depose any person who has been identified as an expert whose opinions may be presented at trial. If Rule 26(a)(2)(B) requires a report from the expert, the deposition may be conducted only after the report is provided.

(B) *Trial-Preparation Protection for Draft Reports or Disclosures.* Rules 26(b)(3)(A) and (B) protect drafts of any report or disclosure required under Rule 26(a)(2), regardless of the form in which the draft is recorded.

(C) *Trial-Preparation for Communications Between a Party's Attorney and Expert Witnesses.* Rules 26(b)(3)(A) and (B) protect communications between the party's attorney and any witness required to provide a report under Rule 26(a)(2)(B), regardless of the form of the communications, except to the extent that the communications:

(i) relates to compensation for the expert's study or testimony;

(ii) identify facts or data that the party's attorney provided and that the expert considered in forming the opinions to be expected; or

(iii) identify assumptions that the party's attorney provided and that the expert relied on in forming the opinions to be expressed.

(D) *Expert Employed Only for Trial Preparation.* Ordinarily, a party may not, by interrogatories or deposition, discover facts known or opinions held by an expert who has been retained or specially employed by another party in anticipation of litigation or to prepare for trial and who is not expected to be called as a witness at trial. But a party may do so only:

(i) as provided in Rule 35(b); or

(ii) on showing exceptional circumstances under which it is impracticable for the party to obtain facts or opinions on the same subject by other means.

(E) *Payment.* Unless manifest injustice would result, the court must require that the party seeking discovery:

(i) pay the expert a reasonable fee for time spent in responding to discovery under Rule 26(b)(4)(A) or (D); and

(ii) for discovery under (D), also pay the other party a fair portion of the fees and expenses it reasonably incurred in obtaining the expert's facts and opinions.

(5) *Claiming Privilege or Protecting Trial-Preparation Materials.*

(A) *Information Withheld.* When a party withholds information otherwise discoverable by claiming that the information is privileged or subject to protection as trial-preparation material, the party must:

(i) expressly make the claim; and

(ii) describe the nature of the documents, communications, or tangible things not produced or disclosed—and do so in a manner that, without revealing information itself privileged or protected, will enable other parties to assess the claim.

(B) *Information Produced.* If information produced in discovery is subject to a claim of privilege or of protection as trial-preparation material, the party making the claim may notify any party that received the information of the claim and the basis for it. After being notified, a party must promptly return, sequester, or destroy the specified information and any copies it has; must not use or disclose the information until the claim is resolved; must take reasonable steps to retrieve the information if the party disclosed it before being notified; and may promptly present the information to the court under seal for a determination of the claim. The producing party must preserve the information until the claim is resolved.

(c) **Protective Orders.**

(1) *In General.* A party or any person from whom discovery is sought may move for a protective order in the court where the action is pending—or as an alternative on matters relating to a deposition, in the court for the district where the deposition will be taken. The motion must include a certification that the movant has in good faith conferred or attempted to confer with other affected parties in an effort to resolve the dispute without court action. The court may, for good cause, issue an order to protect a party or person from annoyance, embarrassment, oppression, or undue burden or expense, including one or more of the following:

(A)   forbidding the disclosure or discovery;

(B)   specifying terms, including time and place, for the disclosure or discovery;

(C)   prescribing a discovery method other than the one selected by the party seeking discovery;

(D)   Forbidding inquiry into certain matters, or limiting the scope of disclosure or discovery to certain matters;

(E)   designating the persons who may be present while the discovery is conducted;

(F)   requiring that a deposition be sealed and opened only on court order;

(G)   requiring that a trade secret or other confidential research, development, or commercial information not be revealed or be revealed only in a specified way; and

(H)   requiring that the parties simultaneously file specified documents or information in sealed envelopes, to be opened as the court directs.

(2)   ***Ordering Discovery.*** If a motion for a protective order is wholly or partly denied, the court may, on just terms, order that any party or person provide or permit discovery.

(3)   ***Awarding Expenses.*** Rule 37(a)(5) applies to the award of expenses.

(d)   **Timing and Sequence of Discovery.**

(1)   ***Timing.*** A party may not seek discovery from any source before the parties have conferred as required by Rule 26(f), except in a proceeding exempted from initial disclosure under Rule 26(a)(1)(B), or when authorized by these rules, by stipulation, or by court order.

(2)   ***Sequence.*** Unless, on motion, the court orders otherwise for the parties' and witnesses' convenience and in the interests of justice:

(A)   methods of discovery may be used in any sequence; and

(B)   discovery by one party does not require any other party to delay its discovery.

(e)   Supplementing Disclosures and Responses.

(1)   *In General.* A party who has made a disclosure under Rule 26(a)—or who has responded to an interrogatory request for production, or request for admission—must supplement or correct its disclosure or response:

(A)   in a timely manner if the party learns that in some material respect the disclosure or response is incomplete or incorrect, and if the additional or corrective information has not otherwise been made known to other parties during the discovery process or in writing; or

(B)   as ordered by the court.

(2)   *Expert Witness.* For an expert whose report must be disclosed under Rule 26(a)(2)(B), the party's duty to supplement extends both to information included in the report and to information given during the expert's deposition. Any additions or changes to this information must be disclosed by the time the party's pretrial disclosures under Rule 26(a)(3) are due.

(f)   Conference of the Parties; Planning for Discovery.

(1)   *Conference Timing.* Except in a proceeding exempted from initial disclosures under Rule 26(a)(1)(B) or when the court orders otherwise, the parties must confer as soon as practicable—and in any event at least 21 days before a scheduling conference is to be held or a scheduling order is due under Rule 16(b).

(2)   *Conference Content; Parties' Responsibilities.* In conferring, the parties must consider the nature and basis of their claims and defenses and the possibilities for promptly settling or resolving the case; make or arrange for the disclosures required by Rule 26(a)(1); discuss any issues about preserving discoverable information; and develop a proposed discovery plan. The attorney of record and all unrepresented parties that have appeared in the case are jointly responsible for arranging the conference, for attempting in good faith to agree on the proposed discovery plan, and for submitting to the court within 14 days after the conference a written report outlining the plan. The court may order the parties or attorneys to attend the conference in person.

(3)   *Discovery Plan.* A discovery plan must state the parties' views and proposals on:

(A)   what changes should be made in the timing, form, or requirement for disclosures under Rule 26(a), including a statement of when initial disclosures were made or will be made;

(B)   the subjects on which discovery may be needed, when discovery should be completed, and whether discovery should be conducted in phases or be limited to or focused on particular issues;

(C)   any issues about disclosure or discovery of electronically stored information, including the form or forms in which it should be produced;

(D)   any issues about claims of privilege or of protection as trial-preparation materials, including—if the parties agree on a procedure to assert these claims after production—whether to ask the court to include their agreement in an order;

(E)   what changes should be made in the limitations on discovery imposed under these rules or by local rule, and what other limitations should be imposed; and

(F)   any other orders that the court should issue under Rule 26(c) or under Rule 16(b) and (c).

(4)   *Expedited Schedule.* If necessary to comply with its expedited schedule for Rule 16(b) conferences, a court may by local rule:

(A)   require the parties' conference to occur less than 21 days before the scheduling conference is held or a scheduling order is due under Rule 16(b); and

(B)   require the written report outlining the discovery plan to be filed less than 14 days after the parties' conference, or excuse the parties from submitting a written report and permit them to report orally on their discovery plan at the Rule 16(b) conference.

(g)   Signing Disclosures and Discovery Requests, Responses, and Objections.

(1)   *Signature Required; Effect of Signature.* Every disclosure under Rule 26(a)(1) or (a)(3) and every discovery request, response, or objection must be signed by at least one attorney of record in the attorney's own name—or by the party personally, if unrepresented—and must state the signer's address, e-mail address, and telephone number. By signing, an attorney or party certifies that to the best of the person's knowledge, information, and belief formed after a reasonable inquiry:

(A)   with respect to a disclosure, it is complete and correct as of the time it is made; and

(B)   with respect to a discovery request, response, or objection, it is:

(i) consistent with these rules and warranted by existing law or by a nonfrivolous argument for extending, modifying, or reversing existing law, or for establishing new law;

(ii) not interposed for any improper purpose, such as to harass, cause unnecessary delay, or needlessly increase the cost of litigation; and

(iii) neither unreasonable nor unduly burdensome or expensive, considering the needs of the case, prior discovery in the case, the amount in controversy, and the importance of the issues at stake in the action.

(2) *Failure to Sign.* Other parties have no duty to act on an unsigned disclosure, request, response, or objection until it is signed, and the court must strike it unless a signature is promptly supplied after the omission is called to the attorney's or party's attention.

(3) *Sanction for Improper Certification.* If a certification violates this rule without substantial justification, the court, on motion or on its own, must impose an appropriate sanction on the signer, the party on whose behalf the signer was acting, or both. The sanction may include an order to pay the reasonable expenses, including attorney's fees, caused by the violation.

A.2   Federal Rules of Civil Procedure, Rule 30

Rule 30. Depositions by Oral Examination

(a)   When a Deposition May Be Taken.

(1)   *Without Leave.* A party may, by oral questions, depose any person, including a party, without leave of court except as provided in Rule 30(a)(2). The deponent's attendance may be compelled by subpoena under Rule 45.

(2)   *With Leave.* A party must obtain leave of court, and the court must grant leave to the extent consistent with Rule 26(b)(2):

(A)   if the parties have not stipulated to the deposition and:

(i) the deposition would result in more than 10 depositions being taken under this rule or Rule 31 by the plaintiffs, or by the defendants, or by the third-party defendants;

(ii) the deponent has already been deposed in the case; or

(iii) the party seeks to take the deposition before the time specified in Rule 26(d), unless the party certifies in the notice, with supporting facts, that the deponent is expected to leave the United States and be unavailable for examination in this country after that time; or

(B)   if the deponent is confined in prison.

(b)   Notice of the Deposition; Other Formal Requirements.

(1)   *Notice in General.* A party who wants to depose a person by oral questions must give reasonable written notice to every other party. The notice must state the time and place of the deposition and, if known, the deponent's name and address. If the name is unknown, the notice must provide a general description sufficient to identify the person or the particular class or group to which the person belongs.

(2)   *Producing Documents.* If a subpoena duces tecum is to be served on the deponent, the materials designated for production, as set out in the subpoena, must be listed in the notice or in an attachment. The notice to a party deponent may be accompanied by a request under Rule 34 to produce documents and tangible things at the deposition.

(3)   *Method of Recording.*

(A)   *Method Stated in the Notice.* The party who notices the deposition must state in the notice the method for recording the testimony. Unless the court orders otherwise, testimony may be recorded by audio, audiovisual, or stenographic means. The noticing party bears the recording costs. Any party may arrange to transcribe a deposition.

(B)   *Additional Method.* With prior notice to the deponent and other parties, any party may designate another method for recording the testimony in addition to that specified in the original notice. That party bears the expense of the additional record or transcript unless the court orders otherwise.

(4)   *By Remote Means.* The parties may stipulate—or the court may on motion order—that a deposition be taken by telephone or other remote means. For the purpose of this rule and Rules 28(a), 37(a)(2), and 37(b)(1), the deposition takes place where the deponent answers the questions.

(5)   *Officer's Duties.*

(A)   *Before the Deposition.* Unless the parties stipulate otherwise, a deposition must be conducted before an officer appointed or designated under Rule 28. The officer must begin the deposition with an on-the-record statement that includes:

(i) the officer's name and business address;

(ii) the date, time, and place of the deposition;

(iii) the deponent's name;

(iv) the officer's administration of the oath or affirmation to the deponent; and

(v) the identity of all persons present.

(B)   *Conducting the Deposition; Avoiding Distortion.* If the deposition is recorded nonstenographically, the officer must repeat the items in Rule 30(b)(5)(A)(i)–(iii) at the beginning of each unit of the recording medium. The deponent's and attorney's appearance or demeanor must not be distorted through recording techniques.

(C)   *After the Deposition.* At the end of a deposition, the officer must state on the record that the deposition is complete and must set out any stipulations made by the attorneys about custody of the transcript or recording and of the exhibits, or about any other pertinent matters.

(6)   *Notice or Subpoena Directed to an Organization.* In its notice or subpoena, a party may name as the deponent a public or private corporation, a partnership, an association, a governmental agency, or other entity and must describe with reasonable particularity the matters for examination. The named organization must then designate one or more officers, directors, or managing agents, or designate other persons who consent to testify on its behalf; and it may set out the matters on which each person designated will testify. A subpoena must advise a nonparty organization of its duty to make this designation. The persons designated must testify about information known or reasonably available to the organization. This paragraph (6) does not preclude a deposition by any other procedure allowed by these rules.

(c) **Examination and Cross-Examination; Record of the Examination; Objections; Written Questions.**

(1) *Examination and Cross-Examination.* The examination and cross-examination of a deponent proceed as they would at trial under the Federal Rules of Evidence, except Rules 103 and 615. After putting the deponent under oath or affirmation, the officer must record the testimony by the method designated under Rule 30(b)(3)(A). The testimony must be recorded by the officer personally or by a person acting in the presence and under the direction of the officer.

(2) *Objections.* An objection at the time of the examination— whether to evidence, to a party's conduct, to the officer's qualification, to the manner of taking the deposition, or to any other aspect of the deposition—must be noted on the record, but the examination still proceeds; the testimony is taken subject to any objection. An objection must be stated concisely in a nonargumentative and nonsuggestive manner. A person may instruct a deponent not to answer only when necessary to preserve a privilege, to enforce a limitation ordered by the court, or to present a motion under Rule 30(d)(3).

(3) *Participating Through Written Questions.* Instead of participating in the oral examination, a party may serve written questions in a sealed envelope on the party noticing the deposition, who must deliver them to the officer. The officer must ask the deponent those questions and record the answers verbatim.

(d) **Duration; Sanction; Motion to Terminate or Limit.**

(1) *Duration.* Unless otherwise stipulated or ordered by the court, a deposition is limited to 1 day of 7 hours. The court must allow additional time consistent with Rule 26(b)(2) if needed to fairly examine the deponent or if the deponent, another person, or any other circumstance impedes or delays the examination.

(2) *Sanction.* The court may impose an appropriate sanction— including the reasonable expenses and attorney's fees incurred by any party—on a person who impedes, delays, or frustrates the affair examination of the deponent.

(3) *Motion to Terminate or Limit.*

(A) *Grounds.* At any time during a deposition, the deponent or a party may move to terminate or limit it on the ground that it is being conducted in bad faith or in a manner that unreasonably annoys, embarrasses, or oppresses the deponent or party. The motion may be filed in the court where the action is pending or the deposition is being taken. If the objecting deponent or party so demands, the deposition must be suspended for the time necessary to obtain an order.

(B) *Order.* The court may order that the deposition be terminated or may limit its scope and manner as provided in Rule 26(c). If terminated, the deposition may be resumed only by order of the court where the action is pending.

(C) *Award of Expenses.* Rule 37(a)(5) applies to the award of expenses.

(e) **Review by the Witness; Changes.**

(1) *Review; Statement of Changes.* On request by the deponent or a party before the deposition is completed, the deponent must be allowed 30 days after being notified by the officer that the transcript or recording is available in which:

(A) to review the transcript or recording; and

(B) if there are changes in form or substance, to sign a statement listing the changes and the reasons for making them.

(2) *Changes Indicated in the Officer's Certificate.* The officer must note in the certificate prescribed by Rule 30(f)(1) whether a review was requested and, if so, must attach any changes the deponent makes during the 30-day period.

(f) **Certification and Delivery; Exhibits; Copies of the Transcript or Recording; Filing.**

(1) *Certification and Delivery.* The officer must certify in writing that the witness was duly sworn and that the deposition accurately records the witness's testimony. The certificate must accompany the record of the deposition. Unless the court orders otherwise, the officer must seal the deposition in an envelope or package bearing the title of the action and marked "Deposition of [witness's name]" and must promptly send it to the attorney who arranged for the transcript or recording. The attorney must store it under conditions that will protect it against loss, destruction, tampering, or deterioration.

(2) *Documents and Tangible Things.*

(A) *Originals and Copies.* Documents and tangible things produced for inspection during a deposition must, on a party's request, be marked for identification and attached to the deposition. Any party may inspect and copy them. But if the person who produced them wants to keep the originals, the person may:

(i) offer copies to be marked, attached to the deposition, and then used as originals—after giving all parties a fair opportunity to verify the copies by comparing them with the originals; or

(ii) give all parties a fair opportunity to inspect and copy the originals after they are marked—in which event the originals may be used as if attached to the deposition.

(B) *Order Regarding the Originals.* Any party may move for an order that the originals be attached to the deposition pending final disposition of the case.

(3) *Copies of the Transcript or Recording.* Unless otherwise stipulated or ordered by the court, the officer must retain the stenographic notes of a deposition taken stenographically or a copy of the recording of a deposition taken by another method. When paid reasonable charges, the officer must furnish a copy of the transcript or recording to any party or the deponent.

(4) *Notice of Filing.* A party who files the deposition must promptly notify all other parties of the filing.

(g) **Failure to Attend a Deposition or Serve a Subpoena; Expenses.** A party who, expecting a deposition to be taken, attends in person or by an attorney may recover reasonable expense for attending, including attorney's fees, if the noticing party failed to:

(1) attend and proceed with the deposition; or

(2) serve a subpoena on a nonparty deponent, who consequently did not attend.

A.3   Federal Rules of Civil Procedure, Form 52

Form 52. Report of the Parties' Planning Meeting.

(Caption—See Form 1.)

1. The following persons participated in a Rule 26(f) conference on _ date _ by *state the method of conferring*:

2. Initial Disclosures. The parties [have completed] [will complete by _ date _] the initial disclosures required by Rule 26(a)(2).

3. Discovery Plan. The parties propose this discovery plan:

   (Use separate paragraphs or subparagraphs if the parties disagree.)

   a) Discovery will be needed on these subjects: (*describe*)

   b) Disclosures or discovery of electronically stored information should be handled as follows: (*briefly describe the parties' proposals, including the form or forms for production.*)

   c) The parties have agreed to an order regarding claims or privilege or of protection as trial-preparation material asserted after production, as follows: (*briefly describe the provisions of the proposed order.*)

   d) (Dates for commencing and completing the discovery, including discovery to be commenced or completed before other discovery.)

   e) (Maximum number of interrogatories by each party to another party, along with dates the answers are due.)

   f) (Maximum number of requests for admission, along with the dates responses are due.)

   g) (Maximum number of deposition for each party.)

   h) (Limits on the length of deposition, in hours.)

   i) (Dates for exchanging reports of expert witnesses.)

   j) (Dates for supplementation under Rule 26(e).)

4. Other Items:

   a) (A date if the parties ask to meet with the court before a scheduling order.)

   b) (Requested dates for pretrial conference.)

c) (Final dates for the plaintiff to amend pleadings or to join parties.)

d) (Final dates for the defendant to amend pleadings or to join parties.)

e) (Final dates to file dispositive motions.)

f) (State the prospects for settlement.)

g) (Identify any alternative dispute resolution procedure that may enhance settlement prospects.)

h) (Final dates for submitting Rule 26(a)(3) witness lists, designations of witnesses whose testimony will be presented by deposition, and exhibit lists.)

i) (Final dates to file objections under Rule 26(a)(3).)

j) (Suggested trial date and estimate of trial length.)

k) (Other matters.)

(Date and sign—see Form 2.)

APPENDIX B

B.1   **Sample Notice of Nonparty Deposition on Oral Examination**

IN THE UNITED STATES DISTRICT COURT

FOR THE EASTERN DISTRICT OF VIRGINIA

(ALEXANDRIA DIVISION)

MORLAND CORPORATION,

         Plantiffs,

v.   Civ. Action No. 12-PTH-1212 (E.D.Va.)

JOHNSON COMPANY, INC.,

         Defendant.

NOTICE OF DEPOSITION OF JONATHAN K. SWIFT

To: Counsel for Defendant,

The Plaintiff Morland Corp., by its counsel, notices the Defendant, Johnson Company, Inc., that Plaintiff will take the deposition on oral examination of Jonathan K. Swift, director of the Miasma Corporation, on March 23, 2013, at the offices of Plaintiff's counsel, Flotsam, Jetsam, Sandbar & Quagmire, 1411 Buena Vista Ave., Suite 2700, McLean, Virginia, 22101, beginning at 9:00 a.m. A subpoena *ad testificandum* has been served on the deponent, and a copy is attached. Defendant, by counsel, is entitled to appear and participate as provided by Federal Rules of Civil Procedure 26 and 30.

This deposition will be recorded by video and by stenographic transcription, by the Arnoldson Reporting Company of Arlington, Virginia.

By: *James F. Cooper*
James F. Cooper (Va. Bar #112-A-47405)
Flotsam, Jetsam, Sandbar & Quagmire
1411 Buena Vista Ave., Suite 2700
McLean, VA 22101
703-555-0105
Attorneys for the Plaintiff

B.2   **Sample Notice of Nonparty Deposition on Oral Examination (seeking both testimony and production of documents)**

IN THE UNITED STATES DISTRICT COURT

FOR THE EASTERN DISTRICT OF VIRGINIA

(ALEXANDRIA DIVISION)

MORLAND CORPORATION,

           Plaintiffs,

v.   Civ. Action No. 12-PTH-1212 (E.D.Va.)

JOHNSON COMPANY, INC.,

           Defendant.

NOTICE OF DEPOSITION OF JONATHAN K. SWIFT

To: Counsel for Defendant,

The Plaintiff Morland Corp., by its counsel, notices the Defendant, Johnson Company, Inc., that Plaintiff will take the deposition on oral examination of Jonathan K. Swift, of the Miasma Company, on March 23, 2013, at the offices of Plaintiff's counsel, Flotsam, Jetsam, Sandbar & Quagmire, 1411 Buena Vista Ave., Suite 2700, McLean, Virginia, 22101, beginning at 9:00 a.m. A subpoena *duces tecum* and *ad testificandum* has been served on Jonathan K. Swift, and a copy is attached to this Notice. Defendant, by counsel, is entitled to appear and participate as provided by Federal Rules of Civil Procedure 26 and 30.

This deposition will be recorded by video and by stenographic transcription by the Arnoldson Reporting Company of Arlington, Virginia.

By: *James F. Cooper*
James F. Cooper (Va. Bar #112-A-47405)
Flotsam, Jetsam, Sandbar & Quagmire
1411 Buena Vista Ave., Suite 2700
McLean, VA 22101
703-555-0105
Attorneys for the Plaintiff

B.3   Sample Notice of Deposition on Oral Examination of Witness Controlled by Defendant

IN THE UNITED STATES DISTRICT COURT

FOR THE EASTERN DISTRICT OF VIRGINIA

(ALEXANDRIA DIVISION)

MORLAND CORPORATION,

              Plantiffs,

v.   Civ. Action No. 12-PTH-1212 (E.D.Va.)

JOHNSON COMPANY, INC.,

              Defendant.

NOTICE OF DEPOSITION OF HENRIETTA LONGFELLOW

To: Counsel for Defendant

The Plaintiff Morland Corp., by its counsel, notices the Defendant, Johnson Company, Inc., that Plaintiff will take the deposition on oral examination of Henrietta Longfellow of the Johnson Company, on March 23, 2013, at the offices of Plaintiff's counsel, Flotsam, Jetsam, Sandbar & Quagmire, 1411 Buena Vista Ave., Suite 2700, McLean, Virginia, 22101, beginning at 9:00 a.m.

This deposition will be recorded by video and by stenographic transcription, by the Arnoldson Reporting Company of Arlington, Virginia.

By: *James F. Cooper*
James F. Cooper (Va. Bar #112-A-47405)
Flotsam, Jetsam, Sandbar & Quagmire
1411 Buena Vista Ave., Suite 2700
McLean, VA 22101
703-555-0105
Attorneys for the Plaintiff

B.4   Sample Notice of Rule 30(b)(6) Deposition on Oral Examination

IN THE UNITED STATES DISTRICT COURT

FOR THE EASTERN DISTRICT OF VIRGINIA

(ALEXANDRIA DIVISION)

MORLAND CORPORATION,

         Plantiffs,

v.   Civ. Action No. 12-PTH-1212 (E.D.Va.)

JOHNSON COMPANY, INC.,

         Defendant.

<u>**NOTICE OF RULE 30(b)(6) DEPOSITION**</u>

To:Counsel for Defendant

The Plaintiff Morland Corp., by its counsel, notices the Defendant, Johnson Company, Inc., that Plaintiff will take the **Rule 30(b)(6) deposition** on oral examination of Johnson Company, Inc., by its designee(s), on March 23, 2013, at the offices of Plaintiff's counsel, Flotsam, Jetsam, Sandbar & Quagmire, 1411 Buena Vista Ave., Suite 2700, McLean, Virginia, 22101, beginning at 9:00 a.m. and continuing until completed.[1] Plaintiff Morland Corporation requests that the Defendant Johnson Company advise plaintiff, at least ten days before March 23, 2013, of the number and identities of its Rule 30(b)(6) designees who will provide testimony pursuant to this Notice. The topics for the examination are identified in the attached statement, as required by Rule 30(b)(6).

---

1. This language is appropriate because multiple designees may justify multiple seven-hour periods under Fed R. Civ. P. 30(b)(6). The Advisory Committee's Notes indicate that questioning of each designee is considered a separate deposition, and each may therefore extend for seven hours. Obviously, the language in this footnote is not to be included in the Notice of a Rule 30(b)(6) Deposition.

This deposition will be recorded by video and by stenographic transcription, by the Arnoldson Reporting Company of Arlington, Virginia.

By: *James F. Cooper*
James F. Cooper (Va. Bar #112-A-47405)
Flotsam, Jetsam, Sandbar & Quagmire
1411 Buena Vista Ave., Suite 2700
McLean, VA 22101
703-555-0105
Attorneys for the Plaintiff

Specifications Attached

Specifications for F.R.C.P. 30(b)(6) Deposition of
Defendant Johnson Company

"Ari-Vederci" as used in these specifications includes "Ari-Vederci CR" and "Ari-Vederci ER," or other sleep aids whose active ingredients are the same as those of Ari-Vederci. At the deposition of Defendant Johnson Company, currently noticed for March 23, 2013, pursuant to Federal Rule of Civil Procedure 30(b)(6), Plaintiff Morland Corporation will depose the Defendant's designees on the following topics, among other topics related to this litigation:

1. The document retention or destruction policies and procedures of the Johnson Company in effect at the New York City, New York, headquarters office and at the Schenectady regional office in Schenectady, New York, for the period from January 1, 1999, through and including the date of this deposition.

2. The persons involved in any way in the decision to market the drug Ari-Viderci (chemical name 4-trichlor-5-dimethyl-2-monocyclene) as "approved" for use as a diuretic and weight-reducing compound or formulation for sale through retail and online pharmacies, their responsibilities for that compound, and their role in the decision to market.

3. All steps taken to obtain information relating in any way to the preparation of designees to respond to this Notice of Deposition and these Specifications, including the collection of information by other persons for the purpose of providing that information to the designees.

4. The topics in these Specifications to which each different designee will testify at the noticed deposition.

5. All factors considered by Johnson Company and any of its officials or employees in making the decision referenced in Specification 2, above.

6. The pricing decision for the drug or compound or formulation known as Ari-Viderci and any generic compounds advertised or referred to as equivalents in therapeutic effect and chemical composition to Ari-Viderci.

7. All information considered, obtained, or utilized by Johnson Company in marketing or selling Ari-Viderci that relates in any way to the sale or planned sale by other companies of generic products that are, or are claimed to be, equivalent in therapeutic effect or chemical composition to Ari-Viderci, including marketing plans, market analyses, and any other plans of any sort; and clinical evaluations and trials.

B.5 Sample Subpoena to Nonparty Deponent Residing in Another District

IN THE UNITED STATES DISTRICT COURT

FOR THE EASTERN DISTRICT OF PENNSYLVANIA

MORLAND CORPORATION,

        Plantiffs,

v.   Civ. Action No. Misc. 13-457

                (Re: Civ. Action No. 12-PTH-1212 (E.D.Va.)

JOHNSON COMPANY, INC.,

        Defendant.

SUBPOENA TO TESTIFY AND

TO PRODUCE MATERIALS AT DEPOSITION

To: Edward F. Horton
       134 Rosecroft Road
       Bensonville, PA 19743

You are commanded to appear at 9:00 a.m. on April 12, 2013, at the law offices of Ohlbaum & Natali, 149 N. Broad St., Suite 1500, Philadelphia, PA 19701, to testify at a deposition to be taken in a civil action pending in the Eastern District of Virginia between Morland Corporation, PLAINTIFF, and Johnson Company, DEFENDANT. This deposition will be recorded by video and by stenographic transcription by the Smith Reporting Company of Philadelphia, PA.

You must **BRING WITH YOU** to the deposition, or produce prior to the deposition to counsel whose signature appears below, the following documents, electronically stored information, or objects, and permit their inspection, copying, testing, or sampling:

1. Any and all materials relating in any way to the invention, discovery, or development of the compound known as Ari-Vederci.

2. Any and all materials relating in any way to plans for selling, marketing, or providing Ari-Vederci and its generic equivalents to retail drug outlets of any type, online or otherwise, during the period from 1999 through 2007.

3. Any and all materials relating in any way to the wholesale and retail pricing of Ari-Vederci and its generic equivalents during the period from 1999 through 2007.

The provisions of Federal Rule of Civil Procedure 45(c), (d), and (e) apply to your rights and duties in responding to this subpoena and to the potential consequences of not responding. A copy of this rule is attached to this subpoena.

A copy of this subpoena has been provided to counsel for the Defendant Johnson Company by electronic mail and by delivering it by messenger, as agreed between the parties.

Date: March 4, 2012

By: *James F. Cooper*
James F. Cooper (Va. Bar #112-A-47405)
Flotsam, Jetsam, Sandbar & Quagmire
1411 Buena Vista Ave., Suite 2700
McLean, VA 22101
703-555-0105
Attorneys for the Plaintiff Morland Corporation

(Proof of Service Attached)

B.6   Sample Privilege Log

[CASE CAPTION]

PLAINTIFF'S PRIVILEGE LOG

COMES NOW the Plaintiff and identifies the following documents withheld from production in response to Defendant's Request for Production dated May 5, 2012:

LOG NUMBER :   2736
[OR EXHIBIT NUMBER]

Identity and Position of Author   Elliot Milstein

(and sender if different):   President & Chief Executive Officer

                                                           Minicom, Inc.

Identify and Position of Recipients: Nicholas Vanderhagen

                                                           Attorney, Vanderhagen & Jones, LLP

                                                           Attorney for Plaintiff

Document Title: Letter

Date: June 3, 2011

Description: Letter describing legal problem and seeking legal advice.

Privilege Claimed: Attorney-Client Privilege

Present Location: Files of Nicholas Vanderhagen, Attorney for Plaintiff

[Repeat same information for other documents withheld]

[Signature]

APPENDIX C

C.1 The *Daubert* Deposition Dance: Retracing the Intricacies of the Expert's Steps

By David M. Malone and Ryan M. Malone

After the decision in *Daubert v. Merrill Dow*[1] there was some question about whether the gatekeeping responsibilities of the federal trial courts extended to all expert testimony or merely to "scientific" expert testimony. Even among circuits that believed that only scientific testimony was covered, there was confusion as to what was scientific testimony and what was "technical or other specialized" testimony. The *Kumho Tire*[2] case resolved that confusion by clearly stating that the methodologies underlying *all* expert testimony must be evaluated for reliability.

This decision therefore clarified the occasions for application of the *Daubert* approach, although it compounded any remaining problems by increasing the number of cases covered. Chief among those remaining problems is the need for trial practitioners and trial courts to develop a coherent body of analytic tools by which methodological reliability can be measured with some confidence by lawyers and judges without formal training in the specialized fields. For example, how does the trial judge assess the reliability of methodologies employed by the astrophysicist, since it is unlikely that the trial judge coincidentally has been trained in astrophysics.[3]

Although the Supreme Court in *Daubert* and again in *Kumho Tire* emphasized that the four criteria—publication in a peer-reviewed journal; known or knowable error rate; general acceptance in the relevant scientific community; and testability or replicability (including the concept of "falsifiability"[4])—were not exclusive (indeed, none of the four is even

---

1. *See* Daubert v. Merrill Dow Pharmaceuticals, Inc., 509 U.S. 579 (1993).

2. *See* Kumho Tire Co. v. Carmichael, 526 U.S. 137 (1999).

3. Some suggest that the court could overcome this problem by obtaining its own expert (at the parties' expense, of course). This is not a solution, however, because the question of the reliability of expert methodologies would then legitimately be directed toward the court's expert and her methodologies. Pundits might suggest that another court-retained expert could be consulted, and then another, until we complete some regression back to a Prime Expert.

4. A premise is "falsifiable" if it can be proven wrong, usually through direct experience. For instance, the premise "all ravens are black" is falsifiable, since it can be proven wrong by the discovery of a white raven. On the other hand, the premise "everything in the universe doubles in size for a second, and then it halves in size the next second" is not falsifiable, since it is impossible to disprove through direct experience. (If everything is alternating in doubling and halving in size, it remains *relatively* the same size, and therefore the difference is impossible to measure.) Scientific premises are tentative and falsifiable, while some other premises are not. It is common for creationists to point out that evolutionary biologists often contradict parts of evolutionary theory. However, the testing of evolutionary theory by its subscribers, which the creationists see as a weakness of that theory, is actually proof positive that the theory is scientific. *See, e.g.,* ROBERT T. PINNOCK, TOWER OF BABEL: THE EVIDENCE AGAINST THE NEW

required), there seems to be some belief among attorneys and judges that we must measure reliability by those criteria alone. In an earlier article,[5] the authors suggested a number of additional, objective criteria that could be utilized in conducting this analysis, beyond those four mentioned in *Daubert*. Abstract criteria, whether four or fourteen, are not easily applied in discovery depositions, however, and we must recognize that it is in deposition that the foundation for challenge to an expert's methodology is uncovered. We therefore thought it might be useful to examine some specific questions that an attorney can ask at deposition to explore these various concepts of reliability, with follow-up and rationale explained as we go along.

1.   *Publication in a Peer-Reviewed Journal*

This criterion of reliability actually has two prongs to it: an article describing the methodology must have been published, which subjects it to scrutiny by whatever readership the journal has; and the article must have been reviewed, pre-publication, by "peers" in the particular field of knowledge, who ostensibly would scrutinize it for errors and challenge any unsupported conclusions. It is objective because it does not require the application of judgment to determine whether it has been satisfied—only examination of the literature. Deposition questions that examine whether this criterion has been satisfied are rather easy to create, but the exercise is useful:

    a.   *Where has this methodology been published?*

    b.   *Who published it?*

    c.   *What is the process for pre-publication review?*

    d.   *What are the credentials of the reviewers (sometimes called "referees")?*

    e.   *What criticisms or suggestions did the reviewers make?*

    f.   *What changes were made as a result of those suggestions?*

CREATIONISTS, xvi (MIT Press 2000): "Science imposes severe constraints upon itself to ensure that its conclusions are intersubjectively testable, constraints that require that it not appeal to supernatural hypotheses or allow the citation of special (private) revelations as evidence. The new creationists, including Johnson and philosophers such as Alvin Plantinga, reject these constraints and share the view that supernatural explanations should be admitted into science."

5. *See* David M. Malone & Ryan M. Malone, *The Zodiac Expert: Reliability After Kumho,* 22 The Trial Lawyer Magazine 265 (Fall 1999).

g.   *What other changes were made?*

h.   *What comments were received post-publication?*

i.   *What is known of the credentials of those persons providing comments?*

j.   *What changes in methodology were made as a result of those comments?*

k.   *Have you, or has anyone else, published additional articles on this methodology?*

2.   *Known or Knowable Error Rate*

This criterion requests the expert to provide information about the likelihood that the methodology will produce incorrect results. It does not establish a threshold of correctness for admissibility, but it is difficult to believe that a court would admit an expert's opinions after hearing in limine testimony that a methodology may produce wrong results half the time. In the world of commercial litigation, economists and financial analysts may be the experts most susceptible to challenge based on a failure to satisfy this criterion; in truth, are they able even to assess their error rates when they conclude that a particular market structure is more competitive than another?

a.   *Identify studies that have calculated error rates for this methodology.*

b.   *Describe how you yourself would determine the error rate.*

c.   *What mechanisms are available for reducing or eliminating errors?*

d.   *Is there a particular aspect of the methodology (e.g., data collection, data input, interpretation of results) that is more likely to produce errors?*

e.   *How would someone employing this methodology know that an error had occurred?*

f.   *What types of errors can occur?*

g.   *What effect would those errors have on the utility or correctness of your opinion?*

3.   *General Acceptance in the Relevant Scientific Community*

This is the (previously) well-established *Frye*[6] test. The weakness of this test was not that it asked an irrelevant question—the question is indeed relevant—but rather that it depended on the expert for an opinion on the reliability of the methodology, rather than seeking objective information. As a sole criterion, however, it also assumes that the court could identify the relevant scientific community. Today, with specialists within specialties within sub-areas within practice areas within medical board areas, as an example, the nests of Russian dolls prevent any court from knowing, on its own, whether this is a "relevant scientific community" or a sub-specialty that should be evaluated according to standards from a larger group or merely a fringe group of radicals. Furthermore, while mechanical engineering methodology may quite reasonably be scrutinized by application of the standards of mechanical engineering, as it was in *Kumho Tire*, we are not so confident that aromatherapist methodology should be evaluated only by application of the standards of aromatherapists. There is a skepticism here that we recognize and believe to be appropriate, even while we understand that we must be able to distinguish it from mere bias or prejudice.

> a.   *What evidence is there that practitioners in your field generally accept this approach?*
>
> b.   *How do you define your field?*
>
> c.   *What other approaches are utilized in that field?*
>
> d.   *What approach is utilized most often?*
>
> e.   *What are the advantages and disadvantages of the main methodologies?*
>
> f.   *Why did you choose to use this methodology?*
>
> g.   *When was this methodology developed?*
>
> h.   *What effect did introduction of this methodology have on the acceptance of other methodologies?*

4.   *Testability or Replicability*

It is not sufficient for a researcher to state that she has discovered a relationship between certain effects and a purported cause. She must specify that relationship in a sufficiently specific way that other researchers can

---

6. *See* Frye v. United States, 293 F. 1013 (D.C. Cir. 1923).

examine it for themselves. If their examinations corroborate her results, then the hypothesis may become accepted. Without such corroboration, however, her hypothesis stands as no better than conjecture. For example, several years ago at the National Heart, Lung, and Blood Institute, a researcher noted a statistically significant correlation between people who ate sandwiches for lunch and people who developed serious heart disease. The researcher spelled out his methodology in sufficient detail that other researchers could review his approaches and data; they discovered that sandwiches and heart disease were not directly related to each other, but each was instead related to hurried meal times, a characteristic of Type A personalities at high risk for heart disease because of multiple stress factors. The original researcher's problem of *multicolinearity* would not have been observed if the original hypothesis had not been stated with sufficient specificity to permit test and replication.

    a.   *Step by step, how have you conducted your tests or examinations?*

    b.   *Identify all of your data sources.*

    c.   *Provide all of your laboratory or session notes.*

    d.   *Beginning with a particular item of raw (empirical) data, show us how it is treated or manipulated by the methodology.*

    e.   *What tests did you do yourself to confirm that the methodology produced parallel results for parallel inputs? (If your methodology is addition and you input [2, 2] and get 4, then when you input [4, 4] you should get 8.)*

    f.   *What tests did you do to confirm that disparate inputs would yield disparate results? (If the factor of few firms in an industry is said to lead to high profits, then we should not observe industries with many firms also enjoying high profits. For a simpler analogy, if a friend says that a black box will light a red light when salted pretzels are inserted, it is not a sufficient test to insert salted pretzels and watch for the light; we must also insert unsalted pretzels and stale Gum-miBear candies and watch for the light. Otherwise, we might merely have a machine (methodology) that turns on a light when anything is inserted.)*

5.   **Development and Use of the Methodology in Nonlitigation Contexts**

The Ninth Circuit, on remand in the *Daubert* matter, grafted an additional criterion onto the four suggested by the Supreme Court: Was the methodology developed for nonlitigation purposes?[7] Questioning on this criterion should be reasonably straightforward because it asks the expert for historical facts, not scientific opinions or relationships. If the methodology was developed solely (or, logically, primarily) for the purpose of supporting a particular side in litigation, we are more skeptical about its objectivity.

    a.   When was this methodology developed?

    b.   Who was the developer?

    c.   What was the original purpose of its development?

    d.   Are you using any modifications that were developed for litigation?

    e.   Why were modifications made to the original methodology?

    f.   Is the methodology still being used for its original purpose?

    g.   Has it been partially or largely supplanted?

    h.   What methodologies have supplanted it? Why?

6.   *Sufficiency to Explain the Salient Facts*

The Supreme Court in *Kumho Tire* expressed skepticism that a practitioner of a legitimate methodology ("visual and tactile tire failure analysis") could not evaluate whether an apparently salient fact was present (whether the tire had traveled 50,000 miles or more).[8] This does involve the a priori belief on the part of the Court that this factor is significant; nevertheless, the expert should at least have been able to provide a reasonable explanation for his inability to determine this fact.

    a.   Describe all of the categories of information that were available to you for this analysis (or that are generated by the event being analyzed: profits, margins, gross sales revenue, industry concentration, firm rank, unit sales, advertising-to-sales ratios, advertising expenditure ramps, etc.).

    b.   Rank those categories of data from most to least significant, and explain the ranking.

    c.   Show us where each of those categories was used.

---

7. *See* Daubert v. Merrill Dow Pharmaceuticals, Inc., 43 F.3d 1311 (9th Cir. 1995).
8. *See Kumho Tire*, 526 U.S. at 254.

d. *Tell us why some categories of data were not used.*

e. *Tell us how you adjusted for your inability to obtain some data (e.g., tire travel miles).*

f. *Have you considered different data in other cases? Why?*

g. *Do other researchers consider other data or rank the data differently in importance?*

h. *Have you ever reached conclusions without data from each category?*

7.   *Quantitative Sufficiency of the Data Employed*

In an industrial conveyor belt failure case,[9] the court was concerned that the mechanical engineer was relying on a very small sample to provide data points for his analysis: a few bolts from a very large conveyor assembly. While testimony from someone trained in statistical methods might satisfy the court that the data were sufficient for conclusions at a reasonable level of certainty, the mechanical engineer could not provide that foundation, and the court was uncomfortable with the minimal basis.

a. *What were your sources of data?*

b. *How much data was available from each source?*

c. *Was there richer data available elsewhere?*

d. *Was a statistical analysis performed to determine the adequacy of the data for the purpose of drawing conclusions?*

e. *At what confidence level did the data allow you to draw your conclusions?*

f. *At what confidence level do you typically operate in nonlitigation activities in your profession?*

g. *In your last published article, what confidence level did you employ?*

h. *In the last article that you read or refereed, what confidence level was employed?*

---

9. Watkins v. Telsmith, 121 F.3d 984 (5th Cir. 1997).

> i. *If the data points were increased by a factor of two, how would the confidence level have been affected? If the points were increased tenfold?*

> j. *If one-third of the data you used were determined to be unreliable, would your conclusions still be sound, at the same level of confidence?*

8.   Qualitative Sufficiency of the Data Employed

In some cases, we can imagine that the data are quantitatively sufficient (we have enough data points to satisfy the statisticians among us), but we are troubled by the quality of the data or its sources. For example, in child abuse cases, experts sometimes are willing to testify based in part on their experiences with descriptions of abuse and its sequela from numerous children. The sample may be sufficient in size; even the simple hearsay nature of the bases may be so commonly encountered that it does not disqualify the testimony; but the impressionable nature of the sources—children interviewed under unknown and perhaps uncontrolled circumstances, having been subjected to unrevealed pressures or influences—renders them suspect and may impel a court to exclude the expert testimony.

> a. *What were the sources of your data?*

> b. *Who collected the data?*

> c. *Who supplied the data to the persons collecting it?*

> d. *What prior experience have you had with this methodology for data collection?*

> e. *What tests did you conduct to determine that your data were accurate?*

> f. *What motivations were provided to the sources to encourage accurate reporting?*

> g. *Were there any penalties for inaccurate reporting by the sources to your collectors?*

> h. *What were the sources told about the purposes of the data collection?*

> i. *What were the collectors told about the purposes?*

> j. *What were the criteria for including and excluding sources of data?*

9. *Consistency with General Methodology*

Methodologies should be reliable regardless of the context-based biases or prejudices of the persons employing them. For example, the methodology the expert uses to determine the quality of structural steel should be the same, whether that examination is being done as quality control for an industry member, as consultant to a plaintiff in a contract suit, or as consultant to a defendant in a products liability suit. Of course, the general approach should be identified first at deposition, before questioning about specifics; otherwise, the description of what is generally done will be adjusted to match what the witness already said was done in this case. In *Kumho Tire* itself, the Court was interested in the fact that the expert said that his approach involved analysis of four "visual and tactile" aspects of the failed tire and, if any two were present, concluding that the failure was the result of owner abuse rather than manufacturing defect. The expert then found two factors to be present (apparently one just a little bit), but he nevertheless concluded that the failure resulted from defect. This departure from his general methodology may have been fatal to his opinion.[10]

> *a.* *Tell me the steps in using this analysis in your everyday, nonlitigation work.*
>
> *b.* *What are the uses of such analysis?*
>
> *c.* *What data do you obtain; from what sources?*
>
> *d.* *Who assists you? Why? How?*
>
> *e.* *When have you used this analysis before?*
>
> *f.* *Did you follow the general methodology you have just described?*
>
> *g.* *In this litigation, what steps do you perform in this analysis?*
>
> *h.* *Who assisted you? Why? How?*
>
> *i.* *Was it necessary to depart from the general approach in any way? Why?*
>
> *j.* *What precautions did you take to insure that those departures would not inappropriately affect the results of the analysis?*
>
> *k.* *What authority did you have for believing those precautions were sufficient?*

---

10. *See Kumho Tire*, 526 U.S. at 254–55.

> *l.   What other steps did you take that were different from your general approach or methodology?*

10.   *Existence of a Body of Literature on the Particular Methodology*

If there is no body of literature on the methodology that the expert is recommending, and the explanation for such absence is not apparent or the expert cannot or does not explain the absence of such literature, then the court is justified in exercising skepticism about the reliability of the methodology. (Of course, other factors would be affected also, such as "general acceptance in the relevant scientific community"; how would such acceptance be evidenced if there is no literature?) Of course, if the field of expertise would not be expected to generate such a body of literature ("the adequacy of methods for cleaning tomato sauce spills in supermarket aisles"), the court might well ignore this factor. A faulty syllogism could lead people to believe that because there is a body of literature on an approach, it represents a reliable methodology; it may merely mean that there are lots of unreliable adherents who write lots of unreliable stuff.[11] The field of astrology, as an example, has generated thousands of books and articles over centuries (or millennia, if Druidic runes qualify).

> *a.   How does one learn about this methodology?*

> *b.   How do you keep up with changes and improvements in the methodology?*

---

11. To be certain that we can identify faulty syllogisms, let us look at a correct syllogism and a faulty syllogism:
   - Correct syllogism A: (1) All frogs are green; (2) Clyde is a frog; therefore (3) Clyde is green.
   - Correct syllogism B: (1) All frogs are green; (2) Clyde is not green; therefore (3) Clyde is not a frog.
   - Incorrect syllogism C: (1) All frogs are green; (2) Clyde is green; therefore (3) Clyde is a frog.

This is incorrect because Clyde could be something else that is green but not a frog, such as a pet lime. Now, applying this syllogistic template to the *Daubert* methodology questions:
   - Correct syllogism D: (1) Reliable methodologies are likely to generate relatively substantial literature; (2) this is a reliable methodology; therefore (3) it is likely to generate (or to have generated) a relatively substantial body of literature.
   - Correct syllogism E: (1) Reliable methodologies are likely to generate relatively substantial literature; (2) this methodology has not generated relatively substantial literature; therefore (3) this is not a reliable methodology (or, even more correctly, this is *not likely to be* a reliable methodology).
   - Incorrect syllogism F: (1) Reliable methodologies are likely to generate relatively substantial literature; (2) this methodology has generated a relatively substantial body of literature; (3) therefore this is a reliable methodology.

c.   *What are the principal journals or publications in this field?*

d.   *Who contributes to them?*

e.   *Who referees or edits them for methodological correctness?*

f.   *Do noted scientists contribute or subscribe? (e.g., do astronomers subscribe or contribute to the "Astrologers' Journal"?)*

g.   *Do contributors or editors appear in journals of related and accepted fields? (e.g., do astrologers get published in the "American Journal of Astronomy"?*

f.   *How long have the main journals in the field been published?*

11.   Logical Derivation of the Methodology

Experience suggests that the scientific progress is, indeed, progressive; that is, new developments build in some recognizable and articulable way on past, related explorations: blood-letting did not lead immediately to heart transplantations; green Post-It™ notes followed yellow Post-It™ notes; and the methods for putting a human on the moon depended on the development of methods for putting a human in Earth orbit. As a general, a priori principle that makes us comfortable—few steps are skipped. When steps are skipped in such normally evolutionary change, so that it becomes revolutionary, we look for explanations, and we expect the proponent of the new theory to provide those explanations.

a.   *Describe the derivation of the methodology that you used.*

b.   *What prior methodology is this one most closely related to?*

c.   *Describe the similarities between them. Describe the differences.*

d.   *What problems or factors led to the change from the old to the new methodology?*

e.   *Who were the foremost proponents of the prior methodology?*

f.   *Who initiated, sponsored, or championed the change to the new methodology?*

g.   *What role did you have in this change?*

> h.   *In what circumstances would the two methodologies yield different results?*

> i.   *What specific differences in the methodologies lead to those different results?*

> j.   *Why is the new methodology superior?*

Conclusion

The Supreme Court in *Kumho Tire* emphasized that it would be fruitless to attempt to list all criteria for assessing reliability of experts' methodologies because they are as numerous as the fields of human knowledge.[12] The purpose of this article is obviously not to disagree with the Court on this point, but rather to suggest ways of thinking about reliability, approaches to assessing methodologies, that can be used across fields of expertise and that do not depend on requiring the lawyers or the judges to develop competence in the field being assessed. As we consider these legal questions (both the question of how to determine reliability and the questions being suggested here as part of a solution), we are in fact considering questions of much broader application to the human condition: How do we learn? How do we know when we know? How can we learn what someone else *actually* knows? If we were concerned only with the question—trivial in this context—of determining the credibility of an expert, traditional tools are available: cross-examination, impeachment, learned treatises, omissions, and so forth. Instead, in considering *Daubert-Kumho Tire* issues, we must concern ourselves with the possibility of truth-telling witnesses, armed with patently impressive credentials, whose science may represent the future, but whose testimony should not be presented in court.

---

12. *See Kumho Tire*, 526 U.S. at 251.

Index

E

I